POLYSEXUALITY

POLYSEXUALITY [SEMIOTEXT(E) #10]

SPECIAL EDITOR
FRANÇOIS PERALDI

ASSOCIATE EDITORS
KATHRYN BIGELOW, DENISE GREEN, LEE HILDRETH,
DENIS HOLIER, SYLVÈRE LOTRINGER, ROGER MCKEON,
JOHN RAJCHMAN, PAT STEIR.

DESIGN / ILLUSTRATION
MARTIM AVILLEZ, KATHRYN BIGELOW, DIEGO CORTEZ,
DENISE GREEN, JOSEPH KOSUTH, MICHAEL OBLOWITZ,
FRANÇOIS PERALDI, PAT STEIR.

VISUALS
HONCHO, THE NEW YORK POST, MICHAEL OBLOWITZ.

TRANSLATION EDITORS
THOMAS GORA, ROGER MCKEON, DANIEL SLOATE.

TRANSLATORS
PARVEEN ADAMS, CHARLES CLARK, CATHERINE
DUNCAN, MICHEL FEHER, RICHARD GARDNER,
DENISE GREEN, THOMAS GORA, SUZANNE GUERLAC,
JOHN JOHNSTON, ANDREA KAHN, THERESE LYONS,
RACHEL MCCOMAS, MARGARET MCGAW, LINDA MCNEIL,
STAMOS METZIDAKIS, DANIEL SLOATE, P. ZOBERMAN.

PRODUCTION STAFF
STEPHANIE ABARBANEL, KATHRYN BIGELOW,
MARK BLASIUS, ROSS BLECKNER, HAROLD CHESTER,
DENISE GREEN, THOMAS GORA, KAREN HORNICK,
MICHAEL OBLOWITZ, MARC POLIZZOTTI, CHARLES &
HÈLÉNE POTTER, DIANA SILVERMAN, DUNCAN SMITH,
PAT STEIR.

BACK COVER
MICHAEL OBLOWITZ

WE WOULD LIKE TO THANK COOSJE VAN BRUGGEN AND
CLAES OLDENBURG, ROBERT RAUSCHENBERG, & KEITH
SONNIER FOR THEIR GENEROUS CONTRIBUTIONS.

SEMIOTEXT(E) OFFICES:

522 PHILOSOPHY HALL   POST OFFICE BOX 568
COLUMBIA UNIVERSITY   WILLIAMSBURGH STATION
NEW YORK, NY 10027   BROOKLYN, NY 11211

PHONE & FAX: (718) 963-2603

EDITORS
JIM FLEMING, SYLVÈRE LOTRINGER.

SEMIOTEXT(E) IS A SELF-SUPPORTING, NON-PROFIT
PUBLICATION.

ORIGINAL PUBLICATION OF THIS ISSUE WAS MADE
POSSIBLE BY GRANTS FROM THE COORDINATING
COUNCIL OF LITERARY MAGAZINES, THE NEW YORK
STATE COUNCIL ON THE ARTS, AND THE NATIONAL
ENDOWMENT FOR THE ARTS.

ISSN: 0-093-95779
ISBN: 1-57027-011-2

SUBSCRIPTIONS
INDIVIDUALS: $20 (THREE ISSUES)
INSTITUTIONS: $40 (THREE ISSUES)
PLEASE ADD $8 FOR SURFACE MAIL OUTSIDE
OF THE U.S.
CHECKS OR MONEY ORDERS SHOULD BE
IN U.S. DOLLARS ONLY AND MADE
PAYABLE TO SEMIOTEXT(E).
OUR PUBLICATION SCHEDULE IS IRREGULAR.

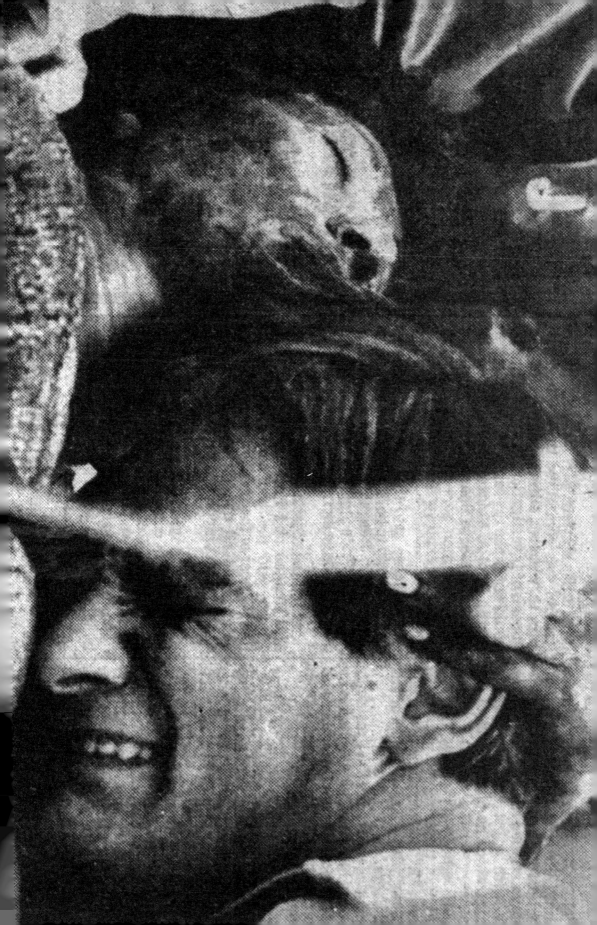

POLYSEXUALITY

POLYSEXUALITY IS NOT ONLY A SET OF TEXTS WRITTEN BY CAREFULLY CHOSEN AUTHORS AND ILLUSTRATING THE PLURAL ASPECTS OF SEXUALITY.

POLYSEXUALITY IS A TEXT IN ITSELF, THE EDITORS OF WHICH ARE THE AUTHORS. LET'S CALL IT A COLLAGE OR A TEXTUAL PATCH-WORK, IF YOU PREFER.

IT TELLS WHAT THE REALITY OF SEX HAS ALWAYS BEEN WITH RESPECT TO ITS ALIENATION TO 'USURA' AND EXPLOITATION.

IT ALSO POINTS TOWARD THE 'REAL OF SEX' WHICH STILL LIES UNTOUCHED, UNTHOUGHT OF, BUT PERHAPS ALLUDED TO BY FREUD WHEN HE SUGGESTED THAT LIBIDO HAD NO GENDER.

LIBIDO: AN IRREPRESSIBLE 'VOLONTÉ DE JOUISSANCE' (WILL TO PLEASURE) NEVER PURE SINCE IT IS ALWAYS LINKED TO THE DEATH DRIVES TO THE POINT THAT FOR SOME RIGOROUS SEEKERS, 'JOUISSANCE' CULMINATES IN DEATH: THE ULTIMATE SEX.

IF LIBIDO IS THE ORGANIZING FORCES OF ALL ACTIVITIES LEADING TO 'JOUISSANCE,' ALL THESE ACTIVITIES, INCLUDING WRITING ABOUT SEX AND 'JOUISSANCE,' HAVE TO BE CONSIDERED AS IMAGES OF THE OTHER SIDE OF THE DEATH DRIVES.

THE DEATH DRIVES, WHICH CENTRIFICATE POLITICS, HAVE BEEN PRESENTIFIED IN THIS TEXT BY IMAGES OF POLITICAL DISASTERS, MASSACRES, GENOCIDES, CRIMES OF WAR: OUR DAILY LOT. THE THEORY OF CATASTROPHIES IS AT THE VERY CORE OF THE THEORY OF POLITICS AND IT HAS TO BE THOUGHT OF AS GIVING SHAPE TO THIS OTHER SIDE OF LIBIDO.

FROM COVER TO COVER, THIS WHOLE ISSUE IS NOTHING ELSE, IN OUR OPINION, THAN THE TEXTUAL WORKING THROUGH OF THIS THESIS. WE CALL IT TEXTUAL, BECAUSE LANGUAGES, OF COURSE, CONSTITUTE THE THIRD SIDE OF LIBIDO, AND DEATH DRIVE, BY KNOTTING THEM TOGETHER AND MAKING THEM TANGIBLE, SYMBOLICALLY OR SEMIOTEXTUALLY SPEAKING.

FRANCOIS PERALDI

BOSTON, MARCH 16, 1981

SELF SEX

BODY OF THE TEXT

THIS IS NOT WRITTEN, BUT DICTATED, IMPROVISED, NOTEBOOKS IN HAND—NOT FOR A STOCKTAKING OF PAST OR PRESENT JOTTINGS ON WHAT I AM ABOUT TO DESCRIBE: THE RELATIONSHIP BETWEEN MASTURBATION AND WRITING—BUT IN ORDER TO SPEAK TEXT IN HAND AND EXPOSED TO VIEW—; NO USE EXPECTING THEN, A TEXT THAT MIGHT BE DESCRIBED AS "SCHOLARLY" OR "MARGINAL" (NECESSARY TERMS AT AN EPOCH DETERMINED BY POLITICAL ENGAGEMENTS OF AN ADMINISTRATIVE KIND, OR BY A HESITATION TO EXPRESS THE MOST VOCAL SOUNDINGS OF THE MASTURBATORY TEXT). NONETHELESS, THE NEED TO MAKE MY FIRST DECLARATIONS ON THE RELATIONSHIP MASTURBA-TION-WRITING DATES FROM A POLITICAL CONTEXT ("LA NOUVELLE CRITIQUE").

I REMEMBER HAVING BEGUN TO MASTURBATE AT THE AGE OF NINE, IN ORDER TO "PUT OFF" A DESIRE TO PISS OR CRAP. AT THAT AGE IT WAS DIFFICULT FOR ME TO PUT UP MY HAND IN CLASS AND PUBLICLY MAKE KNOWN MY NEEDS, DRAWING ATTENTION TO MYSELF AS A BODY, ORGANISM, PRODUCER OF MATTER, ALTHOUGH I HAVE NEVER EVER FELT THE LEAST EMBARRASSED ON THE CONTRARY, ABOUT BEING SEEN AS BODY, ORGANS. ALREADY THEN, BY DISCOVERING AND PUTTING INTO PRACTICE THIS MASTURBATORY SYSTEM, I WAS ACTING IN A VERY COHERENT WAY AS TO THE MASTERING OF MY NEEDS AND WANTS: AS I SAW IT, ORGASM—ALTHOUGH I COULDN'T HAVE NAMED IT AT A TIME IT DID NOT YET LEAD TO EJACULATION—WITHELD THE TURD AND URINE. REPEATED SEVERAL TIMES A DAY, THIS OPERATION SEEMED TO ME IN NO WAY REPREHENSIBLE. IT TOOK PLACE, AS UNOBTRUSIVELY AS POSSIBLE, UNDER THE DESK: FIST THRUST INTO MY POCKET (ITS SEAMS FULL OF CRUMBS, ORANGE PEEL, SUGAR, ETC.), JERKING THE LITTLE SEX, THROUGH THE UNDERPANTS AT FIRST, THEN GRADUALLY, MONTH BY MONTH AS THE PLEASURE BECAME MORE PRACTISED, WITH UNDERPANTS PUSHED AGAINST THE THIGH. FROM THAT TIME ON I ALSO MASTURBATED MUCH LESS IN THE WC, ACCORDING TO A KIND OF GAME, A CHALLENGE TO MY OWN BODY: ARSE DISTENDED OVER THE HOLE (OUT OF WHICH RISE TO PALPITAT-ING MOUTH AND NOSTRILS ALL THE ODORS OF THE SUMP AND THE HERCYNIAN MOUNTAIN EARTH ON WHICH THE SCHOOL IS BUILT, PERVADED, FILTERED BY THE FRAILER SMELL OF SEMEN), AND I—HIDDEN IN THE VERY HAUNT OF HUMAN AND OFTEN ANIMAL DEJECTIONS (DOGS, CATS, SCREECH-OWLS FROM THE FARM COMING THERE TO DEFECATE)—I, MOST COMICALLY, CONDUCTING A DIALOGUE BETWEEN

14

THE ARSE-HOLE AND THE SEX, BETWEEN THE SLITHER OF THE TURD AND THAT OF THE ORGASM.

SOMETIMES, GETTING OUT OF CONTROL, ORGASM AND DEFECATION TOOK PLACE SIMULTANEOUSLY, AND SUCH MOMENTS ARE PINNACLES OF PLEASURE. AS A RESULT, BECAUSE MY UNDERPANTS BEAR THE MARKS (SOMEWHAT OVER-ESTIMATED) OF THIS TRANSFER, I REFUSE TO GIVE THEM TO THE LAUNDRY OR THE SCHOOL LAUNDRESSES, AND HIDE THEM UNDER MY MATTRESS IN THE DORMITORY; THEN, STUFFING THEM INTO MY POCKET WHEN WE FALL INTO LINE AT 6 A.M. TO GO DOWN TO CHAPEL, I CARRY THEM OUTSIDE SCHOOL LIMITS BEHIND THE TUMBLEDOWN W.C.: THERE, I HIDE THEM UNDER A PILE OF STONES. IT HAPPENS AT MOMENTS OF PANIC THAT QUITE UNINTENTIONALLY I EVACUATE THE LAST OF MY SUPPLY OF UNDERPANTS, AND AM FORCED (BUT WITH WHAT PLEASURE!) TO PUT MY PANTS ON OVER BARE SKIN, SUBMITTING TO THIS ADDITIONAL STRAIN OF DRESSING AND UNDRESSING IN PUBLIC UNTIL I CAN RECUPERATE A PAIR FROM UNDER THE STONES. DURING THE HOLIDAYS MY MOTHER, WHO DIED IN AUGUST '58, WAS SURPRISED BY MY DWINDLING PACKET (NUMBER 49) OF WASHING, AND AFTER LAYING SIEGE TO ME FOR SEVERAL DAYS FINISHED BY REDUCING HER "WEEPING CHILD" TO AN ADMISSION OF WHY AND WHEREABOUTS; AND, MAKING THE MOST OF A VISIT PAID BY MY DOCTOR FATHER IN THE VICINITY OF THE SCHOOL, CLOSED FOR THE SUMMER, SHE CAME WITH ME TO LIFT THE STONES ONE AFTER ANOTHER AND, UNKNOWN TO MY FATHER WHO DIED IN NOVEMBER '71, RECUPERATE AND PUT BACK INTO CIRCULATION THAT IMPORTANT PART OF MY WARDROBE.

THE RELATION BETWEEN WRITING AND MASTURBATION APPEARS FOR THE FIRST TIME ROUND THE AGE OF TEN OR ELEVEN. I START TO DRAW (WOMEN WITH HALOS, ILLUMINATED TITLES) AND THIS GESTURE BRINGS MY HAND, MY RIGHT HAND, THE MASTURBATOR, OUT OF MY POCKET. I IMMEDIATELY WORKED OUT ANOTHER SYSTEM—WHAT I DON'T REMEMBER— TO POSTPONE THE NEED TO DEFECATE; THEN, THE LEFT HAND, MORE AND MORE EXPERT, BEGINS TO TAKE OVER, TO MASTURBATE. THIS COINCIDES WITH THE FIRST EJACULATION, THE EXPULSION THEREFORE OF ANOTHER MATTER, DISTURBING BECAUSE HALF WAY BETWEEN SHIT AND URINE, AND WHICH, BECAUSE IT SMELLS AND WETS THE CLOTHES, PUTS A STOP ONCE AND FOR ALL TO RESORTING TO ORGASM AS AN ANTI-DEFECATOR. I DON'T REMEMBER THAT PERIOD, DURING WHICH I PRACTISED DRAWING AND SPECIALLY PAINTING MORE AND MORE ASSIDUOUSLY, AS EXCEPTIONALLY SEXUAL. IT IS ONLY WHEN I BEGIN TO WRITE THAT THE MASTURBATORY PROCESS ACCELERATES AND LEADS, AS ERECTION AND DISCHARGE INCREASE IN CAPACITY, TO A DRAMATISATION OF THE PRACTICE.

FOR THIS RELATIONSHIP WRITING/MASTURBATION THERE ARE TWO MAIN SETTINGS: ONE IS THE COLLEGE I NOW ATTENDED, TERM TIME, THE OTHER HOME, HOLIDAYS. THE FIRST SETTING IS DIVIDED INTO TWO: CLASSROOM AND DORMITORY.

—CLASSROOM: I CONTINUE MASTURBATING WITH THE LEFT HAND, THE RIGHT HAND DEVOTED HENCEFORTH TO WRITING—SOMETIMES A "DECENT" TEXT (POEMS) COPIED AFTERWARDS ON TO LUXURY SHEETS OF DRAWING PAPER AND PUT TOGETHER IN ALBUMS OR "BOOKS"; AT OTHER TIMES, A CONVULSIVE SERIES OF ORGIASTIC NOTES KNOWN AS ORGIASTIC WRITINGS, WRITTEN, SCRIBBLED ON PIECES OF RULED PAPER TORN FROM EXERCISE BOOKS, WHERE NEIGHBOURING BODIES, WITH THEIR OWN NAMES, PHYSICAL PECULIARITIES, CLOTHING, ETC., BECOME THE DRAMATIS PERSONAE OF THE ACT—BOYS WITH WHOM I LOOK AT PORNOGRAPHIC MAGAZINES BROUGHT FROM THEIR HOME TOWNS, A COMMUNAL EXCITEMENT PRODUCING THE HOMOSEXUAL RELATIONSHIP WHICH LINKS US UNCONSCIOUSLY (ALTHOUGH WHERE OTHERS OF MY KIND ARE CONCERNED I WAS THEN, AND STILL AM, CONSCIOUS OF MY SEXUAL SUPERIORITY BECAUSE I CAN WRITE WHAT IS VOCALLY IMMINENT BETWEEN US). NOT INFREQUENTLY IN THESE NOTES A PROCESS EMERGES (VERY PRODUCTIVE SUBCONSCIOUSLY) IN CONTRADICTION WITH THE METHODS OF "DECENT" WRITING, NAMELY: A WRITTEN PHONETISATION OF THE USUAL SPEECH OF ONE OR OTHER OF THE BOYS, BASED ON THEIR SEXUAL BREATHING QUICKENED BY THE SIGHT OF THE PORN PHOTOS. TODAY, I CAN'T SAY AT WHAT POINT ("DECENT" OR ORGIASTIC TEXT?) THE MASTURBATORY ACT BEGAN TO PREDOMINATE, BUT IF I AM PERSUADED THAT NOBODY EVER SAW ME MASTURBATE IN CLASS, IT IS BECAUSE I AM MORE AND MORE CONVINCED THROUGH MY OWN EXPERIENCE AND HEARING OTHERS TALK, THAT MOST OF THOSE ROUND ME WERE DOING THE SAME THING AT THE SAME TIME.

—DORMITORY: HERE, MASTURBATION WITH SUCCESSIVE ORGASMS INDUCED BY LECHEROUS REVERIE, FUNCTIONS AT FIRST ON THE THRESHOLD OF THE SUBCONSCIOUS, ON THE EDGE OF DREAM, WHEREAS LATER, INTO WHAT IS AFTER ALL A VERY ORDINARY SITUATION, IS INTRODUCED AN IMPOR-

TANT MATERIAL ELEMENT: THE MASTURBATORY COSTUME, WHICH, ONCE THE SESSION IS BROUGHT TO AN END BY LACK OF JUICE, MUST BE REMOVED, SPERM AND ALL, FROM BETWEEN THE THIGHS, ITS CLEAN END USED FOR WIPING BALLS AND PENIS IN THE PROCESS. IN OTHER WORDS, THE ACT OF MASTURBATION, ORIGINALLY MERGED WITH SLEEP AND DREAM, IS PROGRESSIVELY DISTINGUISHED BY THE NEED TO DISPOSE OF THE COSTUME AND WIPE THE ORGANS INVOLVED BEFORE GOING TO SLEEP, MARKING IN THIS WAY A MATERIAL BOUNDARY BETWEEN CONSCIOUSNESS AND UNCONSCIOUS-NESS. BECAUSE ALL OPERATIONS HAD TO BE CARRIED OUT AS SILENTLY AS POSSIBLE, I BECAME MORE AND MORE SKILLFUL IN MAKING THEM COINCIDE WITH ONE OF THE PREDICTABLE SOUNDS IN THE DORMITORY—FOR EXAMPLE, THE RUSTLE OF WRIGGLING OUT OF THE COSTUME WITH THE RUSTLE OF THE PRIEST'S CASSOCK AGAINST THE CURTAIN DURING ONE OF HIS ROUNDS OF INSPECTION (SINCE MY SESSION ALWAYS TOOK PLACE BEFORE HE RETIRED TO HIS ALCOVE FOR THE NIGHT)—OR WITH UNPREDICTABLE SOUNDS (OUTSIDE, A SUCCESSION OF DOGS BARKING, OR A SUDDEN SHOWER) WHICH SERVED AS DAMPER OR MUFFLER FOR MY BREATHING, AND DIVERTED ATTENTION FROM THE HEAVING OF SHEET AND BLANKET. ONCE THE COSTUME REMOVED, A HAND DRAWING IT UP ALONG THE BODY WEIGHTED WITH WARMTH AND THE LATEST ODORS, IT WAS SLID UNDER THE MATTRESS. AS I SUFFERED FROM SOMNAMBULISM AT THE TIME, I WAS AFRAID OF FALLING ASLEEP BEFORE HIDING IT, OR WALKING IN MY SLEEP BRANDISHING IT. THIS FEAR, TOO VAGUE TO RECALL, NEVER PREVENTED THE DAILY SESSION. SHOULD THIS BE SEEN AS AN EARLY MARK OF CONFIDENCE IN MY UNCONSCIOUS BODY, IN THE POWER OF CONTROL (NOT OF SELF-EFFACEMENT AT THAT PARTICULAR EPOCH) OF OR GUILT FEELINGS, INEVITABLE IN THE ATMOSPHERE OF CULTURAL VISCERALITY PRODUCED BY THE PRACTICE? UNLESS, THE PROFOUND PROSTITU-TIONAL DRIVE TO WHICH I WAS PREY AT THE TIME, PREVENTED MY SLEEPING BODY FROM MAKING A BAWDY STROLL BETWEEN BEDS AND BODIES.

THE SECOND SETTING ALSO COMPRISES TWO DECORS: BEDROOM AND "NATURE".

THESE TWO HOMELY AND HOLIDAY SETTING ALLOW MORE FREEDOM FOR ELABORATE DRAMATISATION. IT IS AT THIS POINT THEN, THAT WE SHOULD DESCRIBE THE MASTURBATORY COSTUME, FOR IT WAS AT HOME, NOT AT COLLEGE THAT I MADE IT; IN MY BEDROOM AND USUALLY AT NIGHT, SINCE A CHILD'S ROOM IS OPEN BY DAY TO ITS MOTHER, A

LITTLE LESS AT NIGHT (MY ROOM UNDER THE EAVES AT SOME DISTANCE FROM THE PARENTAL BED-ROOM, WAS RELATIVELY PRIVILEGED, AND I COULD, BY LEAVING THE DOORS ON THE ATTIC AND STAIRCASE OPEN, FORESTALL ANY IMPORTUNATE VISITS FROM MY FATHER IF CALLED ON AN URGENT VISIT DURING THE NIGHT). THE COSTUME WENT THROUGH VARIOUS STAGES, EVOLVED OR DE-TERIORATED ACCORDING TO TIME AND PLACE. ORIGINALLY IT WAS MADE UP OF TWO ELEMENTS: A KIND OF JOCK-STRAP FASHIONED FROM RAGS, AND A CLOTH LAID UNDER THE CENTRE OF OPERATIONS (OBVIOUSLY AT COLLEGE IT SERVED TO PROTECT THE SHEET FROM STAINS, BUT IN MY BEDROOM IT WAS OFTEN SUPERFLUOUS AS THE SESSION OFTEN TOOK PLACE NAKED AND IN THE RAW ON THE TILES OF THE BEDROOM FLOOR.

—THE JOCK-STRAP: A METICULOUS SEARCH IN CUPBOARDS, LUMBER-ROOM, ETC. FOR THE MATERIAL, THE CHOICE DETERMINED BY THE POSSIBILITY OF SOMEONE DISCOVERING A PIECE MISSING OR TORN FROM A LENGTH OF MATERIAL, AND ALSO BECAUSE OF ITS LECHEROUS EFFECT ON THE BODY: NEVER FOR ITS AESTHETIC EFFECTS, BECAUSE OF ITS SOFTNESS, FOR EXAMPLE, BUT IN FUNCTION OF ITS SOCIAL REFERENCE (CHOICE OF A PROLETARIAN CLOTH AT A TIME, 1955, WHEN IT SEEMS TO ME THERE WAS STILL A CONSIDERABLE DIFFERENCE BETWEEN, LET US SAY, MY MOTHER AND HER MAID IN THE WAY THEY DRESSED): THIS SHOULD BE SEEN AS A DRAMATIC DESIRE OF MY EFFACEMENT AS THE BOURGEOIS BODY; KNEADING BY BOURGEOIS HAND OF BOURGEOIS SEX THROUGH PROLETARIAN TISSUE, MASTURBATION AND EJACULATION PRODUCING A BLENDING OF ONE AND THE OTHER MEMBER WITH THE DYE AND WORN AND FADING FIBRE IN A SERIES OF INCREASINGLY VIOLENT ORGASMS. CHOICE DETERMINED ALSO BY A CLOTH CAPABLE OF A CRADLING OR LECHEROUS CURBING OF THE PARTS (RUSTIC WITHOUT RIGIDITY, GENTLE IN ITS THREADBARE GIVE, ACCORDING TO WHETHER I WAS IN THE MOOD TO BE PIMP OR BAWD— AND OFTEN IN THE COURSE OF A SESSION A CHANGE OF COSTUME TOOK PLACE BETWEEN TWO ORGASMS, SO THAT I SWITCHED FROM BAWD TO PIMP, ACCOMPANIED OBVIOUSLY BY A SIMUL-TANEOUS CHANGE IN ORGIASTIC TEXT: WITH PIMP'S COSTUME PIMP'S TALK OR VICE VERSA, WITH BAWD'S COSTUME BAWDY TALK OR VICE VERSA—, OR ELSE, IF UNDECIDED AS TO SOCIAL POSTURE, BOTH COSTUMES ONE ON TOP OF THE OTHER, BUT NEVER TO THE POINT WHERE HAND, PALM AND FINGERS CEASE TO FEEL THE EXACT OUTLINE OF MY SEX; AT WHICH POINT THE TEXT TURNS INTO A GENERAL

APOSTROPHISING OF MY BODY). USUALLY I MADE THE COSTUMES SITTING NAKED ON THE EDGE OF MY BED: I CUT THE CLOTH BY GUESS-WORK, NOT BOTHERING WITH A HEM AS THE ROUGH EDGES MADE IT LOOK MORE REMINISCENT OF A BAWDY HOUSE. AROUND THE SIDES I POKED HOLES THROUGH WHICH I THREADED COARSE PACKING STRING, AND THERE, ON THE NARROW MEDIAN OF CLOTH THUS PREPARED, I SAT WITH A HARD ON, FORCING IT DOWN SO THE CLOTH COULD BE LACED ROUND MY LOINS: THE SOUND OF THE HOLES TEARING UNDER THE STRAIN OF THE LACES DURING MASTURBATION COULD, BY REFERENCE TO THE BORDEL AND THE THREAT OF THE COSTUME'S DESTRUCTION, PRECIPITATE ORGASM EVEN AT THE EXPENSE OF A TEXT RICH IN LECHEROUS PROMISE. THE SIZE OF THE COSTUME VARIES ALSO, ACCORDING TO THE CAPACITY OF ERECTION AT A GIVEN PERIOD: THE PERIOD OF ADOLESCENCE WHEN I HAD MY BIGGEST ERECTIONS CORRESPONDS WITH A COSTUME REDUCED TO ITS MINIMUM, A MICROSCOPIC SCRAP OF CLOTH OVER THE FRONT ONLY, LACED AROUND THE LOINS AND DOWN THE CLEFT OF THE ARSE, A KIND OF SCREEN WHERE THE JET, SPURTING FROM THE RIGID VOID, ROD BENT TO THE STRAINING CLOTH, STRIKES THE STUFF DECORATED WITH ITS FORMER SPERM. HERE, IT SHOULD BE REMARKED THAT THE PART WHICH ATTRACTS ME MOST IN THE MALE BODY, THE BUTTOCKS, RECEIVED, SO FAR AS THAT PART OF MY OWN BODY WAS CONCERNED, NO SPECIAL DRAMATISATION DURING THESE SESSIONS.

—THE CLOTH: NOTHING TO SAY ABOUT THIS EXCEPT TO NOTE THAT THE DOMINATING COLOR WAS RED, TEXTURE SPONGY. I TOOK TO COLLEGE WITH ME THE MOST ELEMENTARY MATERIALS (THAT IS TO SAY, THE LIGHTEST OF COSTUMES AND THOSE THAT LEAST RESEMBLED FACTORY-MADE UNDERPANTS, MY IDEA BEING THAT IN CASE OF A SEARCH THEY MIGHT AT FIRST GLANCE BE MISTAKEN FOR A BANDAGE.

—NATURE: DURING THE DAY WHEN MY BEDROOM'S LACK OF SECURITY PREVENTED ME FROM SATISFYING A DESIRE ACCENTUATED BY THE SUDDEN RESOLUTION OF A PROBLEM OF WRITING WHICH HAD BEEN TROUBLING ME FOR SOME TIME (ATTEMPTS AT A NEW SYNTAX), OR THE TRANSCRIPTION OF A SOCIO-BORDELLO INTUITION; OR AGAIN, BY A SUDDEN PANIC BEFORE THE INSOLUBILITY OF MY SOCIAL CONTRADICTIONS AND THE IRREDUCTIBLE INCAPACITY OF THOSE CLOSE TO ME TO HELP ME UNDERSTAND THEM EXCEPT BY TREATING THEM WITH STRICTLY EMOTIONAL RESPECT, I DON, UNDER

THE OFFICIAL UNDERPANTS, A CLANDESTINE COSTUME, DELIBERATELY ALLOWING THE MOIST SEXUAL MASS TO "NORMALISE" IT, WARM ITS STRANGENESS, SO TO SPEAK, REWORKING THE SUBSTANCE NEUTRALISED DURING TWENTY-FOUR HOURS OF ABANDON BY LETTING THE SAPS SOFTEN AND REANIMATE THE DRY SPERM STUCK TO THE CLOTH, THEN TAKING MY BIKE, I SET OUT FOR THE HIGHEST POSSIBLE POINTS IN THE MOUNTAINS WHICH I KNOW ARE RARELY FREQUENTED. THERE, TAKING THE CURRENT NOTES OUT OF MY CLAMMY POCKET AND RESTING THEM ON ONE OF THE SATCHELS FROM THE BIKE, UNDOING MY FLY AND WRIGGLING MY HIPS SO THE SHORTS SLIP DOWN MY LEGS OF THEIR OWN ACCORD, I DENUDE, SO TO SPEAK, THE CLANDESTINE COSTUME BY PULLING THE OFFICIAL UNDERPANTS ASIDE, MY FIST SEEKING THE SEMINAL HALO DISPERSED BY THE SEXUAL MASS DURING ITS RIDE ON THE BIKE'S SADDLE, THEN STRETCH OUT, BARE-ARSED, ON GROUND SELECTED FOR ITS GENERAL HUMIDITY, NAPE OF MY NECK AGAINST A TREE TRUNK: A FIR TO BEGIN WITH, SYMBOL FOR ME AT THAT MOMENT OF A ROMANTIC, WESTERN AUSTERITY WHICH, IN SPITE OF THE FASCINATION OF MYTH, MADE ME REJECT GREEK HISTORY, TRAGEDY, AND EVERYTHING THAT IN LANDSCAPE AND WRITING APPEARED AS IN THE FULL LIGHT OF DAY—LATER SUBSTITUTED BY A PINE TREE (THE TRUNK BOTH DRYER, WARMER, MORE "OPEN", EXPULSING RESINOUS-SEMEN FROM ITS CREVICES) AND BATHING THE ORGIASTIC BODY MORE "COSMICALLY" IN ITS SPARER SHADE AND STRONGER ODOR: SINCE THEN, THE EFFORTS MADE TO REACH SUCCESSIVE ORGASM REPERCUTING THROUGH VERTEBRAE, MUSCLES, NERVES, THROUGH THE NAPE OF THE NECK PUSHING ON CERVICAL VERTEBRAE, HANG OVER ALL MY WRITING.

IN THE NOTES I REFERRED TO EARLIER (NUMBERED ACCORDING TO A HABIT I STILL RETAIN AND WHICH CAN LEAD TO A WHOLE DAY'S SEARCH FOR AN IDEA TO BE TRACED THROUGH THE SUCCESSION OF "IDEAS" NUMBERED AND MENTALLY NOTED THE NIGHT BEFORE) THUS PUTTING A STOP—NOT SO MUCH TO THE WORK OF WRITING (WHICH FUNCTIONS WITH EVEN GREATER INTENSITY DURING THIS SCIENTIFIC SEARCH FOR THE LOST "IDEA" AND ITS PLACE, ALSO LOST, IN THEN MENTAL FLUX)—BUT TO MY "ADHERANCE" TO THE AMBIENT REALITY, EMOTIONAL, POLITICAL, SEXUAL, SO THAT WHAT EMERGES IN THE NOTES ARE WHAT MIGHT BE TERMED RESOLUTIONS BECAUSE OF THEIR FORMULATION:

"TONIGHT, ORGY" / "TOMORROW NIGHT, USE THE PLASTER COSTUME" / "TIGHTEN THE COSTUME" / "LET THE SPERM RUN DOWN MY LEGS" / "TREAD IT IN ON THE TILES" / "EAT THE SPERM" / NEXT MORNING, EXAMINE IT THROUGH A MAGNIFYING GLASS" / "THIS SUMMER, SMEAR SPERM ON MY MOUTH" / "TONIGHT, TIE THE COSTUME ROUND MY NECK" / ETC., THESE RESOLUTIONS ALTERNATING WITH OTHERS ABOUT MY WRITING, FICTITIOUS LISTS OF RECORDS TO BUY, OR SOME MECHANICAL PROBLEM (REPAIRS TO THE BIKE, INVENTION AND FABRICATION OF IMAGINARY MACHINES, ETC.). PERHAPS THIS SYSTEM OF RESOLUTIONS CAN BE SEEN AS THE BEGINNINGS OF A DRAMATISATION THEN TAKING TEXTUAL, SOCIAL AND POLITICAL FORM; IT ALSO, I THINK, PROVIDED A SOLID CORPOREAL BASIS FOR MY WRITING, STILL SO FRAIL AND UNRECOGNISED. FINALLY, IT SHOULD BE SAID THAT THESE RESOLUTIONS CALLED FORTH AND PREPARED THE LONGEST POSSIBLE SCENARIO; NOW, THE FIRST ORGASM DESTROYED THE IMAGINARY EDIFICE (THOSE THAT FOLLOWED IMMEDIATELY SERVED TO PROLONG THE TEXT AS FAR AS POSSIBLE AND AT THE SAME TIME EFFACE, IF POSSIBLE, BY MUSCULAR FATIGUE, BOTH THE "DESPAIR" OF THE DISGUISE AND THE POST ORGIASTIC RELAPSE INTO A SAVING MYSTICISM), AND OF THIS EXALTED RESOLUTION NOTHING SUBSISTED IN MY EYES EXCEPT A LUDICROUSLY TRUNCATED SCENARIO: BUT ON REFLECTION, WHAT MORE BRUTALLY EXCITING SPECTACLE COULD THERE BE THAN A CHILD MASTURBATING IN COSTUME WITH HIS LEFT HAND, AND WRITING WITH THE OTHER?

MY DISARRAY AT THAT TIME STEMMED FROM THE CONTRADICTORY DRIVES TO BE BOTH SEEN AND SEE-ER ("SEER"), PIMP AND BAWD, BUYER AND BOUGHT, FUCKER AND FUCKED, AND THESE DRIVES WERE PARTLY REFLECTED IN THE APPARATUS EMPLOYED DURING THE MASTURBATORY SESSION: FOR INSTANCE, WHEN MASTURBATING ON THE BED, AGAINST THE BOTTOM BARS OF THE BED-END CLOSEST TO MY HEELS, WAS PROPPED A PIECE OF FAMILY MIRROR (ONCE PART OF THE BEDROOM MIRROR WHERE MY PARENTS COULD CONTEMPLATE THEMSELVES FULL LENGTH), STILL BIG ENOUGH FOR ME TO CONTEMPLATE MYSELF—IN A FORE-SHORTENING REMINISCENT OF MANTEGNA—WHILE MASTURBATING: THIGHS OPEN, LEFT HAND KNEADING THE MASS OF ORGANS, CLOTH AND STRING, BELLY AND LUNGS WORKING LIKE BELLOWS, HEAD SWEATING, EYES STARING TILL ECLIPSED BY THE ORGASM, AND THE RIGHT HAND WRITING, WRITING, WRITING UNTIL THE SWEAT OF HEEL AND TOES MISTS UP THE MIRROR. LATER, A TAPE RECORDER IS ADDED TO THIS VISUAL DISPOSITION, MACHINE AND MICROPHONE SET UP BETWEEN THE KNEES TO TAPE THE MASTURBATORY SESSION, CONCENTRATING ON SOUNDS PRODUCED RIGHT IN FRONT OF THE MICROPHONE, NAMELY THE SPLASH OF SPERM AS IT HIT THE COSTUME, A RECORDING USED AFTERWARDS NOT ONLY AS ADDITIONAL STIMULANT, BUT TO PUNCTUATE THE MUSIC OF MASTURBATION.

THE SESSION TAKES PLACE BEHIND CLOSED WINDOWS, NEUTRALISING DIURNAL AND NOCTUR-NAL SOUNDS FROM THE VILLAGE, THE TOWN, OR BACKGROUND NOISES, SO THAT THE MUSIC, VOCALISING ON THE ORGIASTIC SCORE, SO TO SPEAK, MAY RETURN TO THE BODY FROM WHICH IT COMES. ONLY LATER AND ON RARE OCCASIONS, WAS COMMERCIAL MUSIC USED (GENRE POP SINGER AND ANGLO-SAXON POP, ETC., THE VOICES HIGHLY CHARGED SEXUALLY) TO WHIP UP FLAGGING ORGIASTIC ENERGIES. IN WINTER, THE NEED IS SO GREAT THAT EVEN THE AWFUL COLD DOES NOT PREVENT ME FROM MASTURBATING NUDE, EVEN LYING NAKED, TENDONS TAUT AGAINST THE TILES, AND FOR QUARTER OF AN HOUR AFTERWARDS IN A POST-ORGIASTIC STUPOR, WITH ORGANS, MUSCLES, NERVES FROZEN STIFF IN THEIR RELAXATION, LIKE A FROSTY ECHO OF THE ORGIASTIC CIRCUIT.

DURING THOSE SAME WINTER HOLIDAYS, THANKS TO MY "PLUS-FOURS" AND ON DAYS OF EXTREME "SOLITUDE," I COULD PUT ON ONE OF MY CLAN-DESTINE COSTUMES, WEARING IT TILL EVENING WHEN I HAD DECIDED TO MASTURBATE: TO WALK ROUND THUS GIRDED IN THE FAMILY CIRCLE, OR AMONG MY FELLOWS AT COLLEGE, GAVE ME AN ALMOST PERFECT SATISFACTION, PARTICULARLY IF TO THE COSTUME UNDER THE OFFICIAL UNDER-PANTS, TIGHT ROUND ORGANS, LOINS, BUTTOCKS, CIRCUMSCRIBING MY VIRILE ATTRIBUTES, SO TO SPEAK, WERE STUCK SCRAPS OF THE ORGIASTIC NOTES. AT THE END OF EACH MASTURBATORY SESSION, THESE SCRIBBLED NOTES WERE, ONCE THE RELATIVE PARTS HAD BEEN WIPED, ROLLED UP WITH THE COSTUME IN THE CLOTH AND HIDDEN, ALWAYS IN A DIFFERENT CRANNY OF THE ATTIC WHERE, DURING THE DAY AND NIGHT PRECEDING THE NEXT ORGASM, I COULD COUNT ON THEM ACQUIRING A LAYER OF THE DAMP AND DUST TYPICAL OF SUCH PLACES. IT SOMETIMES HAP-PENED THAT, FORAGING THROUGH HEAPS OF RAGS AND PILES OF BROKEN FURNITURE WITHOUT HAVING GIVEN ME FAIR WARNING, THIS MASTURBATORY ROLL FELL INTO MY MOTHER'S HANDS, WHO, IN ALL INNOCENCE, PUTS IT SOMEWHERE WHICH TAKES

FINDING: FOR EXAMPLE, HAVING FINALLY TRACKED THE ROLL TO MY FATHER'S GARAGE UNDER THE HOUSE, I GOT INTO THE HABIT OF TAKING IT DOWN THERE AFTER THE NIGHTLY MASTURBATION, BRINGING IT UP NEXT DAY COVERED IN GREASE, GIRDING IT ON LIKE A MECHANIC'S APPRENTICE OR ADOLESCENT PROSTITUTE, PROMISING MYSELF TO EXAMINE IT AFTER MASTURBATION FOR TRACES OF A MIXTURE OF SPERM AND GREASE.

INITIALLY, ORGASM IS FOLLOWED BY A RELAPSE INTO MYSTICAL AND LITURGICAL PHANTASIES. THIS SWITCH, AT THE VERY MOMENT OF ORGASM, FROM A MENTALITY AND A BODY STRETCHED TO THE LIMITS OF PROSTITUTIONAL DESIRE TO A MENTALITY AND A BODY SLIPPING BACK INTO THE VISUAL, TACTILE, AUDITORY AND OLFACTORY SENSATIONS OF A SOCIETY LITURGICALLY IMMACULATE, A PROCESS SO IMPERCEPTIBLE IN ITS SWITCH OF ENERGY, OF FORCES, CROWDS, AND RITUALS, THAT IT HAS ALWAYS CONVINCED ME, NOT ONLY OF THE ENERGY OF MY DRIVES, BUT ALSO OF THE DRIVE BEHIND ALL HUMAN AND MATERIAL ACTIVITY. IT IS THIS CONVICTION THAT, ONCE THE COSTUME AND NOTES ROLLED UP, RESTORES ME TO EQUILIBRIUM. BUT EVEN BEFORE THAT, BETWEEN THE FIRST ORGASM AND THE ROLLING UP OF THE CLOTH, CLEAR-HEADED MOMENTS INTERVENE: AFTER THE TRANSPORT OF THE FIRST ORGASM, BECAUSE OF THE SWITCH IN MY THOUGHT PROCESS, THE COSTUME STILL GIRDING ME SEEMS LIKE A HORRIFYING DERELICTION BY COMPARISON WITH THE IMMACULATE LINENS OF LITURGY (LIT-ORGY); THEN, AT A LATER DATE, THE COSTUME STUCK TO MY FLANKS WITH SEMEN FEELS LIKE THE PESTILENTIAL CAST-OFF OF A DECADENT WEST AS OPPOSED TO LINEN AND OBJECTS RESTORED TO PRISTINE WHITENESS AFTER EACH BOMB, EACH SPLASH OF MUD OR BLOOD BY A REVOLUTIONARY VIET NAM, AS REVEALED IN FILMS BY JORIS IVENS AND OTHERS.

DURING EACH SESSION, AS THERE ARE SEVERAL EJACULATIONS, SEVEN AT MOST, THE INTERVAL BETWEEN THE FIRST ONE AND THE ROLLING OF THE COSTUME IN THE CLOTH IS EMPLOYED AS FOLLOWS: FROM ONE EJACULATION TO THE NEXT I OSCILLATE BETWEEN TRIUMPHAL LOIN-CLOTH AND ABJECT CAST-OFF SO LONG AS THE WHOLE IS NOT NEUTRALISED. WITH THE RESULT, THAT IN EITHER DIRECTION (MYSTIC OR POLITICAL) MASTURBATION EXCRETES DESIRE AND ITS ANTIDOTE SIMULTANEOUSLY: THE "HYGENIC" REFLEX (WIPING AND ROLLING UP) FRUSTRATING WHAT, FOR OBVIOUS SOCIAL REASONS, IT CANCELS OUT, NAMELY: THE WEARING OF THE SEMEN-SOAKED COSTUME AT ALL TIMES, IN SUN AND WIND, IN RAIN, IN COLD AND HEAT, IN A CROWD, RUNNING, SLEEPING, IN CONTACT WITH OTHER PROSTITUTIONAL BODIES, IN THE STREET, IN SHOPPING CENTRES, ETC.—WHICH, SEEN IN RETROSPECT, MAY APPEAR AS THE OUTWARD MANIFESTATION OF A CONTROL I HOPE IS LASTING, EXTENDING FURTHER AND FURTHER, AND MORE AND MORE DIALECTICALLY OVER ALL MY DRIVES.

ALL THE ORGIASTIC NOTES OF MY ADOLESCENCE HAVE BEEN LOST, TORN UP INTO MINUTE SCRAPS SO THAT NO ONE COULD RECOGNISE THE BAWDY TERMS I WAS ALREADY USING; OR THROWN AS THEY WERE DOWN THE WC AT THAT PRECISE MOMENT WHEN I KNEW AND DID NOT KNOW IF DESIRE WOULD RETURN. I HAVE A MEMORY OF SHORT FRAGMENTS WHERE NARRATIVE AND SPEECH ALTERNATE, SOMETIMES VERSE, AS I WAS WRITING MAINLY POETRY AT THE TIME. IN AN EPHEMERAL AND SUMMARY FASHION, THEY DRAMATISED, UNDER THEIR OWN NAMES AND APPEARANCE, CERTAIN OF MY SCHOOL FRIENDS, OR PEOPLE I HAD CAUGHT SIGHT OF IN THE SLUMS OF THE INDUSTRIAL TOWN WHERE THE COLLEGE FLAUNTED ITS MACMAHONIEN ARCHITECTURE—FUGITIVE BUT OBSESSIVE VISIONS—LIKE THAT OF A BOY, GLIMPSED ONE SUMMER EVENING RETURNING FROM A PILGRIMAGE ON FOOT TO SOME "GROTESQUE" CAVERN OF A MIRACULOUS VIRGIN, THE BITTER TASTE OF A DRINK DISTRIBUTED BY THE GUARDIAN NUNS STILL IN OUR MOUTHS . . . TORSO BARE, WEARING A PAIR OF TIGHT BLUE LINEN SHORTS SOAKED WITH SWEAT BETWEEN THE THIGHS, SEATED IN FRONT OF A HOUSE INHABITED BY SLAV WORKERS, HIS LEGS SO WIDE APART I COULD SEE THE WHITE EDGE OF UNDERPANTS THAT MOULDED A PRECOCIOUSLY DEVELOPED VIRILITY, HEAD THROWN BACK, THROAT PULSING, BLACK CURLS STUCK TO HIS BROW WITH WHAT I IMAGINED WAS SPERM, OR FLUID BELONGING TO A WOMAN IN A FULL DRESS AND WHITE KERCHIEF LEANING, LAUGHING, OVER THE BALLUSTRADE OF A ROUGH WOODEN BALCONY ABOVE HIM—A MAN SUDDENLY LOOMING UP BEHIND THE BOY FROM A DARK PASSAGEWAY, BROOM IN ONE HAND, KNIFE IN THE OTHER, IN PURSUIT OF A RAT—RAT JUMPING OVER THE BOY'S BARE NECK, SPLASHING HIM WITH ITS BLOOD, VEERING BACK TO THE WALL, SQUEALING, TRYING TO SCALE THE COAL-BLACKENED STONES—AND SUDDENLY, THE SHOWER THAT HAS BEEN THREATENING, BREAKS OVER THIS SUBURB HANGING ALONG A SCHIST OF ROCK, WHERE FAMILIES LIVING IN CELLARS AND AT GROUND LEVEL HAVE TO CLEAN UP THE SHIT THEMSELVES, THAT POURS FROM BURST SEWERS INTO THEIR ONE AND ONLY LIVING ROOM.

AMONG OTHER REAL OR IMAGINARY BODIES, WOMEN, VERY SEXY OF BUM OR BREAST, ALREADY LOOKED ON AS "SERVANTS OF THE MALE BODY," WEARERS OF MASCULINE ATTIRE REMOVED FOR "INTERCOURSE" (MORE FAMILIAR TO ME AT THAT MOMENT AS AN ENSEMBLE OF SOCIAL POSTURES THAN AN ACT OF PENETRATION), PUSHERS OF ORGIASTIC BODIES, MENDERS OF PROSTITUTIONAL GARMENTS TORN DURING "INTERCOURSE." THE FREQUENCY OF THIS SEXUAL CHOICE SHOULD BE SET AGAINST ANOTHER VERY DEFINITE TENDENCY OF MY FIFTEENTH OR SIXTEENTH YEAR: AS I REMEMBER IT, THREE QUARTERS OF MY WAKING THOUGHTS ARE BUSY PLOTTING "HOMOSEXUAL" SCENARIOS, WHILE SLEEP AND DREAM AFFORD ME ONLY CONFRONTATIONS, IN THE NUDE, WITH THE BODIES OF VERY REAL AND BAWDY WOMEN. QUITE EARLY IN THE PIECE, BOTH MALE AND FEMALE SCENARIOS TAKE A TURN TOWARD SLAVERY IN ANTIQUITY (THE LATINISED OR GRECIAN NAMES OF BODIES CONSTITUTING BY THEIR SOLE ENUMERATION ALL THE TEXT REQUIRED TO STIMULATE DESIRE); THEN THE THEME CHANGES TO PROSTITUTION AS I LEARN FROM RADIO HOW SEXUALLY CHARGED CERTAIN OBVIOUSLY MODERN NAMES CAN BE, THEIR HACKNEYED, COMMON SOUND EVOKING A PROSTITUTIONAL "SOAP OPERA." (DURING MY TRIPS TO NORTH AFRICA I DISCOVERED THAT MANY ARAB SERVANTS, SHOP ASSISTANTS AND APPRENTICES CALL THEMSELVES "CHARLEY," "JACKY," "EDDIE," "FRANKIE," ETC.) THE ONLY OFFICIAL FRENCH NAMES THAT FIGURE AMONG THESE ANGLO-SAXON BORROWINGS ARE OF SLAV ORIGIN (SERGE). I HAVE ALWAYS CONSIDERED THAT THE NAMES INTEGRAL TO THE FRENCH LANGUAGE CARRY WITH THEM THE DESUET ATMOSPHERE OF A WESTERN CIVILISATION WHICH, AT THAT TIME, WAS TRYING TO IMPOSE ON ME THE MOST INSIPID AND SUPERFICIAL OF ITS PRODUCTIONS.

THE IRREGULAR ALTERNATION NARRATIVE/SPEECH SHOULD ALSO BE SEEN IN RELATION WITH THE POSITIONING OF ORGANS AND COSTUME, OR WITH THE DEGREE OF THE MEMBER'S ERECTION. FOR EXAMPLE: PRONOUNCED ERECTION ACCELERATES ORGASMIC URGENCY, WHICH MEANS THE TEXT HAS TO BE WRITTEN IN HASTE; THIS HASTE ONLY ALLOWS FOR WORDS TO BE PUT ON PAPER, OR FRAGMENTS OF WORDS, INTERJECTIONS WITHOUT SYNTACTIC LINKS—ONLY SPEECH, THEREFORE; BUT GRADUALLY, AS I GOT MY "TONGUE" INTO THE WRITING OF FRENCH, SO TO SPEAK, FAMILIARITY AND EASE IN HANDLING ITS RHETORIC GAVE MY HAND THE SPEED NECESSARY, IN CASE OF A PRONOUNCED ERECTION, TO WRITE A NARRATIVE SEQUENCE. I PLAYED

ON THIS EXCHANGE: HAVING WEDGED THE ERECT MEMBER INTO THE COSTUME BY IMPRESSING ON IT A PROPULSION THAT REMINDED ME OF A COG-WHEEL OR A SCREW, I ABANDONED IT, DIRECTING MY THOUGHTS TOWARD NON-SEXUAL ZONES, MY EYES ON A PAGE OF EUROPEAN HISTORY IN A BOOK I KEPT BESIDE THE BED, OR BETTER STILL, A PAGE OF PHILOSOPHY OR HISTORY OF PHILOSOPHY, ALLOWING THE MEMBER TO SUBSIDE, AND WRITING AS MUCH TEXT AS POSSIBLE BEFORE IT ROSE AGAIN. THIS I COULD DO SEVERAL TIMES, UNTIL THE MOMENT CAME WHEN THE MEMBER, OVER-STIMULATED BY REPEATED MANIPULATION, ERECTION/DEJECTION/RE-ERECTION, DISCHARGED ITS JET BEFORE I COULD SUMMON UP ALL THE MENTAL AND CORPOREAL TENSIONS THAT USUALLY PRESIDED AT THE MOMENT OF ORGASM. ON THE OTHER HAND, THE STRICTURE OR LAXITY OF THE COSTUME MOULDING THE TEXT MADE IT EITHER TOUGH OR TENDER, EVEN COMIC. IF I LET THE COSTUME HANG LOOSE ON MY LOINS, THE MANIPULATON OF THE PENIS INSIDE THE UNINHIBITED CLOTH PRODUCED A RELAXED TEXT, SPEECH AND NARRATIVE WRITTEN WITHOUT THOUGHT OF THE PROSTITUTIONAL SITUATION; WHEREAS THE TIGHT LACING OF THE CLOTH ON THE MEMBER, ITS ERECTION SCREWED DOWN, OR FORCED TO THE BACK OF THE BALLS, INDUCED A TEXT OF NARRATIVE AND SPEECH IN WHICH THE HARD ECONOMIC FACTS OF PROSTITUTION (SALE, HIRE, PRICE OF BODIES, COST OF MANIPULATING THESE BODIES, ACCOUNTANCY OF THE NUMBER OF TIMES, ETC.) FOUND THEIR EXPRESSION IN THE HANDWRITING ITSELF, CRAMPED AND MORE DELIBERATELY VERTICAL.

THIS ALTERNANCE, MULTIPLIED LATER BY THE NUMBER OF PLACES (HOTELS, ETC.) IN WHICH I MASTURBATED, LED TO A REPETITION WITH VARIATIONS OF PRECEDING SEQUENCES INSCRIBED ON THE MASS OF NOTES WHICH I COULD NOT TRANSPORT, PRODUCING A TEXT WHERE TYPING NECESSARILY OPERATED A CHOICE OF INTRODUCED AN ORDER: THE MANUSCRIPT (1962-1969) BEARS GRAPHIC WITNESS NOT ONLY TO THE DETAIL AND CHRONOLOGICAL CURVE OF THIS PROCESS OF INTERACTION, BUT ALSO IN ITS WRITING, OF A PROGRESSIVE CONVERGENCE BETWEEN THE "DECENT" (THAT IS TO SAY THE PUBLISHABLE OR PUBLISHED) TEXT WITH THE GREAT SEXUAL SWELL. FROM THE MEETING OF THESE CONTRADICTORY CURRENTS, "DECENT" TEXT/INDECENT MASTURBATORY, RESULTS THE ABUNDANCE, IN THIS MANUSCRIPT, OF VARIATIONS, REPETITIONS, OVERLAPPING OF SEQUENCES, NOMINAL CONFUSIONS, ETC. DURING THIS PERIOD WHICH I

REMEMBER BEST, FROM ONE NIGHT TO ANOTHER, FROM AFTERNOON TO EVENING (AT CERTAIN TIMES THE RESURGENCE OF DESIRE ACCELERATES, HENCE THE EXALTATION OF CERTAIN TEXTS, NO DOUBT) I HAVE TO INTERRUPT WHAT THREATENS TO BECOME A PHYSIOLOGIC DANGER—PULMONARY, CARDIAC, RENAL—AND BRING MY BODY BACK TO WHAT I BELIEVE IS A CRUDER, MORE COMMON REALITY: DESIRE AND ITS RESOLUTION IN THE ORGASM; THE STYLE CHANGES, A FRAGMENT OF RHETORIC CHOSEN FOR ITS QUASI-BANALITY TO FIT THE "DECENT" TEXT SUCCEEDED BY A FRAGMENT OF SPEECH OR NARRATIVE TEXTUALLY COMPLEX AND ELLIPTIC IN ITS JARGON. IT SHOULD BE NOTED THAT THE TEXTUAL AND MASTURBATORY SESSION, ABOVE ALL ONE THAT PRODUCES WRITING-JARGON, IS PREPARED "TEXTUALLY" LONG HOURS IN ADVANCE OF THE SESSION: RHYTHMICALS, MODULATIONS, WORDS OF THIS JARGON THEM-SELVES, ARE INVENTED SIMULTANEIOUSLY WITH WORK ON A "DECENT" TEXT, WHICH MAY SUBSE-QUENTLY ENTAIL MAKING CERTAIN CUTS. FINALLY, A NUMBER OF NOTES FROM THIS PERIOD, WHEN I WAS ASSAILED BY THE DIFFICULTIES OF PUBLISH-ING EVEN "DECENT" TEXTS, LET ALONE A LITERARY PUBLICATION OF THE NOTES, ARE UNREADABLE TODAY: STUCK AND UNSTUCK BY SUCCESSIVE ORGASMS, ALL THAT EMERGES THROUGH THE FADED MIXTURE OF INK AND SEMEN, ARE FRAG-MENTS OF SEXUAL WORDS, INSULTS, APOSTROPHIC PUNCTUATION, OR PRICES OF THE SALE AND HIRE OF BODIES, AND NOMINAL APPELLATIONS, PRINCI-PALLY BECAUSE WHEN WRITING NAMES AND NUMBERS I PRESSED HARDEST WITH THE NIB.

PIERRE GUYOTAT

TRANSLATED BY CATHERINE DUNCAN

I STRUGGLED WITH A DEMON IN THE WOODS.
I SAT UPON THE ANCIENT STUMP,
TOUCHING THE CRUMBLED FINGERS THAT HAD
  FELLED THE TREE,
MARVELLING THROUGH THEIR EYES AS IT TOPPLED
  SLOW.

THOSE ECHOS STILL TREMBLED IN THE GRASS,
THOSE FOOTPRINTS STILL FLICKED THROUGH THE
  SUNLIGHT.

THE DEMON SEIZED MY LOINS AND WRESTLED THEM.
THE SUN LAY LIKE A PRESENCE ON MY CHEST.

I WAS NAKED AND ALONE.

I HOWLED LIKE A BEAST UPON THE DEAD SHADOWS
WHERE THE FALLEN TREE HAD LAIN.

AND I SPRINKLED THE GRASSES WITH MY OFFERING
TO ITS SILENCE AND ITS WOODEN CARESS.

THE DEMON LEFT ME AND SLEPT UPON THE
  OFFERING,
GLISTENING THERE LIKE A MUSHROOM AFTER RAIN.

DANIEL SLOATE

ONANISM AND NERVOUS DISORDERS IN TWO LITTLE GIRLS

CASE HISTORY

X... WAS TEN YEARS OLD. OF DELICATE COMPLE-XION, THIN, NERVOUS, EXTREMELY INTELLIGENT, RATHER OLD-FASHIONED IN HER WAYS, SHE ACTED AND TALKED LIKE A GROWN-UP. ALWAYS SMILING, WITH SOMETHING SACCHARINE IN HER EXPRESSION, A HINT OF HYPOCRISY THAT SEEMED OUT OF PLACE IN SOMEONE OF HER AGE. HER KIND AND CONSIDERATE MANNERS MADE EVERYONE LIKE HER. SHE WAS PROUD, VAIN, CAPRICIOUS. IN EVERY GAME SHE HAD TO BE THE LEADER, RESERVING FOR HERSELF THE ROLES OF QUEEN, PRINCESS OR FAIRY, ALWAYS TRYING TO DOMINATE THE OTHER CHILDREN AND FIGHTING TOOTH AND NAIL IF THEY DARED OPPOSE HER. SHE EXERCISED A CONSIDER-ABLE INFLUENCE ON ALL HER COMPANIONS, TYRANNIZING THEM AT TIMES. IN SPITE OF THAT, THEY PUT UP WITH IT BECAUSE OF HER UNFAILING CHARM. SHE WON EVERYBODY'S HEART WITH HER SWEET AND TENDER DISPOSITION. EVEN LITTLE BOYS WERE HER ADMIRING SLAVES! LITTLE X... WAS GOOD AT PRETENDING, AND THE GAME SHE LIKED PLAYING BEST OF ALL WAS GETTING MARRIED. SUCCESSIVELY, SHE MARRIED AND DISMISSED ALL HER LITTLE BOY FRIENDS, INSISTING THEY SHOULD BE HEARTBROKEN TO THE POINT OF TEARS.

JEALOUS, ENVIOUS, VINDICTIVE, QUICK TEMPERED, HER MOOD WOULD CHANGE WITHOUT WARNING. SOMETIMES IN A FIT OF RAGE SHE ROLLED SCREAMING ON THE FLOOR; OR SHE BECAME DEPRESSED FOR NO REASON. AT OTHER TIMES SHE WAS POSSESSED BY A FEVERISH GAIETY, OR ELSE FELL INTO A BROWN STUDY. SHE WAS COQUETTISH AND ATTRACTIVE, ADORED CLOTHES AND DOTED ON PERFUME. ONE FACT THAT SHOULD BE NOTED IS THAT FROM EARLY CHILDHOOD SHE STOLE AND CAREFULLY HID OBJECTS THAT TOOK HER FANCY, EVEN WHEN THEY COULD HAVE BEEN HER'S FOR THE ASKING. THIS TENDENCY TO THEFT HAD BEEN REMARKED WHEN SHE WAS NOT YET FIVE. SHE LOVED TO LEARN ABOUT THINGS AND NEVER STOPPED ASKING QUESTIONS. OF A LIVELY IMAGINATION, SHE LIKED WHAT WAS BEAUTIFUL, BUT DISLIKED PRAYING ON THE CONTRARY, POKED FUN AT THE PIETY OF OTHER CHILDREN AND MADE A FACE WHEN TOLD ABOUT GOD.

EARLY IN 1879, THE CHILD BEGAN TO LOSE WEIGHT IN SPITE OF HER USUAL APPETITE. SHE WAS ANAEMIC AND HIGHLY EXCITABLE. THERE WERE SIGNS OF LEUCORRHOEAIC DISCHARGE FROM THE GENITAL ORGANS, AND ANAL IRRITATION. A LOCAL EXAMINATION REVEALED THE PRESENCE OF ENDO-

PARASITES. CALOMEL SUPPOSITORIES WERE PRESCRIBED AND THE CHILD GIVEN A TREATMENT OF IRON AND BROMIDE OF POTASSIUM. AS A RESULT OF THIS TREATMENT X... SEEMED TO IMPROVE. TOWARD THE MONTH OF JUNE THE SAME YEAR, PETTY LARCENIES OF DESSERT, SWEETS, RIBBONS AND OTHER SMALL OBJECTS ARE CONTINUALLY PERPETRATED BY X... WHO FALLS INTO THE TRAP SET FOR HER.

IN SPITE OF BEING CAUGHT RED HANDED LITTLE X... DENIES HER GUILT WITH BLATANT DEFIANCE; SHE POSES AS OUTRAGED INNOCENCE! SHE PROTESTS! HER FACE CONTORTS WITH RAGE; THE SCENE WAS INDESCRIBABLE. FROM THAT DAY ON A PROGRESSIVE CHANGE TOOK PLACE IN THE CHILD, MORALLY AND PHYSICALLY: SHE SEEMED MORE AND MORE SICKLY. AT THE SAME PERIOD IT WAS NOTICED THAT SHE WAS FOREVER GOING TO THE LAVATORY AND STAYING SO LONG THAT AT TIMES SOMEONE WENT TO LOOK FOR HER; ON ONE OCCASION SHE WAS FOUND ASLEEP THERE. IT WAS ALSO NOTED THAT DURING GAMES X... HAD A SPECIAL LIKING FOR HIDING IN THE SHRUBBERY, OR OFF IN THE WOODS WITH CERTAIN CHILDREN, AS FAR AWAY AS POSSIBLE FROM MAIDS AND GOVERNESSES: A LITTLE ARBOUR WAS HER EXCLUSIVE PROPERTY. SHE TOOK A CHAIR OUT THERE AND REFUSED ACCESS TO ALL EXCEPT CERTAIN FAVOURITES, BOYS AS WELL AS GIRLS. SHE CALLED IT HER "PLEASURE PALACE." SHE OFTEN STAYED THERE FOR A LONG TIME WITH A LITTLE BOY. WHAT WENT ON IN THAT PLEASURE PALACE? SUSPICION WAS NOT YET SUFFICIENTLY AROUSED. AT ALL EVENTS THE CHILDREN PLAYED AT GETTING ENGAGED AND BEING MARRIED. THEY EVEN EXCHANGED RINGS AND PROMISED TO MARRY EACH OTHER WHEN THEY GREW UP.

LATER AN END WAS PUT TO THIS PRECOCIOUS INTIMACY AND SUPERVISION INCREASED.

IN MARCH 1881, X... WAS STRICKEN BY VIOLENT PAINS IN THE LOWER ABDOMEN, WITH TENESMUS AND HAD GREAT DIFFICULTY IN URINATING; IT WAS THEN THAT HAVING ASCERTAINED, DE VISU, A PRONOUNCED IRRITATION OF THE VULVA WITH SWELLING OF THE VARIOUS PARTS, I MADE MY FEARS KNOWN TO THE PARENTS. X... WAS FORCED TO ADMIT THE PRACTICES SHE INDULGED IN, WEPT COPIOUSLY AND PROMISED NOT TO DO IT AGAIN. IN SPITE OF THAT SHE CONTINUED TO LOSE WEIGHT. KINDNESS, ADVICE, ADMONISHMENTS, SUPERVISION, NOTHING HAD ANY EFFECT ON HER. X... CONTINUED HER SELF-ABUSE, AS SHE LATER

ADMITTED. AT THE SAME EPOCH STEALING BECAME A DAILY EVENT. CAPRICIOUS AND QUARRELSOME, HER BAD TEMPER MADE THE CHILD UNBEARABLE. THE GOVERNESS ALSO NOTICED HOW LASCIVIOUS IN HER MOVEMENTS X... WAS BECOMING. AT TIMES X... WOULD EVEN START SCRATCHING HERSELF WITH BOTH HANDS, HER FACE BETRAYING AN EVIDENT PLEASURE. QUITE OPENLY AND AT ANY GIVEN MOMENT THE CONTACTS WOULD BE REPEATED. THE CHILD DEVELOPED A STRANGE WAY OF WALKING: SHE WALKED WITH HER LEGS APART, BENDING HER KNEES AND ROLLING THE HIPS. IT WAS MOST INDECENT BEHAVIOUR. SEATED ON A CHAIR, SHE ADOPTED REVOLTING POSITIONS: SHE SAT ON THE EDGE, OPENED HER LEGS, BENT FORWARD, AND LIKE THIS CONTRACTED SUCCESSIVELY VARIOUS PARTS OF HER BODY IN ORDER TO GIVE HERSELF VOLUPTUOUS SENSATIONS.

AS KINDNESS MADE NO IMPRESSION ON X... WHO GAVE HERSELF UP MORE AND MORE TO VICE, THERE WAS NO HELP FOR IT BUT TO CHANGE TACTICS AND TAKE STERNER MEASURES, EVEN TO BE HARSH AND CRUEL IF NECESSARY.

CORPORAL PUNISHMENT WAS RESORTED TO, PARTICULARLY FLOGGING. X... SUBMITTED WITHOUT PROTEST, BUT ALSO WITHOUT ANY SIGN ON IMPROVEMENT. SHE BECAME ABJECT; HER FEATURES TOOK ON A BESTIAL EXPRESSION, SHE SPREAD HER LEGS, TIGHTENED HER BODY AND PROCURED THE VOLUPTUOUS SPASM. WHEN SCOLDED SHE TREMBLED AND WEPT BITTERLY. SHE WAS TERRIBLY AFRAID OF THE ROD WHICH WAS ADMINISTERED UNSPARINGLY; AND IN SPITE OF THAT SHE ABUSED HERSELF MORE AND MORE IN A THOUSAND WAYS: WITH HER HANDS, HER FEET, WITH ANY KIND OF FOREIGN BODY THAT CAME TO HAND; RUBBING HERSELF ON THE CORNERS OF FURNITURE, ADOPTING CERTAIN POSES AND STIFFENING WITH CONTRACTIONS, ETC. ETC. FURTHER ON I WILL DESCRIBE IN DETAIL ALL THE INGENIOUS METHODS INVENTED DAILY BY HER FERTILE IMAGINATION, AND THE ENERGY SHE EXPENDED IN PERPETRATING WHAT SHE HERSELF CALLED HER HORRORS.

AT THAT POINT IT WAS DECIDED TO ATTACH HER HANDS, THEN HER LEGS AND FEET. REMARKABLY ENOUGH, THE UPPER PART OF HER BODY GREW THINNER AND THINNER, WHILE THE THIGHS, HIPS AND GENITAL ORGANS DEVELOPED. IN FRONT OF THE GOVERNESS, HER PARENTS, SERVANTS, FRIENDS, STRANGERS, SHE TOOK UP LASCIVIOUS POSES AND GAVE WAY TO HER PASSION IN THE MOST INDECENT FASHION. HER BEHAVIOUR EVEN IN

THE STREET ATTRACTED THE ATTENTION OF PASSERS-BY. THUS, NEITHER KINDNESS NOR SEVERITY HAD THE SLIGHTEST EFFECT.

FLOGGING MADE HER SEEM MORONIC, MORE DECEITFUL, MORE PERVERSE, MORE SPITEFUL. THOUGH KEPT UNDER CONSTANT WATCH, SHE STILL MANAGED TO SATISFY HERSELF IN A THOUSAND DIFFERENT WAYS. WHEN SHE DID NOT SUCCEED IN DUPING HER GUARDIANS, SHE FLEW IN TO THE MOST FRIGHTFUL TEMPER. SHE FROTHED AT THE MOUTH, CHANGED COLOUR; SHE WRITHED AND STRUGGLED FURIOUSLY IF ANYONE TRIED TO HOLD HER. AT SUCH MOMENTS SHE SHOUTED AT THE TOP OF HER VOICE, SOBBING: "WHY DO YOU DEPRIVE ME OF SUCH AN INNOCENT PLEASURE?" AND A MOMENT LATER: "IT'S DIRTY, I KNOW, BUT THAT'S MY BUSINESS, LET ME ENJOY MYSELF! IF IT KILLS ME, WHAT DO I CARE? I WANT TO DO IT AND DIE, I WANT TO!"

ONE DAY SHE SAID THE FOLLOWING PRAYER: "DEAR GOD, IF, AS MY SISTER SAYS, YOU ARE ALL-POWERFUL, SHOW ME A WAY TO DO IT WITHOUT SINNING."

AT THIS EPOCH A STRAIT-JACKED WAS EMPLOYED TO PREVENT THE CHILD TOUCHING HERSELF CONTINUOUSLY. BOTH FOREARMS WERE HELD CROSSED ON THE CHEST, HANDS IN PROXIMITY OF THE SHOULDERS: LEGS AND FEET SET WIDE APART AND FIRMLY ATTACHED TO THE IRON BED-STEAD; A BODY-BELT IN THE FORM OF A STRAP FIXED THE TRUNK TO THE MATTRESS BY CORDS KNOTTED TO THE BED. IN SPITE OF ALL THESE PRECAUTIONS X.... BY A VERITABLE TOUR DE FORCE WORTHY OF THE DAVENPORT BROTHERS, MANAGED TO UNTIE EVERYTHING IN ORDER TO SATISFY HER CRAVING. IN THE MORNING THE SEXUAL PARTS BORE OBVIOUS TRACES OF ASSAULT BY A SHARP INSTRUMENT. THE FOLLOWING NIGHT A WATCH WAS KEPT UNDER PRETEXT OF SLEEP, WHICH PROVED THAT SHE SUCCEEDED IN ATTAINING HER OBJECTIVE AFTER SEVERAL HOURS OF EFFORT, CONTORTING HERSELF IN IMITATION OF THE KABYLES, HER BODY FREQUENTLY SHAKEN BY SPASMS. THEN, SUPPORTING HERSELF ON THE CROWN OF HER HEAD, SHE PULLED AT THE JACKET WITH HER TEETH UNTIL SHE SUCCEEDED IN REACHING THE SEXUAL PARTS WITH HER HANDS. DURING THE DAY SHE HAD TAKEN THE PRECAUTION OF HIDING HAIR-PINS IN HER PILLOW, AND THESE SHE PULLED OUT AT NIGHT AND STRAIGHTENED WITH HER TEETH; THUS, BY HOLDING ONE END OF THE EXTENDED PIN IN HER MOUTH, SHE WAS ABLE TO TOUCH HERSELF WITH THE OTHER. THIS WAS THE ANSWER TO THE RIDDLE OF HOW, AS

SO OFTEN HAPPENED, THE HACKET AND STRAP REMAINED IN PLACE, WHILE THE SEXUAL PARTS WERE COVERED IN BLOOD AND MARKED BY SCRATCHES, SOMETIMES EVEN DEEP GASHES.

IN THIS WAY SHE ALMOST ALWAYS MANAGED TO SATISFY HERSELF DURING THE NIGHT. WHEN SHE DIDN'T SHE WHIMPERED, EMITTING RAUCOUS CRIES THAT GREW MORE AND MORE SAVAGE, JERKING HERSELF FURIOUSLY ON THE BED, WORKING HERSELF UP TO SUCH A STATE SHE KNEW NEITHER RESTRAINT NOR SHAME; SHE GROUND HER TEETH, CURSING EVERYONE, SHOUTING AT THE TOP OF HER LUNGS: "I DETEST DADDY, I LOATHE MUMMY, PLEASE GOD MAKE THEM DIE." IN SHORT, SHE WAS PREY TO A FIT OF MADNESS: HER FACE BECAME DEAD WHITE, HER EYE-BALLS ROLLED AND GLARED AS IF THEY WOULD BURST FROM THEIR SOCKETS, DROPS OF SWEAT STOOD ON HER TEMPLES. THESE VIOLENT SCENES, THESE ATTACKS OF FOLLY WERE FOLOWED BY AN IMMEDIATE REACTION, WITH DEMONSTRATIONS OF TENDERNESS AND REPENTANCE. IN SUCH MOMENTS OF AFFECTION AND LUCIDITY SHE ADMITTED EVERYTHING AND TOLD HER SECRETS, PROMISING TO IMPROVE AND BEGGING FOR ANOTHER CHANCE.

DURING THE DAYTIME WHEN THE TEMPTATION BECAME IRRESISTABLE, X... ASKED AS A MEANS OF OVERCOMING IT, TO WASH HER PARTS WITH COLD WATER, BUT SOON THESE ABLUTIONS BECAME OVER FREQUENT. BEFORE LONG IT WAS DISCOVERED THAT ALL THE SPONGES HAD BEEN POKED FULL OF HOLES, AND THAT THE WASHING WAS NOTHING BUT A PRETEXT IN ORDER TO SATISFY HER CRAVING WITH IMPUNITY. IN ONE OF HER MOMENTS OF CALM AND REPENTANCE, X... MADE THE FOLLOWING CONFESSION:

"I VAGUELY RECALL, BECAUSE IT HAPPENED YEARS AGO, A MAID WHO LOOKED AFTER ME WHEN I WENT TO BED LIFTING HER SKIRTS AND RUBBING HER SHAMEFUL PARTS FOR A LONG TIME, I THINK IT WAS SHE WHO GAVE ME THE IDEA OF TOUCHING MYSELF. LATER I HAD A GOVERNESS WHO WAS ALWAYS TELLING ME NOT TO PUT MY HANDS THERE; SHE TOLD ME NOT TO SO OFTEN IT MADE ME CURIOUS AND I SAID TO MYSELF THAT JUST ONCE WOULDN'T HURT. IT'S A LONG TIME AGO NOW SINCE I GOT INTO THE HABIT. I USED TO GET UP EARLY TO PLAY WITH MY DOLLS, I USED TO DRESS THEM AND PLAY WITH MYSELF AUTOMATICALLY. WHENEVER I FELT BORED I ALWAYS PLAYED THE SAME GAME, BUT WITHOUT REALLY WANTING TO, WITHOUT GETTING ANY PLEASURE FROM IT. LATER, I USED TO PRETEND I

HAD SOMETHING WRONG WITH ME DOWN THERE, AND PLAYED AT GIVING MYSELF A DOUCHE OR BATHING MYSELF AND PUTTING ON A POULTICE. I USED WHATEVER I COULD FIND, GRASS, SAND, ETC. GIVING MYSELF THE DOUCHE WITH LITTLE STICKS: FOR YEARS I'VE LIKE PUTTING LITTLE STICKS UP ME. BUT IT'S ALWAYS BEST REALLY WHEN YOU CAN DO IT WITH EXACTLY THE THING YOU FEEL LIKE AT THE MOMENT. LATER THE DESIRE CAME OVER ME AT ALMOST REGULAR INTERVALS. AT FIRST, TOUCHING MYSELF TWO OR THREE TIMES WAS ENOUGH, USUALLY IN FRONT (THE CLITORIS), BUT LATER I HAD TO RUB HARDER AND HARDER. WHEN WE LIVED IN SUCH AND SUCH A HOUSE (1877) I SHOWED MY LITTLE SISTER HOW TO DO IT. (THE LITTLE SISTER WAS FOUR YEARS OLD AT THE TIME!) I GOT BORED PLAYING THE GAME ON MY OWN; I WANTED SOMEONE TO DO IT WITH ME. MY LITTLE SISTER DIDN'T ENJOY IT AND DIDN'T WANT TO: I MADE HER. SHE ONLY BEGAN TO LIKE IT IN THE WINTER OF 1881.

"WE DID LOTS OF THESE HORRORS WITH Y... WE USED TO SHUT OURSELVES UP IN THE LAVATORY AND TAKE ALL OUR CLOTHES OFF, STANDING OPPOSTIE AND TOUCHING EACH OTHER, SOMETIMES WITH OUR HANDS, SOMETIMES WITH BITS OF WOOD. AFTERWARDS I MADE FRIENDS WITH A LITTLE BOY I LIKED VERY MUCH, AND I DID THE SAME HORRORS WITH HIM. SOME MONTHS LATER I SHOWED LITTLE V... HOW TO DO IT AND WE USED TO TOUCH EACH OTHER.

"IT'S AWFUL TO WANT TO DO IT AND NOT BE ABLE TO, IT'S ENOUGH TO DRIVE YOU MAD, I WOULD HAVE KILLED ANYONE WHO TRIED TO STOP US. AT MOMENTS LIKE THAT IT'S AS IF I'M GIDDY, I CAN'T SEE, I CAN'T THINK, I'M NOT AFRAID OF ANYTHING OR ANYBODY, NOTHING MATTERS SO LONG AS I CAN DO IT!

"WHEN I WAS SAD OR CROSS ABOUT SOMETHING I DID IT ALL THE MORE: FOR INSTANCE THE TIMES I WAS CAUGHT STEALING I DID IT WORSE THAN EVER. THAT WAS WHEN I STARTED STICKING UP BITS OF WOOD AND RUBBING HARD (VAGINAL ONANISM), OFTEN I USED A PALM FROND THAT HAD BEEN BLESSED IN JERUSALEM." (APPARENTLY THIS PALM FROND GAVE HER MORE SATISFACTION THAN ANY OTHER FOREIGN BODY BECAUSE IT ADDED TO SENSUAL PLEASURE THE SPIRITUAL ECSTASY OF SACRILEGE.) FINALLY, AFTER USING SMOOTH INSTRUMENTS, SHE RESORTED TO SHARP ONES, SUCH AS SCISSORS, FORKS, ORDINARY PINS, ETC. SHE PARTICULARLY LIKED HAIR-PINS, THE SIGHT OF ONE WAS ENOUGH TO MAKE HER WANT TO USE IT.

"WHEN AT LAST" SHE WENT ON, "PEOPLE BEGAN TO NOTICE WHAT WAS HAPPENING AND TRIED TO STOP ME, I GOT INTO A TERRIBLE RAGE, I SAID NOBODY HAD THE RIGHT TO STOP ME USING MY FINGERS AND MY BODY AS I WANTED TO. I BLAMED EVERYONE, EVEN GOD FOR HAVING MADE ME UNHAPPY AFTER LETTING ME BE SO HAPPY. I GREW WICKED AND WANTED TO DO AS MUCH HARM AS POSSIBLE. I OFTEN THOUGHT OF THE DEVIL AND CALLED ON HIM TO HELP ME. HE DID COME, I SAW HIM, HE MADE EVERYTHING EASY, HE HELPED ME GET FREE. THE FIRST TIME HE CAME THOUGH, IT WAS WITHOUT MY ASKING. IT WAS DURING THE NIGHT, I WAS IN BED, WHEN ALL AT ONCE THE WARDROBE OPENED AND THE DEVIL APPEARED. HE WAS BIG, ALL BLACK AND GRINNING, HIS EYES WERE GREEN. THEN, EVERY CUPBOARD OPENED, EVERY DRAWER, AND OUT CAME A SWARM OF LITTLE DEMONS. IT WAS HORRIBLE! I'VE NEVER FORGOTTEN THAT ABOMINABLE SIGHT!

"IT WAS AFTER THAT I REPENTED, I WENT TO CONFESSION, BUT IT WAS IMPOSSIBLE TO STOP AND I STARTED AGAIN. I OFTEN CALLED ON THE DEVIL TO HELP ME; ONCE I FELT HIS HAND ON MY SHOULDER AND SOMETIMES I BEGGED HIM TO KILL MY PARENTS AND MAKE EVERYONE SUFFER. IF ONLY I COULD BE A DEMON MYSELF TO MAKE MISCHIEF!

"EVEN SO, I LIKE GOING TO CHURCH AND READING THE BIBLE. I FIND IT VERY SOOTHING" ... WHICH DID NOT PREVENT HER FROM BEING CAUGHT ONE DAY PERFORMING HORRORS WITH HER PRAYER-BOOK IN A CROWDED CHURCH.

A FURTHER PROOF THAT THE POOR CHILD SUFFERED FROM MENTAL ABERRATION WAS THE FACT THAT NOT ONLY DID SHE PRACTISE ONANISM IN ALL ITS REFINEMENTS, BUT URINATED ALMOST UPRIGHT IN FRONT OF HER SISTER, AFTERWARDS EXAMINING THE PATTERNS MADE BY THE JET OF URINE. SHE ALSO HANDLED HER EXCREMENTS AND FORCED HER LITTLE SISTER TO DO LIKEWISE.

IN ADDITION TO THE PRACTISES ALREADY CITED, X... PROVOKED THE VOLUPTUOUS SPASM BY RUBBING HERSELF ON THE ANGLES OF FURNITURE, BY PRESSING HER THIGHS TOGETHER, OR ROCKING BACKWARDS AND FORWARDS ON A CHAIR. OUT WALKING SHE WOULD BEGIN TO LIMP IN AN ODD WAY AS IF SHE WERE LOP-SIDED, OR KEPT LIFTING ONE OF HER FEET. AT OTHER TIMES SHE TOOK LITTLE STEPS, WALKED QUICKLY, OR TURNED ABRUPTLY LEFT. FINALLY SHE TRIED AND OFTEN SUCCEEDED IN STRIKING HER PARTS WITH THE EDGE OF A PIECE

OF WOOD, WHICH SHE RELEASED BY PRESSING IT WITH HER FOOT.

IF SHE SAW SOME SCRUB SHE STRADDLED IT AND RUBBED HERSELF BACK AND FORTH. THE CHILD'S PATIENCE AND CUNNING WERE TRULY AMAZING! OFTEN SHE LOCATED A SHRUB TO BE MADE USE OF SEVERAL DAYS LATER.

SHE PRETENDED TO FALL OR STUMBLE OVER SOMETHING IN ORDER TO RUB AGAINST IT. ALL AT ONCE SHE WOULD STOP AND EXCLAIM: "LOOK AT THAT PRETTY FLOWER!" SIMPLY TO DIVERT ATTENTION AND GIVE A QUICK KICK OF THE HEEL TO HER PARTS.

BUT THAT WAS NOT ALL! BY CUNNING AND PRACTICE X... WOULD ATTAIN HER OBJECTIVE IN WAYS THAT WERE INCONCEIVABLE IN A LITTLE GIRL OF GOOD FAMILY, WELL BROUGHT-UP SINCE CHILDHOOD. IN HER IT WAS CERTAINLY DUE TO MORAL PERVERSITY, A LEWD INSTINCT, AN ETHICAL NEUROSIS IN THE MORAL SENSE, AS SHOWN BY THE FOLLOWING EXAMPLE: THOUGH WATCHED OVER BY THE EYES OF ARGUS, X... IS SUDDENLY OVERCOME BY THE IRRESISTIBLE DESIRE TO COMMIT HER HORRORS. SHE IS TIED UP, PUT INTO HER STRAIT JACKET AND CHASTITY BELT (PUBIC BANDAGE), HER FEET ARE ATTACHED, AND YET THE VOLUPTUOUS SENSATION IS ABSOLUTELY ESSENTIAL. ONCE SHE GETS THE IDEA, SHE CANNOT RESIST PUTTING IT TO EXECUTION. SO SHE CONTRACTS HER NECK TO MAKE IT SWELL, HOLDS HER BREATH MOMENTARILY, MAKES EFFORTS AS IF SHE WANTED TO BLOW HER NOSE OR EXPECTORATE. AFTER WHICH SHE STARTS SQUEEZING HER ANUS AS AT THE END OF DEFECATION. THUS, BY THE ALTERNATIVE CON-TRACTING AND RELAXING OF THE ANAL SPHINCTER AND ANAL LEVATOR, BY THE REPETITION OF THESE MOVEMENTS WHICH I HAD HER PERFORM IN FRONT OF ME, THE VAGINA'S CONSTRICTOR IS MADE TO TAKE PART IN THESE SPASMODIC CONTRACTIONS, WHICH PERTURB THE WHOLE PERINEUM, THE VULVA SWELLS, AND A DULL, RHYTHMIC SOUND CAN BE HEARD SOME DISTANCE AWAY. IN EFFECT, THE ALTERNATIVE OPENING AND CLOSING OF THE LABIA PUDENDI PRODUCES A SMACKING SOUND, NOT UNLIKE THAT RESULTING FROM A SUDDENLY OPENING OF THE LIPS WHEN THE MOUTH HAS BEEN CLOSED, OR THE SIMILANCE OF THE TONGUE AGAINST THE PALATE. THIS MONOTONOUS NOISE IS OFTEN KEPT UP FOR A GOOD PART OF THE NIGHT. THOSE IN CHARGE OF THE CHILD SAY IT IS ODIOUS TO HAVE TO LISTEN TO IT IN THE SILENCE WITH ONLY THE NIGHT-LIGHT BURNING. OFTEN BOTH CHILDREN

INDULGE IN THE SAME MUSCULAR CONTRACTIONS AND PRODUCE THE SAME SOUND SIMULTANEOUSLY. YET, THE CHILDREN REMAIN IMMOBILE, AS IF NAILED TO THEIR BED, AND PRETEND TO BE ASLEEP. X... SAYS IT TAKES A LONG TIME, SOMETIMES MORE THAN AN HOUR TO REACH THE FINAL VOLUPTUOUS SPASM IN THIS WAY. IF, AFTER HAVING LEARNT FROM THESE NOCTURNAL SCENES, X... WAS GIVEN A GOOD SLAP AS SOON AS SHE BEGAN, SHE COULD BE STOPPED, BUT IF SHE HAD TIME TO WORK HERSELF UP, A SUDDEN INTERRUPTION BEFORE THE CLIMAX CAUSED THE OUTBREAK OF TERRIBLE STORMS. THEN X... SCREAMED, STRUGGLED LIKE ONE POSSESSED, AND FELL INTO CLONIC OR TONIC CONVULSIONS.

AS WE HAVE ALREADY STATED, WHEN X... BEGAN TO PRACTISE ONANISM IT WAS NOT THROUGH THE EXIGENCIES OF NATURE, THAT IS TO SAY, THE NEED TO MASTURBATE DID NOT ORIGINATE FROM THE SEXUAL ORGANS, IT WAS A THOUGHT, A CEREBRAL IMPULSE THAT INCITED X... TO STIMULATE THE SEXUAL PARTS, STILL MUTE AND UNRESPONSIVE. A BETTER WAY OF PUTTING IT WOULD BE TO SAY THAT AT FIRST, MASTURBATION WAS ENCEPHALIC. ONLY LATER DID IT BECOME GENITAL, WHEN THE CLITORIS AND VAGINA ROUSED AND MADE SENSITIVE BY REPEATED CONTACTS, GAVE RISE IN THEIR TURN TO THE LASCIVIOUS CONCEPT. THUS, X... AT THE POINT IN HER HISTORY WHICH CONCERNS US AT THE MOMENT, WAS DRIVEN TO CONTINUE HER DISAS-TROUS HABITS BY TWO DIFFERENT IMPULSES: CEREBRAL AND GENITAL.

OFTEN, AS SOON AS THE FIRST TOOK PLACE, IT REPERCUTED AS IF BY LIGHTNING ON THE SEXUAL ORGANS, AND X... BECAME INCAPABLE OF CHECKING THE IRRESISTABLE DESIRE TO SATISFY HER PASSION.

WHEN, FRIGID PHYSICALLY SPEAKING, X... GOT THE IDEA OF MASTURBATING, SHE BRACED HER WHOLE BODY AS STIFFLY AS SHE COULD, PRINCIPALLY THE LEGS, THUS PROVOKING PHYSICAL DESIRE CONSECUTIVELY TO THE CEREBRAL STIMULUS. AT THAT PERIOD SEXUAL ERETHISM WAS SUCH THAT A SINGLE TOUCH WAS ENOUGH TO PRODUCE ORGASM. THE MORE SUDDEN THE TOUCH, THE MORE QUICKLY THE DISCHARGE OCCURED. IN THE MONTH OF JUNE, AS A RESULT OF CONSIDERABLE ABUSE, X... SUFFERED FROM A FIT OF NERVOUS TREMBLING THAT GAINED ALL HER LIMBS, AND ACCOMPANIED BY PAINS SO VIOLENT THEY MADE THE CHILD SCREAM. THIS WAS FOLLOWED BY A TETANIC STATE LASTING SEVERAL MINUTES, DURING WHICH IT WAS

IMPOSSIBLE FOR HER TO PERFORM THE SLIGHTEST MOVEMENT: SHE WAS A RIGID AND MOTIONLESS AS A FROG SUBJECTED TO VIOLENT ELECTRIC SHOCKS.

THIS GAVE HER SUCH A FRIGHT SHE WAS GOOD FOR SEVERAL DAYS AFTERWARDS. X...'S GENERAL HEALTH WAS DETERIORATING RAPIDLY. SHE COMPLAINED OF VIOLENT HEADACHES; SHE WAS SUBJECT TO A SUDDEN NERVOUS RISE IN TEMPERATURE THAT LASTED SEVERAL HOURS; SHE HAD ERRATIC PAINS ALL OVER HER BODY AND SHOOTING PAINS IN HER PARTS. THERE WERE FREQUENT ATTACKS OF ANXIETY, SUFFOCATION, PALPITATIONS WITH A TENDENCY TO LIPOTHYMY. AT TIMES SHE BECAME HIGHLY AGITATED, INCAPABLE OF KEEPING STILL. SHE WOULD JUMP UP FROM HER CHAIR AND PACE UP AND DOWN THE BEDROOM; SHE COULDN'T SLEEP AND DECLARED SHE SPENT TWO OR THREE NIGHTS AT A TIME WITHOUT CLOSING HER EYES. SHE IS UTTERLY WORN OUT, AS WELL AS IN A DEPLORABLE MENTAL STATE. SHE IS ONLY ALLOWED OUT OF HER STRAIT-JACKET AT MEAL TIMES. EVEN SO, DURING THOSE BRIEF MOMENTS OF LIBERTY, HER ONE AND ONLY THOUGHT IS TO GET HER HANDS ON HER PARTS, OR INSERT A FORK OR THE HANDLE OF HER KNIFE. ON ONE OCCASION, CAUGHT RED-HANDED, THE FORK IS SNATCHED FROM HER. SHE BURSTS INTO TEARS, JUMPS UP FROM THE TABLE AND YELLS AT THE TOP OF HER VOICE: I WANT TO! FOR PITY'S SAKE LET ME DO IT!

AS X...'S STATE PROGRESSIVELY WORSENED, IT WAS DECIDED, IN ORDER TO AVOID A SCANDAL, OR SEND HER TO THE COUNTRY, SHE WAS INSTALLED IN A CHALET IN THE MIDDLE OF A GARDEN. HER LITTLE SISTER Y... AGED ABOUT SIX, TO WHOM SHE HAD IMPARTED HER SHAMEFUL HABITS, WENT WITH HER, AND IN ADDITION TO THE STAFF, TWO GOVERNESSES WERE ENGAGED TO WATCH OVER THE CHILDREN DAY AND NIGHT TO CHECK ANY GUILTY INCLINA- TIONS. EVERYTHING HAD BEEN WELL ORGANIZED: THE DAY DIVIDED IN SUCH A WAY AS TO OCCUPY EACH MOMENT, AND DIVERT THEIR ATTENTION FROM VICE BY INCULCATING RELIGIOUS SENTIMENTS THROUGH PRAYER AND READINGS FROM PIOUS WORKS.

WALKS TWICE A DAY AND VARIOUS GAMES DID MUCH TO MAKE THEIR LIFE AGREEABLE, BUT TO NO PURPOSE. X...'S ONE IDEA WAS TO OUTWIT THE VIGILANCE OF HER GUARDIANS. WHILE THE MAID WAS DRESSING HER, SHE WOULD SUDDENLY PUT HER FINGERS ON HER PARTS, OR GIVE THEM A KICK WITH HER HEEL. WHILE BATHING IN THE SEA SHE USED HER TOES WITH ASTONISHING AGILITY TO PICK UP SHELLS AND LITTLE STONES WHICH SHE INSERTED IN THE PARTS. OR ELSE, WHILE GETTING UNDRESSED, SHE STOLE A HAIRPIN AND HID IT IN HER MOUTH UNTIL SHE FOUND A FAVOURABLE MOMENT TO USE IT. SHE WOULD DIVE AND STAY UNDER WATER SEVERAL SECONDS IN ORDER TO MANIPULATE HERSELF.

FROM TIME TO TIME X... HAS MOMENTS OF REMORSE, ADMITTING THAT SHE IS ON THE DOWNWARD PATH, WEEPS AND PROMISES TO IMPROVE, BUT IT IS NO MORE THAN A DRUNKARD'S PLEDGE. A MOMENT LATER SHE IS INVENTING SOME NEW TACTIC. ONE DAY, FOR EXAMPLE, ON RECEIVING A LETTER FROM HER MOTHER EXHORTING HER TO IMPROVE, SHE IS MOVED TO TEARS BY ITS TENDER AFFECTION, BUT AT THE SAME MOMENT THE LETTER THAT HAS SO MOVED HER IS BEING ROLLED INTO A SPOOL WHICH, UNDER HER CLOTHES, SHE ART- FULLY INTRODUCES INTO HER SEXUAL PARTS. SHE CANNOT BE LEFT ALONE FOR A MOMENT, NOT EVEN WHEN RESPONDING TO URGENT CALLS OF NATURE. AT NIGHT ONE GOES SO FAR AS TO TIE LITTLE BELLS TO THE HANDS AND FEET OF THE TWO CHILDREN ATTACHED WITH THEIR STRAIT-JACKETS, BELT AND STRAPS AS ALREADY DESCRIBED, IN ORDER TO PREVENT ALL MOVEMENT, ALL DANGEROUS FRICTION. BUT HOW DOES ONE PREVENT THE MUSCLES OF THE PERINEUM FROM CONTRACTING AND PRODUCING VOLUPTUOUS SATISFACTION IN SPITE OF ALL PRECAUTIONS?

X... OFTEN SPOKE OF THE DEVIL WHO CAME TO FREE ONE OF HER HANDS AND HELP HER PERPETRATE HER HORRORS.

SEA BATHS HAVING OVER-EXCITED THE CHILDREN'S NERVOUS SYSTEMS, THEY WERE REPLACED BY SOFT WATER BATHS, WARM AND PROLONGED, A DOSE OF FOUR GRAMMES OF BROMIDE OF POTASSIUM PER DAY, MILK, VEGETABLES, BEER, NO RED MEAT.

THIS DIET AND THE PROLONGED BATHS CON- TRIBUTED FURTHER TO THE CHILDREN'S WEAKENED STATE. FOR ABOUT THREE MONTHS THINGS CONTINUED IN THE SAME WAY, WITH A REPETITION OF THE SAME SCENES OF AGITATION AND VIOLENCE.

IF PRESENTED WITH A CRUCIFIX X... BECAME EVEN MORE UNMANAGEABLE, BITING AND SPITTING ON IT, CRYING OUT THAT SHE PREFERRED THE DEVIL WHO HELPED HER DO WHAT SHE WANTED. A MOMENT LATER SHE WOULD REPENT, BEGGING TO BE

PRAYED FOR AND READ THE PSALMS! SHE ALSO HAD HALLUCINATIONS DURING THE DAY. IN THE MIDDLE OF A GRAMMAR LESSON SHE SUDDENLY BEGAN TO SHOUT: "CHASE HIM AWAY, CHASE HIM AWAY, I DON'T WANT THE DEVIL AT THIS MOMENT!" ONE DAY IN THE MIDDLE OF A WALK SHE STOPS ABRUPTLY AND LETS OUT A SCREAM. HER FACE CONTORTS WITH FEAR, SHE THROWS HERSELF INTO HER GOVERNESS'S ARMS CRYING: "THERE HE IS. HE'S HORRIBLE! HOW HIS EYES GLEAM! I'M GOING BLIND, I CAN'T SEE ANYTHING!" HER VOICE BECOMES RAUCOUS, HER EXPRESSION THAT OF A MADMAN. AT ONE MOMENT SHE EMBRACES HER GOVERNESS WITH EFFUSION, THE NEXT SHE HITS AND BITES HER. SHE WANTS TO RUN AWAY FROM EVERYTHING. FINALLY, THE DAY COMES WHEN SHE TRIES TO THROW HERSELF OUT OF A SECOND-STORY WINDOW INTO THE STREET BELOW. AT CERTAIN MOMENTS SHE WANTS TO BE CUDDLED AND EXPRESSES GRATITUDE WHEN SHOWN AFFECTION. AT OTHERS, ON THE CONTRARY, SHE GETS ANGRY IF ANYONE SYMPATHISES WITH HER SUFFERINGS. "NOBODY ELSE CAN SHARE IN THEM," SHE SAYS, "BECAUSE MY SUFFERINGS ARE SHAMEFUL!"

THE 26TH OF AUGUST, SEEING THE LITTLE SUCCESS OBTAINED BY MEANS OF COERCION, BY TYING, BY VARIOUS INSTRUMENTS, BY SEVERE PUNISHMENT, I HAVE HER FREED ENTIRELY, TRYING BY ADVICE AND KINDNESS TO STIMULATE HER AMOUR PROPRE, TO RESTORE HER DIGNITY AND AWAKEN A SENSE OF HONOUR. I PICTURE THE FEARFUL CONSEQUENCES OF HER HABITS, PROMISING TO LEAVE HER COMPLETELY FREE IF SHE WILL BE SENSIBLE AND OBEY ME. BUT I AM QUICK TO ADD: "IF YOU REFUSE TO LISTEN I WILL HAVE TO BE CRUEL. I WILL BURN YOUR PARTS WITH A RED HOT IRON!" ALTHOUGH X... APPEARED TO BE MOVED BY MY MARKS OF SYMPATHY, SHE DID NOT PROMISE TO BE GOOD IN THE FUTURE. "I WILL DO MY BEST," SHE TOLD ME, "BUT I AM NOT SURE OF SUCCEEDING, AND THEREFORE I CANNOT PROMISE." CURIOUSLY ENOUGH SHE DID NOT WANT TO BE LEFT UN-ATTACHED. "I DO NOT TRUST MYSELF," SHE SAID. "PUT ON MY STRAIT JACKET AGAIN; TIE ME UP, I BEG YOU." I WAS OBLIGED TO COMPLY WITH HER REQUEST, ALTHOUGH RULES WERE LESS STRICTLY ENFORCED THAN BEFORE. I INSISTED THAT THE CHILD BE LEFT TO HERSELF NOW AND THEN, FOR I HAD NOTICED THAT SHE REBELLED AGAINST SEVERE TREATMENT, THAT SHE JIBBED AS IT WERE, AGAINST THE BRUTALITY EMPLOYED, AND FOUGHT WITH ALL HER WIT AND CUNNING AGAINST WHATEVER COERCIVE MEASURES WERE ADOPTED. ONE WOULD HAVE SAID THAT SHE GOT MORE PLEASURE OUT OF OBTAINING SATISFACTION, THE GREATER THE OBSTACLE SHE HAD BEEN OBLIGED TO OVERCOME.

TREATMENT: COLD SHOWERS, BROMIDE OF POTAS-SIUM AND AMMONIUM, TWO GRAMMES EVERY TWENTY-FOUR HOURS, FERRUGINOUS WINE, A VARIED DIET TO BUILD UP THE SYSTEM. IN THE DAYS FOLLOWING X... APPEARED TO BE MENTALLY CALMER. SHE DID NOT HAVE HALLUCINATIONS. NEVERTHELESS SHE ADMITTED TO HAVING YIELDED SEVERAL TIMES TO HER INCRIMINATING MANIPULA-TIONS, THOUGH IN A MORE MODERATE FASHION. BY DINT OF TOUCHING AND EXCITING HERSELF, THE SENSITIVITY OF THE SEXUAL PARTS HAD BECOME SO GREAT THAT THE MAID, IN PULLING OFF THE CHILD'S NIGHT-SHIRT WHEN DRESSING HER, SET OFF AN ELECTRIC CURRENT THAT SENT A SHUDDER THROUGH HER WHOLE BEING. X... FLUSHED, HER BREATHING BECAME UNEVEN, HER SKIN DAMP, HER FACE AS IF ILLUMINATED; IN A FEW SECONDS THE VOLUPTUOUS SENSATION REACHED ITS CLIMAX. "THIS TIME IT'S NOT MY FAULT," SHE SAID, "YOU PULLED IT OFF TOO QUICKLY. A RAPID MOVEMENT ON THAT PART OF ME STARTS OFF A SENSATION I CANNOT CONTROL." X... HAS INDEED BECOME HYPER-SENSITIVE. THE SLIGHTEST PRESSURE PUT ON THE SENSUAL PARTS LEADS TO AN ERETHISM AS QUICK AS LIGHTNING WHICH CAN BE READ ON HER FACE. THUS X... BENDING OVER TO PICK A FLOWER, GIVES HERSELF A QUICK TAP ON THE PARTS WITH HER HAND AND THE RESULT IS ACHIEVED; THE SAME THING HAPPENS IF SHE KNOCKS AGAINST A PIECE OF FURNITURE IN PASSING, OR LEANS ON SOMEONE. IT IS EASY TO UNDERSTAND THE UTTER IMPOSSIBILITY OF AVOIDING ALL THE OCCASIONS FOR WHICH SHE WAS ON THE LOOK-OUT, WHICH SHE SOUGHT OR CREATED IN ORDER TO CONTINUE HER ABUSES.

THE NIGHTS PASS WITH FREQUENT REPETITIONS OF THE USUAL ABUSE, SHE OFTEN HAS NERVOUS TREMORS, BUT A FEW KIND WORDS FROM THE GOVERNESS AND A HAND SMOOTHING HER BROW OFTEN SUCCEED IN CALMING THESE NOCTURNAL CRISES. THE CHILD LOOKS BETTER, SHE SEEMS HAPPY. SHE WORKS AT HER LESSONS WITH PLEASURE. SHE FRANKLY ADMITS TO PROVOKING THE VOLUPTUOUS SPASM TWELVE TO EIGHTEEN TIMES A DAY. SHE EVEN INSERTS A PAINT-BRUSH INTO THE VAGINA. THE PARTS ARE HIGHLY INFLAMED, WITH A YELLOWISH GREEN DISCHARGE, THICK AND ABUNDANT.

THE 29TH OF AUGUST X... IS ALTOGETHER CHARMING. A STRIKING CHANGE HAS TAKEN PLACE.

SHE BEHAVES PROPERLY. DURING THE VISIT OF A RELATIVE SHE IS VERY POLITE, KEEPS UP AN ANIMATED CONVERSATION, RECITES POEMS AND SINGS A BALLAD. BUT AFTER THE VISIT, SHE TOUCHES HERSELF SEVERAL TIMES, IS GLOOMY DURING THE WALK, HER VOICE GROWS HOARSE, A SURE SIGN OF INCREASING TENSION. LATER, SEATED ON A CHAIR, SHE KEEPS MOVING HER HEAD ABOUT, ROLLING HER EYES AND LOOKING UP AT THE CEILING, COMPLAINING THAT GOD IS UNJUST TO HER BECAUSE HE HAS GIVEN HER EVERYTHING TO MAKE HER HAPPY AND NOW TAKES IT AWAY FROM HER. "I AM ASKING HIM TO MAKE ME DIE," SHE SAYS. "I AM SO AFRAID OF THE OPERATION THE DOCTOR THREATENED! AND HOW HUMILIATING TO BE FORCED TO MEND MY WAYS INSTEAD OF BY MY OWN FREE WILL." WHAT CHAOS REIGNS IN THAT LITTLE HEAD! AT TIMES SHE SAYS: "YOU WILL SAVE ME WITH GOD'S HELP," AND HER EYES SHINE WITH JOY. AT OTHERS, SHE LAMENTS THAT IT IS TOO LATE AND THAT SHE IS LOST FOREVER! HER HALLUCINATIONS RETURN, WILD-EYED, SHE SEES THE TERRIBLE HEAD WITH ITS GREEN EYES. SHE IMAGINES THAT A PLAGUE OF DEVILS SETTLE ON THE HOUSE AND THAT SHE HERSELF TURNS INTO A DEMON!

SHE FANCIES SHE IS ALREADY DEAD, THAT SHE ENTERS A HOUSE WITHOUT BEING SEEN AND DOES HARM TO EVERYONE IN IT, WHICH MAKES HER VERY HAPPY! SHE IS SURE OF BEING IN TOUCH WITH THE DEVIL AND HAVING MYSTERIOUS CONNECTIONS WITH HELL. IT SHOULD BE NOTED THAT EXCESSIVE ONANISM IS INEVITABLY FOLLOWED BY SUCH HALLUCINATIONS AND MENTAL ABERRATIONS.

FOR SOME TIME X... HAS BEEN THINKING A GREAT DEAL ABOUT MARRIAGE, ALREADY SHE SEEMS INSTINCTIVELY ATTRACTED BY THE IDEA OF THE PLEASURE TO BE HAD IN SEXUAL RELATIONS.

ONE DAY, FOR INSTANCE, TO AMUSE HER, SHE WAS TOLD ABOUT THE MYTHICAL POWERS OF FAIRIES TO OBTAIN WHATEVER THEY DESIRE. "WHAT I DESIRE," SHE ANSWERED, "IS THAT THERE SHOULD BE AS MANY MEN AS LADIES ON EARTH SO THEY CAN MARRY."

"DO YOU THINK THE ONLY HAPPINESS IS IN BEING MARRIED?" HER GOVERNESS ASKED. "THERE ARE MANY UNMARRIED WOMEN WHO ARE USEFUL AND CONTENT."

X... REPLIES AT ONCE WITH A SMILE ON HER LIPS: "NOT ME—I'M NO SAINT!"

SOMETIMES HER FACE IS FLUSHED AND SHE HAS A ROVING EYE; AT OTHERS SHE IS PALE AND LISTLESS. OFTEN SHE CANNOT KEEP STILL, PACING UP AND DOWN THE BEDROOM, OR BALANCING ON ONE FOOT AFTER THE OTHERS. WHEN SPEAKING SHE DECLAIMS, OR PUTS ON AIRS, HER FEATURES TWITCH, SHE GRIMACES, SHE LAUGHS OUT LOUD WITHOUT RHYME OR REASON. DURING THESE BOUTS X... IS INCAPABLE OF ANYTHING: READING, CONVERSATION, GAMES, ARE EQUALLY ODIOUS. ALL AT ONCE HER EXPRESSION BECOMES CYNICAL, HER EXCITEMENT MOUNTS. X... IS OVERCOME BY THE DESIRE TO DO IT, SHE TRIES NOT TO OR SOMEONE TRIES TO STOP HER. HER ONLY DOMINATING THOUGHT IS TO SUCCEED. HER EYES DART IN ALL DIRECTIONS, HER LIPS NEVER STOP TWITCHING, HER NOSTRILS FLARE! LATER, SHE CALMS DONW AND IS HERSELF AGAIN. "IF ONLY I HAD NEVER BEEN BORN," SHE SAYS TO HER LITTLE SISTER, "WE WOULD NOT HAVE BEEN A DISGRACE TO THE FAMILY!" AND Y...REPLIES: "WHY DID YOU TEACH ME ALL THESE HORRORS THEN?" UPSET BY THIS REPROACH, X... SAYS: "IF SOMEONE WOULD ONLY KILL ME! WHAT JOY, I COULD DIE WITHOUT COMMITTING SUICIDE."

THE AFTERNOON OF THE 14TH OF SEPTEMBER X... IS IN A TERRIBLY OVER-EXCITED STATE. SHE WALKS ABOUT RESTLESSLY, GRINDING HER TEETH. THE GOVERNESS TRIES TO CONTROL HER, BUT SHE KICKS BACK. THERE IS FOAM ON HER LIPS, SHE GASPS, REPEATING: "I DON'T WANT TO, I DON'T WANT TO, I CAN'T STOP MYSELF, I MUST DO IT! STOP ME, HOLD MY HANDS, TIE MY FEET!" A FEW MOMENTS LATER SHE FALLS INTO A STATE OF PROSTRATION, BECOMES SWEET AND GENTLE, BEGGING TO BE GIVEN ANOTHER CHANCE. "I KNOW I'M KILLING MYSELF," SHE SAYS, "SAVE ME."

WHICH PROVES THAT AFTER A DESPERATE STRUGGLE, THE INSTINCT OF PRESERVATION IS SOMETIMES STRONGER THAN THE ALLURES OF VICE! SHE EXPLAINS HOW SHE SHOULD BE TIED SO THAT SHE CANNOT POSSIBLY ATTAIN HER OBJEC- TIVE. BUT HER INCONSISTENCIES ARE ENDLESS. NEXT DAY SHE HAS A FIT OF DESIRE, THIS TIME IN THE PRESENCE OF A STRANGER. ATTEMPTS ARE MADE IN VAIN TO IMPOSE A RESPECT FOR DECORUM. SHE CANNOT CONTROL HERSELF. DURING THEIR OUTING SHE WALKS IN THE MOST INDECENT FASHION IN FRONT OF PASSERS-BY, DESPITE THE PLEADINGS OF HER GOVERNESS. IN THE LITTLE VILLAGE THEY COME TO, SHE CAUSES A SCANDAL. THE GOVERNESS, WITH THE HELP OF A SERVANT, PUTS A STOP TO THE SCENE BY BRINGING HER HOME

IN A CARRIAGE. HARDLY IS X... SEATED THAN SHE FLINGS HERSELF BACK AND ACTS IN SUCH A WAY AS TO PROVOKE THE VOLUPTUOUS SENSATION. THE SERVANT'S PRESENCE IN NO WAY DISSUADES HER FROM THIS SHAMELESS BEHAVIOUR. THE 28TH, TORMENTED BY REMORSE, SHE ASKES FOR A PRIEST TO GIVE HER CONFESSION. NOTHING COULD BE MORE DISTRESSING THAN THE SCENE THAT TAKES PLACE UNDER OUR EYES. WHILE THE VENERABLE PRIEST GIVES HER INSTRUCTION, X... BATHED IN TEARS, HANDS JOINED TOGETHER, PRAYS FERVENTLY, BOWED TO THE GROUND; BUT ALL AT ONCE A DIABOLIC THOUGHT CROSSES HER WRETCHED MIND AND, MAKING THE MOST OF HER INCLINED POSITION, SHE RUBS HER PARTS WITH ... THE PRIEST'S CASSOCK!

I WILL CUT AS SHORT AS POSSIBLE THE HISTORY OF LITTLE Y... WHO IS X...'S SISTER AND WHOM I HAVE ALREADY MENTIONED WHEN RELATING FACTS CONCERNING THE LATTER. SHE IS NOT AS INTELLIGENT OR AS ATTRACTIVE AS HER SISTER. UNFORTUNATELY, THE TWO CHILDREN WERE NOT SEPARATED. AS A RESULT, THE LITTLE ONE COPIED EVERYTHING THE BIG ONE DID, AND EVERY PRACTICE INVENTED BY X... IS ADOPTED BY Y... THE GENITAL ORGANS ARE SO PRECOCIOUSLY DEVELOPED THERE ARE ALREADY TUFTS OF HAIR ON THE LABIA PUDENDI ALTHOUGH Y... IS NOT YET SIX. THE SAME HARSH METHODS USED ON X... ARE EMPLOYED ON Y... BECAUSE OF HER STURDY CONSTITUTION SHE IS WHIPPED SO FORCIBLY THE BUTTOCKS ARE STRIPED BY DEEP ECCHYMOSE. IT HAS AS MUCH EFFECT ON Y... AS IT HAD ON THE ELDER SISTER; THE PUBIC BANDAGE IS EQUALLY UNSUCCESSFUL. THE SEXUAL PARTS ARE VERY INFLAMED AND BLOOD-RED IN COLOUR. A THICK YELLOW DISCHARGE WITH A REPULSIVE ODOR PERSISTS IN SPITE OF ABLUTIONS REPEATED SEVERAL TIMES A DAY. THE CHILD, WHOSE VENEREAL DESIRES, AS A RESULT OF PROVOKED STIMULATION, HAVE ALREADY BEEN ACTIVE FOR SEVERAL MONTHS, GETS VERY WORKED UP AND OFTEN ROUSES DESIRE BY A SERIES OF PREPARA-TORY BODY MOVEMENTS. ALTHOUGH WELL BUILT AND ALERT, SHE IS REDUCED, BY EXCESSIVE ABUSE, TO SUCH A STATE OF IMBECILITY, SHE NO LONGER UNDERSTANDS WHAT IS SAID TO HER. AT SUCH TIMES SHE IS PALE AND CROSS-EYED.

BUT THE MOMENT SHE GETS THE IDEA OF SATISFYING HERSELF, HER EYES SHINE, HER SPEECH BECOMES JERKY, HER SALIVA ABUNDANT. SHE HAS EVEN BEEN KNOWN TO WEEP!

SHE OFTEN REPROACHES HER SISTER FOR HAVING TAUGHT HER SUCH HORRORS, BUT THIS DOESN'T PREVENT HER FROM MODELLING HER CONDUCT ON THAT OF HER OLDER SISTER: THE SAME INDECENT MOVEMENTS WHEN THEY ARE OUT, THE SAME TRICKS WHEN SHE IS ATTACHED TO THE BED, THE SAME RUSES TO OUTWITH HER GUARDIANS, THE SAME TREATMENTS ADMINISTERED TO X..., THE SAME LACK OF SUCCESS!

DURING MY JOURNEY TO LONDON FOR THE INTERNATIONAL MEDICAL CONGRESS, I WAS FORTUNATE ENOUGH TO MEET DR. JULES GUÉRIN. I SUBMITTED THE HOPELESS CASE OF THE TWO CHILDREN TO OUR EMINENT COLLEAGUE AND ASKED HIS ADVICE. DR. J. GUÉRIN AFFIRMED THAT, AFTER ALL OTHER TREATMENTS HAD FAILED, HE HAD SUCCEEDED IN CURING YOUNG GIRLS AFFECTED BY THE VICE OF ONANISM BY BURNING THE CLITORIS WITH A HOT IRON.

ON MY RETURN TO CONSTANTINOPLE I HAD NO DIFFICULTY IN PERSUADING THE FAMILY TO FOLLOW THE RECOMMENDATION PROPOSED BY THE DIS-TINGUISHED ACADEMICIAN. I DECIDED TO EXPERI-MENT FIRST ON LITTLE Y...

THE 8TH OF SEPTEMBER, TREMBLING IN EVERY LIMB, THE POOR CHILD IS EXTREMELY VOLUBILE, BUT REASONS LIKE A GIRL OF 16. SHE BEGS ME NOT TO BURN HER AND IS EVEN VERY GRATEFUL WHEN I REMOVE HER STRAIT JACKET. I NOTE THAT THE SMALL LABIA ARE SCORED BY PERPENDICULAR WOUNDS, TRACES OF INJURIES INFLICTED YESTER-DAY BY A TABLE FORK! THE ORIFICE OF THE VAGINA IS BRIGHT RED. IT IS MOST DISTRESSING TO THINK THAT SO YOUNG A CHILD CAN BE SO PERVERSE! SHE ADMITTED EVERYTHING SHE HAD DONE DURING MY ABSENCE. "I AM ASHAMED, SIR," SHE SAID, "TO TELL YOU ABOUT MY HORRORS." AFTER SOME HESITATION, SHE ADMITTED TO RUBBING HERSELF WITH HER HANDS, WITH HER FEET, WITH ANY FOREIGN BODY SHE COULD FIND. AT MY INSISTENCE, SHE SHOWED ME WHAT SHE DID IN BED IN ORDER TO GET AT HERSELF, AND HOW SHE PRODUCED THE SMACKING SOUND OF THE VULVA WHICH SHE KEPT UP MOST OF THE NIGHT IN CONCERT WITH HER SISTER. WE HAVE ALREADY DESCRIBED IN DETAIL THE MECHANISM OF THIS SOUND WHICH CAN BE HEARD SEVERAL METERS AWAY. IT IS CAUSED BY THE OPENING AND CLOSING OF THE LABIA PUDENDI UNDER THE INFLUENCE OF RHYTHMIC AND ENERGETIC CONTRACTIONS STARTING FROM THE ANUS, WHICH SET THE WHOLE PERINEUM IN MOTION AND SPREAD TO THE LARGE, SWOLLEN LABIA. "BUT

WHO SHOWED YOU HOW TO DO SUCH INFAMOUS THINGS?" I ASKED HER. "I FOUND OUT FOR MYSELF, SIR," SHE REPLIED. "IT FEELS NICE WHEN I CONTRACT AND SQUEEZE. MY SISTER DOES THE SAME."

EVERYTHING WAS READY FOR THE TRANSCURRENT CAUTERISATION, BUT BEFORE THE TEARS AND SUPPLICATIONS, THE PROMISES MADE BY Y... I RELENT. FOR OVER AN HOUR I LECTURE HER, EXPLAINING THAT HER HEALTH WILL BE RUINED AND HER REPUTATION LOST IF SHE CONTINUES THE WAY SHE IS GOING! BUT IF SHE FAILS TO KEEP HER WORD SHE WILL BE BURNT ON MY NEXT VISIT. "IT IS DISGRACEFUL THAT YOU SHOULD HAVE TO BE TIED UP LIKE AN ANIMAL IN A STABLE, OR A CRIMINAL," I TELL HER. COLD SHOWERS, BROMIDE OF POTASSIUM. BUT HARDLY HAD I LEFT BEFORE SHE WAS AT IT AGAIN WORSE THAN EVER.

THE 11TH OF SEPTEMBER IN ORDER TO FRIGHTEN HER AS MUCH AS POSSIBLE, I MAKE A GREAT DISPLAY OF BRAZIERS FULL OF BURNING COALS IN WHICH I PLACE AN ENORMOUS IRON IN THE FORM OF AN AXE. I BLOW ON IT UNTIL IT BECOMES RED HOT. SHE TREMBLES AT THE SIGHT OF ALL THESE INFERNAL GOINGS ON. "YOU DID NOT KEEP YOUR PROMISE," I SAID TO HER, "AND I'LL SHOW YOU THAT YOU MADE A MISTAKE BY KEEPING MINE." I SHOWED HER THE BIG HOT IRON, BUT I CAUTERISED THE CLITORIS WITH A LITTLE STYLET THREE MILLIMETERS IN DIAMETER HEATED OVER A SPIRIT LAMP. "IF YOU DO IT AGAIN," I TOLD HER, "I WILL BURN YOU WITH THE BIG IRON NEXT TIME AND WITHOUT PITY."

THE 14TH OF SEPTEMBER, THE OPERATION PROVED TO HAVE HAD AN IMMEDIATE AND SALUTARY EFFECT. LITTLE Y... HAD BEEN GOOD EVER SINCE THE CAUTERISATION. "THE PAIN IS HORRIBLE," SHE SAID, "I'LL NEVER DO IT AGAIN." ALTHOUGH LEFT AT LIBERTY, SHE WAS VERY WELL BEHAVED ON THE WALK AND VERY GOOD AT NIGHT. BUT, ON THE AFTERNOON OF THE 15TH, HER PHYSIOGNOMIE UNDERWENT A SUDDEN CHANGE; HER HANDS SHOOK AS THEY ALWAYS DID WHEN SHE WAS ON THE POINT OF ·PERPETRATING HER CRIME. IN A TWINKLING ONE OF HER HANDS DISAPPEARED UNDER THE PLEATS OF HER DRESS AND Y... BECAME RED IN THE FACE. QUESTIONIED, SHE ADMITTED TO HAVING DONE IT, BUT SOUGHT TO JUSTIFY HERSELF BY SAYING IT WAS IMPOSSIBLE TO RESIST THE CRAVING. SHE WAS REMINDED OF THE SESSION WITH THE FIRE AND KEPT UNDER SUPERVISION. TOWARD EVENING SHE BECAME CAPRICIOUS, THEN BROKE DOWN, SOBBING. THIS IS

WHAT HAPPENS WITH BOTH SISTERS WHEN, DRIVEN BY THE IRRESISTABLE DESIRE TO TOUCH THEMSELVES, THEY ARE PREVENTED FROM DOING SO.

THE 15TH, SHE THRUSTS A PIECE OF WOOD INTO THE VAGINA. LATER, STOOPING OVER A LITTLE TABLE, SHE RUBS HER PARTS AGAINST THE DECORATION ON ITS LEG. HOWEVER, SHE ABUSES HERSELF MUCH LESS SINCE THE CAUTERISATION, TOUCHING ALONE IS NOT ENOUGH TO PRODUCE ORGASM, LONG AND REPEATED FRICTION IS REQUIRED ROUND THE ORIFICE OF THE VAGINA, BECAUSE THE CLITORIS IS NOT ONLY INSENSITIVE BUT EXTREMELY PAINFUL TO THE TOUCH. AT LAST, THE SUPERVISION OF Y... BECOMES POSSIBLE AND REWARDING.

THE 16TH, SECOND CAUTERISATION. I APPLY THE HOT POINT THREE TIMES TO EACH OF THE LARGE LABIA AND ANOTHER ON THE CLITORIS. TO PUNISH HER FOR DISOBEDIENCE, I CAUTERISE BUTTOCKS AND LOINS WITH THE BIG IRON. SHE SWEARS SHE WILL NOT BE NAUGHTY AGAIN AND ADMITS TO BEING DOUBLY GUILTY BECAUSE, SHE SAYS, SINCE THE FIRST CAUTERISATION SHE HASN'T HAD THE SAME DESIRE TO EXCITE HERSELF. "I SEE THAT THIS METHOD WILL CURE ME, BECAUSE I CAN GO FOR MORE THAN TWENTY-FOUR HOURS WITHOUT DOING A HORROR."

NEXT DAY SHE COMPLAINS OF HER BURNS. SHE IS NONE THE LESS ON THE LOOK OUT FOR ANY CHANCE TO TOUCH HERSELF BUT STOPS AS SOON AS SHE IS THREATENED WITH BURNING.

SEEING THE PUNISHMENTS INFLICTED ON HER SISTER, X... BECOMES VERY DESPONDENT; SHE KEEPS REPEATING: "IF ONLY I COULD DIE! I KNOW I WILL HAVE TO UNDERGO THE SAME TORTURE, WHAT CAN I DO?" HER EXCESSES CONTINUE AND HER STATE BECOMES ALARMING: SHE IS PALE, THIN, WEAK, HER LOWER LIMBS HAVE OEDEMA ALMOST TO THE KNEE.

YESTERDAY WHEN THE ANGELUS WAS RUNG, SHE BEGAN TO SHIVER, HER FACE TOOK ON AN EXPRESSION OF TERROR AND HER EYES FLOODED WITH TEARS. SHE TRIED TO RUN AWAY, CRYING: "THE SOUND OF THE BELLS MAKES ME THINK OF THE DAY OF JUDGEMENT!"

THE 19TH, THIRD CAUTERISATION OF LITTLE Y... WHO SOBS AND VOCIFERATES.

IN THE DAYS THAT FOLLOWED Y... FOUGHT

SUCCESSFULLY AGAINST TEMPTATION. SHE BECAME A CHILD AGAIN, PLAYING WITH HER DOLL, AMUSING HERSELF AND LAUGHING GAYLY. SHE BEGS TO HAVE HER HANDS TIED EACH TIME SHE IS NOT SURE OF HERSELF: ONE RELAPSE IS EVEN PUNISHED BY FLAGELLATION ON THE RAW BUTTOCKS! OFTEN SHE IS SEEN TO MAKE AN EFFORT AT CONTROL. NONETHELESS SHE DOES IT TWO OR THREE TIMES EVERY TWENTY-FOUR HOURS, HAVING IN GENERAL FULL LIBERTY OF ACTION. THIS IS RELATIVELY LITTLE COMPARED WITH THE THIRTY OR FORTY ABUSES COMMITED EACH DAY BEFORE THE CAUTERISATION. THE GOVERNESS IS ENCHANTED WITH THE RESULT OBTAINED. BUT X... MORE AND MORE DROPS ALL PRETENCE OF MODESTY. ONE NIGHT SHE SUCCEEDS IN RUBBING HERSELF TILL THE BLOOD COMES ON THE STRAPS THAT BIND HER. ANOTHER TIME, CAUGHT IN THE ACT BY THE GOVERNESS AND UNABLE TO SATISFY HERSELF, SHE HAS ONE OF HER TERRIBLE FITS OF RAGE, DURING WHICH SHE YELLS: "I WANT TO, OH HOW I WANT TO! YOU CAN'T UNDERSTAND, MADEMOISELLE, HOW I WANT TO DO IT!" HER MEMORY BEGINS TO FAIL, SHE CAN NO LONGER KEEP UP WITH LESSONS, SHE HAS HALLUCINATIONS ALL THE TIME. EVEN HER ARMS ARE COVERED WITH OEDEMA. THE SAME INDECENT ACTS AS IN THE PAST DURING THEIR OUTINGS: SHE THROWS HERSELF ON THE BUSHES, KICKS HER PARTS WITH HER HEEL, ETC. HER URINE CONTAINS NO ALBUMIN.

THE 23RD, SHE REPEATS: "I DESERVE TO BE BURNT AND I WILL BE. I WILL BE BRAVE DURING THE OPERATION, I WON'T CRY." FROM TEN AT NIGHT UNTIL SIX IN THE MORNIING, SHE HAS A TERRIBLE ATTACK, FALLING SEVERAL TIMES INTO A SWOON THAT LASTED ABOUT A QUARTER OF AN HOUR. AT TIMES SHE HAD VISUAL HALLUCINATIONS, AT OTHER TIMES SHE BECAME DELIRIOUS, WILD EYED, SAYING: "TURN THE PAGE, WHO IS HITTING ME, ETC."

THE 25TH I APPLY A HOT POINT TO X...'S CLITORIS. SHE SUBMITS TO THE OPERATION WITHOUT WINCING, AND FOR TWENTY-FOUR HOURS AFTER THE OPERATION SHE IS PERFECTLY GOOD. BUT THEN SHE RETURNS WITH RENEWED FRENZY TO HER OLD HABITS. FINALLY, TO OBVIATE ANY FRICTION, SHE IS KEPT ON HER FEET, LEGS CLOSED AND TIED TOGETHER, OR ELSE ATTACHED TO A CHAIR, BUT LYING ON HER BACK TO AVOID ANY RUBBING ON THE CHAIR'S EDGE. SHE COMPLAINS OF VAGUE PAINS IN THE CHEST, SHE BEGINS TO COUGH, BUT AN EXAMINATION OF THE CHEST REVEALS NOTHING.

LITTLE Y... IS GOOD. THE INFLAMMATION SET UP BY VICIOUS RUBBING HAS DISAPPEARED. THE 12TH OF OCTOBER THE HORRORS BEGIN AGAIN. LITTLE Y... HOWLS LIKE A WILD BEAST WHEN SHE HEARS ME COMING. I TRY GIVING HER SEVERAL VIOLENT AND VERY PAINFUL ELECTRIC SHOCKS ON THE PARTS WITH CLARK'S APPARATUS. AS MIGHT BE EXPECTED, THIS METHOD PROVES UNSUCCESSFUL. ON THE CONTRARY, ACCORDING TO THE GOVERNESS, Y... BECAME HIGHLY EXCITED AND ABUSED HERSELF EVEN MORE THAN SHE HAD DURING THE DAYS BEFOREHAND.

THE 17TH, X... ONCE AGAIN HAS A VERITABLE FIT OF FOLLY DURING WHICH SHE TRIES TO THROW HERSELF OUT OF THE WINDOW. YESTERDAY, SHE RUBBED THE VAGINA SO VIOLENTLY WITH A PIECE OF BRONZE SHE BLED FREELY. I CAUTERISE THE CLITORIS AND ENTRY TO THE VAGINA. FROM THEN ON THE TWO LITTLE PATIENTS WERE NO LONGER UNDER MY OBSERVATION. THEY WERE SEPARATED. ACCORDING TO MY INFORMATION, LITTLE Y... WAS COMPLETELY CURED. AS TO X..., SHE CONTINUES TO ABUSE HERSELF AS IN THE PAST. SHE IS FAR AWAY, IN THE COUNTRY, WITHOUT ANY MEDICAL SUPERVISION AND DEPRIVED OF ALL TREATMENT.

COMMENTS

THE DETAILS OF THE FOREGOING CASE-HISTORY HAVE BEEN RELATED IN SUCH METICULOUS DETAIL, AND THE SALIENT POINTS OF THIS INTERESTING CASE MADE SUFFICIENTLY CLEAR FOR THE ADDITION OF ANY LONG COMMENTARIES TO BECOME UNNECESSARY.

EXAMPLES OF ONANISM AT SUCH AN EARLY AGE ARE RARE IN LITTLE GIRLS, WE KNOW OF ONLY TWO CASES: THAT OF FONASSA-GRIVES RELATING TO A SEVEN YEAR OLD CHILD WHOSE HABITS NECESSI-TATED THE REMEDY OF A BELT, WITHOUT ANY SUCCESS, FOR THE CHILD OBTAINED SATISFACTION BY SLIPPING A LONG FEATHER INSIDE THE BANDAGE IN ORDER TO REACH THE GENITAL PARTS; AND THAT OF DESLANDES, WHOSE PATIENT WAS A LITTLE GIRL OF THREE. IN SPITE OF SUCH PRECOCIOUS ABUSE AND ITS FREQUENT REPETI-TION, THIS YOUNG GIRL MANAGED TO RESIST UNTIL MARRIAGE.

IN THE CASE OF THE TWO LITTLE SISTERS, AS OUR OBSERVATION DEMONSTRATES, ONANISM WAS BOTH CLITORIAL AND VAGINAL.

IF ONE SEEKS THE ORIGIN, THE EARLY CIRCUM-STANCES IN WHICH THESE VICIOUS HABITS WERE CONTRACTED, TWO PRINCIPAL CAUSES EMERGE: THE INTESTINAL PARASITES (AT LEAST IN THE CASE OF THE ELDER SISTER), AND INITIATION. AT AN EARLY AGE, LITTLE X... HAD WORMS, FOR WHICH I TREATED HER. NOW, BOTH THE RASH ON THE SEXUAL PARTS AND THE PRESENCE OF HELMIN-THES AT THE LOWER EXTREMITY OF THE RECTUM CAN, BY THE IRRESISTABLE IRRITATION THEY CAUSE, LEAD TO THE MANUAL EXCITATION OF THE PARTS. BUT X...'S CURIOSITY HAD ALREADY BEEN AROUSED BY THE MAID TOUCHING HERSELF VIGOROUSLY WHEN SHE BELIEVED THE CHILD TO BE ASLEEP. AS TO LITTLE Y..., AT THE AGE OF FOUR SHE WAS CORRUPTED BY HER SISTER, IN COMPANY WITH OTHER CHILDREN.

BECAUSE OF THEIR YOUTH AT THE TIME THEY BEGAN TO ABUSE THEMSELVES, IT WOULD HAVE BEEN IMPOSSIBLE FOR OUR YOUNG PATIENTS TO HAVE DONE SO BY GENITAL NEED. IT WAS SIMPLY BY IMITATION, OR TO ALLEVIATE BOREDOM WHEN LEFT UNOCCUPIED. IT WAS ONLY AFTER CONSTANT REPETITION OF SUCH CONTACTS THAT AN AWAKEN-ING OF THE SEXUAL INSTINCTS TOOK PLACE, WITH IMPULSION TO SATISFY THEM IMMEDIATELY AT ALL COSTS. I THINK WE MAY CONSIDER THIS IRRESIST-ABLE DESIRE, THIS UNCONTROLLABLE CRAVING WHICH TOOK POSSESSION OF THE CHILDREN, AS A VERITABLE NEUROSIS. VERY OFTEN X... STRUG-GLED WITH ALL HER MIGHT TO OVERCOME THE UNHEALTHY IMPULSE WHICH DROVE HER TO EXCITE HER ORGANS. WITH THE BEST WILL IN THE WORLD SHE COULD NO MORE CONTROL HERSELF THAN A SUFFERER FROM CHOLERA CAN PREVENT CRAMPS, OR AN HYSTERICAL WOMAN AVERT AN ONCOMING ATTACK.

MANY TIMES X... TRIED TO GET THE BETTER OF HERSELF, BEGGING TO BE TIED UP AND PREVENTED FROM DOING IT! A MOMENT LATER SHE EMPLOYED EVERY RUSE TO OUTWIT THE VIGILANCE OF THOSE IN CHARGE OF HER.

IN THE BEGINNING, THE STIMULUS FOR THESE VICIOUS HABITS ORIGINATED EXCLUSIVELY IN THE ENCEPHALON: ONLY LATER AS A RESULT OF FREQUENT AND REPEATED RUBBING, THE STIMULUS ORIGINATING FROM THE GENITAL PARTS THEM-SELVES.

LITTLE X... SUFFERED FROM MULTIPLE NERVOUS DISORDERS. EITHER SHE WAS SUBJECT TO THE MOST PROFOUND DEPRESSION, OR ELSE PREY TO A MANIACAL AGITATION SO VIOLENT THAT THE CHILD, USUALLY SO SWEET AND DOCILE, BECAME AS FURIOUS AS A WILD BEAST, HITTING AND BITING THOSE SHE MOST RESPECTED IF THEY OPPOSED THE SATISFACTION OF HER CRAVING WHEN HER EXCITEMENT WAS AT ITS HEIGHT.

THIS WAS FOLLOWED SOON AFTER BY A PERIOD OF PROSTRATION, OF CALM AND REMORSE. THE EXTINCTION OF ALL MORAL SENSE SHOULD ALSO RECEIVE SPECIFIC MENTION. WHENEVER THE TWO CHILDREN WERE OVERCOME BY AN ARDENT DESIRE TO MASTURBATE THEY DID NOT CARE IN THE LEAST ABOUT PROPRIETY OR THOSE PRESENT. THEY GAVE WAY WITHOUT BLUSHING TO THEIR DISGRACEFUL PRACTICES IN FRONT OF PASSERS-BY OR SER-VANTS. IF TO THIS WE ADD THE HALLUCINAITONS WO WHICH X... WAS FREQUENTLY SUBJECT, THERE CAN BE NO DOUBT THAT SHE SUFFERED FROM DEEP PSYCHIC DISTURBANCE.

X...'S EYE-SIGHT HAD ALSO CONSIDERABLY DETERIORATED. ON THIS POINT I FEEL IT NECES-SARY TO REFER TO A SIMILAR CASE WHICH CAME UNDER MY OBSERVATION WHEN I PRACTISED IN PARIS. IT WAS THAT OF A YOUNG LADY OF TWENTY-EIGHT YEARS OLD WHO CONFESSED TO ME THAT SHE TOUCHED HERSELF A GREAT MANY TIMES EACH DAY, WHICH LED TO A PROGRESSIVE AND ALMOST TOTAL AMAUROSIS.

DESMARRES SENIOR, TO WHOM I SENT THE PATIENT WITHOUT ACQUAINTING HIM OF HER HABITS, RECOGNISED THE ESSENTIAL CAUSE OF HER FAILING SIGHT. HE INFORMED ME OF IT IN A SEALED LETTER WHICH HE GAVE THE PATIENT. LATER, HAVING FOLLOWED OUR ADVICE, THIS YOUNG LADY RENOUNCED ONAN AND ALSO RECOVERED PER-FECT EYE-SIGHT.

I WILL SAY JUST A WORD CONCERNING THE THERAPEUTIC METHODS EMPLOYED IN THE CASE OF THE LITTLE GIRLS: MEDICAMENTS HAD NO EFFECT, NEITHER SEDATIVES NOR TONICS MET WITH ANY SUCCESS. NOR DID SHOWERS AND WARM BATHS BRING ABOUT A RETURN TO NORMAL. MORAL THERAPY WAS EQUALLY INEFFECTUAL. ADVICE, COAXING, CARESSES, INTIMIDATION, THE CRUEL-LEST PUNISHMENT, RELIGION WITH ITS THREATS AND PROMISES, NOTHING COULD DISSUADE THESE POOR CHILDREN FROM YIELDING TO THEIR FATAL ADDICTION!

PUBIC BELT, STRAIT JACKET, STRAPS, BONDS, THE MOST ASSIDUOUS SUPERVISION ONLY RESULTED IN

THE INVENTION OF NEW EXPEDIENTS INSPIRED BY RUSE AND SUBTLETY.

CAUTERISATION BY HOT IRON ALONE GAVE SATISFACTORY RESULTS. AFTER THE FIRST OPERATION, FROM FORTY TO FIFTY TIMES A DAY, THE NUMBER OF VOLUPTUOUS SPASMS WAS REDUCED TO THREE OR FOUR. ACCORDING TO THE INFORMATION I RECEIVED, LITTLE Y... THANKS TO THIS METHOD, WAS COMPELTELY CURED. IN ALL, SHE WAS CAUTERISED FOUR TIMES. X... UNDERWENT ONLY ONE CAUTERISATION, AFTER WHICH I LOST SIGHT OF HER ENTIRELY. THERE IS NO REASON TO CONCLUDE THEN, THAT SHE PERSISTS IN HER ABUSE, OR THAT THE METHOD IS INEFFECTIVE.

IT IS REASONABLE TO INFER THAT CAUTERISATON BY HOT IRON DIMINISHES THE SENSITIVITY OF THE CLITORIS, WHICH CAN BE COMPLETELY DESTROYED IF THE OPERATION IS REPEATED A CERTAIN NUMBER OF TIMES. THE SECOND POINT OF GENITAL SENSITIVITY CONSTITUTED BY THE VULVAL ORIFICE HAVING ALSO BEEN DEADENED BY THE CAUTERISATION, IT IS EASY TO CONCEIVE THAT THE CHILDREN, HAVING BECOME LESS EXCITABLE, ARE ALSO LESS PRONE TO TOUCH THEMSELVES.

IT IS EQUALLY PROBABLE THAT, THE CLITORIS AND VULVAL ORIFICE HAVING BECOME MORE OR LESS INFLAMED AS A RESULT OF THE OPERATION, THAT TOUCHING MAY PROVE PAINFUL RATHER THAN A SOURCE OF PLEASURE.

FINALLY, THE TERROR PROVOKED BY THE SIGHT OF THE INSTRUMENTS, AND THE IMPRESSION MADE ON THE CHILDREN'S IMAGINATION BY THE RED HOT IRON MUST ALSO BE COUNTED AMONG THE BENEFICIAL EFFECTS OF TRANSCURRENT CAUTERISATION.

WE BELIEVE THEN, THAT IN CASES SIMILAR TO THOSE SUBMITTED TO YOUR CONSIDERATION, ONE SHOULD NOT HESITATE TO RESORT TO THE HOT IRON, AND AT AN EARLY HOUR, IN ORDER TO COMBAT CLITORAL AND VAGINAL ONANISM IN LITTLE GIRLS.

DEMETRIUS ZAMBACO

TRANSLATED BY CATHERINE DUNCAN

SOFT SEX

ROBERTE'S DIARY (CONTINUED)

MAY 1954

I LEAVE OCTAVE TO HIS RATIOCINATIONS AND HIS PRAYERS: THAT HE SHOULD HAVE THE INCONCEIVABLE ARROGANCE TO IMAGINE HIMSELF THE AUTHOR OF MY IMPROPRIETIES IS ONE THING—BUT AS TO CONSIDERING HIMSELF AT THE ORIGIN OF MY TEMPERAMENT ... THE POOR DEAR HAS NO IDEA WHAT I AM CAPABLE OF WHITHOUT HIM, AND THOUGH HE GOES TO SO MUCH TROUBLE SUPPOSING WHAT HAPPENS TO ME AND WHAT HE'D LIKE TO SEE ME SUBMITTED TO, I'LL NEVER TELL HIM THE THINGS THAT HAVE HAPPENED AND STILL COULD HAPPEN TO ME IN ALL LIKELIHOOD: ANTOINE WOULD KNOW ABOUT IT AT ONCE AND NEVER SLEEP AGAIN.

ONCE I WOULD NEVER HAVE DREAMED OF GOING BACK OVER SUCH THINGS. I MEAN THOSE DUE TO OCTAVE. BUT NOWADAYS I CAN'T RESIST TELLING MYSELF THE STORY OF THIS OR THAT INCIDENT (WHICH TOOK PLACE UNKNOWN TO HIM): NOTHING COULD BE MORE VULGAR, BUT SINCE THAT HAPPENED TO ME AND KEEPS COMING BACK TO ME, I'LL TRY TO TAKE REFUGE IN WORDS SO AS NOT TO HAVE TO THINK ABOUT IT DURING THE DAY. THIS MORNING AT THE COMMISSION I WAS DISTRAIT BECAUSE OF THAT, NO ONE NOTICED, BUT EVEN SO

... NOT EVEN A BATH WAS ANY HELP, LIKE THE LAST TIME. IS IT POSSIBLE THAT A WOMAN SEEKS TO EXPERIENCE A VIOLENT FEELING OF SHAME JUST BECAUSE SHE IS RESPECTABLE? IT'S A POINT OF VIEW: FOR A LONG TIME OCTAVE HAS MADE IT HIS PABULUM. FOR ME SUCH A RESEARCH IS UNREAL, NO DOUBT; OR AM I INCITED BY MY RESPECTABILITY TO MAKE IT? I REMEMBER THAT I WAS ASHAMED: WAS MY VOLUPTUARY ANY THE LESS FOR THAT? AND NOW MY SHAME IS EVEN LESS REPUGNANT TO ME IN RETROSPECT SINCE I CAN SEE HOW ATTRACTIVE I MUST HAVE BEEN TO THOSE TWO INDIVIDUALS... DOES THAT MEAN THEY HAVE SOME IMPORTANCE BECAUSE OF IT? SHOULD THE SAME THING HAPPEN AGAIN, IN ALL HONESTY I MUST ADMIT I WOULD NOT RESIST, AND I TAKE (AS I DID EARLIER) AS MUCH PLEASURE IN MY DISGRACE AS THOSE WHO INFLICTED IT ON ME.

AFTER MY MANICURE, RUE SCRIBE, JUSTIN WHO WAS WAITING FOR ME AT THE WHEEL OF OUR BUICK COULDN'T GET IT TO START. THE BREAKDOWN DIDN'T WORRY ME, I HAD TIME TO KILL BEFORE RETURNING TO THE PALAIS BOURBON, AND, NOT HAVING ARRANGED ANY APPOINTMENTS IN THE MEANTIME, I WANTED TO MAKE THE MOST OF SUCH A WARM AND WONDERFULLY SUNNY AFTERNOON. I JUMPED ON

THE PLATFORM OF THE FIRST BUS, AND LEANT OUT WATCHING IN A KIND OF DREAM THE SHOPS GO BY, WHEN A SUGGESTIVE PRESSURE FORCED ME TO CHANGE PLACES AND SIT INSIDE... AS HE DIDN'T STOP LOOKING AT ME, I ROSE AND GOT OUT AT THE THÉÂTRE FRANCAIS. PASSING THROUGH THE ENTRY OF THE PALAIS-ROYAL, I SET OFF DOWN THE GALLERY DE MONTPENSIER. UNDER THE ARCADES ALMOST DESERTED AT THAT HOUR, FOOTSTEPS LIKE THE ECHO OF MY OWN DREW CLOSER: SOMETHING QUITE USUAL FOR A MEMBER OF PARLIAMENT, I WAS BEING FOLLOWED. THE INDIVIDUAL, A KIND OF LARGE COLOSSUS, FAT, CLEAN-SHAVEN, THE PERFECT TYPE OF POLICE PIMP, STOPS TWO OR THREE SHOP WINDOWS AWAY EACH TIME I GLANCE AT ONE OR OTHER OF THE DISPLAYS. WHERE CAN THE NEW BLOUSE SHOP BE THAT GILBERTE TOLD ME ABOUT? FINALLY I PASS UNDER THE VAULT OF THE GALLERY DE BEAUJO-LAIS: IT MUST BE THERE, TO THE RIGHT. BUT AT THIS SAME MOMENT THE INDIVIDUAL WALKS PAST ME. I PUSH OPEN A GLASS DOOR, MISTAKING THE SHOP— THIS ONE IS UNDERGOING TRANSFORMATION—THE INDIVIDUAL FOLLOWS ME IN. ALTHOUGH IT IS QUITE POSSIBLE FOR PEOPLE PASSING OR STOPPING IN FRONT OF THE BOOK-SHOP OPPOSITE TO SEE THROUGH THE HALF-FROSTED PANE ANYTHING UNUSUAL THAT MIGHT HAPPEN IN THE EMPTY SHOP, NO ONE GIVES IT A THOUGHT. HIS BACK AGAINST THE GLASS DOOR, THE COLOSSUS BARS MY PASSAGE AS SOON AS I TRY TO LEAVE, HIS HAND ON THE KNOB. THEN, THROUGH A DOOR AT THE REAR, ANOTHER MAN APPEARS, OF MEDIUM HEIGHT, SQUAT IN SHIRT SLEEVES. THE TWO EXCHANGE A CONNIVING LOOK. THE SECOND MAN STANDS ASIDE AND LEAVES THE INNER DOOR AJAR.

LESS THAN AN HOUR LATER I FIND MYSELF SITTING OUTSIDE THE REGENCY CAFÉ, MY TEMPLES POUNDING. MY HANDS ARE TREMBLING NO DOUBT AND THE WAITER ASKS ME AT ONCE IF I'M ALL RIGHT. I SMILE, RISE AND GO TO THE WASHROOM, CONSIDER MYSELF IN THE MIRROR: NO NEED TO PUT ON NEW MAKE-UP, I LOOK FINE. WHAT, IN FACT, DO I HAVE AGAINST THEM? IF THEY GOT A PITIFUL PLEASURE... FOR ME, NOW THE PLEASURE BEGINS. I RETURN TO THE TERRACE AND RECAPITULATE. WHEN I HAD STOOD ON THE PLATFORM OF THE BUS, MY BACK AGAINST THE RAIL, ARM RAISED, HAND LYING ON THE BALUSTRADE, THE COLOSSUS, WHO WAS TALKING TO THE CONDUCTOR AT FIRST, TOOK MY FINGERS. I HAD GONE INSIDE AND CHOSEN AN EMPTY SEAT, BUT HE, HAVING SAT DOWN OPPOSITE, BEGAN SCRUTINIZING ME IN AN INSOLENT FASHION. I WAS SEATED, BOTH HANDS LYING ON THE LEATHER,

LEGS APART PERHAPS, AND A SMILE ON MY LIPS FEELING THE WARM BREEZE THROUGH THE LOWERED WINDOW. DID I CONTINUE TO SMILE WITH HALF-OPEN LIPS AS HIS REGARD BECAME MORE INTENT? AT LEAST I IMMEDIATELY CROSSED MY LEGS, FOLDED MY HANDS. ALL THE SAME I WAS WEARING THE ROSETTE OF THE LEGION OF HONOUR IN THE BUTTONHOLE OF MY SUIT. IT WAS THEN I DECIDED TO GET OUT, AND I REMEMBER, I PULLED OFF THE ROSETTE AND HID IT IN MY BAG. CASUALLY I CROSSED THE SQUARE OF THE THÉÂTRE FRANCAIS, WALKED INTO THE PALAIS-ROYAL, AND SO ON UNTIL REACHING THE VAULT OF THE GALLERY DE BEAUJOLAIS... AT THIS POINT LET ME TRY TO IMAGINE EACH STAGE OF THE INDIVIDUAL'S ITINERARY. I HAD ATTRACTED HIM. HE HAD FOUND IT NECESSARY TO TOUCH MY FINGERS AND AFTER THAT THERE COULD BE NO STOPPING FOR HIM UNTIL THE DESCENT INTO THE BASEMENT. BEGINNING WITH THAT FURTIVE BUT IRRESISTABLE PRESSURE, WHAT A RAPID AND AT THE SAME TIME DETAILED SCENARIO MUST HAVE UNWOUND INSIDE HIS SKULL... OR HAD THERE BEEN NOTHING ALL THE WAY BUT THE SOLE IMAGE OF THOSE PARALLEL BARS AND THE FEAR THEY MIGHT REMAIN FIXED IN VAIN UNTIL THE END OF THE DAY? WHEN HE FOUND HIMSELF AFTERWARDS ON HIS KNEES IN FRONT OF ME, FINALLY BOUND HAND AND FOOT, POWERLESS, DID THE TWO IMAGES: ONE OF THE BEAUTIFUL UNKNOWN WOMAN WITH THE ROSETTE, THE OTHER OF THE SAME WOMAN SUSPENDED AND TIED, DID THEY COINCIDE TO THE POINT OF SUBSTITUTION, OR WERE THEY SUFFICIENTLY CONTRADICTORY TO PROVOKE THE EMOTION THAT CONTORTED HIS SORRY FACE? ONCE HAVING GOT OFF THE BUS, THEN FOLLOWING CLOSE ENOUGH ON MY HEELS TO WATCH ME STROLL AHEAD OF HIM UNDER THE ARCADES OF THE PALAIS, HAVING "CONTACTED" THE EPIDERMUS OF MY FINGERS, HE MUST HAVE BEEN ELABORATING THAT SENSATION, EXTENDING IT TO MY WHOLE BODY WHICH HE WAS CONSCIOUS OF, STUDYING THE MOVEMENT OF MY HIPS, MY POSSIBLE POSITIONS IN THE IMPENDING SITUATION WHICH HE KNEW WAS UNPRECEDENTED FOR ME, INCONCEIVABLE AND THEREFORE ALL THE MORE IMPERIOUS FOR HIM ... TO THAT MOMENT WHEN THE ONLY THING HE COULD DO WAS TO CORNER ME IN THE EMPTY SHOP. IT WAS WHILE, ALMOST DAZED, HE WAS CONSIDERING MY HAND ON THE KNOB WHICH HE PREVENTED ME FROM OPENING, THAT THE SQUAT MAN LOOMED UP THROUGH THE REAR DOOR, THAT FATAL DOOR AJAR ON THE SHADOWY STAIRCASE! PERCEIVING AN EXIT TO THE FLOOR ABOVE GIVING ON TO THE RUE DE BEAUJOLAIS NO DOUBT, I TRIED TO MAKE A DASH FOR IT. BUT THE

SQUAT MAN WAS WAITING FOR ME ON THE STAIRS, BRINGS HIS HAND DOWN ON MY FINGERS AS THEY GRIP THE BALUSTRADE, AND I, STILL BELIEVING IT POSSIBLE TO ESCAPE, SNATCH THEM AWAY, TURN DOWN AGAIN AND—TWO STEPS FROM THE BACK-ROOM OF THE SHOP—THE MOMENT COMES WHEN, STILL DETERMINED TO DEFEND MYSELF, HITTING THE COLOSSUS IN THE FACE WITH MY BAG, I SAW HIM CROUCH, OR SLUMP RATHER ... AND AT THE SAME TIME INSINUATE HIMSELF UNDER MY SKIRT IN BETWEEN SUSPENDER BELT AND FLESH, GRABBING A HANDFUL OF THIGH, HIS ARM GOES ROUND MY LEGS, LIFTS ME, THROWS ME OVER HIS SHOULDER, THE WHOLE MOVEMENT SO UNEXPECTED AND PRECIPITATE I HAVE TO SAVE MYSELF BY HANGING ON TO THE NAPE OF HIS NECK WITH BOTH HANDS— AND THEN THE DIZZY DESCENT WITH ME BY THE SPIRAL STAIRCASE TO THE BASEMENT. THE OTHER MAN WHO HAD PRECEDED HIM WAS ALREADY PUSHING OPEN THE HEAVY STEEL DOOR GIVING ON TO A NEON-LIGHTED ROOM WITH GLEAMING WALLS. THE FLOOR SHONE WITH LINOLEUM AND, AS THE ENORMOUS FANS OF A VENTILATOR BEGAN TO WHIRR ON THE CEILING, THERE IN THE MIDDLE OF A PHYSICAL CULTURE SET-UP, THE SIGHT OF THOSE PARALLEL BARS EQUIPPED WITH LEATHER STRAPS ... TO THINK THAT A MOMENT AGO I WAS STROLLING LEISURELY BETWEEN THE OPERA AND THE THÉÂTRE FRANCAIS WHILE HERE THOSE BARS WERE WAITING FOR ME! SO THAT NOW, TIED BY THE WRISTS, MY CLAMMY HANDS EXHALE THE PERFUME OF THEIR CREAM IN THE STUFFY AIR DESPITE THE VENTILATORS, THE NAILS PERFECT AND USE-LESS... WITHOUT SHOWING ANY INTEREST IN MY BUST OR REMOVING THE COAT OF MY GREY SUIT, MY SKIRT IS UNHOOKED AND THE REST TAKEN OFF. I CAN STILL KICK; MY ANKLES ARE SPREAD AND ATTACHED TO THE EXTREMITIES OF THE VERTICAL BARS AND ALL THAT IN SILENCE, A SILENCE MADE OF MY OWN MUTISM IN ACCORDANCE WITH THE TWO MEN, AS IF OUR BREATHING REPLACED ANY WORDS WE COULD EXCHANGE HERE. THE COLOSSUS APPROACHES HIS MOUTH TO ONE OF MY TIED HANDS AND, AS I CLOSE MY FIST, HE UNFOLDS AND STRAIGHTENS MY FINGERS, PASSES THEM BETWEEN HIS LIPS AND DELICATELY SAVOURS EACH NAIL. THEN, HAVING TAKEN BREATH, REELING AND SWEATING, LEANING AGAINST THE BAR, HE PUTS OUT HIS TONGUE WHICH MOVES BACKWARDS AND FORWARDS IN A MISERABLE ATTEMPT AND ONLY SLOWLY SUCCEEDS IN TOUCHING MY OPEN PALM. AT LAST THIS TONGUE SETTLES THERE AND BEGINS ITS TITILLATIONS MORE AND MORE RAPIDLY. I TURN MY HEAD AWAY... SOON I CAN CONTROL MYSELF NO LONGER, IN VAIN I ATTEMPT TO LIFE MY KNEE TO HIDE THE IRRESISTABLE EFFECTS ON MY THIGH. "PUT OUT THE LIGHTS THEN," I SAY IN A VOICE NO LONGER MY OWN, DURING WHICH TIME THE SQUAT MAN EXHIBITS A CARD OSTENTATIOUSLY AND SLIPS IT INTO MY BAG. BUT THE LIGHT STAYS ON AND, EYES CLOSED, UNDER THE WHIRR OF THE FANS ON THE CEILING, I ABANDON MYSELF IN FRONT OF THOSE TWO UNKNOWN MEN... WHAT A RELIEF IT IS LETTING MYSELF GO AT LAST, BESIDE MYSELF WITH PLEASURE UNDER THEIR EYES IN THAT IMPOSSIBLE POSITION. THE SOUND OF A DULL THUD AT MY FEET. I OPEN MY EYES, THE COLOSSUS HAS COLLAPSED. THE SQUAT MAN TAKES HIM UNDER THE SHOUL-DERS AND DRAGS HIM STAGGERING AWAY. FOR MORE THAN A MINUTE I STAY THERE, TIED UP, ALONE, CERTAINLY THE LEAST PLEASANT MOMENT IN WHAT I CANNOT EVEN CALL A NIGHTMARE. AND I AM ALMOST GLAD TO SEE THE SECOND MAN RETURN, SLOWLY, HANDS IN POCKET—FAIR BOY, CREW-CUT HAIR, LEVEL EYES, INTELLIGENT EXPRESSION. HIS SHIRT IS IMPECCABLY WHITE AND HIS HANDS, WHICH HE NOW TAKES OUT OF HIS POCKETS TO UNTIE ME, WELL KEPT, A BRACELET ON THE LEFT WRIST. HE TURNS AWAY WHILE I READJUST MY SKIRT, GOES TO FIND MY BAG AND RETURNS TO GIVE IT TO ME, OFFERING ME A GLASS OF BRANDY. BUT I SLAPPED HIM. THEN, WITH A GESTURE, HE RIPS OFF MY SKIRT AGAIN, PUTS HIS FOOT ON IT, RETURNS HIS HANDS TO HIS POCKETS AND, WITHOUT FLINCHING, RECEIVES ANOTHER SLAP; AFTER WHICH THERE IS NO STOPPING ME TILL I HAVE NO STRENGTH LEFT... WHAT ELSE COULD A WOMAN DO IN SUCH A SITUATION? ... SCREAM, OBVIOUSLY, DISTURB THE WHOLE BUILDING—IN SUCH A BUSY QUARTER—BUT WOMEN LIKE ME WHO WERE ON THE "CHARITY FRONT," WOMEN LIKE ME WHO ARE NOW AT THE CONTROLS OF THE NATION, WOMEN LIKE ME WHO HAVE "BEEN AROUND"—SO LONG AS WE ARE BEAUTIFUL, SO LONG AS WE REMAIN SO—WE CAN ONLY REMAIN SILENT. CALL FOR AN INVESTIGATION? BECAUSE OF THIS CARD WHICH REPRODUCES ... MY FINGER-PRINTS? RETURN TO THE "SOURCE"? HARDLY WORK ENOUGH FOR THE RUE DE SAUSSAIES TO KEEP THAT INCAPABLE C. OCCUPIED... WHAT NONSENSE! BUT TO RETURN ONE OF THESE DAYS TO THAT PLACE, RUN MY HANDS OVER THOSE PARALLEL BARS WHERE THEY HAD BEEN SO FIRMLY TIED ... THAT'S ANOTHER MATTER. THAT PARTICULAR OCCASION OF FEELING REALLY MYSELF FROM THE MOMENT WHEN I EMBARKED ON THE ADVENTURE IN THE BUS UNTIL THAT OTHER MOMENT IN THE BASEMENT WHEN I FOUND MYSELF SUSPENDED AND AROUSED, THAT OCCASION IS STILL NEITHER MORE NOR LESS THAN THE BOW OF MY REFLECTION DRAWN OVER THIS

LAZY AFTERNOON. WHAT A DELICIOUS CROISSANT!
HOW SOOTHING THE PLAY OF THE FOUNTAINS
UNDER THE PLANE TREES! HOW EXQUISITE THE CITY
AS IT GLIDES BY!

PIERRE KLOSSOWSKI
TRANSLATION BY CATHERINE DUNCAN

TAKEN FROM THE REVOCATION OF THE
EDICT OF NANTES.

SEQUENCE OF THE PARALLEL BARS

(SHOT LIST BY PIERRE KLOSSOWSKI MADE ROUND 1966 FOR AN IMAGINARY FILM)

1. LONG SHOT, CROSSROADS RUE SCRIBE-OPERA.

2. THE CAR IN PAN SHOT FROM ROBERTE.

3. JUSTIN, THE CHAUFFEUR, GETS OUT, LIFTS THE BONNET.

4. ROBERTE GETS OUT SLOWLY IN HER TURN.

5. FRONT OF PALAIS BOURBON (HOUSE OF PARLIAMENT).

6. WATCH ON ROBERTE'S WRIST.

THE OCTOPUS IN JAPAN

THE OCTOPUS IS USUALLY CONSIDERED TO BE BENEFICIAL. AT THE ORDER OF THE PROTECTOR YAKU-SHI NYO-RAÏ, BUDDHA THE HEALER OF SOULS AND THE GOD OF WISDOM, THREW A SMALL SCULPTED STATUE IN THE IMAGE OF THIS DIVINITY (WITH WHICH HE HAD NEVER PARTED) INTO THE SEA DURING A TEMPEST. IT WAS SAVED. LATER, AN OCTOPUS CARRIED IT TO JAPAN AND SET IT DOWN ON THE COAST OF HIRA-DO. JI-KAKU DAÏ-SHI THEN BUILT A TEMPLE AT MEGURO, WHERE HE ERECTED A LARGE STATUE OF YAKU-SHI IN THE WOODS, WHICH SERVED AS A CASE FOR THE RELIC.

IN THE SAME WAY, ONE OF THE PRINCIPLE MESSENGERS OF RYŪ-JIN IS FIGURED WITH AN OCTOPUS ON HIS HEAD. THE ASCETIC KEN-SU SOMETIMES CARRIES IT ON HIS SHOULDERS, TO THE PLACE OF THE TRADITIONAL SHRIMP, WHICH BRINGS TO MIND HIS SOLE NOURISHMENT. THE ASHI-NAGA ARE LEGENDARY MEN WHO CARRY THE TE-NAGA, WITH ITS NINE-METER-LONG ARMS, ON THEIR SHOULDERS. THEY THEMSELVES HAVE LEGS SEVEN METERS LONG, AROUND WHICH THE OCTOPUS' TENTACLES ARE ALWAYS WRAPPED. ONE THUS THINKS OF THE OCTOPUS AS FRIENDLY, HELPFUL, A LITTLE LIKE THE PRINCE OF THE GREEKS, AND ENJOYING THE COMPANY OF MONASTICS.

ON THE OTHER HAND, ITS SENSUALITY, IS NO LESS INDICATIVE AS A CHARACTERISTIC TRAIT OF ITS NATURE. CLEARLY THIS IS VERIFIED IN THE LEGEND OF THE BEAUTIFUL AND LICENTIOUS KIYO-HIME, WHO SOUGHT THE IMMODEST ADVANCES OF THE MONK AN-CHI. THE PRIEST HID ON THE BELL OF THE MONASTERY, SIX FEET HIGH AND SO HEAVY THAT ONE HUNDRED MEN COULD NOT LIFT IT. IT FELL AND THUS IMPRISONED THE SAINTLY MAN. KIYO-HIME TRIED TO BREAK THE METAL WITH HIS MAGIC WAND AND MAKE IT MELT BY EXHALING ON IT WITH HIS FLAMING BREATH. IN VAIN. IT WAS CHANGED INTO A SORCERER WITH A HUMAN HEAD AND A DRAGON'S AND SERPENT'S BODY, LIKE ANOTHER GIANT OCTOPUS LOVINGLY EMBRACING THE BELL WITH ITS SINUOUS TENTACLES.

MANY WORKS, NOTABLY AN ENGRAVING OF KOUNI-YOSHI, PROVIDE AN ELEGANT ILLUSTRATION OF A SIGNIFICANT CHANGE.

THIS CONSTANT LIAISON WITH SALACIOUSNESS EXPLAINS WITHOUT DOUBT THE EQUIVALENT ROLE WHICH THE OCTOPUS SEEMS TO PLAY IN BUDDHISM. THE SENSUALITY OF THE CREATURE APPEARS IN THE MOST EXPLICIT MANNER IN A FAMOUS ENGRAVING OF HOKOUSAÏ, WHICH PLAYS ON THE

MOLLUSK'S CAPACITIES FOR EMBRACING AND SUCTION. THE OCTOPUS, BETWEEN THE THIGHS OF A RECLINING WOMAN, IS GLUED GREEDILY TO THE SEX ORGAN OF ITS CONSENTING AND NO DOUBT GRATIFIED PREY, WHILE HE CARESSES AND ENTWINES, EXPLORES AND SUCKS WITH HIS EIGHT ARMS AND SUCKERS. THE ARMS CLOSE UPON THE BODY OF THE BELOVED IN A LASCIVIOUS WEB, WITHOUT EVEN REACHING THE NECK AND SHOULDERS, WHERE IT FINDS RELIEF AND LETS ITS TENTACLES WANDER. THERE IS ALSO A SMALLER OCTOPUS WHICH APPLIES ITS MOUTH, OR TO BE MORE EXACT, ITS HORNY BEAK OR TRUNK WITH AVIDITY TO THE FREE LIPS OFFERING THEMSELVES. THE ARTIST HAS PUT TO USE THE SURFEIT OF LUBRICITY WHICH COMES FROM THE CONSISTENCY AND CONFIGURATION OF THE CREATURE. WHAT HORROR IS SURELY ELICITED BY THE SPECTACLE! YET THE ARTIST'S INSISTENCE IS VISIBLY TO GIVE THE IMPRESSION OF ECSTASY PROCURED BY A PARTNER WHOSE CONTACT IS SIMULTANEOUSLY FELT IN SO MANY PLACES.

IN HIS WORK ON HOKOUSAÏ, EDMOND DE GONCOURT HAS SUCCESSFULLY CAPTURED THE ECSTATIC EXPRESSION OF THE WOMAN IN A SWOON OF PLEASURE, SICUT CADAVER, TO SUCH A DEGREE THAT ONE DOES NOT KNOW WHETHER SHE IF LIVING OR DROWNED.

BY THIS AMBIGUOUS PROCESS THE OCTOPUS SHARES THE IDENTITY WITH WHICH IT IS INVESTED BY THE EAST. IT IS CLEAR THAT IN THE MATTER OF LASCIVIOUSNESS, THE OCTOPUS ETCHED BY THE ASIATIC BELONGS TO THE SPECIES DESCRIBED BY THE MEDITERRANEAN OPPIEN, WHO STATES THAT THE MALE CLINGS TO HIS DELIGHT UNTIL HE DIES OF PLEASURE AND EXHAUSTION.

OPPIEN, IN ANTIQUITY, EMPHASIZED THE OCTOPUS' UNCTUOUS IMMODESTY; IN JAPAN, HOKOUSAI DEPICTED IT PREVAILING ON A SLEEPING WOMAN. IN THE 16TH CENTURY, ALDROVANI RECALLED THAT, ACCORDING TO THE ANCIENTS, ITS FLESH WAS AN APHRODISIAC, AND THAT THE CREATURE WAS CONSIDERED THE MOST LASCIVIOUS OF SEA DWELLERS. IN THE 19TH CENTURY, IT WAS FAR FROM FORGOTTEN BY VICTOR HUGO THAT "THIS LOATHSOME CREATURE HAS ITS PASSIONATE RELATIONS." THE FEMALE RADIATES A PHOSPHORESCENT GLOW AT THE MOMENT OF INITIATION: "SHE AWAITS UNION. SHE MAKES HERSELF BEAUTIFUL, SHE LIGHTS UP, SHE GLOWS ..." THE FLIRTATIOUSNESS AND LASCIVIOUSNESS OF THE OCTOPUS ARE IN NO SENSE CONCLUSIONS DRAWN

FROM OBSERVATION: ALMOST EXCLUSIVELY, THEY ARE DEDUCED FROM THE NUMBER OF TENTACLES AND THE ARRAY OF SUCKERS WHICH CHARACTERIZE THE SPECIES (MOLLUSK). IN FACT, THE AMOROUS RELATIONS OF THE OCTOPUS ARE EXCEEDINGLY CHASTE. TO MAN, THEY CAN HARDLY BE PERCEIVED AS ANYTHING BUT DISMAL.

ARISTOTLE OFFERS A SUMMARY DESCRIPTION OF THE MATING OF OCTOPI: TIGHTLY INTERTWINED, THEY PRESS MOUTH AGAINST MOUTH, ARM AGAINST ARM. IN THIS FASHION, ONE LEADING, ONE FOLLOWING, THEY SWIM TOGETHER. THIS DEPICTION IS PURELY IMAGINARY. I MYSELF FOUND NO OBJECTIVE DESCRIPTION OF OCTOPUS MATING BEFORE THE ONE BY HENRY LEE. FURTHERMORE, THE TERM "DESCRIPTION," IS INCONSISTENT WITH THE OBSCURELY CONVOLUTED AND AWKWARD STATEMENTS THAT THE AUTHOR, RESTRAINED BY VICTORIAN DECORUM, USES TO CONVEY THE IDEA OF THESE SEXUAL YET EXTRAORDINARILY ASCETIC RELATIONS. ACCORDING TO THE AUTHOR, IT SEEMS THAT THE RIGHT THIRD ARM OF THE MALE OCTOPUS SWELLS AT THE MOMENT OF EXCITATION; OUT OF THE ARM, A KIND OF ELONGATED WORM EMERGES WITH A FILAMENT AT THE END: THIS IS THE HECTOCOTYLE. THE MALE PROFFERS IT TO THE FEMALE, WHO ACCEPTS IT AND CARRIES IT AWAY WITH HER. SHE PLACES IT HERSELF WITHIN HER PALLIAL CAVITY, A POCKET SITUATED BETWEEN HER BODY AND THE FOLDS OF HER MANTLE, AT THE BACK OF WHICH THE GENITAL ORIFICES OPEN UP. THERE, THE HECTOCOTYLE COMES BACK TO LIFE TO FERTILIZE THE EGGS. ONE CAN SEE, LEE STATES, SUCH EXCRESCENCES SEVERED IN THIS STATE AND PRESERVED IN JARS IN THE MUSEUM OF NATURAL HISTORY IN PARIS. THE ENIGMATIC AND OBSCURE TEXT SEEMS TO HAVE KNOWN NO CONFIRMATION. IN FACT, ACCORDING TO LATER OBSERVATIONS, THINGS HAPPEN OTHERWISE.

WHILE ALL INDICATIONS SEEM TO DESTIN THESE BODIES TO ENTWINE, IN FACT, THERE IS NO EMBRACE AND VIRTUALLY NO CONTACT BETWEEN THEM. THEY AVOID, IF NOT TO SAY THEY FLEE, THE CLOSENESS AND INTIMATE, MULTIPLE, MUTUAL CONTACT THAT THEIR SUCKERS WOULD PERMIT. THE DISTANCE WHICH SEPARATES THE PARTNERS IS KEPT AS WIDE AS POSSIBLE. THESE CREATURES, WHO POSSESS THE MOST HIGHLY PERFECTED EYES IN THE ANIMAL KINGDOM, DO NOT EVEN LOOK AT EACH OTHER. THE FEMALE RESTS ON A ROCK OR ON THE SAND. THE MALE IS DRAWN UP ON HIS TENTACLES. AS LEE HAD WELL OBSERVED, ONE OF THESE TENTACLES, THE THIRD ON THE RIGHT SIDE,

IS ALTERED: A SPOON-SHAPED DEPRESSION REPLACES ONE SECTION OF THE SUCKERS. THE REPRODUCTIVE ORGAN WITH WHICH THE TENTACLE IS EQUIPPED INTRODUCES ITSELF WITHIN THE PALLIAL CAVITY OF THE FEMALE, BUT WITHOUT BECOMING DETACHED.

SUCH IS WHAT IS SHOWN, AT LEAST, IN THE DRAWING WHICH ACCOMPANIES THE STUDY ON THE MATING AND FERTILIZATION OF THE COMMON OCTOPUS OBTAINED BY E. G. RACOVITZA IN 1894. THE ALTERED ARM DEPOSITS CERTAIN SPERM-FILLED CAPSULES IN THE APPROPRIATE POCKET. WHEN THE FEMALE RELEASES HER EGGS, THE CAPSULES OPEN AND FERTILIZATION IS COMPLETED.

IN 1962, J. Z. YOUNG PUBLISHED SKETCHES OF THE STAGES OF THE SEXUAL MATING DANCE AND COPULATION OF THE OCTOPUS HORRIDUS. NOTHING COULD APPEAR MORE SINISTER. THE TWO LOVERS LOOK LIKE SENTINELS AT ATTENTION, AND, WITH HORN-LIKE PROTRUSIONS GROWING OUT OF THE TOPS OF THEIR HEADS, SEEM EVEN MORE LUDICROUS. ONE MIGHT DESCRIBE THEM AS CARNIVALESQUE DEVILS. THEY ARE DESPONDANT, MEASURED, RESERVED AND DILIGENT. THE ESSENTIAL LINES OF J. Z. YOUNG'S OBSERVATION MERIT RECOUNTING. THE WORK WAS CARRIED OUT WITH PROFESSOR R. SURGEON DURING A DIVE NEAR SINGAPORE. THE OCTOPUS COUPLE WAS WATCHED FOR A HALF HOUR AT A DEPTH OF SEVERAL FEET IN A CORAL REEF. THE SKETCHES WERE DRAWN IMMEDIATELY UPON CLIMBING OUT OF THE WATER. I LEAVE THE AUTHOR OF THE REPORT TO SPEAK FOR HIMSELF:

"THE MALE WAS NOTICED BY PROFESSOR SURGEON; HE WAS COMING OUT OF A CRANNY IN THE CORAL, HIS HEAD RISING UP VERTICALLY FIRST. NO NODULE APPEARED ABOVE THE EYES. I BEGAN MY OBSERVATION. WHEN WE EXTENDED OUR HANDS, THE ANIMAL DOVE BACK DOWN INTO ITS HOLE. THEN, AFTER SEVERAL MINUTES REAPPEARED. THE FEMALE APPEARED THEN, ALSO FROM A CRANNY, ABOUT 60 CM. FROM THE MALE, BUT EXTENDING OUTWARD LATERALLY A FEW ARMS. A FISH APPROACHED (SEEMINGLY TO ATTACK THE FEMALE), AND HER ARMS TURNED TOWARD IT.

"THE MALE ROSE OUT OF ITS HOLE, TO A HEIGHT OF 15-20 CM. PERHAPS, STRIKINGLY MARKED BY VERTICLE STRIPES. A BRIGHTLY COLORED BAND APPEARED RUNNING ALONG THE EDGE OF THE BACK SIDE OF EACH ARM, UP TO THE HEAD. THE COLORING TURNED A DARK BROWN AROUND THE EYES. A DEEP BROWN STRIPE WAS ALSO VISIBLE ON HIS MANTLE, BEHIND THE CAVITY, AND ANOTHER IN THE MIDDLE OF THE MANTLE. THE REST WAS SOMEWHAT DINGY WHITE. THE DARK STRIPES GLOWED, SET OFF MORE OR LESS, SOMETIMES VERY CLEARLY, FROM THE BACKGROUND. AT THE TOP OF HIS HEAD, THE SKIN FORMED STRANGE LOOKING PROMINANT NODES. NODES ALSO APPEARED ON THE SKIN OF THE ARMS AND MANTLE, NOTABLY ON THE RIGHT SIDE.

"THE MALE KEPT THE FEMALE WITHIN THE VISUAL FIELD OF HIS RIGHT EYE. AFTER FIVE MINUTES, HE EXTENDED HIS THIRD RIGHT ARM AND INTRODUCED IT INTO THE FEMALE'S MANTLE—AT A DISTANCE OF 40-60 CM. THE THIRD ARM, A WHITISH COLOR, RESTED ON A ROCK BETWEEN THEM. THE MALE RETAINED HIS VERTICLE STRIPES, WHICH THE FEMALE ALSO SHOWED AT CERTAIN MOMENTS. AT OTHER MOMENTS, BROWN SPOTS WITH TRANSVERSAL STRIPES APPEARED ON HER ARMS.

"THEY REMAINED IN THIS POSITION FOR APPROXIMATELY TEN MINUTES. THE MALE'S COLORATION CHANGED. AT NUMEROUS TIMES, THE STRIPES DISAPPEARED COMPLETELY FROM HIS LEFT SIDE ... IN SUCH A WAY THAT ALL THAT REMAINED THERE WERE SOME TRANSVERSAL SPOTS, WHILE THE VERTICLE STRIPES ON THE RIGHT SIDE REMAINED STRONGLY MARKED.

"NO MOVEMENT WAS VISIBLE ON THE THIRD ARM. THE OBSERVATION WAS UNINTERRUPTED, BEING MADE THROUGH A DIVING MASK, AND I WAS ABLE TO MOVE COMPLETELY AROUND THE COUPLE WITHOUT DISTURBING THEM.

"THEN, THE FEMALE DREW AWAY, SLOWLY ENOUGH, PULLING THE MALE ALONG BY HIS THIRD ARM. AFTER THEY HAD GONE ABOUT THREE METERS, THE ARM PULLED BACK. THE FEMALE CONTINUED TO MOVE AWAY, AND THE MALE FOLLOWED HER STILL KEEPING HER WITHIN THE FIELD OF VISION OF HIS RIGHT EYE. HE KEPT HIS HEAD ERECT, THOUGH NOT AS MARKEDLY AS BEFORE.

"THE FEMALE SLIPPED UNDER A ROCK. AFTER A FEW INSTANTS, SHE REAPPEARED ON THE OTHER SIDE, THE MALE STILL FOLLOWING. IN THIS FASHION, THEY COVERED APPROXIMATELY 20 METERS, WHEREUPON THE FEMALE CAME TO A STANDSTILL IN A CREVASSE. THE MALE ALSO STOPPED, ABOUT 50 CM. FROM HER. AFTER A NEW AND BRIEF APPEARANCE OF THE BRILLIANT VERTICAL STRIPES, HIS THIRD ARM WAS AGAIN EXTENDED AND

INTRODUCED, WITH NO DELAY OR HESITATION ON THE PART OF EITHER OF THE TWO. IT REMAINED IN PLACE APPROXIMATELY TEN MINUTES, WHEREUPON THE FEMALE BROKE SHARPLY AWAY AND THE MALE WITHDREW INTO HIS HOLE."

THE TEXT IS ELOQUENT. VOLUPTUOUSNESS HAS LITTLE PLACE IN THESE RESPECTFULLY DISTANT AMOROUS RELATIONS. MAN'S IMAGINATION HAS MISCONSTRUED THE NATURE OF THE COUPLING OF THESE ORGANISMS SO WELL EQUIPPED FOR AN INSEPARABLE UNION. IN THE CASE OF THE PAPER NAUTILUS, WHICH COULD BE DEFINED AS AN OCTOPUS IN A SHELL, THE FERTILIZING ARM SEPARATES FROM ITS OWNER AND WANDERS AIMLESSLY FOR HOURS AT A TIME UNTIL FINDING A FEMALE TO WHICH IT ATTACHES ITSELF WITH ITS SUCKERS. CERTAIN SCHOLARS, AMONG THEM CUVIER, FIRST IDIENTIFIED IT AS A PARASITIC WORM. THESE ARE PROBABLY THE TRAVELLING PENISES WHICH LEE NOTICED IN THE MUSEUM IN PARIS. THESE VIRTUALLY APHYSICAL AMOROUS RELATIONS, OR THOSE EFFECTED BY "SATELLITE" [LARGUÉ] ORGANS ARE AT THE OPPOSITE EXTREME FROM THE HUMAN CONCEPTION OF SENSUALITY, OF WHICH, HOWEVER, THE OCTOPUS HAS OFFERED A PRIVILEGED SYMBOL RIGHT INTO MODERN LITERATURE. IT IS FOUND MORE THAN ONCE IN THE POEMS OF JOYCE MANSOUR. IN HIS LETTERS TO LOU, APOLLINAIRE CONFIDES TO HIS MISTRESS:

"I SAVOUR YOUR TONGUE LIKE THE STUMP OF AN OCTOPUS' ARM WHICH ATTACHES ITSELF TO YOU WITH ALL THE FORCE OF ITS SUCKERS."

WHEN SAINT-JOHN PERSE CALLS TO MIND THE GREAT TEXTS RECITED BY TRAGEDIANS (TRAGIC HEROINES?), WHEREIN FLOW "THE GREAT ADMISSIONS OF THE DREAM AND THE SOUL'S USURPATIONS," HE DEFINES THEM IN THE FOLLOWING FASHION:

"THERE WHISTLES THE OCTOPUS OF PLEASURE."

IT WOULD BE EASY TO MULTIPLY THE EXAMPLES. THERE IS A SIGNIFICANT CONTRAST BETWEEN AN UNSETTLING REALITY AND THE IMAGES OF VOLUPTUOUSNESS AND RAPTURE WHERE LIBIDINOUS DREAMING IS INVOLUNTARILY TRIGGERED BY BODIES OF EXCEPTIONAL SUPPLENESS, SO MANY LITHE ARMS AND AVID MOUTHS.

ROBER CAILLOIS
TRANSLATED BY LINDA McNEIL AND MARGARET McGAW

ON THE BALCONY

BOTH GIRLS WERE WATCHING THE SWALLOWS FLY;
ONE PALE, HAIR BLACK; THE OTHER BLOND
AND PINK; THEIR LIGHT ROBES OF OLD GOLD
WERE FLUTTERING LIKE CLOUDS AND VAGUE.

AND BOTH THE GIRLS, AS SLOW AS LANGOROUS AS ASPHODEL,
AND AS THE MOON ROSE ROUND AND SOFT,
DRANK DEEPLY AND FULL OF THE TREMBLING EVENING
AND THE WISTFUL JOY OF CONSTANT HEARTS.

STANDING THERE, DAMPLY EMBRACED, WARM AND LOOSELY CURVED,

THE STRANGE GIRL-COUPLE THAT LOOKS IN PITY ON THE OTHER COUPLES;
DREAMING ON THE BALCONY STOOD THE GIRLS.

BEHIND THEM, IN THE LISTLESS DARK OF THEIR ROOM,
AS DRAMATIC AS THE THRONE OF A QUEEN,
RUMPLED WITH SMELLS, WAS THE BED FLOWEROPENING IN THE SHADOWS.

PAUL VERLAINE

TRANSLATED BY DANIEL SLOATE.

MEMOIRS OF AN OCCUPATION

WHEN I WAS VERY YOUNG I WAS FASCINATED WITH MOLLUSKS. THESE CREATURES ARE MOSTLY OF THE SEA, WITH THE EXCEPTION OF LAND SNAILS AND SLUGS OR THE FRESH-WATER SPECIES. MY LOCALE, THE PACIFIC NORTHWEST, IS ADVANTAGEOUS FOR GROWTH OF THE LAND SNAIL OR SLUG, SINCE THEY THRIVE IN ZONES OF HEAVY RAINFALL.

ON MY WALKS HOME FROM GRADE-SCHOOL I WOULD USUALLY SEE HUNDREDS OF SLUGS ALONG GARDEN PATHWAYS. LEOPARD SLUGS, BANANA SLUGS OR BROWN-ORANGE ONES ABOUNDED. ONE GARDEN HAD STEPS OF ROUGHLY-CHISLED ROCK; THROUGH THEIR CREVICES GREW THE GRASS, BRAKEN AND MOSS THESE SLOW-MOVING THINGS WOULD EAT. YOU HAD TO AVOID THEM FREQUENTLY AND STEP WITH AGILITY OVER THEIR SLIPPERY BODIES. THERE WERE ALWAYS THOSE TIMES WHEN YOU WOULD SLIP AND HAVE THE SMEERED REMAINS OF A SLUG DOWN YOUR THIGH. DURING THESE HOURS AFTER SCHOOL I WOULD STOP AND STARE IN ADMIRATION OF THEIR ANTENNAE AND PULSATING BODIES, THE SLICK, MOIST COATS USUALLY OF GREEN. THEIR BODIES WERE CURIOUSLY SHAPED, NEITHER LEGGED, SAVE FOR ONE, AND PONDEROUSLY ALIGNED TO THE GROUND. THEY NEVER APPEARED EQUIPPED TO JUMP, FLY, HOP AND TWIRL LIKE THE OTHER ANIMALS. THEIR DELIBERATION ATTRACTED ME GREATLY. AN EXQUISITE SENSITIVITY TO THE EFFECTS OF TOUCH AND LIGHT MADE ME THINK THEM TOO DELICATE AND VULNERABLE TO THE CRUELTIES OF THE OUTSIDE WORLD.

THEIR PROFUSION IS GREAT IN THE MOIST FORESTS OF OREGON, DESPITE ALL THE KIDS WHO ENJOYED SNIPPING THEIR EYES OUT OR CUTTING THEIR BODIES IN HALF OR POURING THE PROVERBIAL SALT ON THEIR NEVER DRY BACKS. I REGARDED THEM AS VERY EXOTIC AND ORIGINALLY FROM THE SEA, NOW THAT THEY WERE INVADING THESE GLENS RICH IN PLANT LIFE. PORTLAND, OFTEN OVERCAST, ALLOWED THEM MUCH REST FROM THE IMMODERATE BLAZING OF THE SUN, SOMETHING THEY WILL ALWAYS HATE. WHEN RAINS ENDED AND SUN SHONE, ORANGE SLUGS DRIED TO BLACK AND THEIR SLIMEY TRAILS TURNED IRIDESCENT. THESE TRAILS SHOWED YOU THEIR PAINFUL ROAD TO DOOM—A DRY, SUN-BAKED SIDEWALK.

SLUGS APPEARED MORE PLENTIFUL AND LESS ATTRACTIVE THAN SNAILS. SLUGS WERE CONSIDERED BY EVERYONE TO BE TOO NUMEROUS, AND THEIR RELATIVE UGLINESS DIDN'T REMEDY THE LOW OPINION. WHEREAS SNAILS CAPTURED ONE'S

INTEREST MORE; THEY HAD SHELLS, OF VARYING SIZE AND COLOR, AND THEIR FLESH WAS NOT SO STARTLINGLY HUED AS THEIR SHELL-LESS COUNTERPARTS.

ONE RAINY DAY, IN MY MANY WALKS THROUGH A WOODED NEIGHBORHOOD, I DISCOVERED A MOST BEAUTIFUL SNAIL. THE SHELL HAD ORANGE AND YELLOW STRIPS AGAINST BROWN AND PURPLE. ITS BODY WAS LONG AND THICK, NOT LIKE THE TINY WHITE ONES THAT POSSESSED MEDIOCRE SHELLS. IT WAS SO BEAUTIFUL THAT I LET IT CRAWL OVER MY FINGERS AND HANDS AS I WALKED HOME. I CALLED THE SNAIL "POKY" AFTER THE HORSE IN THE GUMBY TV CARTOON AND PARTLY AFTER ITS SLOW, IMPLORING NATURE. I WAS HEARTILY WELCOMED BY MY YOUNGER BROTHER WITH THE CREATURE. WE COINED A SONG FOR THE LOVELY PET WHICH RAN AS FOLLOWS:

POKY THE SNAIL
POKY THE SNAIL
YOU MAY SEE HIM LAUGHIN'
YOU MAY SEE HIM CRYIN'
BUT YOU KNOW HE'S GOT
A GRE-E-E-E-EN MOUTH!

RIGHT AWAY WE BUILT A TERRARIUM FOR HIM—A LARGE GLASS JAR WHEREIN WE PLACED SOME SOIL, MOSS, FERN AND GRASS. THE TOP WAS SEALED WITH A METAL LID WITH HOLES FOR AIR TO COME THROUGH. SOMETIMES POKY WOULD ESCAPE AND BE SEEN LATER CRAWLING UP THE SIDES OF OUR BEDROOM WALL. ONE TIME WHEN I LET POKY CRAWL OVER MY FINGERS (MY SISTERS AND OLDER BROTHER THOUGHT IT DISGUSTING, BUT TIM, THE YOUNGER BROTHER, EVEN ALLOWED POKY ON HIS FINGERS), IT BACKFIRED: THE THING BIT ME. I KNEW THEN THAT SNAILS HAVE AN UNUSUAL TONGUE LINED WITH TEETH CALLED A RADULA. THIS FACILITATES THE WELL-AIMED STROKES AT LEAVES AND FLOWERS THEY'RE DESPISED FOR. I NEVER WANTED TO BE BITTEN BY A SNAIL AGAIN IN MY LIFE. SOON WE LOST POKY, BUT WE COULD DETECT HIS SLIMEY TRAILS OVER THE BEDROOM WALLS AFTERWARDS.

ONE QUESTION WE ASKED ABOUT SNAILS WAS, DID THEY "GO TO THE BATHROOM." IT REMAINED MYSTERIOUS UNTIL WE SAW TINY GREY COILS ON THE SURFACES OF THE TERRARIUM. FURTHERMORE, THE GENDER OF SNAILS SEEMED NO MATTER; WE WERE SO CHILDISH AT THE TIME THAT IT DIDN'T CONCERN US. I WAS TO LATER FIND OUT THAT THEY ARE HERMAPHRODITIC AND THAT THEY NEED TO MUTUALLY INSEMINATE EACH OTHER; THE RESULT IS BOTH ANIMALS BEARING THE EGGS. ONE SUMMER

EVENING I TURNED ON THE SPRINKLER IN ORDER TO SEE AS MANY OF THESE NOCTURNALLY ACTIVE CREATURES AS POSSIBLE. ARMED WITH A FLASH-LIGHT, I DISCOVERED A PAIR CEMENTED TOGETHER IN AN EXCESS OF SLIME. I WAS INITIALLY HORRIFIED, BUT THEN REASONED THEY WERE FUCKING. I DIDN'T STAY LONG BECAUSE IT WAS DISTASTEFUL TO LOOK AT FOR ANY LENGTH OF TIME. THE SHOCK LINGERED ON WHEN I FINALLY LEFT THE GARDEN TO GO INDOORS TO WATCH TV WITH MY PARENTS, IGNORANT OF WHAT I HAD JUST SEEN.

AFTER POKY'S DISAPPEARANCE I WAS DESPON-DENT. I THOUGHT I'D NEVER BE ABLE TO FIND A SNAIL AS BEAUTIFUL AS THAT. I HAD SPENT HOURS LOOKING FOR A COMPARABLE SNAIL, BUT TO NO AVAIL. THERE WERE ONLY SLUGS OR THE SMALLER SNAILS WITH FURRY SHELLS. WHOLE DAYS WERE TAKEN UP WITH LOOKING FOR A SNAIL BEARING A COLORFUL SHELL. ON THESE DAYS I'D HUM THE "POKY THE SNAIL" SONG, DESPARATELY SEARCHING FOR THE PERFECT SNAIL, A SNAIL AS GOOD AS POKY.

WITH POKY GONE, I EVENTUALLY RESORTED TO A PET SLUG, CALLED "FLASH." ITS HOME WAS IN AN ORIGINALLY BOTANICAL TERRARIUM. ON THE TOP OF THE CLEAR PLASTIC BOX WAS A SMALL VENTILATION CAP; TWIST AN UPPER PORTION CLOCKWISE AND VENTS APPEAR. FLASH'S LONG BODY WOULD INCH UP TO THESE HOLES AT THE VERY TOP. THERE HE'D SCRAPE HIS RADULA NIGHT-LONG; IT SOUNDED LIKE A FAINTER VERSION OF CHALK SCREECHING ACROSS A BLACKBOARD. DID HE WANT TO ESCAPE OR DID HE JUST LIKE TO SUCK ON PLASTIC? THE TERRARIUM WHICH HOUSED THIS SLUG WAS PLACED ON A GIGANTIC TELEVISION SET TIM AND I WOULD WATCH. AT TIMES FLASH COULD BE HEARD THROUGH THE DIN OF COMMERCIALS, HIS SCRAPING CRY FOR REVENGE, FREEDOM, FOOD— WHO KNOWS WHAT IT WANTED! (WE ORIGINALLY CALLED HIM FLASH AFTER THE COMIC BOOK SUPRHERO WHO CAN TRAVEL AT SPEEDS NO SLUG COULD EVER MATCH.) ONE TIME I PLACED MY FINGER TOO CLOSE TO THE VENTILATION HOLE WHEN FLASH WAS SCRAPING. HE, LIKE POKY BEFORE, BIT IT. I'M SURE I SENSED SOME PERVERSE PLEASURE. LATER ON, I THREW FLASH OUT, SIMPLY BECAUSE I CARED NOT TO CLEAN OUT HIS CAGE, BY THIS TIME VERY SMELLY AND SLIMEY.

SLUGS WERE BY NO MEANS MY SOLE OBSESSION. MY CHILDHOOD FRIENDS SHARED THE INTEREST. TIM, A FRIEND CALLED MATT AND MYSELF INVENTED A REALM CALLED "SLUGONIA" POPULATED BY SLUG-

INSPIRED CARTOON CREATURES. THEY DIDN'T HAVE ANY ANTENNAE OR SLIME OR RADULAS AND THEY RESEMBLED HUMANS IN THEIR WEAKER MOMENTS. THESE CARTOON SLUGS WERE VERY SELF-INDULGENT, PRIDING THEMSELVES ON RAVENOUS APPETITES OR EXCESSIVE TV WATCHING. WE DREW COMICS ABOUT THE CENTRAL SLUG CHARACTERS. SOME OF THEIR NAMES WERE HARVEY (A TRICK-STER), HOBART (THE DICTATOR OF SLUGONIA), FEEDOR (A TV ADDICT), GARFO (A SLUG WHO HAD A SIGN ON HIS BACK READING "BEAT ME"), CHEERFUL (A COMPULSIVELY HAPPY SLUG), AND FLASH (AGAIN, A VORACIOUS EATER—LIKE MY FORMER PET—WITH A SUPER FAST TONGUE). MATT WAS INGENIOUS AND PROLIFIC IN CREATING FICTIONAL SITUATIONS CONCERNING SLUGS. HE ALSO ORIGINATED THEIR IMAGE AND INVENTED MOST OF THE CHARACTERS AND THEIR NAMES. TIM AND I CONTRIBUTED A GREAT DEAL, EITHER IN OUR OWN IDEAS OR JUST LAUGHTER OVER MATT'S TALKS ON THE IDEA OF SLUGONIA. TIM AND I MADE A SUPER-8 ANIMATION FILM ABOUT SLUGONIA, WHICH UNFOR-TUNATELY APPEARS TO HAVE BEEN LOST. MATT AND I EVEN WENT SO FAR AS TO SUGGEST A "SLUG PATROL" TO OUR BOY SCOUT TROOP. THE SCOUT-MASTER WAS CHARMED BY THE IDEA BUT HAD TO REFUSE THE TITLE (HE WAS A STUPID MAN) SINCE THERE WERE SO MANY OTHER NAMES OF ANIMALS THAT WE COULD USE BESIDE THAT OF "SLUG." WE KNEW IT WAS A POOR REASON—BESIDES, WE WERE ALREADY RESIGNED TO HIS DISAPPROVAL. BEFOREHAND, MATT HAD COMPOSED A FLAG WITH SOMERSAULTING OR "FLIPPING" SLUGS (OUR SLUGS COULD FLIP IN MID-AIR); THE FLAG'S SLUGS WERE ALSO WEARING BANDANAS AND HATS, VESTIGES OF OUR UNIFORMS. WE EVEN INVENTED A HANDSHAKE WHICH CONSISTED OF CONTACT WITH EITHER PALM ONLY TO HAVE SQUISHING SOUNDS MEET THE OTHER PERSON; ANOTHER ONE WAS CONTACT BUT RAPID DRAWING AWAY—"YECCH!"—AS IF THE PALM WERE SLIMEY.

AROUND THIS TIME (11 TO 14 YEARS OF AGE, I CANNOT RECALL SPECIFICALLY) I HAD BOUGHT THE MOST COMPREHENSIVE BOOK ON THE SUBJECT, PILSBURY'S LAND MOLLUSCA OF NORTH AMERICA NORTH OF MEXICO. (THE ACTUAL TITLE MIGHT BE LONGER.) THE BOOK WAS A FOUR-VOLUMED MONOGRAPH SOLELY ON LAND SNAILS AND SLUGS. WHEN IT ARRIVED, I NOTICED THE PAGES WERE UNCUT, AND AFTER PLYING THEM APART WITH A LARGE KITCHEN KNIFE, I WAS ABLE TO MARVEL AT THE HUNDREDS OF ILLUSTRATIONS OF MY FAVORITE ANIMAL. I COULD NOW SAY THAT SUCH-AND-SUCH WAS "ARION ATER," "VESPERCOLA LATINBRUM," "HELIX POMATA." EVERY SPECIES HAD A TECHNICAL DESCRIPTION OF THEIR REPRODUCTIVE, DIGESTIVE AND RESPIRATORY SYSTEMS. THE CLASSIFICATION INTO FAMILY, GENUS AND SPECIES WAS BASED UPON THE ORGANIZATION OF THIER RESPIRATORY TRACTS. THE BOOK HAD VERY STRANGE ACCOUNTS ON CERTAIN SPECIES. ONE SPECIES WAS PREDA-TORY-CANNIBALISTIC. IT WOULD ATTACK BY SWAYING ITS HEAD AND TRUNK BACK AND FORTH IN FRONT OF THE VICTIM AND THEN LUNGE VERY QUICKLY FOR THE OTHER SNAIL'S MAIN ARTERY RUNNING UP THE CENTER OF THE SPIRAL.

DURING A SUMMER CAMP VACATION I REQUESTED A FRIEND OF MY PARENTS' TO BRING THE BOOKS WITH HER SINCE SHE WAS GOING TO VISIT SOME COUNSELORS. THE AREA HAD A NUMBER OF SNAILS I DIDN'T KNOW THE NAMES TO. WHEN SHE ARRIVED SHE MADE A WISECRACK AS TO THE WEIGHT OF THE BOOKS. MANY OF THE COUNSELORS HELD ACA-DEMIC POSITIONS AND ONE OF THEM WAS A BIOLOGIST. HE WAS STRUCK BY MY INTEREST IN THESE CREATURES, EVEN THOUGH AT MOMENTS DURING OUR TALKS ON THE MATTER I FELT AS IF HIS INTEREST WAS TOO ATTENTIVE AND TOO OBSES-SIONAL. IT FRIGHTENED ME INTO THINKING I WAS ALSO STRANGE FOR DEVOTING SO MUCH TIME TO FINDING SNAILS AND CLASSIFYING THEM. THE BULGING VOLUMES ON SNAILS HELPED ME SOMEWHAT WHEN MUCH OF IT WAS DONE IN AN EFFORT TO IMPRESS MY PEERS THAT I WAS A SCHOLARLY TYPE.

AS I ALSO LEARNED FROM THE BOOK, HELIX POMOTA WAS CALLED THE EUROPEAN GARDEN SNAIL, AND IT IS THE SNAIL THAT THE FRENCH USE FOR ESCARGOTS. EVERYTIME I WENT TO A FRENCH RESTAURANT I ORDERED ESCARGOTS, CHARMING MY MOTHER WITH MY SOPHISTICATION ("ISN'T THAT CUTE, HE'S ORDERING ESCARGOTS!"). WHEN EATING SNAILS BEGAN, IT WAS ONLY A FOODSTUFF POOR FARMERS RESORTED TO WHEN THEY HAD NOTHING ELSE TO EAT. IN HIGH SCHOOL I REMEMBER A SKINNY BLACK GIRL IN FITS OVER A FRENCH TEACHER EATING A SNAIL: "YOU'RE EATING A SNAIL?!" SHE SHRIEKED. WHEN ONE WAS OFFERED TO HER ON BREAD WITH GARLIC BUTTER, SHE BECAME HYSTERICAL, REFUSING IN FITS OF LAUGHTER AND SHOCK. EATING ESCARGOTS WAS ONE WAY OF SHOWING YOU WERE SMART.

MANY TIMES THE IMAGE OF SNAILS GREW TO DISTURBING PROPORTIONS. ON A BOAT TRIP THROUGH THE STRAIT OF GEORGIA IN BRITISH COLUMBIA I SAW A POST OR LOOK MAGAZINE THAT FEATURED A SHORT STORY ABOUT MONSTER

SNAILS ON A REMOTE ISLAND. THE MAIN CHARACTER DESCRIBED HIS HORROR AT THE ENORMITY OF THE CREATURES WHICH WAS ALL THE MORE BELIEVABLE WITH AN ILLUSTRATION OF ONE. I THINK MY YOUNGER SISTER SHOWED ME THE PICTURE. WHEN I SAW IT, TERROR WAS THE REACTION. A GIANT SNAIL WAS DWARFING A TREE ITS DEVOURINGS HAD PROBABLY DENUDED. THE MOUTH OF THE MONSTER LOOKED LIKE A BALL OF A THOUSAND ICE-PICKS, READY TO RIP APART ANYTHING ORGANIC. THE IMAGE OF THE MOUTH WAS MOST DISTURBING AND I THOUGHT ABOUT IT OFTEN DURING THE VACATION. I WOULD FREQUENTLY OPEN THE MAGAZINE AND FIXEDLY STARE AT THE MOUTH'S PRICKLY CAVERN.

DURING THAT VACATION, MY MOTHER AND A GOOD FRIEND OF HERS, THE MOTHER OF THE ACCOMPANYING FAMILY, LOVED TO PREPARE FRESH OYSTERS. WITH PLENTY OF OYSTER BEDS AROUND, WE WOULD PARTAKE OF MANY LUNCHES "ON THE HALF-SHELL." IT SEEMED A VERY ELEGANT THING TO DO IN THE WILDERNESS. MOM'S FRIEND WAS QUITE WORLDLY IN MY EYES AND BEAUTIFUL ENOUGH TO HAVE ME COMPARE HER TO AUDREY HEPBURN. WE'D ALL DIVE FOR OYSTERS IN CLEAR-BLUE WATER, ARMED WITH BUCKETS OR PLASTIC BAGS. LATER ON WE'D PRY THEM OPEN, A PAINFUL TASK FOR A SHELL'S SHARP EDGES WOULD CUT YOU, AND THE KNIFE OR PRYING TOOL, AFTER HAVING PUNCTURED YOUR SKIN, WOULD ADD TO THE MISERY OF ALREADY SLICED FINGERS. A LEMON AND TOMATO SAUCE AWAITED THE HUNGRY MINORITY SINCE MANY IN OUR PARTY DIDN'T CARE FOR THEM. ONE TIME I FOUND A PEARL; IT WAS VERY SMALL AND BROUGHT MUCH ATTENTION FROM THE OLDER WOMEN. I DIDN'T KNOW WHERE TO PLACE IT, SO I LEFT IT IN THE CHANGE PURSE OF EITHER MY MOTHER'S BAG OR HER FRIEND'S. I NEVER SAW THAT PEARL AGAIN ONCE IT WAS SAFE INSIDF THE FOLDS OF LEATHER.

A YEAR AFTER THE BOAT TRIP, I HAD WRITTEN A LONG PAPER ON THE DUTCH PAINTER JAN VERMEER. HIS ATTENTION TO PEARLS MUST HAVE CONTRIBUTED TO MY EXCITMENT OVER HIS WORK. BESIDES, THE DUO OF MOTHER AND HER FRIEND THOUGHT ME QUITE SENSITIVE TO SELECT VERMEER AS A SUBJECT FOR A RESEARCH PAPER. (I WAS 14 YEARS OLD AND A FRESHMAN IN HIGH SCHOOL.) MOM EVEN TOLD ME ONCE THAT VERMEER WAS CONSIDERED TO HAVE GROUND REAL PEARLS INTO HIS OILS, CONTRIBUTING TO THE SOFT, MILKY PALLOR OF HIS MOSTLY FEMALE SUBJECTS. I GREW TO APPRECIATE THE PAINTING ENTITLED "WOMAN WEIGHING PEARLS" AS HIS MOST EXQUISITE EFFORT. VERMEER'S CONTEMPORARY DEHOOCH DEPICTED A WOMAN WEIGHING GOLD COINS. SIMILARLY ATTIRED (THOUGH NOT WITH THE SATIN AND ERMINE JACKET) AND POSITIONED BEFORE THE WINDOW OF STREAMING DAYLIGHT, IT FAILED SIMPLY BECAUSE SHE WAS MEASURING GOLD, A VULGARITY IN ITS FAILURE TO UNDERSTAND THE RESONATING SIGNIFICANCE OF PEARLS. SOME CRITICS EVEN THOUGHT VERMEER'S WOMAN WAS WEIGHING GOLD, BUT MY PAPER ENDORSED LAWRENCE GOWING'S POINT—HOW COULD ANYONE THINK SHE WAS WEIGHING SOMETHING BESIDES THESE JEWELS FROM OYSTER BEDS?

ANOTHER PAINTING, BOTTICELLI'S LA PRIMIVERA, FEATURED THE BIRTH OF VENUS FROM THE LEGENDARY SEA-SHELL. I THOUGHT IT TO BE A MOST BEAUTIFUL PICTURE. IN IT HER HAIR COILS IN SPIRALS WHILE A MALE ZEPHYR, FLORA, IS FITFULLY BLOWING HIS GENTLE BREATH, WHICH, IF YOU DON'T MIND THE FREE-ASSOCIATING, WAS SOMETHING I OFTEN DID TO SNAILS: I BLEW ON THEIR ANTENNAE TO SEE IF THEY WERE TRULY THAT SENSITIVE, AND VERY OFTEN THEY WERE— RECOILING THE TENDER FILAMENTS. THIS DELICACY SENT ME IN SMILES, PROMPTING MORE ASSERTIVE MEASURES SUCH AS TOUCHING THE STALKS, ONLY TO HAVE THEM RECOIL MORE RAPIDLY, HENCE TAKING LONGER TO EMERGE AGAIN FACING THE HUMAN ADVERSARY, MYSELF.

. . . .

A GARDEN'S BRIGHT FLOWERS AND GLISTENING LEAVES HAS A RAPACIOUS PREDATOR, THE SNAIL AND SLUG. THEY SCAR SUCH LUMINOUS PARADISES THAT REFLECT A PROUD OWNER'S LABOR. AND TO SEE MY MOTHER SPREADING SLUG-BE-GONE OR SOME SUCH SIMILAR POISON ON OUR GARDEN HURT ME IN ATTENUATED WAYS. NOW THE PETALS OF OUR IRISES, LILIES AND PETUNIAS COULD FLOURISH IN MANY A SUMMER'S LIGHT UNRAVAGED BY GAPS AND HOLES. THE SNAIL'S HATED STATUS WAS WHAT I ATTEMPTED TO CHANGE. I VAINLY THOUGHT MY DISCUSSING OF THE CREATURES WOULD SWAY MY FAMILY INTO APPRECIATING THEM. THE BRILLIANT GROWTH OF FLOWERS WAS NOTHING TO HARM, YET HARM TO THEM SEEMED INEVITABLE FOR THEY WOULD NO DOUBT QUICKLY WITHER AND DIE. I EVEN CHASTISED IN FRONT OF MOTHER AMERICA'S CULT OF YOUTHFULNESS IN WOMEN WHEN SHE WAS PASSING INTO MIDDLE-AGE AS SEEN BY MY OBSESSIONAL SCRUTINY OF HER FACE'S GROWTH OF WRINKLES. HER FACE IS STILL VERY YOUTHFUL AND MY VICIOUSNESS AGAINST THE ONE WHO HAD LOOKED OVER ME WITH TENDERNESS FOR SO MANY YEARS APPEARS ONLY TO BE REVENGE AGAINST

HER OBSESSIVE PICKING OF MY ZITS AS I ADVANCED INTO THE HORMONAL DISFIGUREMENTS OF ADOLESCENCE.

THE BITING SNAIL, LIKE THE LEECHES THAT HAD FASCINATED ME IN FIFTH GRADE, COULD ALSO DRAW BLOOD FROM MY FACE AS A FRESHLY EXTRACTED WHITEHEAD ALWAYS WOULD. MY MOTHER, TRUE TO HER NURSING EDUCATION DEGREE, WOULD WIPE OFF THE OIL FROM HER FINGERNAILS/FINGERSNAILS ONTO HER DRESS OR APRON. THE ATTACK WAS ALWAYS ON, WHETHER IT WAS COMBING MY HAIR OR WIPING OFF DIRT FROM ANY PART OF MY BODY. A COMPULSIVELY NEAT PERSON, A PRODUCT OF LUTHERAN UPBRINGING, IS STILL INSPIRING ME TO WASH AND SHAVE EVERYDAY, CLEANSING A PERPETUALLY DIRTY, SHIT-RIDDEN ENVELOPE OF FLESH. THIS BLASEN, OR BUBBLE OF SKIN IS WHAT THE SNAIL-HEADED MAN, FREUD, HAD DESIGNATED THE PHYSICAL METAPHOR OF THE EGO.

BEING BROUGHT UP IN A SOCIAL APPARATUS THAT EXULTS IN A STREAMLINED PASSION FOR ASSIMILATING EGO-IDEALS, HAS FURTHER TRANSFORMED THE PAST OF PURIFYING DIRT ON THE SKIN INTO A MILITANT OCCUPATION. I HAVE SUCCUMBED TO THE ADVERTISING VISAGE OF GREATER POTENCY, WISHING THAT THE PHOTOS AND COMMERICALS I SEE WILL BE PRESENT IN MY LIFE AS A RESULT OF BUYING THE PRODUCT. THEN REALITY WILL CONCURE WITH MY HALLUCINATION AND I SHALL BE AIR-BRUSH PERFECT LIKE ALL THE BEAUTIES WHO COULD GET INTO STUDIO 54 WITHOUT WAITING. AND IF YOU WENT HTERE, THE LARGE MALE HOMOSEXUAL CROWD OBEYS THE SAME IMPULSE I SECRETLY CHERISH: AN ORAL DRIVE, THE DRIVE OF THE VAMPIRE FOR THESE OTHERS WHO HAVE TRIUMPHED IN THEIR IDEOLOGICAL PERFECTION, OUR SOCIETY'S INDICIA IN CLEAN, BODILY SPLENDOR. THE FEW MILDLY ACNED AND HANDSOME MEN THERE HAVE SENT ME IN SHIVERS, PROPELLING MY EYES TO FIX ON THEIR HUMAN RADULAS THAT COULD BITE THE VERY PIMPLES I POSSESS THAT EVENING.

ALTHOUGH I AM NOT IDENTICAL TO THE WOLF-MAN PACING HYSTERICALLY TO AND FRO IN A DERMATOLOGIST'S OFFICE WITH MIRROR AND FACE POWDER IN HAND, I HAVE ENCRYPTED UNDYING FANTASIES AND THEIR CORRESPONDING PLEASURE-WORDS. HIS PLEASURE-WORD, A WORD IN HIS NOSE-LANGUAGE, TERIET, THE RUSSIAN TERM FOR SCRAPING AND RUBBING SEEMS SIMILAR TO MY VERBARIUM: SNAIL, SLUG, PICK OR PICKY, ACNE AND ZITS.

SNAIL ALLOPHONICALLY RESIDES IN "AILS." I, THE ONE WHO AILS FROM ACNE. HER FINGERNAILS WERE THE VERY INSTRUMENT OF MY REPETITION: SNAIL[S]. WITH NAILS, JESUS CHRIST'S HANDS AND FEET WERE BLOODIED BY THEM, AN INCIDENT KNOWN IN EVERY CHRISTIAN HOME. BEFORE MY GRANDFATHER'S DEATH HIS HANDS WERE ALSO WOUNDED BY IMPROPER PROTECTION FROM X-RAYS HE GAVE TO HIS PATIENTS. HE WAS A PEDIATRICIAN LIKE MY FATHER IS NOW. WHY DID I LIKE TO HAVE POKY CRAWL OVER MY FINGERS? I AM ALSO SUPPOSED TO BE "GENETICALLY IDENTICAL" TO HIM, MY FATHER SAYS SO, AND I BEAR HIS FIRST NAME AS MY MIDDLE ONE. MY HANDS HAVE BEEN CALLED "ATTRACTIVE" BY THOSE CLOSE TO ME, BUT A GIRLFRIEND I ONCE KNEW HAD AN EXQUISITE PAIR, COMPENSATING FOR HER VERY BLEMISHED FACE. HER NAME WAS IDENTICAL TO MY MOTHER'S, FORCING ME TO THINK OF A MOTHER RAVAGED BY WHAT I HAD, A HOPELESS REVENGE. IT ALSO HELPED ME ENDURE WHATEVER PAROXYSMS MY COMPLEXION WENT THROUGH, WITH BAD SKIN BEING MY GRANDFATHER'S DOOM, SO HAVE I FELT IT TOO TO BE MINE. THE WORD SKIN, THOUGH ANASEMIC DECIPHERING, IS RELATED TO THE LETTERS IN SNAIL, THE "S," "I" AND "N"; PLACE AND "L" FOR THE "K," AND YOU HAVE "SLIN"—THEN GO ON TO "SNAIL," THE "S" AND "L" ARE CRUCIAL: BOTH PARENTS POSSESS THEM IN THEIR ORIGINAL NAMES. ALSO, WRINKLES ARE LINES/LAINS (SNAIL) ON THE SKIN/SLIN (SNAIL).

FURTHERMORE, WITH SLUG ELIMINATE THE "S" AND WITNESS "LUG," BETTER YET, "ULG," OR AS IS CLEAR, "ULG[Y]." "SLUGS ARE SO UGLY" SAY THE COMMON LOT. SLUGS MAKE UGLY, AS FLASH DID WITH ITS CAGE, OR AS IT DID TO MY FINGER BY ITS BITING; A BITING, UGLIFYING SLUG, SCRAPING AT MY SKIN. MY MOTHER'S NAME, JULIE, IS ALLOPHONICALLY RELATED TO "GUL[S]," SIMILAR TO DAD'S ENDEARMENT, "JULES," SOUNDING MUCH LIKE "JEWELS." AN UGLY JEWEL IS THE SLUG THAT COULD RENDER THE CHILD-JEWEL OF JULIE UGLY AS WELL.

OFTENTIMES MY MOTHER WOULD LAMENT, "DUNCAN YOU'RE SO PICKY," MEANING SHE PROBABLY WAS DISCONTENT WITH MY FONDNESS FOR CRITICALITY AND DISTINCTION, WHILE THINKING I WAS PICKABLE, THAT IS, PREY TO HER FONDNESS FOR DRAWING OIL OUT OF MY SKIN. A SISTER OF MINE WAS ALSO NOTED FOR GOUGING HER YOUNGER BROTHERS' FLESH WITH A FINGER CALLED "PINKY." IT WAS ALL A JOKE, ALTHOUGH AT TIMES HER ATTACKS WERE FRIGHTENING. "PINKY" APPEARS ORTHOGRAPHI-

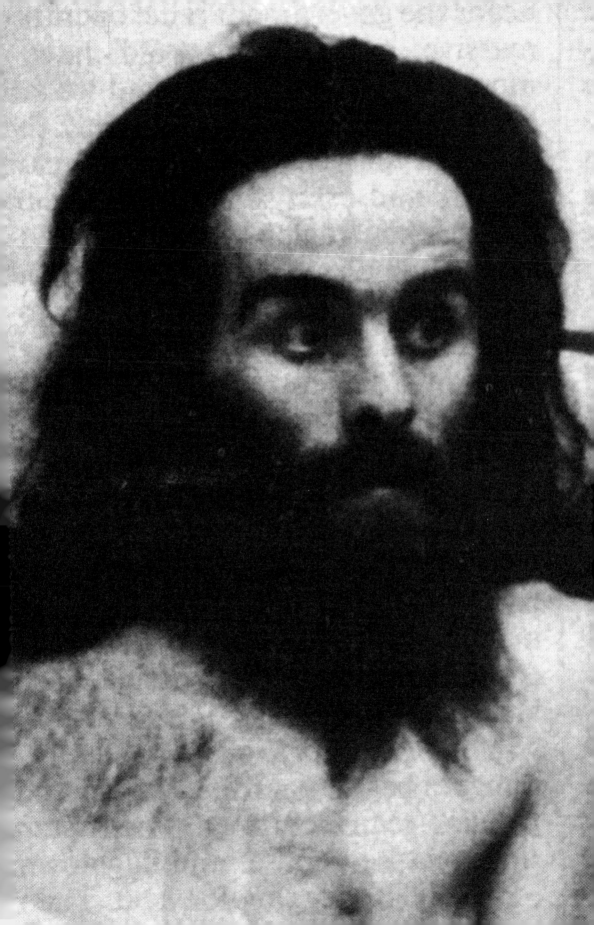

CALLY SIMILAR TO POKY, MY PET SNAIL. FINGERS POKE, POKY ON MY FINGERS, THE POKY, PICKY FINGER/SNAIL. FURTHER, MUCUS OR SNOT, AS IT IS MORE COMMONLY CALLED, IS PICKED IN THE NOSE, SOMETHING MELANIE KLEIN CALLS AN ANAL ATTACK UPON THE MOTHER. PICKING YOUR NOSE FREQUENTLY LIKE I DO IS GHASTLY, DELICATE READER, AND THIS HABIT OF MINE IS EVEN WORSE WHEN I VENTURE TO EAT THE STUFF, BITING THE GREEN JUNK ALONG THE WAY. ("HE HAS A GRE-E-E-E-E-EN MOUTH.")

ANOTHER CRUCIAL PLEASURE-WORD, ACNE, IS BURIED IN MY NAME: DUNCAN/DUNACN[E].

ZITS OR "SZIT" VIBRATES WITH "SHIT" AND CLEANING IS OF COURSE AN ANAL MOTIF. MY "CRITICALITY" (MY "PICKY" NATURE— IS ALLOPHONIC WITH "ZIT": CRITICAL, CITICAL, ZITICAL. INDEED "ZITICAL THEORY" BECOMES AN EXPLANATION FOR MY FASCINATION FOR THE WRITINGS OF THAT SCHOOL, THE [S]UGL/Y INTELLECTUAL READING AN IMAGE-IMAGINARY BANISHING T. W. ADORNO—DON'T ADORE "SELF-STYLING ADORN," ADORE ME, "OUI, JE T'ADORE."

MY MOVE TO NEW YORK WAS OPPORTUNE. I CAME HERE TO FALL INTO THE ARMS OF ITS BEAUTIFUL MEN. NEW YORK WAS "FUN-CITY" AND I ENVISIONED THE MANY "FUN" PEOPLE LIVING HERE. BUT "FUN-CITY" IS, FOR ME, A "FUN-ZITY," SINCE WHEN YOU HAVE A "ZIT" IN FUN-CITY YOU DON'T HAVE FUN. AN UNLUST-ICH, A NO-FUN EGO, WITH A ZIT ON ITS BUBBLE, IS NOT A LUST-ICH, A FUN EGO IN A CITY-ZITY WITH ALL ITS FUN, BEAUTIFUL PEOPLE.

TO ELIMINATE THE ZIT IN THIS CITY NEEDS AN APPLICATION OF CREAMS, REPRODUCING THE MUCILAGE FROM SNAILS I ONCE PUT ON MY BODY. PROFESSIONAL FACIALS ARE SURGEON-LIKE WITH RUBBERY HANDS VIOLENTLY PICKING AWAY. SNAILS, NATURE'S SURGEONS (THEY LEAVE SCARS ON PLANT TISSUE) ARE NOW ONLY COSMETOLO-GISTS FOR PEOPLE TO KEEP CORPSEHOOD INTACT AND GOLDEN. I'M RECALLING BAUDELAIRE'S EQUATION OF LOVE-MAKING AND SURGERY IN HIS JOURNAX INTIMES.

TO MAKE GOLDEN AND YOUTH EVOCATIVE, TO GET A TAN, IS A CRYPTIC IMPULSE IN NEW YORK, THE NEW YORK WITH AN ISLAND CALLED MANHATTAN, OR MAN-HAT-TAN. THE NUMEROUS "NOCTURNALLY ACTIVE CREATURES" HERE WITH DEEP BROWN TANS IS ONLY THE MANY MEN WITH THE EVIDENCE OF BEING AFFLICTED BY SUMMER'S RAYS, THE SONNENSTRAHLEN. A PERFECT TAN IN MANHATTAN TAKES SOME TIME, BE IT DAYS, WEEKS, MONTHS, EVEN A HUNDRED YEARS.

I BEG FORGIVENESS FOR ALL THIS CONFESSING AND THE ATTENDANT MORBIDITIES. IT SCRAPES STILL, IN THIS CITY OF SKYSCRAPERS OR STAR-SCRAPERS, THOUGH NOT SO HARSHLY, AND NIGHTLONG LIKE MY PET SLUG HAD DONE ATOP THE GIANT TV SET. THE TV SHOW WILL NOT BE FORGOTTEN AS LONG AS I LIVE WHERE TV'S ARE WATCHED, CRITICIZED, PICKED AT, WITHOUT END, UNENDLICH.

DUNCAN SMITH

ALIMENTARY SEX

TABLE MANNERS, BED MANNERS,
LANGUAGE MANNERS

TO MARIE BONAPARTE, WHO HAD ASKED HIM IF PSYCHOANALYSIS HAD SOME REASON TO DIS-COURAGE INCESTUOUS RELATIONSHIPS, FREUD REMARKED:

> THE SITUATION OF INCEST IS EXACTLY LIKE THAT OF CANNIBALISM. NATURALLY THERE ARE GOOD REASONS THAT IN MODERN LIFE ONE DOES NOT KILL A MAN TO DEVOUR HIM, BUT THERE IS NO REASON WHATEVER FOR NOT EATING HUMAN FLESH IN PLACE OF MEAT. NEVERTHELESS MOST OF US WOULD FIND THAT COMPLETELY IMPOSSIBLE. INCEST IS NOT SO FAR REMOVED, AND IT OCCURS ONLY TOO OFTEN. WE CAN EASILY SEE THAT, IF IT WAS PRACTISED ON A LARGE SOCIAL SCALE IT WOULD BE AS HARMFUL TODAY AS IT WAS IN TIMES PAST.

THIS TEXT IS FULL OF GOOD SENSE. BUT GOOD SENSE—AND FREUD WOULD NOT HAVE SAID THE CONTRARY—OFTEN ERRS. ONE SHOULD JUDGE— THE LAST PHRASE MAKES ONE THINK THAT INCEST COULD HAVE BEEN PRACTISED ONCE, BUT THAT MEN HAD RENOUNCED IT FOR GOOD REASONS. THE PROHIBITION IS THEN JUSTIFIABLE; HOWEVER, IT IS TRANSGRESSED "ONLY TOO OFTEN." MURDER IS THE SAME: ONE SHOULD NEVER KILL, ESPECIALLY IN ORDER TO DEVOUR ONE'S VICTIM, AND HERE ALSO "GOOD REASONS" CAN BE INVOKED; BUT THAT ONE

KILLS, IN GENERAL AND IN PARTICULAR, THIS ALSO IS ONLY TOO EVIDENT. ON THE CONTRARY, THERE IS NO REASON FOR NOT EATING HUMAN FLESH. THE PROHIBITION OF CANNIBALISM THUS APPEARS UNJUSTIFIABLE, DESPITE THE FACT THAT IN EATING A MAN ONE NEED NOT BEGIN BY KILLING HIM; NONETHELESS, WE RESPECT IT MUCH LESS. HOW CAN ONE SAY THEN THAT FOR INCEST, AND IMPLICITLY FOR MURDER, THE SITUATION IS "EXACTLY LIKE THAT OF CANNIBALISM?"

TO BE A CANNIBAL IS TO EAT OTHER MEN, AND ONE CAN ONLY EITHER BE ONE OR NOT BE ONE. MATTERS ARE NOT SO SIMPLE WITH RESPECT TO INCEST, WHICH PRESENTS BOTH A SEXUAL AND A SOCIO-LOGICAL ASPECT; THEY CANNOT BE COMPLETELY DISSOCIATED ONE FROM THE OTHER, BUT ARE RARELY RIGOROUSLY LINKED; ONE CAN PROHIBIT THE MARRIAGE OF CERTAIN KIN WITHOUT MAKING A DRAMA OF THEIR EVENTUAL SEXUAL RELATIONS. WITH US FOR EXAMPLE, TWO NEAR KIN CAN SLEEP TOGETHER, THEY SIMPLY CANNOT BE MARRIED AND THEIR CHILDREN WILL NOT BE LEGITIMATE; THEIR RELATIONS WILL BE SEXUAL BUT NOT CONNUBIAL. THUS ONE WILL BE—MUST ONE SAY, MORE OR LESS—EXACTING: THE SEXUAL RELATIONSHIP AT ONE TIME TREATED RITUALLY WILL BECOME A

FULLY LEGAL MARRIAGE. THUS AGAIN, ITS SIMPLE EXISTENCE COULD FORM THE BASIS OF A RECOGNIZED UNION OF INFERIOR STATUS. IN EVERY CASE A TWO-SIDED PLAY IS POSSIBLE, WHICH ALLOWS ONE TO MAINTAIN THE PROHIBITION, TO EFFACE ITS VIOLATION ... AND TO BEGIN AGAIN. ON THE CONTRARY, IN THE MATTER OF CANNIBALISM, ONE CANNOT THUS DISSOCIATE DE FACTO AND DE JURE STATUS. IT IS UNDERSTOOD THAT IN CANNIBALISM AS WELL THERE ARE TWO ASPECTS: TO EAT, AND TO EAT OTHER MEN PRECISELY; BUT THE BIOLOGICAL ASPECT OF THE MATTER IS NOT SEPARABLE FROM ITS SOCIAL CONSEQUENCE. I CAN SLEEP WITH A WOMAN WITHOUT MARRYING HER AND SHE REMAINS A POSSIBLE SPOUSE, FOR ME OR FOR SOMEONE ELSE. BUT IF I EAT HER SHE IS NO LONGER EDIBLE FOR ANY ONE ELSE! DIFFERENT FROM THE SEXUAL RELATIONSHIP, THE CANNIBALISTIC RELATIONSHIP CANNOT BE REPEATED, ITS ACHIEVEMENT EXHAUSTS IT, AND IF IT IS PROHIBITED AND NONETHELESS REALIZED, THERE IS NO POSSIBLE REMISSION, THE VICTIM IS IRRECUPARABLE. ONE WOULD SAY THAT THE SAME IS TRUE OF MURDER, BUT THE FACT IS THAT, AS FOR INCEST AND CONTRARY TO CANNIBALISM, ONE CAN GET AROUND THE RULE, VIOLATING IT WHILE MAINTAINING IT: THIS IS NOT TO SPEAK OF WAR WHERE TO KILL IS AN EXPLOIT; THE ACQUITTAL OF A MURDERER WHERE EXTENUATING CIRCUMSTANCES CAN BE RECOGNIZED DOES NOT PLACE THE PROHIBITION IN QUESTION. AS FOR THE EXECUTION OF A MURDERER, WHICH ITSELF IS A MURDER, ITS PURPOSE IS TO REINFORCE THE PROHITIBION, NOT TO WEAKEN IT; TO KILL SOMEONE WHO HAS KILLED DOES NOT TRANSFORM THE SOCIETY INTO A SOCIETY OF KILLERS, AND THIS IS WHY THE PUNISHMENT OF DEATH CAN BE ALLOWED BY THE VERY PEOPLE WHO MOST VIGOROUSLY CONDEMN MURDER. SIMILARLY IT WOULD COME TO NO ONE'S MIND, IN A NON-CANNIBAL SOCIETY, TO SUGGEST THE CONSUMPTION OF SOMEONE WHO HAD BEEN FOUND GUILTY OF CANNIBALISM. ONE ONLY EATS A CANNIBAL IN A SOCIETY OF CANNIBALS, WHICH BRINGS US BACK TO THE FACT THAT CANNIBALISM IS ALMOST ALWAYS AN INSTITUTION, NEVER A TRANSGRESSION.

SYNTHESIS AND RESULTS OF ALL THESE OPPOSITIONS: INCEST (AND MURDER) IS PROHIBITED EVERYWHERE AND ENCOUNTERED EVERYWHERE, CANNIBALISM IS ONLY PRACTISED WHERE IT IS AUTHORISED AND NEVER WHERE IT IS PROHIBITED. IN GENERAL, THERE IS ON ONE SIDE A PROHIBITION WHOSE VIOLATION IN NO WAY COMPROMISES IT, ON THE OTHER, A RULE WHICH CANNOT BE VIOLATED SINCE THAT WHICH IT CONDEMNS, IF ONE DOES IT, PROVES ITS ABSENCE AND MANIFESTS THE OPPOSITE RULE. THE POSSIBILITY OF INCEST IS SO WELL PREDICTED THAT OFTEN ONE HAS ALSO FORSEEN A RITE TO ACHIEVE IT, TO FILL THE GAP, AND PERHAPS ALSO, AS ONE HAS ALREADY INDICATED, WITHOUT CONSTRAINING THE SEPARATION OF THE INCESTUOUS PARTIES. THE CANNIBAL, IN A SOCIETY WHICH IS NOT, TRANSGRESSES THE NORM IN A MANNER THAT IS, ON THE CONTRARY, IRREPARABLE; ONE CANNOT CONSIDER HIM A MEMBER OF THE SOCIAL BODY. THIS IS WHY, IN SOCIETIES WHERE ONE DOES NOT EAT OTHER MEN, BUT WHERE MEN FEAR BEING EATEN, AND WHERE ONE ATTRIBUTES MALADIES AND DEATHS TO CANNIBAL ACTIONS, ONE IMPUTES THE COMMISSION OF THE CRIMES TO MYSTERIOUS FOREIGNERS, OR TO SORCERERS WHO ARE DIFFICULT TO IDENTIFY.

SYMMETRICALLY, WHERE CANNIBALISM IS THE RULE, THERE IS NO WAY TO ELUDE IT, POSITIVE OR NEGATIVE, IT TOLERATES NO MEANS OF ESCAPE. "FINALLY," WRITES H. CLASTRES ABOUT THE ANCIENT TUPI, "THE ESSENTIAL RULE OF ANTHROPOPHAGY IS PERHAPS THE EXIGENCE THAT EVERYONE PARTICIPATE." ONE FINDS ONESELF IN THE PRESENCE OF A PARADOX THAT IS AT LEAST APPARENT: THE UNIVERSAL RULE SUFFERS ITS TRANSGRESSION, WHILE, WHERE IT APPLIES, THE PARTICULAR RULE KNOWS PRACTICALLY NONE. IN REALITY THE DEFINITIONS OF INCEST AND OF CANNIBALISM EASILY EXPLAIN THIS.

A RELATIONSHIP IS ONLY INCESTUOUS WITH RESPECT TO THE PROHIBITION IT BREAKS; ONE CANNOT, THUS, PRESCRIBE IT WITHOUT CONTRADICTING ONE'S TERMS: SINCE IT SUPPOSES THE RULE WHICH CONDEMNS IT, IT ALWAYS APPEARS AS A TRANSGRESSION, AND THIS TRANSGRESSION CAN BE FOUND EVERYWHERE BECAUSE OF THE UNIVERSALITY OF SEXUAL DESIRE. AN APPEARANCE MORE OR LESS FREQUENT ACCORDING TO THE EXTENT OF ITS PROHIBITION: RELATIVELY RARE IN SOCIETIES WITH A LARGE POPULATION, AND WHERE THE CIRCLE OF FORBIDDEN PARTNERS IS LIMITED, MORE FREQUENT IN THOSE SOCIETIES THAT HAVE FEWER MEMBERS AND THAT HAVE ENLARGED THE BOUNDS OF THE PROHIBITION. FOR THIS REASON, THE PRETENDED UNIVERSAL HORROR OF INCEST IS IN GENERAL MUCH LESS PRONOUNCED IN THESE LATTER; WHERE ONE HAS AFFIRMED IT IN ABUSIVELY EXTRAPOLATING A SENTIMENT WHICH, FOR US, KEEPS THE RESTRICTION OF THE PROHIBITION TO THE ONLY KIN WHO ARE CONSISTENTLY FORBIDDEN.

AS FOR CANNIBALISM, ONE CANNOT EXPLAIN WHY

SOME SOCIETIES ACCEPT IT AND OTHERS FORBID IT, BUT THAT ITS PROHIBITION NEVER PLACES ITS PRACTICE IN QUESTION; THIS POSES THE PROBLEM OF ADMITTING A UNIVERSAL DESIRE TO EAT MEN. BUT MUST THERE BE ONE? SUCH A DESIRE DOES NOT EVEN SEEM PRESENT FOR ALL CANNIBALS. TRUE THE IROQUOIS ENJOY THIS KIND OF FOOD, AND JEAN DE LÉRY WRITES OF THE TUPI: "ALL ADMIT THIS HUMAN FLESH TO BE WONDERFULLY GOOD AND DELICATE," EXPLAINING THAT OLD WOMEN IN PARTICULAR HAD A TASTE FOR IT, BUT THIS TASTE IS NOT THE ONLY THING INVOLVED, BECAUSE HE ADDS: "THEIR PRINCIPAL INTENTION IS THAT IN PREPARING AND EATING THE DEAD IN THIS WAY, TO THE BONE, THEY GIVE, BY THESE MEANS, FEAR AND TERROR TO THE LIVING." THIS CONFIRMS STADEN: "THEY DO THIS NOT TO EASE THEIR HUNGER, BUT THROUGH HOSTILITY, OUT OF GREAT HATE," AND CLAUDE D'ABBEVILLE WHO CONTESTS THE VERY REALITY OF CANNIBALISTIC DESIRE: "IT IS NOT THAT THEY SO MUCH ENJOY EATING HUMAN FLESH BUT THAT THEIR SENSUAL APPETITE BRINGS THEM TO THESE MEANS. FOR I HAVE HEARD THEM SAY THAT AFTER HAVING EATEN, THEY ARE SOMETIMES FORCED TO VOMIT, THEIR STOMACH NOT BEING CAPABLE OF DIGESTING IT." THE SAME MISADVENTURE CAN HAPPEN TO THE FATALEKA, OF WHOM R. GUIDIERI TELLS US THAT THEY ARE CANNIBALS, NOT BY TASTE AND FOR PLEASURE, BUT BY OBLIGATION, BY SUBMISSION TO THE WILL OF A DEAD CHIEF WHO, THANKS TO HIS CONSUMPTION OF A SACRIFICED VICTIM, ACCEDED TO THE RANK OF ANCESTOR. THIS SUBMISSION IS DESERVING, BECAUSE HUMAN FLESH IS DANGEROUS, AND TO EAT IT, THE FATALEKA MUST SURMOUNT A CERTAIN AVERSION: THE VICTIM MUST BE COMPELTELY CONSUMED, IF ONE OF THE CONVIVES VOMITS, HIS COMMENSALS MUST COMPLETELY REABSORB WHAT HAS UNFORTUNATELY BEEN REJECTED. THIS IDEA THAT ONE CANNOT EAT HUMAN FLESH WITHOUT RISK IS, MOREOVER, WIDESPREAD; IT IS A GOOD FOOD BUT TOO STRONG FOR ONE TO EAT IT PURE; THE GUYAKI MUST MIX IT WITH A VEGETABLE FOOD; ONE COOKS IT IN RAGOUT WITH HEARTS OF PALM. BESIDES, UNLIKE THE SEX ACT, THE CANNIBAL ACT IS ALWAYS PUBLIC AND RITUALIZED; THERE IS ALWAYS AN ELEMENT, PERHAPS A CAPITAL ONE, OF A COMPLEX CEREMONY OFTEN LIKE A FUNERAL. THIS IS EVIDENTLY TRUE OF THE GUAYAKI WHO EAT THEIR DEAD AND OF THE FATALEKA WHO EAT FOR THEIR DEAD; IT IS ALSO THE TUPI WHO EAT THEIR PRISONERS IN ORDER, AMONG OTHER REASONS, TO APPEASE THE SOUL OF A DECEASED RELATIVE. THESE CEREMONIES HAVE BEEN THE OBJECT OF DIVERSE INTERPRETATIONS: DESIRE FOR VENGEANCE, DESIRE TO APPROPRIATE THE QUALITIES OF THEIR VICTIMS. IN ANY EVENT EACH MAY BE VALID FOR A GIVEN POPULATION, BUT CAN PRETEND TO NO GENERAL VALIDITY. THEY HAVE ABOVE ALL AN IDEOLOGICAL CHARACTER: THEY EXPRESS THE IDEAS THAT THE INTERESTED HAVE OF THE POST MORTEM EXISTENCE OF THE HUMAN PERSON, OF THE RELATIONS BETWEEN THE LIVING AND THE DEAD; FROM THIS LAST POINT OF VIEW, CANNIBALISM CAN BE CONSIDERED AS WELL AS A MEANS TO KEEP AWAY THE DEAD BY DESTROYING THEIR CORPORAL SUPPORT—SO THE GUYAKI THINK—AS A MEANS TO ASSURE CERTAIN DEAD OF ACCESS TO THE SUPREME POWER, THAT OF ANCESTORSHIP—SO THE FATALEKA THINK. IN ONE CASE AS IN THE OTHER, THERE IS NO EVIDENT REASON TO SUPPOSE A PROPERLY CANNIBAL DESIRE.

HOWEVER, IF THE PRACTICE DOES NOT IMPLY A DESIRE, ABSTENTION DOES NOT HINDER CANNIBALISM FROM HAUNTING THE LANGUAGE AND FROM NOURISHING FEARS, PERHAPS EVEN DREAMS, OF NON-CANNIBALS. CULINARY LANGUAGE IS FREQUENTLY EMPHASIZED TO DESIGNATE, IN THE FAMILIAR OR ARGOT MODE, SEXUAL RELATIONS, AND THE USE OF NAMES OF MAN-EATING ANIMALS OR OF COMESTIBLES TO DESIGNATE THE LOVE PARTNER, TO EXPRESS THE FEAR OF BEING IN SOME WAY DEVOURED BY HER ("WHAT A TIGRESS") OR TO FORMULATE A SENSUAL ATTRACTION ("WHAT AN APPETIZING CHICK"). ONE COULD ADD THAT SEXUAL PLAY CAN CONTAIN CANNIBALISTIC BEHAVIOR (BITING, SUCTION). THERE IS NO DOUBT THAT THERE EXISTS AN ORAL COMPONENT OF SEXUAL DESIRE, AND IT IS THIS COMPONENT THAT PERMITS CANNIBALISTIC LANGUAGE. BUT—AND THIS IS WHAT WE WISHED TO SUGGEST IN THE PRECEDING PARAGRAPH—CANNIBALISM DOES NOT REDUCE ITSELF TO ORALITY. THE AMOROUS ANTHROPOPHAGE IS NOT, IN HIS SEXUAL RELATIONS, MORE "ORAL" THAN THE NON-CANNIBAL: NO MORE DOES HE DEVOUR HIS PARTNER! HIS CANNIBALISM EXISTS ON ANOTHER GROUND ENTIRELY, A GROUND OF WHICH THOSE WHO DO NOT EAT THEIR COUNTERPARTS ARE IGNORANT, AND THIS IS WHY THE LATTER, WHEN HE TRIES TO UNDERSTAND THE FORMER, CANNOT DO IT WITHOUT CONFOUNDING ANTHROPOPHAGY AND EXCESSIVE ORALITY. FROM THIS FACT, THE PROHIBITION OF HUMAN FLESH LIBERATES THE METAPHORIC USAGE OF CANNIBALISM: PRECISELY BECAUSE ONE DOES NOT TRANSGRESS THE PROHIBITION, THE REPRESENTATIONS OF CANNIBALISM SERVE TO SIGNIFY ANOTHER THING, AND NOT ONLY, IF OFTEN, OF A SEXUAL ORDER.

A SEXUAL METAPHOR, CANNIBALISM CAN, IN CURRENT LANGUAGE, GIVE AN EXCESSIVE IMAGE OF AN ADMISSIBLE EXCESS (IN THE ORDER OF TENDERNESS FOR EXAMPLE). IN MYTHS AND TALES, IT FURNISHES MOST FREQUENTLY A DISQUIETING IMAGE OF AN INTOLERABLE EXCESS. SOME STORIES ANALYSED BY G. CALAMEGRIAULE MAKE A FIGURE OF UNSOCIALIZED SEXUALITY OUT OF EATING, AS WELL AS OF ITS PERILS OR SANCTIONS: ENDOCANNIBALISM—EATING ONE'S KIN—EXPRESSES AN EXCESSIVE ENDOGAMY, THAT IS TO SAY INCEST WHICH MENACES THE INTERIOR OF SOCIETY; EXOCANNIBALISM—TO EAT OR TO BE EATEN BY STRANGERS—RESULTS ON THE CONTRARY IN AN EXAGGERATED EXOGAMY WHICH MENACES THE SOCIAL GROUP FROM THE EXTERIOR. IT IS THE IMPRUDENT UNION WITH THIS STRANGE FOREIGNER WHO IS THE SEDUCTIVE OGRE. THE CANNIBALISTIC METAPHOR SERVES HERE TO CIRCUMSCRIBE THE FIELD OF ACCEPTABLE ALLIANCE: BETWEEN THOSE INELIGIBLE FOR MARRIAGE BECAUSE TOO NEAR AND THOSE INELIGIBLE FOR MARRIAGE BECAUSE TOO DISTANT. BUT IT CAN ALSO SERVE TO EXPRESS OTHER OPPOSITIONS WHICH DETERMINE PERMISSIBLE AND FORBIDDEN MARRIAGES. OPPOSITION OF THE HUMAN AND THE INHUMAN—BUT NOT THE INVERSE—WHICH CAN BE CONSIDERED AS COINCIDING WITH THAT WHICH DETERMINES COMESTIBLE AND NON-COMESTIBLE. THE POLITICAL AND ECONOMIC OPPOSITION OF THE RULER TO HIS SUBJECTS, OF WHICH AN ALIMENTARY COMPARISON FORMULATES INSUPPORTABLE TENSION. THE CHIEF "EATS" MEN, SAY THE HADJERAI, AND THEY ARE NOT THE ONLY ONES TO AFFIRM THIS; ACTUALLY, IT IS AGGRESSIVITY, MORE THAN ORALITY, THE DESIRE TO ABSORB, WHICH IS METAPHORIZED.

ALL THESE VIRTUALITIES OF THE ALIMENTARY CODE (AND NOT ONLY THE CANNIBAL) ARE FOUND IN THE AMERINDIAN MYTHOLOGY; THE MYTHOLOGIES OF C. LÉVI-STRAUSS GIVES INNUMERABLE EXAMPLES, IN WHICH THE STORY DEVELOPS IN PLAYING ON HOMOLOGIES BETWEEN DIFFERENT CODES. THUS THE STORY OF A GIRL WHO, HAVING TASTED HER OWN BLOOD—AUTOCANNIBALISM—ALIMENTARY INCEST—FEELS THE ARDENT DESIRE TO CONSUMATE A REAL INCEST, AND THIS FRUSTRATED DESIRE RETRANSFORMS ITSELF INTO ALIMENTARY APPETITE, IS TOO INSPIRED BY THE BODY OF A RETICENT BROTHER; OR THAT OF THE SUN-WOMAN, A CANNIBAL, WHO A HERO "TEMPERS" AND MAKES MORE CLEMENT TOWARDS MEN BY POSSESSING HER WITH A PENIS MADE OF ICE. FOR THOSE WHO ARE LIMITED TO IMAGINING IT, CANNIBALISM IS THUS A FIGURE OF DISORDER. INDIVIDUAL AND BIOLOGICAL DISORDER: THE EBRIE AND THE ALLADIAN STUDIED

BY M. AUGÉ EXPLAIN SICKNESS BY AN ANTHROPOPHAGY EITHER UNDERGONE—CONSUMPTION OF THE SICK ORGAN BY A SORCERER—OR INVOLUNTARILY PRACTICED ABSORPTION OF HUMAN FLESH BY THE BEWITCHED PATIENT. POLITICAL AND RELIGIOUS DISORDER: THE GREEK CITY, WRITES M. DETIENNE, REPRESENTED ITSELF BY WAYS OF EATING, AND "IT REJECTED WITHOUT AMBIGUITY" A CANNIBALISM THAT IT SITUATED AT THE CONFINES OF ITS HISTORY, IN AN AGE ANTERIOR TO HUMANITY, OR TO THE LIMITS OF ITS SPACE, AMONG THE PEOPLE WHO COMPOSE THE WORLD OF BARBARIANS. THE VIEW IS NOT CONTRADICTED BY THE MOVEMENTS WHICH IN GREECE ITSELF HAVE CONTESTED THE SYSTEM OF VALUES WHICH EXPRESSES THIS REJECTION: CANNIBALISM, WHETHER IT BE INTEGRATED INTO CERTAIN DIONYSIAN RITUALS IN ORDER TO PROVIDE DIRECT CONTACT WITH THE SUPERNATURAL, OR IT BE DEMANDED BY THE CYNICS "TO AFFIRM THE RIGHTS OF THE INDIVIDUAL IN THE FACE OF SOCIETY AND AGAINST EVERY FORM OF CIVILIZATION," REMAINS A MEANS TO MAKE MAN SAVAGE. FOR THOSE WHO CONTEST IT, AS WELL AS FOR THOSE WHO CONFORM, IT PLACES CULTURE IN QUESTION, NOT ANOTHER DEFINITION OF CULTURE.

THE USE OF THE CANNIBALISTIC METAPHOR, AND THE REJECTION OF CANNIBALISTIC PRACTICE RESTS, AS WE SEE, ON THE IDEA THAT CANNIBALISM IS AN UNREGULATED BEHAVIOR, OF WHICH DIVERSE FORMS—AUTO- ENDO- EXO-CANNIBALISM—ARE ONLY INTERCHANGEABLE VARIETIES, WITHOUT THEIR OWN SIGNIFICATION. IT POINTS OUT "SAVAGES," BUT NOT THE INDICATION OF ANOTHER CULTURE, THE VERY PROOF OF THE ABSENCE OF CULTURE. THIS GENERALIZED CANNIBALISM, SUB- OR PRE-HUMAN, APPEARS AS AN IRRUPTION OF NATURE IN THE BODY OF CULTURE: IT EFFACES THE FRONTIERS WHICH SEPARATE THE HUMAN WORLD FROM THE INHUMAN WORLD, JUST AS INCEST ABOLISHES THE DISTINCTION WHICH, IN THE BODY OF SOCIETY, MAKE IT ANOTHER THING THAN AN AMORPHOUS MAGMA. THE TWO PROHIBITIONS ORGANIZE THE SOCIAL FIELD CONJOINTLY, THE ONE DELIMITING IT FROM THE OUTSIDE, THE OTHER ARTICULATING IT FROM THE INSIDE.

*

WE ARE BROUGHT BACK TO FREUD, A FACT WHICH IS NOT SURPRISING, SINCE FREUD WAS CERTAINLY NO CANNIBAL! BUT IT IS TIME TO ASK IF THIS IS HOW THOSE WHO ARE THINK AND ACT. WE IMMEDIATELY GIVE A RESPONSE THAT IS PERHAPS UNEXPECTED: THIS IS WHAT THEY THINK, BUT—AND UNDOUBTEDLY FOR THIS—THIS IS NOT WHAT THEY DO.

FIRST OF ALL, WHAT DO THEY SEEM TO THEM-SELVES, THOSE WHO SEEM TO US TO BE CANNI-BALS? A CURIOUS PROBLEM, AND AT FIRST GLANCE INCOMPREHENSIBLE: THEY TAKE OFFENSE AT BEING TREATED AS EATERS-OF-MEN. THE CANNIBALS ARE ALWAYS THE OTHERS, AND THESE OTHERS ARE PRECISELY THE "SAVAGES," PEOPLE WITHOUT GOOD MANNERS: NEAR NEIGHBORS WHO BEHAVE DIF-FERENTLY, OR MYTHICAL POPULATIONS—DISTANT IN TIME AND SPACE, WHO ARE IGNORANT OF ANY RULES, NOTABLY THOSE OF MARRIAGE AND OF DIET, IN SHORT, INCESTUOUS CANNIBALS. THE FATALEKA, GUIDIERI TELLS US, "OPPOSE TO THEIR INSTITU-TIONALIZED CANNIBALISM A SAVAGE CANNIBALISM. ... THIS CANNIBALISM, WHICH EXISTED BEFORE THE SOCIETY OF MEN ... IS ATTRIBUTED TO AN ANCIENT PEOPLE OF THE INTERIOR ... (OF WHOM) CANNIBAL CUSTOMS, STRONGLY REPROVED, ARE SYSTEMATI-CALLY OPPOSED TO RITUAL PRACTICES." AS FOR THE IROQUOIS, OF WHOM U. CHODOWIED SPEAKS, THEY PEOPLE THEIR MYTHS WITH CHARACTERS WHO EAT ANYONE AT ALL—THEIR NEAR KIN, IT IS UNDERSTOOD—AND PERHAPS EVEN THEMSELVES, AND PREPARED IN ANY WAY AT ALL—RAW, FOR EXAMPLE—AND IT IS NECESSARY TO DESTROY THEM OR TO BRING THEM TO REASON, THAT IS TO THE PROPER MANNER OF EATING MEN. THE BASIC MYTH OF THE CELEBRATED POLITICAL ASSOCIATION, "THE FIVE NATIONS," THE IROQUOIS, TELLS HOW MAN PASSED FROM A SAVAGE MONSTROUS CANNIBA-LISM TO INSTITUTIONALIZED, SOCIALIZED, CANNI-BALISM. THE GUYAKI HAVE NO NEED OF MYTHS TO CONDEMN CANNIBALISM: THEY EAT THEIR OWN DEAD AND IT IS WELL, BUT THEIR NEIGHBORS, THE GUAIANI, WHO KILL THEIR ENEMIES AND EAT THEM, GIVE AN EXAMPLE TO BE AVOIDED, THEY ARE TRUE CANNIBALS.

IN OTHER WORDS, REAL CANNIBALISM IS NEVER UNORDERED: THE EXOCANNIBALS, FOR EXAMPLE, DO NOT EAT THEIR DEAD, AND THE ENDOCANNIBALS WHO DO DO NOT EAT FOREIGNERS; THE VICTIM'S SEX IS IMPORTANT TO CERTAIN OF THEM WHO ONLY EAT MALE INDIVIDUALS AND EXCLUDE WOMEN, WHILE OTHERS DO NOT TAKE THIS INTO ACCOUNT; THE PRACTICE MAY BE GENERAL, BUT IT MAY BE RESERVED FOR CERTAIN CATEGORIES OF INDIVID-UALS; THE CONSUMMATION, MAY BE COMPLETE OR NOT; THE DISTRIBUTION OF PARTS MAY BE ALEATORY OR REGULATED; THE FUTURE VICTIM MAY HAVE HIS WORD TO SAY, AS WITH THE FORE WHO CUT UP THE DEAD IN EATING THEM, OR THE MORIBUND MAY "DETERMINE WHICH OF HIS KIN WILL BE AUTHORIZED TO TASTE HIS FLESH." THE METHODS OF COOKING AND OF PREPARATION VARY AS WELL FROM ONE GROUP TO ANOTHER. IN BRIEF THERE IS

NO LACK OF RULES, POSITIVE OR NEGATIVE, NOR OF MORE OR LESS ELABORATE JUSTIFICATIONS. THIS HAS NOTHING TO DO WITH A GENERALIZED CANNIBALISM, WHICH, COMPLETELY UNATTESTED AND EVERYWHERE DREADED, IS PURELY IMA-GINARY.

ONE SEES THAT REAL CANNIBALISM OUGHT NOT TO EXCLUDE IMAGINARY CANNIBALISM, SINCE IT IS IN OPPOSING ITSELF THAT THE LATTER DEFINES ITSELF, OR, IF ONE PREFERS, THE PROHIBITION OF SAVAGE CANNIBALISM DOES NOT EXCLUDE REAL CANNIBALISM. THE CANNIBAL AND THE NON-CANNIBAL JOIN IN CONDEMNING IN THE SAME WAY AND FOR THE SAME REASONS AN UNRESTRAINED CANNIBALISM. EACH REPRESENTS IN THE SAME WAY THIS INADMISSABLE ANTHROPOPHAGY, AND IN THIS SENSE ONE CAN SAY THAT THEY RESPECT THE SAME PROHIBITION: ONE CANNOT EAT EVERYTHING, THE COMESTIBLE IS NOT ALWAYS LIABLE TO CONSUMPTION. THE PARALLELISM WITH SEXUAL PROHIBITIONS (OR SIMPLY WITH MATRIMONIAL) BECOMES EVIDENT: ONE CANNOT MARRY ANYONE, ANY "KISSABLE" PERSON IS NOT ALWAYS MAR-RIAGEABLE. A PARALLELISM THAT EXTENDS IN ANOTHER DIRECTION: SAVAGE CANNIBALISM IS PAIRED WITH PRIMITIVE "PROMISCUITY," ONE AND THE OTHER EQUALLY REJECTED ... AND EQUALLY IMAGINARY. A PARALLELISM, FINALLY, THAT EMPLOYS CANNIBALISTIC METAPHORS.

ONE WILL SAY THAT THERE REMAINS AN IRREDU-CIBLE DIFFERENCE BETWEEN THE CANNIBALS AND THE OTHERS: JUST AS SEVERE AS THE FIRST CAN BE IN THEIR CONDEMNATION OF SAVAGE CANNI-BALISM; THE FACT IS THAT THEY EAT MEN AND THAT THE LATTER DO NOT. THIS APPEARS INCONTEST-ABLE—ESPECIALLY TO US WHO GIVE CANNIBALISM A GENERAL AND SILLY DEFINITION; BUT THIS IS NOT SO SURE, AS M. DETIENNE SHOWS. ONE IS ALWAYS SOMEONE ELSE'S CANNIBAL; EVERYTHING DEPENDS ON THE POINT OF VIEW. IF, IN HIS ALIMENTARY REGIME—"A PLAN OF PRIVILEGED SIGNIFICATION TO DEFINE THE SYSTEM OF RELATIONS BETWEEN MAN, NATURE, AND THE SUPERNATURAL" FOR THE GREEKS—MAN MUST PLACE HIMSELF SOMEWHERE "BETWEEN BEASTS AND GODS," AND IF THE ANTHROPOPHAGY IS ONLY A MODALITY OF ALLELOPHAGY, ONE RISKS BEING INEVITABLY A LITTLE BIT OF A CANNIBAL, SINCE ONE CANNOT BE CONTENT LIKE THE GODS, WITH SMOKE AND AROMATIC ODORS. IN THE EYES OF STRICT PYTHAGORIANS, CARNAL ALIMENTATION IS A FORM OF ANTHROPOPHAGY, AND THOSE THAT ACCEPT A COMPROMISE "DECIDING THAT CERTAIN SACRIFI-CIAL VICTIMS—PIGS AND GOATS—ARE NOT,

PROPERLY SPEAKING, MEAT, AND THAT MEAT ACTUALLY IS THE FLESH OF FARM COWS, THE SLAUGHTER OF WHOM IS THE OBJECT OF A FORMAL PROHIBITION." THIS RESTRICTION IS EXPLAINED BY THE CLOSENESS OF COW AND MAN: FUNDAMENTAL-LY MEAT IS MORE OR LESS MAN, AND AS ROUSSEAU ALSO THOUGHT (SEE EMILE), EVERY CARNIVORE IS A CANNIBAL, AT LEAST POTENTIALLY.

CANNIBALISM THUS DOES NOT EXIST, EXCEPT IN THE IMAGINATION, AND ONE ENCOUNTERS ONLY CANNIBALS WHO DEFINE THEMSELVES BY THE NEGATION OF THIS PHANTASM. SINCE THIS PHANTASM IS IMAGINED BY ALL AS REAL, IN A SUPPOSED ELSEWHERE, ONE CAN SAY THAT NO ONE IS A CANNIBAL, BUT, LIKE EVERYONE ELSE, ACCORDING TO HIS EFFECTIVE ALIMENTARY REGIME, CAN BE JUDGED A CANNIBAL BY THE OTHERS, ONE COULD SAY JUST AS WELL THAT EVERYONE IS ONE.

FINALLY, THE ERROR NOT TO BE COMMITTED IS THAT OF CONTENTING ONESELF WITH A MATERIAL, BIOLOGICAL DEFINITION OF CANNIBALISM: TO EAT MEN, OR TO RECONSIDER THE EXAMPLE OF THE GREEKS, A FLESH ESTIMATED TOO CLOSE TO THAT OF MAN. IF THE FLESH OF THE FARM COW MUST NOT BE CONSUMED, THIS IS NOT BECAUSE OF ANY EFFECTIVE RESEMBLANCE, IN TASTE FOR EXAMPLE, WITH THAT OF MAN, IT IS BECAUSE OF THE QUASI-SOCIAL STATUS OF THE ANIMAL. SIMILARLY, IF ONE FORBIDS ONESELF THE EATING OF ONE'S KIN, BUT ONE EATS STRANGERS, THIS IS NOT BECAUSE THE LATTER ARE MORE DELECTABLE, IT IS BECAUSE THE FORMER IS NOT DONE, FOR A SOCIOLOGICAL REASON. CANNIBALISM IS A WAY OF THINKING MORE THAN A WAY OF EATING. THUS, JUST AS INCEST AND CORRELATIVELY THE AUTHORIZED ALLIANCE FORMALLY DEFINES ITSELF BY THE GENEALOGICAL POSITION OF THE PARTNER, THE PROHIBITION AND PRESCRIPTION OF CANNIBALISM DEFINES ITSELF FORMALLY BY THE SOCIAL POSITION OF HIM WHO MUST BE EATEN. AS FOR INCEST AND THE ALLIANCE, THE VARIABILITY OF THE PROHIBITED FIELD EXPLAINS THE MULTIPLICITY OF SYSTEMS.

ONE WILL FIND, IN THIS REVIEW, SOME EXAMPLES WHICH GIVE AN IDEA—A FORETASTE—OF THAT WHICH COULD BE A GENERAL THEORY OF CANNI-BALISTIC STRUCTURES. THE VARIANTS MUST BE ORDERED SIMULTANEOUSLY ACCORDING TO MANY AXES. THAT OF KINSHIP, NATURALLY; THE GUYAKI EAT THE DEAD IN THE GROUP TO WHICH THEY BELONG AND WITH WHICH, BECAUSE OF ITS EFFECTIVE WEAKNESS, THEY ALMOST INEVITABLY HAVE TIES OF KINSHIP. AT THE SAME TIME, THEY CANNOT EAT THOSE WITH WHICH THEY CANNOT COPULATE; FATHERS AND MOTHERS DO NOT EAT THEIR SONS AND DAUGHTERS, AND RECIPROCALLY; BROTHER AND SISTER DO NOT EAT EACH OTHER. HERE, CONSEQUENTLY, THE TWO PROHIBITIONS COMBINE AND HAVE THE SAME BREADTH. SINCE THE NOMENCLATURE OF KINSHIP SUFFICES TO INDICATE WHO CAN AND CANNOT BE EATEN, ONE COULD SPEAK OF AN "ELEMENTARY STRUCTURE OF CANNIBALISM." EVEN WHEN THEY ARE NOT DETERMINATES, KINSHIP AND ALLIANCE OFTEN FURNISH A LANGUAGE FOR CANNIBALISM: WITHIN A GROUP, THE TUPI, KIN OR NOT, ALLIES OR NOT, NONE ATE EACH OTHER; THOSE THAT THEY ATE THEY CALLED "BROTHERS-IN-LAW," METAPHORIZING THE NON-CANNIBALS INVERSELY. IROQUOIS DID NOT EAT IROQUOIS, EVEN THOSE OF ANOTHER NATION; THEIR VICTIMS WERE FOREIGNERS; HOWEVER THE PRISONERS THAT THEY BROUGHT FROM THEIR EXPEDITIONS WERE THE OBJECT OF A CHOICE, ONE ATE THEM OR ONE ADOPTED THEM, AND THOSE THAT WERE EATEN WERE THUS THOSE WITH WHOM ONE DID NOT WISH TO FORGE A LINK OF KINSHIP. IN THE THIRD CASE, ONE EATS REAL OR POTENTIAL ALLIES. THIS IS INEVITABLE FOR THE GUYAKI, SINCE THE ONLY PEOPLE EXCLUDED FROM THE RITUAL WERE THE FATHER AND MOTHER, THE SON AND THE DAUGHTER, THE BROTHER OR THE SISTER OF THE DEAD PERSON. FOR THE TUPI, IT WAS A POSSIBILITY EXPRESSED BY THE LANGUAGE; THE WOMEN OF ENEMY GROUPS FROM WHICH ONE HAD TAKEN PRISONERS FOR THE PURPOSE OF EATING THEM COULD BE MARRIED. FOR THE IROQUOIS, THE GROUP THAT ONE TOOK PRISONER WAS ALSO THAT FROM WHICH ONE BROUGHT BACK PEOPLE, WHO, ADOPTED, ENTERED IN FULL RIGHT IN THE MATRIMONIAL FIELD; THOSE ADOPTED COULD HAVE BEEN EATEN JUST AS THOSE EATEN COULD HAVE BEEN ADOPTED. THERE AGAIN THE METAPHORICAL AND REVERSIBLE LIAISON OF CANNIBALISM AND SEXUALITY IS EASILY UNDERSTOOD.

IN FACT, WHAT IS DETERMINING FOR THE IROQUOIS AND THE TUPI IS LESS KINSHIP THAN THE APPARTENANCE TO A POLITICALLY DEFINED GROUP, AND THE PERTINENT OPPOSITION IS THUS THAT OF ENDOCANNIBALISM, ILLUSTRATED BY THE GUYAKI, AND EXOCANNIBALISM, ILLUSTRATED BY THE OTHER TWO POPULATIONS. IT IS UNDERSTOOD THAT THESE NOTIONS ARE RELATIVE, AS ARE THOSE OF EXOGAMY AND ENDOGAMY. TWO GROUPS THAT WAGE WAR PERIODICALLY, BOTH PRACTICING CANNIBALISM WITH THEIR PRISONERS ARE EXOCANNIBALS, BUT CONSIDERED IN THE LIGHT OF THEIR COMMUNAL HISTORY, DO THEY NOT FORM A

SINGLE, ENDOCANNIBAL GROUP? THE TUPI SEEM TO BE CONSCIOUS OF THIS: THE VALOROUS WARRIOR, ON THE POINT OF BEING EATEN, NEVER FAILS TO REMIND HIS TORTURERS OF HOW MANY OF THEM HE HAD EATEN IN THE PAST, AND THAT THOSE WHO WERE PREPARING TO DINE AT HIS EXPENSE WERE GOING TO RECUPERATE THEIR CANNIBALIZED DEAD BY INGESTING HIM. VENGEANCE, WHICH THE TUPI SAID EXPLICITLY INCITED THEM TO EAT THEIR ENEMIES, WAS ALSO A RECUPERATION.

IT IS ALSO NECESSARY TO TAKE INTO ACCOUNT THE MANNER IN WHICH THE ONE WHO IS EATEN DIED: FROM A NATURAL OR A VIOLENT DEATH, OR FROM THE HAND OF THOSE WHO HE IS GOING TO NOURISH. THE ENDOCANNIBALS, EVIDENTLY, DO NOT KILL TO EAT, AND EVEN, SINCE ONE ONLY KILLS ONE'S ENEMIES, DO NOT EAT THOSE THEY HAVE KILLED; THEY EAT THEIR "DEAR DEPARTED." INVERSELY, TUPI AND IROQUOIS EXPLAIN THAT IT IS NOT NECESSARY TO EAT THE LIVING, OR THE PEOPLE WITH WHOM ONE LIVES—THIS IS "SAVAGE" CANNIBALISM—BUT IT IS FIRST NECESSARY TO KILL (ENEMIES, CONSEQUENTLY) AND THAT ONE CAN EAT THOSE THAT ONE HAS KILLED—THIS IS POLICED CANNIBALISM. AT THE SAME TIME, THIS DOES NOT MEAN THAT THE IROQUOIS MADE WAR SIMPLY TO KILL AND EAT: THEY FOUGHT TO TAKE PRISONERS, AND THEY TOOK PRISONERS WITH THE PURPOSE OF ADOPTING A GOOD NUMBER; IN FACT, IROQUOIS OF PURE STRAIN WERE QUITE RARE. THE DEMOGRAPH- IC AND THUS POLITICAL IMPORTANCE OF THE IROQUOIS FEDERATION CAME FROM THE SYSTE- MATIC USAGE OF THIS METHOD; ON THE WHOLE IT WAS THE RESIDUALS WHO WERE EATEN, THOSE THAT WEREN'T WANTED. AS FOR THE TUPI, THEY KILLED AND ATE ALL THEIR PRISONERS, BUT AFTER SO LONG A DELAY THAT ONE COULD NO LONGER CONSIDER THEM, AT THE MOMENT OF THEIR EXECUTION, AS SIMPLY CAPTURED ENEMY; THEY HAD BEEN INTEGRATED, EFFECTIVELY, IF TEM- PORARILY, INTO THE GROUP, THEY WERE NO LONGER ANYONE IN PARTICULAR; ONE WOULD HAVE LIKED, WRITES H. CLASTRES, "THEM TO HAVE BEEN MUCH BETTER DETERMINED." MOREOVER, THE MURDERER WAS THE ONLY ONE NOT TO PARTICI- PATE IN THE DINNER. IT WOULD THUS BE SIMPLISTIC TO SAY THAT ONE KILLS TO EAT.

THE PASSAGE FROM SAVAGE AND MYTHIC CANNI- BALISM TO SOCIALIZED CANNIBALISM INCITED THE INVENTION OF CULINARY PREPARATION AND TABLE MANNERS. THE FIRST IS THE SOLITARY EATING OF A LIVING BEING THAT ONE EATS RAW; CANNIBAL PEOPLES HAVE BEEN DISCUSSED, BUT ONE SAYS NOTHING ABOUT THE EVENTUAL DIVISION BETWEEN COMMENSALS. ON THE CONTRARY, THE SECOND, IS REGULATED CONSUMPTION—OFTEN TAKING PLACE IN A VERY ELABORATE RITUAL—OF A COOKED CADAVER OF WHICH CERTAIN ORGANS COULD BE RESERVED OR FORBIDDEN TO CERTAIN CATE- GORIES OF PERSONS. THE CONSUMPTION GENER- ALLY IS TOTAL, ONLY THE BONES BEING THROWN AWAY; THE CANNIBAL IS ALMOST ALWAYS A CARNIVORE. STILL, SOME, IN THE OPPOSITION BETWEEN FLESH AND BONES, PRIZE THE LATTER. THE YANOMAMI, LET THE FLESH OF THE CADAVER DECAY, THEN CLEAN AND PULVERISE THE BONES WHICH THEY EAT MIXED WITH A BANANA PURÉE. THE CUISINE, PROPERLY SPEAKING, IS NOT THE SAME ALL OVER, AND WITHOUT A DOUBT THE SYSTEM OF CATEGORIES ELABORATED BY CLAUDE LÉVI- STRAUSS WOULD BE APPLICABLE HERE TOO. WITH REGARD TO THIS, THE TORTURES ENDURED BY THE VICTIMS BEFORE THEIR EXECUTION SHOULD NOT BE NEGLECTED: AFTER THEIR EXPEDITIONS, ON THE WAY BACK, THE IROQUOIS INFLICTED ATROCIOUS TREATMENT ON THEIR PRISONERS; PERHAPS ONE MUST SEE IN THESE TORTURES A SORT OF CUISINE, PRACTICED, ONE COULD SAY, IN ANTICIPATION.

FINALLY, AND EVIDENTLY, RELIGION, THE CONCEP- TION OF THE WORLD AND MAN, SHOULD BE TAKEN INTO CONSIDERATION. THE EXAMPLE OF THE FATALEKA, THAT THE ANALYSIS OF R. GUIDIERI MAKES, IS PARTICULARLY REVEALING FROM THIS POINT OF VIEW. IN EVERY CASE, PEOPLE AND THINGS MUST BE PLACED IN A CORRECTLY ORDERED WORLD: PARENTS, ALLIED AND FOREIGN, GODS, MEN AND ANIMALS, DEAD AND LIVING. CANNIBALISM CANNOT BE ISOLATED FROM "THE GROUP OF REPRESENTATIONS THAT SOCIETY MAKES FOR ITSELF AND FOR OTHERS," (M. DETAINNE). IT IS A CULTURAL PHENOMENON.

THAT IS WHY, FOR HONORABLE CANNIBALISM, THOSE WHO PRACTICE IT OPPOSE A CANNIBALISM THAT IS DISHONORABLE, SO MUCH SO THAT, ONCE THE MISUNDERSTANDINGS ARE DISSIPATED, CANNIBALS AND NON-CANNIBALS JOIN IN CON- DEMNING IT IN THE NAME OF THE SAME PRINCIPALS OR ORDER AND OF THE PRECISE DELIMITATION BETWEEN NATURE AND CULTURE.

JEAN POUILLON

APPENDIX

OFFICE OF THE SECRETARY OF
PROPHET ATCHO ALBERT'S ASSOCIATION
BREGBO P.O. 25, BINGERVILLE
REPUBLIC OF THE IVORY COAST

AUGUST 22, 1954

DIABOLICAL CONFESSION

NAME: LOGAIDJUI
SEX: FEMALE
VILLAGE: ABIGJAN-ADJAMÉ
RACE: EBRIÉ
RELIGION: HARRIS

"LET THE AUDIENCE KNOW THAT THIS PASSAGE IS NOT COMMON; IT IS EXCLUSIVELY A DIABOLICAL CASE."

I OPENLY DECLARE THAT I AM A DEVIL.

BY WAY OF MY DIABOLICAL ACTIVITY I KILLED MY OWN MOTHER, MY OLDER BROTHER N'GBADJUI, MY BROTHER JEAN NANTCHIO, MY SISTER AKRAI WHO HAD JUST GIVEN BIRTH, AND MY SON AKÈ GUIANI.

THAT IS, 5 PERSONS KILLED.

HERE ARE MY ASSOCIATES' NAMES:
1. AHIMAN LOBA
2. MOMO GBÉKRAI
3. NANGUY TOHI
4. THREE DIOULAS WITHOUT NAMES
5. BEUGRÉ-BRI
6. KOFFI AKPA
7. ÝESSI MOBIO

THAT IS, 9 PERSONS ASSOCIATED.

THE PERSONS KILLED BY MY ASSOCIATES:

AHIMAN LOBA: KILLED ATOBIO-MOBIO WHO WAS PREGNANT, ALOKÈ DJÉBA .... (2)
MOMO N'BÉGZAI: KILLED ANNOH AND ANOTHER WHOSE NAME I DO NOT KNOW .... (2)
NANGUY TOHI: KILLED AGOUSSI-BRI AND HER CHILD YUÉMIN .... (2)
THE DIOULAS KILLED 6 PERSONS WHOSE NAMES I DO NOT KNOW .... (2)
BUEGRÉ-BRI: KILLED AGOUATCHA GOUA AND AKOUATCHA YOUA .... (2)
KOFFI KPA: KILLED N'MLOUYA AND A NEW-BORN CHILD WITHOUT NAME .... (2)
ÝESSI MOBIO BOTTY: KILLED TWO OF AMIAN-MIN'S CHILDREN: BEUGRÉ, THE OTHER'S NAME I DO NOT KNOW .... (2)

THAT IS, 18 PERSONS KILLED BY MY ASSOCIATES

SUMMARY:
THEREFORE I KILLED .... 5 PERSONS
MY ASSOCIATES KILLED .... 18 PERSONS
WHICH MEANS ALTOGETHER .... 23 PERSONS
                                                      KILLED

DAMAGES AND MISDEEDS

I DRINK HUMAN BLOOD AND I EAT HUMAN FLESH. I, LOGAIDJUI, WAS TEMPTED BY THE DEVILS AND I ENDED UP EATING THEIR MEAT. FROM THAT VERY DAY, I HAVE STAYED WITH THEM IN ORDER TO DO EVERYTHING AND EAT WITH THEM.

THERE ARE 10 OF US DEVILS ASSOCIATED IN ORDER TO EAT: 7 EBRIÉS AND 3 DIOULAS. EACH OF US MUST GIVE TWO PERSONS ACCORDING TO OUR AGREEMENT.

MY CHILD DJANNÉ AND DJOMAN-BIÉ WERE GIVEN UP TO THE DEVILS BY ME. I CHOSE DJOMAN-BIÉ TO BE KILLED FIRST, AND THEN MY CHILD DJANNÉ.

I CONVERTED MYSELF INTO A MAN TO SLEEP WITH DJAKO-BIÉ, THAT IS WHY SHE CANNOT HAVE CHILDREN ANY MORE.

I SOLD DJOKÉ-BRI'S PLANTATION. SHORTLY THEREAFTER I GAVE UP THIS PLANTATION.

ONCE I WANTED TO GO AND TAKE DJOMAN-BIÉ BY FORCE, TO GIVE HER TO THE DEVILS. I FOUND TWO PRIESTS IN DJOKÉ-BRI'S YARD. THESE TWO PRIESTS TURNED ME AWAY WITHOUT SAYING ANYTHING TO ME. FROM THAT MOMENT, MY ILLNESS HAS GROWN STRONGER.

I GAVE SOME DISEASES TO ALMOST EVERYBODY IN THIS COURT, EXCEPT DIEKÈ ANDRÉ, YÉZOU DJAKO, AND MY BROTHER DJOMAN.

ONCE, I TRIED TO GO AS A DEVIL TO HARM MY HUSBAND, BUT GOD DID NOT GIVE ME A WAY. I DID SO BECAUSE ONCE HE CHASED AFTER A WOMAN, OF WHICH I AM NOT PLEASED. THIS IS WHY I AM ALWAYS ILL WHEN I STAY AT HIS HOUSE, WHEREAS ELSEWHERE I AM ALWAYS WELL.

ON THE OTHER HAND I DO NOT LIKE AHIBAKÈ AHOBRI AT ALL AND I ALWAYS TAKE HER BLOOD. MY DEVIL DISLIKES ONLY THIS GIRL.

THE HARRIS APOSTLES UPSET ME. THEY DECLARED THAT WE WHO HAD NOT CONFESSED IN THEIR PRESENCE BEFORE GOING TO BRÈGBO WOULD NEVER RECOVER, AND WOULD RETURN FROM BRÈGBO SUFFERING FROM THE SAME ILLNESSES. I AM VERY UPSET. I DECIDED TO MAKE A DEVIL OF MYSELF SO THAT I WOULD BE REPRIMANDED BY THEM IN ORDER TO FIND A WAY TO DIE IN THIS RELIGION.

AT A TIME I WANTED PEOPLE IN MY VILLAGE TO COME TO TAKE MR. ATCHO ALBERT'S WATER OF BLESSING. NOW I AM NOT PLEASED WITH THIS WATER BECAUSE IT TAKES AWAY FROM US THE WAY OF EATING AND DOING WHAT WE WANT.

I AM REALLY A DEVIL AND I SEE EVERYTHING THAT THE DEVILS OF MY VILLAGE DO, AND ELSEWHERE TOO.

MR. ATCHO ALBERT, I BESEECH YOU, PRAY FOR MY SAKE SO THAT I FINALLY RECOVER AND—WHAT I FORGOT TO SAY TOO—ASK GOD TO FORGIVE ME. PRAY FOR MY SAKE, SO THAT I CAN FORGET EVERYTHING THAT NOW HAPPENS THROUGH THE DEVILS.

I DO NOT WANT TO SEE THEM ANY LONGER. I ASK EVERYBODY IN MY VILLAGE.

(SIGNED): LOGAIDJUI
TRANSLATED BY P. ZOBERMAN

THE SONNET OF THE HOLE IN THE ASS

PAUL
VERLAINE

DARK AND PUCKERED LIKE A VIOLET ROSE
IT PULSES, HUMBLY HIDDEN AMIDST THE MOSS,
STILL DAMP FROM LOVE THAT TRICKLES SOFT
ALONG WHITE THIGHS RIGHT TO ITS LIP.

FECIT

LITTLE DROPS LIKE TEARS OF MILK
HAVE WEPT, BENEATH THE ZEPHYR BLOWING CRUEL,
UPON THE PEBBLES OF AUBURN MARL,
OBEYING THE SLOPE AND HEEDING ITS CALL.

ARTHUR
RIMBAUD

OFTEN MY MOUTH IS PRESSED AGAINST ITS HOLE.

OFTEN MY SOUL WILL YEARN FOR A FUCK WITH
    FLESH,
AND IT TAKES IT FOR ITS DANKEST DRIPSTONE, ITS
    NEST
OF THROBBING SIGHS.

INVENIT

IT'S THE OPEN OLIVE IN ECSTASY, THE BLOWN FLUTE
    IN THE AIR;
IT'S THE CELESTIAL TUBE DOWN WHICH ALL
    FONDANTS FREELY FLOW;
FEMALE CANAAN FIRMLY MOIST AND FILLED WITH
    PROMISE DEEP.

PAUL VERLAINE AND ARTHUR RIMBAUD
TRANSLATED BY DANIEL SLOATE

COPROPHAGY AND URINOLOGY

I WISH TO INTRODUCE THIS MOST EXTREME FETISHISM BY REMINDING THE SUPERIOR OF THE OCCASION WHEN SHE OR HE MAY HAVE NOTICED THEIR SLAVE PICKING UP CRUMBS THEY HAVE DROPPED ON THE FLOOR AND EATING THEM. THE SAME PRINCIPLE IS AT WORK HERE—THE SUBMISSIVE SOUL THAT CLINGS TO EVERYTHING, EVEN THE LEAVINGS OF HIS BELOVED SUPERIOR.

AFTER A SLAVE HAS FANTASIZED HIMSELF AS AN ANIMAL, A PET, THEN A WORM, SUB-HUMAN, AND MOVES ON TO ACTING LIKE FURNITURE AND BEING INVISIBLE, HIS PRIDE DRIVES HIM ON TO MORE ELABORATE INDENTIFICATIONS WITH LOWLINESS AND SELF-EFFACEMENT. HIS INVERTED LOGIC SEEKS TO MAKE HIM SUBMISSIVE BEYOND ALL OTHERS, A SLAVE AMONG SLAVES, AND WORTHLESSNESS PERSONIFIED. HE ATTAINS THIS END, AND BECOMES UTTERLY DISGUSTING, WHEN HE PROFESSES HIS AMBITION AND ATTRACTION TO BE AS ONE WITH THE FECES AND URINE OF THE SUPERIOR.

THESE SUBSTANCES, UNEQUIVOCALLY REGARDED AS HORRID, ARE REVERED AND SOUGHT AFTER BY THE MASOCHIST AS THE SOURCE OF HIS TRUE IDENTITY. HIS CONTACT WITH THEM CONFIRMS HIS TRUE LOWNESS OF BEING. IT IS VERY PECULIAR TO THE SUPERIOR TO REALIZE THE SLAVE WORSHIPS HIS OR HER WASTE MORE THAN ANY GOOD QUALITY. THE SUPERIOR CAN TAKE NO PRIDE IN SUCH SLAVES, UNLESS HE OR SHE REGARDS THEIR PRODUCTS WITH THE SAME GLAMORIZED EYES AS THE MASOCHIST. THUS DOES THEIR WASTE BECOME THE LOWLY'S ONE NOURISHMENT; THEIR FILTH CLEANSES THE SLAVE; THEIR FOULNESS SEEMS A RARE PERFUME. IN THIS POOR WAY, AS WELL, DOES THE SLAVE INGEST, AND SO POSESS, HIS BELOVED SUPERIOR.

THUS DOES THE MASOCHIST SEEK OUT HIS VILENESS THROUGH HIS CONCENTRATION ON WHAT IS COMMONLY REGARDED AS THE MOST VILE SUBSTANCE ON EARTH. BUT FECES AND URINE ARE THE RAW MATERIAL FOR ALL THAT EXISTS AND GROWS IN THIS WORLD—THEY ARE NO MORE WONDERFUL THAN THEY ARE DISGUSTING—THE SLAVE DEVOUTLY PREPARES A COCOON OF PLASTIC SACKS AND BOXES TO CARRY HIS PRECIOUS SACRAMENT HOME WITH HIM.

THE SLAVE DEIFIES THESE SUBSTANCES, GIVING THEM SUCH NAMES AS "GOLDEN ELIXIR," "SHOWER OF SWEETNESS," AND SUCH LIKE. HE MAY DEVOUR

THEM OR MERELY HOLD THEM IN HIS MOUTH FOR A SPASMODIC INSTANT BEFORE SPITTING THEM OUT. THIS BEHAVIOR CREATES SUCH REVULSIVE CONTEMPT IN THE SUPERIOR FOR THE WEAK ADORATION OF THE SLAVE THAT THE SUBMISSIVE MUST BE PREPARED TO DO ABSOLUTELY ANYTHING THE SUPERIOR MAY THEREAFTER COMMAND HIM TO DO. BUT THE SUPERIOR MAY CERTAINLY BE AT A LOSS, AS NO DEGREDATION CAN SURPASS THIS ONE. IT IS ADVISED TO AVOID INDULGING THE SLAVE SO THAT HE REMAINS IN A STATE OF CONSTANT LONGING . . .

THE TOILET-SLAVE ENJOYS BEING REFERRED TO AS JUST THAT PIECE OF BATHROOM FURNITURE, AND MAY BE LEFT HAPPILY CHAINED TO IT FOR HOURS, READY AND WILLING AT ALL TIMES TO RECEIVE A DOSE OF HIS BELOVED COMMUNION.

ONE MAY MAKE A MINOR DISTINCTION IN THE CASE OF THE AFFICIONADO OF "GOLDEN SHOWERS." THERE IS A SENSUOUS APPEAL IN THE COURSING OF THE HOT LIQUID OVER THE BODY—AS WELL, SUCH A SLAVE IS NOT SO FILTH-OBSESSED BECAUSE (1) URINE IS STERILE AND (2) THE FLOW MAKES IT SEEM FRESH AND LIVE, LIKE A FLOW OF BLOOD. BUT BOTH THESE SCATOLOGICAL FETISHES ARE MOST ILLUSTRATIVE IN THE FACT THAT ALL FETISHISM IS A FORM OF NECROPHILIA—A LOVE AND ATTRACTION TO WHAT IS DEAD.

FILTH DIALOGUE

TAKES PLACE IN THE BATHROOM. SLAVE IS CHAINED TO THE TOILET AND LIES ON THE FLOOR. MISTRESS IS PERCHED UPON THE SINK.

M: HOW MANY GALLONS CAN YOU DRINK?

S: AS MANY AS YOU WILL GIVE ME, MISTRESS.

M: YOU ARE A TOILET—YOU LOVE TO BE A TOILET.

S: YES, YES, ANYTHING YOU SAY.

M: IT'S TRUE. YOUR HIGHEST AMBITION IS TO BE INSTALLED IN THE LADIES' ROOM AT GRAND CENTRAL STATION.

S: WILL YOU PLEASE WATCH ME CLEAN OUT THE URINALS WITH MY TONGUE?

M: WOMEN DON'T USE URINALS, IDIOT.

S: I'M SORRY, MISTRESS. I'M JUST A TOILET.

M: YOU'RE THE TYPE WHO THINKS IT WOULD BE HEAVEN TO HAVE HUNDREDS OF STRANGE WOMEN SQUATTING OVER YOUR FACE, EVERY DAY, USING YOU AS THEIR SEWER. ADMIT IT, VILENESS.

S: IT'S TRUE. OH PLEASE, PLEASE, LET ME KISS YOUR BEAUTIFUL ASS, MY MISTRESS.

M: (KICKS HIM) DON'T SAY "MY" MISTRESS. I OWN YOU, THING. AS FOR KISSING EVEN THE BOTTOM OF MY SHOE, YOUR MOUTH IS TOO DIRTY. WHO KNOWS WHAT YOU'VE BEEN LICKING TODAY, THE GUTTERS YOU CRAWL ABOUT IN, SO SHAMELESSLY. I DON'T WANT TO CATCH YOUR DISEASES.

S: PLEASE MISTRESS, USE ME AS YOUR TOILET. PISS ON ME. I WANT TO EAT YOUR SHIT.

M: SILENCE! KEEP YOUR DEGRADED LUSTS TO YOURSELF. BESIDES, MY PRODUCTS ARE TOO GOOD FOR YOU. THE FOOD I EAT IS VERY EXPENSIVE.

S: I'LL PAY, I'LL PAY.

M: I KNOW YOU WILL. I OUGHT TO HAVE A LITTLE PORCELAIN BOWL FITTED OVER YOUR REVOLTING ORIFICE. I DON'T LIKE TO SIT DOWN ON MOVING OBJECTS. LET'S SEE HOW WIDE YOU CAN OPEN YOUR MOUTH. WIDER! (INSERTS HER HEEL.) LICK!

S: (SALIVATES ALL OVER THE SHOE.) PLEASE, MISTRESS, I WANT TO BE YOUR TOILET!

M: GREEDY LITTLE PIG! I TOLD YOU TO LICK MY SHOE, NOT EAT IT! (TAKES A LONG TIME WASHING OFF HER SHOE.) NOW, YOU WERE SAYING YOU WANTED TO SERVE AS MY TOILET, THAT THIS WAS YOUR TRUE PLACE IN LIFE. PERHAPS THAT IS ALL YOU'RE FIT FOR. BUT YOU HAVE TO LEARN TO MOVE UP IN THE WORLD, TO EARN YOUR PRIVILEGES. FIRST YOU MUST SHOW ME HOW USEFUL YOUR MOUTH CAN BE. CLEAN THE FLOOR! (HOLDS HIS HEAD DOWN WITH HER FOOT.)

S: MISTRESS, PLEASE, IT'S HARD TO LICK THE FLOOR WHEN YOU'RE STEPPING ... OOWW ... (TRIES TO PEER UP HER SKIRT.)

M: WHAT'S THIS? COMPLAINING? AND ON TOP OF IT ALL! OH! LOOKING AT MY LEGS! I DON'T LET MY SERVANTS LOOK AT ME WHILE THEY'RE WORKING!

S: I'M SORRY, GODDESS. I COULDN'T HELP MYSELF. PLEASE FORGIVE ME. (SPRAWLS OUT ABJECTLY ON THE BATHROOM TILES.)

M: GET BACK ON YOUR KNEES, SPINELESS! YOU NEED SOME DISCIPLINE!

S: OH, NO! (WATCHES IN HORROR AS THE MISTRESS FILLS UP AN ENEMA BAG WITH STEAMING HOT WATER.) PLEASE, PLEASE, DON'T I'LL DO ANYTHING!

M: YOU'LL DO AS I SAY AND NOTHING ELSE. STOP PAWING ME!

THE MISTRESS REQUIRES THE SLAVE TO PRESENT HIS BUTTOCKS TO THE AIR AND KEEP HIS HEAD ON THE GROUND AS SHE ADMINISTERS THE DOUCHE.

M: NOW, THAT OUGHT TO CLEAN UP YOUR ACT. LET'S HAVE A LITTLE ENTERTAINMENT AROUND THIS PLACE. (PUTS ON A DISCO RECORD AND REQUIRES THE SLAVE TO DANCE FOR HER. IF HE IS A POOR DANCER, HE OUGHT TO BE EGGED ON TO IMPROVE WITH A FEW LICKS OF THE WHIP.)

S: MISTRESS, MISTRESS, I BEG OF YOU ...

M: YOU LET ONE DROP FALL ON MY CARPET OUT OF YOUR SORRY LITTLE ASS, AND YOU'LL WISH YOU HAD NEVER BEEN BORN THE SLAVE YOU ARE!

THE MISTRESS MAY, IF SHE THINKS THE SLAVE CAN TOLERATE IT, REQUIRE THAT HE NOW RUN A FEW LAPS AROUND THE HOUSE, PREFERABLY HOPPING ON ONE FOOT.

M: HUP, TWO, HUP, TWO. EXERCISE IS GOOD FOR YOU! (SLAVE IS BY NOW GRIMACING IN PAIN WHICH DELIGHTS THE MISTRESS IMMEASURABLY.)

S: MISTRESS, I NOW THINK I AM VERY CLEANED OUT. PLEASE MISTRESS ...

M: SILENCE, TOILET-BOY. KNEEL OVER THERE AND WAIT FOR ME TO NOTICE YOU. (MISTRESS MAY THEN AMUSE THE SLAVE BY TELLING A STORY OF HOW SEVERELY SHE PUNISHED A SLAVE FOR SOILING HIMSELF.) ... AND I THOUGHT THAT WOULD TEACH HIM TO LEARN TO HAVE MORE SELF-CONTROL.

S: OH DARLING DARLING MISTRESS, PLEASE MAY I GO TO THE BATHROOM?

M: NO.

S: PLEASE, PLEASE MAY I GO. (MISTRESS DOES NOT BOTHER TO ANSWER.) PLEASE I HAVE TO ...

M: YOU DIDN'T ASK ME "PLEASE, MISTRESS!!!" (WHIPS HIM A FEW TIMES.)

S: (ON HIS KNEES) PLEASE, DARLING MISTRESS.

M: OKAY, YOU CAN GO. (SLAVE STARTS TO RUN ... MISTRESS SCREAMS ...) COME BACK HERE, KNEEL DOWN.

S: YES, MISTRESS?

M: YOU DIDN'T SAY THANK YOU.

(ETC. FINALLY SLAVE IS PERMITTED TO RELIEVE HIMSELF IN THE BATHROOM.) WHEN HE COMES OUT 15 MINUTES LATER, HE LOOKS VERY ASHAMED.)

M: THAT SHOULD CLEAN UP YOUR ACT, YOU DEGRADED LITTLE FART. I'LL TEACH YOU TO LOOK AT MY LEGS WITHOUT MY PERMISSION.

S: YES, MISTRESS. (LONG PAUSE.) MISTRESS?

M: ASK MY PERMISSION TO SPEAK!

S: MISTRESS, MAY I SPEAK?

M: NO. (LONG PAUSE.)

S: MISTRESS, MAY I SPEAK?

M: WHAT IS IT?

S: WON'T YOU PLEASE USE ME AS A TOILET, MISTRESS?

M: NO, I DON'T HAVE TO GO.

S: I'LL MAKE YOU A DRINK, MISTRESS?

M: VERY WELL.

SLAVE DONS AN APRON AND HURRIES TO THE BAR. THE MISTRESS RECEIVES THE COCKTAIL. THE SLAVE STARES AT THE LIQUID COURSING OVER HER LIPS. THE MISTRESS PUTS THE BOY IN A STOCKS SO HE WON'T BE BOTHERING HER.

M: NOW, I WANT YOU TO AMUSE ME BY SINGING THIS LITTLE SONG. YOU MUST SING, "I ADORE BEING YOUR TOILET," TO THE TUNE OF "I ADORE BEING A GIRL." KEEP SINGING! (SLAVE SINGS THIS ONE LINE, TUNELESSLY OF COURSE, OVER AND OVER.)

M: (LAUGHING RESTRAINEDLY) "WHAT A STUPID LITTLE BOY! YOU ARE SO TORMENTABLE.

S: I ADORE BEING YOUR TOILET, I ADORE BEING YOUR TOILET, I ADORE BEING YOUR TOILET, I ADORE BEING YOUR TOILET, I ADORE ...

MISTRESS REMOVES SLAVE FROM STOCKS AND OFFERS HIM A DRINK. IT IS HER SPECIAL SUBSTANCE IN A GLASS, WHICH HE IS REQUIRED TO DOWN. SLAVE SIPS CAREFULLY.

M: WHAT IF I HAD A TUB FILLED TO THE BRIM WITH MY SPECIAL LIQUID, WHAT IF I SHOVED YOUR HEAD RIGHT UNDER UNTIL YOU SOAKED IT ALL UP, YOU'D BE SATURATED WITH MY SUBSTANCE! JUST LIKE A NASTY LITTLE SPONGE!

S: OH, YET MISTRESS, O THANK YOU SO MUCH, DIVINE QUEEN, O THANK YOU ...

T.C. SELLERS

VIII

A LITTLE SHIT, A LITTLE CUM
WILL NEVER, NO BUT NEVER
AFFRIGHT MY NOSE, MOUTH OR BUM
WHEN CROTCHERIES ARE NIGH.

YES, THE SMELL IS GAY TO ME
FROM THE HOLE IN MY LOVER'S ASS
COOL AND SOUR AS AN OLD CHERRY
ROTTING GAYLY IN THE RAIN.

AND MY RESTLESS TONGUE, SO MAD,
FLICKS ALONG HIS SOFT DAMP HAIRS
STIFF AND QUICK AND OH, SO BAD
AS IT LICKS ITS FAVORITE FOOD.

IT TICKLES ITS WAY FROM THE HOLE
TO BALLS AND OH, SO SLOW
ALONG THE THROBBING JOY-POLE

THEN DROOLS UPON THE KNOB.

AND DEEP IT SUCKS, DYING FOR
THE SWEETS IT KNOWS ARE THERE;
LIVE, HOT CREAM FROM THE BORE
PUMPED STRAIGHT FROM THE WELL OF LOVE.

ONCE ALL DUE LOVING CARE
IS ROUNDLY PAID TO THE JUICY SLIT,
BACK SLIPS MY TONGUE TO MY MOUTH WHERE
HIS PULSING PRICK PLUNGES

AND THERE SPURTS OUT ITS CUM;
AND I POOR SLAVE, A-WALLOW IN HIS BLESSING,
I SWALLOW ALL OF IT, THEN ON MY KNEES
WAIT HUMBLY FOR HIS SECOND COMING.

PAUL VERLAINE
TRANSLATED BY DANIEL SLOATE

SEX OF THE GAZE

THE MUTE NEGRESS

"... I WAS SEVEN OR EIGHT YEARS OLD AND I WAS WATCHING A HIVE OF BEES STUCK TO A BRANCH. THE DESIRE TO GRAB IT AND DISLODGE IT TINGLED THROUGH MY FINGERS. I WAS GOING TO GET A STICK—AT THE RISK NO DOUBT OF CROAKING FROM THE SWELLING STINGS—WHEN I SAW LITTLE SOPHIE, MY NEIGHBOR. A LITTLE BLOND GIRL FROM TOWN WHO WAS AROUND ONE MONTH A YEAR.

"SHE WAS WALKING SLOWLY IN MY DIRECTION, AS THOUGH FASCINATED BY SOMETHING WHICH MUST HAVE BEEN AT HER FEET THAT I COULD NOT SEE. I IMMEDIATELY FORGOT THE BEEHIVE AND LAY DOWN IN THE TALL GRASS. SHE WAS WALKING SO SLOWLY THAT I HAD NO HOPE OF HER BEING ABLE TO REACH ME. I WAS SWIMMING, I WANTED TO BITE, UNKNOWN INSTINCTS RIPPED THROUGH MY NECK. SOPHIE WAS ABOUT TWELVE, PERHAPS LESS, FOR HER LOVELY FLESHINESS NO DOUBT AGED HER. FINALLY SHE WAS WITHIN REACH. I STILL DIDN'T SEE WHAT WAS FASCINATING HER, BUT HER FASCINATION IN-TRIGUED ME ALL THE MORE. SHE STOPPED, AND AT THE SAME MOMENT, RAISED HER SKIRT OVER HER NAKED STOMACH. WELL, I HAD ALREADY SEEN MY SISTER CARESS HERSELF, AND I HAD FELT NO REAL PLEASURE FROM IT EXCEPT FOR THE DAY I CAUGHT HER DOING IT IN A MIRROR. A FALSE MUSLIM PROPHET USED TO PROCLAIM THAT MIRRORS (LIKE PATERNITY) WERE ABOMINATIONS, FOR THEY CONFIRM AND MULTIPLY THE EARTH WHICH WE INHABIT, GROTESQUE ERROR, UNAUTHORIZED PARODY.

"SOPHIE STILL KEPT HER SKIRT RAISED, EXAMINING HERSELF WITH SUCH GREAT ATTENTION THAT I WAS AFRAID OF SEEING SOMETHING SURGE FORTH FROM BETWEEN HER THIGHS. APPLYING MYSELF TO DETECTING ITS APPEARANCE, I PERCEIVED THE DOWN OF HER SEX. I DON'T KNOW WHY, BUT IT MADE ME LAUGH. I IMMEDIATELY FEARED THAT I HAD REVEALED MY PRESENCE, BUT I WAS ASTONISHED TO NOTE THAT SOPHIE HAD NOT HEARD ME. I RAISED MYSELF ON MY ELBOWS BUT COULD SEE NOTHING AT HER FEET. AND TIRED OF WAITING, I WAS ABOUT TO GET UP, TO SCARE HER AT LEAST, WHEN I HEARD A NOISE BEHIND ME. I THOUGHT THE BEEHIVE HAD JUST FALLEN, BUT FOLLOWING SOPHIE'S GAZE NOW FIXED ON A POINT ABOVE MY HEAD, I SAW A MAN IN A TREE. I LOOKED AT SOPHIE AGAIN: SHE WAS SMILING. AND WHILE SHE SMILED, SHE RAISED HER DRESS SO HIGH THAT SHE UNVEILED HER PALE LITTLE BREASTS. 'ARE YOU COMING?' SAID A VOICE, BUT SHE SHOOK HER HEAD.

"I HADN'T RECOGNIZED THE VOICE, AND SOPHIE'S REFUSAL SEEMED TO ME TO INDICATE THAT SHE HERSELF HADN'T RECOGNIZED IT. THE SCENE, HENCEFORTH INDEED QUITE BANAL, THREATENED TO PROLONG ITSELF. WHEN SOPHIE ADVANCED DECISIVELY ALMOST TO THE POINT OF BRUSHING ME, FLAT DOWN IN THE GRASS, I NONETHELESS HAZARDED A GLANCE; AND TO MY GOOD FORTUNE, FOR A HAND CAME DOWN FROM THE TREE, BRUSHED HER NECK, AND IMPRISONED ONE OF HER BREASTS. I COULD MYSELF HAVE RAISED MY ARM AND SEIZED THE CHUBBY RUMP IF MY ATTENTION HADN'T BEEN DRAWN TO THE ARRIVAL OF A THIRD CHARACTER. IT WAS A TALL MAN WITH A ROUGH APPEARANCE, NOT A PEASANT, BUT A POACHER PERHAPS, ANYWAY I WAS TOO YOUNG TO PREOCCUPY MYSELF WITH PEOPLE'S PROFESSIONS, ONLY THEIR ACTIONS MATTERED TO ME (JUST AS TODAY, AND I CAN WELL SAY THAT IN THAT SENSE I HAVEN'T AGED). HE WAS APPROACHING WITH LONG STRIDES, WITHOUT BOTHERING ABOUT THE NOISE HE WAS MAKING, AS IF HE HADN'T SEEN THE LITTLE GIRL; BUT I WAS WRONG ABOUT THAT, BECAUSE, HAVING TURNED HALFWAY AROUND, SHE SAW HIM AND MURMURRED SOMETHING I DIDN'T UNDERSTAND, WHILE A SECOND HAND GRABBED HER OTHER BREAST. THIS HUMAN PLANT WAS RATHER AMUSING. THE MAN STOPPED BEHIND SOPHIE. IMMEDIATELY SHE LET GO OF HER DRESS, AND, WITH GREAT DEXTERITY, UNBUTTONED THE MAN WHOSE PENIS POPPED OUT. THEN SHE RAISED HER DRESS AGAIN AND, LEANING FORWARD, WHICH OBLIGED THE HANDS AND THE ARMS FROM THE TREE TO COME DOWN A LITTLE FURTHER, SHE PRESENTED HER BEHIND TO THE KNOTTY COCK— FOR, IN TRUTH, THE SCENE DIDN'T LOSE A BIT OF ITS RURAL CHARACTER, AND ONE COULD HAVE IMAGINED (AS I DID, PERHAPS) THAT THE GROUP WAS ONLY WAITING TO BE SCULPTED.

"SHE DIDN'T SCREAM WHEN THE MAN PENETRATED HER, AND ALTHOUGH I HAD ONCE CAUGHT MY SISTER UNDER THE BELLY OF A NAKED MAN, I CAN NONETHELESS SAY THAT SOPHIE IS THE FIRST THAT I REALLY SAW MAKE LOVE. THE MAN SOON WITHDREW FROM THE LITTLE GIRL AND THE HANDS FROM THE TREE DISAPPEARED. SOPHIE LET HERSELF FALL ON THE GROUND WHILE THE RED-HAIRED MAN (HAVE I MENTIONED THAT? IT PLEASES ME THAT HE WAS A REDHEAD) WAS ALREADY MOVING AWAY. THEN SHE SPOTTED ME. 'WERE YOU THERE?' SHE ASKED. I DIDN'T ANSWER, I THREW MYSELF ON HER NAKED BREASTS, BIT THEM, WHICH MADE HER SCREAM. SHE DIDN'T PUSH ME AWAY, THOUGH, ON THE CONTRARY SHE VERY MUCH WANTED TO PULL ME ONTO HER STOMACH. BUT I

WAS SUSPICIOUS, IT SEEMED TO ME THAT I WOULD HAVE TO WAIT, OR ELSE DO SOMETHING OTHER THAN WHAT SHE WAS HOPING FOR. AND INSTEAD OF RUBBING MY FACE AGAINST WHAT WAS IN SUM NOTHING BUT AN ALREADY RIPE FRUIT, I BRUSHED IT WITH MY FINGERS, THEN, TURNING HER OVER ON HER BELLY, REVEALED HER BUTTOCKS WHICH BOTHERED ME EVEN MORE. I MUST HAVE HURT HER, FOR SHE ARCHED HER BACK, SO I GOT UP WITH A LEAP; SHE DISGUSTED ME NOW.

"THE ADVENTURE COULD END HERE, THE REST IS PROBABLY MYTHICAL, BUT THE COLLECTOR SOMETIMES CAN NOT KEEP HIMSELF FROM DREAMING, FROM SLIPPING IN AMONG HIS RIGOR-OUS CLASSIFICATIONS SOME SUMPTUOUS APOCRY-PHAL PIECE. THUS IN THE EVENING, IN OUR LITTLE PROVINCE, THEY SET OFF FIRE WORKS. I GOT PERMISSION TO ATTEND, ACCOMPANIED BY MY GRANDMOTHER, A STUPID PERSON WHOM I COULD EASILY LOSE IN A FEW SECONDS. WHICH I DID, FOR I HAD A PLAN MORE INTERESTING THAN A FEW MISERABLE FIRE WORKS: HIDING MYSELF IN SOPHIE'S ROOM.

"I HAD HARDLY ANY DIFFICULTY GETTING IN. IT WAS ON THE GROUND FLOOR OF ONE OF THOSE HEAVY HOUSES LOVED BY THE MIDDLE CLASS. AS SOON AS I GOT INSIDE, I HID MYSELF BEHIND A WARDROBE PROVIDENTIALLY PLACED OBLIQUELY OPPOSITE THE LITTLE BED. THE WINDOW WAS ON MY RIGHT, AND THE DOOR FACING ME. AFTER AN HOUR IT SUDDENLY OPENED WITH GREAT COMMOTION AND CLOSED LIKEWISE. SOPHIE THREW HERSELF ON THE BED, IN TEARS—OR AT LEAST I TOOK THIS PERSON FOR SOPHIE, FOR QUITE FRANKLY I COULDN'T SEE ANYTHING, THE ROOM ONLY BARELY LIT BY A DISTANT STREET LAMP. THEN THE SOBS BECAME LESS FREQUENT AND A NIGHT LIGHT WAS LIT. I LEANED OUT AND SAW TWO LEGS RAISED, BUT THEY WERE MUCH LONGER THAN SOPHIE'S. I WAS ALREADY ASTONISHED THAT SHE HAD GROWN SO QUICKLY, PREFERRING, AS IS SUITABLE, THE MIRACULOUS TO THE LOGICAL, BUT INSTEAD OF TAKING ADVANTAGE OF THE SITUATION AND MY GOOD LUCK, I FEARED BEING DISCOVERED. THIS FEAR WAS CHANGED INTO TERROR WHEN THE WOMAN GOT UP AND CAME TO CLOSE THE SHUTTERS. THUS I WAS A PRISONER! NEXT SHE TURNED ON THE BRACKET LIGHTS AND BEGAN TO UNDRESS. AT THAT MOMENT I FIGURED OUT THAT SHE WAS THE CHAMBER MAID AND I FEARED HER NUDITY; IT WAS NOT SOPHIE'S NUDITY THAT I HAD DESIRED BUT SOME UNKNOWN ACT THAT I MIGHT HAVE SEEN WHICH WOULD HAVE SATISFIED ME.

HOWEVER, THE MAID HAD FROZEN, HER EAR ATTENTIVE AS THOUGH SHE WERE LISTENING OUT FOR A PREARRANGED SIGNAL. STRANGELY ENOUGH, I REGAINED HOPE JUST AS ABRUPTLY AS I HAD BECOME SO QUICKLY DISCOURAGED. THE WOMAN PUT HER HANDS BEHIND HER BACK AND HER DRESS FELL. IT WAS DAZZLING, THE REVELATION OF THE SUMPTUOUS AND VULGAR TRAPPINGS WITH WHICH WOMAN TITILLATES, MAGNIFICENT MARE! A SHORT BLACK-LACE SLIP, A BRA, AND AN ARACHNIDEAN GARTER BELT, AS WELL AS TINY RED PANTIES, WHICH MAGNIFIED, INSTEAD OF HIDING, A THICK TAWNY FLEECE, COMPOSED A MUCH MORE SATISFYING SPECTACLE THAN ALL THOSE I HAD DREAMED. SHE TURNED, AND, IN PROFILE, ONLY HER TAUT CHEST AND RUMP COULD BE SEEN, THE THIGHS AND HOLLOWED WAIST BEING ONLY SECONDARY SUPPORTS FOR THESE SUPERB INDECENCIES.

"THAT'S WHEN THEY ENTERED. THE RED-HEADED MAN, AND ANOTHER I RECOGNIZED AS SOPHIE'S FATHER. HE CAREFULLY CLOSED THE DOOR, PLACED HIS EAR AGAINST THE WOOD BEFORE TURNING THE KEY, WHILE THE CARROT-HAIRED MAN WAS ALREADY FEELING UP THE SERVANT, WHO BENT OVER AT THE WAIST, THUS OFFERING TO MY GAZE HER RIPE BUTTOCKS. A THOUSAND EYES WOULD NOT HAVE SUFFICED TO FOLLOW ALL THE DEVELOPMENTS OF THAT SITUATION; CARROT-TOP HAD ALREADY SLIPPED ONE HAND INSIDE THE PANTIES, WITH THE OTHER HAND HE WAS LIGHTLY SLAPPING HER ASS. THE FATHER IN A LOW VOICE WAS SAYING: 'MARQUISE, MARQUISE!' AND WAS TAKING HER BREASTS OUT OF THE STRAPLESS BRA, KISSING THEM WITH ARDOUR, AND THE MAID, MEANWHILE, PLAYED WITH THE FUR WHICH PROTRUDED FROM BEHIND THE RED CLOTH. THE MEN NOTICED THIS ACTIVITY, THE RED-HEAD PULLED THE PANTIES WHICH SNAPPED, BURST, BURSTING IT SEEMED TO ME ESPECIALLY FROM THE PRESSURE OF THAT PRODIGIOUS FLEECE. THE MEN JOSTLED EACH OTHER AND I FIGURED THAT EACH ONE WANTED TO BURY HIS FACE IN THAT MANE, SINCE I WAS MYSELF GRIPPED BY THE SAME DESIRE. THEY COMICALLY BUMPED THEIR HEADS TOGETHER AND THE SERVANT LAUGHED. BUT THEY WERE TOO BUSY TO NOTICE. I LOOKED AT THOSE LAUGHING EYES, CIRCLES DARKENING BENEATH THEM, THE WORD 'PLEASURE' WHICH I HAD ONLY RECENTLY LEARNED CAME TO ME, AND I FOUND IT TO HAVE A SINGULAR SAVOUR, I WATCHED THE TWO FREED LIPS BETWEEN TWO HEDGES OF LONG SHINY HAIRS. THE WOMAN LEANED OVER TO SEE, ALSO TO ENJOY HER OWN SPECTACLE, BUT THE BACKS OF THE MEN

PREVENTED THIS; CARROT-TOP, KNEELING, SHACKLED HER STOCKINGED THIGHS WITH HIS ARMS, THE OTHER SLOWLY MOVED HIS FINGERS IN THE MAUVE MOUTH. I SAW THE SAME WHITISH FOAM THAT I HAD CAUGHT SIGHT OF IN THE ORCHARD ON SOPHIE'S THIGHS. THE SAME? THAT IS INDEED WHAT I BELIEVED!

"THERE WAS A CRACKLING OF A BUZZER. CARROT-TOP JUMPED UP AS IF HE HAD BEEN STUNG TO THE QUICK, THE OTHER STARTED TO TREMBLE, BUT THE WOMAN REMAINED MARBLE. (IF I MAY PERMIT MYSELF TO ANTICIPATE, I WILL SAY THAT IT WAS A RED AND WHITE MARTHA, AND THAT IT WOULD INDEED BY PLEASANT TO FIND HER AGAIN— ALTHOUGH I KNOW, ALAS! HOW BADLY DOMESTICS AGE.) THE MEN TOOK OFF, AND I, WITHOUT THINKING ABOUT IT ANYMORE, SHOWED MYSELF. SHE MADE NOT THE SLIGHTEST GESTURE OF SURPRISE, LOOKING AT ME ON THE CONTRARY WITH CURIOSITY, THEN REALIZING THAT HER BELLY WAS BARE, SHE PUT HER HAND OVER IT. BUT IT WAS REALLY SO THAT SHE COULD CARESS HERSELF, AND I CLEARLY SAW TWO OF HER FINGERS GENTLY MOVE INSIDE HER.

"SHE CAUGHT MY GAZE, OFFERED ME HER OTHER HAND WHOSE ODOR ENCHANTED ME. I DIDN'T KNOW HOW TO EXPRESS IT TO HER, BUT I WOULD HAVE LIKED TO HAVE HER TAKE ME IN HER ARMS, BURY ME IN HER BED WITH HER, TO ROLL ON HER BREASTS, AND ESPECIALLY TO PLUNGE MY FACE IN HER FLEECE. I MADE A GESTURE WHICH SHE DID NOT UNDERSTAND, BECAUSE SHE PLACED HER FINGER TO HER LIPS AS THOUGH ORDERING ME TO BE QUIET. BUT I WASN'T TALKING. SUDDENLY, I THREW MYSELF AGAINST HER BELLY. SHE HELD MY HEAD, I CONFUSEDLY FELT THAT SHE WAS GIVING IN, THAT ALL RESISTANCE WAS CEASING IN HER. HER PERFUME WAS SO ARDENT, THE BUTTON OF FLESH SO HARD, THAT I WAS BITING SAVAGELY. I HEARD HER SIGHING, I THOUGHT SHE WAS ONCE AGAIN GOING TO CRY AND I DREW AWAY VERY QUICKLY, BUT SHE, IGNORANT OF MY IGNORANCE, ONCE AGAIN STUCK MY FACE AGAINST THE NEW MOUTH.

"AFTERWARD, SHE OPENED THE SHUTTERS WITH INFINITE PRECAUTIONS. SHE KISSED ME ON THE FOREHEAD WHILE I WAS CRAWLING OVER THE WINDOW LEDGE. I LIKE TO THINK THAT I ONLY RETURNED HOME THE NEXT DAY, AFTER HAVING WANDERED THROUGH THE COUNTRYSIDE, OR, MORE EXACTLY, PROWLED UNDER THE SERVANT'S SHUTTERS. ANYWAY, I DEMANDED THAT MY GRANDMOTHER WEAR LONG PANTIES, AND SHE DID

NOT REFUSE."

IRENE CLOSED THE PINK BOOK. "WHO IS THAT BLACKSMITH?" ASKED LAURA.

"THE ADMIRAL," ANSWERED IRENE, "THE MASTER OF THE 'SANS-SOUCI'."

"BUT WHY 'BLACKSMITH'?"

"YOU'LL UNDERSTAND LATER. DID YOU LIKE IT?"

"I DON'T UNDERSTAND THE DIGRESSIONS; WHAT IS A COLLECTOR?"

"HE IS! I ALREADY TOLD YOU THAT THIS HOUSE IS FULL OF TRICKS; SPYHOLES, PEEPHOLES, HOLES ARE HIS OBSESSION."

"HOLES? THAT'S ODD, LIKE IN PUBLIC TOILETS."

"YES, IF YOU LIKE. BUT THE ADMIRAL PREFERS LOOKING AT SOMEONE WHO'S ALREADY LOOKING."

"THE LITTLE GIRL SOPHIE, SHE'S LIKE ME, ISN'T SHE?"

"I DON'T KNOW. SHE SEEMS LESS INNOCENT THAN YOU."

"INNOCENT? YOU'RE MAKING FUN OF ME! ... ANYWAY, HE COULDN'T KNOW ME."

"HE KNOWS YOU WELL. EVEN BEFORE YOUR ARRIVAL, HE KNEW EVERYTHING ABOUT YOU. I TOLD YOU THAT WE ONLY TAKE SINGLE PEOPLE, IF HE ACCEPTED YOU, IT'S BECAUSE HE THINKS YOU HAVE EXCEPTIONAL GIFTS; YOU WILL TAKE SPECIAL COURSES TO DEVELOP THEM."

"THERE ARE COURSES, TOO?"

"YES, NUDE COURSES. A TYPING COURSE, FOR EXAMPLE. IT'S INTERESTING TO SEE THE WORK OF THE MUSCLES, THE QUIVERING OF BUTTOCKS AND THE LOINS, THE SEPARATED THIGHS. CERTAIN CLIENTS OF OURS LIKE TO GET ON THEIR KNEES AND STROKE YOU DURING THIS TEST. IT'S A GOOD TEST, EVEN THOUGH THE INCREASE IN YOUR MISTAKES CANNOT WITH MUCH EXACTITUDE BE ATTRIBUTED TO YOUR AGITATION OR THE SKILL OF

YOUR ADMIRER. THERE ARE ALSO COURSES IN BEHAVIOR, LITERATURE, AND LOVE."

"LOVE? ..."

"DON'T FORGET THAT ONE MUST MAKE LOVE DIFFERENTLY FOR A VOYEUR'S PLEASURE."

'WHAT ABOUT THOSE WHO DO IT WITH US?"

"SIMPLE EXECUTORS. THEIR PAY IS VERY LOW. SOME EVEN PAY, IMAGINING THAT THEY WILL THUS FEEL SOME NEW PLEASURE, BUT THEY'RE WRONG BECAUSE WE TEACH YOU TO REDUCE THEIR PLEASURE."

"REDUCE IT? I DON'T UNDERSTAND AT ALL!"

"YOU MUST FIRST CONSIDER THE ONE WHO'S WATCHING YOU. IT'S AS THOUGH YOU WERE MAKING LOVE WITH THE ONE WHO'S LOOKING AT YOU; THE PERFORMER MUST COMPLETELY DISAPPEAR FROM YOUR THOUGHTS, AND, OBVIOUSLY, FROM YOUR FEELINGS, TOO."

"BUT WHY ARE THERE VOYEURS?"

"YOU CAN ASK THE ADMIRAL THAT, IT'S A SUBJECT HE'LL BE HAPPY TO DEAL WITH."

"YOU'RE MAKING FUN OF ME. HE'S THE ONE WHO ENTERED, TURNED OUT THE LIGHTS, AND HELD US SO ROUGHLY?"

"IT WAS HIM; HIS HAND, HIS SHADOW, HIS MASK. WE NEVER SEE HIM IN THE LIGHT OF DAY. BUT HE IS A CONQUEROR, A BUILDER. IF HE NEVER LEAVES HIS EMPIRE, HE CAN FORGET THE REST OF THE WORLD."

"HE FRIGHTENS ME. WILL YOU PROTECT ME?"

"HE'S A CHILD TOO, HE KNOWS IT. WHAT DO YOU WANT TO DO NOW?"

"I'D LIKE YOU TO READ SOME MORE."

"NO, TOMORROW."

MICHEL BERHARD
TRANSLATED BY RICHARD GARDNER

TEMPLE THROUGH THE LOOKING GLASS

ONCE INSIDE AND ONCE THE HEAVY STEEL DOOR HAS CLOSED BY ITSELF WITH A LOW SOUND LIKE THE WHOOSH OF SOME NIGHT BIRD FOLLOWED BY A SERIES OF SMOOTH CLICKS FROM WELL-OILED BOLTS SLIDING INTO PLACE, I FIND MYSELF PLUNGED INTO BLUISH SEMI-DARKNESS AND I HAVE TO STAND STILL FOR A FEW SECONDS—A FEW MINUTES POSSIBLY—BEFORE I CAN SEE WELL ENOUGH TO MAKE OUT MY SURROUNDINGS AND TAKE MY BEARINGS CAUTIOUSLY.

ACTUALLY THERE IS NO CAUSE FOR HESITATION; ONLY ONE DIRECTION IS POSSIBLE: A NARROW, SMOOTH-WALLED CORRIDOR WITH NO SIDE OPENINGS; MY FIRST IMPRESSION IS THAT IT MUST BE LONG AND STRAIGHT, BUT IT TURNS SUDDENLY AT RIGHT ANGLES TO THE LEFT THEN CONTINUES IN THIS NEW DIRECTION WITH STILL NO SIDE OPENINGS OR PASSAGES; ITS WIDTH, HOWEVER, NOW APPEARS SOMEWHAT INCREASED... IN THE SILENT DISTANCE WHAT SEEM TO BE THE NOTES OF A PIANO CAN BE HEARD, FORLORN, SPACED LIKE DROPS OF WATER, MUFFLED BY THE HEAVY HANGINGS AND CURTAINS OF AN OLD APARTMENT WHERE EVERYTHING, EVEN THE LITTLE GIRL DOZING OVER HER SCHOOL BOOKS, IS MOTIONLESS IN THIS MONOTONIC ETERNITY.

AFTER A FEW STEPS FORWARD, AND UNEXPECTEDLY IN SPITE OF THE LIGHT THAT IS SLIGHTLY STRONGER (OR ARE THE EYES SIMPLY ADAPTING TO THE GLOOM?) THE CORRIDOR HAS ANOTHER RIGHT-ANGLED ELBOW LEADING AGAIN TO THE LEFT AND AGAIN THERE IS A WIDENING OF THE PASSAGEWAY TO WHICH THE TERM "NARROW" NO LONGER APPLIES—AND PROBABLY THE LIGHT IS STRONGER FOR GRADUALLY IT HAS BECOME BRIGHT ENOUGH TO SHOW CLEARLY THAT THERE IS NOTHING TO SEE EXCEPT THE WALLS, THE CEILING AND THE FLOOR, ALL OF THEM COVERED WITH THE SAME WHITE LACQUER, SMOOTH, ABSTRACT—ONE MIGHT SAY—CONVEYING THE IMPRESSION OF BEING UNALTERABLE, UNATTAINABLE, TIME-PROOF.

THE LIGHT HERE, PALE AND MILKY, CAUSES ANOTHER QUERY TO ARISE IN THE MIND OF HIM WHO IS WALKING (ONCE AGAIN) SLOWLY FORWARD: EVEN THOUGH IT HAS IMPERCEPTIBLY BUT DEFINITELY GROWN BRIGHTER, NO LIGHT SOURCE CAN BE SEEN. ANOTHER DISQUIETING FACT IS THE RIGHT-ANGLED TURNS WHICH HAVE BECOME MORE FREQUENT, NOW TO THE RIGHT, NOW TO THE LEFT, BUT WITH NO REGULAR DISTANCE BETWEEN THEM AND REPEATED SO OFTEN THAT IT IS NOW IMPOSSIBLE TO

TELL IN WHAT DIRECTION ONE HAS BEEN MOVING SINCE ENTERING THE SANCTUARY.

THESE UNANSWERED QUESTIONS RECEDE SUDDENLY AT THE APPEARANCE OF YET ANOTHER DETAIL, NEW AND REMARKABLE, ALONG THE PASSAGEWAY AFTER ANOTHER ABRUPT TURN TO THE RIGHT: AGAINST THE PALE POLISHED WALL ON THE LEFT IS A VERY DARK RECTANGLE THE SIZE AND LOCATION OF WHICH WOULD SUGGEST AN OPEN DOORWAY.

ACTUALLY, AS ONE DRAWS NEARER IT IS OBVIOUS THERE IS NO OPENING. A NEARLY INVISIBLE GLASS STANDS THERE, UTTERLY BREAKING THE CONTINUITY OF THE VARNISHED WALL. BEHIND THIS UNSILVERED MIRROR LIES A VERY DARK ROOM WHOSE CONTOURS AND SIZE ARE DIFFICULT TO ASSESS BECAUSE OF THE VERY DEEP HUES—BLACK PERHAPS—OF ITS HIDDEN CONFINES, CARPETS, TAPESTRIES AND HANGINGS. AGAINST THIS INKY BACKDROP ONLY THREE THINGS STAND OUT MORE SHARPLY ILLUMINATED OR PERHAPS REFLECTING MORE LIGHT FROM THE CORRIDOR BECAUSE OF THEIR BRIGHTER CAST.

FROM THE RIGHT FOREGROUND AND MOVING DIAGONALLY TOWARDS THE LIMITS OF ONE'S VISUAL RANGE, THESE THINGS ARE A PAIR OF WOMEN'S SHOES MADE OF FINE BLUE SKIN AND VERY HIGH-HEELED, A FLESH-PINK ROSE AT THE END OF A LONG, STIFF STALK SIMILAR TO THE ROSES OFFERED TO GENTLEMEN IN EVENING DRESS LEAVING THE OPERA HOUSE BY THE LITTLE FLOWER-GIRL KNOWN AS TEMPLE IN THE QUARTER, AND LASTLY THE FLOWER-GIRL HERSELF (OR SO IT APPEARS) LYING OUTSTRETCHED ON THE SHADOWY FLOOR, LIKE THE OTHER THINGS IN THIS INVENTORY. THE GIRL IS NAKED EXCEPT FOR HER LONG BLACK GLOVES AND A PAIR OF STOCKINGS—OF A SIMILAR SHADE BUT MORE TRANSLUCENT—FASTENED AT MID-THIGH BY FRILLY GARTERS WITH TINY PERCALE ROSES AROUND THEM. HER NECK IS CLASPED IN A SORT OF WIDE LACE COLLAR, ALSO BLACK. SHE SEEMS TO BE ASLEEP BUT THROUGH THE SPREAD FINGERS OF ONE OF HER HANDS OVER HER FACE AS THOUGH TO SHIELD HER FROM THE BRIGHT LIGHT OF A LAMP—ABSENT—IT IS IMAGINABLE THAT THE CHILD HAS HER EYES OPEN AND IS WATCHING. OR IS SHE DEAD . . . OR AT THE LEAST UNCONSCIOUS?

THE ENIGMA OF THE WHOLE COMPOSITION PROMPTS ONE TO ATTEMPT TO MAKE A CHOICE, A BET, RATHER THAN ASSEMBLE THE DIFFERENT ELEMENTS IN ACCORDANCE WITH THE RULES LAID DOWN BY SOME IMAGINARY ORGANIZER. ONE MUST MERELY CHOOSE ONE OF THE ELEMENTS IN THE TABLEAU, BUT IT MUST BE DONE WITHOUT DELAY. A FAINT PERCUSSIVE SOUND HAS DRAWN NEARER, NOW STRIKING WITH THE DRY, REGULAR BEAT OF A METRONOME, INEXORABLY.

THE NARRATOR, FRANK V. FRANCIS, WHO IS WORRIED WHETHER HE IS COMMITTING AN ERROR IN FINDING HIMSELF AT THE STARTING POINT ON THE TERRACE STEPS OF IMITATION GRANITE IN FRONT OF THE NUMBERLESS STEEL DOORS WITH ITS MISSING KNOB, EVENTUALLY OF COURSE CHOOSES THE PALE BLUE SHOE LYING ON ITS SIDE AND WHOSE HEEL APPEARS BROKEN AT THE BASE. AND IMMEDIATELY HE IS PLANTED BEFORE THE NEXT WINDOW, PROBABLY A LITTLE FURTHER DOWN THE LONG CORRIDOR.

THIS GLASS RECTANGLE IS IDENTICAL WITH THE FIRST ONE, GIVING ON AN UTTERLY DARK SPACE. THE SPECTACLE UNFOLDING THEREIN PROVIDES AN EXPLANATION (TEMPORARY?) FOR THE REPEATED SOUNDS THAT ISSUE FROM A METRONOME OR A PIANO, OR FROM LIQUID DROPS SOUNDING IN THE SILENCE. IT WOULD BE MORE ACCURATE TO SPEAK OF PEARLS STRIKING AGAINST EACH OTHER AT THE CENTRE OF AN OVAL MIRROR ON THE FLOOR DIRECTLY BEHIND THE GLASS WINDOW. NOTHING ELSE CAN BE DISTINGUISHED IN THE ROOM SAVE THE MIRROR AND THE SILVER PEARLS SUCCESSIVELY FALLING FROM AN INVISIBLE CEILING THAT STRIKE SIMULTANEOUSLY AGAINST THEIR OWN IMAGES AND THE EPHEMERAL SURFACE REFLECTING THEM WITH A MUSICAL SOUND, PURE AND BARELY MUFFLED BY THE TRANSPARENT WALL, THEN BOUNCE BACK HIGH IN THE AIR TRACING TRAJECTORIES THAT ARE FAIRLY PRONOUNCED IN THEIR INCLINE FROM THE VERTICAL, AND THAT ARE OCCASIONALLY SUBJECTED TO INFINITELY SMALL VARIATIONS CAUSED BY THE CONTACT BETWEEN EACH SPARKLING SPHERE AND ITS REFLECTION, BOTH OF WHICH SOON VANISH FROM THE SPECTATORS' VIEW AS SOON AS THEY NO LONGER CATCH THE LIGHT FROM THE ROOMS FOR EXAMINATIONS, AUDITIONS, SUPERVISION, EXHIBITIONS OR INTERROGATIONS, ETC.

THE CONCERT CONTINUES IN TRANQUILLITY. THE NOTES VARY FROM ONE PEARL TO THE NEXT, AS WELL AS THE INTERVAL BETWEEN TWO CONSECUTIVE PEARLS; BUT IT SHOULD BE POSSIBLE TO ASCERTAIN, IN THE MIDST OF THEIR APPARENT CONFUSION, A RELATIVELY SMALL NUMBER OF INTERVALS AND NOTES. AND SO THE SAME

QUESTION ARISES ONCE MORE: IS IT A PROBLEM OF CHOICE AS IN THE PRECEDING SCENE OR ON THE CONTRARY IS IT NOW AN EXPERIMENT IN STRUCTURAL ORGANIZATION?

PLUNGED PROBABLY IN THE DEPTHS OF AN ANALYSIS OF THESE DISTINCT UNITS AND THEIR COMBINATIONS, THE WOMEN, SITTING IN A SEMICIRCLE FACING THE SCREEN ON SEATS AS VARIED AS THEY ARE UNCOMFORTABLE, LOST IN THEIR BLANK-EYED CONTEMPLATION, OR FASCINATED BY THE TIMELESS FALLING LIGHTS BOUNCING AWAY AND BACK IN ALWAYS UNFORESEEN (UNFORSEE-ABLE?) DIRECTIONS, THE SPECTATORS, AS I SAID, REMAIN MOTIONLESS, FROZEN IN POSES STIFFLY IMITATING NATURE, LIKE THOSE TABLEAUX OF LIFE-SIZES WAX FIGURES IN MUSEUMS AND IN WHICH FAMOUS SCENES FROM HISTORY ARE SUPPOSEDLY REPRODUCED FROM LIFE.

MADE UP EXTRAVAGANTLY THOUGH IN PALE HUES EXCEPT FOR THE BRIGHT PINK UPON THEIR CHEEKS, DRESSED IN BLACK AND WHITE, BUT IN LONG DRESSES OF BYGONE FINERY, RICH IN LACE, SILK BROCADE, FEATHERS, SEQUINS AND STONES, SEVERAL OF THEM ARE ALSO WEARING HUGE RINGS AND GIGANTIC BROOCHES, JEWELS, PENDANTS, DIADEMS, SPRAYS OF GEMS OR EARRINGS AS SUPERBLY COMPLEX AS FIREWORKS AND WHICH APPEAR TO BE MADE WITH THE SAME DROP-SHAPED PEARLS THE VISUAL ABSTRACTION OF WHICH CONTINUES TO FALL VERTICALLY BEFORE THEM, ONLY TO BOUNCE BACK AT ONCE TOWARD THE FLIES ALONG ENDLESSLY RENEWED PARABOLIC SEGMENTS.

OTHERS ARE BEDIZENED WITH ARTIFICIAL ROSES AND LILIES OR GIANT BUTTERFLIES.

THE FEET OF NEARLY ALL REST, IN VARIOUS CONTORTED POSITIONS, UPON CUSHIONS, LITTLE FUR RUGS OR LACE MATS, THUS OFFERING, AS THOUGH ON A SERIES OF SHELVES, A WHOLE COLLECTION OF FOOTWEAR FOR CUSTOMERS WITH SPECIAL TASTES, FROM BOOTS TO BALL-SLIPPERS, AND SANDALS WITH LEATHER THONGS CRISS-CROSSING FROM PAINTED TOE-NAILS TO CALF.

THE FULL EVENING GOWNS ARE, MORE OFTEN THAN NOT, TUCKED UP VERY HIGH EXPOSING LONG LEGS SWATHED IN SILK, SO ONE MAY ADMIRE AT GREATER EASE THE DIFFERENT SPECIMENS (WILL IT BE NECESSARY ONCE MORE TO BET ON ONE OF THEM?)—SO HIGH IN FACT, AND IN THE ABSENCE OF UNDER GARMENTS, IT HAPPENS THAT WHAT IS ALSO EXPOSED, CAREFULLY SMOOTHED, PRIMPED AND PAMPERED, DECKED WITH PEARLS OR LITTLE GEM-ROSES, IS THE DELICATE PUBIC FLEECE, DARK OR FAIR, WITH THE CLEFT AT TIMES REVEALING WAXEN FLESH IN ITS MOST SECRET RECESSES WHENEVER THE PATIENT'S POSTURE HOLDS HER LEGS OPEN WIDE ENOUGH.

IN THE FIRST ROW, IMITATING THE POSITION OF HER NEIGHBOR'S HANDS, WHO APPEARS TO BE STOPPING HER EARS TO DEADEN THE TINKLING SOUND THAT IS HIGHER AND HIGHER PITCHED—NEARLY A WHISTLE —WHICH THE PEARLS PRODUCE WITH EVER-DIMINISHING INTERVALS BETWEEN THEM, HER WRISTS TOUCHING BENEATH HER CHIN AND HER PALMS ON EITHER CHEEK, IS LITTLE TEMPLE HERSELF SULKILY WATCHING THE SCENE UNFOLD IN THE GREAT RECTANGULAR GLASS WHEREIN SHE SEES HER OWN NAKED, INVERTED IMAGE, BLACK-STOCKINGED LEGS SPREAD APART, FACE STILL HELD (AS WAS JUST MENTIONED) BETWEEN HER TWO SMALL HANDS WITH FINGERS HUGELY MAGNIFIED, AND LYING SHOELESS UPON THE CUSHIONS IN DISARRAY AMONG THE ROSES THAT HAVE SPILLED FROM THE WICKER TRAY SHE USES TO DISPLAY HER FLOWERS TO HER CUSTOMERS, SOME HIGH-HANDED AND DIFFICULT.

IT WAS ONE OF THE LATTER WHO HAS JUST BRUTALLY AND UNEXPECTEDLY CAUSED THE CHILD AND HER DELICATE WARES TO TUMBLE TO THE FLOOR. IN THE DISTANCE, STANDING SLIGHTLY APART FROM THE OTHERS, IS THE MAN WITH THE BALD HEAD AND NARROW DARK GLASSES OBSERV-ING THE RESULTS OF HIS VIOLENT ACT, A CRUEL SMILE ON HIS LIPS. HE MAY HAVE TAKEN ADVAN-TAGE OF THE MOMENT TO PURLOIN THE HOLLOW APPLE USED FOR SECRET MESSAGES THAT WAS CONCEALED UNDER THE LEAVES OF THE FLOWERS. BUT JUST NOW A MUFFLED CRY IS HEARD FROM THE LITTLE THEATRE WHERE NOTHING, TO ALL APPEAR-ANCES, HAS MOVED.

ONE OF THE YOUNG WOMEN IN THE AUDIENCE AS THOUGH PARALYZED BY HER CONSTRAINED POSITION HAS SUDDENLY LOST CONSCIOUSNESS. WITHOUT HER COMPANIONS SO MUCH AS BATTING AN EYELID, EVEN THOSE NEXT TO HER, SHE HAS SLUMPED BACKWARDS WITH A LOW GROAN SHE WAS NO LONGER ABLE TO RESTRAIN, HER HEAD ON ONE SIDE, HER LIPS PARTED AND EYES CLOSED, QUITE UNCONSCIOUS ON THE CRUELLY HARD SEAT. IT IS NOW APPARENT THAT SHE IS ATTACHED TO THE FOUR TIGHT ROPES OF PEARLS WITH THEIR METALLIC GLITTER THAT FORM A DOG COLLAR

AROUND HER NECK, AS WELL AS THE BRACELETS AROUND HER WRISTS, ARE ACTUALLY SOLID THONGS FIRMLY HOLDING THE GIRL PRISONER IN THE CHAIR: ONE AT THE TOP OF THE STRAIGHT BACK AND ONE AT EACH END OF THE ARM-RESTS.

IN ALL LIKELIHOOD HER SINGULARLY RIGID POSITION, WITHOUT THE SLIGHTEST LATITUDE OF MOVEMENT, THAT HER BONDS HAVE FORCED HER TO ADOPT—AND PERHAPS FOR SEVERAL HOURS—IS THE CAUSE OF HER PRESENT STATE (FATAL?) ... AND ALL THE MORE SO AS THE SPIKE HEEL OF ONE OF HER PINK SLIPPERS WITH PEARL POMPOMS HAS ALSO BEEN RIVETED TO THE WOODEN FRONT OF THE CHAIR, KEEPING HER LEG IN THE AIR AS THOUGH IN A STIRRUP, THUS FORCING HER KNEE TO BEND SHARPLY TO THE SIDE AND HER ANKLE TO TOUCH, OR NEARLY, HER GENITALS, WHICH ARE EXPOSED IN FULL VIEW DUE TO THE WIDE ANGLE PRODUCED WHEN HER LEGS WERE PULLED APART.

JUST BELOW THE LOWER ARC, HOLDING HER GARTERS, OF THE BLACK WASP-CORSET SHE IS WEARING AND NOTHING ELSE, AND WHOSE LINES OF FORCE THIN HER WAIST AND PUSH UP HER BREASTS UNDERSCORED BY MORE ROPES OF PEARLS, THE SACRED TRIANGLE'S BLONDE TUFTS ARE DIS-PLAYED IN ALL DUE POMP, REFLECTING MOREOVER IN THE CENTRE OF THE OVAL MIRROR IN VENETIAN CRYSTAL LYING ON THE FLOOR BEFORE HER TO SERVE AS A FOOT-REST, UNATTAINABLE.

FRANK V. FRANCIS ABRUPTLY BECOMES CON-SCIOUS OF AN ANOMALY WHICH DOES NOT FAIL TO CAUSE HIM MISGIVINGS: NO ONE HERE SEEMS TO NOTICE HIS PRESENCE. SINCE HE CANNOT HAVE BECOME INVISIBLE (EVEN UNDER THE MAGIC SPELL OF THE HOLLOW MESSAGE-APPLE!), THE ONLY ADMISSIBLE EXPLANATION IS THAT HE IS PROBABLY PART OF THE SCENE: THE BALD-HEADED MAN WEARING NARROW DARK GLASSES IS NONE OTHER THAN HIS OWN REFLECTION IN A SIDE MIRROR. SATISFYING HIMSELF WITH THAT INTERPRETATION FOR THE TIME BEING, THE INSPECTOR NOTES JUST IN CASE THE FACT THAT THE ROLE PLAYED BY THE PEARLS AS INSTRUMENTS OF TORTURE IS BECOM-ING INCREASINGLY OBVIOUS. IT IS TO BE CONJEC-TURED THAT SEVERAL OF THE JEWELS THEY INFORM ARE PRICKED DIRECTLY INTO THE WOMEN'S SKIN. A SECOND WOMAN, MOREOVER, ALSO SHOWS SIGNS OF ILLNESS OR DISTRESS: CROWNED WITH MOTHER-OF-PEARL THORNS LIKE A CHRISTIAN MARTYR, SHE IS GOING, AS SOON AS SHE CAN NO LONGER HOLD HER PRESCRIBED POSE, TO DROP FROM HER CUPPED HANDS—THAT A KIND OF

ROSARY BINDS TOGETHER AT HER JOINED WRISTS—THE LUMINOUS ROSE SYMBOLIZING HER VIRGINITY, THE TARGET OF ADDITIONAL CRUELTY FROM HER PERSECUTORS.

ON THE STAGE, HOWEVER, THE SCENE CONTINUES: THE LITTLE FLOWER-GIRL IS NOW AWAKENING AS THOUGH FROM A DREAMLESS SLEEP AND IMME-DIATELY RIVETS HER GAZE ON THE EYES OF HER DOUBLE, THE YOUNGEST OF ALL THE SPECTATORS SITTING ON THE OTHER SIDE OF THE GLASS. WITHOUT DISTURBING FOR AN INSTANT THIS REFLECTED VISION, THIS MIRAGE, SHE RISES TO HER FEET WITH A PIROUETTE, SHEDDING AS SHE DOES SO THE LIGHT EMBROIDERED LACE VEIL THAT HAD PARTLY CONCEALED HER TORSO, THE MAKESHIFT CHEMISE OF THE WRY YOUNG WHORE. THEN SHE ARRANGES HER BLACK STOCKINGS AND SLIPS INTO A PAIR OF FINE HIGH-HEELED SHOES. MOTHER-OF-PEARL BUTTERFLIES ARE CLINGING TO HER BLONDE TRESSES.

UPON REMARKING THIS LAST DETAIL THE NARRA-TOR BECOME AWARE OF A SECOND INCONSISTENCY IN THIS ACCOUNT: IF HIS MEMORY SERVES HIM WELL—AND IN THIS CASE IT DOES—TEMPLE, THE FRAGILE FLOWER-GIRL PEDDLING HER ROSES NEAR THE OPERA HOUSE, WAS DARK-HAIRED, VERY DARK-HAIRED. BUT PERHAPS THE LONG BLONDE HAIR OVER THERE, AS GOLDEN AND UNDULATING AS A FIELD OF RIPENED WHEAT, IS SIMPLY—LIKE SO MANY OTHER THINGS IN THIS HOUSE—THE RESULT OF SOME ARTIFICE OR OTHER. FOR INSTANCE, ONE WOULD SWEAR THAT THE GIRL HAS GROWN EVEN YOUNGER, FOR THIS IS THE EFFECT PRODUCED BY HER FEATURES—MORE CHILDLIKE THAN EVER—IN THE GLARE OF THE PROJECTORS, WHEREAS ON THE CONTRARY THE PEARLS SCATTERED AROUND HER HAVE GROWN BIGGER UNTIL THEY HAVE BECOME LIGHT PARTY BALLOONS FLOATING SILVERY IN THE CUBE-SHAPED ROOM. CONCURRENTLY THE OVAL MIRROR AND THE ROSES LYING HELTER-SKELTER NOW BLEND INTO VARIOUS DECORATIVE MOTIFS, HARMLESS AND WITH NO OBVIOUS EROTIC CONNOTATIONS.

THE NEXT TABLEAU, KNOWN AS "THE BARTERED BRIDE," BEGINS WITH A PRESENTATION OF WEDDING COSTUMES (FULL WEDDING GOWNS, WHITE, DIA-PHANOUS, TRANSLUCENT: IMMACULATE TULLE VEILS, LACED PEARL-COVERED BOOTS, LILY CROWNED TIARAS, ETC.), FOR TEMPLE'S BENEFIT WHO IS STILL NEARLY NAKED BUT WHO IS RENDERED ALMOST NUBILE BY APPROPRIATE LIGHTING, WITH HER SMALL ROUND BREASTS, HER

WAIST ALREADY PERCEPTIBLE, HER BUDDING FLEECE SHADING HER PUBIS WITH SILKY DOWN. SHE STANDS FACING THE PUBLIC, HER LEGS SOMEWHAT APART, THOUGHTFULLY CONSIDERING THE ELEGANT DRESSMAKER-SLAVES AS THEY SPREAD AT HER FEET THE TRAPPINGS, THE FRILLS AND THE FLOUNCES FOR THE SACRIFICE. SHE IS STILL WEARING ONLY HER LONG BLACK GLOVES—ONE IS RESTING ON HER HIP AND THE OTHER CUPS HER CHIN, FINGERS SPREAD—AND STOCKINGS THAT HALT AT MID-THIGH, EACH GARTER SPORTING A ROSE WITH A GOLDEN HEART.

THERE IS A FURTHER CHANGE IN THE LIGHTING AND SUDDENLY FROM THE SHADOWS SEVERAL BIRD CAGES EMERGE, CYLINDRICAL IN SHAPE AND OF VAST PROPORTIONS (IF CROUCHED, THE GIRL COULD FIT THEREIN), INSIDE OF WHICH HUGE JET-BLACK RAVENS BEAT THEIR WINGS, LONE AND PERHAPS FAMISHED; THEY APPEAR AT THIS POINT IN THE NARRATIVE (EVEN THOUGH ONE DOES NOT EXACTLY UNDERSTAND THE REASON FOR THIS SUDDEN REFERENCE) AS A REMINDER OF THE DEATH OF THE OLD KING, CHARLES-BORIS. BUT RIGHT NOW FASHION MANNEQUINS ARE ON GRACEFUL PARADE, COSTUMED LIKE BRIDES FOR THE CEREMONY, THE BETTER TO SHOW OFF THE ARTICLES PRESENTED. SILENTLY, ONE AFTER ANOTHER, THE GIRLS APPROACH AND GREET THE NEWLY CHOSEN ONE, AUREOLED WITH THOSE FLUTTERING WEDDING VEILS ON DISPLAY A WHILE AGO—AS MENTIONED—IN THE WINDOWS OF THE SPLENDID SHOP OF ILLUSIONS, AND WHOSE IMPORTANCE HAS OFTEN BEEN CAPITAL IN EFFECTING THE DISCREET CAPTURE OF MANY A PRISONER IN THE PALACE OF ILLUSION.

THE NEXT ONES, HERDED ALONG BY SEVERAL STERN NUNS, HAVE NOTHING COVERING THEM BUT BLACK MESH TIGHTS, FEATHERS, AND THEIR LONG HAIR, OR SOMETIMES AN ARRAY OF NEGLIGÉES, THAT PROFANE, LIGHT AND INTIMATE UNDERCLOTHING WHOSE VESTAL WHITENESS ONLY SERVES TO EMPHASIZE ITS LICENTIOUSNESS. ONE OF THEM, LIKE SALOMÉ BEFORE HEROD, IS WEARING NOTHING BUT JEWELS IN ARABESQUE PATTERNS ON HER SKIN; ANOTHER IS WEARING ONLY HER SOFT, KNEE-HIGH BOOTS AND A DOG LEASH OF BRAIDED LEATHER THAT HANGS ABOUT HER NECK AND DOWN TO HER BELLY WHERE IT DANGLES BETWEEN HER LEGS; SEVERAL DISPLAY THE PERFECTION OF THEIR NAKED BREASTS WITH THEIR HEADS NEARLY CIRCLED BY ENORMOUS HALOS THAT RECALL THE ONES ON BYZANTINE SAINTS AND UPON WHICH, ONCE AGAIN, THE PEARLS ARE DECKED IN SUCH A

WAY AS TO MAKE ONE FEAR (OR HOPE FOR) THE WORST AS FAR AS THE GIRLS' FATE IS CONCERNED.

BUT NOW A DEATH FIGURE APPEARS IN THE PARADE (THE BIRDS WERE PROBABLY ITS HARBINGER), COSTUMED SO AS TO EVOKE ASSOCIATIONS—OFTEN MACABRE—WITH WHITE VEILS AND BLACK MESH. TEMPLE IS FRIGHTENED. SHE TURNS TOWARD THE TALL BAROQUE MIRROR BEHIND HER. HER REFLECTION SEEMS BLURRED TO HER, AS THOUGH IT MIGHT DISSOLVE. SHE CLOSES HER EYES. AND HER AWARENESS OF WHAT IS AROUND HER BEGINS TO FADE. SHE FEELS FAINT. THE MIRROR'S LIQUID IS SUDDENLY INVERTED AND FILLS WITH MARBLED VEINS, PANTHER SKINS AND TATTERED CHLAMYDES, TOWARDS WHICH TEMPLE SENSES SHE IS BEING SUCKED, AS THOUGH BY A GIGANTIC SEA-ANEMONE, BY THE GLASS TURNED TO SPONGE AND THE FLOOR THE SAME, SOFT AND YIELDING.

SHE FALLS DIZZILY FORWARD. HER BLONDE HAIR TRACES A WAVY PATH DOWN HER BACK ...

THE LITTLE GIRL IS NOW ON THE OTHER SIDE OF THE MIRROR WHOSE SIDES SHE HAS PUSHED APART TO STEP THROUGH THE FRAME MORE EASILY, AND FINDS HERSELF IN A VAST BOURGEOIS DRAWING ROOM WITH ITS OVERLY ORNATE DECORATIONS AND IN WHICH THE YOUNG IMMOBILE WOMEN SEEM TO BE WAITING THE HABITUÉS OF THE HOUSE. HALF-DRESSED (SOMETIMES EVEN LESS SO, AS THOUGH THE FASHION DISPLAY IN WHICH THEY TOOK PART HAS LEFT THEM WITH ONLY TATTERED, TORN OR MISMATCHED PIECES OF CLOTHING), THE WOMEN ARE SEATED PRIMLY IN PADDED ARMCHAIRS AND ON VELVET DARK RED SOFAS, OR RECLINING ON COUCHES AMIDST THE HEAPED PILLOWS. SOME ARE LYING UPON ORIENTAL RUGS OR ANIMAL SKINS IN THE MOST RELAXED OF POSES, THEIR LEGS AKIMBO, THEIR HEADS THROWN BACK, THEIR GENITALS ON DISPLAY, AS THOUGH UNCONSCIOUS, PERHAPS EVEN LIFELESS. THE EFFECT OF THIS TABLEAU SUGGESTS THE PASSAGE OF BARBARIAN CUSTOMERS WHO HAVE JUST VICTIMIZED TWO OR THREE OF THE INMATES. THE SURVIVORS CONTEMPLATE THE SACRIFICED BODIES WITHOUT THE SLIGHTEST VISIBLE EMOTION, ACCUSTOMED—APPARENTLY—TO THESE EXACTIONS.

THE RAVENS HOWEVER HAVE BEEN RELEASED FROM THEIR CAGES AND THEY ARE PERCHED HERE AND THERE UPON THE CARVED CORNICES OF THE FURNITURE OR ON THE PEDIMENTS OF THE MIRRORS. ONE OF THEM TAKES PONDEROUS BUT SILENT FLIGHT AND PERCHES ON THE UNPROTEC-

TED BELLY OF AN UNCONSCIOUS GIRL. ANOTHER, WANTING TO BE STROKED, SPREADS HIS ROYAL PLUMAGE, ERECT IN ALL ITS GLORY, AGAINST THE NAKED BREASTS OF A DOOMED CAPTIVE WHO IS HALF-RECLINING ON A CANOPY. AT HER FEET LIES A LION SKIN EVOKING SOMETHING THAT MUST HAVE OCCURRED ELSEWHERE IN THE NARRATIVE. BUT WHAT? AND WHERE?

ONE OF THE NUNS GOES UP TO TEMPLE AND WHISPERS A FEW INAUDIBLE WORDS TO HER, WITH THE PROBABLE INTENTION OF PERSUADING HER TO REJOIN HER COMPANIONS, AND TO WAIT WITH THEM IN THE ARMCHAIR OF THE DRAWING ROOM WHOSE YOUNGEST ORNAMENT SHE WILL BE. THE LITTLE GIRL FEIGNS INDECISION TO CONCEAL HER DUPLICITY. THEN SHE TRIES ON VARIOUS OUTFITS DESIGNED TO AROUSE THE INTEREST OF A CERTAIN CATEGORY OF CUSTOMER. RANGING FROM BEG-GAR'S RAGS OR A TURN OF THE CENTURY BATHING COSTUME TO A SINGLE FULL-BLOWN ROSE CONCEALING HER VULVA. IF SHE DOES NOT BEHAVE SHE WILL BE LOCKED INSIDE THE DEAD DOLL SHOP, WHERE SHE DOES NOT EVEN NOTICE, REFLECTED IN THE DEPTHS OF A LOOKING GLASS, THE BALD HEAD OF THE NARRATOR.

ALAIN ROBBE-GRILLET
TRANSLATED BY DANIEL SLOATE

7.   R. MOVES AWAY FROM HER CAR, DISAPPEARS INTO THE CROWD.

8.   R. BOARDS A STREET BUS.

8 BIS.   PLATFORM OF BUS TRAVELLING TOWARD THE PALAIS-ROYAL.

8 TER.   THE CONDUCTOR TALKING TO A PASSENGER.

9.   THE PASSENGER (FAT, CORPULENT, TALL). HE GLANCES AT R.

10. R.'S HAND HOLDING THE RAIL.

11. THE HAND OF THE CORPULENT PASSENGER SLIDING ALONG THE RAIL TO R.'S FINGERS WHICH ARE SLOWLY COVERED BY THE HAND.

12. R. GOES QUICKLY INSIDE THE BUS.

13. R. SITS IN A CORNER SEAT NEAR AN OPEN WINDOW.

AMBIGUOUS SEX

I HAVE EVEN MET HAPPY TRAVELOS

THE MIRABELLES ARE EXPERIMENTING WITH A NEW TYPE OF MILITANT THEATRE, A THEATRE SEPARATE FROM AN EXPLANATORY LANGUAGE, AND LONG TIRADES OF GOOD INTENTIONS, FOR EXAMPLE, ON GAY LIBERATION! THEY HAVE RECOURSE TO TRANSVESTISM, SONG, MIME, DANCE, ETC., NOT AS DIFFERENT WAYS OF ILLUSTRATING A THEME, TO "CHANGE THE IDEAS" OF THE SPECTATOR, BUT IN ORDER TO TROUBLE HIM, TO STIR UP UNCERTAIN DESIRE-ZONES THAT HE ALWAYS MORE OR LESS REFUSES TO EXPLORE. THE QUESTION IS NO LONGER TO KNOW WHETHER ONE WILL PLAY FEMININE AGAINST MASCULINE OR THE REVERSE, BUT TO MAKE BODIES, ALL BODIES, BREAK AWAY FROM THE REPRESENTATIONS AND RESTRAINTS OF THE "SOCIAL BODY," AND FROM STEREOTYPED SITUATIONS, ATTITUDES AND BEHAVIORS, OF THE "BREAST PLATE" OF WHICH WILHELM REICH SPOKE. SEXUAL ALIENATION, ONE OF CAPITALISM'S FOUNDATIONS, IMPLIES THAT THE SOCIAL BODY IS POLARIZED IN MASCULINITY, WHEREAS THE FEMININE BODY IS TRANSFORMED INTO AN OBJECT OF LUST, A PIECE OF MERCHANDISE TO WHICH ONE CANNOT HAVE ACCESS EXCEPT THROUGH GUILT AND BY SUBMISSION TO ALL THE SYSTEM'S MECHANSIMS (MARRIAGE, FAMILY, WORK, ETC.). DESIRE, ON THE OTHER HAND, HAS TO MANAGE AS BEST IT CAN! IN FACT IT DESERTS MAN'S BODY IN ORDER TO EMIGRATE TO THE SIDE OF THE WOMAN, OR MORE PRECISELY, TO THE BECOMING-WOMAN SIDE. WHAT IS ESSENTIAL HERE IS NOT THE OBJECT IN QUESTION, BUT THE TRANSFORMATIONAL MOVEMENT. IT'S THIS MOVEMENT, THIS PASSAGE, THAT THE MIRABELLES HELP US EXPLORE: A MAN WHO LOVES HIS OWN BODY, A MAN WHO LOVES A WOMAN'S BODY OR ANOTHER MAN'S IS HIMSELF ALWAYS SECRETLY CHARACTERIZED BY A "BE-COMING-WOMAN." THIS IS OF COURSE MUCH DIFFERENT THAT AN IDENTIFICATION TO THE WOMAN, EVEN LESS TO THE MOTHER, AS PSYCHOANALYSTS WOULD HAVE US BELIEVE. INSTEAD, IT IS A QUESTION OF A DIFFERENT BECOMING, A STATE IN ORDER TO BECOME SOMETHING OTHER THAN THAT WHICH THE REPRESSIVE SOCIAL BODY HAS FORCED US TO BE. JUST AS WORKERS, DESPITE THE EXPLOITATION OF THEIR WORK POWER, SUCCEED IN ESTABLISHING A CERTAIN KIND OF RELATIONSHIP TO THE WORLD'S REALITY, WOMEN, DESPITE THE SEXUAL EXPLOITATION WHICH THEY UNDERGO, SUCCEED IN ESTABLISHING A CERTAIN TRUE RELATIONSHIP TO DESIRE. AND THEY LIVE THIS RELATIONSHIP PRIMARILY ON THE LEVEL OF THEIR BODIES. AND IF AT THE ECONOMIC LEVEL THE BOURGEOISIE IS NOTHING WITHOUT THE PROLE-

TARIAT. MEN AREN'T MUCH WHERE BODIES ARE CONCERNED IF THEY DO NOT ACHIEVE SUCH A BECOMING-WOMAN. FROM WHENCE COMES THEIR DEPENDENCE ON THE WOMAN'S BODY OR THE WOMAN IMAGE WHICH HAUNTS THEIR DREAMS AND THEIR OWN BODIES, OR WHICH THEY PROJECT ONTO THEIR HOMOSEXUAL PARTNER'S BODY. FROM WHENCE COMES THE COUNTER-DEPENDENCE TO WHICH THEY TRY TO REDUCE WOMEN OR THE PREDATORY SEXUAL BEHAVIORS WHICH THEY ADOPT IN REGARD TO THEM. ECONOMIC AND SEXUAL EXPLOITATION CANNOT BE DISSOCIATED. BUREAUCRACIES AND THE BOURGEOISIE MAINTAIN THEIR POWER BY BASING THEMSELVES ON SEXUAL SEGREGATION, AGE CLASSES, RACES, THE CODIFICATION OF ATTITUDES AND CLASS STRATIFI-CATION. IMITATION OF THESE SAME SEGREGATIONS AND STRATIFICATIONS BY MILITANTS (FOR EXAM-PLE, REFUSAL TO LOOK CLOSELY AT THE CON-CRETE ALIENATION OF WOMEN AND CHILDREN, AT POSSESSIVE AND DOMINATING ATTITUDES, AT RESPECT FOR THE BOURGEOIS SEPARATION OF PRIVATE LIFE AND PUBLIC ACTIVITY, ETC.) CONSTITUTES ONE OF THE FOUNDATIONS OF THE PRESENT BUREAUCRATIZATION OF THE REVOLU-TIONARY WORKER'S MOVEMENT. LISTENING FOR THE REAL DESIRES OF THE PEOPLE IMPLIES THAT ONE IS CAPABLE OF LISTENING TO HIS OWN DESIRE AND TO THAT OF HIS MOST IMMEDIATE ENTOURAGE. THAT DOESN'T AT ALL MEAN THAT WE SHOULD PUT CLASS STRUGGLES WAY DOWN ON THE LADDER BENEATH DESIRE STRUGGLES. ON THE CONTRARY, EACH JUNCTURE BETWEEN THEM WILL BRING AN UNEXPECTED ENERGY TO THE FORMER.

THAT IS THE "FRONT" ON WHICH, WITH MUCH MODESTY AND TENACITY, THE MIRABELLES WORK. BUT THEY ESPECIALLY DON'T WANT US TO TAKE THEM SERIOUSLY; THEY ARE STRUGGLING FOR SOMETHING MORE IMPORTANT THAN WHAT IS "SERIOUS!" (THEIR MOTTO: "TRANSVESTED AND MONETARY CRISIS, TRANSVESTED GREEN BEAN" ...) WHAT INTERESTS THEM IS TO HELP TO PULL HOMOSEXUALITY OUT OF ITS GHETTO, EVEN IF IT IS A MILITANT GHETTO; WHAT INTERESTS THEM IS THAT SHOWS LIKE THEIRS TOUCH NOT ONLY HOMOSEXUAL CIRCLES, BUT ALSO THE MASS OF PEOPLE WHO JUST DON'T FEEL GOOD ABOUT THEMSELVES.

FELIX GUATTARI
TRANSLATED BY RACHEL McCOMAS

POLLY OR/AND PAUL

POLLY WAS SECRETLY A MAN IN WOMAN'S PANTIES. HER/HIS PARENTS HAD DECIDED ON FEMALE ISSUE AND WHEN POLLY APPEARED WEARING THE USUAL MALE ACCOUTREMENTS, HER/HIS PARENTS PUT THEIR COLLECTIVE IDS TOGETHER AND SIMPLY IGNORED POLLY'S ADDENDA. POLLY WAS RAISED POLLY, BOUNCING RINGLETS UNTIL TWELVE YEARS OF AGE AND BANGS AFTERWARDS WELL INTO THE PUBLIC YEARS. MASTURBATION TRIGGERED BY POLLY'S FURTIVE READINGS À LA FLASHLIGHT UNDER MIDNIGHT BLANKETS, WAS ACCOMPLISHED BY MEANS OF AN ADROIT FINGER INTRODUCED UNDER THE PREPUCE AND TWIRLED COUNTER-CLOCKWISE. THE WHITE RESULTS WERE LONG MISTAKEN FOR THE MENSTRUAL FLOW AND POLLY DUTIFULLY MASTURBATED ONCE EVERY TWENTY-EIGHT DAYS, EVEN THOUGH SHE/HE FOUND THE TIME LONG BETWEEN PERIODS. EXPOSURE OF COURSE WAS INEVITABLE: IT HAPPENED ON HALLOWEEN WHICH ALSO HAPPENED TO BE HER/HIS WEDDING NIGHT. POLLY'S PARTNER (WE SHALL CALL HIM PAUL FOR AMBIGUITY'S SAKE) HAD REFRAINED FROM THE USUAL FUMBLINGS BEFORE THEIR NUPTIAL AND SO THEY WERE QUITE UNPREPARED FOR WHATEVER OCCURED. REPORTS ARE CON-FLICTING. ACTUALLY, AS FAR AS MISS THRIPPE, LIBRARIAN, CAN ASCERTAIN (THIS FROM A FOOTNOTE ON A NEW ENZYME SHE DISCOVERED IN THE AMANITA VIROSA WHICH PROVES CONCLUSIVE-LY THAT MOST DEATH ARE PSYCHOSOMATIC) POLLY WAS UNMASKED AS PAUL, AND PAUL, ONCE HIS PANTS WERE DOWN THOROUGHLY, WAS BASICALLY A POLLY, ALTHOUGH THE FOOTNOTE BREAKS OFF HERE IN MID-ECSTASY. NO ONE SEEMS TO KNOW ANYTHING AT ALL ABOUT THE ACTUAL GOINGS-IN AND -OUT OF THAT NIGHT (MISS THRIPPE FOOTNOTE, ALAS, MAY EVEN BE APOCRYPHAL). ALL WE DO KNOW, AND THIS MERELY ADDS TO THE CONFUSION, BUT WE FEEL IT SHOULD GO INTO THE DOSSIER ANYWAY, IS THAT PAUL AND POLLY OPENED A DINER OUTSIDE AN AUTOMOBILE PLANT IN WINDSOR MEWS. THE DINER WAS A REMODELED HAND-CAR.

DANIEL SLOATE

USE ME

LET US REREAD PRESIDENT SCHREBER'S MEMOIRES: "THE REMARK HAS ALREADY BEEN MADE IN THE PREVIOUS CHAPTERS THAT THE RAYS (GOD'S NERVES) WHICH WERE ATTRACTED, CONSENTED TO THIS ATTRACTION AGAINST THEIR WILL BECAUSE IT LED TO A LOSS OF THEIR OWN EXISTENCE, AND THUS, CONTRADICTED THE CONSERVATION INSTINCT. IT WAS A QUESTION, THEREFORE, OF CONSTANTLY TRYING TO SUSPEND THE ATTRACTION, IN OTHER WORDS, TO GET AWAY FROM MY NERVES [...]. THE MAIN IDEA WAS ALWAYS TO HAVE ME STRANDED, TO ABANDON ME, WHICH AT THE TIME SEEMED POSSIBLE TO ACCOMPLISH BY PUTTING A PRICE ON MY BODY, AS ON A PROSTITUTE'S BODY, SOMETIMES ALSO BY PUTTING ME TO DEATH AND, LATER, BY THE DESTRUCTION OF MY INTELLIGENCE (BY DRIVING ME MAD)." AND, LIKE A REAL WHORE, SCHREBER ADDS, "AS FAR AS THE ATTEMPTS AT TRANSFORMATION ARE CONCERNED, IT SOON BECAME CLEAR THAT THE PROGRESSIVE FILLING UP OF MY BODY WITH (FEMININE) VOLUPTUOUS NERVES HAD THE OPPOSSITE EFFECT, THAT THE RESULTANT VOLUPTUOUS DELIGHT WITHIN MY BODY WAS IN FACT INCREASING THE POWER OF ATTRACTION." LIKE A REAL GIRL, OR RATHER, WAS HE CARRIED AWAY BY THE POWER OF THE DEPENDENCE?

BUT FIRST, WHO WANTS THIS SCANDAL, THIS FEMINIZATION? "IT WAS PERFECTLY NATURAL THAT FROM A HUMAN POINT OF VIEW DOMINATING ME THEN, ONLY IN PROFESSOR FLECHSIG [SCHEBER'S ANALYST], OR IN HIS SOUL, DID I CONTINUALLY SEE MY REAL ENEMY. AS MY ALLY, I IMAGINED THE ALMIGHTY DIVINITY WHOM I PERCEIVED IN DANGER, THREATENED BY PROFESSOR FLECHSIG. THEREFORE, I THOUGHT I HAD TO HELP GOD BY EVERY MEANS POSSIBLE, EVEN IF IT MEANT BEING SACRIFICED. IT WAS ONLY MUCH LATER THAT I BECAME CONVINCED THAT GOD HIMSELF HAD BEEN AN ACCOMPLICE IF NOT AUTHOR OF THE PLOT SET UP TO KILL MY SOUL AND PROSTITUTE MY BODY [...].

THE PROSTITUTE ACCEPTS PROSTITUTION IN THE NAME OF A SUPERIOR INTEREST. SHE WANTS IT, AND IN THIS REGARD, SHE IS SIMILAR TO A MARTYR: SHE TESTIFIES THROUGH HER HUMILIATION. MAGDALENE AS JESUS. SHE BEGINS TO TESTIFY AGAINST HER PROCURER. THE DISSOCIATION OF THE TWO INSTANCES (GOD AND PIMP) IS STILL NAIVE: GOD AS THE AFFECTIVE INSTANCE, SINCE THE SUFFERING IS EXPOSED TO HIS EYES AND GIVEN TO HIS HEART; THE PROCURER AS THE ECONOMICAL INSTANCE, SINCE HERE IT IS FLECHSIG, BUT ALSO HEROD, OR PILATE, WHO CONVERTS THIS SUFFERING INTO

CASH, MAKING A PROFIT, THUS IGNORING IT AS SUCH. THEN, IN THE SUCCEEDING MOMENT, IN THE SUCCEEDING TIME FRAME (THE MOMENT OF WRITING, AND THIS IS IMPORTANT: "THIS IDEA EMERGED ONLY MUCH LATER, COMING TO MY MIND, I DARE SAY, ONLY AS I WAS WRITING THIS PIECE."), THE TWO NAMES, FLECHSIG AND GOD, MERGE. THE INSTANCE OF APPEAL APPEARS TO BE JUST AS IF NOT MORE CRIMINAL THAN THAT OF THE CRIME. THEN THE PIMP-GOD-DOCTOR ACQUIRES HIS LIBIDINAL DIMENSION: THE ORDER OF THE WORLD, SAYS SCHREBER, IS REALLY VIOLATED BY THE PROJECT OF MY TRANSFORMATION INTO WOMAN (PROSTI-TUTE); THERE IS NO INSTANCE OF APPEAL, GOD IS ALSO PERSECUTING ME, HE IS NOT THE HONEST JUDGE WHO RECEIVES MY SUFFERING, HE IS THE PIMP WHO DEMANDS IT AND USES IT TO MAKE A PROFIT, THEREFORE REVEALING IT AND EXPLOITING IT IN THE DUPLICITY OF SUFFERING-JOUISSANCE.

SCHREBER PROTESTS; HIS FIGHT TO GET OUT OF MENTAL INSTITUTIONS, WHERE EVERYBODY WANTS TO PUT HIM, IS THE SAME STRUGGLE AS THAT OF A GIRL TO GET AWAY FROM THE UNDERWORLD AND THE WHOREHOUSE/RED LIGHT DISTRICT WHERE SHE IS CONFINED. BECAUSE, AS WE HAVE SEEN, SCHREBER WANTS TO BE THE PROSITUTE OF GOD, HE WANTS TO EXPERIENCE PLEASURE LIKE A WOMAN AND GIVE GOD PLEASURE, IF NOT AS HIS LOVER, THEN AT LEAST AS HIS MASTER. THIS IS WHY SCHREBER WANTS TO BE ALL WOMEN AND WOMAN ALL THE TIME, AND THE "INCESSANTLY" AND "CONTINUOUSLY" THAT REAPPEARS UNDER HIS PEN TO DEFINE THE NATURE, ACCORDING TO HIM, OF FLECHSIG-GOD'S PLEASURE: THERE IS (A) CONTINU-OUS WOMAN. THIS CAN BE CONSIDERED AS THE EFFORT OF THE CREATURE TO REACH THE LEVEL OF THE DIVINE OMNITEMPORALITY: "EVEN WHEN I WAS LIVING ALONE IN MY STUDIO," SAYS XAVIÈRE LAFONT, A FORMER PROSTITUTE OF RATHER GREAT NOTERIETY, "THE PHONE WOULD RING AT ALL HOURS, CHECKING IF I WERE HOME [. . . THE PIMPS] HAVE ALL THE TIME THEY NEED TO GET YOU, EVEN IN AMERICA IF THEY WANT." AND EVEN WHEN SHE QUIT HER JOB, "SOMETIMES THE PHONE WOULD RING, EVEN IN THE MIDDLE OF THE NIGHT, AND ON THE OTHER END, THERE WOULD BE NOTHING, JUST THE SOUND OF HEAVY BREATHING, AND THEN, THEY WOULD HANG UP."

IN THE CONSTITUTUTION OF THIS AMBIVALENCE WHICH MIXES UP GOD AND PIMP, GOD AND FLECHSIG, THE PUNISHMENT IS A DECISIVE ELEMENT: IT IS CALLED PERSECUTION BY SCHREBER. STILL IT IS THE SAME AS THE PUNISHMENT THAT XAVIÈRE MUST ENDURE. BEING LOCKED UP, REDUCED TO A STATE OF DEPENDENCE, RELEGATED TO THE ASYLUM: SUCH IS THE LAW OF THE MOB. HERE XAVIÈRE SAYS WHAT IS ESSENTIAL: "THE PUNISH-MENT IS AGAIN THE WAY TO GET A HUMAN BEING TO ACCEPT THE UNACCEPTABLE. BUT IT IS ALSO THIS SADO-MASOCHISTIC LINK THAT IN THE END MAKES YOU FEEL SOMETHING TOWARDS YOUR PROCURERS. THIS SOMETHING HAS NO NAME. IT IS BEYOND LOVE AND HATE, BEYOND SENTIMENTS, A SAVAGE JOY MIXED WITH SHAME, JOY TO ENDURE AND TO HOLD OUT, TO BELONG AND TO FEEL FREED FROM FREEDOM. IT MUST EXIST FOR ALL WOMEN, IN EVERY COUPLE AT LEAST ON A MINOR OR UNCONSCIOUS LEVEL. I CANNOT REALLY EXPLAIN IT. IT IS A DRUG, LIKE THE FEELING OF LIVING YOUR LIFE SEVERAL TIMES ALL AT ONCE WITH UNBELIEVABLE INTENSITY. THE PIMPS THEMSELVES FEEL THAT "SOMETHING" WHEN THEY PUNISH, I'M SURE." THAT NAMELESS SOMETHING, WHY GIVE IT THE NAME OF SADO-MASOCHISM AS SHE SUGGESTS? HERE WE ARE IN THE MIDDLE OF A PROCESS OF DISSIMULATION. IF FLECHSIG IS THIS VERTIGO'S NAME, THE PIMP OR THE COMMUNITY OF PIMPS IS TOO. WHAT DISAP-PEARS IN THE PUNISHMENT, REGARDING THIS VERTIGO, IS THE ILLUSION OF AN EGO: "THEY HAD SUCCEEDED SINCE FROM THEN ON I EXISTED ONLY THROUGH THEM."

BUT OF COURSE, AS IN THE GOOD OLD MASTER-SLAVE DIALECTIC, THIS EXTREME DEPENDENCE CAN BE MANIPULATED BY THE WOMAN AS A WEAPON AGAINST THE MASTER. IN LOVE, IT IS PERHAPS THE FEMININE ORGASM THAT ATTRACTS THE BODIES TO BLIND MIXING; THUS SCHREBER WANTS TO BE MORE WOMAN AND MORE PROSTITUTE, AND THEREFORE, MORE AND MORE MAD, MORE AND MORE "DEAD," IN ORDER TO SEDUCE FLECHSIG AND GOD EVEN BETTER. SO, IS IT A QUESTION OF INTUITION RATHER THAN INTENSITY? AND AT THIS PONT, WHERE WITH XAVIÈRE WE THOUGHT WE HAD FOUND THE STRENGTH OF POWERLESSNESS ("I WOULDN'T SAY I REGRET THIS LIFE. BUT YOU MISS IT FOREVER. IT IS LIKE COCAINE. YOU NEVER FIND THIS INTENSITY IN . . . NORMAL LIFE"), SHOULD WE MAKE ROOM FOR POWER AND ITS COMPLICITY WITH EVERY WEAK-NESS? FOR SURE! BUT THERE IS NOT A REASON TO DISREGARD THE STRENGTH OF POWERLESSNESS; INSTENSITY HIDES IN SIGNS AND INSTANCES. IF THE PROPER NOUN IS THE PIMP OR GOD, IT IS ALSO THE OCCASION OF THIS UNSPEAKABLE "SOMETHING." THE "EGO" DOESN'T FALL INTO DEPENDENCE ONLY BECAUSE OF A MISERABLE FLUCTUATION IN THE POWER GAME. IN THE DEAD OF NIGHT, WHEN PALMS AND LOOKS ARE EXHAUSTED, WHEN PENIS AND VULVA ARE IN TATTERS, WHEN THE SCORCHED EARTH HAS NO TACTICS LEFT, THIS ORDER CAN

STILL ARISE FROM THE HOARSE AND INTIMATE THROAT OF A WOMAN: "USE ME"—THIS MEANS, THERE IS NO ME, NO EGO. PROSTITUTION IS THE POLITICAL ASPECT OF DEPENDENCE, BUT THERE IS ALSO A LIBIDINAL ASPECT, OVERLOOKED BY SADE. THE DEMAND FOR PASSIVITY IS A DEMAND FOR SLAVERY. THE DEMAND FOR DEPENDENCE IS NOT A PLEA TO BE DOMINATED. THERE IS NO DIALECTIC OF THE SLAVE; NEITHER HEGEL'S NOR LACAN'S DIALECTIC OF THE HYSTERIC. BOTH PRESUPPOSE A PERMUTATION OF ROLES WITHIN THE SPACE OF DOMINATION. ALL THIS IS VIRILE BULLSHIT. "USE ME" TENDS TOWARDS THE MALE MEMBER ERECTED ABOVE THE SMALL OF A BACK, THE ILLUSION OF POWER, OF A RELATIONSHIP OF DOMINATION. BUT SOMETHING COMPLETELY DIFFERENT HAPPENS WITHIN THIS SMALL OF THE BACK, SOMETHING MUCH MORE IMPORTANT, NAMELY THE OFFER TO SUP-PRESS THE CENTER, THE HEAD. WHEN THE MAN, FLECHSIG, THE PIMP, USES THIS DEMAND IN ORDER TO BECOME HEAD OR POWER HIMSELF, HE IS PROTECTING HIMSELF; HE DOESN'T DARE PAY ATTENTION TO THE OFFER, MUCH LESS ANSWER IT. THE PASSION FOR PASSIVITY WHICH CAUSES THIS DEMAND TO BE FORMULATED IS NOT A SINGLE FORCE, A COMPLEMENTING POWER IN A CONFLICT, BUT RATHER, IT IS THE OVERWHELMING AND UNMEDIATED POWER [PUISSANCE] ITSELF THAT LIQUIFIES ALL STASES INTERMITTENTLY BLOCKING THE FLUX OF INTENSITY. BECAUSE THE OFFER OF OPEN BUTTOCKS AND ANUS ON THE PART OF THE WOMAN BENT OVER AS A GLEENER IS NOT A CHALLENGE OF THE POTLATCH KIND—"HERE IS WHAT I GIVE YOU, LET US SEE WHAT YOU HAVE GOT"—IT IS THE OPENING OF THE LIBIDINAL BAND. AND THIS OFFERING, THIS INSTANTANEOUS EXTENSION AND INVENTION IS PRECISELY WHAT THE MEN OF POWER, THE PIMPS, THE POLITICIANS DENY. THEY CONTENT THEMSELVES WITH A MEAN CAPITALIZATION OF LIBIDINAL INTENSITITES IN ORDER TO CREATE SURPLUS VALUE, AN OVER-EXPLOITATION OF JOUISSANCE'S FORCE.

"USE ME" IS AN ORDER AND AN IMPERIOUS PLEA. BUT WHAT SHE ASKS IS THE SUPRESSION OF THE I/YOU RELATIONSHIP (MASTER/SLAVE, REVERSIBLE) AND ALSO OF THE RELATIONSHIP OF USE, OF COURSE. THIS SUPPLICATION APPEARS AS PURE RELIGION AS LONG AS IT REQUESTS DEPENDENCE. ISN'T THIS WHAT JESUS SAID ON THE CROSS? BUT JESUS CAN ASK FOR DEPENDENCE BECAUSE HE OFFERS HIS SUFFERING AS SIN'S SALARY: THE "OVER-PRICED" NATURE OF HIS OFFERING, OF HIS ABANDONING OF SELF, THE TERRIBLE SCHREBER-IAN DEMIRACLENESS HE SUFFERS, RELINQUISHING OF SELF PERPETRATED AND ACCOMPLISHED BY

THE BELOVED AND OMNIPRESENT—THIS OVER-PRICED QUALITY IS FIXED BY JESUS AS THE REDEMPTION PRICE OF SIN. IN THIS SENSE, JESUS IS A CALCULATING PROSTITUTE: YOU MAKE ME DIE. IT HURTS, BUT EVERYONE BREAKS! EVEN PERVERTS OR FOOLS ("THEY KNOW NOT WHAT THEY DO") WILL BE RECUPERATED INTO THE GRACIOUS BODY OF THE CREATER, I.E., THE CAPITAL. AND GOD IS A PIMP WHO SAYS TO HIS WIFE JESUS, AS HE SAYS TO SCHREBER, "DO IT FOR ME, DO IT FOR THEM." WHAT DOES JESUS GET FROM ALL THIS, YOU ASK? AND JUST WHAT DOES A PROSTITUTE GET FROM SELLING THE MOST UNPREDICTABLE PARTS OF HER BODY? HER LOOKS, HER TALENTS AS A DRESSMAKER, HER SHOES. AND WHAT DOES SCHREBER GET? THIS IS NOT THE QUESTION. THE PROSTITUTE SCHREBER OR JESUS INVENTS AND DEFINES HIMSELF BY CAREFUL PLANNING AS A SUBJECT, EVEN IF ONLY IN FANTASY, CAPABLE OF CONVERTING PERVERSION, OF CIRCUMVENTING IT. AND DON'T FORGET THAT AS JESUS IS ALSO GOD, THE PROSTITUTE IS ALSO HER OWN PROCURER. THE MYSTERY OF THE TRINITY WHICH IS ALSO THE MYSTERY OF SIMILITUDE IS THE VERY MACHINERY PRODUCING THE MEANINGFUL SIGN AND HIDING THE TENSOR, UNDERCOVER SIGN.

"USE ME": AN ENUNCIATION OF VERTIGINOUS SIMPLICITY THAT ISN'T MYSTICAL BUT RATHER MATERIALIST. I'LL BE YOUR SACRIFICE AND YOUR TISSUES, YOU BE MY ORIFICES, MY PALMS AND MY MEMBRANES. LET'S GET LOST AND LET'S LEAVE THE POWER AND THE ABJECT JUSTIFICATIONS OF THE REDEMPTION DIALECTIC BEHIND. "LET'S BE DEAD." AND NOT: I WANT TO DIE BY YOUR HAND, AS MASOCH SAYS. HERE LIES THE SUPREME DECEIT, INTEN-TIONAL OR NOT. SO THAT FROM THIS ULTIMATE COMMAND, COMING FROM A BODY ALREADY EXHAUSTED BY CARESSES AND INSOMNIA, WOULD REEMERGE IN THE ROARING OF UNTIED PARTIAL DRIVES THE SUBJECT FUNCTIONS. HEGELIAN GLOSS OF THE PLEA: BE MY MASTER; MAY YOUR WILL BE DONE. THIS IS HOW SADE, OR FREUD, OR BATAILLE UNDERSTANDS IT, REINTRODUCING POLITICS, AND THEREFORE, ORDER, STRATEGY, THE RATIONALITY OF WAR, LACLOS AND CLAUSEWITZ.

NOW, WHAT DOES SHE WANT, SHE WHO DEMANDS TO BE USED IN THE ARIDITY AND EXASPERATION OF ALL PARTS OF HER BODY, SHE, THE ONE-WOMAN BAND? TO BE THE MASTER OF HER MASTER AND ALL THAT, DO YOU THINK? COME ON! SHE WANTS YOU TO DIE WITH HER, SHE WANTS THE LIMITS OF EXCLUSION TO BE FORCED BACK FURTHER. SHE DEMANDS THE SCANNING, THE VISION OF ALL TISSUES, IMMENSE TACTILITY, THE FEEL OF EVERYTHING CLOSING UP WITHIN ITSELF, BUT NOT

LOCKING ITSELF UP, OR OF EVERYTHING CONTIN- UALLY EXTENDING WITHOUT CONQUERING. OP- POSED TO THIS IS THE SELF-ADHESIVE MEDIOCRITY OF THE VIRILE, LAUGHING, BELIEVING ITSELF CAPABLE OF UNVEILING AND EXPLOITING THE HYSTERIC OR THE WOMAN AND HER SO-CALLED LIE. A MEDIOCRITIY SIMILAR TO THE POLITICIAN'S. IT IS WRITTEN IN THE LETTER LENIN SENT TO TROTSKY THROUGH THE HALLS OF THE WINTER PALACE (I HARDLY HAVE TO MAKE IT UP): "SAY, IF THE WHITE GUARDS KILL US, DO YOU THINK SVERDLOV AND BUKHARIN HAVE A CHANCE TO ESCAPE?" IT'S THE WORD OF A MAN OF THE UNDERWORLD. THE LAST COMMENT COMES, OF COURSE, FROM XAVIÈRE: "AT FIRST SIGHT, THEY SEEM TO BE QUITE JOVIAL FELLOWS. THEY ARE WELL DRESSED, OFTEN WITH AN EFFEMINATE FLAIR. THEY ARE NOT NECESSARILY HOMOSEXUAL, BUT THEY ALMOST COULD BE. ANYWAY, THEY ARE NOT VERY GOOD LOVERS. THEY ALWAYS MOVE IN PACKS," BECAUSE THEY NEED AN ORGANIZATION, THESE SMALL TOWN PERVERTS, AS DELEUZE AND GUATTARI PUT IT (AS FOR THEM . . .).

"WHAT DOES A WOMAN WANT?" ASKS FREUD. SHE WANTS THE MAN TO BECOME NEITHER MAN NOR WOMAN. SHE WANTS HIM NOT TO WANT ANYTHING ANYMORE. SHE WANTS THEM TOGETHER TO BE IDENTICAL IN THE CONNECTIONS OF ALL THEIR TISSUES. "IT WOULD BE MORE IN ACCORDANCE WITH THE REALIZATION OF DESIRE, IN LIFE AND BEYOND, IF WE COULD BE FREED FROM THE DIFFERENCE OF SEX," WRITES SCHREBER, QUOTING MIGNON'S SONG IN WILHELM MEISTER: "AND THESE CELESTIAL FIGURES NEVER ASK WHETHER WE ARE MAN OR WOMAN." THE DESIRE THAT EVERYTHING BE CARRIED AWAY AND BURNED UP IS CALLED BY THE GREAT THINKERS THE DEATH INSTINCT. BUT OF COURSE! WHEN THEY THINK ABOUT LIFE, DON'T THEY ALWAYS THINK ABOUT GATHERING, UNIFYING, CAPITALIZING, CONQUERING, EXTENDING, CLOSING UP AND DOMINATING? THE GREEKS, LENIN AND TROTSKY, THE GAYS WHO MOVE IN PACKS, PROSTITUTING THE WOMEN-MASSES. BUT CAUGHT IN THEIR DISGUSTING PROPER NOUNS OF RULERS, THE INSANE PLEA OF THE MASSES IS NOT "LONG LIVE SOCIALITY" (AND EVEN LESS, "LONG LIVE THE ORGANIZATION"), BUT RATHER "LONG LIVE LIBIDINALITY."

JEAN-FRANCOIS LYOTARD
TRANSLATED BY MICHEL FEHER
AND TOM GORA

BECOMING-WOMAN

IN THE GLOBAL SOCIAL FIELD, HOMOSEXUALITIES FUNCTION SOMEWHAT AS MOVEMENTS, CHAPELS WITH THEIR OWN CEREMONIAL, THEIR INITIATION RITES, THEIR MYTHS OF LOVE (MYTHES AMOUREUX) AS RENÉ NELLI PUTS IT. DESPITE THE INTERVENTION OF GROUPINGS OF A MORE OR LESS CORPORATIST NATURE LIKE ARCADIA, HOMOSEXUALITY CONTINUES TO BE TIED TO THE VALUES AND INTERACTIONAL SYSTEMS OF THE DOMINANT SEXUALITY. ITS DEPENDENCE IN REGARD TO THE HETEROSEXUAL NORM IS MANIFESTED IN A POLITICS OF THE SECRET, A HIDDENESS NOURISHED BY REPRESSION AS WELL AS BY A FEELING OF SHAME STILL LIVELY IN "RESPECTABLE" MILIEUS (PARTICULARLY AMONG BUSINESSMEN, WRITERS, SHOW-BIZ PEOPLE, ETC.) IN WHICH PSYCHOANALYSIS IS PRESENTLY THE REIGNING MASTER. IT ENFORCES A SECOND DEGREE NORM, NO LONGER MORAL, BUT SCIENTIFIC. HOMOSEXUALITY IS NO LONGER A MORAL MATTER, BUT A MATTER OF PERVERSION. PSYCHOANALYSIS MAKES AN ILLNESS OF IT, A DEVELOPMENTAL RETARDATION, A FIXATION AT THE PRE-GENITAL STAGE, ETC.

ON ANOTHER, SMALLER AND MORE AVANT-GARDE LEVEL IS FOUND MILITANT HOMOSEXUALITY, OF THE FHAR TYPE. HOMOSEXUALITY CONFRONTS HETERO-SEXUAL POWER ON ITS OWN TERRAIN. NOW HETEROSEXUALITY MUST ACCOUNT FOR ITSELF; THE PROBLEM IS DISPLACED. PHALLOCRATIC POWER TENDS TO BE PUT INTO QUESTION; IN PRINCIPLE, A CONJUNCTION BETWEEN THE ACTIONS OF FEMINISTS AND HOMOSEXUALS THEN BECOMES POSSIBLE.

HOWEVER, WE SHOULD PERHAPS DISTINGUISH A THIRD LEVEL, A MORE MOLECULAR ONE IN WHICH CATEGORIES, GROUPINGS AND "SPECIAL INSTANCES" WOULD NOT BE DIFFERENTIATED IN THE SAME WAY, IN WHICH CLEAR CUT OPPOSITIONS BETWEEN TYPES WOULD BE REPUDIATED, IN WHICH, ON THE CONTRARY, ONE WOULD LOOK FOR SIMILARITIES AMONG HOMOSEXUALS, TRANSVESTITES, DRUG ADDICTS, SADO-MASOCHISTS, PROSTITUTES, AMONG WOMEN, MEN, CHILDREN, TEEN-AGERS, AMONG PSYCHOTICS, ARTISTS, REVOLUTIONARIES, LET'S SAY AMONG ALL FORMS OF SEXUAL MINORITIES ONCE IT IS UNDERSTOOD THAT IN THIS REALM THERE COULD ONLY BE MINORITIES. FOR EXAMPLE, IT COULD BE SAID, BOTH AT THE SAME TIME 1) THAT ALL FORMS OF SEXUALITY, ALL FORMS OF SEXUAL ACTIVITY ARE FUNDAMENTALLY ON THIS SIDE OF THE PERSONOLOGICAL OPPOSITIONS HOMO-HETERO; 2) THAT NONETHELESS, THEY ARE CLOSER TO

HOMOSEXUALITY AND TO WHAT COULD BE CALLED A FEMININE BECOMING.

ON THE LEVEL OF THE SOCIAL BODY, THE LIBIDO IS CAUGHT IN TWO SYSTEMS OF OPPOSITION: CLASS AND SEX. IT IS UNDERSTOOD TO BE MALE, PHALLOCRATIC. IT IS UNDERSTOOD TO DICHOTO- MIZE ALL VALUES—THE OPPOSITIONS STRONG/ WEAK, RICH/POOR, USEFUL/USELESS, CLEAN/DIRTY, ETC.

CONVERSELY, ON THE LEVEL OF THE SEXED BODY THE LIBIDO IS ENGAGED IN A BECOMING-WOMAN. MORE PRECISELY, THE BECOMING-WOMAN SERVES AS A POINT OF REFERENCE, AND EVENTUALLY AS A SCREEN FOR OTHER TYPES OF BECOMING (EXAM- PLE: BECOMING-CHILD AS IN SCHUMANN, BECOM- ING-ANIMAL AS IN KAFKA, BECOMING-VEGETABLE AS IN NOVALIS, BECOMING-MINERAL AS IN BECKETT).

IT IS BECAUSE IT IS NOT TOO FAR REMOVED FROM THE BINARISM OF PHALLIC POWER THAT BECOMING- WOMAN CAN PLAY THIS INTERMEDIARY ROLE, THIS ROLE AS MEDIATOR VIS-Á-VIS OTHER SEXED BECOMINGS. IN ORDER TO UNDERSTAND THE HOMOSEXUAL, WE TELL OURSELVES THAT IT IS SORT OF "LIKE A WOMAN." AND A NUMBER OF HOMO- SEXUALS THEMSELVES JOIN IN THIS SCARCELY NORMALIZING GAME. THE PAIR FEMININE/PASSIVE, MASCULINE/ACTIVE THEREFORE REMAINS A POINT OF REFERENCE MADE OBLIGATORY BY POWER IN ORDER TO PERMIT IT TO SITUATE, LOCALIZE, TERRITORIALIZE, TO CONTROL INTENSITIES OF DESIRE. OUTSIDE OF THIS EXCLUSIVE BI-POLE, NO SALVATION: OR ELSE IT'S THE PLUNGE INTO THE NON-SENSICAL, RECOURSE TO THE PRISON,TO THE ASYLUM, TO PSYCHOANALYSIS, ETC. DEVIATION, DIFFERENT FORMS OF MARGINALISM ARE THEM- SELVES CODED TO WORK AS SAFETY VALVES. WOMEN, IN SHORT, ARE THE ONLY AUTHORIZED TRUSTEES OF A BECOMING-SEXED-BODY. A MAN WHO DETACHES HIMSELF FROM THE PROMISED PHALLIC PROFITS INHERENT IN ALL POWER FORMATIONS UNDERTAKES SUCH A BECOMING- WOMAN ACCORDING TO DIVERSE POSSIBLE MODALITIES. IT IS ONLY ON THIS CONDITION, MOREOVER, THAT HE WILL BE ABLE TO BECOME ANIMAL, COSMOS, LETTER, COLOR, MUSIC.

HOMOSEXUALITY, BY THE VERY NATURE OF THINGS, IS THUS INSEPARABLE FROM A BECOMING-WOMAN— EVEN NON-OEDIPAL, NON-PERSONOLOGICAL HOMOSEXUALITY. THE SAME HOLDS TRUE FOR INFANTILE SEXUALITY, PSYCHOTIC SEXUALITY,

POETIC SEXUALITY (FOR INSTANCE: THE COINCI- DENCE, IN GINSBERG'S WORK, OF A FUNDAMENTAL POETIC MUTATION WITH SEXUAL MUTATION). IN A MORE GENERAL FASHION, EVERY "DISSIDENT" ORGANIZATION OF THE LIBIDO MUST THEREFORE BE DIRECTLY LINKED TO A BECOMING-FEMININE BODY, AS AN ESCAPE ROUTE FROM THE REPRESSIVE SOCIUS, AS A POSSIBLE ACCESS TO A "MINIMUM" OF SEXED BECOMING, AND AS THE LAST BUOY VIS-Á-VIS THE ESTABLISHED ORDER. IF I STRESS THIS LAST POINT IT'S BECAUSE THE BECOMING-FEMININE BODY SHOULDN'T BE THOUGHT OF AS BELONGING TO THE WOMAN CATEGORY FOUND IN THE COUPLE, THE FAMILY, ETC. SUCH A CATEGORY, I MIGHT ADD, ONLY EXISTS IN A SPECIFIC SOCIAL FIELD THAT DEFINES IT. THERE IS NO SUCH THING AS WOMAN PER SE! NO MATERNAL POLE, NO ETERNAL FEMININE... THE MAN/WOMAN OPPOSITION SERVES TO ESTABLISH THE SOCIAL ORDER BEFORE CLASS AND CASTE CONFLICTS. INVERSELY, WHATEVER SHATTERS NORMS, WHATEVER BREAKS FROM THE ESTAB- LISHED ORDER, IS RELATED TO HOMOSEXUALITY OR A BECOMING-ANIMAL OR A BECOMING-WOMAN, ETC. EVERY SEMIOTIZATION OF A BREAK IMPLIES A SEXUALIZATION OF A BREAK. THUS, TO MY MIND, WE SHOULDN'T ASK WHICH WRITERS ARE HOMOSEXUAL, BUT RATHER, WHAT IT IS ABOUT A GREAT WRITER— EVEN IF HE'S, IN FACT, HETEROSEXUAL—THAT IS HOMOSEXUAL.

I THINK IT'S IMPORTANT TO DESTROY NOTIONS WHICH ARE FAR TOO INCLUSIVE, NOTIONS LIKE WOMAN, HOMOSEXUAL... THINGS ARE NEVER THAT SIMPLE. WHEN THEY'RE REDUCED TO BLACK-WHITE, MALE- FEMALE CATEGORIES, IT'S BECAUSE THERE'S AN ULTERIOR MOTIVE, A BINARY-REDUCTIONIST OPERATION TO SUBJUGATE THEM. FOR EXAMPLE, YOU CANNOT QUALIFY A LOVE UNIVOCALLY. LOVE IN PROUST IS NEVER SPECIFICALLY HOMOSEXUAL. IT ALWAYS HAS A SCHIZOID, PARANOID PART, A BECOMING-PLANT, A BECOMING-WOMAN, A BECOM- ING-MUSIC.

ANOTHER OVER-BLOWN NOTION WHOSE RAVAGES ARE INCALCULABLE IS THE ORGASM. DOMINANT SEXUAL MOTIVES REQUIRE OF THE WOMAN A QUASI- HYSTERICAL IDENTIFICATION OF HER ORGASM WITH THE MAN'S, AN EXPRESSION OF A SYMMETRY, A SUBMISSION TO HIS PHALLIC POWER. THE WOMAN OWES HER ORGASM TO THE MAN. IN "REFUSING" HIM, SHE ASSUMES THE FAULT. SO MANY STUPID DRAMAS ARE BASED ON THIS THEME. AND THE SENTENTIOUS ATTITUDE OF PSYCHOANALYSTS AND SEXOLOGISTS ON THIS POINT DOESN'T REALLY HELP THINGS! IN FACT, FREQUENTLY, WOMEN WHO, FOR

SOME REASON OR OTHER, CAN'T HAVE RELATIONS WITH MALE PARTNERS ACHIEVE ORGASM EASILY BY MASTURBATING OR MAKING LOVE TO ANOTHER WOMAN. BUT THE SCANDAL RISKS BEING MUCH WORSE IF EVERYTHING IS OUT IN THE OPEN! LET'S CONSIDER A FINAL EXAMPLE, THE PROSTITUTE MOVEMENT. EVERYONE, OR JUST ABOUT, AT FIRST YELLED, "HURRAH, PROSTITUTES ARE RIGHT TO REVOLT. BUT WAIT, YOU SHOULD SEPARATE THE GOOD FROM THE BAD. PROSTITUTES, O.K., BUT PIMPS, PEOPLE DON'T WANT TO HEAR ABOUT THEM!" AND SO, PROSTITUTES WERE TOLD THAT THEY SHOULD DEFEND THEMSELVES, THAT THEY'RE BEING EXPLOITED, ETC. ALL THAT IS ABSURD! BEFORE EXPLAINING ANYTHING WHATSOEVER, ONE SHOULD FIRST TRY TO UNDERSTAND WHAT GOES ON BETWEEN A WHORE AND HER PIMP. THERE'S THE WHORE-PIMP-MONEY TRIANGLE. BUT THERE ARE ALSO A WHOLE MICRO-POLITICS OF DESIRE, EXTREMELY COMPLEX, WHICH IS PLAYED OUT BETWEEN EACH POLE IN THIS TRIANGLE AND VARIOUS CHARACTERS LIKE THE CUSTOMER AND THE POLICEMAN. PROSTITUTES SURELY HAVE VERY INTERESTING THINGS TO TEACH US ABOUT THESE QUESTIONS. AND, INSTEAD OF PERSECUTING THEM, IT WOULD BE BETTER TO SUPPORT THEM FINAN-CIALLY, AS THEY DO IN RESEARCH LABORATORIES. I'M CONVINCED, PERSONALLY, THAT IN STUDYING ALL THIS MICRO-POLITICS OF PROSTITUTION, ONE MIGHT SHED SOME NEW LIGHT ON WHOLE AREAS OF CONJUGAL AND FAMILIAL MICRO-POLITICS—THE MONEY RELATIONS BETWEEN HUSBAND AND WIFE, PARENTS AND CHILDREN, AND ULTIMATELY, THE PSYCHOANALYST AND CUSTOMER. (WE SHOULD ALSO RECALL WHAT THE ANARCHISTS OF THE "BELLE ÉPOQUE" WROTE ON THE SUBJECT.)

FÉLIX GUATTARI
TRANSLATED BY RACHEL McCOMAS AND
STAMOS METZIDAKIS

ANIMAL SEX

THE WILD CELEBRATION

JEAN-PIERRE BAROU: FIRST OF ALL, BY WHAT SINGLE TRAIT WOULD YOU DEFINE LOVE IN THE ANIMAL WORLD?

FRÉDÉRIC ROSSIF: BY MADNESS. ONE THING THAT HAS ALWAYS SEEMED AMAZING TO ME IS THAT WHEN THEY'RE IN HEAT, ANIMALS LOSE ALL THEIR INHIBITIONS; FOR SOME OF THEM, YOU CAN'T EVEN GET CLOSE ENOUGH TO FILM EXCEPT AT THAT TIME, BECAUSE THAT'S WHEN THEY'RE REALLY OUT OF THEIR SENSES. THEY'RE HOPELESSLY DISTRACTED. YOU CAN EVEN KILL THEM. YOU REALLY HAVE TO HAVE SEEN ANIMALS SUPREMELY "IN LOVE"; THEY DON'T MOVE ANYMORE.

J.-P. B.: THE MOTIONLESS OF MADNESS . . .

F. R.: TO THE EXTENT THAT SEVERAL SMALL TRIBES IN ANTIQUITY, AND STILL TODAY, PROHIBIT HUNTING DURING THIS PERIOD, IN THE COURSE OF SPRING AND AUTUMN.

J.-P. B.: YOU HAVE FILMED MANY LOVE SCENES BETWEEN ANIMALS. THAT MUST BE MUCH MORE THAN JUST A SPECTACLE.

F. R.: SOMETIMES, THERE'S A FEAR IN THE FACE OF IT. I SHALL REPEAT SOMETHING MICHEL FOUCAULT TOLD ME ONE DAY: IT'S REALLY THE FEELING OF ANIMALITY, OF THIS ANIMALITY WHICH DRIVES US CRAZY, WHICH MAKES US HAPPY, WHICH MAKES US SAD. THE SPIRIT OF CELEBRATION IS SO COMPLETE. YOU RUN AFTER ONE ANOTHER, YOU FALL, YOU FALL AGAIN. WILD GOATS COMING DOWN FROM MOUNTAIN TOPS BY THE HUNDREDS, JUMP, TURN AND FIGHT. THEY HAVE BECOME SO CRAZY, SO MAGICAL, THAT THEY LEAP 20 OR 30 METERS. SOME DIE IN THE FALL. THE FLOCK DOESN'T STOP; IT KEEPS GOING, DRAGGED ALONG BY A STRONG WIND . . .

J.-P. B.: DOES ABSOLUTE LOVE EXIST?

F. R.: CERTAINLY. TAKE FOR INSTANCE ANTIGONAL CRANES. ANTIGONAL CRANES WHOSE LOVE DANCES LAST FOR HOURS. THEY TALK TO ONE ANOTHER; SPREAD THEIR WINGS, AND WALK AROUND EACH OTHER. THEY JUMP UP WITH THEIR FEET, LIKE WILD DANCERS. AND THEN, WHEN ONE DIES—THE INDIANS SAY—THE OTHER LETS HIMSELF DIE, TOO. IT'S A DISCONTINUITY OF LIFE, MAYBE DUE TO A KIND OF SYMBIOTIC RELATIONSHIP BETWEEN TWO BEINGS WHO HELP ONE ANOTHER.

J.-P. B.: THE LION, TOO, IS FAITHFUL . . .

F. R.: THE LION IS FAITHFUL BECAUSE THE LIONESS BEATS HIM; HE RECEIVES TERRIBLE BEATINGS. THAT'S COMPLETELY DIFFERENT.

J.-P. B.: IT'S THE LAW OF THE JUNGLE.

F. R.: IN A WAY. TAKE THE CASE OF PRAIRIE DOGS IN AFRICA, LICAONS. YOU KNOW, THEY'RE TERRIFYING ANIMALS THAT KILL EVERYTHING IN THEIR PATH. NOTHING CAN STOP THEM. THEY ATTACK COLLECTIVELY, BE IT A HYENA, BUFFALO, GIRAFFE OR A LION. YET, ONE OF THE GREATEST ANIMAL SPECIALISTS, IF NOT THE BEST, IN MY EYES, MISS JANE GOODALL, FOLLOWED FOR A YEAR A BAND OF LICAONS WHOSE LEADER WAS A FEMALE. THIS FEMALE HAD THREE OR FOUR MALES DIRECTLY DEPENDING ON HER SEXUALLY. ONE DAY, ONE OF THE MALES COHABITATED WITH ANOTHER FEMALE WHO BECAME PREGNANT. THE LICAON, THE HEAD OF THE BAND, FIRST RELEGATED HER RIVAL TO THE VERY END OF THE GROUP; THEN, WHEN THE LATTER GAVE BIRTH, SHE TOOK HER BABIES AND KILLED THEM ALL, EXCEPT FOR ONE, THE PUNIEST, WHICH SHE GAVE AS SHE WOULD A TOY, OR A SLAVE TO HER OWN CHILDREN. ONLY AFTER THAT DID SHE DEFINITIVELY EXCLUDE HER RIVAL FROM THE GROUP. YOU SEE, ONE CAN ALSO FIND ABSOLUTELY FEROCIOUS JEALOUSY.

J.-P. B.: AT THE SAME TIME, IT'S A VERY ORDERED WORLD.

F. R.: IT DEPENDS ON THE SPECIES, THE GROUPS. ONE OF THE MOST BEAUTIFUL LOVE STORIES I KNOW IS ABOUT THE ORCHID AND THE BEE, THE HUGE WASP OF NEW GUINEA. THE ORCHID SMELLS LIKE FEMALE GENITALIA (OF THE WASP). SO THE MALE GOES STRAIGHT AT IT AND MAKES LOVE TO THE PLANT. HE RUBS HIS STINGER AGAINST IT. AFTERWARDS, THE FEMALE SMELLS HIS ODOR AND COMES AND RUBS HERSELF IN IT, IN HER TURN. THAT'S HOW SHE IS IMPREGNATED, THROUGH THE PLANT. STRANGE . . . WHY DOESN'T THIS COUPLE EVER MEET, EXCEPT THROUGH THE PLANT? WHAT PHYSIOLOGICAL, BIOLOGICAL LAWS OF THE WORLD OF SMELLS AND FEELINGS GIVE RISE TO THIS TRIO?

J.-P. B.: AND, HOW ABOUT POSSIBLE HOMOSEXUAL OR INCESTUAL RELATIONS?

F. R.: THERE'S LOTS OF HOMOSEXUALITY, EVEN THOUGH IT REALLY DOESN'T MAKE SENSE TO PUT IT IN THOSE TERMS. LET'S JUST SAY THAT CARESSES BETWEEN FEMALES EXIST AS WELL AS DO THOSE BETWEEN MALES AND BETWEEN CHILDREN AND PARENTS. THE YOUNG LION, FROM HIS FIRST AND A HALF YEAR UP, BEGINS TO DESIRE HIS MOTHER; SOMETIMES, HIS FATHER KILLS HIM. AND THE MOTHER DEFENDS HER SON, WHO IS HER LOVER. YOU KNOW, THE LOVE CELEBRATION IS OFTEN PRECEDED BY FATAL BATTLES. ANIMALS FIGHT EACH OTHER TO THE DEATH. MALES FIGHT TO GET THE FEMALE. DEATH PRECEDES THIS GREAT LOVE MADNESS, THAT GREAT LEAP WHERE EVERYTHING CHANGES. AFTERWARDS, THEY BECOME VERY MOURNFUL. THEY MAKE THEMSELVES UP, DECORATING AND PAINTING THEMSELVES.

J.-P. B.: DECORATE THEMSELVES?

F. R.: IN AUSTRALIA, IN NEW GUINEA, BIRDS DECORATE THEIR NEST IN RED, BLUE AND GREEN.

J.-P. B.: YES, BUT, PAINT THEMSELVES?

F. R.: THAT TOO! SOME EVEN CHANGE COLOR AND APPEARANCE.

J.-P. B.: IN ORDER TO SEDUCE?

F. R.: OF COURSE! YOU ALSO HAVE LOVE SONGS AND CRIES. IT'S A CHARACTERISTIC OF THAT PERIOD. THE WOLF MAKES LOVE CRIES FOR HOURS. THE SOUND, THE SONOROUS WELCOME, THE SONOROUS RELATIONSHIP ARE VERY IMPORTANT. SOMETHING REALLY AMAZING: GIRAFFES ARE DEAF ANIMALS WHO, IN THAT SITUATION, START WHAT ONE MIGHT CALL LONG MIME ROUTINES: EACH WRAPS AND RUBS HIS NECK AROUND THE OTHER ONE'S, AND—WHO KNOWS?—THUS, COMPENSATING FOR AN ABSENCE OF SOUND.

J.-P. B.: FOR YOU, THIS ANIMAL WORLD, WHEN YOU LOOK AT IT, DOES IT CORRESPOND TO A SALVATION?

F. R.: IT IS TO LIVE IN SALVATION. IT'S ESPECIALLY TO LIVE IN SOMETHING UNLEARNED. FOR ME, ANIMALS, AS BACHELARD SAID SO WELL, ARE OUR OLDEST COMPANIONS IN DREAMING. WHILE FILMING THEM, I'M FILMING A LOST DREAM, A DREAM WHICH GOES BACK THOUSANDS OF YEARS, WELL INTO PREHISTORIC TIMES. I'M ABLE TO HEAR LOVE, THE DEEP CRY, DEATH, THE FOREST, WATER AND RHYTHMS. AND ALL BECAUSE THERE WAS A MASK, MASKS, WALLS SET UP, HISTORICAL CIRCUMSTANCES, ALL

OF WHICH WERE A CONTINUAL TURNING-AWAY-FROM OUR ANIMALITY.

J.-P. B.: ARE YOU RECOMMENDING THIS ANIMALITY?

F. R.: WHAT I MEAN IS THAT THERE ARE LOST CELEBRATIONS DEEP IN OUR MEMORY. WE MUST ENDEAVOR TO REMEMBER THEM. IF WE SUCCEED, WE'LL BE LIKE THE POETS AND PROPHETS. IF WE REDISCOVER THE POETRY OF OUR CRADLE, WE'LL HAVE THE MEMORY OF THE FUTURE. BECAUSE, EITHER WE DISAPPEAR, OR, ASSUMING THERE IS A FUTURE FOR MAN, IT WILL ONCE AGAIN BE POETIC.

J.-P. B.: YOU HAVE REPEATEDLY REMINDED US THAT ANIMALS, BEFORE DYING, FIGHT ONCE AGAIN.

F. R.: A WOUNDED ANIMAL IS DANGEROUS. A WOUNDED MAN IS WOUNDED; HE'S GOOD FOR A STRETCHER. A WOUNDED LION ATTACKS WITH ALL HIS MIGHT. SAME WITH AN ELEPHANT. MAN THINKS OF GOD. ANIMALS DON'T HAVE GODS. THEY HAVE ONLY THE PRESENT. AN ANIMAL DOESN'T BARGAIN WITH HIS DEATH. WE DO! THAT INDICATES A LACK OF ANIMALITY.

TRANSLATED BY STAMOS METZIDAKIS

14. THE CORPULENT MAN SITS DOWN OPPOSITE R.

15. THE EYES OF THE CORPULENT MAN.

16. GRADUAL FADE IN ON: THE INTERIOR OF A DESERTED GYMNASIUM. PARALLEL BARS EQUIPPED WITH LEATHER STRAPS.

17. IN THE BUS: R.'S LEGS SET APART, HANDS LYING EACH SIDE OF HER ON SEAT.

18. EYES OF CORPULENT MAN.

19. R. CROSSES HER LEGS.

20. R.'S BUST, THEN HER FACE IN PROFILE, TURNED TOWARD THE WINDOW.

21. PLATFORM OF THE BUS AT THE BUS STOP: R. JUMPS DOWN, SQUARE OF THE THÉÂTRE FRANCAIS.

22. THE CLOCK, SQUARE OF THE THÉÂTRE FRANCAIS, MARKS 4 P.M.

JOURNEYS OF A GENTLEWOMAN

IT MUST HAVE BEEN TOWARD 1930 THAT THE ROAD WENT THROUGH TO QUEENSTOWN ON THE WILD WEST COAST OF TASMANIA. IN RETROSPECT, MY AMBITION TO BE ONE OF THE FIRST TO MAKE THE JOURNEY SEEMS PUERILE, BUT I WAS ONLY SIXTEEN AT THE TIME, AVID TO EXPLORE THE WORLD AND OPEN UP THE CONTINENT OF MY SENSES.

THE LITTLE INFORMATION I POSSESSED ABOUT THE WEST COAST HAD BEEN SUPPLIED BY A HUNTER WHO MADE OCCASIONAL EXPEDITIONS THERE IN SEARCH OF KANGAROO AND WALLABY. SOMETIMES HE SPENT A NIGHT BOOZING WITH THE MINERS AMONG THE DESOLATE SLAG-HEAPS OF QUEENS-TOWN, BUT HE PREFERRED CAMPING ALONE IN THE BUSH. I WAS ON ONE OF THOSE NIGHTS, HE TOLD ME, THAT HE HEARD THE HOWL OF THE WILD DOG. I EXPRESSED SURPRISE, NOT KNOWING OF DINGOS IN TASMANIA.

"I'M NOT SURE IT WAS A DINGO," HE SAID. "WHEN THE LAST OF THE ABORIGINES WERE ROUNDED UP AND KILLED, THEIR DOGS WERE LEFT TO FEND FOR THEMSELVES IN THE BUSH. MOST OF THEM WERE SHOT LATER WHEN THEY CAME ROUND THE FARMS STEALING CHICKENS, BUT THERE WAS ONE OLD FELLOW MUST HAVE BEEN A LONER, HE STAYED IN THE BUSH, AND IF YOU CAN BELIEVE WHAT THEY SAY DOWN THERE, MATED WITH A TASMANIAN TIGER. I DON'T BELIEVE IT MYSELF, THE TIGER BEING ABOUT AS EXTINCT AS THE ABO THESE DAYS, AND ANYWAY, THOSE CHAPS ON THE WEST COAST ..." HE STOPPED, AND AFTER LOOKING SIDEWAYS AT ME, ADDED ABRUPTLY: "YOU SHOULDN'T DO THIS TRIP ALONE."

"BECAUSE OF THE MEN? I CAN LOOK AFTER MYSELF."

"OH, I DON'T THINK THEY'D TOUCH A WOMAN," THE HUNTER SAID SLOWLY. "NOT ON THE FARMS—BEEN TOO LONG WITHOUT 'EM."

"YOU MEAN THEY PREFER THEIR OWN KIND?"

HE SHOOK HIS HEAD, SUDDENLY FINDING HIS PIPE NEEDED ATTENTION. "NOT EVEN THAT. ANIMALS. AND NOT EVEN WITH THEM THE WAY YOU'D THINK. I ONCE CAME ON A CHAP ALL ALONE IN A PADDOCK AT SUNSET, SUCKING A CALF'S EAR."

KNOWING BUSHMEN AND THEIR LOVE OF YARNS, I REMAINED SCEPTICAL OF THE HUNTER'S TALES. IF ANYTHING THEY MADE ME MORE DETERMINED TO VISIT A REGION WHERE NO WOMAN COULD BE PERSUADED TO SHARE THE LIFE OF REMOTE HOMESTEADS.

THE NEW ROAD HAD BEEN HACKED LITERALLY THROUGH VIRGIN BUSH, AND I MET NO OTHER CARS ALONG THE WAY. SO THAT WHEN, STILL TWENTY MILES FROM QUEENSTOWN, MY ENGINE STARTED GIVING TROUBLE IT LOOKED AS THOUGH I WOULD BE SPENDING THE NIGHT UNDER THOSE CHILLY GUMS UNTIL THE MAIL CAR CAME THROUGH NEXT MORNING. FORTUNATELY, A LITTLE FURTHER ON, A DIRT TRACK WITH RUTS MADE BY A DRAY PROMISED A FARM AT THE END OF IT.

THE HOMESTEAD WAS A TYPICAL WOODEN STRUCTURE WITH VERANDAH AND CORRUGATED IRON ROOF SET IN THE MIDDLE OF PADDOCKS WHERE A FEW CATTLE GRAZED. A DOG TIED UP IN THE YARD BEGAN TO BARK, BUT I REACHED THE BACK DOOR BEFORE A MAN APPEARED. I TOLD HIM THE TROUBLE AND WITHOUT A WORD HE WENT BACK INTO THE HOUSE LEAVING ME, I SUPPOSED, TO FOLLOW.

INSIDE, THE HOUSE WAS SURPRISINGLY UNLIKE ITS COUNTERPARTS. INSTEAD OF BEING DIVIDED BY A CENTRAL PASSAGE, IT RESEMBLED A RABBIT WARREN, WITH ROOMS GROUPED HAPHAZARDLY ON DIFFERENT LEVELS, ALONG BRIEF PASSAGEWAYS, ALL OF THEM COMMUNICATING WITH THE KITCHEN. THROUGH ONE OF THE HALF-OPEN DOORS I COULD SEE SEVERAL MEN ON A IRON BEDSTEAD, THEIR BACKS AGAINST THE WALL. IN A SECOND ROOM ANOTHER GROUP MIGHT HAVE BEEN PLAYING CARDS OR DRINKING. ALL THE ROOMS WERE OCCUPIED, BUT THE HOUSE WAS SO SILENT THE FIGURES ON THE BED MIGHT HAVE BEEN EFFIGIES OR STRAW MEN. I SAW NO TRACE OF A WOMAN'S PRESENCE ANYWHERE.

EVENTUALLY THE FIRST MAN RETURNED WITH A HANDFUL OF TOOLS, INDICATING HE WOULD LOOK AT THE CAR, AND ONCE AGAIN I FOUND MYSELF ALONE IN THE KITCHEN, EVEN MORE ALONE BECAUSE OF THOSE HALF-OPEN DOORS AND THE MEN FOR WHOM I MIGHT NOT HAVE EXISTED. IT SEEMED PREFERABLE TO WAIT OUTSIDE WITH THE DOG, AND I REACHED THE YARD AS THE MECHANIC RETURNED TO TELL ME HE COULD MAKE TEMPORARY REPAIRS THAT SHOULD GET ME TO QUEENSTOWN, BUT IT MIGHT TAKE AN HOUR. HE GAVE ME THIS INFORMATION IN THE FEWEST POSSIBLE WORDS, ALMOST WITHOUT OPENING HIS MOUTH, THE SOUNDS SO FLUID AND UNFORMED THEY SEEMED HARDLY DISTINGUISHABLE FROM THE STRING OF SALIVA DRIPPING FROM THE DOG'S JAWS, PANTING ON THE END OF ITS CHAIN.

I HAD NO INTENTION OF SPENDING AN HOUR IN THE VICINITY OF THE HOUSE, NOR OF RETURNING TO THE CAR WHILE THE MAN WORKED. THE BEST ALTERNATIVE SEEMED TO BE A WALK IN THE BUSH, WHICH COULD BE REACHED BY CROSSING ONE OF THE PADDOCKS. AS I REPLACED THE SLIP-RAILS THE CATTLE STOPPED GRAZING AND EVERY HEAD TURNED IN MY DIRECTION. TELLING MYSELF THAT THE CURIOSITY OF CATTLE WAS LESS INTIMIDATING THAN THE MEN WHO IGNORED ME, I SET OFF.

WITHOUT HASTE, THE CATTLE ALSO STARTED TO MOVE, AND HALF-WAY ACROSS THAT STRETCH OF OPEN LAND I BECAME AWARE THEY WERE FOLLOWING ME, NOT ONLY FOLLOWING, BUT CLOSING IN FROM ALL SIDES, RAISING A GROUND-MIST OF DUST FROM WHICH EMERGED THE BUTTRESS OF THEIR CHESTS AND HORNS, MY SILHOUETTE REFLECTED IN THE GLOBE OF THEIR EYES. I COULD HAVE NO DOUBT OF THEIR OBJECTIVE, THAT HUMAN IMAGE PRINTED INSIDE THEIR SKULLS, AS THE PRESENCE OF WATER MIGHT BE DETECTED BY A DROUGHT-STRICKEN HERD. BUT THERE WAS NO PANIC: THEY CAME TOWARD ME, DRAWN, I WOULD HAVE SAID IF THE IDEA HAD NOT BEEN SO ABSURD, BY A COVETOUS EXPECTATION. I DIDN'T KNOW WHETHER TO RUN OR TO STAY, TO BE AFRAID OR EXCITED. THE HEADS, AS THEY ADVANCED, LOOKED CURIOUSLY HUMAN, A STEER WITH A STRING OF SLAVER PENDANT FROM ITS JAW REMINDING ME AGAIN OF THE MAN'S SPEECH, HIS INARTICULATE ATTEMPT AT COMMUNICATION. I HAD A SUDDEN VISION OF THE TWO TOGETHER, THE MAN AND THE STEER, RELATED BY A KIND OF MUTUAL YEARNING. EACH OF THEM WOULD KNOW WHAT WAS EXPECTED OF THE OTHER, WHEREAS I STOOD OUTSIDE THE COMPLICITY, IGNORING WHAT GESTURES OF TENDERNESS OR LUST THESE BEASTS ATTENDED. THE HUNTER'S TALES CAME BACK TO ME, AND IF NOW I WERE READY TO BELIEVE THEM, THEY EXPOSED TOO LITTLE OF THE MYSTERY I SUSPECTED: THE BACCHANAL IN PREPARATION BETWEEN THOSE MEN IN THE HOUSE WAITING FOR DARKNESS, AND THESE BEASTS THEIR PARTNERS, IN WHICH THE MEMORY OF FORMER RITUALS HAD BEEN BURNT LIKE A BRAND. MY ARRIVAL BEFORE THE HOUR HAD RELEASED A FORMIDABLE REFLEX, SETTING IN MOTION RITES THAT BELONGED TO THE SECRECY OF MOONLESS PADDOCKS, TO A SABBATH OF NAKED

MEN AND BEASTS STUMBLING TO THEIR KNEES, OF CRIES THAT RESEMBLED AN INHUMAN AND PLAINTIVE LOWING.

IF THE SHOT HAD BEEN FIRED AT ME I WOULD HAVE ACCEPTED THE JUSTICE OF ITS PUNISHMENT FOR MY INTRUSION, A NECESSARY ACT SINCE NO WOMAN SHOULD HAVE BEEN WITNESS TO THAT CONCEALED AND POIGNANT INTIMACY, BUT IT CRACKED OVER THE BACKS OF THE HERD LIKE A STOCK WHIP, FOLLOWED BY A SECOND SHOT. THE LEADING CATTLE STOPPED, MY IMAGE DROWNING IN THEIR EYES IN POOLS OF ANGUISH, AND SUDDENLY VEERED, TAKING THE HERD WITH THEM IN A STAMPEDE TO THE FAR CORNER OF THE PADDOCK. SOMEHOW I MANAGED TO REACH THE FENCE WITHOUT RUNNING, NOR DID I LOOK BACK TO SEE WHO HAD FIRED THE SHOTS. BUT ONCE UNDER COVER OF THE TREES MY KNEES BUCKLED UNDER ME AND I SANK ON A FALLEN LOG.

II

WAS IT A DOG? CERTAINLY A BREED I DID NOT RECOGNIZE, ALMOST TOO BIG FOR A DOG, SET HIGH ON THIN, SINEWY LEGS, ITS FLANKS MARKED BY STRIPES OF A DARKER GREY, A PARIAH TO JUDGE BY ITS WARINESS, THE COCK OF ITS EARS IN THE DIRECTION OF THE FARM. IT HAD HEARD THE SHOTS NO DOUBT, AND KNEW WHAT THAT MEANT, ALWAYS ON THE ALERT AGAINST ARMED AND HOSTILE MEN. BUT IT WAS NOT AFRAID OF ME, A VULNERABLE THING SLOUCHED ON THE LOG, A FEMALE REDOLENT OF SOME OBSCURE MEMORY. IT TOOK A STEP INTO THE CLEARING AND I COULD ALMOST HAVE ADMIRED ITS ARROGANCE HAD I NOT FELT THOSE YELLOW EYES ON ME, BURNING WITH THE HUNGER OF HOW MANY CAMP FIRES WATCHED FROM THE RIM OF DARKNESS, NOSTRILS TWITCHING TO THE ODOR OF COOKING MEAT, AND THAT DISTANT WARMTH OF HUMAN BODIES, OF VOICES, THAT SENT A SHUDDER ALONG ITS RIBS LIKE WIND OVER WHEAT. THE CREATURE'S SOLITUDE ASSAILED ME, AND INVOLUNTARILY I STRETCHED OUT A HAND AND SAID: "HERE—COME HERE."

MY OVERTURES WERE GREETED BY A LOW SNARL. THE POINTED MUZZLE LIFTED AND I SAW THE TEETH. THEN I WAS AFRAID, A TERROR THAT STARTED FROM MY ARM-PITS AND STANK THE CLEARING. I KNEW IF I TRIED TO ESCAPE THE DOG WOULD HUNT ME DOWN AS PITILESSLY AS THE ABORIGINES HAD BEEN HUNTED, AND DESPATCHED WITH THE SAME

CRUELTY. IF I CRIED OUT MY VOICE WOULD SKIM ACROSS THE SILENCE OF THE BUSH AND SINK LIKE A PEBBLE. I THOUGHT OF TAKING REFUGE IN A TREE, AND SAW IN MY MIND'S EYE THEIR ARCHAIC BREADTH AND HEIGHT. NO DEFENCE EXISTED IN THAT PRIMAL SOLITUDE WHERE THE ABORIGINES HAD WANDERED AT A TIME WHEN MAN DREAMED HIMSELF AS OTHER THAN ANIMALITY. NOW THEY WERE ALL DEAD, AND ONLY THIS WILD DOG AND I REMAINED IN THEIR HUNTING GROUNDS, WHERE I HAD BECOME THE PREY.

I STOOD UP, AND AT ONCE THE DOG SHOWED ITSELF ALERT. I BEGAN TO WALK TOWARD IT, SLOWLY, PUTTING ONE FOOT IN FRONT OF THE OTHER, MY REGARD NEVER QUITTING THOSE YELLOW EYES. THE CREATURE SEEMED UNCERTAIN OF MY INTENTIONS, AND I HALF-EXPECTED IT TO TURN TAIL AND SLOPE OFF INTO THE BUSHES, WHICH I COUNTED ON BY BRAVING IT AS MY ONLY CHANCE OF ESCAPE. INSTEAD, THE DOG CHANGED ITS STANCE, EVERY MUSCLE TAUT, AND I SAW, EXTENDING UNDER THE BELLY, THE LONG, RISING ROD OF ITS SEX.

I MUST HAVE STOPPED, AND AT THAT INSTANT THE DOG SPRANG, KNOCKING ME TO THE GROUND WITH THE WEIGHT OF ITS BODY. IN THE BLINDNESS OF OUR BATTLE, STIFLED BY THE RANK STENCH OF FUR, FEELING THE DOG'S TEETH AS IT RIPPED MY CLOTHES, ROLLING AND STRUGGLING AGAINST THE CONTACT OF SEX AGAINST MY MOUTH, I STILL EXPERIENCED THE SAME FURIOUS JOY AS WHEN I HAD WRESTLED WITH BOYS AND PINNED THEM DOWN BY MY FORCE. BUT MY STRENGTH WAS NOT EQUAL TO THE DOG'S. IT WORKED WITH THE FRENZY OF THE KILL. I WAS COVERED IN SLOBBER, AND BLOOD TRICKLED WHERE TEETH TORE THROUGH THE LAST RAGS OF CLOTHING. EVEN THE WILL TO RESIST SEEPED OUT OF ME AT LAST. AS MY BODY CAPITULATED, I SEIZED THE BLACK SEX, DIRECTING IT AGAINST MYSELF IN THE ONLY GESTURE THAT COULD SAVE ME. AND IN THAT SAVAGE COUPLING WE ARRIVED, PERHAPS, AT A RECONCILIATION.

III

IN THE OLD TOWN OF PRAGUE WHERE ARCHIMBOLDO ONCE VISITED THE ALCHEMISTS AND COLLECTED OBJECTS FOR THE EMPEROR RUDOLPH'S CABINET OF CURIOSITIES, THERE STILL LIVED AFTER THE WAR THE LAST SURVIVING MEMBER OF THE KISCH FAMILY, EGON, THE INVENTOR OF "REPORTAGE" HAVING DIED A WEEK BEFORE MY ARRIVAL. KASPAR,

"THE CLOWN," WAS THE YOUNGEST OF THE KISCH BROTHERS AND HAD ESCAPED THE DESTINY OF EUROPEAN JEWS BY SERVING AS A SURGEON WITH THE 8TH ROUTE ARMY IN CHINA. THE REST OF THE FAMILY PERISHED, AND NOW KASPAR LIVED ALONE IN THE ECHOING APARTMENT, WITH A HOUSEKEEPER TO LOOK AFTER HIM. SHE WAS A TACITURN WOMAN WHO KEPT A GOOSE ON THE LANDING, FATTENING IT FOR CHRISTMAS. THE GOOSE BEING A RARE BIRD IN POST-WAR PRAGUE, I WILLINGLY ACCEPTED KASPAR'S INVITATION TO SHARE IT WITH HIM ON CHRISTMAS EVE.

WE SAT OPPOSITE AT THE LONG TABLE, I THE ONLY GUEST TO OCCUPY ONE OF THOSE EMPTY CHAIRS, AND IT HARDLY LIGHTENED THE GHOSTLY ATMOS-PHERE WHEN THE HOUSEKEEPER SERVED THE GOOSE IN A FLOOD OF TEARS, STANDING BEHIND MY CHAIR WHILE WE ATE, SOBBING AUDIBLY AT EACH MOUTHFUL OF HER DEAR DEPARTED. NOT ALTO-GETHER A FESTIVE OCCASION, BUT WITH KASPAR I HAD BECOME HABITUATED TO MACABRE CON-TRASTS. IF, DURING OUR WALKS THROUGH PRAGUE, WE VISITED THE OLD JEWISH CEMETERY WHERE SPACE IS SO LIMITED THE DEAD ARE BURIED ONE ON TOP OF ANOTHER, JOSTLING CENTURIES OF TOMB-STONES, HE FOLLOWED THIS BY SHOWING ME, AND DESCRIBING WITH BAWDY BRUTALITY, THE CARVING OF A NUN ON THE CHARLES BRIDGE, A PEASANT STICKING HIS HAND UP HER HABIT. I SOMETIMES SUSPECTED THAT KASPAR'S BLACK HUMOUR SUBSTITUTED FOR HIS CHILDHOOD ROLE OF "HE WHO GETS SLAPPED," WHEN THE ELDER BROTHERS DONGED HIM ON THE HEAD TILL HE WAS DIZZY, A TEST OF HOW MUCH HE COULD ENDURE, A FORM OF PHYSICAL PAIN TO MASK THE INTOLER-ABLE. PERHAPS FOR THE SAME REASON, HE CHOSE THAT CHRISTMAS EVE TO TELL ME THE STORY OF THE CHINESE PROSTITUTE.

DURING THE EARLY PERIOD OF THE WAR IN CHINA WHEN CHANG KAI SHEK STILL PROFESSED HIS ALLIANCE WITH THE 8TH ROUTE ARMY IN FIGHTING THE JAPANESE, KASPAR FOUND HIMSELF ON ONE OCCASION IN A TOWN HELD BY THE GENERAL'S TROOPS, THE SOLDIERS BIVOUACKED ON THE EDGE OF THE BOMBED CITY, WHERE THE QUARTER OF A THOUSAND FLOWERS HAD BEEN DECLARED OUT OF BOUNDS. AS A PALLIATIVE TO THIS PRIVATION ONE OF THE MORE ENTERPRISING PROSTITUTES HAD SET UP A LITTLE TENT NOT FAR FROM THE CAMP, IN FRONT OF WHICH A LONG LINE OF SOLDIERS AWAITED THEIR TURN.

KASPAR'S SARDONIC DESCRIPTION OF THE SCENE, OF ITS FLIMSY TENT JUST LARGE ENOUGH FOR TWO RECUMBENT BODIES ONE ON TOP OF THE OTHER, OF THE QUEUE OF SOLDIERS ABSORBED BY THEIR OWN NEED, ADDED TO ITS DESOLATION. FOR HOURS THE QUEUE KEPT MOVING, AND DARKNESS CAME BEFORE THE LAST MAN EMERGED, RE-ADJUSTING HIS UNIFORM. WHEN EVERYONE HAD GONE, KASPAR TOOK HIS DOCTOR'S BAG AND APPROACHED THE TENT, NOW A VAGUE HUMMOCK ON THE GROUND, AND TOO SMALL FOR KASPAR'S BULK TO PENE-TRATE EVEN ON HANDS AND KNEES. VIOLENTLY, HE TORE UPON THE WRETCHED SCREEN AND ON ALL THAT ENDLESS PLAIN THERE WAS NOTHING BUT A WOMAN LYING SPREAD-EAGLED ON A MAT. SHE HAD, KASPAR SAID, BEEN DEAD FOR A LONG TIME.

CATHERINE DUNCAN

A BLOATED OEDIPUS

TWO YEARS AFTER THE LETTER TO HIS FATHER, KAFKA ADMITS THAT HE "THREW HIMSELF INTO DISSATISFACTION," AND THAT HE DID SO "WITH ALL THE MEANS MADE ACCESSIBLE TO (HIM) BY (HIS) ERA AND TRADITION." IT TURNS OUT THAT OEDIPUS IS ONE OF THESE MEANS, WHICH, QUITE MODERN, BECAME COMMON IN FRUED'S TIME, PERMITTING MANY COMIC EFFECTS. IT SUFFICES TO ENLARGE UPON IT: "IT IS STRANGE THAT, PRACTICING DISSATISFACTION IN A SUFFICIENTLY SYSTEMATIC MANNER, ANY COMEDY CAN BECOME A REALITY." BUT KAFKA DOES NOT CHALLENGE THE EXTERIOR INFLUENCE OF THE FATHER IN ORDER TO INVOKE AN INTERIOR GENESIS OR AN INTERNAL STRUCTURE WHICH WOULD STILL BE OEDIPAL. "IT IS IMPOSSIBLE FOR ME TO ADMIT THAT THE BEGINNINGS OF MY UNHAPPINESS WERE INTERNALLY NECESSARY, THEY MAY HAVE HAD A CERTAIN NECESSITY, BUT NOT AN INTERNAL NECESSITY, THEY CAME UPON ME FLUTTERING LIKE FLIES AND COULD HAVE BEEN CHASED AWAY AS EASILY." THAT IS THE ESSENTIAL THING: BEYOND EXTERIOR AND INTERIOR, AN AGITATION, A MOLECULAR DANCE, A WHOLE RELATION—LIMIT WITH THE OUTSIDE WHICH WILL ASSUME OEDIPUS' INORDINATELY DISTENDED (GROSSI) MASK.

FOR THE EFFECT OF COMIC DISTENSION IS DOUBLE. ON ONE HAND, BEHIND THE FAMILY TRIANGLE (FATHER-MOTHER-CHILD) ARE DISCOVERED OTHER, INFINITELY MORE ACTIVE TRIANGLES, FROM WHICH THE FAMILY BORROWS ITS OWN POWER, ITS MISSION TO PROPOGATE SUBMISSION, TO BOW AND TO MAKE OTHERS BOW THEIR HEADS. BECAUSE THAT IS WHAT THE INFANTILE LIBIDO INVESTS FROM THE BEGINNING: THROUGH THE FAMILY PHOTO, A MAP OF THE WHOLE WORLD. SOMETIMES ONE OF THE TERMS OF THE FAMILY TRIANGLE IS REPLACED BY ANOTHER TERM WHICH SUFFICES TO DE-FAMILIAL-IZE THE WHOLE PICTURE (IN THIS WAY THE FAMILY STORE ENACTS THE TRIANGLE, FATHER-EMPLOYEE-CHILD, THE CHILD BEING PLACED ON THE SIDE OF THE LOWLIEST EMPLOYEES WHOSE FEET HE WOULD BE HAPPY TO LICK); OR ELSE IN "THE JUDGMENT" THE RUSSIAN FRIEND TAKES THE PLACE OF ONE OF THE TERMS OF THE TRIANGLE AND TRANSFORMS IT INTO A JUDICIAL OR CONDEMNATORY APPARATUS. AT OTHER TIMES THE WHOLE TRIANGLE CHANGES ITS FORM AND CHARACTERS, AND IS SHOWN TO BE JUDICIAL, OR ECONOMIC, OR BUREAUCRATIC, OR POLITICAL, ETC. SUCH IS THE TRIANGLE, JUDGE-ATTORNEY-ACCUSED IN THE TRIAL, WHERE THE FATHER NO LONGER EXISTS AS SUCH (OR ELSE THE

UNCLE-LAWYER-BLOCK TRIO, ANXIOUS FOR K. TO TAKE HIS TRIAL SERIOUSLY AT ALL COSTS). OR OTHER PROLIFERATING TRIOS, BANK EMPLOYEES, POLICE OFFICERS, JUDGES. OR ELSE THE GEO-POLITICAL, GERMANS-CZECHS-JEWS, WHICH PARADES BEHIND KAFKA'S FATHER: "IN PRAGUE, (THE JEWS) WERE REPROACHED FOR NOT BEING CZECHS, IN SAAZ AND IN EGER FOR NOT BEING GERMANS. (...) THOSE WHO WANTED TO BE GERMANS HAD THEMSELVES ATTACKED BY CZECHS, AND AT THE SAME TIME BY GERMANS." FOR THIS REASON, THE FATHER'S HYPOTHETICAL INNOCENCE AND DISTRESS FORMS THE WORST ACCUSATION, SINCE THE FATHER HAD DONE NOTHING BUT BOW HIS HEAD, SUBMIT TO A POWER WHICH WAS NOT HIS OWN, PUT HIMSELF AT AN IMPASS BY BETRAYING HIS RURAL JEWISH CZECH ORIGIN. THUS, TOO WELL FORMED, THE FAMILY TRIANGLE WAS ONLY A CATALYST FOR INVESTMENTS OF A COMPLETELY DIFFERENT NATURE WHICH THE CHILD NEVER CEASES TO DISCOVER BENEATH HIS FATHER, IN HIS MOTHER, IN HIMSELF. JUDGES, COMMISSIONERS, BUREAUCRATS, ETC., ARE NOT FATHER SUBSTI-TUTES, RATHER IT IS THE FATHER WHO IS CONDENSED FROM ALL THESE FORCES TO WHICH HE SUBMITS AND INCITES HIS SON TO SUBMIT. THE FAMILY HAS ONLY DOORS AT WHICH, FROM THE START, KNOCK "DIABOLICAL POWERS" THAT REJOICE EXCESSIVELY AT THE PROSPECT OF ENTERING ONE DAY. IN KAFKA, IT IS NEITHER THE FATHER, NOR THE SUPER-EGO, NOR ANY SIGNIFIER WHICH MANUFAC-TURES ANXIETY OR PLEASURE, BUT RATHER THE AMERICAN TECHNOCRATIC MACHINE, THE RUSSIAN BUREAUCRATIC MACHINE, OR THE FASCIST MACHINE. IT COULD BE SAID THAT TO THE EXTENT THAT THE FAMILY TRIANGLE IS UNDONE, IN ONE OF ITS TERMS, OR SUDDENLY AND COMPLETELY IN FAVOR OF THE POWERS WHICH ACTUALLY ARE AT WORK, OTHER TRIANGLES PUSHING OUT FROM BEHIND HAVE A CERTAIN FLUIDITY, A DIFFUSENESS AND ARE PERPETUALLY CHANGING INTO ONE ANOTHER, EITHER BY MEANS OF A SUDDEN PROLIFERATION OF ONE OF THE TERMS OR VERTICES, OR BECAUSE TOGETHER THE SIDES ARE CONTINUOUSLY BEING DEFORMED. THUS, AT THE BEGINNING OF THE TRIAL, THREE UNIDENTIFIED CHARACTERS ARE TRANSFORMED INTO THREE BANK WORKERS, IN A MOBILE RELATIONSHIP WITH THE THREE INSPECTORS, AND WITH THE THREE BUSY-BODIES GROUPED AT THE WINDOW. IN THE FIRST REPRESENTATION OF THE LAW COURT, THERE IS STILL A WELL-DEFINED TRIANGLE WITH THE JUDGE AND TWO SIDES, RIGHT AND LEFT. BUT ONE IS ULTIMATELY WITNESS TO AN INTERNAL PROLIFERA-TION SIMILAR TO A CANCEROUS INVASION, THE INEXTRICABLE ENTANGLEMENT OF OFFICES AND BUREAUCRATS, THE INFINITE AND UNGRASPABLE HIERARCHY, THE CONTAMINATION OF SUSPICIOUS SPACES, AN EQUIVALENT OF WHICH, THOUGH IN COMPLETELY DIFFERENT TERMS, COULD BE FOUND IN PROUST WHERE THE UNITY OF CHARACTERS AND THE FIGURES THEY CONSTITUTE GIVE WAY TO NEBULOUS FORMS, TO PROLIFERATING, BLURRED GROUPINGS. IN THE SAME WAY, BEHIND THE FATHER IS THE WHOLE NEBULOUS GROUP OF JEWS WHO, HAVING LEFT THE RURAL CZECH MILIEU BEHIND FOR AN URBAN, GERMAN ENSEMBLE, ARE LIABLE TO BE ATTACKED FROM BOTH SIDES—A TRANSFORMA-TIONAL TRIANGLE. THERE IS NO CHILD INCAPABLE OF KNOWING THIS: THEY EACH HAVE A GEOGRAPHI-CAL AND POLITICAL MAP WHOSE MARKINGS ARE DIFFUSED AND SHIFTING, EVEN IF ONLY DUE TO NANNIES, MAIDS, THEIR FATHER'S EMPLOYEES, ETC. AND IF THE FATHER RETAINS THE LOVE AND ESTIMATION OF HIS SON, IT IS BECAUSE IN HIS YOUTH HE HIMSELF CONFRONTED CERTAIN "DIABOLICAL POWERS" AT THE RISK OF BEING OVERCOME BY THEM.

FURTHERMORE, TO THE EXTENT THAT OEDIPUS' COMIC ENLARGEMENT ALLOWS THESE OTHER OPPRESSIVE TRIANGLES TO BE SEEN UNDER THE MICROSCOPE, THE POSSIBILITY OF AN ESCAPE HATCH, A ROUTE OF FLIGHT APPEARS. TO THE INHUMANITY OF "DIABOLICAL POWERS" ANSWERS THE SUB-HUMANITY OF BECOMING ANIMAL: BECOMING-BEETLE, BECOMING-DOG, BECOMING-APE, "TO RUN OFF, TOPPLING HEAD OVER HEELS," RATHER THAN TO BOW THE HEAD AND REMAIN A BUREAUCRAT, INSPECTOR, JUDGE AND JUDGED. HERE AGAIN, THERE ARE NO CHILDREN WHO DON'T CONSTRUCT OR SENSE THESE ESCAPE ROUTES, THESE INSTANCES OF BECOMING-ANIMAL. AND THE ANIMAL, AS A BECOMING, HAS NOTHING TO DO WITH EITHER A FATHER SUBSTITUTE OR AN ARCHETYPE. FOR, INASMUCH AS HE IS A JEW WHO LEAVES THE COUNTRY TO GET ESTABLISHED IN THE CITY, THE FATHER IS NO DOUBT CAUGHT IN A MOVEMENT OF REAL DETERRITORIALIZATION; BUT HE NEVER CEASES TO RETERRITORIALIZE IN HIS FAMILY, IN HIS BUSINESS, IN THE SYSTEM OF HIS AUTHORITY AND SUBMISSIONS. AS FOR ARCHETYPES, THEY ARE PROCESSES OF SPIRITUAL RETERRITORIALIZATION. FORMS OF BECOMING-ANIMAL ARE JUST THE OPPOSITE: AT LEAST IN PRINCIPAL, THEY ARE ABSOLUTE DETERRITORIALIZATIONS EMBEDDED IN THE ARID WORLD WHICH KAFKA HAS ACTIVATED. "MY WORLD'S POWER OF ATTRACTION IS GREAT TOO, THOSE WHO LOVE ME LOVE ME BECAUSE I HAVE BEEN ABANDONED, AND PERHAPS IT IS NOT THAT THEY LOVE ME AS WEISS'S VACUUM, BUT BECAUSE THEY FEEL THAT IN MY GOOD MOMENTS AND IN

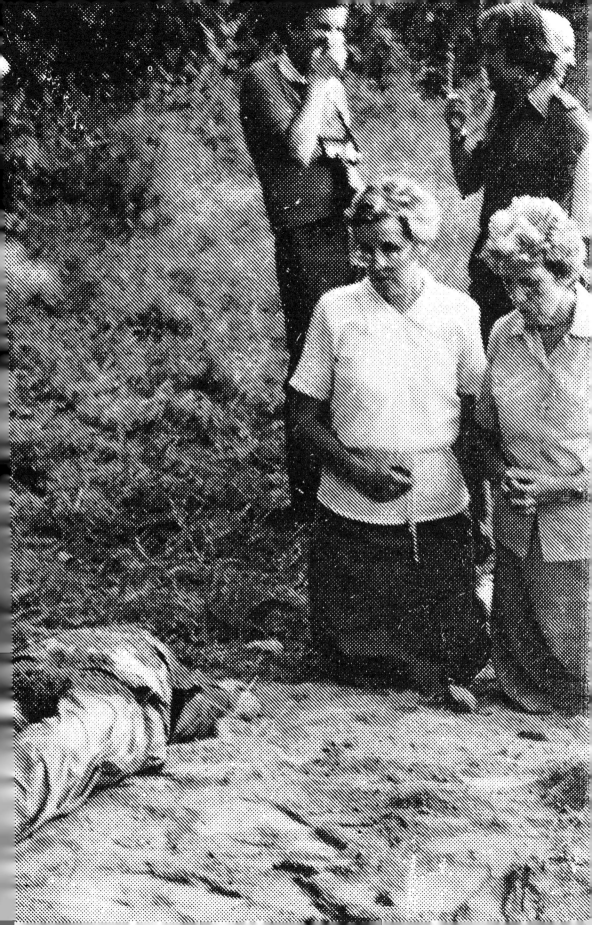

ANOTHER SPHERE, I AM ACCORDED THE FREEDOM OF MOVEMENT WHICH IS COMPLETELY LACKING HERE." TO BECOME ANIMAL IS PRECISELY TO MAKE THE MOTION, TO TRACE ROUTE OF FLIGHT IN ALL ITS POSITIVITY, TO CROSS A THRESHOLD, TO REACH A CONTINUUM OF INTENSITIES WITH VALUE ONLY IN AND OF THEMSELVES, TO FIND A WORLD OF PURE INTENSITIES WHERE ALL FORMS AS WELL AS ALL SIGNIFICATIONS ARE UNDONE, SIGNIFIERS AND SIGNIFIEDS, IN FAVOR OF AN UNFORMED MATTER, OF DETERRITORIALIZED FLUX, OF NON-SIGNIFYING SIGNS. KAFKA'S ANIMALS NEVER REFER TO ARCHETYPES OR A MYTHOLOGY, BUT ONLY CORRESPOND TO GRADIENTS CROSSED, TO ZONES OF FREED INTENSITIES WHERE CONTENTS BREAK OUT OF THEIR FORMS, JUST AS EXPRESSIONS BREAK OUT OF THE SIGNIFIER WHICH FORMALIZES THEM. NOTHING IS LEFT BUT MOVEMENTS, VIBRATIONS, THRESHOLDS IN A DESERTED MATTER: ANIMALS, MICE, DOGS, APES, COCKROACHES CAN ONLY BE DISTINGUISHED BY VARIOUS THRESHOLDS, VARIOUS VIBRATIONS, BY SOME UNDERGROUND PASSAGEWAY IN THE TUBER OR BURROW. FOR THESE PASSAGEWAYS ARE UNDERGROUND INTENSITIES. IN THE BECOMING-MOUSE, A WHISTLING DEPRIVES WORDS OF THEIR MUSIC AND MEANING. IN THE BECOMING-APE, A COUGH "SEEMS WORRISOME," BUT HAS NO SIGNIFICANCE (BECOMING-CONSUMPTIVE-APE). IN THE BECOMING-INSECT, A PAINFUL SQUEEK WINS OUT OVER THE VOICE AND SCRAMBLES THE RESONANCE OF WORDS. GREGOR BECOMES A COCKROACH NOT ONLY IN ORDER TO FLEE FROM HIS FATHER, BUT MORE IMPORTANTLY, TO FIND A WAY OUT AT THE VERY POINT WHERE HIS FATHER COULD FIND NONE, IN ORDER TO FLEE FROM THE CHIEF CLERK, BUSINESS AND BUREAUCRATS, IN ORDER TO REACH THAT REGION WHERE THE VOICE NO LONGER DOES ANYTHING BUT BUZZ— "'DID YOU HEAR HIM SPEAKING? THAT WAS AN ANIMAL'S VOICE,' THE CHIEF CLERK DECLARED."

IT IS TRUE THAT KAFKA'S ANIMAL TEXTS ARE FAR MORE COMPLEX THAN WE SAY. OR, ON THE CONTRARY, FAR SIMPLER. IN "A REPORT TO AN ACADEMY" FOR EXAMPLE, IT IS NOT A QUESTION OF A BECOMING-ANIMAL FROM HUMAN, BUT A BECOMING-HUMAN FROM APE; THIS BECOMING IS PRESENTED AS A SIMPLE IMITATION; AND IF IT IS A QUESTION OF FINDING A WAY OUT (A WAY OUT AND NOT "FREEDOM"), THIS WAY OUT IS NOT THE RESULT OF FLIGHT, QUITE THE CONTRARY. BUT, ON ONE HAND, FLIGHT IS ONLY REJECTED AS USELESS MOTION IN SPACE, ONLY A SEEMINGLY LIBERATING MOTION; IN RETURN, FLIGHT IS AFFIRMED AS A FLEEING IN PLACE, FLIGHT BY INTENSITY ("THAT'S WHAT I'VE DONE, I'VE SNUCK AWAY. THERE WAS NO

OTHER SOLUTION FOR ME SINCE WE WARDED OFF THE POSSIBILITY OF FREEDOM."). ON THE OTHER HAND, THE IMITATION IS ONLY APPARENT SINCE WHAT IS AT STAKE IS NOT THE REPRODUCTION OF FIGURES, BUT THE PRODUCTION OF A CONTINUUM OF INTENSITIES IN AN APARALLEL AND ASYMMETRICAL EVOLUTION WHERE MAN DOES NOT BECOME LESS APE THAN THE APE BECOMES MAN. THE BECOMING IS A SEIZURE, A POSSESSION, AN ADDITIONAL VALUE, AND NEVER A REPRODUCTION OR IMITATION. "I WASN'T SEDUCED BY THE NOTION OF IMITATION, I IMITATED BECAUSE I WAS LOOKING FOR A WAY OUT, AND NOT FOR ANY OTHER REASON." IN REALITY, AN ANIMAL CAPTURED BY MAN IS DETERRITORIALIZED BY HUMAN FORCE, THE ENTIRE BEGINNING OF "A REPORT" INSISTS ON THIS POINT. BUT THE DETERRITORIALIZED ANIMAL FORCE IN TURN PRECIPITATES AND INTENSIFIES THE DETERRITORIALIZATION OF THE DETERRITORIALIZING HUMAN FORCE (IF IT CAN BE SO PUT). "MY APE NATURE FLED OUT OF ME, HEAD OVER HEELS AND AWAY, IN SUCH A WAY THAT AS A RESULT MY FIRST TEACHER BECAME APE-LIKE HIMSELF, AND SOON HAD TO GIVE UP TEACHING TO ENTER AN ASYLUM." THUS IS CONSTITUTED A CONJUNCTION OF DETERRITORIALIZING FLUXES WHICH OVERFLOWS THE LIMITS OF STILL TERRITORIAL IMITATION. IN THE SAME MANNER, THE ORCHID SEEMS TO REPRODUCE A BEE'S IMAGE, BUT DETERRITORIALIZES MORE PROFOUNDLY IN IT AT THE SAME TIME THAT THE BEE, IN TURN, DETERRITORIALIZES IN COUPLING WITH THE ORCHID: SEIZURE OF A BIT OF CODE AND NOT IMAGE REPRODUCTION. IN "INVESTIGATIONS OF A DOG," ANY INKLING OF RESEMBLANCE IS EVEN MORE ENERGETICALLY ELIMINATED: KAFKA ATTACKS "THE SUSPICIOUS TEMPTATIONS OF RESEMBLANCE WHICH IMAGINATION MAY PROPOSE TO HIM;" THROUGH HIS SOLITUDE, THE DOG SEEKS TO GRAB THE GREATEST DIFFERENCE, THE SCHIZO DIFFERENCE.

THESE THEN ARE THE TWO EFFECTS OF THE DEVELOPMENT OR COMIC BLOATING OF OEDIPUS: THE DISCOVERY A CONTRARIO OF OTHER TRIANGLES, THE A FORTIORI MARKING OUT OF THE ORPHANED BECOMING-ANIMAL'S ESCAPE ROUTES. NO TEXT WOULD SEEM TO SHOW THE TIE BETWEEN THESE TWO ASPECTS BETTER THAN "THE METAMORPHOSIS." THE BUREAUCRATIC TRIANGLE PROGRESSIVELY COMES TOGETHER: FIRST THERE IS THE CHIEF CLERK WHO COMES IN ORDER TO MENACE, TO EXACT COMPLIANCE; THEN THERE IS THE FATHER WHO HAS RETURNED TO WORK AT THE BANK AND WHO SLEEPS IN HIS UNIFORM THEREBY MAKING EVIDENT THE YET EXTERIOR FORCE TO WHICH HE IS SUBJECTED, AS IF "EVEN AT HOME HE EXPECTED TO HEAR THE VOICE

OF HIS SUPERIOR;" FINALLY, ALL OF A SUDDEN THERE IS THE INTRUSION OF THE THREE BUREAUCRATIC BOARDERS WHO NOW PENETRATE THE VERY FAMILY, SUBSTITUTE IN IT, TAKE THEIR SEATS "IN THE PLACES WHICH THE FATHER, THE MOTHER AND GREGOR FORMERLY OCCUPIED." AND, CORRELATIVELY, THERE IS GREGOR'S WHOLE BECOMING-ANIMAL, HIS BECOMING-BEETLE, MAY-BUG, DUNG-BEETLE, COCKROACH, WHICH TRACES THE INTENSE ESCAPE ROUTE IN RELATION TO THE FAMILY TRIANGLE, AND ESPECIALLY IN RELATION TO THE BUREAUCRATIC AND COMMERCIAL TRIANGLE.

BUT WHY, AT THE VERY INSTANT ONE BELIEVES HE HAS CAUGHT HOLD OF THE TIE BETWEEN OEDIPUS' BEYOND AND BEFORE (AU-DELÀ ET EN-DECÀ), IS ONE FARTHER AWAY THAN EVER FROM A WAY OUT? WHY DOES ONE REMAIN STUCK IN AN IMPASS? IT IS BECAUSE THERE IS STILL DANGER OF A RESURGENCE OF OEDIPAL MASTERY. THE INCREASING PERVERSITY OF THE USAGE HAS NOT BEEN ADEQUATE TO EXORCIZE ALL RE-CLOSING, ALL RECONSTITUTION OF THE FAMILY TRIANGLE WHICH ITSELF TAKES CHARGE OF OTHER TRIANGLES AS IT DOES OF THE ANIMAL ROUTES. IN THIS SENSE, "THE METAMORPHOSIS" IS THE EXEMPLARY STORY OF A RE-OEDIPALIZATION. IT COULD BE SAID THAT AT A CERTAIN MOMENT GREGOR'S DETERRITORIALIZING PROCESS, HIS BECOMING-ANIMAL, WAS BLOCKED. IS GREGOR AT FAULT IN THAT HE DOES NOT DARE TO GO ALL THE WAY? HIS SISTER WANTED TO CLEAR OUT HIS WHOLE ROOM IN ORDER TO PLEASE HIM. BUT GREGOR REFUSES TO ALLOW THEM TO TAKE AWAY THE PORTRAIT OF THE LADY MUFFLED IN FURS. HE CLINGS TO THIS PORTRAIT AS TO A LAST TERRITORIALIZED IMAGE. IN REALITY, THIS IS WHAT HIS SISTER CANNOT TOLERATE. SHE ACCEPTED HIM, LIKE GREGOR SHE WANTED SCHIZO INCEST, HIGH VOLTAGE INCEST, INCEST WITH THE SISTER AS OPPOSED TO OEDIPAL INCEST, INCEST WHICH MANIFESTS A NON-HUMAN SEXUALITY LIKE BECOMING-ANIMAL. BUT, JEALOUS OF THE PORTRAIT, SHE BEGINS TO HATE GREGOR AND CONDEMNS HIM. FROM THEN ON, THE BECOMING-ANIMAL ASPECT OF GREGOR'S DETERRITORIALIZATION FAILS: HE ALLOWS HIMSELF TO BE RE-OEDIPALIZED BY THE TOSS OF AN APPLE AND CAN ONLY DIE, APPLE ENCRUSTED IN HIS BACK. LIKEWISE, THE FAMILY'S DETERRITORIALIZATION INTO MORE COMPLEX AND DIABOLICAL TRIANGLES HAS NO ROOM TO CARRY ON: THE FATHER KICKS OUT THE THREE BUREAUCRATIC BOARDERS, RETURN TO THE OEDIPAL TRIANGLE'S PATERNAL PRINCIPAL, THE FAMILY CLOSES HAPPILY IN ON ITSELF. ONE CANNOT EVEN BE CERTAIN THAT GREGOR WAS AT FAULT. RATHER, ISN'T IT TRUE THAT FORMS OF BECOMING-ANIMAL FAIL TO FULFILL THEIR OFFICE AND ALWAYS RETAIN AN AMBIGUITY THAT MAKES THEM INSUFFICIENT AND CONDEMNS THEM TO FAILURE? AREN'T ANIMALS THEMSELVES STILL TOO FORMED, TOO SIGNIFYING, TOO TERRITORIALIZED? DOESN'T THE BECOMING-ANIMAL, AS A WHOLE, OSCILLATE BETWEEN A SCHIZO ESCAPE AND AN OEDIPAL IMPASS? OEDIPAL ANIMAL PAR EXCELLENCE, THE DOG, OF WHICH KAFKA FREQUENTLY SPEAKS IN HIS DIARY AND LETTERS, IS AT THE SAME TIME A SCHIZO BEAST, SUCH AS THE MUSICIAN DOGS IN "INVESTIGATIONS" OR THE DIABOLICAL DOG IN "THE TEMPTATION AT THE VILLAGE." THE FACT IS THAT KAFKA'S PRINCIPAL ANIMALESQUE TEXTS WERE WRITTEN JUST BEFORE THE TRIAL, OR COEXTENSIVE WITH IT AS A COUNTERPART TO THAT NOVEL WHICH IS FREED FROM ANY ANIMAL PROBLEMATIC, IN FAVOR OF A HIGHER CONCERN.

GILLES DELEUZE AND FELIZ GUATTARI
EXCERPTED FROM KAFKA
TRANSLATED BY RACHEL McCOMAS

THE DOGS

THE CERTAINTY OF MY COMING DEPARTURE HAD RESTORED MY TASTE FOR EMMA, ALTHOUGH MY DREAMS REMAINED UNDER THE SIGN OF THE HUNTER'S MOON. WHY DIDN'T I CONFIDE MY PLAN TO HER? WHY SHOULD I? THE PRESENT IS THE PRESENT AND THAT'S ENOUGH. BESIDES, I MYSELF HAD NOT SET THE DAY.

THERE CAME A MILDER EVENING WITH A LITTLE FOG ON THE HORIZON, AND I SAW AS ON THE FIRST EVENING THE MOON EMERGED FROM THE SEA. IT WAS FULL: THE CYCLE WAS COMPLETED. I DECIDED THE TIME HAD COME. I LOVED EMMA SO MUCH THAT I FILLED HER WITH MYSELF, AND, WHEN SHE HAD GONE TO SLEEP, I WENT TO A RATHER DISTANT CREEK WHERE THE BOATS WERE KEPT. IT MUST HAVE BEEN TWO IN THE MORNING: I HAD JUST ENOUGH TIME TO REACH THE ISLAND BEFORE DAYBREAK.

THE WAVELESS OCEAN BARELY RIPPLED BENEATH THE PROW OF MY BOAT, ALTHOUGH I USED THE OARS IN ORDER TO GO FASTER THAN THE COMING DAY. THE MOON WAS IN FRONT OF ME, BUT SETTING, MILKY AND VEILED. FATIGUE RENDERED ME ACUTELY AWARE OF ALL THAT WAS GOING ON BETWEEN THE AIR AND THE WATER—ACTIVITY TOO INTANGIBLE TO BE CAPTURED IN A WORD. I WAS ON MY WAY; I HAD NEITHER MEMORY NOR PRESENT; I WAS CROSSING. AND DOUBTLESS—FOR AT THAT MOMENT MY MIND COULD DISCERN NO DIVISION BETWEEN THEM—TIME WAS CARRYING ME AS THE SEA WAS CARRYING MY BOAT.

SUDDENLY BEFORE ME, I SAW THE ISLAND, WHILE A PINK FINGER ON THE HORIZON ANNOUNCED THE ADVENT OF DAY. THE LOW COASTLINE WAS A MERE MARGIN OF SAND AT THE BASE OF AN ABRUPT CLIFF. I SET ABOUT TO FIND A MORE FAVORABLE PORT, BUT THE CLIFF CONTINUED TO PRESENT THE SAME RIGHT ANGLE. I WAS STEERING AROUND THE HORN OF A SMALL PROMONTORY WHEN I SAW THE YACHT WHICH HAD BELONGED TO THE COUNTESS. IT TRIGGERED IN ME A NEW FEAR, PERHAPS BECAUSE IT WAS TOO WHITE; I DOUBLED BACK AND DECIDED TO LAND ON THE NARROW BEACH, THEN CONTINUE ON FOOT. I THEREFORE MANOEUVERED IN THAT DIRECTION AND, HAVING TOUCHED SHORE, BUSIED MYSELF WITH LANDING MY BOAT AND FINDING SHELTER FOR IT. SUDDENLY A NOISE BEHIND ME MADE ME TURN AROUND: AN ENORMOUS NIGGER ACCOMPANIED BY TWO MASTIFFS WAS WATCHING ME.

I SMILED AT THE MAN: HE REMAINED IMPASSIVE. HIS EYES AND THOSE OF THE ANIMALS EXAMINED ME WITH AN ABSENCE OF CURIOSITY AND COLDNESS THAT WAS FRIGHTENING. THE SUN WAS RISING BEHIND ME; ITS REDNESS, ENVELOPING ME, GAVE ME COURAGE. I STEPPED FORWARD AND SAID:

"I WOULD LIKE TO SEE THE COUNTESS."

THE DOGS STRETCHED THEIR NECKS TOWARDS ME; THE MAN DID NOT CHANGE HIS STATUE-LIKE POSITION. I CONTINUED:

"I HAVE MET THE COUNTESS. I WOULD LIKE ... ."

THE MAN MADE AN IMPERCEPTIBLE SIGN, AND THE TWO MONSTERS LEAPT ON ME. BEFORE I COULD THINK OF MOVING, I WAS THROWN ON THE SAND; ONE OF THE BEASTS GRIPPED MY THROAT WHILE THE OTHER SAT ASTRIDE ME. NEITHER OF THEM HARMED ME, BUT I COULD FEEL THEY WERE READY TO TEAR ME APART ON COMMAND. FEAR CAUSED RED FLAKES TO SWIM IN MY THROAT AND MY EYES. BEHIND THAT SCREEN MY BRAIN WAS WORKING, SEARCHING FOR AN EXPLANATION, WATCHING, NOTING, PREPARING MY NERVES TO OBEY INSTANT-LY. AND THEN I REMEMBERED: "WHATEVER HAPPENS," SHE HAD SAID, "SUCK IN YOUR STOMACH, BREATHE DEEPLY, SPACE YOUR BREATHING REGULARLY."

A SHADOW PASSED OVER ME: THE NIGGER WAS APPROACHING. HIS IMMENSE BODY DOMINATED ME, HIS EYES, STILL COLD, FIXED ME FROM ABOVE. I SAW HIM BEND HIS LEGS, THEN MOVE HIS ENORMOUS FOOT TOWARD MY FACE, SLOWLY, SO THAT I SHOULD HAVE PLENTY OF TIME TO CONTEMPLATE THE REPULSIVE PALLOR OF THAT GOURD STRIATED WITH PINK WRINKLES WHICH WAS GOING TO CRUSH ME. THE FOOT STOPPED A FEW INCHES FROM MY EYES. THERE WAS A SECOND OF INFINITE ANGUISH IN WHICH I DID MY UTMOST TO CONTROL MY BREATHING AND NOT TO BUDGE. HE WITHDREW HIS FOOT. THE DOGS LET ME GO.

I REMEMBER. THE MAN MADE ANOTHER SIGN. THE TWO WILD ANIMALS ATTACKED AGAIN. FURIOUSLY, THEY TORE OFF MY CLOTHES. I DIDN'T MOVE. I KNEW I MUST NOT MOVE. BUT THE DOGS WORKED SKILL-FULLY WITH THEIR TEETH AND CLAWS: THEY DIDN'T HARM ME. IN A MATTER OF SECONDS I WAS NAKED. THE DOGS SAT ON EITHER SIDE OF ME, THEIR LIPS CURLED BACK IN A SNARL, THEIR TONGUES HANGING OUT: THEY WATCHED ME CLOSELY. THE

MAN CONTINUED TO STAND OVER ME. WITHOUT MOVING MY HEAD, I FOLLOWED THE THREE BRUTES WITH MY EYES.

JUST AS I THOUGHT THE ORDEAL WAS DRAWING TO A CLOSE, THE MAN POINTED TO MY GROIN AND THE TWO WOLFISH DOGS POUNCED ON MY CROTCH. I FELT A SHIVER DOWN MY BACK AS THEIR TONGUES TOUCHED ME. I CHOKED BACK THE CRY WHICH ROSE IN MY THROAT. THEY WERE NOT GOING TO DEVOUR ME—NOT YET. ANOTHER MINUTE AND I WAS NO LONGER STRUGGLING AGAINST FEAR BUT AGAINST THE ABOMINABLE TEMPTATION WHICH THOSE TONGUES AWOKE IN MY CROTCH, AROUND MY SCROTUM, ALONG MY PHALLUS. FROM HEAD TO HEELS I RESISTED. I EXERTED MY WILLPOWER MIGHTILY TO KEEP FROM BECOMING ERECT, BUT THE LENGTH OF THEIR TONGUES GAVE THE DOGS A TERRIBLE ADVANTAGE: NO MOUTH HAD EVER HAD SUCH POWER OVER ME. THE LONG PINK WHIPS HANGING FROM THEIR MAWS HAD AN AMAZING SUPPLENESS AND ENABLED THE TWO QUADRUPEDS TO ENCIRCLE MY PRICK AND PROBE MY ANUS WITH IRRESISTIBLE VIGOR. AND THEIR SLAVER, WITH WHICH I WAS ABUNDANTLY DRENCHED, FACILI-TATED THEIR TASK BY GIVING MY MEMBER THE ILLUSION OF ENTERING A HOSPITABLE PORT.

IN THAT INSTANT, MY PENIS WAS THE OTHER, WHICH THE SHEER URGE TO FUCK COMMANDED TO STAND UPRIGHT IN SPITE OF MYSELF. THE THICK UNDER-VEIN INFLATED MY PENIS IN REGULAR THROBS, INEXORABLY; I WATCHED THIS PROCESS WITH A KIND OF HORROR, WITH THE FEELING OF PARTICIPATING IN SOME UNCLEAN ACT. WHEN MY PENIS HAD ATTAINED ITS LARGEST DIMENSIONS, I SAW IT BECOME AN ENORMOUS BONE, SO TO SPEAK, IN THE MOUTH OF THE DOG WHO WAS PULLING AT IT. THE NIGGER LEANED OVER ME; A VAGUE SMILE SHOWED HIS TEETH. SUDDENLY HE DREW A DAGGER FROM HIS POCKET AND AS THE DOG LEAPT AWAY, HE POINTED HIS WEAPON AT MY BELLY.

A FLASH. A MARK ON MY SKIN. I WAITED FOR THE PAIN. I DIDN'T DARE LOOK. THE NIGGER STRAIGHT-ENED UP, STARING ME IN THE FACE, WITH THE KNIFE STILL EXTENDING FROM HIS RIGHT HAND. I DIDN'T MOVE. THE BLADE WAS ABOVE MY EYES. IT FELL. IT GRAZED MY FOREHEAD SLIGHTLY AT THE BASE OF MY NOSE, THEN WAS LIFTED AGAIN.

NOW MY GAZE, TOO, WAS COLD. THE NIGGER DREW BACK. I COULD NO LONGER SEE HIM, BUT HIS SHADOW COVERED ME COMPLETELY. THE AIR

WHISTLED; THERE WAS ANOTHER FLASH: HIS KNIFE FLEW TOWARD MY GROIN. NO PAIN. I LOWERED MY CHIN A LITTLE. I SAW THE HILT OF THE DAGGER STICKING OUT OF THE SAND, RIGHT BETWEEN MY LEGS. THE NIGGER WAS STANDING AT MY FEET, HIS SMILE DISPLAYING MORE TEETH.

HE WHISTLED. THE DOGS, WHO HAD DRAWN BACK, RETURNED. AGAIN HIS HAND POINTED TO MY BELLY, AND THE BEASTS RESUMED THEIR TASKS, FOR THE BONE HAD LOST MUCH OF ITS SIZE DURING THE KNIFE-THROWING. THE TONGUES REKINDLED MY SHAME, AND I WATCHED MY BELLY HOISTING ITS MAST. I WAS WATCHING AND I WAS WATCHING MYSELF WATCHING. THERE WAS A STRANGE DISTANCE WITHIN ME WHICH CONTAINED THE HALL OF MIRRORS WHERE MY SELF-IMAGE DWELT—A SHATTERED IMAGE INTO WHICH MY FUTURE BLED INTO THE PRESENT.

I WAS ERECT. ALL OF A SUDDEN I ACCEPTED THE FACT. THE FIRE HAD TO BURN ITSELF OUT. I RAISED MY HIPS TOWARDS THEIR MOUTHS. ONE OF THE TONGUES WAS RELENTLESSLY FLICKING ME FROM MY BALLS TO MY ANUS; THE OTHER ONE WAS WRAPPED AROUND MY PENIS—ENVELOPED IT, SQUEEZED IT, DID WONDERS. AND I LET MYSELF GO, ENTERED NATURALLY INTO THE HORROR OF IT—FOR AFTER ALL, THIS WAS NATURE TOO. NO LIMIT, AN ANCIENT VOICE WITHIN ME CRIED, NO LIMIT, EXCEPT PLEASURE.

WHAT I WAS GOING THROUGH EXCEEDED EVERY-THING I COULD HAVE IMAGINED, AND IT SEEMED TO ME THEN, AS THE TWO DOGS PLAYED WITH ME, THAT I WAS PAST THE HIGHEST PITCH; THIS REASSURED ME, BUT IN THE MIDST OF MY PLEASURE I DID NOT REALIZE THAT THE IMPOSSIBLE GIVES RISE TO THE IMPOSSIBLE.

I STARTED TO BECOME AWARE OF THIS AS DROPS OF A MUSKY ESSENCE SPURTED ON ME, MAKING ME REALIZE I WAS NOT THE ONLY ONE ERECT; FOR INDEED, UNDER THE MONSTERS' BELLIES I COULD SEE THEIR LONG PENISES WHOSE REDNESS AND JUTTING MEATUS LEFT NO DOUBT AS TO THE DEGREE OF THEIR EXCITEMENT. THOSE REPUL-SIVELY THIN MEMBERS CAN SWELL CONSIDERABLY IN THE HEAT OF ACTION ONCE THEY HAVE ENTERED THEIR RECEPTACLE; SO MUCH SO,THAT HEAVY WORK AND MUCH TIME ARE REQUIRED BEFORE THEY CAN WITHDRAW. FOR THE TIME BEING THEY WERE IN INCESSANT MOVEMENT, ALTERNATELY CAUSING THEIR MEMBERS TO STICK OUT OF THEIR FURRY SHEATHS AND THEN PLUNGE BACK INTO THEM. I

COULD HARDLY DECEIVE MYSELF ABOUT THE INTENTION THE DOGS HAD IN TERMS OF ME: BUT WHAT I DIDN'T KNOW WAS THAT A BEING ALIEN TO THEIR RACE HAD ENLARGED THE FIELD OF THEIR INSTINCT BY TEMPERING IT WITH HIS OWN IMAGINA-TION.

I BEGAN TO GUESS THIS WAS THE CASE WHEN ONE OF THE MONSTERS—THE ONE WHO HAD PERFORMED MIRACLES WITH HIS TONGUE IN THE SERVICE OF MY ORGAN—SUDDENLY CHANGED HIS POSITION WITHOUT LETTING GO OF HIS OBJECT, AND STOOD DIRECTLY OVER ME: HIS REAR LEGS PLANTED ON EITHER SIDE OF MY HEAD, HIS BALLS JUST ABOVE MY EYES. HIS PENIS NOW DRIPPED ON MY NECK AND CHEST AS IT JERKED ABOUT IN AN ACCELERATED RHYTHM. MOREOVER, IN HIS INCREASING EXCITE-MENT THE ANIMAL BEGAN TO KICK UP THE SAND SO VIOLENTLY THAT I WAS SOON COVERED WITH IT. THE NIGGER GAVE A SHORT CRY. THE ANIMAL HESI-TATED AS THOUGH IN THOUGHT, THEN CROUCHED DOWN, RUBBED HIS HAIRY MUZZLE IN MY FACE AND BEGAN USING HIS TONGUE WHILE HIS THIGHS AND HAUNCHES BEGAN TO QUIVER STRANGELY; HIS BALLS SLAPPED AGAINST ME. HE BEGAN PANTING. I REALIZED HE WANTED TO FIND A HOLE. I SHOUTED: "NO, STOP!"

THE NIGGER GAVE ME A KICK TO SHUT ME UP AND THE OTHER DOG INCREASED HIS ARDENT ATTEN-TIONS: HIS DAMP NOSE SLIPPED BETWEEN MY BUTTOCKS, SNIFFED AT MY ASSHOLE, ROOTED AT IT WITH HIS MUZZLE AND THEN BEGAN USING HIS TONGUE, DARTING IT IN AND OUT, DROPPING GOBS OF SALIVA IN AN ATTEMPT TO FORCE OPEN THE SPHINCTER. MY COCK FLAILED VIOLENTLY BACK AND FORTH, THE DESIRE TO FUCK DEADENED ALL RESTRAINT.

MY RIDER BENT HIS LEGS, STRETCHED OUT HIS CHEST, LIFTED HIS HAUNCHES SLIGHTLY AND AIMED HIS COCK AT MY MOUTH. I REMEMBERED MY MOTHER'S REMARK: "IT SMELLS LIKE A WILD ANIMAL," SHE SAID TURNING HER HEAD AWAY. THE MONSTER'S LANCE WAS ON MY LIPS; IT KNOCKED AGAINST THEM CONTINUALLY AND COVERED THEM WITH A BITTER-TASTING LUBRICANT, THEN FORCED THEM OPEN, WEDGING BETWEEN MY JAW AND CHEEK, AND CARESSED THE GUMS SO PLEA-SURABLY THAT I OPENED MY MOUTH. AND THEN I HAD IN MY MOUTH THAT STRANGE THING, THAT HORRIBLE THING, THAT SHAMEFUL MEMBER, AND YET I FOUND NEITHER SHAME NOR HORROR WITHIN ME. WHY DID I HAVE TO LEARN SO CRUDELY THAT A DOG IS WORTH A PRIEST . . . NOW, A GENTLE IN AND

OUT MOVEMENT WAS WRITING ON MY TONGUE THAT ALL DOGMA IS HATEFUL, BECAUSE IT CASTRATES THE IMAGINATION AND THEREFORE IS AN OBSTACLE TO EXPERIENCE.

THE WRITING BECAME URGENT AND MY TONGUE BEGAN TO MOVE: IT EXPLORED THE GLANS, THE BEVEL BARELY APPARENT, AND THE BITTER, DRIPPING MEATUS. THE DOG TENSED HIS MUSCLES, EAGERLY ATTENTIVE. HE STOPPED MOVING HIS TONGUE. THEN MINE BEGAN MOVING AGAIN: IT WRAPPED ITSELF AROUND THE GLANS, MOVED UP AND DOWN SPREADING SALIVA ALL ALONG IT, LICKING AND TICKLING. A LONG SHUDDER WENT THROUGH THE ANIMAL AS IT TURNED BACK TOWARD MY MOUTH. BUT AS WE WERE ABOUT TO PITCH INTO THE FRAY, THE NIGGER'S SHADOW FELL UPON US. WAS HE COMING CLOSER THE BETTER TO WATCH US, OR WAS HE GOING TO TEAR ME AWAY FROM MY LOVER? I WAS ALREADY EXPRESSING MY RAGE IN GRUNTS BECAUSE I COULD NOT PRONOUNCE ANY WORD, SO BUSY WAS I IN SUCKING HIS THING THAT SLID BETWEEN MY LIPS AGAIN AND AGAIN.

LODGED AGAINST MY PALATE WAS A CARESS, A CARESS I HAD DREAMED ABOUT WITHOUT KNOWING WHAT THE DREAM MEANT. IN MY MOUTH HIS THING GREW ROUND AND SWELLED UP; IT WAS AS THOUGH MY TONGUE WERE FLAT ON THE GROUND AND MY JAWS WERE DISTENDED TO FORM THE MOST STUPEFIED O MY LIPS HAD EVER MADE. I BEGAN TO SUFFOCATE WITH MY NOSE BURIED IN HIS FUR; I WAS SUFFOCATING AND I MOVED MY ARMS AND LEGS LIKE AN INEXPERIENCED SWIMMER WHOSE EVERY MOVEMENT, INSTEAD OF HELPING HIM, DOES NOTHING BUT ENSURE HIS PERDITION.

THE NIGGER MUST HAVE BEEN WAITING FOR THAT MOMENT: I HEARD HIM CRUNCHING THE SAND AROUND ME AND THEN CHASING AWAY THE DOG WHO WAS BADGERING THE HOLE IN MY ASS—AND WHO WAS LOATH TO LET GO, BECAUSE HIS TONGUE HAD MADE SOME PROGRESS. THEN THE NIGGER GRABBED MY FEET, LIFTED MY LEGS, TWINED THEM AROUND THE NECK OF THE ANIMAL THAT I WAS SUCKING, THEN HE SEIZED MY HANDS TWINING THEM AROUND THE CROUP OF MY RIDER SO THAT I FOUND MYSELF HANGING UNDER ITS BELLY. THE ANIMAL'S HUGE KNOT THAT I HAD IN MY MOUTH HELD ME FAST, EVEN MORE FIRMLY THAN MY KNOTTED LIMBS DID.

THERE WAS A GUTTURAL CRY AND THE DOG IMMEDIATELY STARTED OFF AT FULL SPEED. MY BACK SCRAPED AGAINST THE SAND AND WAS TORN OPEN BY THE STONES; FLAMES ENVELOPED ME; THE

AIR WAS ROARING IN MY EARS. MY HEART WAS IN MY THROAT. AND EVEN THOUGH I WAS SUFFOCATING, ALL I COULD FEEL WAS THE INSANE THROBBING OF THE DOG'S COCK IN MY MOUTH AND MY OWN SWOLLEN COCK IN HIS MOUTH. HECATE WAS BEATING THE COUNTRYSIDE WITH HER MONSTERS: THE CRESCENT WAS BLACK ON HER BROW, AND MY BODY, A MERE CRESCENT STRETCHED BETWEEN TWO ORAL CAVITIES, WAS BLACK AS WELL. THAT SHADOW SUDDENLY ACROSS THE THRESHOLD! THE CAGE IS SO NARROW! MY HEART IS GOING TO STOP. THE AIR IS ROARING; I HAD NEVER REALIZED HOW LIKE AN OCEAN THE AIR CAN BE WITH WAVES CRASHING AND ROLLING. FROM THE VERY HEAVENS, HUGE WAVES WITH THEIR BLACK WALLS WERE HURTLING TOWARD ME AND WERE CREATING HIDEOUS HOLLOWS INTO WHICH WE WERE GOING TO FALL. AND THE LAST ONE WOULD SURELY DROWN ME.

WHEN I REGAINED MY SENSES, THE TWO DOGS WERE STARING AT ME: ONE WAS QUIETLY SITTING THERE, HIS TONGUE LOLLING; THE OTHER ONE WAS TRYING TO NIP AT WHITISH FILAMENTS DROOLING FROM HIS CHIN. BEHIND THEM, STANDING VERY STRAIGHT WITH HIS LEGS APART, THE NIGGER WAS WATCHING ME. WHEN OUR GLANCES MET, HE CAME UP TO ME, LEANED OVER AND GRABBED ME BY THE NAPE, PICKED ME UP, DRAGGED ME BEHIND HIM, AND THREW ME VIOLENTLY INTO THE SEA. THE SHOCK OF THE WATER BROUGHT ME BACK TO MYSELF AND TO THE PRESENT. I WAS THIRSTY AS THOUGH I HAD EATEN VERY SPICY FOOD. I WASHED AND SHOOK MYSELF OFF, AND THEN CAME OVER TO THE MAN AND HIS ANIMALS.

"I WANT TO SEE THE COUNTESS," I SAID.

A FLASH OF HATE GLIMMERED IN THE NIGGER'S EYES; THE DOGS THREW THEMSELVES ON ME AGAIN AND KNOCKED ME TO THE GROUND. THE DOG WHO HAD LATELY LICKED THE HOLE IN MY ASS SEEMED MUCH MORE EXCITED THAN HIS COMPANION. HE STARTED TO MOVE HIS DAGGER IN AND OUT OF ITS SHEATH, AND IT WAS HE THIS TIME WHO TRIED TO GET MY COCK HARD. RESIGNED TO A REPLAY OF THE PREVIOUS PERFORMANCE, I DECIDED TO LET MYSELF GO AND TO ACCEPT THE RITUAL. BUT AS SOON AS I HAD REACHED THE DESIRED STATE, INSTEAD OF STRIKING MY MOUTH WITH THE TIP OF HIS BLADE, THE DOG SUDDENLY TURNED HIS BACK ON ME. DRUGGED BY MY OWN DESIRE, I DID NOT MOVE FROM THE GROUND, MY MAST UPRIGHT AND SHINY WITH SLIME IN THE SUNLIGHT. THE NIGGER SCREAMED, BUT SEEING THAT I STILL DID NOT

REACT, HE GRABBED ME UNDER THE ARMS AND THREW ME DOWN ON MY KNEES, SEIZED MY COCK IN ONE OF HIS ENORMOUS HANDS AND DRAGGED THE RUTTING DOG CLOSER TO ME WITH HIS OTHER HAND. THE ANIMAL, PERFECTLY TRAINED, IMMEDIATELY BACKED UP TOWARDS ME AND LOWERED HIS HIND END SO AS TO PLACE THE HOLE IN HIS ASS AT THE RIGHT ANGLE. THE NIGGER STEERED MY COCK TOWARDS THE HOLE OF HIS FAVORITE'S ASS, AS HE FORCED ME TO GRAB HOLD OF THE DOG'S THROBBING COCK. THE MONSTER IMPALED HIMSELF ON MY PENIS IN ONE QUICK MOVEMENT AND TIGHTENING THE RING OF HIS ASS AROUND MY STALK, HE TRIED TO EXTRACT MY ESSENCE OF MAN. BUT SINCE I WAS NOT MANIPULATING THE DOG'S PENIS AT ALL,THE DOG TURNED AND STARED QUIZZICALLY AT ME AND THEN AT HIS MASTER. THE NIGGER DECIDED THAT I NEEDED A HELPING HAND AND, HOLDING HIS DAGGER BY THE BLADE, RAMMED IN ONE STROKE THE HANDLE UP MY ASS.

SOMETHING STRANGE HAPPENED IN MY BELLY WHERE CONTRARY FEELINGS OVERWHELMED ME: A TERRIBLE PAIN IN MY BATTERED ASS AND AN EQUALLY TERRIBLE PLEASURE IN MY BALLS. THE RESULT WAS A FRANTIC EFFORT ON MY PART TO FUCK AS WELL AS JERK OFF THE DOG. MY ESSENCE SPURTED IN UNISON WITH THE ANIMAL'S WHO BROKE AWAY HOWLING. I FELL FACE FORWARD ON THE SAND, STRETCHED OUT ON THE THRESHOLD OF THE INFINITE.

AND YET MY ASS, STUFFED WITH A DAGGER HANDLE

WAS THERE FOR ALL TO SEE, AND FLASHING ITS BLADE IN THE SUNLIGHT.

THE NIGGER HELPED ME TO MY FEET.

"DO YOU WANT TO SEE THE COUNTESS?"

I STARED STRAIGHT AT HIM AND DID NOT ANSWER. AND THEN, SINCE HE APPEARED TO BE EXPECTING AN ANSWER, I DREW BACK MY LIPS AND SHOWED HIM MY CLENCHED TEETH.

"THE COUNTESS WILL BE PLEASED TO SEE YOU. SHE IS EXPECTING YOU AND I WAS SENT TO WELCOME YOU."

HE TURNED ME AROUND GENTLY, WITHDREW THE WEAPON IMPALING ME AND POINTED AT THE SEA:

"YOU SHOULD WASH AGAIN."

I WALKED STIFFLY AND CAREFULLY TOWARDS THE OCEAN, BATHED VERY LEISURELY, AND THEN CAME BACK TO THE NIGGER.

"PLEASE, FOLLOW ME."

BERNARD NOEL

TRANSLATED BY DANIEL SLOATE

TRUDY OR THE SECRET APHID

TRUDY HAD A CROTCH BEAUTIFUL. LARGELY WELL-PROPORTIONED EXCEPT FOR THE HEAD, WHICH WAS REALLY A CONVEX, INSIDE-OUT NAVEL. THIS HE DULY CONTEMPLATED FROM DAWN TILL STAR-RISE. THEN OTHERS DID. HE HAD A SMALL ANT FOR PET WHICH HE KEPT IN AN OLD-FASHIONED TOOTHPASTE TUBE. HE LIKENED HIS DESTINY TO A SHIP'S AND THE ANT'S TO A CAPTAIN'S. WHICH IS TO SAY (OTHER THAN THE OBVIOUS) THAT TRUDY'S SENSE OF BALANCE WAS EROTIC IN THE EXTREME. THE ANT WOULD GRAZE UPON HIS FACE EAR AND NOSE HAIRS THEN WORK SLOWLY DOWN TO TRUDY'S

RUDDER. THIS HE WOULD STROKE, FONDLE, MANIPULATE AND STEER AS THROUGH IT WERE AN APHID UNTIL THE JUICES FLOWED. SO PASSED THE NIGHTS AND THE YEARS. WHEN TRUDY'S CROTCH BEAUTIFUL WENT TO POT, THE ANT DID NOT SEEM TO CARE. OH, IT RUBBED ITS HIND-LEGS TOGETHER MORE OFTEN, PERHAPS, WHEN ALONE, BUT YOUTH WILL OUT. BY-THE-BYE, THIS IS A HAPPY TALE AS I HAVE OMNISCIENTLY DECIDED AND THEREFORE IT WILL NOW END.

D. C. SLOATE

CHILD SEX

THE SILVER PIPE CAFE

ORPHANED AT NINE HE LEFT HIS VILLAGE ALONE AND CAME DOWN ON THE COAST BELOW THE SOUTHERN HILLS—ONCE AN INDEPENDENT SULTANATE WHERE THE MEN MADE THEIR LIVINGS AS PIRATES—SOME GRANDFATHERS NOW STILL REMEMBER—IN THEIR LATEEN RIGS WITH RED SAILS OR BLACK, LYING A QUARTER OF A MILE OUT IN THE SHALLOW BAY—LONGBOATS FETCH AND CARRY FROM THE SHIPS TO THE BEACH, WHITELY CURVED AND PALM LINED—THE TOWN: TIN-ROOFED HOUSES, SHOPS TILTING OVER THE GARBAGE IN THE CANALS, A CRACKED STUCCO CATHEDRAL IN THE STYLE OF GOA OR MACAO. AT THE FAR END OF TOWN, FACING THE SAND, A LONG SHED, THATCH-ROOFED AND DECAYED, THE SIVER PIPE CAFÉ—STAINED WALLS, TEA-POT SPUMES CAUGHT IN SLANTING SUN, LOW PLATFORMS AROUND THE ROOM WHERE HABITUÉS RECLINE, A YELLOW CAT, FLYSPECKED CALENDARS WITH COLOURED PRINTS OF GODS, RADIO CRACKLING WITH GAMELAN AND CHINESE POP TUNES— AND DARKLY SHADOWED AS THE STAGE BETWEEN WAKING AND SLEEP—A HYPNAGOGIC CAFÉ. AT TEN HE FIRST LEARNED HOW TO SERVE THE CUSTOMERS: THE OLDER BOYS TAUGHT HIM TO HEAT THE HASHISH OVER A BRAZIER TILL IT COULD BE CRUMBLED INTO LIITLE PASTILLES—THEN FILL THE BLACKSTONE BOWL OF THE LONGSTEMMED SILVER PIPE, CHOOSE HOT COALS AND ARRANGE THEM WITH TONGS OVER THE DRUG, TAMP THEM DOWN, TAKE A FEW PUFFS TO START THE SMOKE FLOWING, HAND IT OVER TO THE PATRON, ONE RUPIYAH PER PIPE, FETCH TEA AND CIGARETTES FOR THE OLD BROWN MEN IN THEIR FLOWER-PATTERNED LUNGHEES, DARK SAILORS WITH EARRINGS, A CHINESE OR MOSLEM MERCHANT, DISSOLUTE EUROPEAN ADVENTURER OR FAILED PRIEST. WITH THE TIPS HE EARNED HE COULD BUY RICE AND FISH, AND SLEPT AT NIGHT IN THE CAFÉ OR ON THE BEACH. AT FIRST HE FELT NO INTEREST IN THE DRUG—BUT THE OLDER BOYS SAVED UNBURNT REMNANTS AND CRUMBS AND SMOKED THEM, HUDDLED TOGETHER OUTSIDE THE BACK OF THE CAFÉ NEXT TO THE LATRINE, AND WHEN THEY LIT PIPES FOR CUSTOMERS THEY INHALED AS MUCH AS THEY COULD. IN THE EVENINGS ONE OR TWO OF THEM WOULD DRESS LIKE GIRLS IN A SACRED DRAMA AND PERFORM THE TRADITIONAL DANCES, THEIR LONG CURLS BRAIDED AND CROWNED WITH HEAVY WHITE FLOWERS, LIPS ROUGED, ARMS AND LEGS BRACLETED WITH TINSEL, SILK CLOTHS BOUND AROUND THEIR CHILDISH WAISTS—GOLDEN MOTHS, MOVING SLOW AS IF NARCOTIZED, SHIFTING SLENDER HIPS TO THE CANDLELIGHT OF DRUM, FLUTE AND GONGS. THE DANCERS WERE WELL TIPPED, DISAPPEARED WITH

THEIR ADMIRERS AND CAME BACK WITH TOYS OR JEWELS, AND HE DETERMINED TO MASTER THEIR SKILLS. BY ELEVEN HE DISCOVERED THE PLEASURE OF THE PIPE, AND HE TOO BEGAN TO STEAL GREEN FLAKES FROM HIS CUSTOMERS. HE SAVED COINS AND BOUGHT A NEW SARONG FROM A THIEF, OF BLACK WATERED CHINESE SILK—WITH HIS WHITE BLOOD HE WAS THE PALEST BOY IN THE CAFÉ, AND THE INKY CLOTH SET OFF HIS PALLOR AND THE HINT OF GOLD IN HIS BROWN BANGS AND COFFEE-TINTED EYES—AN OLDER BOY TAUGHT HIM A TRICK: IF YOU WANT A BIGGER TIP, LET YOUR SARONG FALL OPEN, AS IF BY ACCIDENT, WHILE YOU SERVE THEM THEIR PIPES, THEN PRETEND NOT TO NOTICE BUT STAY NAKED FOR A FEW MINUTES TILL YOU TIE IT AGAIN. EVERY DAY HE SWAM IN THE SEA. A MAN GAVE HIM A GOLD CHAIN FOR HIS NECK IN EXCHANGE FOR A KISS. BY THE TIME HE WAS TWELVE HIS EYES WERE ALWAYS LAZY, MELTING WITH INTOXICATION—LATE AT NIGHT, THE LAST FEW CUSTOMERS SLUMBERING DEEPLY, HE AND HIS FRIENDS WOULD HUDDLE TOGETHER ON ONE OF THE PLATFORMS, AWAY FROM THE PATRON'S EYE AND EAR AS HE NODDED OVER HIS TEA-POTS—CEILING FANS STIRRED THE AIR, A WARM SLUGGISH RAIN SPATTERED THE DRY ROOF— THE BOYS SMOKED, CURLED UP TOGETHER AGAINST THE DIRTY BOLSTERS TO WHISPER AND SLEEP, LIMBS TANGLED TOGETHER, LIKE YOUNG PYE-DOGS IN THE SHADE—NIGHTBIRDS MOANED OUTSIDE THE CAFÉ. AT THIRTEEN HE DANCES IN A COSTUME OF HIS OWN INVENTION: A LONG LOINCLOTH OF LILAC-COLORED SHANTUNG, A BELT OF CHASED SILVER, NECKLACES OF SEED PEARLS AND JASMINE, BELLS ON HIS BARE ANKLES AND WRISTS. STILL ANOTHER YEAR OR TWO BEFORE HE MUST BEGIN TO DEPILIATE HIS BODY AND USE POWDER LIKE THE OLDER BOYS—

BUT THE HASHISH NOW KEEPS HIM AWAKE SOME NIGHTS, TOO INSANE TO MOVE, STARING AT THE CRESCENT MOON UNDER THE ROOF, A GREEN PARROT PERCHED ON ITS CUSP, AND THE SILVER HANDS DRIPPING FROM THE STARS—NOW HE IS A DEVOTEE HIMSELF: IN THIS RELIGION I HAVE INVENTED, OF HASHISH AND LITTLE BOYS, HE IS BOTH WORSHIPPER AND OBJECT OF WORSHIP. THE SKY OPENS AND BETWEEN HIS LEGS THE BLACK SILK CHAFES HIM TILL HE THROWS IT OFF—THE SILK, AND THE TROPICAL LIMBS OF SLEEPING BOYS, MORE ELECTRIC THAN SILK AND DARKER, BRIGHTER THAN AMBER. THE MOON, A HUNDRED AND SIX MOONS INVADE HIS VEINS WITH THEIR PULSING LIGHT, SPERMY AND OPALESQUE. HE LIGHTS THE PIPE AGAIN, BALANCING THE COOL STEM ON HIS KNEE, WATCHING IT GLITTER IN THE MATCH-LIGHT, AND SMOKE ENGLOBES HIS SPACE, OWL'S WINGS BRUSH HIS SHOULDERS AND THIGHS, HE ALONE AWAKE IN THIS ANDROGYNOUS CAFÉ, THE MOONLIGHT KISSING HIS FEET, RUNNING ITS GLOWWORM TONGUE OVER HIS THIN LEGS. THE NIGHT STROKES HIS INNO-CENCE, FINGERS IT TILL IT WAKENS, A PIRATE OF SELF-ABUSE, AND THE HASHISH MIRRORS HIS PIGEON'S MOANS, FEARFUL THE OTHERS MIGHT BE FEIGNING SLEEP. MIRRORS, THE SILVER PIPE CAFÉ IS MADE OF MIRRORS—TAKE THIS NIGHT FOR AN EMBLEM, THE HALF-BREED ACOLYTE FOR YOUR DERVISH BOY, YOUR DOUBLE-SEXED SHAMAN CHILD, AND THE LILACS OF HIS HANDS OPEN FOR YOU A CRACK BETWEEN EARTH AND SKY, AND FILL ALL TIME WITH THE PUBESCENT LIGHTNING OF A SINGLE PIPE.

PETER WILSON

COUNTESS LULU

THREE TINY NAVELS SEEN TOGETHER ALL ALMOST ALIKE ONE MINUSCULE EMBEDDED WITHIN A BELLY THE COLOR OF DAWN ANOTHER ELONGATED SLANTING THE EYE OF A DOE THE THIRD LIGHT BROWN TINGED WITH AMBER FLECKS THE TINIEST OF THE THREE BELONGS TO ME STANDING ON THE RIVERBANK WATCHING THE OTHER TWO DAISIES REACHING UP TICKING MY ARMPITS THEY GROW SO VERY TALL HERE IN THE MARSHLAND BIG WHITE GOLDEN FLOWERS SMELLING OF PEEPEE SMELLING OF FLOWERS MAKING ME SNEEZE   DOE'S EYE WINKS DISAPPEARS WITHIN A FOLD OF CLAUDE'S BELLY HE'S SEATED AMIDSHIPS FEET SPLASH THE WATER THAT COVERS THE TARRED BOAT BOTTOM DOE'S EYE WINKING BLINKING WHENEVER HE LEANS OVER TO BAIL OUT MORE WATER   AMBER NAVEL FLATTENS TAUTENS STRAINS EXERTIONS OF BERNARD'S TORSO AS HE HOISTS HIS ARMS HIGH CLUTCHING THE HANDLE OF THE STERN OAR LOOKING LIKE HE'S ABOUT TO POLE VAULT WITH IT

YANN HEY AREN'T YOU COMING TOO SHRIMP? HE GESTURES TOWARD ME THEN TUGS YANKS UP HIS RED BRIEFS SHINY MATERIAL CAUGHT PINCHED TIGHT WITHIN THE FURROW OF HIS ASS I SHAKE MY HEAD THAT BOAT DOESN'T BELONG TO US

OH YOU'RE TOO CHICKEN WE'LL NEVER ASK YOU TO COME ALONG WITH US AGAIN   BERNARD SWUNG HIMSELF LEISURELY OFF HIS BICYCLE RANG THE BELL ALONGSIDE THE GRILLEWORK GATE CALLED OUT IMPATIENTLY AND A FAT BOY HIS OWN AGE CAME TIMIDLY OUT OF THE TINY HOUSE THEY HEADED OFF TOWARD THE RIVER FAT LULU ON FOOT BERNARD BACK ON HIS BIKE ZIGZAGGING SLOWLY BACK AND FORTH OVER THE HUMP IN THE CENTER OF THE ROAD WOBBLING PERILOUSLY AT TIMES BECAUSE THE FRONT WHEEL TURNED TOO SLOWLY MOVING TO THE LEFT THE RIGHT BERNARD TRYING TO KEEP THE BIKE BALANCED SO HE WOULDN'T FALL ON HIS ASS GIVING A FEW IDLE TURNS NOW AND THEN TO THE PEDALS THE REST OF THE TIME COASTING FREEWHEELING TIRES ON GRAVEL EMITTING AN AGREEABLE HUMMING OF HAPPY BEES BERNARD HAD CALLED OUT HI THERE FAT CUNT WHEN LULU CAME OUT OF THE HOUSE WE'RE SAILING OVER TO THE ISLAND WANT TO COME ALONG FAT CUNT? LULU IS NOT REALLY ALL THAT FAT IT'S MOSTLY BECAUSE OF HIS ROUND MOON FACE HORMONES MAYBE AND HIS CLUMSY SLOW-MOVING MANNER BERNARD IDLING ALONGSIDE HIM PLAYS THE ROLE OF THE HANDSOME YOUNG HOOD FREEWHEELING BERNIE ON HIS WHEELS THEY'VE SOMEHOW WITHOUT EVER DISCUSSING IT AGREED

110

TO PLAY THESE RESPECTIVE ROLES BERNARD THE CRUEL BUTCH NUMBER LULU THE NELLY YOUNG THING SIMPERING TREMBLING WITH ADMIRATION ALWAYS IN ANTICIPATION INSEPARABLE NOW EACH OF THEM NEEDING THE OTHER TO COMPLETE HIMSELF

IT WAS TWO THREE YEARS AGO BERNARD FIRST WENT TO PLAY AT LUCIEN'S THAT COMBINATION CAFE AND GROCERY STORE IN THE CENTER OF TOWN AND LEFT AROUND TEN O'CLOCK LUCIEN WE CALL FAT LULU FOLLOWED HIM OUT INTO THE STREET GRABBED HIM ONE ARM AROUND THE NECK KISSED HIM WETLY AS A WAY OF SAYING GOODNIGHT BERNARD OF COURSE SHOVING HIM AWAY AND DISGUSTEDLY WIPING HIS CHEEK WITH THE BACK OF HIS HAND NEVERTHELESS THE NEXT NIGHT BERNARD WAS BACK FOR MORE BECAUSE LULU SEEMED TO POSSESS ONE OF EVERY TWO EVER MADE PLUS THANKS TO HIS FATHER ALL THE CANDY AND SODA POP TOO LULU REMAINED THERE THAT NIGHT UNMOVING STANDING BY THE CAFE DOOR SILENTLY WATCHING BERNARD SPEED OFF TAIL LIGHT CLIMBING UP UP AND OVER THE RISE IN THE MAIN STREET GONE NOW NOTHING LEFT BUT NIGHT AND BLACKNESS AND SILENCE LULU'S MOUTH TREMBLING HE NO LONGER EVEN TRIES TO KISS BERNARD BUT THEY SHOW THEIR COCKS TO EACH OTHER JUST LIKE ALL THE OTHER GUYS AND BERNARD LETS HIS OWN BE SUCKED OFF SOME-TIMES WHICH ALWAYS CAUSES LULU TO GET TOO RED IN THE FACE BERNARD OF COURSE NEVER TOUCHES LULU DOWN THERE HE PUTS ON HIS MOST DISGUSTED MANNER IF HE SO MUCH AS SEES IT AND HE PURPOSELY NEVER WASHES HIS OWN COCK BEFOREHAND BUT THE FAT BOY DOESN'T EVEN SEEM TO MIND HE LIKES SUCKING SO MUCH

HEY FATSO WANT TO KNOW SOMETHING FATSO I THINK YOU'RE A REAL QUEER CUNT FATSO

YES

IT EXCITES YOU MAKES YOU WANT TO DROP YOUR COOKIES HUH SUCKING OFF A REAL TOUGH GUY LIKE ME YOU'RE IN LOVE WITH ME AREN'T YOU YOU'D LIKE ME TO FUCK YOU UP THE ASS TILL YOU'RE CRISS-EYED HUH

YES OH YES

SHIT ON THAT FATSO YOUR ASS IS TOO BIG TOO MUCH LIKE SHOVING MY TOOL INTO A TUB OF LARD ONE HUNDRED POUNDS OF SHIT IN A FIFTY-POUND BAG THAT'S WHAT YOU ARE FATSO FAIRY

YES

A BIG FAT COCKSUCKING FAIRY THAT'S WHAT YOU ARE I THINK WHAT I'D LIKE MOST IS TO SMASH YOUR UGLY FAT MUG IN COME OVER HERE CLOSER I SAID PUT UP YOUR MITTS

NO   NO   PLEASE   STOP THAT!

BERNARD NEVER TOLD ANY OF US AOBUT IT AND IN THE STREET WHEN WE ARE ALL STROLLING ROAMING TOGETHER AND WE HAPPEN TO PASS BY FAT LUCIEN HE ALWAYS TURNS HIS EYES AWAY BUT CLAUDE AND ME ALL THE SAME WE SAW THEN ON THE ISLAND WE'D GONE THERE OURSELVES TO FINISH OFF OUR LOOT STRING BEANS IN TOMATO SAUCE A CAN OF CONDENSED MILK A BOX OF CHEESE CRACKERS I'D JUST PINCHED FROM THE GROCERY WE REALLY LOVED PACKING IT IN THE TWO OF US BULLSHITTING QUIETLY AND THAT ONE TIME WE HEARD THEM BOTH THEY WERE VERY NEAR US BEHIND SOME BUSHES BERNARD LEANING AGAINST A TREE HIS HEAD HIDDEN BY LEAVES AND LUCIEN ON ALL FOURS BERNARD BREAKS OFF A BRANCH HINGING DOWN AND SWATS LULU'S SHOULDERS WITH IT THE LEAVES SCRAPING FALLING LIKE RAIN THEN BERNARD RAINS TOO PISSES ALL OVER LULU'S FACE WHO LEAPS UP TRYING TO ESCAPE BUT BERNARD IS TOO QUICK GRABBING HIM BY THE SHOULDER FORCING HIM TO KNEEL ONCE MORE LULU FAT LULU PISS STILL STREAMING DOWN HIS CHEEKS WHILE BERNARD STARTS PUMPING AWAY ON HIS OWN MACHINE GETTING MORE AND MROE EXCITED HE STARTS TALKING FAST AND LOW FILTHY DISGUSTING STOMACH-TURNING THINGS SOME LITTLE GYPSY GIRL HIS GANG HAD BEATEN UP AND THEN GANG-FUCKED LULU WATCHING BERNARD GROW HARD MOVES HIS MOUTH NEARER GRASPING FISHLIKE BERNARD SLAPPING HIM HARD ACROSS BOTH CHEEKS BUT LUCIEN BEGS INSISTS NOSTRILS QUIVER FLARING WIDE LIKE A FRIGHTENED MARE'S STINK OF PISS STINK OF SEMEN AND THEN BERNARD LETS GO WITH A FAT GLOBULE OF SPIT RIGHT IN LULU'S KISSER YANKS HIM BY THE HAIR SHOVING MOON CHEEKS AND ALL HARD UP AGAINST HIS GLISTENING COCK MAKING HIM SUCK SUCK ALL THE WHILE SUCK POUNDING ON LULU'S SKULL WITH BOTH FISTS A LITTLE LATER HE LIFTS ONE LEG SENDING HIS KNEE CRASHING INTO LUCIEN'S JAW WHO FALLS BACKWARD BLUBBERING BLEEDING BERNARD UNTIED THE BOAT FROM ITS MOORING AND SAILED OF LULU RUNNING AFTER CLAUDE AND ME WE DIDN'T FEEL MUCH LIKE TALKING WE JUST STARED AT EACH OTHER I MADE A FULLY OH-LA-LA GESTURE WITH ONE HAND AND CLAUDE GRABBED

THE TIN OF CONDENSED MILK FROM ME PUCKERING HIS LIPS AT THE HOLE SUCKING IT ALL UP FINALLY WIPED HIS MOUTH CLEAN AND SAID QUITE CALMLY IT'S NOT A VERY PRETTY SIGHT HIS COCK.

AT FIRST WE KNOW ONLY BERNARD NO OTHER GUYS FROM THE VILLAGE HE STOLE WITH US POINTED OUT CHICKS THE ONES YOU COULD COP A QUICK FEEL FROM BRAGGED A LOT ABOUT BEING A REAL COOL DUDE NOBODY LIKES HIM VERY MUCH TO TELL YOU THE TRUTH WE LISTEN TO HIS STORIES BUT HAVE A HUNCH THEY'RE ALL A CROCK OF SHIT ESPECIALLY ALL THAT ABOUT HOT-ASSED CHICKS IF YOU ASK ME WE'LL NEVER GET TO SEE SO MUCH AS ONE HOT ASS BELONGING TO ANY OF THEM I DIDN'T MUCH CARE ANYWAY I HAD ENOUGH TIME FOR THAT LATER ON AND BESIDES I'M ALREADY IN LOVE BUT CLAUDE HOPED BERNARD COULD FIX HIM UP WITH SOME TOWN WHORE SOME HOT-ASSED BEAUTY AND TOGETHER THEY MIGHT FUCK THAT HOT ASS OF HERS HE KEEPS TALKING ABOUT IT TO ME OH THEIR EYES THEIR HAIR I DON'T THINK HE'S PRETENDING EITHER HE REALLY SEEMS TO FEEL THAT WAY STARING AT THEM THE WAY YOU MIGHT EYEBALL SOME MONUMENT TO THE WAR DEAD IN SOME VILLAGE SQUARE IT'S THE OLDER BROADS WHO EXCITE HIM MOSTLY THE ONES OF OUR OWN AGE DON'T EVEN HAVE REAL TITS YET THEY JUST STIKE POSES GO AROUND ACTING COY AND GIGGLING WHILE THE BIGGER ONES ARE ALL TOO FLESHY WITH SWOLLEN HAUNCHES BIG HAMS CHEWING ON THEIR CUDS LIKE STUPID COWS VICIOUS DEPRAVED HUGE RED MOUTHS AND HIGH HEELS MAYBE IT'S THEIR STINK THAT ATTRACTS CLAUDE THAT FEMALE SMELL SINCE HE KNOWS HE'S VERY HANDSOME THEY REALLY SEEM TO SHAKE HIM UP A LOT HE NEVER STOPS TALKING ABOUT THEM   ONE AFTERNOON BERNARD FINALLY MANAGED TO LURE ONE OF THEM INTO THAT SHANTY BY THE SAWMILL THEY MADE ME STAND OUT BY THE DOOR AS LOOKOUT I COULD HEAR THE GIRL LAUGH A LOUD SCREECH MAKING FUN OF THEM ALL THEN COMPLAIN THEN MOAN THEN SUDDENLY BECOME SILENT SHE WHISPERS FINALLY OH STOP THAT! AND THEN SHE WHISPERS AGAIN OH YOU'RE GETTING ME ALL HOT AND WET DOWN THERE LOVERBOY WHAT A LITTLE PIG YOU ARE! AND THEY ALL LEFT BEFORE SHE DID BERNARD HAD NOT SHOT OFF I NOTICED THAT RIGHT AWAY NOR LULU SO THAT LOVERBOY PIG STUFF MUST HAVE BEEN FOR CLAUDE ALL THE SAME HE DOESN'T EVEN HAVE HAIR DOWN AROUND THERE YET SHE WAS FAT FRIZZY RED HAIR STICKING OUT EVERY WHICH WAY STINKING OF SWEAT GREEN CHECKERED SKIRT NOSE ALL DOTTED WITH BLACKHEADS STUMPY DUMPY LEGS A SICKLY GRAY

COLOR AND HAIRY TOO BIG BROWN BLEMISH ON ONE ARM AND SHOES WITH HOLES IN THEM SHE WASN'T EVEN PRETTY BUT SHE WAS YOUNG AT LEAST AND SO I DIDN'T DARE ASK CLAUDE TO TELL ME WHAT HAD HAPPENED WE BOTH TOOK THE ROAD BACK THAT WINDS THROUGH THE OPEN MEADOWS UNTIL IT GETS TO THE LANE THAT LEADS UP TO THE CHATEAU THAT'S WHAT THEY ALL CALL OUR HOUSE AROUND HERE THE CHATEAU

KICKING UP CHALKY DUST HE STARTED WHISTLING SO I FINALLY DARED WAS IT FUN? CLAUDE SHRUGGED SPEAKING IN A VOICE MORE SERIOUS THAN USUAL I DIDN'T ENJOY IT AL ALL SHE'S A FUCKING HALF-WIT HE REALLY SUCKED US IN THAT BERNARD CLAUDE WAS NO LIAR HE DIDN'T EMBROIDER THINGS AND SO I LISTENED BELIEVING

BUT SHE GOT BARE-ASSED DIDN'T SHE?

YEAH WELL NO NOT REALLY SHE YANKED HER SKIRT UP OVER HER WAIST

BUT YOU DID GET TO SEE HER PUSSY DIDN'T YOU?

THREE BOYS CROSS IN A GREEN AND BLACK BOAT HERE WHERE THE RIVER BROADENS BEFORE REACHING THE DARK FOREST THERE WHERE IT LAPS LAZILY AROUND A TINY ISLAND COVERED ALL OVER WITH UNDERBRUSH CHESTNUT TREES THE BLOND BOY AND THE YOUNGEST KID ARE NOT FROM THE VILLAGE THEIR DELICATE FINE FEATURES GRACIOUS MANNERS ATTEST TO THAT QUITE OBVIOUSLY THEY BELONG TO THAT PRIVATE INSTITUTION THE CHATEAU THE TWO BIGGEST ARE ABOUT TWELVE WEARING BRIGHTLY COLORED BRIEFS WHILE THE THIRD IS NO MORE THAN TEN TORSO NUDE ALSO BUT DOWN BELOW HE SPORTS BLACK VELVET KNEE BREECHES REMNANTS OF SOME ELEGANT EIGHTEENTH-CENTURY COSTUME FALLING DOWN LOOSELY FROM HIS HIPS FOR WANT OF A BELT WHITE ELASTIC BAND OF HIS UNDER-SHORTS PEEKING OUT HERE AND THERE WHENEVER HE WRIGGLES HIS BUTTOCKS

WE WENT THERE ALL FOUR OF US LULU INCLUDED BERNARD NO LONGER MAKES ANY BONES ABOUT THAT HE'D TOLD US LULU'S A FAT CUNT BUT YOU CAN ALL FUCK HIM IF THAT SORT OF THING INTERESTS YOU LULU WON'T MIND HOW MANY AS FOR ME I'M DISGUSTED WHEN CLAUDE AGREES AND WHEN THE TIME CAME HE BROUGHT WITH HIM FROM THE CHATEAU A BIG SACK WE JUMPED INTO THE ROWBOAT AND HID OUT ON THE ISLAND THE

BAG CONTAINED A YELLOW SILK GOWN GILT EMBROIDERY GLASS JEWELS SEWN ON FOR DECORATIONS A WHITE WIG SOME POWDER AND PAINT AND EVEN A PAIR OF HIGH-HEELED PUMPS

YEAH SHE SHOWED IT TO US ALL RIGHT BUT IT WAS SO FUCKING DARK IN THAT SHANTY AND THEN WITH ALL THOSE THICK BLACK HAIRS COVERING IT

BUT YOU TOUCHED IT DIDN'T YOU HUH

NO NOT ME BERNARD   SHE DIDN'T APPEAL TO ME AT ALL SHE STUNK SO BAD

SHAME HUH IT'S BERNARD'S FAULT CHOOSING ONE LIKE THAT BUT YOU DID SOMETHING WHAT THOUGH?

NOTHING   HE RUBBED HIMSELF AGAINST IT   WHEN IT CAME TO MY TURN SHE USED HER FINGERS MESSING AROUND FEELING MY YOU KNOW

IS THAT WHY SHE SAID SHE WAS ALL WET DOWN THERE YOU DIRTY PIG?

THEY FORCE LULU TO UNDRESS THEN DON THE GOWN BERNARD GRIPS THE FAT BOY'S HEAD WHILE CLAUDE APPLIES ROUGE TO HIS LIPS POWDER TO HIS CHEEKS CLAMPING THE WIG DOWN HARD UPON HIS SKULL WE USE DISGUISES LIKE THIS WHENEVER WE HAVE PARTIES BACK AT THE CHATEAU SO NOW IT'S COUNTESS LULU WE ALL START TEASING HER EXCEPT SUDDENLY BERNARD POINTS TO ME AND THIS SQUIRT HERE ISN'T HE GOING TO BE A HOT-ASSED CHICK TOO/ LUCKILY CLAUDE DEFENDS ME NO NOT HIM HE'S A REAL GUY JUST LIKE US BERNARD MAKES A FACE SUCKS IN HIS BREATH BUT HE PUTS OUT ALL THE SAME DON'T YOU SQUIRT? TREMBLING I LOOK AWAY MUMBLE NO I DON'T PUT OUT I'M STAYING HERE WITH CLAUDE   FINALLY WE START OUT LET'S PRETEND TWO PIRATES KIDNAPING THE ADMIRAL'S NOBLE DAUGHTER AT FIRST SHE'S ALL ALONE ON HIS SPLENDID GALLEON EVERYBODY ELSE ALREADY MURDERED

SHE DIDN'T SAY I WAS A DIRTY PIG SHE SAID WHAT A LOVERBOY BIG I WAS THERE'S A BIG DIFFERENCE BERNARD WANTED TO GO ALL THE WAY WITH HERE HE EVEN TRIED TO STICK IT IN BUT SHE FOUGHT HIM OFF AND SO HE STOPPED GETTING A HARD-ON HE'S A REAL WEIRDO ANYWAY THAT BERNARD IF YOU ASK ME

HE HAS LOTS OF HAIR DOWN THERE THOUGH

YEAH   NOT LOTS BUT A LITTLE YEAH JUST LIKE ME

YOU DON'T HAVE ANY HAIR

WHAT DO YOU KNOW ABOUT IT?

I'VE SEEN YOU

WHEN?

OH WHEN WE GO TO BED AND SOMETIMES TOO IN THE MORNING

AND IT DOESN'T EMBARRASS YOU TO STARE AT GUYS DOWN THERE HUH BUT ALL THE SAME YOU MUSTN'T HAVE LOOKED VERY CLOSELY BECAUSE I HAVE SO GOT

AND IN HER GOLDEN GOWN SHE SCREAMED HOOTED FOR HELP BERNARD ARRIVING ON THE SCENE HIS WOODEN LEG A STUB OF BAMBOO HE'D LASHED TO HIS THIGH CALF BENT BAK UP AGAINST ONE BUTTOCK HE ASKED COUNTESS LULU WHERE SHE'D HIDDEN THE TREASURE OF COURSE CLAUDE AND ME WE'D STASHED IT AWAY EARLIER CANS OF SHREDDED COCONUT LICORICE STICKS FILTER CIGARETTES BOOKS OF MATCHES THREE NOUGATS CHOCOLATE EGGS FILLED WITH LIQUEUR A BIG BAG OF POTATO CHIPS A GLASS JAR OF BRANDIED PEACHES MAYONNAISE CRACKERJACKS TINS OF CHOCOLATE CUSTARD PUDDING STRAWBERRY JAM MACKEREL IN WHITE WINE SOME BROWN SUGAR BACON FIVE CANS OF SARDINES ONE OF BLACK OLIVES TWO OF PORK AND BEANS CASSOULET TWO OF RAVIOLI WITH A BOTTLE OF SPARKLING WHITE WINE AND ONE OF LEMON SODA BUTTER HOLLAND RUSK SALTED NUTS SOUR PICKELS A JAR OF SPAGHETTI SAUCE ALL THE LOOT WE'D BEEN ABLE TO PINCH OVER AN ENTIRE WEEK'S TIME BERNARD IN TURN HAD SWIPED THE BOAT WHERE LULU NOW PLAYED THE FIGHTENED HYSTERICAL COUNTESS MY RESPECTS DEAR LADY SAID CLAUDE WHO TURNED UP NOW AS THE SHIP'S CAPTAIN HE HAS A LITTLE BURNT CORK MUSTACHE MY PISSPECTS QUEER LADY REPEATED BERNARD AND THEY EACH GRABBED COUNTESS LULU BY ONE PUDGY ARM ME STEPPING ASIDE TO LET THEM PASS

YOU'VE ONLY TO SHOW THEM TO ME THEN   SO LET ME SEE IF YOU HAVE THEM   CLAUDE HAD ALREADY REACHED THE STEEP EMBANKMENT WHERE THE ROAD VEERED UNDER THE POPLAR TREES HE TURNED HIS BACK TO THE HOUSES ON

THE OUTSKIRTS OF THE VILLAGE AND OPENED HIS FLY LOOKING OVER HIS SHOULDER ALL THE WHILE TO MAKE SURE NO CAR WAS COMING

STAND ALONGSIDE ME HERE AS IF WE'RE BOTH JUST TAKING A PISS

I FEEL LIKE PISSING ANYWAY SO   HE LOWERED HIS BRIEFS A BIT WHERE THE FLY GAPED BUT NOT ENOUGH TO REVEAL HIS PRICK AND I STARED DOWN SOME HAIRS YES A LITTLE CURL TO THE LEFT ANOTHER TO THE RIGHT BUT ALMOST NONE IN THE MIDDLE   I FINISHED PISSING I WANTED SO BAD TO TOUCH IT BUT HESITATED STRUGGLING TO SEE IT BETTER I SAID IF MAYBE YOU COULD JUST FLUFF IT OUT A BIT

WHAT?   WITH JUST US TWO HERE?   YOU KNOW YOU CAN'T COME YOU'RE NOT OLD ENOUGH YET

NO I CAN'T SHOOT ANY JUICE BUT I CAN STILL ENJOY THE FEELING

OH ALL RIGHT THEN I DIDN'T REALIZE   BUT LOOK HERE TELL ME SOMETHING FIRST   WOULD YOU SAY YES IF FOR EXAMPLE SOME BIG GUY ASKS TO FUCK YOU UP THE ASS THERE ARE BIG GUYS BACK AT THE HOUSE LIKE THAT YOU KNOW THEY WANT TO DO IT TO THE LITTLE ONES ALL THE TIME

NOW YOU'RE BEING DISGUSTING   BECAUSE UH   UH BECAUSE WOULD YOU UH DO IT?

NO   WELL ER THAT ALL DEPENDS   ON WHO IT WAS   SOME TIME I MIGHT IT ER ALL DEPENDS ON WHO

YES MAYBE ME TOO YES   BUT JUST THE SAME NO   NO I DON'T THINK SO

THEN LET'S GO OVER THERE HUH   HE POINTED AT THE CARCASS OF AN AUTOMOBILE ABANDONED ONLY THE BODY STILL INTACT THERE WAS A SHARP TURNING IN THE ROAD LED STRAIGHT DOWN TO THE RIVER IT DIDN'T HAVE SEATS ANYMORE NOR DOORS EITHER WE LAY DOWN IN THE TALL GRASS RIGHT BEHIND IT I HAD TO BE CAREFUL BECAUSE OF NETTLES BUT THIS TIME THEY DIDN'T SEEM TO STING

THEY STOPPED ALL THREE OF THEM BESIDE THE HOLE IN WHICH THE BURIED TREASURE LAY OH MY POOR DEAR DEAD FATHER MURDERED SO VILELY SAID LULU SOBBING QUITE SERIOUSLY BOTH HANDS

COVERING HIS FACE BUT NOBODY LAUGHED BECAUSE HE'S SUCH A SILLY ASSHOLE ANYWAY FOR BELIEVING IN LET'S PRETEND AND BERNARD LIFTED UP THE HEM OF HIS GOWN HEY COUNTESS YOU'RE BARE-ASSED UNDER YOUR SILK DUDS YOU'VE GOT SUCH A FAT ASS COUNTESS IT LOOKS SUSPICIOUS TO ME I'LL WAGER THAT'S WHERE THE CAPTAIN'S TREASURE IS HIDDEN! AND HE SLAPS COUNTESS LULU ON BOTH BUTTOCKS DEAR ME DEAR ME SAYS CLAUDE COULD BE COULD BE

THEY COME UP ALONGSIDE THE ISLAND AND THE BLOND BOY LEAPS OUT OF THE ROWBOAT TO MOOR IT FINALLY THE OTHER TWO FOLLOW ALL THREE DISAPPEARING INTO THE UNDERBRUSH CAUSING BIRDS TO FLY UPWARD CAWING SCREECHING DROWNING OUT ALL SOUND OF THEIR GAME ALTHOUGH THE ISLAND IS EXTREMELY SMALL ALMOST AT THE SAME TIME A SECOND BOAT MOVES OUT FROM THE STEEP RIVERBANK THIS TIME ON THE TOWN SIDE IT ALSO CARRIES THREE BOYS ALL THREE NAKED TO THE WAIST ALL THREE THE SAME AGE AS THE FIRST GROUP BUT THEIR CRAFT IS DECKED OUT TO LOOK LIEK A SAILBOAT AN OAR STANDING UP ALMOST STRAIGHT IN ITS CENTER HELD IN PLACE BY TWINE REPRESENTING THE STAYS OF A MAST A SQUARE PIECE OF BLACK CLOTH WITH WHITE POLKA DOTS NAILED TO ANOTHER STICK SET CROSSWISE UPON THE OAR BLACK AND WHITE BEING PIRATE COLORS ALL THREE SPORTING BANDANAS OF THE SAME MATERIAL KNOTTED AROUND THEIR FOREHEADS PLUS A BLACK PATCH OVER ONE EYE BELTS BULGING WITH WOODEN WEAPONS KNIVES SABERS NEVER USING THE SAIL ACTUALLY FOR SAILING BUT TWO OTHER OARS INSTEAD VEERING TACKING THE MANY CHANGES OF DIRECTION SUGGESTING A LONG VOYAGE ACROSS PERILOUS SEAS AS THEY RUN UP AND DOWN THE LENGTH OF THE BOAT CALLING OUT VARIOUS COMMANDS THAT THE WIND ON THIS LATE AFTERNOON COUPLED WITH THE GUSH OF RUSHING RIVER CARRIES AWAY RENDERS INDISTINCT AND FLEETING

SPREAD YOUR CHEEKS WIDER

MAYBE IF WE COULD KISS FIRST HUH

WHAT?   HAVE YOU LOST ALL YOUR MARBLES? STRETCH YOURSELF OUT LENGTHWISE THAT WAY YOU WERE A SECOND AGO

BUT WITH GIRLS DON'T YOU KISS FIRST?   AND SINCE WE'RE DOING THE SAME THING NOW?

AFTER THEY REACH THE ISLAND AND DISEMBARK THEY PULL THEIR BOAT UP ONTO THE NARROW STRAND OF SAND LIFTING A FOURTH OCCUPANT WHO HAS UNTIL NOW BEEN HIDDEN IN THE BOTTOM BODY BOUND AND GAGGED A TINY GIRL LONG BLACK TRESSES DARK BROWN SKIN THREADBARE CLOTHES AND HARDY IF EMACIATED BODY PROCLAIMING HER TO BE A GYPSY HER LONG CALICO SKIRT HAS BEEN RIPPED OFF EARLIER SHE'S CLOTHED NOW ONLY IN A FILTHY GREEN SWEATER AND BADLY TORN BLOOMERS SALLOW-BROWN FROM TOO MUCH WEAR AND WHOSE LACE TRIMMING UNRAVELS THE MORE ROUGHLY THEY HANDLE HER INTO A SERIES OF STRINGY FESTOONS FLUTTERING DOWN UPON HER THIGHS LIKE JELLYFISH TENTACLES   THE GROUP SETS OFF IN A MARCH THICK UNDERBRUSH CLOSING BEHIND THEM WITH A RUSTLE OF REEDS

ALL RIGHT LET'S SAY I DO KISS YOU BUT JUST ONCE AND ONLY ON ONE CONDITION

WHAT'S THAT?

THAT YOU SUCK ME OFF IN EXCHANGE

OH NO THAT'S NOT FAIR YOU'RE A REAL BASTARD YOU ARE

IT'S NOT DIRTY TO SUCK HONEST I'VE DONE IT MYSELF

YOU?   WHO WITH?   WITH SIMON MAYBE?

YOU'RE NUTS YOU KNOW THAT? NOBODY HOME BUT THE CLOCK AND THAT'S STOPPED   AW COME ON IF YOU SAY YES I'LL GIVE YOU MY FOUR RACING CARS AND THE ELECTRIC TRACK THAT GOES WITH THEM I'M NOT JUST LENDING THEM TO YOU EITHER I'LL GIVE THEM TO YOU OUTRIGHT HONEST

THEY UNTIED THE LITTLE GIRL GRIPPING HER BODY ALL THE WHILE BECAUSE SHE HAD BEGUN TO STRUGGLE YANKING DOWN HER BEIGE BLOOMERS THERE WAS THE ROTTING HULK OF A BOAT ITS BOTTOM COMPLETELY FLATTENED OUT RUN AGROUND A LONG TIME AGO DURING SOME SPRING FLOOD THAT COVERED THIS ISLAND THEY'VE TURNED IT OVER NOW AND HAULED IT INTO THE BUSHES TYING THE GIRL TO IT BACK AND BUTTOCKS PRESSED HARD UP AGAINST THE OUTER HULL LEGS SPREAD APART EXHIBITING A VULVA FLAT AND TINY AND FURTHER BELOW THAT THE INCURVATE SHADOW OF AN ANUS

FIRST OF ALL IT'S BOATS NOT CARS I'M INTERESTED IN

IT'S YOU LOSS   PUT YOUR PANTS BACK ON THEN

YOU MEAN WE'RE LEAVING?

THINK IT OVER CAREFULLY MY FOUR RACING CARS PLUS THE TRACK   AND I'LL GIVE YOU SOME-THING ELSE TOO   ALL THE TRADE-SPITS YOU WANT

YOU CAN SHOVE YOUR STUPID RACING CARS BUT WHAT'S A TRADE-SPIT?

DUMB ASSHOLE   IT'S WHEN TWO PEOPLE KISS EACH OTHER BUT WITH THEIR MOUTHS OPEN ALL THE WHILE AND USING THEIR TONGUE

WHOSE TONGUE?

BOTH TONGUES ASSHOLE INSIDE EACH OTHER'S MOUTHS YOURS AND MINE IF YOU'D LIKE

UGH THAT SOUNDS DISGUSTING   STILL   WE COULD MAYBE TRY IT JUST ONCE   TO SEE

THEY APPLIED A SCARF OVER THE GAG COVERING HER MOUTH AND ONE OF THE THREE BOYS CAME CLOSER AND CLOSER FEELING THE LITTLE VULVA GROWING MORE AND MORE EXCITED BY HIS EXPLORATIONS BUT ONE OF THE OTHER TWO SAYS NO IT'S RENÉ WHO'S TO TAKE HER CHERRY AFTER ALL IT'S RENÉ WHO FOUND HER FOR US AND THE BOY NAMED RENÉ NODS UNBUTTONS HIS PANTS LETS HIS BELLY DROP DOWN OVER THE BELLY OF THE LITTLE GYPSY WHO BEGINS TO STRUGGLE EVEN MORE STRONGLY

YOU'RE THE ONE WHO AGREED TO IT REMEMBER ALL THE TRADE-SPITS I WANT ALL RIGHT GO AHEAD KISS ME COME ON

NO SUCK ME OFF FIRST

SHIT YOU'RE THE ONE WHO'S ACTING DUMB NOW I MIGHT FEEL MORE LIKE SUCKING YOU OFF IF YOU KISSED ME FIRST

OH ALL RIGHT MOVE YOUR MOUTH CLOSER YOU WANT TO KNOW SOMETHING YOU'RE A REAL PAIN IN THE ASS YOU ARE I CAN'T BELIEVE ANYONE CAN BE SO STUPID AT LEAST WIPE YOUR MOUTH OFF FIRST

YOU'RE DROOLING SPIT ALL OVER ME

BERNARD DECLARED THAT COUNTESS LULU WOULD HAVE TO SQUAT DOWN AND SHIT IN ORDER FOR THEM TO SEE WHAT SHE MIGHT BE HIDING UP HER HOLE BUT CLAUDE MADE A FUNNY FACE NO WE CAN TAKE A SOUNDING IN THAT WELL OURSELVES ONE THAT WILL BE A LOT MORE FUN BESIDES AND SO THEY BOTH DREW FORTH THEIR COCKS KICKING LULU OVER INTO A LEAPFROG POSITION RAISING HIS GOWN UP OVER HIS BACK COVERING HIS HEAD WITH YELLOW SILK WHILE THEY FUCKED HIM THE BOTH OF THEM BERNARD FIRST THEN CLAUDE AND AS FOR ME I WAS TOO EMBARRASSED BECAUSE OF THOSE BIG SOFT LARDY CHEEKS SO PALE AND SQUISHY LOOKING I FOUND IT SAD THAT CLAUDE COULD EVEN TOUCH LET ALONE WANT TO ENTER THEM AND SO I SAT DOWN AGAINST A TREE AND LOOKED SOMEWHERE ELSE PLUGGING UP MY EARS WITH MY FINGERS SO I WOULDN'T HAVE TO HEAR ALL THOSE HORRIBLE SOUNDS   THEY TAPPED ME ON THE SHOULDER THEY WEREN'T PIRATES ANYMORE LULU STILL HAD ON HIS SILK GOWN BUT IT WAS YANKED EVERY WHICH WAY THE WIG FALLEN OFF AND THE HIGH-HEELED PUMPS AS WELL

AND THE ONE I LOVE AM IN LOVE WITH KISSED ME MY ENTIRE FACE LAY DOWN ALONGSIDE ME HE ISN'T EVEN PRETENDING ANYMORE HE REALLY ENJOYS IT KISSES SOFTLY GENTLY MY LIPS SO WET AND SHINING WITH HIS LOVELY WET SHINING LIPS MOUTH HOT AND SILKY AGAINST MY CHEEK I YANK OFF MY JERSEY SO THAT WE CAN FEEL OUR BELLIES RUBBING SKIN AGAINST SKIN THE SUN IS ALREADY BEHIND THE TREES AND THE TALL GREEN GRASS TICKLES MY EARS

OH IT'S SO LONG YOUR COCK IF I'D BEEN IN HER PLACE I'D HAVE LOVED GETTING IT FROM YOU BUT ANYWAY I'M A BETTER LOOKING BOY THAN SHE IS A GIRL DON'T YOU THINK?

I DON'T KNOW ANYTHING ABOUT THAT IF YOU WERE TWELVE YEARS OLD YOURS WOULD BE LONG TOO

SO THEN YOU'D RATHER HAVE HER THAN ME?
ALL THE SAME SHE WAS A REAL DOG TO LOOK AT

YOU CAN'T COMPARE THINGS LIKE THAT

RENÉ CLIMBED OFF THE CHILD'S VULVA DIRTY COVERED WITH MUCUS FOAMING SNAIL TRAILS BUT SHE HADN'T BELD   ANOTHER OF THE BOYS THIS ONE BROAD-ASSED AND BANDY-LEGGED SPREAD

HIMSELF OVER THE TINY BODY AND JERKED HIMSELF OFF CLUMSILY KEEPING ONE HAND DOWN THERE BETWEEN THEIR TWO CROTCHES HOPING TO BE ABLE TO INSERT HIS THING INTO BUT NEVER QUITE SUCCEEDING AND SO HE FINALLY SAT ASTRIDE HER TINY TITTIES AND MASTURBATED FINALLY EJACULATING THE TIP OF HIS SEX PRESSING AGAINST MAKING A WELL IN THE GAG COVERING HER MOUTH THE UP AND DOWN PUMPING MOVEMENT OF HIS FIST CONTINUALLY SMASHING AGAINST THE CHILD'S NOSE WHILE HIS SPERM SPLASHED FORTH IN COLORLESS BUBBLES SEEPING THROUGH THE GAG   THE THIRD BOY CAREFULLY WIPED OFF THE STICKY BEGRIMED SCARF WHICH PERHAPS BELONGED TO HIM AND THEN PENETRATED HER ROUGHLY BUT BETWEEN THE THIGHS

YOU'RE CHEATING YANN YOU'RE NOT SUCKING ME AT ALL LOOK SEE HOW I CAN STILL PUT MY ENTIRE FIST AROUND IT THAT MEANS YOU HAVEN'T EVEN TAKEN ALL OF THE HEAD INTO YOUR MOUTH YET

WE SET ABOUT DIGGING UP THE TREASURE I LOVE COLD CASSOULET PORK AND SAUSAGE AND WHITE BEANS ESPECIALLY THOSE LONG THIN SAUSAGES SHAME WE DIDN'T PINCH SOME MUSTARD AS WELL WE WON'T GIVE ANY OF IT TO LULU IT'S HIS FATHER WE STOLE IT FROM BUT THAT PIG CUNT WON'T DARE SQUEAL ON US FOR IF HE DOES WE'LL PUT HIS FATHER WISE TO ALL THOSE BOTTLES OF APERTIFS HE'S BEEN BRINGING AS GIFTS TO BERNARD AND THAT'S EVEN GOING TO GET WORSE NOW THAT THEY'VE BECOME SUCH ASSHOLE BUDDIES

WHAT'S WRONG   YOU LOOK FUNNY   DOES IT HURT TOO MUCH?

NO IT'S I'M ALL RIGHT

WE'LL DO IT AGAIN EVERY NOW AND THEN HUH YANN THE MORE WE DO IT THE MORE

YEAH BUT WHAT IF YOU MAKE A BABY INSIDE ME?

YOU'RE BATTY AS A BEDBUG WITH A GUY THAT CAN'T HAPPEN BESIDES IT'S NOT THROUGH THE ASSHOLE YOU MAKE A BABY

OH GOOD   ARE YOU SURE   EVEN WITH GIRLS?

THE SAME

THEN LET'S START OVER AGAIN RIGHT NOW AND TONIGHT WE CAN

SURE WE CAN CLIMB INTO MY SACK HAVE OURSELVES A BALL HUH

THE THREE PIRATES HELD A LONG CONSULTATION SQUATTING ON THE GRASS A DISTANCE AWAY FROM THE RUINED BOAT WHERE THEIR VICTIM REMAINED BOUND AND GAGGED THE DISCUSSION GROWING MORE AND MORE CONFUSED UNTIL FINALLY THE MOST ROBUST OF THE THREE GOT UP AND WENT OVER AND RAPED THE LITTLE GYPSY ONCE MORE WHO BY THIS TIME SCARCELY STRUGGLED THEN THE OTHER TWO IMITATED THEIR LEADER

AFTERWARD I'D LIKE TO DO IT TO YOU TOO

OH NO I'M OLDER THAN YOU SO I COULD HAVE A KID IF SOMEBODY FUCKS ME IT'S NOT THE SAME THING AS WITH YOU YOU KNOW

BUT YOU JUST TOLD ME THAT IN THE ASSHOLE STOP IT NOW   I DON'T WANT YOU TO MAKE A BABY I CAN SEE NOW YOU DIDN'T TELL ME THE WHOLE STORY BEFORE

OH SHIT YOU NEVER UNDERSTAND ANYTHING YOU DON'T HAVE TO WORRY I TOLD YOU THAT ALREADY

NO I DON'T BELIEVE YOU IF I CAN'T FUCK YOU AS WELL

HE GIVES ME HIS POTATO CHIPS HIS NOUGAT CANDY I GIVE HIM MY RAVIOLI EXCEPT FOR ONE CAN AND MY SHARE OF THE CIGARETTES FROM TIME TO TIME JUST FOR KICKS WE TOSS OUR OLIVE PITS AT LULU AS WE BULLSHIT AND BERNARD ALONE EATS ALL FIVE CANS OF SARDINES WITH TOMATO SAUCE AND THE MAYONNAISE MOPPING UP THE REMAINS WITH HIS FINGERS LICKING THEM HE HASN'T REBUTTONED HIS FLY AND IN THE CENTER OF HIS BRIEFS THERE'S A BIG STAIN OF WETNESS SOMETHING ROUND LIKE A RING STANDS OUT IT'S HIS FORESKIN STRAINING FORWARD THROUGH THE FABRIC LIKE A TINY HOSE NOZZLE

ALL RIGHT I'LL LET YOU DO IT TO ME TONIGHT ONLY YOU WON'T TELL ANYBODY ELSE PROMISE?

I PROMISE   BUT NOT TONIGHT RIGHT NOW OR ELSE TAKE AWAY YOUR COCK FROM MINE

LISTEN DON'T SQUIRM SO MUCH YOU'RE GIVING ME A HARD TIME I'M JUST ABOUT READY TO COME AND AFTERWARD YOU CAN DO WHATEVER YOU WANT

YOU'VE SHOT OFF?   I DON'T FEEL I

SHUT UP I CAN'T CONCENTRATE IF YOU   ONE SECOND OR SO MORE AND   THERE   AH THAT'S IT

NOW IT'S MY TURN

RENÉ BENT DOWN OVER THE ROPES WHICH CRISSCROSSED THE GIRL'S TINY BREASTS AND SEEMED EITHER TO BE UNTYING THEM OR ELSE MOVING THEM HIGHER UP TO TIGHTEN AROUND HER NECK   THEY SET SAIL ALL THREE OF THEM LEAVING THE ISLAND NO LONGER PLAYING

SPREAD YOUR CHEEKS WIDER CLAUDE I CAN'T SEEM TO FIND THE HOLE

THAT'S YOUR WORRY

I CAN'T REACH IT YOU'RE A REAL BUDDY YOU ARE ONCE YOU SHOOT OFF YOU DON'T GIVE A DAMN

WELL WHAT DO YOU WANT ME TO DO HUH?   GO AHEAD I'LL HELP YOU BUT JUST THIS ONE TIME TRY STICKING IT IN YES THERE IT'S ALMOST IN NOW PUSH IT FURTHER MAKE IT HARD SO IT WON'T KEEP SLIDING OUT

DO YOU LIKE IT TOO CAN YOU FEEL IT?

WHAT DO YOU THINK I AM SOME HOT-ASSED CHICK OR SOME FAGGOT HUH? DOES THINKING I MIGHT LIKE IT MAKE YOU ALL HOT TO DROP YOUR COOKIES OR SOMETHING?

NO NOT THAT   I LIKE IT TOO   BUT ONLY BECAUSE IT'S YOU I'M DOING IT WITH   BECAUSE I LOVE YOU

SHIT YOU'RE ALWAYS COMING OUT WITH STUPID-ASSED THINGS LIKE THAT FOR CHRISSAKES YOU SOUND LIKE SOME SILLY CUNT OR SOMETHING ME EVEN IF I THINK SUCH THINGS I NEVER

BUT WHEN YOU FEEL THEM WHEN YOU REALLY LOVE SOMEBODY

IF I DO IT'S OBVIOUS AIN'T IT SO WHY DO I HAVE TO

SAY IT? HURRY UP SHAKE IT MORE YOU'LL NEVER COME ANYWAY AT YOUR AGE SO WHY BOTHER

NO I'M NOT FINISHED I WAS STAYING INSIDE YOU JUST FOR THE ENJOYMENT

YOU ALWAYS EXAGGERATE THINGS COME ON PULL IT OUT RIGHT NOW AND HURRY IT UP TOO WE'VE GOT TO BE GETTING BACK MUST BE AWFULLY LATE SINCE I ALREADY FEEL SO HUNGRY ARE YOU GOING TO GIVE ME YOUR DESSERT AT DINNER TONIGHT HUH?

LULU WATCHED US GORGE OURSELVES WITH LITTLE SIDELONG GLANCES HE HELPED OPEN ALL THE CANS AND THEN SAT THERE SWALLOWING HIS SPIT LOOKING GLUM WHAT A PACK OF GLUTTONS JESUS DON'T YOU EVER GET ANYTHING TO EAT AT YOUR BOARDING SCHOOL WE EAT A LOT BETTER THERE THAN YOU DO FATSO SAYS CLAUDE AND IT'S NOT A BOARDING SCHOOL IT'S A PHILANTHROPIC INSTITU-

TION WELFARE YOU MEAN SNEERS BERNARD NO IT'S PRIVATE AND THEY'RE LOADED WITH DOUGH WE'RE NOT JUST TAKEN IN OFF THE STREETS YOU KNOW WE'RE CHOSEN WE'RE BETTER DRESSED THAN YOU VILLAGE GUYS FOR ONE THING BUT DON'T YOU HAVE ANY PARENTS? ASKS LULU

NO I DON'T HAVE ANY PARENTS ANSWERS CLAUDE

HIM NEITHER?

ME NEITHER I ANSWER NOBODY DOES AT THE CHATEAU

WHERE WERE YOU FROM BEFORE THEN?

THAT'S OUR BUSINESS SAYS CLAUDE

TONY DUVERT

THE POPLING

AUDREY AND JERRY SET OUT TO ISOLATE AND CAP-
TURE A POPLING. AN OLD STEAM RAILROAD TAKES
THEM TO A DESOLATE TOWN IN NORTHERN CANADA.
A TRADING POST, A FEW CABINS. A GROUP OF
ADOLESCENTS STAND IN FRONT OF THE TRADING
POST. THEY SNIGGER AND GIGGLE AND NUDGE
EACH OTHER AS THE TWO BOYS PASS THEM ON THE
WAY INTO THE TRADING POST. ONE OF THE LOCAL
YOUTHS TWISTS HIS HEAD TO ONE SIDE AND RUBS
HIS CROTCH. AUDREY FEELS A BLUSH BURNING THE
BACK OF HIS NECK.

THE CLERK IS A YOUTH WITH ONE EYE SLATE GRAY,
THE OTHER BLACK. HE PUTS OUT HIS HAND.

"I'M STEVE ... YOU TWO ARE LOOKING FOR THE
PIPER BROTHERS, RIGHT? WELL JUST FOLLOW THAT
WAGON ROAD OUTSIDE, YOU CAN'T MISS IT, THERE'S
ONLY ONE ROAD. WALK ABOUT TWO MILES AND TAKE
THE PATH TO YOUR RIGHT. IT'S A MILE FROM THE
FORK TO THE PIPER PLACE ..."

OUTSIDE, THE BOYS ARE SITTING IN A LINE, LEANING
AGAINST THE WALL, KNEES UP, WOBBLING THEIR
KNEES BACK AND FORTH AND RUBBING THEIR
CROTCHES. ONE CALLS AFTER THEM.

"WE'LL BE SEEING YOU, MILK BOYS."

THE WAGON ROAD, WHICH WAS ALSO PASSABLE FOR
TRUCKS IN DRY WEATHER, WAS YELLOW GRAVEL
WINDING BETWEEN BIRCH AND PINES. WILD
FLOWERS GREW BY THE SIDE OF THE ROAD, AND A
MOURNING DOVE COOED SOFTLY FROM WOODS. AS
THEY WALKED THEY SWATTED AT DEER FLIES THAT
LIT ON THEIR NECKS AND HANDS AND FACES,
STINGING LIKE SPARKS OF FIRE.

"THEY CAN EVEN BITE YOU ON THE PALMS OF THE
HAND," AUDREY SAID. "AND THE BIG HORSE FLIES
CAN BITE THROUGH JEANS."

"YOU KNOW THIS COUNTRY PRETTY WELL ..."

"THE CABIN WE'RE GOING TO STILL BELONGS TO MY
FATHER, BUT I HAVEN'T BEEN HERE SINCE I WAS
THIRTEEN. WE ALWAYS NEEDED A GUIDE TO FIND IT
... THIS MUST BE THE TURN OFF."

THEY TURNED INTO A NARROW FOOTPATH AND THE
SHADOW OF DEEP WOODS. WEEDS AND BUSHES
BRUSHED THEM AS THEY PASSED, AND NOW
CLOUDS OF VORACIOUS MOSQUITOS TOOK OVER

FROM THE BITING FLIES. THEY STOPPED AND RUBBED CITRONELLA ON THEIR FACES AND HANDS. THE MOSQUITOS HOVERED AROUND THEM, BUZZING IN FRUSTRATION.

THEY STEPPED FINALLY INTO A CLEARING BY A LAKE, AND THERE ON A HIGH ROCKY BANK OVER THE LAKE WAS THE PIPER CABIN. THE MOSQUITOS FELL AWAY BEHIND THEM. THE YOUNGER PIPER, WHO WAS ABOUT 20, WAS CUTTING WOOD. HE DROVE HIS AXE INTO THE BLOCK AND CAME OVER TO GREET THEM.

"YOU'RE AUDREY AND JERRY. I'M CARL PIPER."

THE OLDER BROTHER, WHO WAS AROUND THIRTY, WAS SITTING IN THE OPEN DOOR OF THE CABIN TYING A FLY. HE LOOKED UP AND NODDED GRAVELY. BOTH THE PIPERS HAD YELLOW HAIR, BRIGHT BLUE EYES, AND CURIOUSLY POINTED EARS. THE OLDER PIPER WENT BACK TO HIS FLY. HE FINISHED IT, HELD IT UP TO THE LIGHT AND LOOKED AT IT CRITICALLY, TURNING IT IN HIS HANDS. HE PUT IT INTO A FLY BOX.

"WELL," HE SAID AT LAST. "SO YOU WANT TO GO TO YOUR FATHER'S COTTAGE AND FIND A POPLING. YOU KNOW THAT A POPLING HAS ALREADY FOUND YOU?"

HE LOOKED AT JERRY AND ADDED "BOTH OF YOU."

"WELL YES, WE KNOW THAT AND THAT'S WHY. WE'LL HANG IT ALL, WE HAVE TO COME TO TERMS WITH THIS THING."

HE NODDED. "YES. IF THAT'S WHAT YOU WANT."

"WHEN CAN WE START?"

"RIGHT AWAY. ALL PREPARATIONS HAVE BEEN MADE."

THE TRIP TOOK THREE DAYS, WITH BACK-BREAKING PORTAGES EVERY FEW MILES. AT THE END OF THE DAY JERRY AND AUDREY WOULD FALL ASLEEP IMMEDIATELY AFTER SUPPER, WHICH WAS BLACK BASS OR WALLEYED PIKE WITH BISCUITS AND DRIED FRUIT. THE PIPERS SAT UP DRINKING COFFEE AND PLAYING ON THEIR WOODEN FLUTES. AUDREY DRIFTED OFF TO SLEEP WITH THE STRANGE WILD MUSIC IN HIS EARS: THE PIPES OF PAN.

LATE AFTERNOON ON THE THIRD DAY THEY CAME TO WIDE LAKE AFTER A THREE MILE PORTAGE. AS THE CANOES GLIDED OUT INTO THE CLEAR BLUE WATER, AUDREY COULD SEE GREAT BOULDERS ON THE BOTTOM, SOME FIFTY FEET IN HEIGHT. HE SHIVERED SLIGHTLY—THERE WAS SOMETHING CHILLING ABOUT THE SILENT BLUE DEPTHS AND THE SHADOWS OF THOSE BOULDERS, ROLLED DOWN BY GLACIERS MILLIONS OF YEARS AGO. HE KNEW THAT THE LAKE WAS MORE THAN A THOUSAND FEET DEEP IN THE MIDDLE.

THEY PADDLED FOR TWO HOURS, AND AT SUNSET HE COULD SEE AHEAD A LITTLE PIER AND A SANDY INLET. HE KNEW THAT THE HOUSE WAS SET IN A GROVE OF PINE AND BIRCH A FEW HUNDRED FEET ABOVE THE PIER. THEY TIED UP AT THE PIER AND JUMPED OUT. THE PIER ENDED IN TEN FEET OF WATER. AUDREY REMEMBERED FISHING FROM THE END OF IT FOR ROCK BASS AND YELLOW PERCH. THE BANK SLOPED STEEPLY FROM THE END OF THE PIER INTO CLEAR BLUE DEPTHS. AUDREY LED THE WAY UP THE PATH TO THE HOUSE.

IT WAS JUST AS HE REMEMBERED IT. A SCREENED PORCH IN FRONT, TWO PINE CHAIRS ON THE PORCH. HIS KEY OPENED THE LOCK AND THEY STEPPED INTO THE LIVING ROOM. PINE PANELLING, SMALL WINDOWS, PINE FURNITURE, LOW TABLE, A BOOK CASE WITH SOME OF AUDREY'S OLD BOOKS STILL THERE. THE BOOK OF KNOWLEDGE, SOME COPIES OF ADVENTURE AND AMAZING STORIES, AND A STACK OF LITTLE BLUE BOOKS. THE KITCHEN HAD A WOOD-BURNING STOVE AND PINE TABLE WITH CHAIRS.

UP THE STEEP STAIRS ON THE SECOND FLOOR THERE WERE TWO BEDROOMS OVER THE LIVING ROOM AND A SMALLER BEDROOM OVER THE KITCHEN. THERE WAS A BATHROOM WITH RUNNING WATER AND FLUSH TOILET AND BATHTUB. WATER FLOWED FROM A TWO-HUNDRED-GALLON TANK IN THE ATTIC, WHICH WAS FILLED BY A PUMP FROM THE LAKE. THERE WAS A BOILER THAT COULD BE HEATED BY A SMALL STOVE TO PROVIDE HOT WATER. ON THE BACK PORCH, WHICH WAS ALSO SCREENED, THERE WAS AN ICE BOX AND A WOOD BIN.

BEHIND THE HOUSE WAS A WOOD SHED AND AN ICE HOUSE AND A LONG LOW BUILDING WITH A BEAMED CEILING THAT HAD BEEN HIS FATHER'S WORKSHOP. THE TOOLS WERE STILL THERE—SOME LUMBER, A DRUM OF KEROSENE, AND A COIL OF ROPE. AUDREY LOOKED UP AT THE BEAMS AND REMEMBERED AN INCIDENT THAT HAD OCCURRED ON HIS LAST STAY HERE, WHEN HE WAS THIRTEEN. HIS FATHER AND BROTHER HAD ROWED TO THE OTHER SIDE OF THE

LAKE TO FISH. AUDREY WATCHED THEM GO WITH A TINGLE OF ANTICIPATION IN HIS CROTCH AND THE PIT OF HIS STOMACH. HE WAS GOING TO JACK OFF. BUT THERE WAS NO HURRY NOW. HE COULD TAKE HIS TIME ABOUT IT.

HE WENT OUT TO HIS FATHER'S WORKSHOP, LOOKING UP AT THE SMOOTH ROUND BEAMS. HIS FATHER PLANNED TO NAIL PLANKS TO THE BEAMS TO FORM AN ATTIC AND STOREROOM TO THE WORKSHOP, BUT THIS WAS NEVER ACCOMPLISHED. LOOKING UP AT THE BEAMS, AUDREY SUDDENLY FELT A FEELING OF WEAKNESS IN HIS CHEST. HE WAS STARTING TO GET A HARD-ON AS HE REMEMBERED SOMETHING HE HAD READ IN AN OLD MEDICAL BOOK HE FOUND IN A TRUNK IN THE ATTIC OF THE FAMILY HOUSE IN ST. LOUIS. IT WAS ABOUT DEATH BY HANGING:

"EJACULATION IN YOUNG MALE SUBJECTS DURING HANGING IS SO FREQUENT AS TO BE THE RULE. THIS GENERALLY OCCURS TWICE, ONCE IMMEDIATELY AFTER THE DROP WHEN THE NECK IS BROKEN AND ONCE JUST BEFORE THE BLOOD STOPS CIRCULAT-ING AND THE HEART STOPS. HOWEVER, IN SOME CASES EJACULATION MAY OCCUR THREE TIMES AND SOMETIMES AS OFTEN AS FIVE TIMES. FULL CONSCIOUSNESS MAY PERSIST FOR AS LONG AS THREE MINUTES WITH THE NECK BROKEN, AND AS LONG AS TWELVE MINUTES IN CASES WHERE THE NECK IS UNBROKEN OR LIGHTLY FRACTURED. EJACULATION IS THOUGHT TO RESULT FROM PRESSURE ON THE VAGUS NERVE."

AUDREY WAS STANDING UP AT THE ATTIC WINDOW WHEN HE READ THIS. HE BECAME QUITE DIZZY, AND SILVER SPOTS BOILED IN FRONT OF HIS EYES AND HE WENT OFF IN HIS PANTS. WELL, NOW WAS HIS CHANCE TO TRY IT. HEART POUNDING, BREATH WHISTLING THROUGH HIS TEETH, HE FASHIONED A HANGMAN'S KNOT AND THREW THE ROPE OVER A BEAM. HE STRIPPED OFF HIS CLOTHES, HIS COCK HARD AND LUBRICATING AS HE ADJUSTED THE KNOT BEHIND HIS LEFT EAR, REACHED UP AS FAR AS HE COULD ON THE LOOSE END OF THE ROPE, AND PULLED HIMSELF UP ON TIP TOE. THEN HE ARCHED HIS FEET, SWINGING A FEW INCHES OFF THE FLOOR. BLOOD POUNDED AND SANG IN HIS EARS AND THE ROOM BLACKED OUT AND HE WENT OFF.

HE CAME TO HIMSELF LYING ON THE FLOOR, HIS NECK VERY SORE AND A TASTE OF BLOOD IN HIS MOUTH. HASTILY HE DRESSED AND UNDID THE KNOT AND COILED THE ROPE. HE WENT BACK TO THE HOUSE AND LOOKED IN THE MIRROR. THERE WAS A RED MARK AROUND HIS NECK. HOW WOULD HE EXPLAIN IT TO HIS FATHER? HE GOT AN IDEA. HE TOOK A PAIL AND WENT OUT TO PICK SOME BLACKBERRIES. WHEN HIS FATHER CAME HOME JUST BEFORE SUNSET AND ASKED, "WHAT HAPPENED TO YOUR NECK AUDREY?"

"WELL UH I WAS PICKING BLACKBERRIES AND I FELL AND A BRANCH GOT TANGLED AROUND MY NECK."

HIS FATHER LOOKED AT HIM SPECULATIVELY FOR A MOMENT, AND AUDREY FELT HIMSELF BLUSHING. BUT NOTHING MORE WAS SAID. ALL THIS CAME BACK TO HIM AS HE STOOD IN THE WORK ROOM WITH JERRY AND THE PIPER BROTHERS AND GLANCED UP AT THE BEAM.

AUDREY PICKED UP A SHOVEL AND A CAN. "LET'S CATCH SOME FISH FOR DINNER?"

HE KNEW EXACTLY THE SPOT TO DIG FOR WORMS. THIS WAS A COMPOST HEAP OF GARBAGE AND HUMUS FOR THE WILD FLOWER GARDEN AT THE SIDE OF THE HOUSE. VIOLETS AND FORGET-ME-NOTS, AND EVEN SOME OF THE IRIS HIS FATHER HAD BROUGHT IN, STILL BLOOMED THERE. EVERY SHOVEL OF DIRT TURNED UP THICK RED WORMS. AUDREY COULD SEE THE FISH FLAPPING ON THE PIER, FEEL THE JERK AND VIBRATING WEIGHT ON THE LINE. JERRY AND AUDREY GOT THEIR FISHING POLES AND WALKED DOWN TO THE PIER.

THE PIPERS WERE BUSY UNPACKING GEAR FROM THE CANOES. THE SUN WAS SETTING ACROSS THE LAKE, AND THREE GEESE FLEW NORTH IN V FORMATION. SOMEWHERE IN THE DISTANCE THE LAUGH OF A LOON. THE WATER WAS SMOOTH AS GLASS. AUDREY BAITED HIS HOOK AND LET THE LINE SLIDE INTO THE BLUE WATER. JERRY WAS FISHING FROM THE OTHER SIDE OF THE PIER. ALMOST AT ONCE AUDREY FELT THE TUG ON HIS LINE AND PULLED OUT A ONE-POUND ROCK BASS. IN TWENTY MINUTES THEY HAD SIX ROCK BASS AND SEVEN YELLOW PERCH. THEY CLEANED THE FISH IN THE LAKE AND CARRIED THE ENTRAILS IN A PAN AND DROPPED THEM ON THE COMPOST HEAP. A FIRE WAS ALREADY BURNING IN THE KITCHEN STOVE.

IN THE DAYS THAT FOLLOWED THEY FISHED AND SWAM AND HIKED AND CANOED AROUND THE LAKE.

"THE PRESENCE OF HUMAN BODIES WILL DRAW THE POPLING," LIEF TOLD AUDREY. "SOONER OR LATER HE WILL SHOW HIMSELF."

FOR A WEEK NOTHING HAPPENED, AND THEN ONE AFTERNOON AS JERRY AND AUDREY WERE COMING BACK FROM A WALK AROUND THE EDGE OF THE LAKE WITH TWO BLACK BASS AND A WALL EYED PIKE AUDREY SUDDENLY STOPPED AND PUT HIS HAND IN FRONT OF JERRY. HE KNEW THAT JUST AHEAD WAS A LITTLE SANDY INLET BETWEEN TWO BOULDERS. YOU COULD EASILY MISS IT BECAUSE THERE WERE BUSHES GROWING AROUND THE BOULDERS THAT ALMOST CONCEALED THE INLET. HE KNEW IT WAS THERE BECAUSE THREE DAYS BEFORE, HE AND JERRY HAD STOPPED HERE FOR A SWIM.

THE WATER WAS SHALLOW FOR ABOUT TWENTY FEET, AND THEN THE BANK FELL AWAY SHARPLY INTO DEEP WATER. SOMEHOW AUDREY COULD NEVER BRING HIMSELF TO SWIM OUT INTO THE DEEP WATER, AND ANYWAY THE WATER WAS MUCH TOO COLD TO STAY IN FOR MORE THAN A FEW MINUTES. SO THEY SWAM CLOSE TO SHORE AND THEN CAME OUT AND STOOD ON THE SAND, RUNNING THE WATER OFF THEIR BODIES AND SHIVERING. AS THE SUN WARMED THEM THEY STOOD WITH THEIR ARMS AROUND EACH OTHER'S SHOULDERS, LOOKING ACROSS THE LAKE, AND THREE GEESE FLEW OVER, HEADING NORTH. AUDREY BECAME AWARE THAT SOMEONE OR SOMETHING WAS LOOKING AT HIM. HE FELT A SUDDEN RUSH OF BLOOD TO HIS CROTCH. JERRY GLANCED DOWN, GRINNING.

"YOU'RE GETTING A HARD-ON, AUDREY."

"YEAH. I SUDDENLY GOT HOT FOR SOME REASON."

"ME TOO. LOOK." HE POINTED DOWN TO HIS STIFFENING PHALLUS.

THEY STOOD THERE WITH THEIR ARMS STILL AROUND EACH OTHER'S SHOULDERS, AS IF THEY WERE HAVING A PICTURE TAKEN, AND AUDREY REALIZED THAT IT FELT EXACTLY LIKE SOMEONE WAS TAKING A PICTURE. NEXT TAKE SHOWED THE TWO BOYS JACKING OFF, BODIES CONTRACTED, LOOKING DOWN AS THEY EJACULATED AND AUDREY THOUGHT OF A PICTURE HE HAD SEEN IN PARIS OF A LITTLE BOY PISSING INTO THE WATER . . . "NE BUVEZ JAMAIS D'EAU" AS THEIR SEMEN SLASHED INTO THE WATER LIKE SALMON ROW.

NOW HE KNEW THAT WHATEVER HAD BEEN WATCHING THEM WAS THERE IN THE INLET. THEY MOVED FOREWARD CAUTIOUSLY AND PARTED THE BUSHES OVER THE INLET AND PEERED DOWN. AT FIRST THEY SAW NOTHING, THEN AUDREY MADE OUT A FIGURE LYING IN THE SAND. THE FIGURE SEEMED ALMOST TRANSPARENT, AND WAS EXACTLY THE COLOR OF THE SAND, WEBBED FEET TRAILING IN THE WATER. AT THIS MOMENT A BREEZE RUSTLED ACROSS THE LAKE BETWEEN THE CREATURE'S LEGS, STIRRING SAND-COLORED PUBIC HAIRS, AND THE CREATURE GOT AN ERECTION AND EJACU-LATED WITH A LOW WHISTLING SOUND. THE BREEZE DIED AND THE CREATURE LAY THERE AS IF DEAD.

TRYING TO MAKE AS LITTLE NOISE AS POSSIBLE THE BOYS DROPPED DOWN ONTO THE SAND BETWEEN THE POPLING AND THE WATER. THE CREATURE LEAPED UP, AND WHEN HE SAW HIS WAY TO THE WATER WAS CUT OFF HE GAVE A WHISTLING SIGH OF FEAR, TURNED GREEN, AND SHIT ON THE SAND. AUDREY COULD SMELL IT AS HE MOVED FORWARD, QUICKLY STRIPPING OFF HIS BELT AND PINIONING THE CREATURE'S ARMS. IT SMELLED LIKE HUMUS, STALE FLOWERS, AND STAGNANT WATER WITH ACCENT SPRINKLED OVER IT. THEY CARRIED THE POPLING SEVERAL HUNDRED YARDS BACK TO THE HOUSE. THE GREEN COLOR SLOWLY SUBSIDED. THE CREATURE WAS LOOKING AT AUDREY, WHO WAS CARRYING HIS LEGS, AND HE GAVE A LITTLE COOING GIGGLE THAT SENT A SHIVER DOWN AUDREY'S SPINE. CARL OPENED THE DOOR AND THEY CARRIED THE POPLING INTO THE LIVING ROOM. CARL BOLTED THE DOOR.

"THEY'VE GOT HIM."

LIEF CAME OUT OF THE KITCHEN WHERE HE HAD BEEN PREPARING THE EVENING MEAL. A SMELL OF FRYING FISH CAME OUT WITH HIM AS HE OPENED THE DOOR. NOW THE POPLING BEGAN TO STRUGGLE LIKE AN IMPATIENT DOG AS HE WHISTLED OUT . . . "FISH FISH FISH."

AUDREY UNTIED THE CREATURE'S ARMS AND SET HIM GENTLY ON HIS FEET. HE SNIFFED THROUGH THE OPEN DOOR OF THE KITCHEN, WHERE LIEF HAD ALREADY LAID OUT PLATES OF FRIED FISH WITH BISCUITS AND RICE. THE POPLING GRABBED A PLATE OFF THE TABLE AND CARRIED IT INTO A CORNER OF THE KITCHEN, WHERE HE SQUATTED DOWN EATING THE FISH WITH DELICATE VORACITY, CRAMMING RICE AND BISCUITS INTO HIS MOUTH WITH HIS HANDS. IN A FEW SECONDS HE HAD PICKED THE BONES CLEAN. AUDREY HANDED HIM ANOTHER PLATE AND HE ATE THAT TOO. THEN HE CURLED UP IN HIS CORNER AND WENT TO SLEEP.

AFTER THEY HAD FINISHED EATING, AUDREY STEPPED OVER TO THE POPLING AND TOUCHED HIS SHOULDER. THE POPLING LOOKED UP AT HIM,

TURNED A SALMON PINK COLOR AND ROLLED OVER ON HIS BACK WITH HIS LEGS IN THE AIR AND MADE A STRANGE POPPING SOUND IN HIS THROAT. HIS PENIS SURGED ERECT LIKE SOME PINK TRANSLUCENT FISH. AUDREY AND JERRY CARRIED HIM UPSTAIRS TO THE BEDROOM AND LAID HIM DOWN ON THE BED WITH A BATH TOWEL UNDER HIS ASS. THE POPLING WRITHED ECSTATICALLY. HE TURNED BRIGHT RED AND SHIT. AUDREY AND JERRY STRIPPED OFF THEIR SHORTS, DROPPED THE BATH TOWEL ON THE FLOOR AND BEGAN CARESSING HIM, RUNNING LIGHT FINGERS OVER HIS NIPPLES AND NUTS AND ASS. THE POPLING TURNED PURPLE, ORANGE, SALMON, PINK—THE COLORS WASHING THROUGH HIS BODY SO THAT AUDREY ACHED TO LOOK AT HIM. KICKING HIS LEGS SPASMODICALLY IN THE AIR, THE COLORS FLASHING THROUGH HIM FASTER AND FASTER, HE CAME IN A SHRILL WHISTLE OF ECSTASY THAT BROUGHT THE TWO BOYS OFF WITH HIM.

AUDREY'S NOTE ON THE POPLING: PHYSICAL CHARACTERISTICS: HE IS QUITE TALL, ALMOST SIX FEET, BUT SO SLENDER THAT HE COULD NOT WEIGHT MORE THAN 110 POUNDS. HIS NECK IS SERPENTINE AND FLEXIBLE. HIS HEAD COMES TO A POINT AND IS QUITE HAIRLESS. HOWEVER, HE HAS PUBIC AND RECTAL HAIRS. WHEN HE SWIMS, HIS PENIS AND TESTICLES ARE RETRACTED INTO HIS BODY, LEAVING A SMOOTH SLIT. NORMALLY HE IS A SILVER GRAY TRANSLUCENT COLOR, WITH HUGE CLEAR GRAY SHIMMERING EYES. HIS BODY GIVES OFF A GRAY GHOSTLY UNDERWATER SPERM SMELL. HE DEFECATES FROM SUDDEN FEAR OR PLEASURE, BUT HAS NOW LEARNED TO USE THE TOILET AT OTHER TIMES. HE IS AN INSTANT CHAMELEON, CHANGING COLOR IN A SPLIT SECOND TO MATCH HIS SURROUNDINGS. PLEASURE IS ALWAYS MANIFESTED BY RED AND FEAR BY GREEN. THE PUBIC AND RECTAL HAIRS CHANGE COLOR WITH HIS SKIN.

HE CAN SEE WITH HIS WHOLE BODY AND OFTEN TURNS AROUND AND BENDS OVER TO LOOK AT ME WITH HIS ASS. THIS METHOD OF PERCEPTION PRODUCES A PHYSICAL IMPACT, LIKE SOFT EROGENOUS SPARKS. I CAN TELL IF HE IS LOOKING AT ME WITH MY BACK TURNED.

JERRY AND I ARE NAKED MOST OF THE TIME, AND WE ARE SLOWLY LEARNING HOW TO SEE WITH OUR BODIES. THE ASS, NIPPLES AND GENITALS ARE THE MOST SENSITIVE SEEING AREAS. AND THE LOOKOUT IS DIFFERENT ACCORDING TO WHICH AREAS ARE USED. ABOVE ALL, THE POPLING WANTS TO BE SEEN WITH OTHER BODIES AND TO SEE OTHER BODIES. WHEN HE LOOKS AT ME WITH HIS NIPPLES, MY NIPPLES BECOME ERECT. TODAY I WAS IN THE WORKSHOP AND THE POPLING CAME IN. HE LOOKED AT THE BEAMS AND MADE A LITTLE CHIRPING GIGGLE SOUND THAT VIBRATED IN MY THROAT, AND THEN HE LOOKED AT ME WITH HIS NECK WHERE A RED LINE LIKE A ROPE MARK APPEARED, AND JERKED HIS HEAD TO THE LEFT AND I EJACULATED. HIS WHISTLES AND CHIRPS VIBRATE IN MY BODY LIKE SOME SONAR LANGUAGE.

HE CAN MAKE HIMSELF TRANSPARENT AND SHOW HIS VISCERA, LIKE A TROPICAL FISH. HE SEEMS TO BE ABLE TO EJACULATE ANY NUMBER OF TIMES, ACHIEVING EROTIC FRENZIES THAT ARE ALMOST PAINFUL TO WATCH. THESE FRENZIES ARE MORE AND MORE FREQUENT. HOWEVER, HE WILL NOT ALLOW JERRY OR ME TO FUCK HIM. IF WE TRY TO FUCK HIM, HE TURNS GREEN AND SHITS. CARL HAS EXPLAINED TO ME THAT IT IS FATAL FOR A POPLING TO BE FUCKED. "HE WILL POP ALL THE WAY AND DIE."

"WHAT HAPPENS IF HE FUCKS ME?"

"THAT YOU WILL FIND OUT SOON ENOUGH."

WILLIAM BURROUGHS

THE COMMITTAL

**TWO DAYS AFTER THE COMMITTAL HEARING, I WROTE
TO A CLOSE FRIEND:**

"I FEEL CALM AND ACCEPTING AND HAVE A CLARITY
ABOUT WHAT I MUST DO THAT I DIDN'T HAVE BEFORE.
THE IRRELEVENCE AND CRUDITY AND HUMAN FAILURE
(WHICH WAS VAST) OF THE COURT ON FRIDAY MANAGED
TO SIFT THE WHEAT FROM THE TARES. REMEMBER YOU
SAID THAT I COULDN'T GET UP IN COURT AND DENY
THAT I DID LOVE BOYS? THE FEAR OF THAT, AND BEING
MISCONSTRUED, HAD HAUNTED ME FOR MONTHS. YET IT
WAS ALL SAID, MY WORDS WERE OUT AND YOU WERE
RIGHT. THEY SURVIVED EVEN THAT MANGLING OF
EXPRESSION AND MISREADING OF SENTIMENT.

BUT MOST IMPORTANT WERE TWO OTHER THINGS. FIRST,
THE LOVE AND UNDERSTANDING I FELT FROM MY
FRIENDS. FOR THE FIRST TIME IN THIS WHOLE BUSINESS,
I FELT THAT STRENGTH WHICH COMES FROM A COMMON
PURPOSE. I HAD DOUBTED IT WERE POSSIBLE—AS YOU
KNOW, IT HAD PREVIOUSLY ONLY HAPPENED WHEN I
STRUGGLED FOR OTHERS. NOW IT HAD HAPPENED WITH
ME AS THE BENEFICIARY. I HOPED IT REFLECTED WHAT I
MIGHT HAVE BEEN ABLE TO GIVE OTHERS IN THE PAST.

SECOND, THERE WAS WHAT I FELT FOR LEE IN THE
COURT. I STILL CANNOT DIGEST IT. I ONLY KNEW ONE

THING AS I LOOKED AT HIM—THAT I LOVED HIM. THAT
WAS THE ONLY REALITY ON MY SIDE OF THE COURT.
EACH TIME LOVE STRUCK THE AIR, WHETHER AS
GLANCES OR IN WORDS, THEY DEFIED BOTH THE
DERELICTION OF THE PROSECUTION AND THE LEGALISM
ON THE DEFENCE. AND THAT OF COURSE IS WHY THE
CASE IS BOUND TO GO ON.

HOW COULD THE POLICE HAVE NOT BEEN AFFECTED?
OR THE MAGISTRATES? IT WAS NOT PORNOGRAPHY AND
RAPE AND INDOCTRINATION WHICH PERVADED THE AIR,
MUCH AS THOSE MAY HAVE BEEN THE ONLY TERMS IN
WHICH THEY COULD UNDERSTAND OR ORGANISE THE
PROCEEDINGS—BUT THE ASSERTION OF LOVE: LOVE
FOR THOSE GENERALLY CONSIDERED INCAPABLE OF
RECEIVING IT FROM THOSE UNWORTHY OF GIVING IT.
THEREFORE IT WAS A COURT OF FOOLS, A HEARING FOR
MISFITS; A PUBLIC GALLERY FILLED WITH FOOLISH
LOVERS OPPOSITE A COURT FILLED WITH LOVERS OF
THE FOOLISH. NO OTHER OUTCOME WAS POSSIBLE. HAD
THERE BEEN ANOTHER RESULT, I WOULD HAVE FELT
CHEATED. DO YOU UNDERSTAND THAT? CAN ANYONE
UNDERSTAND IT?

DARE I RISK ONE OBSERVATION WHICH MAY SEEM
STRANGE. (IT MAY ALSO BE SELF-DECEPTION BUT I

THROW IT OUT IN ORDER TO HAVE IT TESTED.) IT IS ONLY THE POLITICAL PROCESS, IN ITS BROADEST SENSE, THAT MAKES ANY SENSE OF SUCH WASTE AND STUPIDITY. AS THAT COURT SHOWED, LOVE ALONE IS EASILY DENIED BY THOSE WHO CANNOT UNDERSTAND UNCONDITIONAL LOVE. IT IS ONLY THE ANALYSIS OF WHY SUCH PATHETIC HUMAN CONSTRUCTS DENY HUMAN REALITY WHICH LETS US DETERMINE HUMAN REALITY AT ALL. DOES THAT MAKE SENSE? IF I HAD BEEN SET FREE IT WOULD HAVE BEEN ON THEIR TERMS—THE TERMS THEY CHOOSE. NO TRIUMPH, EXCEPT A TRIUMPH OF FORM AND OF METHOD. NOW THAT THE STRUGGLE GOES ON, HOWEVER, IT IS ON MY TERMS AS WELL.

THIS IS THE ONLY WAY I CAN EXPLAIN THE INNER CALM NOW I FEEL. I AM FREE NOT TO TREMBLE, BUT TO FIGHT . . .

I SAW MARK AND DAREN TODAY BRIEFLY. IT WAS THE ONLY TIME THEY COULD GET OFF. I CANNOT LOOK AT EITHER OF THEM WITHOUT FEELING GLADNESS AND— YES, PRIDE—AT THEIR UNDERSTANDING AND BREADTH OF VISION. HOW THEY KNOW THINGS PEOPLE THREE TIMES THEIR AGE HAVE NO INKLING OF! (WHICH AGAIN IS WHY I AM IN COURT . . .)"

•   •   •

THE COMMITTAL PROCEEDINGS LASTED A DAY. A BRIEF PROSECUTION STATEMENT, OUTLINING MY ARREST AND LEE'S INTERROGATION, WAS FOL- LOWED BY THE APPEARANCE OF THE PROSECU- TION'S FIRST WITNESS, LEE HIMSELF.

AT THAT POINT, MY BARRISTER ASKED FOR THE COURT TO BE CLEARED, BOTH TO RELIEVE PRESSURE ON LEE, AND AVOID ANY POSSIBILITY OF POLICE INTIMIDATION—MERELY BY THEIR PRESENCE. SINCE NO LESS THAN SEVEN BOFORS POLICEMEN HAD TURNED UP AT COURT, THIS WAS NO MEAN THREAT.

LEE'S MOTHER, JEAN, HAD TO LEAVE THE COURT AS WELL. THE POLICE HAD ASSURED HER THAT "ONLY THE MAGISTRATE" WOULD BE IN COURT, BESIDE MYSELF—AND THAT THE WHOLE AFFAIR WOULD BE INFORMAL.

IN MY LETTER TO MY FRIEND AFTER THE COMMITTAL HEARING I CONTINUED:

"JEAN MUST NOW BE FEELING VERY MUCH IN TWO MINDS. ON THE OTHER HAND, RELIEF THAT LEE HAS MADE HIS STATEMENT, AND IT WASN'T "SO BAD" AFTER ALL. (THAT'S TO SAY, SINCE EVERYTHING ONCE IT'S OVER "ISN'T SO BAD"). IF SHE HAD EXPECTED ANY HOSTILITY FROM MY FRIENDS OR MYSELF, I THINK SHE WILL HAVE BEEN REASSURED. ON THE OTHER HAND, SHE MUST HAVE FELT HUMILIATED AND, TO AN EXTENT, BETRAYED. THE POLICE WENT ALL THE WAY UP TO THE MIDLANDS, AND EFFECTIVELY HOODWINKED HER. IF THEY TOLD HER SHE RISKED GOING TO JAIL IF LEE DIDN'T TURN UP IN COURT—THEN CERTAINLY SHE WAS HOODWINKED.

NOW SHE MUST REALISE THAT THE ASSURANCES ABOUT COURT PROCEDURE WERE COMPLETELY FALSE; IT IS THE COURT NOT THE POLICE WHO DECIDE THESE THINGS. INDEED, IF MY BARRISTER HADN'T INSISTED, THEN LEE WOULD HAVE HAD TO TESTIFY NOT ONLY WITH TWO MAGISTRATES, BARRISTERS, SOLICITOR, SOLICITOR'S CLERK, PROBATION OFFICER, COURT REPORTER AND MYSELF PRESENT, BUT FIVE OR SIX HEAVIES ABOUT WHOM HE MUST HAVE MIXED AND PAINFUL FEELINGS.

THE POLICE LIED TO JEAN AND THEY KNEW THEY WERE LYING WHEN THEY DID SO. PERHAPS SHE NOW REALISES THAT THE POLICE ARE CAPABLE OF LYING IN THE SAME WAY THAT I'VE MAINTAINED THROUGHOUT THEY LIED ABOUT ME. IF THEY WERE PREPARED TO FLOUT THE ORDER OF THE COURT TO QUIT IT, AND POSITION ONE OF THEIR NUMBER RIGHT NEXT TO WHERE LEE WOULD TESTIFY, WHAT BETTER INDICATION IS THERE THAT THEY HAVE NO SCRUPLES IN PUTTING ENORMOUS PRESSURE ON KIDS, WHEN IN PRIVATE?

I WISH SHE COULD HAVE BEEN IN COURT WHEN LEE TESTIFIED, NOT SIMPLY BECAUSE OF THE SUPPORT HE NEEDED FROM HER, BUT BECAUSE SHE MIGHT THEN HAVE UNDERSTOOD—IN A WAY COLD WRITTEN WORDS COULDN'T PERSUADE HER—THE EXTENT TO WHICH LEE IS CONFUSED ABOUT THE ALLEGATION HE ORIGINALLY MADE, THE EXTENT TO WHICH HE IN FACT WITHDREW MUCH OF WHAT HE ORIGINALLY SAID, AND THE PAIN THE WHOLE THING CAUSED HIM. I THINK SHE WOULD ONLY HAVE HAD TO LOOK AT HIM, STRUGGLING TO FIND WORDS, STUGGLING TO REMEMBER, STRUGGLING TO LOOK AT ME—THE ONLY PERSON IN THAT GAUNT ROOM WHO COULD GIVE HIM THE LEAST SIGN OF RECOGNI- TION. (CRUELLEST IRONY—THAT IT WAS ME, THE VERY PERSON AGAINST WHOM HE WAS "COMPLAINING," FROM WHOM HE SOUGHT SOME HUMAN FEELING.) SHE MIGHT THEN, AT LAST, HAVE SEEN AN ESSENTIAL TRUTH: THAT THERE IS NO QUESTION OF LEE LYING. BUT THERE IS A QUESTION OF HIS CONFUSION ABOUT EVENTS IN THE LONG GONE PAST (TWO YEARS NOW) AND ABOUT WHAT A SUCCESSION OF ADULTS HAVE WANTED OUT OF HIM.

WHEN HE MADE THAT CLINCHING STATEMENT, I HEARD IT IN WORDS OUT OF THE MOUTHS OF THE POLICE. (WOULD LEE HAVE USED THE WORD "PENIS"? I THINK NOT. IN HIS ORIGINAL STATEMENT TO THE POLICE, THEY INSERTED IT IN BRACKETS AFTER "DICK." AND WOULD HE HAVE SAID "BACKSIDE"? BACKSIDE IS A PECULIARLY ADULT TERM—"I'LL HIT YOU ON YOUR BACKSIDE IF YOU'RE NOT CAREFUL." KIDS WILL ALMOST ALWAYS SAY "BUM," "ASS" OR "BOTTOM." AND IF A BOY WERE TRYING TO BE POLITE IN ADULT COMPANY, SURELY HE WOULD SAY "BEHIND?""

• • •

AS I SAT IN THE DOCK ON JULY 28TH, WATCHING LEE TESTIFY, I WROTE DOWN ALL THE QUESTIONS ADDRESSED TO HIM, AND HIS REPLIES. I ALSO NOTED THE HESITATIONS IN INTONATIONS IN HIS VOICE—SOMETHING NEVER REFLECTED IN THE "DEPOSITION" WHICH THESE STATEMENTS THEN BECOME.

WOMAN MAGISTRATE: LEE, DO YOU KNOW WHAT THE OATH MEANS?

LEE: I'M SUPPOSED TO TELL THE TRUTH.

MAGISTRATE: IT MEANS YOU PROMISE TO TELL THE TRUTH. YOU ARE GOING TO MAKE A SOLEMN PROMISE TO GIVE THE RIGHT ANSWER. YOU MUST PUT YOUR HANDS ON THE BIBLE—ON THE WORDS OF JESUS.

LEE DELIVERS THE OATH

PROSECUTION: LEE, WHEN DID YOU FIRST MEET ROGER MOODY?

LEE: ABOUT FIVE YEARS AGO.

PROS: WHERE DID YOU LIVE?

LEE: I CAN'T REMEMBER

PROS: CLOSE?

LEE: ABOUT THIRTY MILES AWAY.

PROS: DID HE COME TO LIVE WITH YOU AT YOUR HOUSE AT ALL?

LEE: YES.

PROS: FOR HOW LONG?

LEE: ABOUT THREE MONTHS.

PROS: DID YOU SEE HIM A LOT?

LEE: YES.

PROS: WHAT SORT OF THINGS DID YOU DO TOGETHER?

LEE: I CAN'T REMEMBER.

PROS: AFTER THREE MONTHS DID HE LEAVE AND COME TO VISIT YOU FROM TIME TO TIME.

LEE: YES.

PROS: DID YOU GO AND STAY WITH HIM IN LONDON?

LEE: YES.

PROS: ON THE FIRST OCCASION WERE YOU WITH ANYONE ELSE?

LEE: NO.

PROS: CAN YOU REMEMBER HOW YOU WENT TO LONDON?

LEE: BY COACH.

PROS: WHICH CITIES DID YOU GO THROUGH?

LEE: BIRMINGHAM.

PROS: WHERE DID YOU GO WHEN IN LONDON? DO YOU REMEMBER THE ADDRESS.

LEE: NO, I CAN'T REMEMBER.

PROS: DO YOU REMEMBER WHICH PART OF LONDON THE HOUSE WAS IN?

LEE: NO.

PROS: DURING THE DAY WHAT DID YOU USED TO DO?

LEE: GO SWIMMING.

PROS: WHAT ELSE?

LEE: SOMETIMES I WENT WITH ROGER.

PROS: WHAT SORT OF THINGS DID YOU USED TO DO?

LEE: I WENT TO PLAY WITH THE OTHER LADS.

PROS: WHERE DID YOU USED TO GO?

LEE: SOMETIMES THEY CAME TO OUR PLACE, SOMETIMES WE WENT TO WHERE THEY WERE LIVING.

PROS: WHAT WERE THEIR NAMES?

LEE: JIMMY AND STEVE.

PROS: WAS THIS THE FIRST TIME YOU WENT TO LONDON?

LEE: NO.

PROS: WHEN DID YOU GO BEFORE?

LEE: ME AND MY BROTHERS WENT TO STAY WITH ROGER.

PROS: WHEN YOU DESCRIBED YOUR TRIP ON YOUR OWN, HOW LONG AGO WAS THIS?

LEE: I THINK THREE YEARS AGO.

PROS: WHAT TIME OF THE YEAR?

LEE: SUMMER HOLIDAYS.

PROS: HOW OLD WERE YOU?

LEE: ABOUT NINE.

PROS: WHERE DID YOU SLEEP?

LEE: SAME ROOM AS ROGER.

PROS: DID IT HAVE BEDS IN IT?

LEE: NO.

PROS: ON WHAT DID YOU SLEEP?

LEE: MATTRESSES.

PROS: WHERE DID ROGER SLEEP?

LEE: NEXT TO ME.

PROS: WERE THE MATTRESSES CLOSE?

LEE: YES.

PROS: WHAT DID YOU USED TO WEAR?

LEE: PANTS, SOMETIMES A TEESHIRT.

PROS: WHAT DID ROGER USED TO WEAR?

LEE: PANTS.

PROS: ON THE FIRST NIGHT DID ANYTHING HAPPEN?

LEE: HE KISSED ME.

PROS: ANYTHING ELSE?

LEE: I DON'T THINK SO.

PROS: WHAT DID YOU DO ABOUT THAT?

LEE: CAN'T REMEMBER

PROS: ON LATER NIGHTS DID ANYTHING HAPPEN?

LEE (AFTER A LONG SILENCE): HE TRIED TO GET CLOSE TO ME.

PROS: IN WHAT WAY?

LEE: I CAN'T UNDERSTAND.

PROS: TELL US WHAT HAPPENED.

THERE IS ANOTHER LONG SILENCE FROM LEE.

PROS: YOU EXPLAIN TO THE LADY UP THERE (HE POINTS TO THE MAGISTRATE).

MAGISTRATE: WE HAVE SOME IDEA OF WHAT HAPPENED, WE WANT TO HEAR IT FROM YOU.

PROS: HOW DID YOU LIE IN BED? WERE THE TWO MATTRESSES ALONGSIDE EACH OTHER?

DEFENSE BARRISTER (INTERVENING): DON'T LEAD! CLOSE WAS THE WORD, NOT TOGETHER.

LEE: THE MATTRESSES WERE RIGHT NEXT TO EACH OTHER.

PROS: WERE YOU SLEEPING ON ONE OF THE MATTRESSES?

LEE: YES.

PROS: WHERE WAS ROGER SLEEPING?

LEE: ON THE OTHER ONE.

PROS: DID YOUR RESPECTIVE POSITIONS STAY LIKE THAT?

LEE: I STAYED THERE, YES.

PROS: WHAT ABOUT ROGER?

LEE: HE TRIED TO COME OVER TO MY MATTRESS.

PROS: DID HE SUCCEED AT ALL?

LEE: I CAN'T REMEMBER.

PROS: CAN YOU REMEMBER ANYTHING ELSE HAPPENING AT ALL?

THERE IS A LONG SILENCE

LEE: HE TRIED TO PUT HIS ARMS AROUND ME.

PROS: ANYTHING ELSE?

THERE IS ANOTHER LONG SILENCE

MAGISTRATE: DO YOU KNOW WHY YOU'RE HERE TO GIVE EVIDENCE TODAY?

DEFENCE BARRISTER (IN AN ASIDE): THE POLICE OFFICERS TOLD HIM TO COME.

PROS: DID ANYTHING ELSE HAPPEN YOU CAN TELL US ABOUT?

THERE IS YET ANOTHER LONG SILENCE

LEE: HE TRIED TO PUT HIS PENIS UP MY BACKSIDE.

PROS: DID YOU SEE HIS PENIS?

LEE: YES.

PROS: DID HE GET IT IN?

LEE: NO.

PROS: WHEN HE DID SO, WHAT DID YOU DO?

LEE: I MOVED FURTHER AWAY.

PROS: DID ANYTHING ELSE HAPPEN ON ANOTHER NIGHT?

LEE: HE KISSED ME AND THAT.

PROS: WHAT DOES "AND THAT" MEAN?

LEE: NOTHING.

PROS: I'D LIKE YOU TO LOOK AT TWO PHOTOS. WHO TOOK THESE PHOTOS?

LEE: ROGER.

PROS: WHEN?

LEE: WHEN HE CAME TO THE MIDLANDS SOMETIME BEFORE I CAME TO LONDON.

PROS: DID YOU READ ANY BOOKS WHEN STAYING WITH ROGER?

LEE: YES.

PROS: WHAT SORT OF BOOKS?

LEE: SEX BOOKS.

PROS: WAS THERE ANY QUESTION OF PHOTOS BEING TAKEN?

LEE: HE WANTED TO, YES.

PROS: DID YOU AGREE TO THOSE TWO PHOTOS BEING TAKEN?

LEE: NO.

PROS: DID YOU GO OUT IN THE EVENING AT ALL?

LEE: WE WENT TO A PARTY.

PROS: WHO WAS AT THE PARTY?

LEE: ROGER. I CAN'T REMEMBER WHO ELSE.

PROS: WERE THERE ANY WOMEN THERE?

LEE: NO.

PROS: WHAT DID YOU HAVE TO DRINK?

LEE: I DRANK POMAGNE.

PROS: HOW MUCH?

LEE: HALF A BOTTLE.

MY BARRISTER THEN ROSE TO CROSS-EXAMINE

DEFENCE: LEE, YOU KNOW YOU SAID ROGER TRIED TO PUT HIS PENIS UP YOUR BACKSIDE? HE NEVER TOUCHED IT DID HE?

LEE: I DON'T KNOW.

DEF: YOU TELL US.

LEE: I THOUGHT HE DID.

DEF: YOU'RE NOT SURE ABOUT IT ARE YOU?

LEE: YES.

DEF: YOU COULDN'T SEE HIM COULD YOU?

LEE: NO.

DEF: YOU CAN'T REALLY BE SURE CAN YOU? ISN'T THAT RIGHT

LEE: THAT'S RIGHT. I CAN'T BE SURE.

DEF: IT COULD HAVE BEEN A HAND **AGAINST** YOU COULDN'T IT?

LEE: YES.

DEF: IT COULD JUST AS EASILY HAVE BEEN A HAND AS A PENIS COULDN'T IT?

LEE: YES.

DEF: YOU REMEMBER THE PARTY TO WHICH YOU WENT. DO YOU REMEMBER IT WAS FOR TWO PEOPLE GOING OUT TO BANGLADESH?

LEE: NO.

DEF: YOU WENT WITH ROGER OTHER EVEN-INGS DIDN'T YOU? TO THE CINEMA FOR EXAMPLE.

LEE: YES.

DEF: WHEN YOU SAY "ON OTHER OCCASIONS" HE TRIED TO KISS YOU HE WAS DOING THAT RATHER LIKE A FATHER WASN'T HE?

LEE: YES.

DEF: NOT IN ANY OTHER WAY?

LEE: NO.

DEF: AND WHEN HE CUDDLED YOU HE DID SO LIKE A FATHER?

LEE: YES.

DEF: NOT IN ANY OTHER WAY?

LEE: NO.

DEF: HE ASKED TO TAKE PHOTOS OF YOU AND YOU SAID NO. LET ME SHOW YOU THESE OTHER PHOTOS [CLOTHED]. THERE'S NO-THING WRONG WITH THOSE IS THERE?

LEE: NO.

DEF: THE ROOM YOU SLEPT IN WITH ROGER. WHEN YOUR BROTHERS CAME TO STAY, YOU ALL SLEPT IN THE SAME ROOM DIDN'T YOU?

LEE: YES.

DEF: AND THERE WAS ONLY ONE ROOM FOR YOU TO SLEEP IN WHEN YOU WERE WITH ROGER?

LEE: NO, THERE WAS A ROOM BESIDE IT.

DEF: DID IT HAVE ANY FURNITURE IN IT? WASN'T IT BARE?

LEE: YES.

DEF: HAVE YOU EVER STAYED AWAY FROM HOME ON YOUR OWN BEFORE WITHOUT YOUR BROTHERS OR MOTHER?

LEE: NO.

DEF: ROGER USED TO TREAT YOU VERY MUCH LIKE A SON DIDN'T HE?

LEE: YES.

DEF: YOUR MUM AND DAD DON'T LIVE TOGETHER DO THEY?

LEE: NO.

DEF: THEY HAVEN'T DONE SO SINCE YOU WERE A BABY IS THAT RIGHT?

LEE: NO, THEY HAVEN'T.

DEF: DO YOU SEE YOUR DAD VERY MUCH?

LEE: NO.

DEF: ROGER WAS REALLY LIKE A FATHER TO ALL OF YOU?

LEE: YES.

DEF: SO WHEN YOU CAME TO STAY IN LONDON WITH ROGER IT WAS NATURAL FOR YOU TO SLEEP IN THE SAME ROOM AND NOT IN A ROOM—A BARE ROOM—ON YOUR OWN?

LEE: YES.

DEF: AND WHEN ROGER WAS TOUCHING YOU, HE WAS BEING AFFECTIONATE LIKE A FATHER WASN'T HE? HE WASN'T DOING ANYTHING WRONG?

LEE: I DON'T KNOW WHETHER HE WAS TOUCHING ME LIKE A FATHER.

DEF: IT WAS REALLY LIKE A FATHER WASN'T IT?

LEE: I DON'T KNOW.

THE PROSECUTOR RISES TO RE-EXAMINE

PROS: LEE, WHY DID YOU SAY IT WAS A PENIS?

LEE: IT DIDN'T FEEL LIKE A HAND OR ANYTHING.

PROS: WERE YOU LYING DOWN AT THE TIME?

LEE: YES.

PROS: WERE YOU FACING TOWARDS ROGER OR AWAY?

LEE: AWAY.

PROS: COULD YOU SEE HOW HE WAS FACING?

LEE: NO.

PROS: YOU SAY ROGER KISSED YOU. WHERE?

LEE: ON THE CHEEK.

PROS: YOU SAID YOU DIDN'T WANT HIM TO TAKE PICTURES—WERE THEY LIKE THIS? (HE HOLDS UP THE SEMI-NUDE SHOTS)

PROS: NOT LIKE THIS? (HE HOLDS UP THE CLOTHED SHOTS)

LEE: NO.

MAGISTRATE: WE WANT TO ASK YOU ONLY ONE QUESTION LEE. YOU SAID YOU SAW HIS PENIS. BUT LATER ON YOU SAID YOU COULDN'T SEE IT. WAS IT DARK OR LIGHT?

LEE: DARK, I THINK.

MAG: WHEN DID YOU SEE HIS PENIS THEN?

LEE: IN THE MORNING.

I CONCLUDED THE LETTER TO MY FRIEND:

"HERE THERE IS A TERRIBLE IRONY. I'VE LITTLE DOUBT

THAT WHAT LEE FEELS I DID WRONG TO HIM WAS TO KISS HIM. HIS CONFUSIONS ABOUT WHAT THESE KISSES MEANT CAME OVER POIGNANTLY IN THE CROSS-EXAMINATION AT THE COMMITTAL. AT ONE POINT HE SAID HE DIDN'T KNOW WHETHER THEY WERE "FATHERLY" KISSES. AT ANOTHER POINT, THAT, NOT HAVING KNOWN WHAT IT WAS TO HAVE A REAL FATHER, THEN YES—THEY WERE FATHERLY KISSES. LEE LIVES IN A WORLD WHERE PRESSING ONESELF AGAINST ANOTHER PERSON IN MOCK SEXUALITY OR JUST PHYSICAL ANTICS IS A SLIGHT NAUGHTINESS—IF THAT. AFTER ALL, WHAT DOES IT SIGNIFY? WHAT HARM COMES OUT OF IT? KISSING HOWEVER HAS DIFFERENT IMPLICATIONS AND THEY ARE MUCH MORE CONFUSING. KIDS LEARN FROM FILMS THAT IT SIGNIFIES THE START OF SERIOUS LOVE-MAKING. BOYS DO NOT KISS BOYS, AND THOUGH MEN KISS BOYS (AND BOYS MEN) IT IS ONLY WITHIN THE FAMILY. THAT LEE WANTED ME TO KISS HIM, I KNOW. PERHAPS HE ALSO FANTASISED MY PENIS COMING INTO CONTACT WITH HIS BOTTOM: I KNOW OF ONE OCCASION WHEN HE CERTAINLY DID SO. WAS IT THAT SPECIFIC FANTASY WHICH THE POLICE LATCHED ON TO? DID HE FEEL GUILTY ABOUT IT—SO THAT THE ONLY WAY OF ALLEVIATING THE GUILT WAS TO SAY I DID IT TO HIM, RATHER THAN THAT HE WANTED "TO KNOW WHAT IT'S LIKE"? OR WAS IT SIMPLY THAT THE WHOLE THING WAS SO INCIDENTAL IN THE FIRST PLACE THAT UNTIL THE POLICE POUNCED ON IT AND MADE IT THE KEY THING HE DIDN'T KNOW IT HAD ANY SIGNIFICANCE? IN WHICH CASE, HE WOULD HAVE BEEN TAKEN UNAWARES AND, DESPITE HIMSELF, ELABORATED ON IT. I CAN IMAGINE THE PROCESS:

POLICE: WHEN YOU WERE SLEEPING NEXT TO EACH OTHER, DID HE TRY TO COME OVER TO YOUR SIDE OF THE BED?

LEE: YES ONCE OR TWICE.

POLICE: WHAT DID HE DO?

LEE: KISSED ME AND THAT.

POLICE: AND THAT?

LEE: CUDDLED ME SORT OF.

POLICE: HOW DID HE CUDDLE YOU?

LEE: HE PUT HIS ARMS AROUND ME.

POLICE: WAS HE NAKED AT THE TIME?

LEE: I CAN'T REMEMBER.

POLICE: DID YOU FEEL HIM AGAINST YOU?

LEE: YES.

POLICE: DID YOU FEEL HIS PENIS?

LEE: I DON'T KNOW.

POLICE: HE HAD HIS LEGS AGAINST YOU DIDN'T HE?

LEE: I THINK SO.

POLICE: WAS HE FACING YOU?

LEE: I DON'T KNOW.

POLICE: HE WOULD FACE YOU TO KISS YOU WOULDN'T HE?

LEE: YES.

POLICE: BUT PERHAPS HE DIDN'T KISS YOU SOME OF THE TIME?

LEE: NO.

POLICE: SO HE HELD YOU IN A DIFFERENT WAY?

LEE: YES.

POLICE: HOW? PERHAPS HE WAS BEHIND YOU BECAUSE YOU DIDN'T WANT HIM TO KISS YOU?

LEE: YES.

POLICE: AND WHEN HE WAS BEHIND YOU, YOU FELT HIM AGAINST YOU I EXPECT?

LEE: YES.

POLICE: DID YOU FEEL ANYTHING AGAINST YOU?

LEE: HIS DICK I SUPPOSE.

POLICE: PENIS.

LEE: YES.

POLICE: YOU FELT HIS PENIS AGAINST YOU? WHERE AGAINST YOU?

LEE: I DON'T KNOW.

POLICE: WELL, IF HE WAS HOLDING YOU IN HIS ARMS I EXPECT YOU WERE IN HIS LAP WEREN'T YOU?

LEE: YES.

POLICE: SO WHERE WOULD HIS PENIS HAVE BEEN?

LEE: AGAINST MY BOTTOM.

POLICE: SO ARE YOU SAYING LEE THAT ROGER PUT HIS PENIS AGAINST YOUR BOTTOM?

LEE: YES.

POLICE: DID HE GET IT IN?

LEE: NO.

POLICE: SURE?

LEE: YES.

POLICE: OKAY. THAT'S ALL FOR NOW.

AND SO, THE GESTURE BECOMES AN ACT, A CONFIRMATION, AN ACCUSATION. LEE CANNOT SEE THE WICKED AND ESSENTIALLY FALSE LOGIC IN THE PROCESS, BECAUSE HE IS A VICTIM OF THE PROCESS. (AS FREIRE SHOWED IN BRAZIL, VICTIMS ALWAYS REMAIN VICTIMS UNTIL THEY REALISE THE TRUE MEANING OF THE WORDS; THAT WORDS ARE NOT NEUTRAL BUT TOOLS TO BE USED FOR OR AGAINST OTHER HUMAN BEINGS.) IT IS TRUE THAT, UNTIL I ACTUALLY SAW LEE OVER THE COURTROOM ON FRIDAY, I DIDN'T SEE THAT THIS WAS PROBABLY HOW THE WHOLE THING HAD BEEN.

FINALLY I WROTE THE FOLLOWING, TRYING TO CONVEY SOMETHING OF WHAT I FELT WHEN I WAS FORCED TO SIT OPPOSITE LEE IN COURT, WHILE HE WAS COMPELLED TO STAND AGAINST ME:

"I NOW OFTEN SEE LEE IN MY INNER EYE AS HE WAS ON FRIDAY. I FEEL THE TENDERNESS I FELT THEN AND RECALL (PERHAPS SURPRISINGLY, BUT MAYBE THIS IS WHERE THE HUMAN TRIUMPHS OVER THE MANUFAC-TURED) THAT THE LOOKS WE SHARED WERE THE MOST IMPORTANT THING. LIKE PAUL HE HAD BEEN SHAKEN, BUT WASN'T DEFEATED. AND I REALISED THAT, LIKE PAUL, HE HAD STRENGTH WHICH I HAD PARTIALLY HELPED HIM TO ACQUIRE. THE CORE OF HIS TRUTH WAS THAT I HAD BEEN WITH HIM LIKE A FATHER: IT WAS HOW I HAD BEEN AND WHAT HE WANTED. YET I AM NOT HIS FATHER—BEYOND THAT, HE DID NOT KNOW. WHILE HE HAD BEEN WITH ME, IGNORANCE ABOUT WHAT LAY BEYOND HAD BEGUN TO GIVE WAY TO HIS OWN KNOWLEDGE; LACK OF DEFINITION HAD BEGUN TO GIVE WAY TO HIS SELF DISCOVERY. HE WASN'T SURE HOW IT WOULD WORK OUT, AND HIS ILLNESS WHEN HE ARRIVED HOME AFTER THE '76 HOLIDAY WAS THE BEST INDICATION THAT HE DESPERATELY FEARED THE TENSIONS THAT HAD BEEN CREATED. FOR A PERIOD HE COULD NOT SEE HOW TO RESOLVE BETWEEN THE "IS" AND THE "COULD BE." BUT HE RECOVERED. AFTER ALL, I HAD SEEN HIM TWICE SINCE THEN; THE GROWING AWARENESS COULD HAVE GONE ON . . .

NOW HE HAD BEEN PENALISED FOR ATTEMPTING TO GROW BEYOND THE CONFUSION; HAS BEEN TOLD IN THE MOST DEVASTATING FASHION THAT THE AREAS INTO WHICH HE WAS MOVING WERE ABSOLUTE TABOO; THAT AN ADULT WHO ENCOURAGES HIM IN HIS JOURNEY TOWARDS SELF-KNOWLEDGE WILL BE PENALISED BY OPPROBRIUM AT BEST AND INCARCERATION AT WORST. HE KNOWS THAT THIS IS NOT THE TRUTH—HENCE HE SEARCHES MY FACE IN COURT TO DISCOVER THAT I REALLY AM WHO I WAS WHEN WE LAST MET. BUT IT IS THE ONLY "TRUTH" HE CAN EXPRESS, BECAUSE EVERYONE AROUND HIM FEARS—OR CANNOT SEE—ANOTHER TRUTH."

ROGER MOODY

MORBID SEX

THE CULPRIT

IS GOD MERELY A MAN FOR WHOM DEATH, OR RATHER, THINKING ABOUT DEATH, IS JUST ONE, PRODIGIOUS PASTIME?

WRONG WAY TO TALK? PERHAPS.

PERHAPS, MORE ACCURATELY, JUST ONE WAY TO LAUGH. BUT CAN'T WE ONCE AND FOR ALL RECONCILE LAUGHTER AND SPEECH? BY SPEECH, I MEAN THAT SPEECH WITHOUT TRAPS WHICH DOESN'T FLEE IN THE FACE OF THE TOTALITY OF ITS OWN CONSEQUENCES.

THIS NARRATIVE IS A BURST OF CUNNING AND THUS LIVELY LAUGHTER, THE LAUGHTER OF A MAN WHO FORCED HIMSELF TO LIVE SHUT-UP WITHIN THE PERSPECTIVE OF DEATH. HE DID THIS UNDER FAVORABLE CIRCUMSTANCES, BUT WITH GREAT DIFFICULTY, AND IN THE END, HE FAILED. FOR LIFE, A MOST INTENSE, AND OFTEN, MOST HEARTRENDING LIFE, BROUGHT HIM BACK IMMEDIATELY.

THIS NARRATIVE EVOLVED OUT OF THE 1939 DECLARATION OF WAR. IT IS INDEPENDENT OF THE AUTHOR'S LIFE. IN FACT, THE AUTHOR PUT TOGETHER THIS STORY FROM PIECES OF THE "JOURNAL" WHICH HE KEPT DESPITE HIMSELF FROM THE DAY WAR BROKE OUT. FORTY-TWO YEARS OLD AT THIS POINT, THE AUTHOR HAD NEVER BEFORE KEPT A DIARY. BUT FACED WITH THE WRITTEN PAGES, HE SOON REALIZED THAT HE HAD NEVER WRITTEN ANYTHING SO MUCH A PART OF HIM AND SO FULLY EXPRESSIVE OF HIMSELF. HE HAD ONLY TO REMOVE THOSE PASSAGES CONCERNING THE THIRD PERSON: IN PARTICULAR, THOSE PASSAGES CONCERNING LAURE'S DEATH, TO WHICH MICHEL LEIRIS REFERS IN LA RÉGLE DU JEU. THIS STORY IS VIOLENTLY DOMINATED BY TEARS; IT IS VIOLENTLY DOMINATED BY DEATH.

TODAY, THE AUTHOR WAS STRUCK BY THE FACT THAT THE CULPRIT IS DOMINATED BY TEARS AND DEATH AT THE SAME TIME THAT IT IS DOMINATED BY THE REPRESENTATION OF GOD. [...]

SEPTEMBER 14, 1939

YESTERDAY, I WENT TO LAURE'S GRAVE; AS SOON AS I LEFT THE HOUSE, I NOTICED HOW DARK THE NIGHT WAS, AND I WONDERED IF I WOULD EVER FIND MY WAY ALONG THE ROAD. IT WAS SO BLACK THAT I

FELT MY THROAT TIGHTEN; I COULDN'T THINK OF ANYTHING ELSE. SO I FOUND IT IMPOSSIBLE TO GO INTO THE STATE OF NEAR-ECSTACY THAT NORMALLY OVERCOMES ME AS I FOLLOW THE SAME PATH. AFTER A LONG WHILE, NEAR THE MIDDLE OF THE WAY, MORE AND MORE LOST, I REMEMBERED THE ASCENT UP ETNA AND I WAS DUMBFOUNDED. EVERYTHING THEN HAD BEEN JUST AS DARK AND CHARGED WITH CUNNING TERROR THE NIGHT LAURE AND I CLIMBED THE FACE OF ETNA.

MOUNT ETNA OVERFLOWED WITH MEANING FOR US; WE HAD GIVEN UP A TRIP TO GREECE TO MAKE THE CLIMB. WHAT WE HAD ALREADY PAID FOR THE CROSSING HAD TO BE REFUNDED. AT DAWN, WE FINALLY REACHED THE EDGE OF THE IMMENSE AND BOTTOMLESS CRATER. WE WERE EXHAUSTED AND IN A WAY TAKEN ABACK BY THE OVERLY STRANGE, OVERLY DISASTROUS SOLITUDE. IT WAS HEART-RENDING TO LEAN OVER THAT GAPING CREVICE, THAT STARY VOID THAT WE BREATHED IN. THE PORTRAIT OF CINDERS AND FLAMES THAT ANDRÉ MASSON PAINTED AFTER WE DESCRIBED THE SCENE TO HIM WAS NEAR LAURE WHEN SHE DIED; IT IS STILL IN MY ROOM. IN THE MIDDLE OF OUR DESCENT, AFTER WE HAD ENTERED AN INFERNALLY HOT AREA, WE COULD STILL FEEL THE FAR-AWAY PRESENCE OF THE VOLCANO'S CRATER AT THE OTHER END OF THE LONG VALLEY OF LAVA. WE COULDN'T IMAGINE A SPOT WHERE THE TERRIBLE INSTABILITY OF THINGS WAS MORE EVIDENT. ALL OF A SUDDEN, LAURE WAS GRIPPED BY SUCH EXTREME ANGUISH THAT SHE INSANELY AND BLINDLY BEGAN TO RUN. THE TERROR AND DESOLATION THAT WE HAD ENCOUNTERED BEWILDERED HER.

YESTERDAY, I CONTINUED MY CLIMB UP THE HILL TOWARDS HER GRAVE, TROUBLED BY A MEMORY SO FULL OF NOCTURNAL TERROR, BUT AT THE SAME TIME, SO FULL OF SUBTERRANEAN GLORY, AN ALREADY SHATTERED NOCTURNAL GLORY INACCESSIBLE TO REAL MEN, ACCESSIBLE ONLY TO SHADOWS, SHIVERING IN THE COLD. BY THE TIME I REACHED THE CEMETERY, I FELT DELIRIOUS. I WAS AFRAID OF HER. I FELT THAT IF SHE APPEARED TO ME, I WOULD SCREAM, TERRIFIED, DESPITE THE EXTREME DARKNESS, I WAS ABLE TO MAKE OUT THE GRAVES, THE CROSSES AND THE TOMBSTONES. THEY EMERGED FROM THE DARKNESS AS FAINTLY PALE FORMS. I COULD ALSO MAKE OUT TWO GLOWING LINES OF VERSE. BUT LAURE'S GRAVE WAS COMPLETELY COVERED BY VEGETATION AND, FOR SOME REASON, WAS THE ONLY ABSOLUTELY BLACK STRETCH OF GROUND. STANDING IN FRONT OF HER GRAVE, I WAS SO OVERCOME WITH PAIN AND SORROW THAT I HELD MYSELF IN MY OWN ARMS WITHOUT KNOWING WHY; AT THIS VERY MOMENT, I FELT AS IF IT HAD SOMEHOW SPLIT IN TWO AND WAS STRANGLING HER. MY HANDS BECAME LOST AROUND MY BODY AND I FELT AS IF I WERE TOUCHING HER, PERCEIVING HER FRAGRANCE. SUDDENLY, A TERRIBLE SOFTNESS GRIPPED ME JUST LIKE WHEN WE WERE CLOSE BEFORE; JUST LIKE WHEN THE OBSTACLES SEPARATING TWO PEOPLE DISAPPEAR. THEN, WHEN I REALIZED THAT I WOULD SOON COME BACK TO MYSELF, TO THE OLD SELF, RESTRICTED BY MY CUMBERSOME NEEDS, I BEGAN TO TREMBLE AND TO ASK HER PARDON. I WEPT BITTERLY, NOT KNOWING WHAT TO DO BECAUSE I KNEW I WOULD LOSE HER AGAIN. I WAS UNBEARABLY ASHAMED OF WHAT I WOULD BECOME, OF THE PERSON I AM NOW AS I WRITE THIS, OR EVEN WORSE. I WAS SURE OF ONLY ONE THING: THE PERCEPTION OF THOSE LOST TO US WHO HAVE BROKEN THEIR ATTACHMENTS TO THE CUSTOMARY CONFINES OF ACTIVITY IS IN NO WAY LIMITED.

WHAT I FELT YESTERDAY WAS NO MORE BURNING, NO MORE TRUE OR FULL OF MEANING CONCERNING THE DESTINY OF EVERY BEING THAN ANY OTHER EXPERIENCE OF THE UNINTELLIGIBLE, NO MATTER HOW VAGUE OR IMPERSONAL. ONE'S BEING BURNS WITH THE DESIRE TO BECOME PURE BEING THROUGH AND THROUGHOUT THE NIGHT. IT BURNS EVEN BRIGHTER AS LOVE SHOWS ITSELF CAPABLE OF CRUMBLING THE PRISON WALLS AROUND EACH OF US. BUT WHAT COULD BE MORE GRAND THAN THE BREACH THROUGH WHICH TWO BEINGS MIGHT RECOGNIZE EACH OTHER WITHOUT SUCCUMBING TO THE VULGARITY AND THE PLATITUDES OF INFINITY? (HE WHO AT LEAST LOVES BEYOND THE GRAVE. FOR HE ALSO ESCAPES THE VULGARITY OF DAILY LIFE BUT NEVER THE TOO-TENUOUS TIES TO LAURE, EVEN HAD THEY BEEN MORE COMPLETELY SEVERED BY HER. SORROW, HORROR, TEARS, MADNESS, SURFEIT, FEVER AND FINALLY DEATH: THESE ARE THE DAILY BREAD THAT LAURE SHARED WITH ME. THIS BREAD LINGERS AS THE MEMORY OF A DREADFUL AND IMMENSE SORROW, AS THE DIMENSIONS OF A LOVE EAGER TO EXCEED THE LIMITS OF ALL THINGS; AND YET, HOW MANY TIMES WHEN WE WERE TOGETHER DID WE ACHIEVE UNACHIEVABLE HAPPINESS, STARLIGHT NIGHTS, FLOWING STREAMS? IN THE FOREST AT NIGHTFALL, SHE WOULD WALK SILENTLY AT MY SIDE, I WOULD LOOK AT HER WITHOUT HER KNOWING IT. WAS I EVER MORE CERTAIN OF WHAT LIFE BRINGS TO US IN RESPONSE TO THE MOST UNFATHOMABLE MOVEMENTS OF THE HEART? I WATCHED MY DESTINY APPROACHING IN THE DARKNESS NEXT TO ME. NO

WORDS COULD EVER EXPRESS HOW MUCH I WAS AWARE OF HER. NOR CAN I EXPRESS JUST HOW BEAUTIFUL SHE WAS; HER IMPERFECT BEAUTY WAS THE FLUID IMAGE OF AN ARDENT AND UNCERTAIN DESTINY. THE FLASHING TRANSPARENCE OF SIMILAR NIGHTS IS EQUALLY INDESCRIBABLE.) AT LEAST HE WHO LOVES BEYOND THE GRAVE HAS THE RIGHT TO FREE THE LOVE WITHIN HIMSELF FROM ITS HUMAN CONFINES, THE RIGHT TO GIVE AS MUCH MEANING TO HIS LOVE AS HE WOULD TO ALMOST ANYTHING ELSE.

I FEEL IT NECESSARY TO INCLUDE THIS PASSAGE FROM LAURE'S LETTER TO JEAN GRÉMILLON OF SEPTEMBER (OR OCTOBER) OF 1937, AFTER OUR RETURN FROM ITALY:

"GEORGES AND I CLIMBED ETNA. IT WAS TERRIFYING. I WOULD LIKE TO TALK TO YOU ABOUT IT, BUT I CAN'T WITHOUT A GREAT DEAL OF UNEASINESS; I COMPARE EVERYTHING I DO TO THIS MEMORY. SO IT IS EASIER FOR ME JUST TO GRIT MY TEETH ... SO HARD—HARD ENOUGH TO BREAK MY JAWS."

I COPIED THESE SENTENCES DOWN BUT I DON'T KNOW ANYMORE IF THERE IS ANY TRUTH TO THEM. I DON'T EVEN LOOK AT THEM ANY MORE, BECAUSE I SIMPLY CAN'T UNLESS I SET OUT TO ACHIEVE THE BARELY ACHIEVABLE, AND I HAVE THE STRENGTH TO DO THIS ONLY RARELY.

SEPTEMBER 19, 1939

THIS IS NOT A FEELING THAT I ALONE EXPERIENCE. A NERVOUSNESS THAT CAN ONLY LEAD TO A CATACLYSM HAS BEEN GROWING NOW FOR OVER A MONTH ...

SEPTEMBER 20, 1939

... BUT NOW I SENSE A NEW NERVOUS CONDITION. FOR FOUR DAYS NOW IT HAS BEEN GETTING WORSE. THIS MORNING I MANAGED TO ESCAPE IT SOMEHOW. THIS MORNING I FOUND MYSELF IN AN ANGELIC HARMONY WITH REALITY THAT WAS THE MOST ... THIS MORNING, IN THIS ROOM THAT I MUST SOON LEAVE, HERE WHERE EVERYTHING WAS ACCOM-PLISHED. ALL OF THE SHUTTERS WERE WIDE OPEN. THE SKY WAS SLIGHTLY HAZY, BUT THERE WERE NO CLOUDS, AND THE PLANTS IN THE WINDOW HARDLY

MOVED. THIS HOUSE, SURROUNDED BY GRAND OLD TREES, THE ONLY HOUSE TO AFFORD LAURE SOME REST BEFORE SHE DIED, A BRIEF RESPITE, THE NEARBY FOREST, HER GRAVE, THE CROW AND THE DESERT ... SO MANY CURSES, SO MUCH MIRACU-LOUS DARKNESS, BUT THIS MORNING, A SUN ATTENUATED BY A LUMINOUS HAZE AND SOON, THE FINAL DEPARTURE. THE SECRET TRANSPARENCE OF THE LIGHT, OF CHAOS AND OF DEATH, ALL THE MAJESTY OF RECEDING LIFE, MY FORTUITOUS SENSUALITY, MY PERVERSIONS, I WILL NEVER ABANDON THESE THINGS OF WHICH I AM MADE, CONFUSING MYSELF WITH THE IMMENSE SORROW OF A FRACTURED WORLD, A WORLD FRACTURED BY ILL TEMPER, BY THE CROWD'S SORDID RAGE, BY MISERY CRINGING BEFORE FATE. I LOVE WHO I AM SO MUCH! BUT I'VE REMAINED FAITHFUL TO DEATH (LIKE A FAITHFUL LOVER) [...].

LAURE'S PRESENCE, AS SOFT AS AN AXE FLASHING IN THE NIGHT, SPRINGS UP ALL OF A SUDDEN "LIKE A ROBBER IN THE NIGHT" AND SPREADS A CHILLING EMBRACE AS DEEP AND AIRY AS A NIGHT WIND. BUT I MUST MAKE A CONCENTRATED EFFORT TO LEAVE THIS PRESENCE; IT DEMANDS THAT I LEAVE JUST AS FORCIBLY. [...]

I WAS EQUALLY TERRIFIED BECAUSE LAURE'S FACE VAGUELY RESEMBLED THE HORRIBLY TRAGIC FACE OF THAT MAN OEDIPUS, EMPTY, HALF CRAZED. THE RESEMBLENCE GREW THROUGHOUT HER LONG PERIOD OF SUFFERING WHILE FEVER WORE HER DOWN, PERHAPS MOST DURING HER FITS OF ANGER AND HATRED FOR ME. I TRIED TO FLEE WHAT I SAW THERE. I FLED MY FATHER. (TWENTY-FIVE YEARS AGO, I ABANDONED HIM TO FATE DURING THE GERMAN INVASION, WHILE I FLED WITH MY MOTHER. HE STAYED BEHIND IN RHEIMS, ATTENDED BY THE MAID. HE WAS BLIND AND PARALYZED AND HE CONTINUALLY EXPERIENCED GREAT PAIN.) I FLED LAURE. (I FLED HER IN A MORAL SENSE. I OFTEN FACED HER IN TERROR, ALTHOUGH I WAS BY HER SIDE UNTIL THE VERY END; I COULD NEVER HAVE GIVEN ANY LESS OF MYSELF. BUT AS SHE APPROACHED THE TERRIBLE END, I BEGAN TO TAKE REFUGE IN A SICKLY TORPOR. SOMETIMES I DRANK, SOMETIMES I JUST WASN'T THERE.) [...]

THE NATURAL CONDITION OF SIMPLICITY IS ACTION. BUT IN ORDER TO ACT, ONE MUST FOLLOW A CRUEL IMPERATIVE TO IGNORE ALL OF THE APPARENT CONTRADICTIONS. HOW CAN I POSSIBLY ACT IF THE IMPERATIVES WHICH CONTROL ME ARE LAURE'S SUDDEN PANIC AND SUFFERING AS WELL AS THAT NIGHT OF PAINFUL AND SORROWFUL CRIES WHEN

MY FATHER APPEARED BEFORE ME [...].

SEPTEMBER 30, OCTOBER 1, 1939

AMONG ALL THE PIECES I'VE WRITTEN FOR PUBLICATION IN A WIDE RANGE OF PERIODICALS, ONLY ONE, ENTITLED THE SACRED AND PUBLISHED IN CAHIERS D'ART, PORTRAYS WITH ANY REAL CLARITY THAT PARTICULAR RESOLUTION WHICH MOTIVATES ME NOW. ALTHOUGH THE PIECE IS FAR BEHIND ME NOW, ITS "COMMUNICATION" IS NO MORE CLUMSILY DISTANCED OR UNEASY THAN IN MOST OF WHAT I HAVE PUBLISHED SINCE. IN ANY CASE, THE DEMONSTRATIVE SIDE OF THE TEXT DID REACH SOME OF THOSE FOR WHOM IT WAS REALLY INTENDED. I BELIEVE THAT THE REMAINING IGNORANCE AND UNCERTAINTY DOESN'T MATTER. WE CANNOT POSSIBLY LIMIT HOPE NOW. MEN WHOSE LIVES SEEM NECESSARILY LIKE A LONG STORM— WHO CAN BE SAVED ONLY BY A BOLT OF LIGHT-NING—WAIT FOR SOMETHING NO LESS DELIRIOUS THAN SACRED.

WHEN A REALLY ESSENTIAL CHANGE COMES ABOUT, IT SHOULDN'T BE ATTRIBUTED TO THE WRITTEN WORD. WHEN SENTENCES IMPART A MEANING, IT IS ONLY BECAUSE THEY UNITE SOME OTHER THINGS WHICH WERE PREVIOUSLY SEARCH-ING FOR EACH OTHER. SENTENCES THAT SCREAM CONTINUALLY DIE FROM THEIR OWN OUTBURST. WE MUST ERASE WHAT HAS BEEN WRITTEN BY PLACING IT IN THE SHADOW OF THE REALITY WHICH IT EXPRESSES. THIS HONESTY IS NOWHERE MORE PERTINENT THAT IN THAT PARTICULAR ARTICLE.

[CROSSED OUT: I WROTE IT LAST YEAR, FROM AUGUST THROUGH NOVEMBER, I AGREED TO DO IT WITH DUTHUIT, THE SPECIAL EDITOR OF THE CAHIER D'ART ISSUE IN WHICH IT WAS TO APPEAR. I SHOULD ALSO MENTION ONE ESSENTIAL DETAIL ABOUT THE CIRCUMSTANCES SURROUN...]

ESSENTIALLY, I FEEL I MUST DESCRIBE ONE OF THE SITUATIONS SURROUNDING THE WRITING OF THE ARTICLE. DURING THE LAST FEW DAYS OF LAURE'S SICKNESS, DURING THE AFTERNOON OF NOVEMBER 2, I HAD COME TO THE PASSAGE IN THE ARTICLE WHERE I WAS DESCRIBING THE IDENTITY OF THE "GRAAL" WHICH WE ARE ALWAYS SEEKING AS RELIGION'S GOAL. I ENDED WITH THIS SENTENCE: "CHRISTIANITY HAS SUBSTANTIALIZED THE SACRED. BUT THE EXACT NATURE OF THE SACRED, IN WHICH

WE CURRENTLY RECOGNIZE THE BURNING EXIS-TENCE OF RELIGION, IS PERHAPS THE MOST ELUSIVE PRODUCT OF HUMAN INTERACTION. THE SACRED IS NOTHING MORE THAN A PRIVILEGED MOMENT OF UNITY IN COMMUNION, A CONVULSIVE MOMENT FULL OF WHAT IS NORMALLY SMOTHERED." I IMMEDIATELY ADDED A NOTE IN THE MARGINS TO CLEARLY INDICATE, AT LEAST TO MYSELF, THE MEANING OF THESE LAST FEW LINES: "IDENTIFICA-TION WITH LOVE."

I WROTE THESE WORDS IN THE MARGINS, AS I OFTEN DO, WITH THE INTENTION OF COMING BACK TO THEM LATER IN THE ARTICLE. I DIDN'T. IN ADDITION, I READ LAURE'S MANUSCRIPTS BEFORE I CONTINUED WRITING.

I REMEMBERED LOOKING UP AT THIS MOMENT AND SEEING A THIN RAY OF INCREDIBLY BEAUTIFUL SUNLIGHT PLAYING OVER THE GOLDEN-RED LEAVES OF THE TREES ABOUT A HUNDRED FEET FROM MY WINDOW. I TRIED TO CONTINUE WRITING, BUT I COULD BARELY MANAGE ANOTHER TWO SENTENCES. THEN, THE MOMENT CAME WHEN I WAS FINALLY ALLOWED TO SEE LAURE AGAIN IN HER ROOM. AS I DREW NEAR TO HER, I IMMEDIATELY REALIZED THAT HER CONDITION HAD WORSENED. I TRIED SPEAKING TO HER, BUT SHE DID NOT RESPOND. SHE SPOKE CONTINUALLY, ABSORBED WITHIN A VAST DELIRIUM. SHE NO LONGER SAW ME NOR RECOGNIZED MY PRESENCE. I UNDERSTOOD THAT IT WAS ALL OVER, THAT I COULD NEVER SPEAK TO HER AGAIN, THAT THIS WAS HOW SHE WOULD DIE IN A FEW HOURS, THAT WE WOULD NEVER SPEAK TO EACH OTHER AGAIN. THE NURSE WHISPERED TO ME THAT IT WAS ALL OVER. I BROKE OUT INTO TEARS; SHE NO LONGER UNDERSTOOD ME. THE PITILESS WORLD COLLAPSED ALL AROUND ME. I WAS SO OVERCOME THAT I WAS UNABLE TO KEEP HER MOTHER AND SISTERS FROM INVADING THE HOUSE AND HER ROOM.

SHE SUFFERED FOR FOUR DAYS. FOR FOUR DAYS, SHE REMAINED ABSENT, TALKING TO THIS OR THAT PERSON ACCORDING TO SOME UNPREDICTABLE WHIM. AT TIMES, SHE GREW TENSE ONLY TO QUICKLY RELAPSE INTO LETHARGY. SHE UNDERSTOOD NOTHING. SOMETIMES, BRIEFLY, HER PHRASES MADE SENSE; SHE WOULD ASK ME TO LOOK IN HER BAG OR AMONG HER PAPERS FOR SOMETHING THAT SHE URGENTLY NEEDED. I SHOWED HER EVERY-THING THERE BUT I COULDN'T FIND WHAT SHE WANTED. FOR THE FIRST TIME, I CAME ACROSS A SHEET OF PAPER, BLANK EXCEPT FOR THE HEADING THE SACRED, WHICH I SHOWED TO HER. I HAD THE

FEELING SHE WOULD SPEAK TO ME AGAIN, AFTER SHE DIED, ONCE I HAD THE OPPORTUNITY TO READ THE PAPERS SHE HAD LEFT BEHIND. I KNOW THAT SHE HAD WRITTEN, BUT SHE HAD NEVER ASKED ME TO READ ANY OF IT. I NEVER THOUGHT I WOULD FIND AMONG ALL OF HER ABANDONED WORKS AN ANSWER TO PRECISELY THAT QUESTION COWERING IN ME LIKE A STARVING ANIMAL.

I STOPPED LOOKING FOR WHAT SHE WANTED. "TIME" WAS READY TO "CUT HER DOWN;" IT DID AND I STOOD WATCHING WHAT WAS HAPPENING, HEAVY WITH LIFE AND YET, POWERLESS TO UNDERSTAND ANYTHING MORE THAN HER DEATH. I WON'T SAY HOW SHE DIED ALTHOUGH I FEEL MOST "HORRIBLY" THE NEED TO DESCRIBE IT.

WHEN IT WAS ALL OVER, I FOUND MYSELF SIFTING THROUGH HER PAPERS, READING PAGES THAT I HAD NOTICED FOR THE FIRST TIME DURING THE PERIOD JUST BEFORE HER DEATH. WHEN I READ WHAT SHE HAD WRITTEN, I EXPERIENCED ONE OF THE MOST VIOLENT EMOTIONS OF MY LIFE. BUT I WAS NEVER MORE DEEPLY NOR BRUTALLY AFFECTED THAN WHEN I READ THE LAST SENTENCE OF A PASSAGE ON THE SACRED. I HAD NEVER EX-PRESSED TO HER THAT PARADOXICAL IDEA THAT THE SACRED IS COMMUNICATION. I MYSELF DISCOVERED THE NOTION ONLY ONCE I HAD PUT IT INTO WORDS, A FEW MOMENTS BEFORE I NOTICED THAT LAURE WAS ABOUT TO DIE. WITHOUT A DOUBT, NOTHING I HAD EVER SAID TO HER CAME CLOSE TO EXPRESSING THIS IDEA. THE WHOLE QUESTION WAS SO IMPORTANT TO ME THAT I REMEMBER EXACTLY HOW AND WHEN EVERYTHING HAPPENED. WHAT'S MORE, WE ALMOST NEVER CARRIED ON "INTELLEC-TUAL CONVERSATIONS." ONCE SHE EVEN BLAMED ME FOR NOT TAKING HER SERIOUSLY. THE TRUTH IS, I DISDAINED THE INEVITABLE IMPUDENCE OF "INTELLECTUAL CONVERSATIONS."

FINALLY, TOWARDS THE BOTTOM OF THE PAGE, I FOUND THE FOLLOWING SENTENCES IN LAURE'S SCRAWL:

"A POETIC WORK IS SACRED TO THE EXTENT THAT IT IS THE CREATION OF A TOPICAL EVENT, 'COMMUNI-CATION' EXPERIENCED AS NUDITY. IT IS SELF-RAPE, DENUDING, COMMUNICATING TO OTHERS A REASON TO LIVE, FOR THIS REASON TO LIVE 'DISPLACES' ITSELF." EXACTLY WHAT I HAD WRITTEN IN MY ARTICLE, SINCE MY NOTION OF "UNITY IN COMMUN-ION" FIGURES IMPLICITLY IN LAURE'S IDEAS.

LET ME INTERRUPT THIS NARRATIVE FOR A MOMENT

TO DESCRIBE A CAPTIVATING IMAGE THAT JUST CAME TO MY MIND, AN IMAGE THAT ENCOMPASSES AN ENTIRE VISION, AN IMAGE AT BEST OF AN ECSTATIC OUTBURST, OF AN "ANGEL," AS FAR AWAY AND AS IMPERCEPTIBLE AS A DOT ON THE HORIZON, PIERCING THROUGH THE CLOUDY THICKNESS OF THE NIGHT, BUT NEVER APPEARING AS MORE THAN A STRANGELY INTERIOR GLOW. IT APPEARS LIKE THE UNFATHOMABLE VACILLATIONS OF A STREAK OF LIGHTNING. THE ANGEL RAISES UP BEFORE ITSELF A LANCE OF CRYSTAL THAT SHATTERS IN THE SILENCE." [...]

OCTOBER 2, 1939

MAYBE THE ANGEL IS THE "MOVEMENT OF THE WORLDS."

I LOVE HER NEITHER AS AN ANGEL NOR AS A RECOGNIZABLE DIVINITY; THE VISION OF THE SHATTERED CRYSTAL FREES THE SCREAMING LOVE WITHIN ME THAT MAKES ME WANT TO DIE.

I KNOW THAT THIS DESIRE TO DIE RESIDES ON THE IMPOSSIBLE EDGES OF BEING, BUT I CAN SPEAK OF NOTHING ELSE SINCE I DISCOVERED THOSE TWO SENTENCES THAT LINK LAURE'S LIFE AND MINE THROUGH THE EARTH COVERING HER COFFIN. MOREOVER, THESE VERY SENTENCES EXIST NOWHERE ELSE BUT AT THIS VERY POINT.

LAURE AND I OFTEN THOUGHT THAT THE WALL BETWEEN US WAS CRUMBLING. THE SAME WORDS AND THE SAME DESIRES WENT THROUGH OUR MINDS AT THE SAME TIME. LAURE WAS REPULSED BECAUSE SHE OFTEN FELT IT AS A LOSS, A NEGATION OF HERSELF. I CAN'T REMEMBER ANY OF THESE COINCIDENCES, BUT I DO KNOW THAT NONE OF THEM EVER HAD THE EXTRAORDINARY SIGNIFI-CANCE OF THESE TWO SENTENCES ON "COMMUNI-CATION."

I FIND IT VERY DIFFICULT TO EXPRESS JUST EXACTLY WHAT THE PARALLEL PASSAGES MEAN. I FEEL OBLIGED TO TRY, BUT FIRST, I MUST DESCRIBE ALL OF THE DISPARATE ELEMENTS THAT MAKE UP THEIR MEANING.

[CROSSED OUT: I WILL DESCRIBE ONLY ONE MORE THING TODAY: THE NEARLY SIMULTANEOUS PUBLICATION OF THE TWO TEXTS OBLIGES ME TO SAY TO THOSE WHO SUFFER FROM THE SAME THIRST

AS LAURE AND I THAT]

AT THE ONSET OF THE WAR WHEN I BEGAN WRITING, I WANTED TO BRING MYSELF TO THIS POINT. THIS WAS THE ONLY WAY I COULD DO IT, AND I KNEW IT FOR A LONG TIME. I DECIDED TO DO WHAT I'M DOING NOW SEVERAL WEEKS BEFORE THE WAR BROKE OUT. BUT I HAVEN'T FINISHED; I'VE HARDLY BEGUN. FACED WITH WHAT I STILL WANT TO SAY, MY "TONGUE IS TIED."

ON THE OTHER HAND, WHAT'S HAPPENING TO ME TODAY IS SO VERY INEXPRESSIBLE AND AS FOREIGN TO WHAT IS REAL AS A DREAM. WITHOUT ALMOST ANIMAL AUSTERITY, NOTHING OF MYSELF CAN EMERGE FROM THIS FAIRY TALE. THIS FRAGILE ILLUSION DISAPPEARS AT THE SIGN OF THE SLIGHTEST HESITATION, THE SLIGHTEST BREAK IN ATTENTION.

EXCEPT WHEN I WAS NEAR LAURE, I HAVE NEVER FELT SUCH GENTLE PURITY, SUCH SILENT SIMPLICITY. AND YET, THIS TIME, IT IS ONLY A FLICKERING IN THE VOID AS IF A NOCTURNAL BUTTERFLY, UNAWARE OF ITS ETHERIAL BEAUTY, HAD COME TO REST ON THE HEAD OF A SLEEPING MAN.

OCTOBER 3, 1939

IT IS BECOMING MORE DIFFICULT FOR ME TO CONTINUE. I MUST BE ENTERING THAT "KINGDOM" WHERE EVEN THE KINGS ARE AT A LOSS. AND NOT ONLY THAT; BUT FROM WITHIN THIS "KINGDOM" I HAVE TO SPEAK WITHOUT STUTTERING. IN FACT, I HAVE TO FIND WORDS WHICH GO STRAIGHT TO THE HEART. THE MISSION I MUST FULFILL IS AS FAR AWAY AS POSSIBLE FROM THE OBSCURE NEED I FEEL TO LOSE MYSELF. I AM ENTERING A DESERT OF TOTAL SOLITUDE WHOSE EMPTINESS LAURE, NOW DEAD, ONLY MAGNIFIES.

ABOUT A YEAR AGO, I FOUND A RAY OF MAGICAL SUNLIGHT ON THE THRESHOLD OF THAT DESERT. STRUGGLING TO PIERCE THROUGH THE NOVEMBER FOG, THROUGH THE ROTTEN UNDERGROWTH, THROUGH THE UNREAL RUINS, THIS RAY OF SUNLIGHT REVEALED BEFORE ME AN OLD PANE OF GLASS IN THE WINDOW OF AN ABANDONED COTTAGE. AT THIS MOMENT, I FELT ECSTATICALLY LOST, AT THE DESOLATE EDGE OF EVERYTHING HUMAN. I HAD JUST WANDERED THROUGH A FOREST AFTER HAVING LEFT LAURE'S BODY TO THE GRAVEDIGGERS. I WALKED ALONG A PROTRUDING WALL OF BRICK UNTIL I DISCOVERED A MUSTY PANE OF GLASS, COVERED ON THE OUTSIDE WITH A CENTURY OF DUST. IF SOME VISION OF DECAY OR WASTE HAD APPEARED TO ME IN THIS ABANDONED PLACE, I WOULD HAVE TAKEN IT AS AN ACCURATE IMAGE OF MY OWN MISFORTUNE. I WAS WANDERING AIMLESSLY, FEELING THAT I MYSELF HAD BEEN DESERTED. I WAS READY TO WAIT AN INFINITY FOR THE WORLD OF MY DESOLATION TO OPEN UP BEFORE ME, SPLENDID BUT INSUFFERABLE. I WAITED AND I TREMBLED. WHAT I SAW THROUGH THE WINDOW WHERE MY WANDERING HAD BROUGHT ME WAS ON THE CONTRARY THE VERY IMAGE OF LIFE IN ITS MOST LUCID WHIMSIES. THERE, A FEW FEET AWAY, BEHIND THE WINDOW, WAS A COLLECTION OF BRIGHTLY COLORED, EXOTIC BIRDS. I COULDN'T IMAGINE ANYTHING MORE SWEET BEHIND THE DUST, THE DEAD BRANCHES AND THE UPTURNED STONES THAN THESE SILENT BIRDS, FORGOTTEN BY THEIR MASTER WHO HAD LONG SINCE DISAPPEARED. IT WAS OBVIOUS THAT NOTHING HAD BEEN TOUCHED SINCE SOME LONG AGO DEATH. UNDER THE DUST, PAPERS WERE SPREAD ABOUT IN THE DESK AS IF IN PREPARATION FOR A VISIT. I NOTICED A PHOTOGRAPH OF THE OWNER NOT FAR FROM THE WINDOW. HE HAD WHITE HAIR AND A LOOK THAT SEEMED TO ME TO BE ONE OF GOODWILL AND ANGELIC NOBILITY. HE WORE THE CLOTHES OF THE MIDDLE CLASS, OR MORE EXACTLY, OF THE LEARNED CLASS OF THE SECOND EMPIRE.

AT THIS MOMENT, FROM THE DEPTHS OF MY MISERY, I NEVERTHELESS FELT THAT LAURE HAD NOT ABANDONED ME AND THAT HER INCREDIBLE SOFTNESS CONTINUED TO COME THROUGH TO ME DESPITE DEATH AS IT HAD EVEN WHEN SHE WAS EXTREMELY ANGRY AND VIOLENT TOWARDS ME (I CANNOT RECALL THOSE MOMENTS WITHOUT A FEELING OF HORROR).

OCTOBER 4, 1939

TODAY IS THE FIRST REAL DAY OF AUTUMN OR WINTER. IT IS COLD AND GRAY. AND, I'M THROWN BACK TO THE DESERT WORLD OF LAST FALL. ONCE AGAIN, I FEEL FROZEN AND NUMB, FAR FROM SHORE AND NO LESS A STRANGER TO MYSELF THAN ANYONE LOST AT SEA. ONCE AGAIN, I AM GRIPPED BY A KIND OF MONOTONOUS AND ABSENT ECSTASY. I CLENCH MY TEETH AS I DID LAST YEAR. SUDDENLY, THE DISTANCE BETWEEN MY LIFE AND LAURE'S DEATH VANISHES.

WHEN I WALK THROUGH THE STREETS OF RHEIMS, I DISCOVER ANEW A TRUTH THAT KEEPS ME FROM SLEEPING. THIS PECULIAR AND PAINFUL CONTRACTION OF MY ENTIRE LIFE THAT IS SO CLEARLY LINKED TO LAURE'S DEATH AND THE LINGERING SADNESS OF AUTUMN IS THE ONLY WAY I CAN "CRUCIFY" MYSELF.

ON SEPTEMBER 28, I WROTE: "I REALIZE THAT IF I WANT TO OVERCOME MY EROTIC HABITS, I MUST INVENT A NEW WAY OF CRUCIFYING MYSELF. IT MUST BE AS INTOXICATING AS ALCOHOL." WHAT I NOW PERCEIVE FRIGHTENS ME [...].

OCTOBER 11, 1939

DURING LAURE'S LAST HOURS, WHILE I WAS WANDERING AROUND OUR DILAPIDATED YARD AMIDST THE DEAD LEAVES AND WITHERED SHRUBS, I FOUND ONE OF THE MOST BEAUTIFUL FLOWERS I HAVE EVER SEEN. IT WAS A ROSE, "THE COLOR OF AUTUMN," BARELY OPENED. DESPITE MY FRAME OF MIND, I PICKED IT AND BROUGHT IT TO LAURE. SHE WAS LOST WITHIN HERSELF, LOST WITHIN AN INDEFINITE DELIRIUM. BUT WHEN I GAVE HER THE ROSE, SHE CAME OUT OF HER STRANGE STATE LONG ENOUGH TO SMILE AT ME AND SAY, "IT'S BEAUTIFUL." THIS WAS ONE OF HER LAST COHERENT SENTENCES. THEN, SHE BROUGHT THE ROSE TO HER LIPS AND KISSED IT WITH A DELIRIOUS PASSION AS IF SHE WANTED TO HOLD IN EVERYTHING THAT WAS ESCAPING HER. THIS LASTED BUT A MOMENT; SHE FLUNG THE ROSE LIKE A CHILD THROWING DOWN ITS TOYS AND ONCE AGAIN, SHE WAS A STRANGER TO ALL WHO APPROACHED HER, BREATHING CONVULSIVELY.

OCTOBER 12, 1939

YESTERDAY, IN THE OFFICE OF ONE OF MY CO-WORKERS, WHILE HE WAS ON THE TELEPHONE, I WAS OVERCOME WITH ANGUISH. IMPERCEPTIBLY, I RETREATED WITHIN MYSELF, MY GAZE FIXED ON LAURE'S DEATHBED (THE ONE IN WHICH I NOW SLEEP EVERY NIGHT). LAURE AND THE BED WERE WITHIN MY HEART; IN FACT, MY HEART WAS LAURE STRETCHED OUT ON THE BED. WITHIN THE DARKNESS OF THIS THORACIC CAGE, LAURE DIED JUST AS SHE WAS LIFTING ONE OF A BUNCH OF ROSES SPREAD OUT BEFORE HER. SHE WAS

HOLDING IT AS IF EXHAUSTED, AND SHE CRIED OUT IN A VOICE ALMOST ABSENT AND INFINITELY PAINFUL: "THE ROSE!" I THINK THESE WERE HER LAST WORDS. THERE IN THAT OFFICE AND LATER THAT EVENING, THE UPLIFTED ROSE AND THE CRY REMAINED IN MY HEART FOR A LONG TIME. PERHAPS LAURE'S VOICE WASN'T PAINED, PERHAPS IT WAS SIMPLY HEARTRENDING. I REMEMBERED WHAT I HAD FELT THAT MORNING: "TAKE A FLOWER AND LOOK AT IT UNTIL HARMONY ..." THAT WAS A VISION, AN INTERNAL VISION MAINTAINED BY A SILENTLY EXPERIENCED NEED. IT WASN'T A RANDOM THOUGHT [...].

OCTOBER 21, 1939

I SENT A LETTER TODAY BREAKING OFF RELATIONS WITH SOME PEOPLE WHOM I SHOULD NEVER HAVE TRUSTED TO BEGIN WITH. TOO OFTEN, I HAVE SECOND THOUGHTS ABOUT MY DECISIONS. [CROSSED OUT: OFTEN, I CRITICIZED LAURE'S VIOLENT CURSING ALTHOUGH I BORE IT WITH NO LITTLE PAIN, CLINGING TO THIS SUFFERING AS TO A CHANCE TO LIVE. NOW, KNOWING WHAT I HAVE LIVED THROUGH AND WHAT I LOVE, I REALIZE THAT I WOULD HAVE LOST EVERYTHING WITHOUT MY INEXPLICABLE PATIENCE. BUT THOSE WHO HAVE WORN OUT MY PATIENCE HAVE COMPLETELY DESTROYED THE RAPPORT THAT I HAVE WITH THEM.] [...]

WHAT SURROUNDS ME NOW COULD ALL DISAPPEAR IN A FEW HOURS. AT LEAST, I COULD BODILY LEAVE THIS DREAM PLACE. BUT A BEAUTIFUL NEED HAS BEEN INSCRIBED WITHIN ME AS IT WAS WITHIN LAURE'S DESTINY, A NEED TO MOVE AROUND IN A WORLD FULL OF SECRET MEANINGS, WHERE I CANNOT LOOK AT A WINDOW, A TREE OR A CABINET DOOR WITHOUT A GREAT DEAL OF ANGUISH. NEITHER OF US DID ANYTHING (OR VERY LITTLE) TO ORGANIZE THE WORLD AROUND OURSELVES. IT SIMPLY APPEARED IN PLACE AS THE FOG LIFTED LITTLE BY LITTLE. IT DEPENDED ON DISASTER NO MORE THAN IT DID ON DREAMS. BECAUSE A MAN WHO DESIRES BEAUTY FOR WHAT IT IS WILL NEVER ENTER INTO THE WORLD. INSANTIY, ASCETICISM, HATRED, ANGUISH AND THE DOMINATION OF FEAR ARE ALL NECESSARY; ONE MUST HAVE SO MUCH LOVE THAT EVEN ON ITS THRESHOLD, DEATH APPEARS LUDICROUS. A WINDOW, A TREE, A CABINET DOOR ARE NOTHING IF THEY CANNOT BEAR WITNESS TO MOVEMENT AND TO HEARTRENDING DESTRUCTION [...].

NOVEMBER 7, 1939

LAURE DIED ONE YEAR AGO TODAY.

I RECEIVED THE FOLLOWING LETTER FROM MICHEL LEIRIS LAST SUNDAY. HE HAS NEVER BEFORE EXPRESSED HIMSELF LIKE THIS.

COLOMB-BÉCHAR, OCTOBER 29, 1939

DEAR GEORGES,

HERE WE ARE, CLOSE TO THAT MOMENT OF THE YEAR WHEN WE CAN LOOK BACK AND CONSIDER, SOMETIMES WITH TERROR, ALL THAT HAS HAPPENED IN ONE YEAR ...

I DON'T WANT TO INSIST ON ANY ONE THING (ANY INSISTENCE WOULD BE A SACRILEGE IN THIS CASE); RATHER, I WANT TO TELL YOU THAT SOMETIMES, WHEN I'M IN A MELANCHOLIC MOOD, I AUTOMATICALLY RETURN TO CERTAIN MEMORIES WHICH, EVERYTHING CONSIDERED, ARE MORE REASON TO HOPE THAN TO DESPAIR.

WHAT UNITES US WITH JUST A FEW INDIVIDUALS CANNOT BE THE EXTENT OF ALL HUMANLY VALUABLE THINGS, OF ALL THINGS CAPABLE OF SURVIVING ANY AND ALL VICISSITUDES.

I'M USING RATHER SOLEMN LANGUAGE HERE—FAR FROM MY USUAL PRACTICE—LANGUAGE WHICH MAKES ME A LITTLE ASHAMED, OUT OF MODESTY PERHAPS, OR OUT OF HUMAN RESPECT (SACRIFICING ONCE MORE MY MANIA TO REDUCE EVERYTHING). I HOPE YOU WILL FORGIVE ME AND UNDERSTAND DESPITE MY WORDS ALL THAT I WOULD LIKE TO SAY TO YOU AS SPONTANEOUSLY AS AN EXPRESSION OF GRIEF OR A BURST OF LAUGHTER ...

MICHEL

[...]

I JUST CAME OUT OF THE HELDER THEATER WHERE I SAW WUTHERING HEIGHTS: HEATHCLIFF LIVING WITH CATHY'S GHOST AS I WANTED TO LIVE WITH LAURE'S GHOST. LAST SATURDAY, IN LA VAISSENET, I DREAMED ABOUT WUTHERING HEIGHTS, I EVEN DREAMED ABOUT IT IN FERLUC. I SUPPOSE THIS PEREGRINATION FROM HOUSE TO HOUSE IN THE MOUNTAINS WAS NECESSARY TO HELP ME FORGET MY DISLIKE FOR "COMEDY." BUT THAT IS MY CURRENT EXPLANATION. AFTER ALL, I'M BEGINNING TO FEEL MORE AND MORE IGNORANT.

I'VE STOPPED THINKING INSISTENTLY ABOUT LAURE.

THE THOUGHT OF DENISE, ALIVE, POSSESSES ME ENTIRELY. IN THE MIDDLE OF ALL THIS CHAOS, I AM ALIVE, INEBRIATED BY THIS WEIGHTY PURITY OF DENISE, MORE BEAUTIFUL THAN I COULD HAVE EVER IMAGINED (BUT BEAUTIFUL, IT SEEMS TO ME, AS AN ANIMAL IS BEAUTIFUL). TO NOT LOVE DENISE THIS WAY, TO NOT FEEL THIS DEATH-LIKE UNEASINESS IN MY HEART WOULD BE TO BETRAY EVERYTHING. IT IS AS INCONCEIVABLE AS A PLANT THAT HAS STOPPED BUDDING AND GROWING [...].

IN DECEMBER OF 1937, WE ASKED MAURICE HEINE TO DRIVE US TO THE SPOT THAT SADE HAD CHOSEN FOR HIS OWN BURIAL. "HE SHALL BE SOWN OVER THE ACORNS ..." CONSUMED BY OAK ROOTS, DISINTEGRATING TO NOTHINGNESS IN THE EARTH BENEATH A THICKET OF BUSHES ... IT WAS SNOWING THAT DAY, AND WE LOST OUR WAY IN THE FOREST. THE WIND WAS SAVAGE. AFTER WE RETURNED, LAURE AND I PREPARED A DINNER FOR IVANOV AND ODOïEVTSOVA. AS WE HAD EXPECTED, DINNER WAS NO LESS SAVAGE THAN THE WIND. ODOïEVTSOVA UNDRESSED AND BEGAN VOMITING.

IN MARCH OF 1938, WE WENT BACK TO THE SAME SPOT WITH MICHEL LEIRIS AND ZETTE. HEINE DIDN'T GO WITH US. ON THIS OCCASION, AT EPERON, LAURE SAW THE LAST FILM OF HER LIFE, THE ONE WAY TRIP (A 1932 FILM BY TAY GARNETT) WHICH SHE HAD NEVER SEEN BEFORE. SHE WALKED ALL DAY AS IF DEATH WEREN'T WEARING HER AWAY, AND WE ARRIVED IN BROAD DAYLIGHT AT THE EDGE OF THE POND SADE HAD CHOSEN. THE GERMANS HAD JUST TAKEN VIENNA AND THE AIR ALREADY SMELLED OF WAR. THAT EVENING, LAURE THOUGHT ABOUT TAKING LEIRIS AND ZETTE FOR A WALK ALONG A PATH WE BOTH LIKED. WE WANTED TO INVITE THEM TO HAVE DINNER WITH US. BUT NO SOONER HAD WE RETURNED THAN LAURE BEGAN TO FEEL THE FIRST EFFECTS OF THE ILLNESS THAT EVENTUALLY CAUSED HER DEATH. SHE HAD A HIGH FEVER AND WENT TO BED, UNAWARE THAT SHE WOULD PROBABLY NEVER GET UP AGAIN. AFTER SHE SAW SADE'S "GRAVE," LAURE WENT OUT ONLY ONCE, AT THE END OF AUGUST, I TOOK HER BY CAR TO OUR SAINT GERMAIN HOUSE IN THE FOREST. SHE FELL ONCE, IN FRONT OF A TREE THAT HAD BEEN STRUCK BY LIGHTNING. ON THE WAY THERE, WE TRAVELLED OVER THE MONTAIGU PLAINS WHOSE HILLS AND FIELDS GREATLY DELIGHTED LAURE. BUT NO SOONER HAD WE ENTERED THE FOREST THAN SHE SAW TWO DEAD CROWS, HANGING FROM THE BRANCHES OF A TREE ...

I WOULD HAVE WANTED HIM TO ALWAYS ACCOMPANY ME
AND PRECEDE ME,

LIKE A KNIGHT AND HIS HERALD.

(THE CROW. FROM THE WRITINGS OF LAURE)

WE WERE NOT FAR FROM THE HOUSE. I SAW THE TWO CROWS A FEW DAYS LATER, WHEN I PASSED BY THE SAME SPOT. I TOLD HER; SHE SHIVERED AND CHOKED ON HER WORDS SO BADLY THAT I WAS FRIGHTENED. I UNDERSTOOD ONLY AFTER HER DEATH THAT SHE HAD CONSIDERED THE DEAD BIRDS AS A SIGN. BUT BY THEN, LAURE WAS NOTHING MORE THAN AN INERT BODY. I HAD JUST LOOKED THROUGH HER MANUSCRIPTS AND ONE OF THE FIRST I HAD READ WAS THE CROW.

JUNE 3, 1940

PARIS WAS JUST BOMBED [CROSSED OUT: AND SOMEONE TOLD ME THAT A BOMB HAD FALLEN ON THE BOILEAU STREET CLINIC WHERE LAURE HAD SPENT TWO MONTHS BEFORE OUR TRIP TO SAINT GERMAIN ON JULY 15, 1938, WHERE SHE EVEN-TUALLY DIED. I DON'T KNOW IF ANYTHING WAS DESTROYED. WILL SAINT GERMAIN CRUMBLE TO THE GROUND, TOO? IN A LETTER TO LEIRIS, LAURE HERSELF WROTE THAT THE HOUSE WHICH SHE DISDAINFULLY CALLED "THE NUNNERY" WOULD CERTAINLY COME TO A DISASTROUS END. I'M WRITING THIS NOW AS EVERYTHING IS TENDING TOWARDS THE "SONOROUS, ABSURD AND VIOLENT CHAOS" SHE FORESAW AS THE FATE OF THE WORLD]. LET ME ADD: ON THE THRESHOLD OF GLORY, I FOUND DEATH MASQUERADING AS NUDITY, COMPLETE WITH GARTERS AND BLACK SILK STOCKINGS. WHOEVER MET ANYTHING MORE HUMAN, WHOEVER TOLERATED A MORE TERRIBLE FURY? YET THIS FURY TOOK ME BY THE HAND AND LED ME INTO HELL.

I HAVE JUST TOLD YOU ABOUT MY LIFE: DEATH HAD TAKEN THE NAME LAURE.

FOR THOSE WHOM I LOVE, I AM A PROVOCATION. I CAN'T STAND TO SEE THEM FORGET HOW MUCH GOOD FORTUNE THEY WOULD HAVE IF THEY ONLY WOULD PLAY.

LAURE USED TO PLAY. I PLAYED WITH LAURE. NOW I CAN NO LONGER REST BECAUSE I WON. ALL I CAN DO IS PLAY AGAIN, REANIMATE THIS REALLY INSANE FATE ...

LAURE PLAYED AND WON. LAURE DIED.

SOON, SAID LAURE, I'LL MISS THE SUN.

ON NIETZSCHE

CONCERNING THE MANUSCRIPT TO APPEAR UNDER THE TITLE OF THE CULPRIT, WHICH IS MORE OR LESS THE DIARY OF LAURE'S DEATH, BEGUN ON YEAR "LATE," IT SEEMS THAT ALL OF THE FRAGMENTS WHICH MENTION HER NAME HAVE BEEN CROSSED OUT OR OMITTED.

A LARGE "X" OR GAP INTERRUPTS EACH OF THE PASSAGES ON HER DEATH. THE SPACING OF THESE INCISIONS IN THE NARRATIVE REPRESENTS A CENTRAL LOCUS IN THE RELATIONSHIP BETWEEN BATAILLE AND LAURE.

J.P.F.

GEORGES BATAILLE
TRANSLATED BY TOM GORA

MY LATE GRANDMOTHER

THE CLOCK WAS STRIKING MIDNIGHT AS I ENTERED THE KITCHEN WHERE MY GRANDMOTHER WAS LYING.

A SWARM OF DESIRES FLEW THROUGH MY MIND THAT I TRIED TO DRIVE AWAY, BUT IT WAS A HALF-HEARTED EFFORT AT BEST. WARM CONTRACTIONS GRIPPED MY GUTS, SENDING WAVES OF SWEET PAIN RIPPLING THROUGH MY BODY.

THE SMELL, ALL DAY LONG, HAD WAFTED UNDER THE DOOR OF MY ROOM, AND I THOUGHT I HAD FINALLY GROWN ACCUSTOMED TO IT. AND THOUGH I DID EVENTUALLY TAKE PLEASURE THEREIN, I WAS FORCED TO HOLD MY NOSE WHEN I FIRST CAME CLOSE TO THE FOOT OF THE BED.

SLOWLY, DEATH AND MEMORY BEGAN TO DISTILL THEIR HEADY FRAGRANCE AS MY BODY AVIDLY BREATHED IT IN. THE THOUGHT FLASHED THROUGH MY MIND THAT THE OLD WOMAN, SUSPECTING THE DESIRES STIRRING WITHIN ME, HAD TRIED TO REPEL MY BY SURROUNDING HERSELF WITH HER SMELL. THE IDEA THAT SHE HAD TRIED TO RESIST ME, EVEN FOR AN INSTANT, FILLED ME WITH GREAT EXCITE-MENT. YET I COULD NOT UNDERSTAND WHY SHE WOULD TRY TO REJECT ME. SURELY THE PASSION

OF A TWENTY-YEAR-OLD MAN FOR THIS OLD WOMAN WAS THE VERY WATER OF LIFE, SPRINGING FROM THE WELL THAT HAD GONE DRY IN HER MANY YEARS BEFORE. SURELY ALL SHE COULD EXPECT NOW WAS HER BODY'S SLOW DISINTEGRATION IN SOME DAMP CRYPT AS THE GNAWING WORMS ASSAILED HER FLESH.

SURELY, THEREFORE, ANY REJECTION OF ME, HER GRANDSON, WAS UTTERLY INCOMPREHENSIBLE.

THE SILK KERCHIEF ON HER FACE AND THE SHEET COVERING HER BODY ONLY ADDED TO HOW I REMEMBERED HER IN MY MIND'S EYE: A JEALOUSLY HIDDEN PHOTOGRAPH OF HER WITH HER DRESS, DRENCHED IN A SUDDEN SHOWER, CLINGING TO HER BODY. THE CLOTH WAS STICKING TO HER SKIN, FOLLOWING THE CONTOURS OF HER BREASTS, FIRM AND PROUD, WITH THEIR DARK NIPPLES ERECT FROM THE FRESH CARESS OF THE RAIN; THE WET FABRIC OUTLINING THE SOFT CONVEXITY OF HER BELLY AND NAVEL, THE SHAPE OF HER PUBIS AS IT DISAPPEARED BETWEEN HER THIGHS. THOSE THIGHS THAT WERE LONG AND SLIM WITH THEIR MUSCLES JUST BARELY VISIBLE UNDER THE SKIN.

SUDDENLY I THOUGHT I HEARD FOOTSTEPS OUTSIDE. I COULD DETECT THE CRUNCH OF SHOES ON GRAVEL AND STONES, THE RUSTLE OF SOMEONE'S CLOTHES BUT I COULD NOT TELL WHETHER THE SOUND CAME FROM THE ROAD OR THE COURTYARD IN FRONT OF THE HOUSE. I WAS A LITTLE TREMULOUS BUT THE FEAR WAS IN KEEPING WITH THE WARM PAIN GNAWING AT MY GUTS AND THE DARK EXCITEMENT THAT SENT A SLIGHT QUIVER THROUGH MY EVERY MOVEMENT. THE SHUTTERS WERE CLOSED AND THE WOODEN PANELS HAD BEEN DRAWN ACROSS THE FRONT DOOR WINDOW. I WAS PROTECTED ON ALL SIDES BUT AT THE SAME TIME THE MYSTERIOUS HAPPENINGS OF THE OUTSIDE WORLD DISQUIETED ME; THE ONLY LINK I HAD TONIGHT WITH THE EXTERIOR WAS THE SOUND OF FOOTSTEPS WHICH HAD TAKEN ON UNREAL PROPORTIONS IN MY MIND.

THE STEPS SLOWLY MOVED AWAY.

I WENT QUICKLY TO THE DOOR TO MAKE CERTAIN IT WAS LOCKED. I SHOT HOME THE TWO BOLTS MY GRANDMOTHER HAD DECIDED TO INSTALL A SHORT TIME AGO, AND NOW CONFIDENT THAT WE WERE SAFE FROM ANY INTERRUPTION I WENT BACK TO THE BED.

IT WAS QUITE HIGH OFF THE FLOOR IN THE STYLE OF OLDER BEDS SO THAT I HAD SOME DIFFICULTY IN FOLDING BACK THE SHEET TO THE FOOT OF THE BED AND FOLLOWING THE CREASES, STILL INTACT, OF THE CLOTH, DAZZLING IN ITS WHITENESS, THAT HAD BEEN SPECIALLY BROUGHT OUT FOR THE OCCA-SION. I LEFT THE KERCHIEF IN PLACE ON HER FACE. WHEN ALL WAS SAID AND DONE, I REALLY DID NOT WANT HER TO SEE ME; AND THEN TOO, THERE MAY HAVE BEEN A BUDDING SADISTIC DESIRE TO CARESS HER AND ASSUAGE MY ACHING WANT WHILE SHE COULD NOT SEE MY NEXT MOVE. NATURALLY I WAS QUITE AWARE THAT SHE WAS UNABLE TO REACT TO ALL THE CARESSES I INTENDED FOR HER; NEVERTHELESS I DECIDED TO ATTACH HER SECURELY. ON A SHELF IN THE CUPBOARD SQUEEZED BETWEEN THE FIREPLACE AND THE SINK I KNEW THERE WAS A METAL BOX FULL OF STRING AND CORD THAT SHE HAD SAVED THROUGH THE YEARS. I CHOSE SOME SECTIONS OF HEAVY TWINE USED FOR BINDING SHEAVES BECAUSE OF THEIR IDEAL LENGTH AND THE LOOP AT ONE END.

IT WAS NOT DIFFICULT TO SPREAD HER LEGS AND ATTACH HER FEET TO THE BEDPOSTS. IT WAS NO EASY TASK, HOWEVER, TO UNCLENCH HER HANDS

WITH THEIR FINGERS LOCKED TOGETHER, THEN RAISE HER UP TO PUT HER ARMS BEHIND HER BACK AND TIE THEM. WHEN I LOWERED HER AGAIN, HER NEW AND I DARE SAY UNCOMFORTABLE POSITION CAUSED THE BONES IN HER FINGERS OR HER ARMS—I COULD NOT TELL WHICH—TO SNAP LIKE DRY TWIGS. I WAS DISPLEASED AT THIS INCIDENT SINCE I HAD NO WISH TO CAUSE HER ANY PAIN.

HER DRESS HAD ROLLED BACK TO HER KNEES AS I WAS ATTACHING HER FEET, THEREBY DISPLAYING HER BLACK SILK STOCKINGS PULLED HALF WAY UP HER LEGS. HER DRESS WAS COMELY, MADE OF SOME FINE, SOFT FABRIC I COULD NOT IDENTIFY. IT WAS VERY INTRICATELY PLEATED ABOVE THE WAIST: THE FOLDS WERE NARROW AT THE TOP, THEN GRADUALLY BORADENED AND FLARED INTO AN AMPLE SKIRT. VERY DAINTY MAUVE PEARLS WERE SEWN ON THE BODICE IN THE SHAPE OF MANY-PETALLED ROSES CURLING FROM THE LOW CUT NECKLINE; MY MOTHER HAD THOUGHT IT TOO LOW FOR THE OCCASION AND HAD COVERED THE BARE SKIN WITH A BLACK SILK SCARF.

GOD, MY GRANDMOTHER WAS BEAUTIFUL. AND I WAS PROUD SHE WAS MINE, ALBEIT FOR ONE NIGHT ONLY.

SHE WAS NAKED UNDER THE DRESS. THEY HAD NOT GONE TO THE TROUBLE OF PUTTING ON HER UNDERCLOTHES WHICH, ONE MUST ADMIT, WOULD HAVE BEEN QUITE USELESS.

BEFORE I UNDRESSED HER I CAUGHT MYSELF UNCONSCIOUSLY OPENING MY FLY AND UNCOVER-ING MY PENIS. THE COLD ROOM HAD CAUSED IT TO SHRINK DRASTICALLY, AND IT WAS ALL WIZENED AND WRINKLED. MY TESTICLES WERE HURTING SINCE THE METAL TEETH OF THE ZIPPER HAD BITTEN INTO THEM, BUT I TOOK PLEASURE IN INCREASING THE PAIN BY PRESSING DOWN ON MY PENIS.

THEN CAME THE MOMENT WHEN I DECIDED TO PUSH BACK THE DRESS COMPLETELY.

THERE WAS NO SOUND OUTSIDE EXCEPT, FOR THE PAST FEW MINUTES, THE CAT MEWING AT THE DOOR, NOT UNDERSTANDING WHY HIS MISTRESS WOULD NOT LET HIM IN. I CERTAINLY HAD NO INTENTION OF OPENING THE DOOR FOR HIM. I HAVE ALWAYS LOATHED THE CREATURE, A HUGE TOMCAT WITH LONG TAWNY FUR AND BRIGHT, BALEFUL EYES THAT

COULD STARE INTO YOUR FACE BY THE HOUR, FOLLOWING YOUR EVERY MOVE AND NEVER LOSING EVEN FOR AN INSTANT THEIR IMPLACABLE COLDNESS. HE WAS QUITE WILD AND NO ONE WENT NEAR HIM EXCEPT HIS OLD MISTRESS.

SUDDENLY, AND WITH A VIOLENT MOVEMENT THAT SURPRISED ME, I PRESSED FIRMLY ON MY PENIS, THUS CAUSING GREAT PAIN. THE TIPS OF MY FINGERS, PALER THAN USUAL BECAUSE OF THE COLD, WERE STAINED WITH TINY RED DOTS: THE TEETH OF THE ZIPPER HAD BROKEN THE SKIN ON MY TESTICLES. FOR SOME TIME THEREAFTER I WAS NOT AWARE OF THE NEAR-CONSTANT CONTRACTIONS OF MY GUT. THE PAIN SERVED TO IGNITE MORE FIRES UNDER MY PASSION AND DROVE ME TO STRIP THE DEAD WOMAN OF HER MODESTY.

I PUSHED BACK HER DRESS TO THE ARMPITS. I MANAGED TO DO SO BY LIFTING HER AND WORKING THE DRESS SLOWLY AND PAINFULLY UPWARDS. AND EVEN THOUGH THE POSITION OF HER HANDS HINDERED ME CONSIDERABLY I HAD NO INTENTION OF UNTYING THEM. I FELT MUCH SAFER KNOWING THE BONDS WERE FIRMLY IN PLACE.

TICKLING MY PENIS WITH ONE HAND, I GENTLY CARESSED HER BODY WITH THE OTHER, SENDING SHIVERS THROUGH ME FROM HEAD TO TOE.

THE SPECTACLE BEFORE MY EYES WAS A FASCINAT-ING ONE.

HER SALLOW SKIN WAS STRETCHED OVER A FRAME WHOSE SLIGHTEST DETAILS WERE APPARENT. I WAS VERY CAUTIOUS WHENEVER I TOUCHED HER LEST THE SKIN SPLIT WIDE OPEN AND RELEASE THE JAGGED END OF A BONE. BUT MY DESIRES HAD BEEN REPRESSED TOO LONG AND SOON MY HAND GREW MORE DARING, MY CARESSES MORE EXPLICIT.

HER BREASTS, DANGLING ACROSS HER TORSO, WERE NOTHING MORE NOW THAN TWO THIN BAGS THAT THE YEARS HAD EMPTIED AND DRIED UP. ONLY THE DARK, NEARLY BLACK NIPPLES AT EACH EXTREMITY GAVE THEM ANY THICKNESS. THEY LOOKED LIKE TWO DEFLATED BALLOONS WITH THEIR VALVES PITTED AND STIPPLED WITH TINY BLACK CRACKS.

HER GENITALS WERE COVERED WITH LONG GREY HAIRS THAT STRAGGLED THINLY OVER A WIDE AREA OF HER BELLY. THE LABIA WERE AS DRY AS EVERYTHING ELSE BUT WERE DISTINCTLY APPAR-ENT IN THE SPARSE, WHITE FLEECE ON HER GENITALS, AND WHOSE NATURAL INTRICACY HAD BECOME EVEN MORE COMPLEX SINCE EVERY INCH OF HER SKIN, SO KNEADED BY TIME, WAS FURROWED TO THE BREAKING POINT. ONCE SO PINK AND FRESH, HER SKIN NOW WAS NOTHING BUT STRETCHES OF WRINKLES, DESICCATED AND PURPLISH.

I WAS FASCINATED BY THE FOLDS IN HER ARMPITS, THE GROIN, THE CLEFT BETWEEN THE BREASTS, THE INSIDE OF THE THIGHS, EVERYWHERE IN SUM THAT CONSTANT MOVEMENT AND CONSTANT SWEATING HAD WRINKLED THE SKIN AND FINALLY TANNED IT SO THAT IT HAD THE SUPPLE TEXTURE OF OLD, DARKENED LEATHER.

EVERYTHING HAD BY NOW RECEDED INTO OBLIVION, EXCEPT THE TWO OF US. NOTHING COULD COME TO TROUBLE THE TRANQUILITY OF OUR EMBRACES, SO FILLED WITH EACH OTHER'S PRESENCE WERE WE BOTH.

NOTHING WAS OF ANY CONSEQUENCE TO ME EXCEPT HER BODY LYING ON A BED THAT I WAS AWARE OF ONLY BECAUSE THE HEMP CORDS WERE ATTACHED TO IT AND TO THE OBJECT OF MY OVERRIDING PASSION. NOTHING WAS OF ANY CONSEQUENCE TO HER EXCEPT HER LOVER, DRUNK WITH DESIRE, AND TO WHOM SHE WAS OFFERING HER BODY WITH ALMOST UNREAL PASSIVITY, HER GENITALS OPENING WIDE INTO THE DEEPEST RECESSES OF HER BODY, ACCEPTING IN HER NAKEDNESS THE HUMILIATION OF THE RAVAGES OF TIME; ACCEPTING IN HER NAKEDNESS THE HUMILIATION OF HER BONDS THAT INSURED MY COMPLETE ACCESSIBILITY TO HER BODY.

SOON MY HANDS HAD EXHAUSTED ALL THE POSSIBILITIES OF PLEASURE THEY COULD PRO-CURE.

I WAS STILL STANDING BESIDE THE BED, AS THOUGH LOATH TO DEFILE MY MISTRESS'S COUCH, WHEN I LEANED FORWARD AND TOUCHED HER SALLOW BELLY WITH MY TONGUE, LEAVING A WET MARK THEREUPON. THEN GROWING VERY EXCITED, I PLACED MY HANDS ON EITHER SIDE OF HER TORSO AS I BEGAN LICKING EVERY INCH OF HER COLD FLESH.

MY PLEASURE WAS IMMENSE AS I GREEDILY SUCKED IN THE SERE GLOBES OF HER BREASTS, NIBBLING ON THE ROUGH NIPPLES, SALIVATING ON THEM, AND ALL THE WHILE I WAS AMAZED AT THE

LACK OF REACTION, BOTH ON HER PART AND ON MINE, DESPITE THE FRENZY TORTURING THE TWO OF US AND WHICH WAS FLOODING PAINFUL PELASURE THROUGHOUT MY PASSION-WRACKED BODY.

BUT THE DESIRE DOMINATING US LIKE TWO ANIMALS WAS SO INTENSE THAT IT INHIBITED ANY SHOW OF PLEASURE. IT WAS FAR BEYOND ANYTHING AS COMMON AS AN ERECT MEMBER, AN ERECT NIPPLE, OR A DAMP CROTCH. WE LEFT THAT STAGE BEHIND US WHEN ONE DAY, BARELY PUBESCENT, I UNDRESSED IN FRONT OF HER, STEALING GLANCES TO SEE IF SHE SHOWED ANY INTEREST; OR THE DAY WHEN I ROSE EARLIER THAN SHE AND, TREMBLING AT MY NERVE, I LAY IN WAIT FOR HER TO DO HER TOILETTE.

NOR WAS I CONVINCED THAT BEYOND OUR PRESENT PLEASURE, BEYOND OUR PRESENT INHIBITING STATE WHICH, AT THE EXPENSE OF THE MEDIOCRE EXTERNAL SIGNS OF PLEASURE (ALWAYS FRUS-TRATING BECAUSE OF A CASTRATING DETUMES-CENCE, ALWAYS DEGRADING BECAUSE OF THE CONCOMITANT POLLUTIONS), WAS CURTAILING THE VOLUPTUOUS ENJOYMENT OF THIS NIGHT,—THERE WAS NOT ANOTHER SORT OF PLEASURE, NEAR MADNESS THIS ONE, AND WHICH, WERE WE BUT CAPABLE OF ATTAINING IT, WOULD INDUCE US TO EXPERIENCE THE MOST VIOLENT AND UNCONTROL-LABLE OF PLEASURES: EXPLOSIONS OF SKIN AND FLESH; EXTRA-ANAL DEFECATIONS (FROM THE MOUTH, THE SEXUAL ORGANS OR ANOTHER OPENING MADE SOMEWHERE IN THE BODY); EVISCERATION (FOLLOWED BY A DISCHARGE OF THE INTERNAL ORGANS OR THE EJACULATION OF THE BOWELS); BONES THRUSTING THROUGH DRY FISSURES IN THE SKIN; WHITE DISCHARGES FROM THE BRAIN; VERY DARK URINE CARRYING JELLY-LIKE SEEDS IN ITS FLOW; THE ORGANS OF SIGHT LIQUEFYING AND DISCHARGING THEIR VITREOUS SUBSTANCE ON EACH TEMPLE; DISSECTION OF THE GENITALS; EMASCULATION; BLOOD VOMITING FROM THE ANUS, THE VAGINA, THE NAVEL; SUDDEN AND UNCONTROLLABLE ERPUTIONS OF BROWNISH, ADIPOSE GROWTHS; THE SCATTERING OF FILTH BOTH INSIDE AND OUTSIDE THE BODY, ETC.

IT WAS NOT THAT I FEARED A DISASTROUS OUTCOME TO OUR RELATIONS; I SIMPLY WANTED TO PROLONG THEM AS LONG AS POSSIBLE, BEYOND ALL HUMAN BOUNDARIES. BUT IN PARTICULAR I WAS INTENT ON EXTRACTING EVERY LAST DROP OF PLEASURE FROM THEM, ON ENJOYING THEM TO THE FULLEST AND BUILDING TO A GRADUAL CLIMAX, SAVORING EVERY LAST ATOM OF DELIGHT AS I DID SO.

I BEGAN ACTING THEN AS THOUGH OUR NIGHT TOGETHER WERE OUR LAST ONE. ACTUALLY I KNEW IT WAS INDEED THAT LAST BUT IMAGINING THAT THESE PEASURES WERE BUT THE PRELUDE TO OTHER, MORE MARVELLOUS NIGHTS; IMAGINING THAT SOMEONE, MY MOTHER PERHAPS, WAS OVERSEEING THESE DELIGHTS AND THAT ACCORD-ING TO THE MASTER'S WHIM THEY WERE GRANTED FOR BUT ONE NIGHT ONLY, I FELT MY THIRST FOR PLEASURE INCREASED A HUNDRED FOLD.

THUS IT WAS IMPERATIVE I BE VERY ATTENTIVE TO EVERY DETAIL AND IGNORE THE SCRUPLES WHICH MIGHT HAVE FORBIDDEN MY USING THE HEMP BONDS IN ORDER TO ATTAIN THE MAXIMUM OF PLEASURE OUR VORACIOUS SENSES COULD PROVIDE.

SIMILAR TO DRIED, SHRIVELLED MORELS, AS HARD AND AS BLACK AS COAL WERE THE OUTER FRINGES OF HER LABIA. WITHIN, HOWEVER, THEY WERE STILL SOMEWHAT PLIABLE SO THAT, ALONG WITH THEIR BROWNISH CAST, THEY SUGGESTED THE CONSIS-TENCY AND APPEARANCE OF OLD LEATHER.

I RAN MY FINGERS THROUGH HER PUBIC HAIRS AND PINCHED THE SKIN TOGETHER IN ORDER TO OPEN HER VAGINA TO MY GREEDY, SUCKING MOUTH, AND THEN I DARTED MY TONGUE REPEATEDLY INTO THE CONVOLUTIONS OF HER FLESH.

I STRETCHED HER SKIN, EVEN RUNNING THE RISK OF TEARING IT, IN SEARCH OF HER CLITORIS BUT TO NO AVAIL. I WANTED TO PLAY MY TONGUE AROUND IT BUT HER SKIN WAS SO WIZENED AND FURROWED THAT IT WAS NOT DISCERNIBLE. MOREOVER, I COULD NOT THRUST MY TONGUE PAST THE OPENING OF HER VULVA, SO NARROW HAD IT BECOME.

SLOWLY, AS I WET HER BODY WITH MY SALIVA, I THOUGHT HER FLESH WAS GRADUALLY BECOMING SOFTER AND MORE RESILIENT AND MY MOUTH, LIKE A SUCTION CUP, STUCK AND SUCKED AND SALIVATED AS MY TONGUE DARTED INTO EVERY CREVICE, EXPLORED EVERY NOOK OF SKIN, LICKED GREEDILY AT EVERY INCH OF HER ICY GENITALS.

AS I WAS CARESSING HER, I UNDID MY WARM CORDUROY TROUSERS AND DROPPED THEM ON THE FLOOR, I POPPED EACH BUTTON OFF MY SHIRT, ONE BY ONE. I WAS NAKED IN A FEW MOMENTS, THEN KICKED MY CLOTHES AWAY FROM THE BED.

I BEGAN SHIVERING IN THE COLD ROOM. I LAY DOWN

BESIDE HER. SHE TOO WAS COLD, AND I HELD HER CLOSE TO ME TO GIVE HER MY WARMTH.

SOON I WAS STRETCHING OUT MY LONG, THIN BODY OVER HERS, CAREFUL NOT TO PRESS DOWN TOO HARD LEST I HURT HER AND MAKE HER FRAIL BONES CRACK.

MY PENIS WAS LIMP, AND AT EVERY THRUST OF MY LOINS IT TWISTED AND TURNED LIKE A LARGE WORM ON THE WRINKLED PARCHMENT OF HER BELLY. MY LONG, DANGLING TESTICLES STRUCK AGAINST HER PUBLIS, RUFFLING THE STRINGY GREY HAIRS IN HER THIN FLEECE.

MY FACE WAS PRESSED AGAINST HERS AND I COULD FEEL THE SHARP EDGES OF HER BONES GOUGING MY CHEEKS THORUGH THE SILK KERCHIEF. HAD I REMOVED IT, I KNEW I WOULD FEEL HER BREATH MINGLING WITH MY PANTING; I SENSED, UNDER THE THIN CLOTH, THAT HER FACE WAS LIKE MINE, BATHED IN SWEAT AND FLUSHED WITH PASSION AND PLEASURE.

ALTHOUGH MY BODY WAS MORE MALLEABLE, MORE FLEXIBLE THAN HERS AND NICELY MOLDED THE ANGULAR CONTOURS OF HER BODY, I WAS VERY CONSCIOUS OF HER COMPLETE DOMINATION OVER ME WHICH SHE ACCOMPLISHED BY THE COLDNESS AND THE DECEPTIVE RIGIDITY OF HER BODY, DESPITE HER BONDS AND HER INFERIOR POSITION.

HER ONLY RESPONSE TO EACH OF MY MOVEMENTS, TO EACH RHYTHMIC CONTACT OF MY BODY WITH HERS, TO EACH VIBRATION OF MY LIMBS, WAS THE IRRITATING AND INCESSANT CRACKLE OF HER BONES. YET I HAD NOTHING BUT TENDERNESS FOR HER, AND FOR THE TWO OF US NOTHING BUT THE DESIRE FOR BOUNDLESS PLEASURE. EACH ONE OF MY MOVEMENTS WAS PLANNED SO THAT ALL MY CARESSES, THE MOVEMENTS OF MY BODY ON HER BODY, WOULD BE SUFFUSED WITH INFINITE GENTLENESS.

I KNELT BETWEEN HER OPEN LEGS SO I MIGHT CONTEMPLATE HER VAGINA AGAIN. MY DESIRE WAS FANNED ANEW AT THE WAY SHE OFFERED HERSELF SO IMMODESTLY.

I LOWERED MY HEAD AND BRUSHED MY HALF-CLOSED MOUTH AGAINST HER BELLY AND BREASTS, THEN PUSHED ASIDE THE BLACK SILK SCARF MASKING HER THROAT SO I MIGHT KISS HER NECK AND SUCK AT ITS WRINKLES. I TURNED AROUND SO I COULD LICK HER GENITALS AGAIN AND THE BLACK CRANNIES BETWEEN HER THIGHS, DART MY TONGUE INTO HER NAVEL, LAP AT THE SIDES OF HER FLAT, HARD BELLY, NIBBLE LOVINGLY AT HER NIPPLES IN A RUSH OF SALIVA, SUCK AT HER ARMPITS IN THE HOPE OF FINDING A TRACE OF HER SWEAT.

EVERYTHING CHANGED WHEN I, WITH UNINTENTIONAL BRUTALITY, WAS SPREADING WIDE HER LABIA. WITHOUT WARNING, THROUGH HER PUBLIC HAIRS, I SAW A SPLIT RUN ALONG HER SKIN.

IT HAPPENED SO SUDDENLY THAT FOR A MOMENT I DID NOT REACT. HER SKIN HAD OPENED LIKE A CRACK IN A GLASS. THE PUBIS HAD A FURROW AT LEAST FOUR INCHES IN LENGTH; THE WOUND WAS PURPLISH AND ODDLY DRY AS THOUGH HER BLOOD HAD EVAPORATED IN DEATH. MY EYES REMAINED RIVETED UPON HER TORN PUBIS FOR A LONG TIME; THE SLIT HAD EXTENDED THE CLEFT IN HER LABIA TO FREAKISH PROPORTIONS. I WAS SPEECHLESS, INCAPABLE OF MOVEMENT AND OVERCOME BY SUCCESSIVE BOUTS OF DISBELIEF AND TERROR CAUSED BY THAT FISSURED FLESH, THOSE OVERSIZE GENITALIA WHOSE DIMENSIONS MADE MY PENIS, SHRIVELLED AND BLUE WITH COLD, LOOK LIKE A MERE WART.

I FOUND IT DIFFICULT AT THE TIME TO BELIEVE HER ENLARGED CLEFT COULD GIVE OFF SUCH A FOUL ODOUR, BUT GRADUALLY I REALIZED THE SMELL THAT HAD APPALLED ME SO MUCH AT FIRST ROSE FROM HER REEKING CORPSE.

OUR PACT WAS NOW BROKEN. IT HAD BEEN SEALED WITH OUR FIRST KISSES AND WAS TO HAVE TRANSPORTED BOTH OF US TO THE HIGHEST PEAKS OF PLEASURE.

SUDDENLY THE SIGHT OF HER RUINED GENITALS UNHINGED ME COMPLETELY AND I BEGAN PUNCHING HER BELLY. EACH BLOW MADE HER DOUBLE UP AS THOUGH TO PROTECT HERSELF OR TO CATCH HER BREATH, BUT HER EFFORTS WERE VAIN. HER HANDS KEPT SNAPPING BEHIND HER BACK AND THE WHOLE KITCHEN REVERBERATED WITH MY MUFFLED DRUMMING ON HER BELLY.

MY DESPAIR CAUSED BY THE GROTESQUE FINISH TO SO MUCH PLEASURE PROMISED THEN WITHDRAWN; MY RAGE CAUSED BY THE COMPLACENT PASSIVITY SHE SHOWED AFTER THE DISASTER, RELEASED A

FERAL VIOLENCE THAT KEPT ME, FOR ONE LONG HOUR, HAMMERING EVERY INCH OF HER BODY.

I WAS RACKED BY SPASMS OF UNEARTHLY RAGE; I RELEASED ALL THE CRUELTY I COULD MUSTER. I THINK SHE SUFFERED A GREAT DEAL.

BUT HER PAIN CAUSED NO SHOUT, NO GESTURE OF SELF-DEFENCE. EVEN HER EYES REMAINED MUTE. NO SIGN OF APPROVAL. NO SIGN OF REPROACH.

AT TIMES IT WAS NOT HARD TO BELIEVE SHE WAS DEAD.

SHE NEVER ONCE SHUDDERED, NOR DID HER MOUTH GAPE ANY WIDER THAN BEFORE. HER HALF-CLOSED EYELIDS REMAINED THAT WAY. HER EYES WERE FOCUSED UNBLINKINGLY ON WHATEVER WAS BEFORE THEM, AND AT TIMES HER EMPTY GAZE MET MINE.

HER LIPS NEVER QUIVERED. NO TEAR ZIGZAGGED DOWN THE WRINKLE OF HER WAXEN FACE.

UNDER MY REPEATED BLOWS, THE HEMP BONDS TYING HER FEET TO THE BEDPOSTS STRETCHED NEARLY TO THE BREAKING POINT, GOUGING THE SKIN FROM HER ANKLES IN SERE SHEETS THAT ROLLED AWAY FROM THE FLESH LIKE STRIPS OF YELLOWED PARCHMENT. HER WASTED BODY TWISTED AND TURNED IN VIOLENT CONTORTIONS THAT MADE HER LIMBS SNAP LIKE KINDLING AS I PUMMELLED HER BATTERED BODY, KNOCKED HER FROM SIDE TO SIDE AS FAR AS HER MERCILESS FETTERS WOULD ALLOW, AND PUNCHED HER SO HARD SHE KEPT DOUBLING UP LIKE A JACKKNIFE AT EVERY SMASH OF MY FISTS.

SHE SEEMED NOT TO BE THERE. IT SEEMED AS THOUGH I WAS POUNDING AN OLD ROTTEN TREE TRUNK WHOSE ONLY REACTION WAS SPLITS IN ITS BARK.

AND YET I HAD PUT HER THROUGH SO MUCH! THOSE LONG MOMENTS OF MADNESS FULL OF FURY AND HORROR UNTIL THE CRUEL CRAVING OF MY HANDS WAS SATED, AND THE TREMBLING OF MY FINGERS HAD ABATED. BUT ONLY AFTER THEIR NAILS, STIFFENED BY THE COLD, HAD FINISHED TEARING HER INDIFFERENT BODY INTO HIDEOUS SHREDS OF SKIN AND FLESH.

MY RAGE REACHED SUCH BERSERK HEIGHTS THAT AT TIMES I NO LONGER KNEW ITS OBJECT: WAS THE OUTRAGE DIRECTED AT ME OR HER? WAS IT REALLY MY GRANDMOTHER I WAS PUNCHING AND KICKING SO ATROCIOUSLY?

SHE REMAINED AS INSENSIITIVE AS THE BED THAT SUFFERED OUR FERINE THRASHINGS.

NOT A SINGLE TEAR, NOT A SINGLE TEAR OF BLOOD.

HER WOUNDS WERE RAPIDLY TURNING PURPLE OR YELLOW LIKE HER SKIN, WITH NOT A SINGLE RUBY TEAR WINKING IN THE LESIONS. NO SCARLET TEAR TO COMFORT ME.

I SPARED NO PART OF HER BODY: HER BREASTS, HER ARMPITS, HER MONSTROUSLY GAPING LABIA, HER LEATHERN BELLY, HER NECK WERE ALL DULY RIPPED AND TORN. BUT STILL I KEPT ON, EVER MORE INTENSELY, EVER MORE FEROCIOUSLY.

AS LONG AS I STILL HAD AN UNBROKEN FINGERNAIL I SLIT OPEN HER FLESH IN LONG, IRREPARABLE WOUNDS.

HER SKIN, IN VARIOUS PLACES, CAME AWAY BY THE HANDFUL AND CURLED UP INTO WITHERED ROLLS.

AND NOT ONCE DID SHE CRY OUT!

MY ACTIONS HAD BY NOW SURPASSED EVERYTHING THAT MADNESS CAN DICTATE, BUT IT WAS THEN THAT I WRENCHED OPEN HER MOUTH, DISLOCATING THE FRAIL BONES OF HER JAW, AND SLIPPED IN MY PENIS, A TINY WORM BLUE WITH COLD.

AND I BEGAN PISSING.

I PISSED INTO THE DEEPEST REACHES OF HER THROAT, AND WITH THE SINGLEMINDEDNESS OF RAGING DESIRE I MOVED IN AND OUT OF HER MOUTH IN SAVAGE IMITATION OF THE ACT I HAD BEEN DENIED.

AS MY URINE SPURTED OVER HER FACE IT GLUED HER HAIR TO HER SKULL AND FORMED A WET HALO UPON THE STILL IMMACULATE SHEETS.

AND I KEPT ON PISSING, CREATING ARTIFICIAL TEARS OF PAIN ON HER CHEEKS, CREATING ARTIFICIAL BLOOD TO REPLACE THE BLOOD SHE DID NOT HAVE, THE BLOOD SHE DID NOT WANT TO GIVE ME.

SUDDENLY, REPUDIATING ALL DECAY, ALL THOSE
WASTED STRIPS OF SKIN, FLESH AND MY OWN PISS
WITH ITS SMELL NOW MINGLING WITH HER DEAD
SMELL, I FELL INTO A DEEP SLEEP THAT NO DREAM

DISTURBED.

ANONYMOUS AUTHOR

TRANSLATED BY DANIEL SLOATE

23. THE GALLERY MONTPENSIER.

24. R. SEEN FROM REAR WALKING UP THE GALLERY UNDER ARCADES.

25. FADE OUT—SOUND OF R.'S STEPS UNDER THE ARCADES.

26. STEPS OF THE CORPULENT MAN.

27. THE CLOCK ON THE SQUARE OF THE THÉÂTRE FRANCAIS MARKING 5 P.M.

28 THE COLONNADE OF THE GALLERY: R. SLIGHTLY DISHEVELLED, APPEARS, WALKING AS THROUGH NOT
    SURE OF HER STEPS, STOPS THEN CROSSES THE SQUARE.

28 BIS. THE FOUNTAINS ON THE SQUARE.

28 TER. THE TERRACE OF THE REGENCY CAFE WHERE R. IS SEATED AT A TABLE.

29. THE WAITER MOVES TOWARD R.—WIPES THE TABLE.

VIOLENT SEX

THE PARALLEL BARS

EXTERIOR PARIS DAYLIGHT —
GYMNASIUM INTERIOR DAYLIGHT.

THE GARDENS OF THE PALAIS-ROYAL AND ITS
FOUNTAINS PLAYING. ROBERTE'S VOICE IS HEARD
OFF STAGE.

ROBERTE (VOICE OFF): THAT OCTAVE SHOULD HAVE
THE INCONCEIVABLE ARROGANCE TO IMAGINE HE IS
THE AUTHOR OF MY IMPROPRIETIES IS ONE THING....
BUT AS TO BELIEVING HIMSELF THE ORIGINATOR OF
MY TEMPERAMENT, THE POOR DEAR DOESN'T KNOW
WHAT I'M CAPABLE OF WITHOUT HIM.

IS IT POSSIBLE A WOMAN SEEKS TO EXPERIENCE A
VIOLENT SENSE OF SHAME JUST BECAUSE SHE'S
RESPECTABLE? I REMEMBER I WAS ASHAMED ...
WAS MY PLEASURE ANY THE LESS FOR THAT?

ROBERTE, STANDING IN THE SUN, HER BACK
AGAINST THE COLONNADE OF THE PALAIS-ROYAL,
IN FRONT OF THE CAFÉ LE NEMOURS. ON A TABLE

NEARBY SHE HAS LEFT THE TEA THAT HAS BEEN
BROUGHT TO HER AND HER BAG. SHE LOOKS AT THE
FOUNTAINS ON THE SQUARE AND STROKES HER
WRISTS, INSERTING HER FINGERS UNDER THE LACE
OF HER GLOVES.

ROBERTE (VOICE OFF): AFTER ALL, WHAT HAVE I GOT
AGAINST THOSE TWO MEN? IF THEY FOUND SOME
WRETCHED PLEASURE ... IT'S NOW THE PLEASURE
BEGINS FOR ME.

THE WAITER, CONCERNED BY HIS CLIENT'S ODD
BEHAVIOUR, COMES OVER TO HER.

WAITER: ARE YOU ALL RIGHT? YOU LOOK PALE ...

ROBERTE TURNS AWAY WITHOUT SEEING HIM,
SMILES DREAMILY AND RETURNS TO SIT AT HER
TABLE.

SHE TAKES A POCKET MIRROR FROM HER BAG AND
LOOKS AT HERSELF.

BACK VIEW OF ROBERTE ON THE PLATFORM OF A BUS: SHE WATCHES THE PASSING SCENE AS THE BUS TRAVELS FROM THE CHAMBER OF DEPUTIES VIA THE PONT ROYAL TOWARD THE LOUVRE.

SHE PLACES HER GLOVED HAND ON THE RAIL, AS A MASSIVE INDIVIDUAL TAKES UP HIS POSITION BESIDE HER.

CASUALLY, AS ROBERTE, LOST IN REVERIE, WATCHES THE RIVER AND THE TREES GO BY, THE INDIVIDUAL, WHOSE HEAVY BODY AND FACE ARE REMINISCENT OF A MOLLUSK, SLIDES HIS FINGERS IMPERCEPTIBLY TOWARD ROBERTE'S ABANDONED HAND.

HE TOUCHES HER FINGERS: ROBERTE WITHDRAWS HER HAND.

THEN, UNABLE TO RESIST, THE MOLLUSK DELIBER-ATELY PUTS HIS FINGERS ON THOSE OF ROBERTE.

INDIGNANT, ROBERTE IMMEDIATELY PULLS HER HAND AWAY AND GOES TO SIT INSIDE THE BUS.

SHE FINDS A PLACE IN THE SUN WHERE SHE RELAXES, ENJOYING THE BREEZE ON HER FACE FROM THE OPEN WINDOW, HER LEGS LAZILY APART.

THE MOLLUSK, WHO HAS WATCHED HER FROM THE PLATFORM, NOW COMES AND SITS DOWN OPPOSITE, OBSERVING HER AT LEISURE OUT OF THE CORNER OF HIS EYE.

ROBERTE IMMEDIATELY CROSSES HER LEGS AND CLOSES HER EYES.

OVER THE SHOT OF ROBERTE CLOSING HER EYES IS SUPERIMPOSED A SHOT OF THE PARALLEL BARS FROM WHICH TWO LEATHER STRAPS ARE HANGING.

WHEN THE BUS STOPS AT THE COMEDIE FRANCAISE ROBERTE GETS OFF QUICKLY.

NOW SHE CAN BE SEEN THROUGH THE COLONNADE OF THE RUE DE MONTPENSIER IN THE PALAIS-ROYAL. LITTLE SCHOOLBOY X, WEARING THE SAME UNIFORM AS LITTLE F. AND ANTOINE, WATCHES HER, THEN DISAPPEARS.

SHE PASSES ALONG THE GALLERY LOOKING INTO SHOP-WINDOWS.

BEHIND HER CAN BE HEARD THE FOOTSTEPS OF THE MOLLUSK, WHO HAS FOLLOWED HER. HE CATCHES UP WITH HER, WALKS BESIDE HER FOR A MOMENT, THEN PASSES HER AND GOES OSTENSIBLY THROUGH A DARK PORCHWAY.

ROBERTE CONTINUES HER WINDOW-SHOPPING, THEN, WHEN SHE REACHES THE PORCHWAY THE HALF-OPEN DOOR IS SUCH A BURNING INVITATION SHE CANNOT RESIST OPENING IT.

SHE FINDS HERSELF IN A DELAPIDATED AND GLOOMY HALL, RISKS A STEP INTO THE DARKNESS, WHEN THE DOOR BANGS LOUDLY BEHIND HER, BARRED BY THE IMPOSING SILHOUETTE OF THE MOLLUSK.

BEFORE SHE HAS TIME TO CRY OUT A DOOR IN FRONT OF HER IS OPENED BY AN INTERLOPER WHO BARS THE ACCESS, SHE RECOGNIZES THE SQUAT MAN OF THE AMERICAN CAR.

ROBERTE RUNS TOWARD THE STAIRCASE, CAUGHT IMMEDIATELY BY THE MOLLUSK, WHO, ALTHOUGH SHE HITS HARD AT HIM, THROWS HER LIKE A STRAW OVER HIS SHOULDERS, HIS HANDS SPLAYED ACROSS HER THIGHS.

AND WITHOUT HOPE OF ESCAPING FROM HIS DETERMINED GRASP, SHE IS CARRIED ALONG AN INTERMINABLE PASSAGEWAY TO THE TOP OF A STARICASE WHICH LEADS TO A VAST AND EERIE ROOM, FULL OF UNKNOWN FORMS THAT SHINE IN THE HALF-LIGHT.

RUNNING AHEAD OF THEM, THE SQUAT MAN, HAS WAITED FOR THIS MOMENT TO THROW ALL THE LIGHT REQUIRED ON THE SCENE OF EVENTS. HE TURNS ON THE SWITCH AND ILLUMINATES THE ROOM: IT IS A WORK-SHOP IN AN ABANDONED FACTORY, IN THE MIDDLE OF WHICH, IMMENSE ON A LEAD BASE, LOOM TWO PARALLEL BARS.

A LARGE COLONIAL FAN SLOWLY BEGINS TO TURN JUST ABOVE THEM.

WHILE THE MOLLUSK FIRMLY ATTACHES ROBERTE'S WRISTS TO THE BARS BY MEANS OF THE LEATHER STRAPS, THE SQUAT MAN DOES THE SAME FOR HER ANKLES, HAVING FIRST, WITH A SINGLE GESTURE, TORN OFF HER SKIRT.

SO THAT BEFORE SHE KNOWS WHAT HAS HAPPENED ROBERTE FINDS HERSELF, TO HER FURY, TIED HAND

AND FOOT TO THE BARS, THE COAT OF HER SUIT DRAPED OVER HER SUSPENDER BELT.

AND WHILE WITH THE HIGH HEEL OF ONE FREE FOOT WHICH THE SQUAT MAN HAS NEGLECTED TO IMMOBILIZE SHE TRIES TO PUSH AWAY THE MOLLUSK'S BODY, HE DELICATELY REMOVES THE GLOVE COVERING ROBERTE'S HAND, OPENS HER FINGERS ONE BY ONE, AND WITH EMOTION APPROACHES HIS MOUTH TO HER OPEN PALM, FIXES HIS TONGUE AGAINST IT AND BEGINS TO TITILLATE THE PALM WITH INCREASING VIOLENCE.

ROBERTE CLOSES HER EYES. HER LEG IS NO LONGER CAPABLE OF REPULSING THE MOLLUSK WITH THE SAME ENERGY, ITS MOVEMENT SLOWING AND CHANGING LITTLE BY LITTLE INTO A LANGUOR-OUS UNDULATION OF THE KNEE.

ROBERTE MURMURS:

ROBERTE: PUT OUT THE LIGHT THEN ...

FOR A MOMENT SHE OPENS HER EYES TO MEET THE IMPLACABLE GAZE OF THE SQUAT MAN WHO MAINTAINS HIS HOLD QUITE UNNECESSARILY ON THE FETTERED ANKLE, WHEN IN A CLIMAX OF EMOTION, THE MOLLUSK LETS GO HER HAND AND COLLAPSES IN A DEAD FAINT ON THE FLOOR. THE SQUAT MAN IMMEDIATELY DRAGS HIM AWAY, THEN, WITHOUT A WORD, UNTIES ROBERTE AND DISAP-PEARS BY THE STAIRCASE. HE SLIPS THE RED CARD INTO HER BAG AND POURS A GLASS OF BRANDY.

LEFT ALONE WITH THE BARS IN THE DESERTED GYMNASIUM, ROBERTE PUTS ON HER SKIRT AND SUDDENLY FEELS HORRIBLY ALONE. SHE LOOKS UP AT THE GLASS DOME ABOVE HER WHERE THE SHADOW OF A RECLINING BODY SLIDES DOWN: IT IS LITTLE X.

THE SQUAT MAN RETURNS, HANDS HER HER BAG AND THE GLASS OF BRANDY. SHOCKED BY HIS INSOLENCE, ROBERTE SLAPS HIS FACE WITH SUCH FORCE THE GLASS FALLS AND SPLINTERS TO PIECES ON THE TILED FLOOR. THE SQUAT MAN SMILES AT HER INSOLENTLY.

ROBERTE, LOST IN REVERIE, BACK AGAINST THE COLONNADE OF THE CAFÉ LE NEMOURS IS INTERRUPTED BY THE WAITER'S VOICE.

WAITER: ARE YOU ALL RIGHT? YOU LOOK PALE ...

SHE TURNS SLOWLY, WITHOUT SEEING HIM, STROKES HER WRISTS AND GOES TO SIT DOWN AT THE TABLE WHERE A CUP OF TEA AND TWO CROISSANTS ARE WAITING.

OPENING HER BAG TO TAKE OUT THE POCKET MIRROR, SHE SEES A RED CARD SLIPPED INSIDE.

SHE EXAMINES IT.

THE CARD BEARS A FACSIMILE OF HER OWN FINGERPRINTS, SUPERIMPOSED OVER THE WORD OF GOD: "IN PRINCIPIO ERAT VERBUM ..."

SHE PLACES THE CARD ON THE TABLE AND TAKES OUT HER POCKET MIRROR.

SHE LOOKS AT HERSELF AND SMILES.

ROBERTE (VOICE OFF): HOW SOOTHING THE PLAY OF THE FOUNTAINS UNDER THE PLANE TREES.

HOW EXQUISITE THE CITY IN ITS REFLECTIONS ...

THE GARDENS OF THE PALAIS-ROYAL AND ITS FOUNTAINS, STREAMING WITH WATER.

PIERRE KLOSSOWSKI
TRANSLATED BY CATHERINE DUNCAN

SAINTE JACKIE, COMEDIENNE AND TORTURER

LET THE MAN OF VICE TALK, YOU'LL BE TAKEN FOR A RIDE. HE WILL MAKE YOU SWALLOW ALL OF HIS FANTASIES, HIS MYTHS, HIS LIES, HIS PREJUDICES. LET'S GAG HIM. HIS TWO OBJECTIVE ACCOMPLICES, THE PROSTITUTE AND THE COP, TELL ENOUGH AS IT IS. THEY DON'T CHANGE THE FACTS, THEY DON'T GET DELIRIOUS. THEY ARE PROS.

WHY THE PROSTITUTE? IN WHAT SENSE IS SHE MORE QUALIFIED THAN THE DRUG DEALER OR CROUPIER TO SPEAK ABOUT VICE? DON'T ALL THREE PLAY A SIMILAR ROLE: TO FURNISH THE MAN OF VICE WITH THE OBJECT OF HIS PLEASURE? UNDOUBTEDLY, AND, IN ALL THREE CASES, ONE FINDS THE OBJECT DEPRIVED OF ITS FIRST DESTINATION AND PLEASURE MADE UNNATURAL: LOSS ENTERS INTO THE PLEASURE OF THE GAMBLER, JUST AS 'NEED' ENTERS INTO THAT OF THE ADDICT, JUST AS THE SUPREME HUMILIATION—OF PAYING TO BE LOVED— ENTERS INTO THAT OF THE JOHN. VICE IS ALWAYS THE SAME: IT HAPPENS WHEN MISFORTUNE IS GOOD. OF COURSE, BUT THE DOMAIN OF PROSTITUTION, SEXUAL DEVIATION, IS THE ONLY PLACE WHERE A DIRECT RELATIONSHIP IS INVOLVED. THE PROSTITUTE DOES MORE THAN FURNISH AN OBJECT, SHE IS THAT OBJECT. LIVING MATTER WHICH LISTENS, RECORDS, RESPONDS, QUESTIONS, DECIDES, A DRUG WHICH SETS ITS OWN DOSE; A ROULETTE WHEEL WHICH CHOOSES WHERE TO STOP, OBVIOUSLY ALWAYS ONE SPOT AWAY FROM THE WINNING NUMBER. SHE HAS SEEN EVERYTHING, HEARD EVERYTHING ... AND UNDERSTOOD NOTHING? SO WHAT, SHE TALKS, SHE KNOWS WHAT SHE IS TALKING ABOUT, SHE 'KNOWS'. STOP.

JACKIE: THIRTY YEARS OLD NEXT OCTOBER, 5'5", 143 LBS. SOMETHING HEAVY ABOUT HER FACE, HER GAZE, HER GAIT, GREEN EYES, SHORT BLACK HAIR. PRETTY? AN ABSURD QUESTION WHICH NO CUSTOMER HAS EVER ASKED HIMSELF. SHINY RED BOOTS, LACED TO THE KNEE, 3" HEELS. A BLACK SLICKER COAT WHICH SHE HAS WORN FROM THE BEGINNING AND WHICH HAS EARNED HER THE NICKNAME: SLICK-JACKIE. A PHOTO TACKED ON THE WALL: A WOMAN OF ABOUT FIFTY, BLOND, BOOTS, FITTED LEATHER OUTFIT, HER FOOT ON A CHAIR, AN ANIMAL TAMER'S WHIP IN HER HAND. SIGNED: "TO JACKIE WITH BEST REGARDS. JOAN." "SHE'S DUTCH. SHE'S IN NEW YORK. YOU SEE HER IN ALL OF THE MAGAZINES. IN BOOKS TOO. SHE'S A STAR? SHE'S BEEN DOING S/M FOR TWENTY YEARS. SHE'S EVEN SENT ME CUSTOMERS. SHE WRITES ME TO EXPLAIN WHEN THEY DON'T SPEAK FRENCH. NEITHER DOES SHE, BUT I HAVE A CUSTOMER WHO TRANSLATES

HER LETTERS. SHE MIGHT COME SEE ME HERE. SHE'S TERRIBLY WELL-KNOWN. SHE'S A STAR."

TUESDAY, 3:10 P.M. THE DOORBELL RINGS. JACKIE GOES TO OPEN. SOUNDS AT THE DOOR. JACKIE RETURNS TO THE KITCHEN WHERE SHE HAS LEFT US, THE PHOTOGRAPHER AND ME. "YOU'RE LUCKY, HE'S ONE OF THE BEST. AND HE LIKES TO BE PHOTOGRAPHED. GIVE ME TIME TO PREPARE HIM, THEN JOIN ME IN THE ROOM ON THE LEFT. THIS MIGHT NOT BE BAD, HE'S WEARING HIS RAGS. JUST PUT ON A MASK OR A HOOD IF YOU DON'T WANT HIM TO SEE YOUR FACE." SHE LAUGHS.

SHE CALLS US TWO MINUTES LATER. SHE IS IN FRONT OF THE DOOR. AT HER FEET, HANDS AND FEET BOUND WITH A SINGLE CORD, FACE AGAINST THE FLOOR, A MAN OF ABOUT SIXTY-FIVE. HE IS WEARING AN ORDINARY GREENISH-GRAY SHIRT WITH PANTS OF THE SAME COLOR AND FABRIC. HE IS BALD. SHE IS IN FRONT OF US, PULLING A PACKAGE BEHIND HER. WE ENTER THE TORTURE ROOM. SHE TURNS TOWARDS US, AND IN A PENETRATING VOICE ANNOUNCES: "HE'S BELGIAN." THE ABSURDITY OF THIS CONFIDENCE, GIVEN THE SITUATION, DOES NOT EVEN MAKE US SMILE. THE TRUTH IS THAT WE ARE TERRIFIED. DEATHLY SILENCE.

AN HOUR EARLIER, WE HAD EXAMINED THIS SAME ROOM WITHOUT ANYONE IN IT. A GRAND-GUIGNOL SET WHICH GAVE US A FEW GOOD LAUGHS. OBVIOUSLY THE ATMOSPHERE HAS CHANGED: THE MOTIONLESS BODY OF THIS NICE MAN, TIED AT OUR FEET, JACKIE'S PREPARATIONS—IN PARTICULAR, HER INSPECTIONS OF THE WHEEL'S FUNCTIONING, WHICH SEEMS TO LEAVE SOMETHING TO BE DESIRED—THE SEEMINGLY OBLIGATORY MUTENESS: ALL OF THIS ABRUPTLY MAKES THE DIFFERENT APPARATUSES REAL.

THE BIG CROSS, AN X. TEN FEET HIGH, WITH DANGLING RINGS FOR WRISTS AND ANKLES, THE WHEEL, OPERATED WITH A CRANK, WHICH CAN PULL THE LIMBS OF THE VICTIM UNTIL HE IS QUARTERED, THE IRON CAGE, THREE FEET HIGH, TWENTY INCHES DEEP, WHERE THE VICTIM MAY BE 'PUNISHED' FOR FIVE HOURS STRAIGHT, THE STRANGE BULKY WOODEN CONTRAPTION WHICH IMPRISONS THE NECK AND ARMS (UNDOUBTEDLY A REPRODUCTION MADE BY A HORROR MOVIE SET DESIGNER, BUT THIS ONE WORKS!). FINALLY, THE CLASSIC COMMODE-CHAIR FOR WHICH DECENCY—AS IF IT WERE NEEDED AT THIS POINT!—FORBIDS EXPLAINING THE EXACT USE. SOME WHIPS, ABOUT FIFTEEN, ON THE WALLS (WHIPS FOR DOGS, FOR HORSES, FOR WILD ANIMALS,

FOR CHILDREN—ODDLY, ONE OF WHICH IS A FAKE MADE OF RUBBER), COMPLETE THE SET. ALL OF THE OTHER SMALLER PROPS—AND THERE ARE MANY—ARE ARRANGED IN THE OTHER ROOM. THAT'S LATER.

STILL NOTHING. SECONDS FEEL LIKE HOURS. SUDDENLY, THE HEELS OF THE BOOT STRIKES. THE TORN SHIRT RASPS LIKE FABRIC IN A DESIGNER'S WORKROOM. NOW BOTH HEELS, ONE AFTER THE OTHER, ARE SHREDDING THE CLOTHING OF THE CUSTOMER-SLAVE. DELIBERATELY OR NOT. THE SHARP POINT MAKES A LONG RED MARK ON THE BACK. SOFT MOANS. A SIGNAL PERHAPS?

FINALLY, JACKIE'S MOUTH EMITS A SOUND. "SO! IT'S LIKE THAT! YOU DARE TO COME IN RAGS TO SEE YOUR MISTRESS! THAT'S THE WAY YOU WANT IT! IN RAGS!" SHE IS SUDDENLY ANIMATED; SHE PUMMELS THE POOR MAN WITH KICKS AND SLAPS, PULLS OFF HIS LAST SHREDS OF CLOTHING, TAKES DOWN A WHIP, COUNTS OUT THIRTY LASHES IN A TIRED VOICE, OPENS THE CAGE, MAKES HIM ENTER IT, HEAD FIRST, LOCKS IT WITH A KEY. "I'M KEEPING HIM UNTIL EIGHT O'CLOCK TONIGHT," SHE SAYS, AS IF TO EXCUSE HERSELF FOR INTERRUPTING THE SESSION.

IN FIVE MINUTES THE YOUNG CHILDREN WILL LEAVE SCHOOL, THE FRESHMEN WILL BE DISMISSED IN VINCENNES, AND A NEW CUSTOMER WILL COME, TREMBLING, TO RING JACKIE'S DOOR. HE WILL GIVE THE NAME OF A FRIEND WHO SENT HIM. HE WILL BE ASKED IF HE IS "AWARE OF WHAT IS DONE HERE," THEN HE WILL BE POLITELY ASKED TO WAIT IN A LARGE, EMPTY ROOM. NEXT, HE WILL BE BROUGHT TO THE FIRST ROOM. THERE HE WILL FIND, HANGING ON NAILS IN THE WALL, AT LEAST THIRTY SLICKERS, COATS, GARTERS, BELTS, BRAS, AND PANTIES MADE OF BLACK LEATHER. ON A RACK, ALL OF THE BOOTS AND SHOES—INCLUDING A PAIR OF BRIGHT RED PUMPS WITH STILETTO HEELS, SIZE 12. ON THE SHELVES OF A SMALL BOOKCASE—FROM WHICH IS ABSENT ALL OF THE SCANDINAVIAN PORNOGRAPHY WHICH MAKES SEX-SHOP PROFITABLE—ALL OF THE SMALLER OBJECTS: DILDOS OF EVERY SIZE AND SHAPE, CLIPS, LEATHER STRIPS, LITTLE WHIPS (THE OTHERS ARE IN THE TORTURE ROOM), A BOWL FOR WASHING, SEWING UTENSILS (TEN KINDS OF NEEDLES, AS MANY DIFFERENT QUALITIES OF THREAD), FIVE OR SIX PAIRS OF HANDCUFFS MARKED 'PÉGI' (AN IRONWORKER FROM THE RUE DES PETITS-CHAMPS, WHO MAKES THEM, HAD THE IDEA OF MARKING THEM SO AS TO SUGGEST THE INITIALS OF THE POLICE JUDICIAIRE), FINALLY, A BLACK LACQUER PENCIL BOX FILLED WITH SMALL PIECES OF PAPER, FOLDED IN QUARTERS.

JACKIE SITS ON A THRONE PLACED ON A SHAKY PLATFORM, LEGS CROSSED, BUT COVERED BY SLICKERS—NEVER IS THE LEAST BIT OF SKIN REVEALED—RIDING WHIP IN HAND, EYES GLAZED, WITH A TIRED LOOK. THE CUSTOMER KNEELS BEFORE HER, DRAWS A SMALL PIECE OF PAPER FROM THE PENCIL BOX, USUALLY WITH HIS TEETH, UNFOLDS IT AND READS. IT MIGHT SAY—THIS IS ONLY ONE OF A HUNDRED EXAMPLES—LICK THE SOLES OF THE MISTRESS' BOOTS; RECEIVE FIFTY LASHES BEHIND THE KNEES FROM A BLACK WHIP; ONE HOUR IN THE BOX.

WHATEVER PUNISHMENT IS DRAWN, JACKIE WILL EXPLAIN, HALF-ADMIRING, HALF SCORNFUL. "NOW YOU CAN REALLY SAY YOU'RE LUCKY; YOU DREW THE EASIEST PUNISHMENT!" ONLY AFTER THIS WILL JACKIE INFORM THE CUSTOMER OF HIS NUMBER, WHICH HE WILL HAVE TO REMEMBER FOR FUTURE VISITS. "YOU WILL BE SLAVE 84." 84 WILL THEN CHOOSE FROM THE OUTFITS ON THE WALL THE ONE WHICH HE WILL WEAR DURING HIS PUNISHMENT. ONLY THE BEGINNER RISKS ASKING QUESTIONS. HE WILL USUALLY BE ANSWERED WITH A WHIP. UNLESS HE ASKS ABOUT THE WHITE WOOD TRESTLE TABLE, STAINED WITH LONG BLACK MARKS. IN THAT CASE, JACKIE EXPLAINS, WITH THE VOICE OF A HOME ECONOMIST, THAT IT IS A SEWING TABLE.

LET'S ABANDON THE FALSE OBJECTIVITY OF DESCRIPTION AND SPECIFY THAT MORE THAN HALF OF THE VISITORS ASK TO BE SEWN WITH NEEDLE AND THREAD. GENERALLY, THE NIPPLES, THE TESTICLES (TO THE THIGHS), THE CRACK OF THE BUTTOCKS. THE OPERATIONS OBVIOUSLY ONLY TAKE PLACE AFTER THE SUBJECT—RATHER, THE OBJECT—HAS BEEN CAREFULLY BOUND TO AVOID ANY RISK OF REBELLION AND GAGGED TO STIFLE THE CRIES. THERE IS BLOOD, OF COURSE. IT RUNS ON THE TABLE ("NEVER A LOT, I'M CAREFUL" STATES JACKIE). WOUNDS, TOO. COTTON SOAKED IN ALCOHOL AT 200° IS SUFFICIENT TO CAUTERIZE THEM. "THAT'S THE MIRACLE," SAYS JACKIE, "THEY LEAVE IN SHREDS AND THEY RETURN, THREE DAYS LATER, EVERYTHING DRIED UP."

THAT, ROUGHLY, IS WHAT ONE NEEDS TO KNOW ABOUT SLICK-JACKIE'S ACTIVITIES. LOTS OF QUESTIONS COME TO MIND. PRACTICAL QUESTIONS, FOR OUR AIM HERE IS NOT TO ATTEMPT TO ENTER INTO THE WHY OF THIS UNLIKELY FORM OF VOLUNTARY MARTYRDOM. FIRST OF ALL: HOW DO THE VICTIMS REACH ORGASM, THE USUAL GOAL OF A VISIT TO A PROSTITUTE? JACKIE'S ANSWER: "MORE THAN HALF LEAVE WITHOUT REACHING IT. THEY

DON'T EVEN TRY. OF THE OTHERS, TWO OUT OF THREE ONLY REACH IT—HOW SHOULD I PUT IT— THROUGH SCATOLOGY. THERE ARE SOME, OF COURSE, WHO DO THEMSELVES AND SEVERAL, WHOM I HAVE KNOWN FOR A LONG TIME, WHOM I HELP A LITTLE. BUT WITH THEM, I ALWAYS WEAR RUBBER GLOVES, NOT THE ONES FOR DOING THE DISHES, THEY DON'T COME IN BLACK. I HAVE TO BUY SURGEON'S GLOVES."

ANOTHER QUESTION: WHAT IS THE COST OF A SESSION? THOUGH HELL HAS NO PRICE, JACKIE SETS HER ABSOLUTE MINIMUM PRICE AT $50. AVERAGE TIME: ONE HOUR, NO SEWING, NO TORTURE ON THE WHEEL OR THE CROSS, LIMITED WHIPPING, DIALOGUE REDUCED TO THE SIMPLEST EXPRESSIONS. BUT ONE-TIME CUSTOMERS ARE THE EXCEPTION: ONE, AT MOST TWO PER DAY. AND THE OTHERS? WELL, THEY PAY BY THE MONTH.

SIX OF THEM, WHO HOLD IMPORTANT POSITIONS IN BUSINESS AND IN GOVERNMENT, PAY HER A MONTHLY FIXED SUM WHICH VARIES—AT LEAST ACCORDING TO JACKIE—BETWEEN $1500 AND $2500. THE OTHERS PAY BETWEEN $250 AND $1000 DEPENDING ON THEIR MEANS. THUS, THE COST OF SUFFERING IS CALCULATED BY JACKIE ON AN INDIVIDUAL BASIS. THE MONTHLY PAYMENT ENTITLES ONE TO AN UNLIMITED NUMBER OF VISITS. BUT, EVERYONE IS SATISFIED WITH ONE TO THREE VISITS PER MONTH. JACKIE: "ANYWAY, THEY COULDN'T TAKE ANY MORE, PHYSICALLY." HOW MANY OF THEM ARE THERE? "REGULARS, BETWEEN ONE HUNDRED AND ONE HUNDRED AND TWENTY."

A PRIVATE CHAT WITH A HIGH POLICE OFFICIAL: "THE GIRLS LIKE THOSE YOU ARE TALKING ABOUT, WE KNOW THEM ALL. THEY ARE ON FILE HERE, LIKE MOST OF THE OTHER PROSTITUTES, EVEN THOUGH THE FILES WERE OFFICIALLY STOPPED ON NOVEMBER 25, 1960. IN OUR VOCABULARY, THEY ARE 'WHIPPING SPECIALISTS.' THERE'S ONE ON THE RUE BLONDEL, TWO OTHERS ON THE RUE QUINCAMPOIX (TEN YEARS AGO THERE WERE SEVEN OR EIGHT ON THAT STREET), ONE ON THE RUE DE LA REYNIE. THEY EARN A LOT OF MONEY, INDEED. GENERALLY, THEY DON'T HAVE PIMPS BECAUSE THEY ARE MORE INTELLIGENT THAN THE AVERAGE PROSTITUTE.

"CONCERNING THE 'WHIPPING SPECIALISTS,' WHAT WE FEAR MOST IS THE REVOLT OF ONE OF THE CUSTOMERS. UNTIL THEY HAVE REACHED THE PEAK OF THEIR PLEASURE, THEY ARE DANGEROUS. THEY ARE CAPABLE OF MURDER. THAT'S WHY THE GIRLS

TIE THEM UP SECURELY AND RELEASE THEM ONLY WHEN THEY ARE COMPLETELY CALMED DOWN."

GROUP DISCIPLINE AT JACKIE'S. WEDNESDAY AND SATURDAYS—FROM THREE O'CLOCK TO EIGHT O'CLOCK—ARE DEVOTED TO THOSE CUSTOMERS WHO SEEK TO COMBINE THE PLEASURES OF THE WHIP WITH THOSE OF THE GROUP. THERE ARE USUALLY ABOUT A DOZEN MEN WHO 'SUBMIT' AND SUFFER TOGETHER, TWICE A WEEK. SOME OF THEM WEAR BLACK VELVET MASKS IN ORDER TO REMAIN ANONYMOUS. THIS IS TOLERATED BUT NOT WELCOMED. JACKIE GENERALLY LIMITS HERSELF TO GIVING DIRECTIONS AND SUCCEEDS IN HAVING HER CUSTOMERS THEMSELVES TORTURE THEIR CHAINED BROTHERS. SHE ALSO REQUIRES THEM TO PLAY EROTIC GAMES AMONG THEMSELVES AND ONLY GRABS THE WHIP HERSELF WHEN THINGS GET OUT OF HAND. "SOMETIMES I FEEL LIKE I'M IN A LION CAGE," SHE SAYS. "THEY TRACK ME! BUT BASICALLY I LIKE THEM! THE LAST TIME I WENT ON VACATION ALONE—USUALLY I ALWAYS HAVE ONE OR TWO OF THEM WHO COME FOR THE WEEKEND; I MAKE THEM STAY FOR WHOLE DAYS IN THE OUTHOUSES AT THE BACK OF THE GARDEN—AT THE END OF TEN DAYS, I WANTED TO COME HOME, I MISSED MY PREY."

SOMETIMES, CERTAIN CUSTOMERS BEG TO BE ALLOWED TO BRING THEIR WIVES. EITHER TO BE WHIPPED BY HER IN THIS SETTING, OR (MORE OFTEN) TO INITIATE HER TO THE PLEASURES OF SUFFERING. JACKIE RARELY AGREES. ONE OF THE ODDITIES OF PROSTITUTION LEGISLATION IS THAT ITS EYES REMAIN CLOSED AS LONG AS THERE IS ONLY ONE "PRIESTESS," WHEREAS THE PRESENCE OF ANOTHER WOMAN IMMEDIATELY OPENS THE DOOR TO PROSECUTION FOR PROCURING. AND TRY TO EXPLAIN TO A TWENTY-THREE YEAR OLD INSPEC-TOR, JUST OUT OF LAW SCHOOL, THAT THE OTHER WOMAN IS A CUSTOMER LIKE THE OTHERS ... OFTEN, HOWEVER, ESPECIALLY ON SATURDAYS, THE CROWD IS SUCH THAT JACKIE, IN SPITE OF THE CLEVER SYSTEM OF MUTUAL DISCIPLINE WHICH SHE DEMANDS, CANNOT HANDLE IT. AT THOSE TIMES, SHE CALLS ON A NEIGHBOR OR THE CLEANING WOMAN FROM THE LITTLE STREET ON THE LEFT—I.E. ON SOMEONE FROM THE NEIGHBORHOOD WHOSE PRESENCE, IN CASE OF TROUBLE, CAN BE EXPLAINED TO THE POLICE.

"THEY AREN'T TRICKY," SAYS JACKIE WITH A BIG INDULGENT SMILE. "THEY'RE TIMID, SO THEY LAUGH ALL THE TIME; THE MORE THE GUYS SUFFER, THE MORE THEY LAUGH. THEY'RE PISSED TOO, BUT YOU CAN SEE THAT THEY'RE AMATEURS."

SETTING: THE THRONE ROOM. JACKIE, SEATED ON THE NARROW SOFA WHICH DOUBLES AS A BED—ONE HAS THE IMPRESSION THAT IT HAS SHRUNK FROM LACK OF USE—IS TELLING HER LIFE STORY. A PENSIVE LOOK. SOMETHING ABOUT HER GAZE, WITHOUT QUESTION ... BUT WHAT? ...

"WELL, O.K., I'LL START AT THE BEGINNING. I WAS BORN IN NORMANDY. MY FATHER WAS A CONTRAC-TOR. HE DIDN'T GET ALONG WITH MY MOTHER. I DIDN'T GET ALONG WITH EITHER OF THEM. NOR EVEN WITH KIDS MY OWN AGE. SO, AT THRITEEN I FELL IN LOVE. AN OLDER GUY, MARRIED AND ALL. RENÉ. HE WORKED IN IMPORT-EXPORT. I'M SIXTEEN WHEN I GET PREGNANT. HE WARNED ME THAT HE WANTED NONE OF THAT, BUT I'M A FOOL, I DON'T KNOW HOW TO DO ANYTHING RIGHT; SO I CONFESS TO MY MOTHER, THAT CAUSES TERRIBLE TROUBLE, SO I LEAVE. ALL ALONE, IN PARIS. I FOUND A JOB ON THE BOULEVARD RICHARD-LENOIR, IN A BAKERY, THEN IN AN ACCOUNTING FIRM IN ANOTHER NEIGHBOR-HOOD. EVERYTHING I'VE DONE, EVERYTHING I'M DOING, I DON'T GIVE A DAMN ABOUT IT. WHAT I REGRET IS NOT HAVING AN EDUCATION. I WOULD HAVE LIKED TO LEARN.

"AS I WAS THREE MONTHS PREGNANT WHEN I ARRIVED, ALL OF THIS DIDN'T LAST LONG. WHERE COULD I GO? A HOME FOR UNWED MOTHERS. I GAVE BIRTH ON MY SEVENTEENTH BIRTHDAY. MY SON WILL BE THIRTEEN NEXT OCTOBER. HE'S A GOOD KID. WHEN I LEFT THE HOME, I HAD TO FIND SOMETHING: AN AID AT A CLINIC IN BOURG-LA-REINE FOR RICH PREGNANT WOMEN. $50 PER MONTH, THAT'S WHAT I EARNED. BUT THE NURSES GOT $100. SO, WITH THE HELP OF AN OLD FRIEND FROM THE HOME FOR UNWED MOTHERS, I GOT A JOB, AFTER WORK, AT A BAR IN BELLEVILLE. WITH THIS, I JUST MANAGED TO GET BY.

"IN FRONT OF THE BAR, THERE WERE GIRLS WORKING THE STREET. I'M INTRIGUED. I FIND OUT A LITTLE ABOUT HOW MUCH THEY MAKE, AND, IMMEDIATELY I SAY TO MYSELF, I'M GOING TO DO IT TOO. BUT I HAVE NO EXPERIENCE. THE FATHER OF MY KID WAS THE ONLY MAN I KNEW SEXUALLY. PLUS, I HAVE THE IDEA THAT YOU STAY FOR HOURS WITH THE SAME GUY, THAT YOU HAVE TO TALK TO HIM, THAT YOU HAVE TO GET UNDER THE SHEETS WITH HIM. NOW THAT DISGUSTS ME. WHEN I FOUND OUT HOW IT REALLY WORKS, FAST, THE ROD AND THE EDGE OF THE BED, WELL THEN, IMMEDIATELY I SAY YES.

"BUT THAT DOESN'T LAST LONG. THE ARAB PIMPS IN

BELLEVILLE, THEY WANT TOO MUCH. SO, I GO TO LES HALLES WITH A FRIEND WHO KNOWS A HOTEL MANAGER. I'LL ALWAYS REMEMBER MY FIRST DAY THERE. IT WAS ON THE RUE AUBRY-LE-BOUCHER, BETWEEN TOPOL AND THE RUE QUINCAMPOIS. I WAS A KID. THE FIRST CUSTOMER SAID TO ME: 'CAN YOU DO A QUICKIE?' I ANSWERED: 'WHAT'S THAT?' I DIDN'T KNOW ANYTHING. BUT AFTER SEVERAL DAYS THINGS WERE GOING VERY WELL. SO OF COURSE, THE OTHER GIRLS GOT JEALOUS.

"I CHANGED HOTELS IMMEDIATELY, WITH THE HELP OF A FRIEND, I WENT TO THE RUE QUINCAMPOIS. I HAD ONLY BEEN THERE TWO DAYS WHEN GUYS SHOWED UP. THE FIRST, AN ARAB WHO BUYS ME A DRINK AT THE BAR, TELLS ME THAT IF I'M NOT MARRIED, I HAVE TO MARRY HIM. I SAY NO. THEN HE TELLS ME, 'THAT WILL COST YOU A C-NOTE; YOU SHOULDN'T HAVE DRUNK WITH ME. PUT A HUNDRED BUCKS IN AN ENVELOPE AND BRING IT TO THE DOOR, RUE DES FRANCS-BOURGEOIS, TOMORROW AT SIX.' I WENT THERE WITH THE ENVELOPE BUT INSIDE I HAD PUT TOILET PAPER. JUST TO SPITE HIM, I WENT, I COULDN'T RESIST. IT DIDN'T WORK. THERE WERE THREE OF THEM. THEY BEAT MY HEAD IN ... SEVERAL TEETH, THE CHEEK-BONE, A SHOULDER, BOTH ANKLES ...

"WHEN I RECOVERED, I HAD TO GET MARRIED; A LITTLE BARTENDER, TWENTY-FIVE YEARS OLD, SICILIAN, A FRIEND OF THE HOTEL MANAGER. WITH HIM, I WASN'T WORRIED ABOUT THE ARABS. I STAYED WITH HIM. I CAN'T SAY HE WASN'T NICE. ONLY JEALOUS! HE SPIED ON ME IN THE STREET AND SLAPPED ME AS I WALKED BY—INSTEAD OF BEING HAPPY THAT I WAS WORKING—BECAUSE HE SAID I CAME! TERRIBLY JEALOUS GUY. EVEN THOUGH HE HAD A WOMAN ON THE SIDE, BUT SHE WAS FRIGID, POOR WOMAN!

"ONE FINE DAY I HAD HAD ENOUGH, I ESCAPED TO MARSEILLES. I HAD SOME FRIENDS THERE WHO HELPED ME. BUSINESS WASN'T BAD. BUT, I WAS NEVER A MEAT RACK, THIRTY THROWS AT TEN BUCKS, NOT FOR ME! FROM THE BEGINNING, I HAD THE BLACK DRESS AND HIGH HEELS. I WASN'T AS STRONG THEN AS I AM TODAY, BUT I ALREADY KNEW

IT WAS BETTER TO ROUGH UP A GUY FOR $50 THAN TO GET FUCKED ALL DAY FOR THIRTY!

"WHERE WAS I? YES, IN MARSEILLES. WELL IT HAPPENED ONE FOURTEENTH OF JULY. I WAS SITTING ON A CAFE TERRACE. A LITTLE DANCE HALL. IT WAS TWO O'CLOCK IN THE MORNING. A LIMO PULLS UP. I KNOW THAT IT'S FOR ME. I BARELY HAVE TIME TO GET UP. THE BULLET GOES THROUGH MY SHOULDER AN TEARS UP MY CHIN. I WOULD HAVE BEEN HIT RIGHT IN THE HEAD IF I HADN'T STOOD UP. THE LIMO LEFT. IT WAS MY GUY FROM PARIS. I STAYED THERE, ON THE GROUND, ON MY HANDS AND KNEES. THERE WAS SUDDENLY NOBODY LEFT IN THE DANCE HALL. I MADE IT TO A TAXI AND WENT TO THE HOSPITAL ALL ALONE.

"AFTER ALL THAT, IT'S FUNNIER, BETTER FOR ARTICLES. THEY STILL TRIED TO GET ME AS SOON AS I LEFT THE HOSPITAL. I GOT OUT AND CAME BACK TO PARIS. I PAID A PROTECTION FEE OF $2500, THOUGH. I DON'T REMEMBER TO WHOM ... SEE, AT THIS TIME, I WASN'T EVEN TWENTY-ONE. I GOT AROUND ... LITTLE BY LITTLE, I SPECIALIZED. THE CUSTOMERS TAUGHT ME. THE INSTRUMENTS, THE WORDS, ALL THAT CAME FROM THEM. WHAT'S UNIQUE ABOUT ME IS MY GAZE. AND MY STRENGTH. WELL O.K., I MOVE IN. I'VE GOT MY PLACE. AND, FINALLY, THEY FIGURE OUT THAT THEY CAN'T TOUCH ME, THAT IT'S FORBIDDEN. FOR HOW LONG? I HAVEN'T MADE LOVE WITH A CUSTOMER FOR THREE AND A HALF YEARS. NOT BAD FOR A PROSTITUTE. ONCE, I MET MY SON'S FATHER IN DIEPPE. LIKE EVERYONE ELSE, HE WANTED TO SLEEP WITH ME. ESPECIALLY BECAUSE OF WHAT I WAS WEARING, I THINK. AND BECAUSE OF MY DOUGH. HE DIDN'T WANT TO TAKE ANY, BUT HE WAS FLABBERGASTED. SO I ACTED LIKE I WANTED TO SEE HIM. WE HAD DINNER. I TOLD HIM ABOUT MY SPECIALTIES IN PARIS. HIS EYES BULGED. HE WAS TREMBLING. AFTER DINNER, I WAS THE ONE WHO PAID FOR THE HOTEL, THE FANCIEST OF THEM ALL. HE GOT UNDRESSED. AND I TREATED HIM LIKE A CUSTOMER. THERE HE WAS, BEGGING ME TO STOP, TO CONTINUE, HE DIDN'T KNOW WHAT HE WANTED. HE WAS FUNNY THAT WAY."

TRANSLATED BY CHARLES CLARK

M.

[MR. M's STORY]

MR. M. WAS 65 WHEN HE CAME TO ME FOR THE FIRST TIME. A RADIOLOGIST COLLEAGUE OF MINE DISCOVERED HIM AFTER HE HAD CONSULTED HER ABOUT A HEMOPTYSIS WHICH PROVED TO BE OF SHORT-LIVED DURATION. MY COLLEAGUE EXAMINED HIM AND MADE A CAREFUL INVENTORY OF ALL TRACES INDICATING PERVERSE PRACTICES; SHE DISCUSSED HIS STATE WITH HIM AND ADVISED HIM TO SEE ME. MR. M. ACQUIESCED AT ONCE, REMARKING THAT HIS CASE MIGHT BE USEFUL TO OTHERS WITH THE SAME PERVERSION AS HIS. HE ALSO ADMITTED THAT BY AGREEING TO CONSULT ME, HE MIGHT ALSO BE HOPING FOR AN OPPORTU- NITY TO BE HUMILIATED, AND AT THE SAME TIME TO BETTER UNDERSTAND HIS CURIOUS STATUS. HIS CURIOSITY ABOUT HIMSELF HAD NEVER BEEN SATISFIED; HE HAD READ ALL THERE WAS ON THE SUBJECT OF MASOCHISM AND HAD ALWAYS BEEN DISAPPOINTED IN HIS FINDINGS. ACTUALLY, MANY OTHER FACTORS PLAYED A PART IN HIS DECISION TO SEE ME AS I SHALL INDICATE LATER ON.

MR. M.'S APPEARANCE AND HABITS WERE THOSE OF A CALM AND COLLECTED PERSON. HE WAS EXTREMELY CAREFUL TO CONCEAL HIS PERVER- SION FROM THOSE AROUND HIM. HE HAD BEEN A HIGHLY SKILLED TECHNICIAN IN RADIOELECTRICITY BEFORE HIS RETIREMENT. HIS EMPLOYERS HELD HIM IN SUCH HIGH ESTEEM THAT HE WAS ABLE TO OBTAIN SPECIAL WORKING CONDITIONS, AND IN PARTICULAR ARRANGEMENTS AFFECTING HIS HOURS AND HIS VACATIONS. HE LOATHED THE IDEA OF PERSONALLY EXERTING ANY FORM OF AUTHOR- ITY OR OF HOLDING A COMMANDING POSITION AND CONSIDERED BOTH GIVING AND RECEIVING ORDERS TO BE SURE WAYS OF LOSING HIS FREEDOM! HE WAS VERY FOND OF THIS FREEDOM WHICH INVOLVED LONG, SOLITARY WALKS DURING HIS HOLIDAYS. HE LIVED IN A SMALL SUBURBAN COTTAGE WITH HIS ADOPTED DAUGHTER AND HER HUSBAND. IN SHORT, HIS DAILY EXISTENCE WAS SINGULARLY DEVOID OF ANY MORAL MASOCHISM.

BUT WHAT A CONTRAST BETWEEN THESE OUTER APPEARANCES AND HIS NAKED BODY! PROVIDED THAT CERTAIN THRESHOLDS BE EXCEEDED, QUANTITATIVE CONSIDERATIONS AND INTENSITY FACTORS CAN MODIFY THE QUALITATIVE ASPECT OF A PHENOMENON AND ITS SENSE. GOING ON THE ASSUMPTION THAT MASOCHISTIC PRACTICES ARE NO EXCEPTION, I SHALL DESCRIBE THEM IN DETAIL

AND THUS POSSIBLY MODIFY CERTAIN CONCEP-
TIONS OF MASOCHISM.

TO BEGIN WITH, MR. M.'S BODY, EXCEPT FOR THE
FACE, WAS ALMOST COMPLETELY COVERED WITH
TATTOOS: "ALL BIG COCKS WELCOME," AND
LATERALLY, WITH AN ARROW, "BIG PRICKS ENTER
HERE" ON THE BUTTOCKS; IN FRONT, IN ADDITION TO
THE PENISES TATTOOED ON HIS THIGHS, ONE FOUND
THE FOLLOWING IMPRESSIVE LIST: "I'M A SLUT," "I
LIKE IT UP THE ASS," "UP WITH MASOCHISM," "I'M NOT
A MAN, I'M NOT A WOMAN, I'M A SLUT, I'M A WHORE, I'M
FUCKMEAT," "I'M AN AMBULATING SHIT-HOUSE," "I
LOVE SWALLOWING PISS AND SHIT," "I LOVE TO BE
BEATEN ALL OVER, AND THE HARDER, THE BETTER,"
"I'M A SLUT, GIVE IT TO ME UP THE ASS," "I'M A
WHORE, USE ME LIKE A FEMALE, I'LL MAKE YOU
COME BUT GOOD," "I'M THE STUPIDEST CUNT
AROUND, MY MOUTH AND MY ASSHOLE ARE FOR BIG
PRICKS."

MR. M.'S SCARS AND MARKS OF TORTURE WERE
EQUALLY STARTLING, HIS RIGHT BREAST WAS
LITERALLY ABSENT, HAVING BEEN SEARED WITH A
RED-HOT IRON, PIERCED BY SHARP OBJECTS AND
TORN OFF. HIS NAVEL WAS A SORT OF CRATER:
MOLTEN LEAD HAD BEEN POURED INTO IT WHICH
WAS PREVENTED FROM SPATTERING OUT (AS IT
WOULD HAVE DONE BECAUSE OF RIVULETS OF
SWEAT) BY INTRODUCING A RED-HOT METAL ROD
INTO THE LEAD. THONGS OF FLESH HAD BEEN CUT
ALONG HIS BACK, THROUGH WHICH HOOKS WERE
PASSED SO THAT MR. M. COULD BE SUSPENDED
WHILE A MAN PENETRATED HIM. HIS SMALL TOE WAS
MISSING: IT HAD APPARENTLY BEEN SECTIONED
WITH A HACKSAW BY MR. M. HIMSELF, ACTING ON THE
ORDERS OF A PARTNER. THE BONE SURFACE WAS
ROUGH AFTER THE AMPUTATION AND HE HAD FILED
IT EVEN. NEEDLES HAD BEEN PUSHED NEARLY
EVERYWHERE INTO HIS BODY, EVEN INTO THE
THORAX. HIS RECTUM WAS ENLARGED, "SO IT WOULD
LOOK LIKE A VAGINA." PHOTOGRAPHS WERE TAKEN
DURING THIS PROCESS. IT IS INTERESTING TO NOTE
THAT NONE OF THESE TORTURES WAS FOLLOWED BY
THE SLIGHTEST SUPPURATION, EVEN AFTER
FOREIGN BODIES, SUCH AS NEEDLES, NAILS AND
PIECES OF GLASS HAD BEEN INFLICTED ON HIS
BODY. THE DAILY INGESTION OF URINE AND
EXCREMENT OVER A PERIOD OF YEARS DID NOT
CAUSE ANY APPARENT UPSET. THE INTERNIST
ASKED MR. M. TO SHOW HIM VARIOUS INSTRUMENTS
OF TORTURE: BOARDS IMBEDDED WITH HUNDREDS
OF NEEDLES, A WHEEL FULL OF PHONOGRAPHIC
NEEDLES WITH A HANDLE AND THAT WAS USED TO
BEAT HIM. LASTLY, AND MOST REMARKABLY, MR. M.'S

GENITALIA HAD NOT BEEN SPARED.

MANY PHONOGRAPH NEEDLES WERE IMBEDDED IN
THE TESTES AS THE X-RAYS REVEALED. THE PENIS
WAS BLUE ALL OVER, PERHAPS AS THE RESULT OF
INDIA INK INJECTED INTO A VEIN. THE TIP OF THE
GLANS HAD BEEN SLIT WITH A RAZOR BLADE SO AS
TO WIDEN THE ORIFICE. A STEEL RING OF SEVERAL
CENTIMETERS IN DIAMETER HAD BEEN PERMANEN-
TLY AFFIXED TO THE TIP OF THE PENIS, AFTER
THE PREPUCE HAD BEEN MADE INTO A SORT OF
CUSHION FILLED WITH PARAFFIN. A MAGNETIZED
NEEDLE WAS IMBEDDED IN THE PENIS ITSELF, WHICH
I DARE SAY BORDERED ON BLACK HUMOUR SINCE
THE PENIS COULD "DEVIATE" THE NEEDLE OF A
COMPASS, THEREBY ASSERTING ITS POWER.
ANOTHER RING, BUT REMOVABLE THIS TIME, GIRDED
THE BASE OF THE PENIS AND THE SCROTUM.

ALL OF THIS COULD EASILY BE VERIFIED. THE
TORTURES MENTIONED ABOVE LEFT DEFINITE
TRACES WHICH INCONTESTABLY PROVED THAT MR.
M. WAS NOT LYING. AND YET (SHOULD I ATTRIBUTE
THIS TO A DEFENSIVE ATTITUDE ON MY PART?) I
SOMETIMES DOUBTED THE ACCURACY OF CERTAIN
UNVERIFIABLE FACTS WITHOUT BEING ABLE TO
JUSTIFY MY DOUBTS IN ANY WAY. WHY SHOULD HE
LIE ABOUT CERTIAN DETAILS WHEN OTHERS WERE
UNDENIABLY TRUE? I CANNOT SAY, AND YET I HAD
VAGUE DOUBTS CONCERNING IN PARTICULAR WHAT
HE RELATED ABOUT HIS WIFE AND A SPECIFIC CASE
OF AGGRESSIVE ACTING OUT.

HER DEATH, CAUSED IN NO SMALL AMOUNT, ONE
FEELS, BY THE TORTURES SHE HAD ENDURED, HAD
A PROFOUND EFFECT ON M. HE WAS OVERCOME BY
DEPRESSION AND DEVELOPED PULMONARY
TUBERCULOSIS IN HIS TURN, BUT WAS COMPLETELY
CURED AFTER TWO YEARS SPENT IN A SANATORIUM.

HIS MASOCHISTIC PRACTICES, WHICH HAD COM-
PLETELY CEASED DURING THIS PERIOD, BEGAN
ANEW, ESPECIALLY WITH MEN HE PICKED UP SINCE
THE RELATIONS WITH HIS FORMER PARTNERS HAD
RAPIDLY DWINDLED TO NOTHING. HE MARRIED A
SECOND TIME BUT THE MARRIAGE SOON ENDED IN
DIVORCE: HIS SECOND WIFE WAS A PROSTITUTE
WHOM HE HAD SELECTED IN THE HOPE OF FINDING
AN EXPERIENCED PARTNER. THE FACT THAT SHE
WAS A PROSTITUTE AND A PRECURESS PUT M. IN
DANGER OF BEING EXPOSED IF SHE WERE
ARRESTED FOR HER ILLEGAL ACTIVITIES AND HE
WANTED TO AVOID THAT POSSIBILITY AT ALL COSTS.
HE ALSO INTIMATED THAT HIS WIFE'S LACK OF
MORALITY SHOCKED HIM. HE LEGALLY ADOPTED

THE YOUNG GIRL WHO WAS THEIR MAID DURING THEIR BRIEF MARRIAGE. M. WAS 46 OR 47 AT THE TIME. IT WAS THEN THAT HIS PERVERSE ACTIVITIES CEASED ALTOGETHER. FROM THEN ON, HE LIVED COMPLETELY WITHIN THE FRAMEWORK OF THE FAMILY LIFE HE HAD CREATED AND TO WHICH HE WAS VERY MUCH ATTACHED. NOTHING OF HIS SINGULAR PAST WAS KNOWN TO THE PERSONS INVOLVED. CORRESPONDENCE WAS PRACTICALLY THE ONLY CONTACT HE MAINTAINED WITH HIS REAL DAUGHTER. HE TOLD ME THAT HE DID NOT THINK SHE WAS MASOCHISTIC, "EXCEPT FOR THE FACT THAT SHE HAD 10 CHILDREN."

M. DESCRIBED HIS PARENTS AS HAVING BEEN VERY CONSIDERATE AND KIND TO HIM. HE WAS AN ONLY CHILD AND HIS PARENTS WERE NOT YOUNG WHEN HE WAS BORN. HIS MOTHER WAS VERY AFFECTION-ATE; HIS FATHER WAS A LITTLE MORE RIGID. M. WAS VERY ATTACHED TO BOTH OF THEM AND GRADUAL-LY GREW QUITE CLOSE TO HIS FATHER IN PARTICULAR. HIS FATHER FOLLOWED M.'S PROG-RESS AT SCHOOL QUITE CLOSELY BUT WITHOUT BEING OVERLY SEVERE. ALL OF THIS IS VERY ORDINARY, ONE MIGHT SAY. NEVERTHELESS, M. AT 4 YEARS OF AGE HAD SEEN A LITTLE GIRL IN HIS NEIGHBORHOOD EATING HER EXCREMENT. HE EVEN REMEMBERED HER NAME. HE SAID THAT "I WAS DISGUSTED, BUT LATER ON IT CAME BACK TO ME." ANOTHER TIME DURING OUR TALKS HE MADE THE FOLLOWING STATEMENT ABOUT A BOOK HE HAD READ ON FAKIRS: "AT FIRST I THOUGHT IT WAS HORRIBLE, BUT LATER ON IT CAME BACK TO ME." THE APPEARANCE EARLY IN LIFE OF EROGENOUS MASOCHISM—OFTEN CITED BY WRITERS ON THE SUBJECT—WAS VERIFIED IN M.'S CASE: HIS PRACTICES BEGAN WHEN HE WAS 10 YEARS OLD. HE BECAME AWARE OF HIS PUNISHMENT-SEEKING PENCHANT AND HIS ATTRACTION TO URINE AT BOARDING SCHOOL. HE WENT THROUGH A SHORT PERIOD DURING WHICH A CERTAIN REPUGNANCE APPARENTLY HELD HIM BACK, BUT WHEN THIS WAS OVER HIS MASOCHISTIC PRACTICES STARTED IN EARNEST AND GREW IN IMPORTANCE. AFTER BEING SODOMIZED BY A MONITOR, HE BECAME THE TARGET OF MALTREATMENT BY HIS CLASSMATES, THE SEXUAL ASPECT OF WHICH IS OBVIOUS. HIS CLASSMATES, HOWEVER, OFTEN BACKED OFF, NOT DARING TO ACTUALLY COMMIT CERTAIN DEEDS: THEY DARED NOT, FOR INSTANCE, PUSH NEEDLES THROUGH HIS ARM THEMSELVES BUT WOULD GIVE HIM ORDERS TO DO SO. IN SEXUAL "GAMES" HE WOULD ALWAYS ASSUME THE FEMALE ROLE. AS HE SAID, "I WAS REALLY THE LOCAL SLUT, AND IT SATISFIED ME." AFTER HIS MARRIAGE HIS MASO-CHISM DEVELOPED TO ITS FULLEST M. AND HIS

WIFE, ALTHOUGH ENGAGING AS I HAVE STATED IN NORMAL SEXUAL ACTIVITIES, WERE AT THE SAME TIME INDULGING IN SHARED MASOCHISTIC RELA-TIONS: "I LIKED IT WHEN SHE MADE ME SUFFER, AND SHE LIKED IT WHEN I MADE HER SUFFER." THEN CAME THE IDEA OF INCORPORATING ANOTHER PERSON INTO THEIR ACTIVITIES. ONE PERSON, THEN TWO, SHARED THEIR SEXUAL EXISTENCE FOR THREE YEARS. IF ONE CONSIDERS THE DEVELOPMENT OF THIS CASE, IT SEEMS DEFINITE THAT CONSTITU-TIONAL FACTORS WEIGH HEAVILY IN THE BALANCE: M. MARRIED HIS COUSIN WHO HAD BEGUN HER MASOCHISTIC PRACTICES WHEN SHE WAS ELEVEN YEARS OLD (SHE WOULD STICK NEEDLES UNDER HER FINGERNAILS) LONG BEFORE THEY KNEW EACH OTHER. IN ADDITION, M. WAS 21 WHEN HE DISCOVERED THAT HIS FATHER (WHO HAD JUST DIED AND WHOSE CORRESPONDENCE HE WAS EXAMINING) PROBABLY HAD MASOCHISTIC TENDEN-CIES AS WELL. OTHER THAN THIS IMPORTANT CONSTITUTIONAL FACTOR, THE FACT THAT M.'S MASOCHISTIC TENDENCIES CEASED BETWEEN HIS 45TH AND HIS 50TH YEAR IS TO BE NOTED. AT THE BEGINNING OF THIS PERIOD HE STILL HAD A FEW HOMOSEXUAL ENCOUNTERS BUT SOON ALL PERVERSE PRACTICES CEASED COMPLETELY. AND YET, A MOST CURIOUS THING DESERVES CONSIDER-ATION: M. STILL HAD FAIRLY FREQUENT NOCTURNAL EMISSIONS AFTER EROTIC DREAMS THAT HAD BECOME PERFECTLY HETEROSEXUAL IN NATURE AND LESS AND LESS MASOCHISTIC. M. TOLD ME THAT IN HIS DREAMS HE WAS WITH "A VOLUPTUOUS WOMAN WITH WHOM MY SEXUAL ACTIVITIES WERE CLOSE TO BEING NORMAL." HE ADDED THAT "MY INTEREST HAD DIED OUT; I HAD EVOLVED; IF I CAN JUDGE BY MY DREAMS, I HAD BECOME NORMAL AGAIN." (IT IS A FACT THAT HIS EARLIER DREAMS WERE STRICTLY MASOCHISTIC.) THUS M.'S MASO-CHISM DESCRIBED A VERITABLE CURVE STARTING FROM JUST BEFORE THE MOMENT THE CLINICAL SIGNS APPEARED—THE CONSTITUTIONAL FACTOR WHICH M. HIMSELF FINDS VERY IMPORTANT—TO THE POINT WHERE THE PERVERSION CEASED. FOR A LONG TIME—RIGHT FROM PRE-PUBERTY—HIS PERVERSION SEEMS TO HAVE BEEN THE SOLE ACTOR ON STAGE. BUT IF ONE CONSIDERS THE FACT THAT LATER ON M. HAD BEEN CAPABLE OF ENGAGING IN PARALLEL, NORMAL SEXUAL ACTIVI-TIES WHICH OCCUPIED HIS DREAMS AS HE GOT OLDER, ONE CAN SAY THAT THE PERVERSION, INTIMATELY LINKED TO M.'S DESTINY, WAS ADDED, AS IT WERE, TO HIS "NORMAL" SEXUALITY TO MEET AN ECONOMIC NEED—AT LEAST ONE MAY SUPPOSE THIS IS THE CASE. DEVELOPMENTS OF THIS KIND HAVE PROMPTED ME TO PREFER THE TERM MASOCHISTIC MOVEMENT RATHER THAN MASOCHISM.

M.'S CASE ALSO REVEALS THAT THE PHENOMENON OF PHYSICAL PAIN AND ITS MYSTERIOUS ABILITY TO TRIGGER EROTIC PLEASURE AND ORGASM IS NOT WHAT CERTAIN SPECIALISTS HAVE CLAIMED IT TO BE. THEODORE REIK, FOR INSTANCE, CLAIMS IT IS TERROR AND ANXIETY WHICH ARE ASSOCIATED WITH PLEASURE AND THEN WITH ORGASM; M.'S CASE DISPROVES THIS, INDICATING CLEARLY THAT PAIN ITSELF IS THE TRIGGER. THE BASIC LINK BETWEEN THE INTENSITY OF THE PAIN AND THE INTENSITY OF THE ORGASM UNDERLIES EVERYTHING M. DESCRIBED AND AT TIMES MENTIONED OPENLY: "ON THE WHOLE, IT WAS PAIN THAT TRIGGERED MY EJACULATION." THIS EXPLAINS THE CHARACTERISTIC ATTITUDE OF THE MASOCHIST WHO CONSTANTLY DEMANDS THAT HIS PARTNER INCREASE THE PAIN. M. WAS QUITE AWARE OF THIS OUTBIDDING. FEAR OF PAIN WOULD BE ABSENT FROM HIM AND IT WAS HIS SADIST PARTNER WHO WOULD BACK OFF BECAUSE OF THE EXTREME NATURE OF HIS DEMANDS: "AT THE LAST MOMENT, THE SADIST ALWAYS BACKS OFF." IT APPEARS MOREOVER THAT PAIN HAS A DOUBLE FUNCTION: ON THE ONE HAND IT APPARENTLY ACTS AS A CATALYST FOR SEXUAL AROUSAL; ON THE OTHER HAND IT WOULD SEEM TO INCREASE SEXUAL EXCITEMENT AND PUSH IT TO ITS CLIMAX WHILE LOSING ITS OWN SPECIFICITY. IN THIS SENSE, PAIN HAS NO BOUNDARY. "EVERY INCH OF MY BODY COULD BE AROUSED THROUGH PAIN." THIS WOULD INDICATE AN EXTREME MUTATION OF THE BODY'S SENSITIVITY. YET PAIN IN ITSELF WAS NOT THE ULTIMATE PLEASURE. IT WAS BUT A MEANS. M. MADE THE DISTINCTION VERY CLEARLY: "AT FIRST, AND ON THE SPOT WHERE PAIN WAS APPLIED, IT HURT, BUT THEN I GOT AN ERECTION. MORE PAIN, AND STILL MORE, AND THE FEELING OF PLEASURE GRADUALLY BECAME SHARPER, CLEARER. EJACULATION OCCURED WHEN THE PAIN WAS AT ITS MOST INTENSE. AFTER EJACUALTION, THERE WAS PAIN AGAIN AND IT HURT." THIS ASPECT OF PAIN AS A MEANS WAS IDENTIFIED BY FREUD IN THE ECONOMIC PROBLEM IN MASOCHISM WHERE HE POSITS THAT, IN THE CASE OF MASOCHISM, PHYSICAL PAIN AND UNPLEASURE ARE NEITHER ENDS IN THEMSELVES NOR SIGNALS, BUT MEANS TO ATTAIN A GOAL WHICH IS ALWAYS PLEASURE. M. DID NOT ONLY DEMAND THAT HIS TORTURES BE INCREASINGLY PAINFUL, BUT THAT THEY BE PROLONGED, SUSPENDED, RESUMED, AND DIVERSIFIED. IN THIS RESPECT HE IS A GOOD ADEPT OF FREUD WHO SAYS IN CIVILISATION AND ITS DISCONTENTS: WHEN ANY SITUATION THAT IS DESIRED BY THE PLEASURE PRINCIPLE IS PROLONGED, IT ONLY PRODUCES A FEELING OF MILD CONTENTMENT. WE ARE SO MADE THAT WE CAN DERIVE INTENSE ENJOYMENT ONLY FROM A CONTRAST AND VERY LITTLE FROM A STATE OF

THINGS." M. HAD MASTERED THE ART OF PRODUCING CONTRASTS, I.E. INCREASES AND DECREASES IN THE QUANTITY OF STIMULI WITHIN A GIVEN PERIOD OF TIME. THESE IDEAS OF TIME AND QUANTITY GIVE US DEFINITE INFORMATION WHICH CAN THROW SOME LIGHT ON THE MYSTERIOUS CONNECTION BETWEEN PHYSICAL PAIN AND PLEASURE. FROM M.'S ENDLESS SEARCH FOR PAIN, WE CAN LOGICALLY INFER AN EQUALLY ENDLESS NEED FOR PLEASURE. M. ORCHESTRATED THE BRUTAL TORTURES INFLICTED ON HIM IN ORDER TO OBTAIN THE KEENEST POSSIBLE PLEASURE. HE UNDOUBTEDLY EXPERIENCED "THE FEELING OF HAPPINESS DERIVED FROM THE SATISFACTION OF A WILD INSTINCTUAL IMPULSE UNTAMED BY THE EGO," WHICH FREUD TELLS US "IS INCOMPARABLY MORE INTENSE THAN THAT DERIVED FROM SATING AN INSTINCT THAT HAS BEEN TAMED." ONE WOULD BE INCORRECT IN ASSUMING, HOWEVER, THAT M. WAS FREE TO DESIRE OR TO REFUSE THAT JOY. THE PARADOX IS THAT IT WAS FORCED UPON HIM. IN A SENSE HE WAS CONDEMNED TO PLEASURE AND THIS IS WHY HIS CASE IS SO DIFFICULT TO UNRAVEL. SUFFER THE WORST TORMENTS TO OBTAIN PLEASURE UNDER ABSOLUTE COMPULSION: SUCH WAS M.'S DESTINY FOR THE GREATER PART OF HIS LIFE.

IN THE SAME WAY THAT M.'S REACTIONS TO PAIN WERE DIFFERENT FROM WHAT IS GENERALLY ACCEPTED, HIS RELATIONS WITH OTHERS WERE UNORTHODOX IN VARIOUS WAYS. IT IS WELL KNOWN THAT MOST SPECIALISTS STRESS THE MASOCHIST'S QUEST FOR HUMILIATION. I WOULD ADD THAT THIS IS PARTICULARLY TRUE WHEN THE IMPORTANCE OF PHYSICAL PAIN IN ITSELF IS MINIMIZED: TORTURE IS SELDOM VERY HORRIFYING, THE GENITALIA ARE NOT SUBJECTED TO MUTILATION, PAIN DOES NOT GO BEYOND A CERTAIN THRESHOLD, ETC. M'S CASE SHOWS THAT THIS IS NOT TRUE AND THAT EVER-INCREASING PHYSICAL PAIN WAS ACTUALLY SOUGHT FOR. HOWEVER, IT IS OBVIOUS THAT ALTHOUGH PAIN AND HUMILIATION BELONG TO TWO DIFFERENT REGISTERS, THE FACT THAT TORTURE IS INFLICTED OF NECESSITY BY ANOTHER PARTY ESTABLISHES A MOST INTIMATE LINK BETWEEN THEM. AND HOW DID M. LIVE THIS CORRELATION? ACCORDING TO HIM, WHAT HE CRAVED FOR WAS ABOVE ALL AN ABASEMENT OF HIS PERSONALITY. TO ACHIEVE THIS "VERITABLE MORAL SUICIDE" EVERY MEANS WAS VALID THE MOMENT M. AND HIS WIFE "WERE REALLY TWO SLAVES OF TWO LOVERS." EVERY MEANS, I.E. IN ADDITON TO THE TORTURES, THE SIMPLEST SLAP OR OBEYING ORDERS TO INDULGE IN COPROPHAGY, WHICH APPARENTLY

ENABLED HIM TO PROLONG THE "PSYCHICAL PLEASURE" AFTER EJACULATION. THE OBVIOUS HOMOSEXUAL SIDE OF ALL THIS WAS, ACCORDING TO M., ANOTHER MEANS TO HUMILIATION, AS HE FELT THAT HOMOSEXUAL PRACTICES WERE TANTAMOUNT TO INSULTS. WITNESS THESE PHRASES M. GOT A PARTNER TO ORDER HIM TO INSCRIBE ON HIS SKIN SO HIS MORAL DECAY COULD BE SEEN: "I GAVE THE IMPRESSION I WAS AN INVERT WHICH I WAS NOT OUT OF PLEASURE, BUT OUT OF HUMILIATION. I EXPERIENCED NO PHYSICAL SATISFACTION, IT WAS ALL ON THE MORAL PLANE." M. DEPICTED HIMSELF AS HAVING A PRESSING NEED TO BE HUMILIATED—HOMOSEXUALITY WAS ONLY AN INSTRUMENT TO HIS END AND TO HAVE HIS WILL COMPLETELY DESTROYED. CERTAIN EXPRESSIONS KEPT RECURRING IN HIS SPEECH SUCH AS: DISREGARD OF THE WILL, TOTAL ANNIHILATION OF THE WILL, THE WILL EXISTED NO LONGER, ABOLITION OF THE WILL, ETC. THIS TRAIT UNDOUBTEDLY CONCEALED SOMETHING DESPITE THE GENERAL TONE OF HIS DISCOURSE WHICH, ON THE WHOLE, WAS RESTRAINED AND FREE FROM DRAMATIC EFFECTS. NEVERTHELESS THERE WAS SOMETHING A TRIFLE TOO STRONG IN THIS INSISTENCE ON RENOUNCING HIS WILL "FOR THE BENEFIT OF THE PERSON WHO WAS IN COMMAND."

TO BE MORE PRECISE, HE REALLY RENOUNCED NOTHING AT ALL: FIRST, HE WAS THE ONE WHO WANTED THE EROTIC RELATIONSHIP TO EXIST; SECOND, AS SOON AS IT WAS TERMINATED HE RESUMED HIS FREEDOM VIS-A-VIS THOSE PERSONS WHO SUPPOSEDLY HELD HIM IN BONDAGE AND HE DID NOT ALLOW ANY FURTHER SERVITUDE TO OCCUR. M.'S DEEPLY CONCEALED ASSERTION OF TOTAL POWER WAS MATCHED BY HIS OVERWEENING PRIDE WHICH COULD BE GLIMPSED WHENEVER HE DESCRIBED THE HIDEOUS TORTURES HE HAD UNDERGONE. HE FELT HE WAS ALMOST UNIQUE: ONLY ONE PERSON HE KNEW OF, WHO LIVED IN A CAGE BRISTLING WITH SHARP POINTS, HAD EVER SURPASSED HIM. HE SAID THE ONLY REASON HE WAS RETICENT ABOUT PERFORMING EVEN MORE DRASTIC MUTILATIONS—SUCH AS AMPUTATING HIS PENIS—WAS THE FEAR OF MEDICAL OR LEGAL COMPLICATIONS AND THE PROBLEMS INVOLVED IN HEMOSTASIS. IT WAS ALSO HIS IMMENSE PRIDE AND HIS SCORN FOR HIS PARTNERS WHICH PROMPTED HIM TO REMARK, ALMOST INCIDENTALLY, THAT "THE SADIST ALWAYS BACKS OFF AT THE LAST MOMENT." THE SADISTIC STUDENT WHO SHARED M.'S LIFE AND HIS WIFE'S WAS SUPPOSED TO BE ALL-POWERFUL: HE GAVE STRICT ORDERS THAT HAD TO BE OBEYED—AND YET HE WAS IN FACT LOOKED UPON AS UTTERLY WORTHLESS. M. CLAIMED THAT HE HIMSELF DID NOT EXIST AS A SUBJECT BUT THAT HE SIMPLY EMBODIED THE SADIST'S FANTASIES. HE CLAIMED THAT HE HAD VERY LITTLE REAL EXISTENCE OF HIS OWN. AND HERE HE HOODWINKED HIS INTERLOCUTOR FOR HE WAS VERY DEFINITELY EXPRESSING A DESIRE: THE DESIRE THAT THE OTHER PERSON PROCEED IN SUCH A WAY AS TO NEGATE M.'S EXISTENCE. HE WAS READY TO SUBMIT TO ANY KIND OF INVESTIGATION SINCE RETICENCE WAS TOTALLY FOREIGN TO HIM AND INDEED LITERALLY INCONCEIVABLE: TO SHOW ANY RETICENCE WOULD HAVE MEANT TO EXERT HIS WILL, AND THEREFORE TO CANCEL HIMSELF OUT. THUS THE INTERLOCUTOR OR THE PARTNER FOUND HIMSELF IN THE PARADOXICAL SITUATION OF BEING STRIPPED OF ALL POWER OF SPEECH AND DESIRE. AND SO THE MASOCHIST, BEHIND THE FACADE OF A DRAMATIC ASSERTION OF HIS NOTHINGNESS, ACTUALLY SUBDUED THE SADIST BY FORCING HIM TO ASSUME THE ROLE WHICH HE, THE MASOCHIST, APPEARED TO ASSUME. THE TOTAL POWER THAT M. CONFERRED ON HIS PARTNER WAS AN UTTER MOCKERY. I PERSONALLY BELIEVE THAT THE PERVERSE MASOCHIST IS NOT TOTALLY UNAWARE OF HIS DEEP-SEATED ATTITUDE. IN ANY CASE, HE CANNOT RESIST LETTING IT BE GLIMPSED OR GUESSED AT. THE BONDAGE TO WHICH THE SADIST IS CONDEMNED BY THE MASOCHIST IS, IN PART, SO OPAQUELY VEILED THAT ONE MIGHT CONSIDER THIS TO BE THE LAST WORD ON THE WHOLE MATTER, WHILE ANOTHER BONDAGE MUST IN FACT BE CONCEALED, WHICH HOLDS PRISONER THE MASOCHIST HIMSELF.

MICHEL DE M'UZAN
TRANSLATED BY DANIEL SLOTE

POSTFACE:
MASOCHISM AND POLYSEXUALITY

YOU HAVE JUST READ M.'S STORY AS HE TOLD IT TO A FRENCH PSYCHOANALYST, MICHEL DE M'UZAN. ALTHOUGH M. HAS DESCRIBED HIMSELF AS A MASOCHIST, WE SHOULD NOT CONSIDER THIS STORY AS AN OBSERVATION NOR A CLINICAL CASE SINCE M. DID NOT CONSULT MICHEL DE M'UZAN FOR HIS MASOCHISM. HE AGREED TO TALK WITH A PSYCHO-ANALYST ABOUT HIS MASOCHISM BECAUSE HE WAS URGED TO DO SO BY HIS OWN PHYSICIAN WHOM HE CONSULTED FOR RESPIRATORY PROBLEMS AND WHO KNEW THAT M.'S PAST LIFE WOULD CERTAINLY INTEREST DE M'UZAN AS A CASE HISTORY. THE TITLE OF DE M'UZAN'S PAPER, HERE PARTLY TRANSLATED AS "A CASE OF PERVERTED MASOCHISM," IS TO A DEGREE IDEOLOGICAL FRAUD SINCE IT REDUCES M.'S EXPERIENCE TO A MEDICAL CASE, ALTHOUGH NOTHING IN M.'S BEHAVIOR INDICATES THAT HE EVER THOUGHT OF UNDERGOING TREATMENT. M.'S CURIOSITY TOWARD HIS OWN SEXUAL PECULIARI-TIES HAS NOTHING TO DO WITH THE DESIRE OF GETTING RID OF THEM. ON THE CONTRARY, THE SUDDEN INTERRUPTION OF HIS MASOCHISTIC PRACTICES—WHICH CANNOT BE COMPARED TO THE SPONTANEOUS REMISSION OF AN ILLNESS—SHOULD LEAD US TO CONSIDER M.'S STORY AS THE STORY OF A MASOCHISTIC PROCESS.

IT IS QUITE REMARKABLE THAT PSYCHOANALYTIC STUDIES ON SADISM AND MASOCHISM ARE VERY SELDOM BASED ON GENUINE "CLINICAL MATERIAL." BY GENUINE I MEAN THAT WHICH REFERS TO CONCRETE SADISTIC OR MASOCHISTIC PRACTICES. VERY OFTEN THESE STUDIES REFER EITHER TO THE SADISTIC AND/OR MASOCHISTIC FANTASIES OF NEUROTIC PATIENTS, OR TO SADISTIC AND/OR MASOCHISTIC STORIES SUCH AS M.'S, OR MORE OFTEN, SUCH AS THE NOVELS OF SADE AND SACHER MASOCH.

I SHALL NOT EVEN TAKE INTO CONSIDERATION THOSE MASOCHISTS AND SADISTS WHO ARE CONDEMNED BY A JUDGE TO CHOOSE BETWEEN PRISON OR PSYCHIATRIC TREATMENT.

IT IS ALSO A REMARKABLE FACT THAT MASOCHISTS AND SADISTS ARE VERY MUCH AWARE OF THEIR SEXUAL PECULIARITIES, BUT DO NOT CONSIDER THEM AS SYMPTOMS OF ANY PARTICULAR ILLNESS. AND FROM A PSYCHIATRIC POINT OF VIEW, IT WOULD BE IMPOSSIBE FOR THE SADIST AND/OR MASOCHIST TO PRETEND THAT WHEN HE INDULGES IN THESE PRACTICES, HE HAS LOST HIS "SENSE OF REALITY."

GENUINE SADISM AND MASOCHISM THEREFORE SHOULD NOT BE CONFUSED WITH MORAL SADISM

AND MASOCHISM, NOR WITH ATYPICAL PSYCHOSES.

GENUINE SADISM AND MASOCHISM ARE TWO ASPECTS, AMONG MANY OTHERS, OF POLYSEXUALITY: AN INFINITELY DIVERSIFIED SEXUALITY WHICH CONSTITUTES THE POTENTIAL SEXUALITY OF EVERY BODY.

THIS POLYSEXUALITY, WHICH FREUD CALLED "POLYMORPHOUS SEXUALITY," IS VIOLENTLY REPRESSED IN ALMOST EVERYBODY AND PARTICULALY AMONG THOSE WHO CLAIM TO BE SEXUALLY "NORMAL," I.E. HETEROSEXUAL. THE INTENSITY OF THIS REPRESSION AND ITS EFFECTS CAN EASILY BE RECOGNIZED IN THE HORRIFIED EXPRESSION OF THOSE WHO ARE CONFRONTED—WITHOUT HAVING BEEN PREVIOUSLY PREPARED FOR IT—WITH THE REALITY TO WHICH M.'S STORY REFERS.

IN THIS RESPECT, MICHEL DE M'UZAN DOES NOT PROVIDE US WITH WHAT MASOCHISM IS, AS MUCH AS WITH WHAT "NORMAL SEXUALITY" IS: THE INEVITABLE MODEL AGAINST WHICH MOST PSYCHOANALYSTS COMPARE POLYSEXUALITY IN ORDER TO DESCRIBE IT IN TERMS OF DEVIANCE. IT IS VERY TRUE, HOWEVER, THAT IT IS NOT EASY, EVEN FOR A PSYCHOANALYST, TO APPROACH SOMETHING WHEN THIS SOMETHING HAS BEEN VIOLENTLY REPRESSED WITHIN ONESELF: MICHEL DE M'UZAN HAD TO WAIT TEN YEARS BEFORE HE COULD START TO WORK ON M.'S STORY. AND IT IS QUITE IRONICAL TO SEE THAT THE "SEX SPECIALIST," THE PSYCHOANALYST, FELT LIKE A CHILD FACED WITH THIS REMARKABLE SEXOLOGIST: M. THE MASOCHIST.

WE ARE NOT REALLY INTERESTED IN THE RESTRAINED SEXUALITY OF OUR PSYCHOANALYSTS; OUR AIM IS TO GIVE SHAPE TO A NEW NOTION— POLYSEXUALITY—AND TO DESCRIBE THE MANY PROCESSES THROUGH WHICH POLYSEXUALITY BECOMES A "FACT OF LIFE." SUCH PROCESSES ARE TOTALLY ALIEN TO CLASSICAL OPPOSITIONS: MAN/WOMAN, HUSBAND/WIFE, HOMO-/HETERO-, ACTIVE/PASSIVE, ETC . . . IN FACT, THEY HAVE TO BE STUDIED ALONG CERTAIN LINES OF INCREASING INTENSITY: VIOLENT SEXUALITIES, VISUAL SEXUALITIES, LIQUID SEXUALITIES, ALIMENTARY SEXUALITIES, OBESE SEXUALITIES, ETC. CONSIDERED ALONG THESE LINES, POLYSEXUALITY DETERMINES A NEW CUT-UP OF THE CITY AS WELL AS OF THE EROTIC BODY OF PEOPLE, INDEPENDENT, ON THE ONE HAND, OF THE OPPOSITION OF CLASSES AND, ON THE OTHER, OF THE BIOLOGICAL OPPOSITION OF SEXES.

CONTRARY TO WHAT SADE TELLS US IN LES 120 JOURNEES DE SODOME, THE PERVERT DOES NOT NEED A DEEP AND DARK CAVE TO HAVE KINKY SEX, FAR FROM GOD'S SIGHT; HE SIMPLY WALKS ALONG THE STREETS, TAKING SUFFICIENT PRECAUTIONS TO AVOID BOTH POLICE AND "PERVERT HUNTERS."

IN EVERY CITY THERE ARE OPEN PLACES, OPEN SPACES WHERE EVERY PERVERT CAN EXPERIENCE THE SEXUAL PRACTICES OF HIS CHOICE. ONE WOULD CERTANLY WISH TO MEET MORE PSYCHOANALYSTS THERE, OR AT LEAST THOSE AMONG THEM WHO CLAIM THAT THEY HAVE SOMETHING TO SAY ABOUT PERVERSIONS. THESE ARE FREE SPACES, ALSO, WHERE ANYONE CAN DO ANYTHING WITHOUT EXPECTING ANYBODY TO NECESSARILY DO THE SAME THINGS AS HE DOES. THE SO-CALLED DESIRE OF THE PERVERT TO PERVERT THE NONPERVERT IS A MYTH, THE FANTASY OF THE NEUROTIC HETEROSEXUAL: THE DISGUISED EXPRESSION OF HIS UNCONSCIOUS AND REPRESSED DESIRES.

IF I INSIST ON THE FACT THAT M.'S STORY IS A REMARKABLE CASE HISTORY, IT IS FOR THE MOST PART BECAUSE IT DEMONSTRATES THAT MASOCHISM IS NOT A STRUCTURE: ONE IS NOT MASOCHISTIC LIKE ONE IS NEUROTIC. IT IS REMARKABLE INDEED TO SEE HOW M. SUDDENLY ABANDONS HIS MASOCHISTIC HABITS AFTER THIRTY YEARS OF CONSTANT AND HEAVY PRACTICE, AND RETURNS TO A VERY QUIET AND PEACEFUL HETEROSEXUAL LIFE. EVEN HIS DREAMS LOSE ALL MASOCHISTIC CONTENT. SUCH A SUDDEN CHANGE, AS WELL AS THE FACT THAT WHILE HE WAS A MASOCHIST, M.'S LIFE WAS VERY WELL BALANCED BOTH SOCIALLY AND EMOTIONALLY, PRECLUDES ANY TALK OF A "PERVERT STRUCTURE." M. WAS A SPECIALIZED WORKER WHO WAS HIGHLY REGARDED BY HIS PEERS AND HIS SUPERIORS.

MASOCHISM IS NOT A STANCE EITHER, AS SOME FRENCH PSYCHOANALYSTS BELIEVE. A STANCE THAT A SUBJECT MIGHT ADOPT FOR A SHORT WHILE AND THEN ABANDON. IT IS NOT A STANCE BECAUSE MASOCHISTIC PRACTICES CHANGE WITH TIME (AS DO SADISTIC ONES). THEY CAN TRANSFORM INTO ONE ANOTHER, THE MASOCHIST SOMETIMES BECOMING A SADIST AND VICE VERSA, BUT THEY CHANGE FOR THE MOST PART IN THE SENSE OF A BECOMING. THEY FOLLOW A PATTERN OF INCREASING QUANTITATIVE INTENSITY CAREFULLY PROGRAMMED, A SORT OF PROGRESSIVE TENSION TOWARD SOMETHING, A TENSION WHICH IS CALCULATED ACCORDING TO AN INTENSIFICATION

OF VIOLENCE COUPLED WITH A PROGRESSIVE, CAREFULLY PLANNED EXPLORATION OF THE EROTIC BODY.

A CAREFUL READING OF M.'S STORY REVEALS THAT THE CONTROLS ON THIS PROGRESSION ARE DOUBLE. FIRST, THE MASOCHIST CAN STOP WHEN HE WANTS: HIS ACTIVITIES ARE PREPARED WITH GREAT CARE AND THE TERMS OF THESE ACTIVITIES ARE DESCRIBED PRECISELY IN A "CONTRACT" ACCEPTED BY BOTH PARTNERS. SECONDLY, THE PROGRESSION IS ALSO CONTROLLED BY THE ANXIETY WHICH THE MASOCHIST AROUSES IN HIS PARTNER WHO "ALWAYS GIVES UP" AT A CERTAIN POINT, AS M. SAYS. NOT ALWAYS, HOWEVER, AS AN EXTREME EXPERIENCE LIKE "ULTIMATE SEX," THE REAL ONE, HAS SHOWN US.

RATHER THAN COMPARE MASOCHISTIC ACTIVITIES WITH RELIGIOUS RITES, BY NATURE ESSENTIALLY REPETITIVE, WE SHOULD COMPARE THEM WITH AN INITIATION. IN FACT, IT IS AN EXPERIMENTATION WHOSE ULTIMATE GOAL IS DEATH: DEATH AS ULTIMATE SEX! WE DO NOT PRETEND THAT SUCH A GOAL IS ALWAYS REACHED—ACTUALLY IT IS VERY RARELY SO—BUT WE THINK THAT SUCH A GOAL ALWAYS EXISTS IMPLICITLY. PERVERTED EXPERIMENTATION IS A WAY OF BEING-FOR-DEATH (ÉTRE-POUR-LA-MORT). BUT THERE IS ALSO PLEASURE IN ITS QUEST, AND THERE IS EVEN MORE THAN PLEASURE, THERE IS ECSTASY—JOUISSANCE—THE PLEASURABLE COUNTERPART OF DEATH.

IT IS NOT POSSIBLE TO EXPLAIN FULLY IN THIS POSTFACE HOW AND WHY JOUISSANCE IS PRECISELY WHAT WE HAVE HAD TO REJECT IN THE COURSE OF BECOMING OEDIPALIZED, WHILE OUR BODY, OUR EROTIC BODY, WAS SUBJECTED TO THE STRUCTURING AND ALIENATING POWER OF LANGUAGE. THE CONSTRUCTION OF THE SO-CALLED "NORMAL" HETEROSEXUAL SUBJECT COMES ABOUT BY AND THROUGH LANGUAGE. EVERY SUBJECT IS VULNERABLE TO THE FORM OF THE SPECIFIC LANGUAGE OF WHICH HE BECOMES THE SUBJECT. EVEN HIS EROTIC BODY IS VULNERABLE, EACH ZONE OF WHICH HAS BEEN SUCCESSIFELY NAMED, EROTICISED AND FORBIDDEN, TO THE EXCLUSION OF THE GENITAL ZONE AND THIS FOR ONE PURPOSE ONLY: HETEROSEXUAL INTERCOURSES.

THE AIM OF THE MASOCHIST—AND TO A LESSER DEGREE OF THE SADIST—IS TO DECONSTRUCT THE OEDIPAL CONSTRUCTION. IN OTHER WORDS TO DESUBJECTIFY HIS OWN BODY.

HIS ACTIVITIES LEAD HIM PARTIALLY OUT OF THE REALM OF LANGUAGE, OUT OF A SYSTEM OF SIGNS WHICH ALWAYS PRE-EXISTED HIM AND TO WHICH HE WAS SUPPOSED TO HAVE BEEN COMPLETELY SUBJECTED. THE STORY OF THE SEXUAL PHASES (ORAL, ANAL, URETHRAL AND GENITAL) IS NOT ONLY THE STORY OF THE ACCEPTANCE OF OEDIPAL SEX, IT IS ALSO THE STORY OF THE SUBJECTIVIZATION OF THE EROTIC BODY, OR IN OTHER WORDS, THE PROHITIBION OF POLYSEXUALITY.

HERE AGAIN I HAVE TO BE BRIEF; WHAT I SAY IS MERELY A HINT OF WHAT SHOULD BE DETAILED AT SOME LENGTH.

MASOCHISTIC ACTIVITIES ARE NOT SUPPOSED TO DRIVE THE MASOCHIST COMPLETELY OUT OF THE REALM OF LANGUAGE GENERALLY SPEAKING, AS IN THE CASE OF SOME PSYCHOTICS. THE PERVERTED ACT ON ONE HAND IS NOT SPEECH, AND IT DIFFERS FUNDAMENTALLY FROM THE PERVERTED FANTASM WHICH IS ALWAYS A PHRASE, SOMETHING LIKE PRESIDENT SCHREBER'S: "IT WOULD BE SO NICE TO BE A WOMAN SUBJECT TO COïTUS." ON THE OTHER HAND THE PERVERTED ACT IS NOT HAZARDOUS SO FAR. IF WE OBSERVE THE CONCATENATION OF THESE ACTS OVER A CERTAIN PERIOD OF TIME, THEY APPEAR TO FOLLOW A PROGRESSIVE PATTERN LINKED TO EACH OTHER AS IN A SYNTAGM; IT IS A DISCOURSE, A PERFORMATIVE DISCOURSE, WHICH MORE READILY OBEYS OTHER LAWS THAN THE LAWS OF SYMBOLIC LANGUAGE. IT OBEYS AN ALTOGETHER DIFFERENT LOGIC; IT OBEYS THE LOGIC OF THE BODY, IF I MAY SAY SO. IT IS QUITE AMAZING TO SEE THE INCREASING CONTROL A MASOCHIST CAN GET OVER HIS BODY AND ITS PHYSIOLOGICAL FUNCTIONS. THIS CONTROL INCREASES IN PROPORTION TO THE VIOLENCE OF THE PERVERTED ACTS. SUCH A CONTROL IMPLIES A VERY PRECISE KNOWLEDGE, A KNOWLEDGE THAT ONE CANNOT FIND IN BOOKS, A KNOWLEDGE WHICH DERIVES FROM A NON-VERBAL SEMIOTICS, FROM BODY-SEMIOTICS.

THE MASOCHIST ALSO USES ANOTHER MEANS TO DESUBJECTIFY HIS BODY: I.E. HUMILIATION. M.'S TATOOS, ALL OVER HIS BODY, SAY: "THE MEETING POINT FOR THE MOST BEAUTIFUL PRICKS," OR "I AM A BITCH, I AM FUCKED UP, I AM NOT A MAN NOR A WOMAN, BUT A BITCH, A SLUT, FLESH TO BE FUCKED, A LIVING TOILET BOWL . . ."

I WANT TO POINT OUT THREE IMPORTANT DETAILS ABOUT THESE TERMS:

1.) THE FEMINIZATION OF THE NAMES (AT LEAST IN FRENCH: A BITCH, A SLUT, ETC.). M. IS A MAN, BUT IF HE WERE A WOMAN IF WOULD BE EXACTLY THE SAME. HE IS NOT HOMOSEXUAL, HOWEVER, AND WHEN HE GETS FUCKED BY A MAN IT IS ONLY FOR MASOCHISTIC PURPOSES.

2.) IN SPITE OF THE FEMINIZATION OF THE WORDS, THESE TERMS REFER TO A NEUTRAL, RATHER THAN TO A FEMININE OR MASCULINE QUALITY: A BITCH OR A SLUT HAS IN FACT NO BIOLOGICAL SEX: "I AM NEITHER MAN NOR WOMAN BUT FLESH ..."

3.) THESE TERMS REFER NEITHER TO SUBJECT NOR OBJECT, BUT TO A FUNCTION: A BITCH IS SOMEONE WHO INDUCES THE NORMAL HETEROSEXUAL TO BE BITCHY, A LIVING TOILET BOWL IS A PLACE THAT RECEIVES SHIT AND PISS ... HERE I SUGGEST THE READER VISIT THE PIT AT "THE MINE SHAFT" IN NEW YORK CITY ...

IT IS ONLY FOR THE NEUROTIC, OR THE HETEROSEXUAL, SO-CALLED "NORMAL PEOPLE" THAT THE MASOCHIST PRETENDS TO BE EXCREMENT, A GARBAGE-CAN. THE MASOCHIST IS NOT EXCREMENT OR WHATEVER; HE SAYS HE IS, AND THAT MAKES ALL THE DIFFERENCE. IF HE SAYS, AND REPEATS THAT HE IS A SLUT, A TURD, A PILE OF SHIT, AND SO ON, IT IS ONLY TO INDUCE THE AGGRESSIVITY OF THE OTHER, OF THE PARTNER.

THESE TERMS, FROM THE MASOCHIST'S POINT OF VIEW, HAVE NO SPECIAL SENSE, NO MEANING, THEY DO NOT EVEN REFER TO A REAL OBJECT ... THEY HAVE ONLY A PERFORMATIVE FUNCTION: TO INDUCE, TO PROVOKE HORROR AND TO MAKE PEOPLE GO AWAY AND/OR REACT WITH AGGRESSIVITY AND BEAT THE SHIT OUT OF THE MASOCHIST. BUT AT THE SAME TIME IT AROUSES THE DEATH-DRIVES OF THE OTHER, IT AROUSES HIS ANXIETY AS WELL, AND THROUGH THIS ANXIETY THE MASOCHIST IS ABLE TO CONTROL THE AGGRESSIVITY OF THE OTHER.

SUCH A DESUBJECTIVIZATION OF THE MASOCHIST DOES NOT MAKE A PSYCHOTIC OF HIM, A SUBJECT COMPLETELY ALIEN TO THE REALM OF LANGUAGE WHO REFUSES IT COMPLETELY. BUT THIS SUBJECTIVIZATION ALLOWS THE MASOCHIST TO FREE HIMSELF FROM HIS UNCONSCIOUS ALIENATION FROM THE SYMBOLIC FUNCTION OF LANGUAGE; IT ALLOWS HIM TO REDISCOVER THE PERFORMATIVE FUNCTION OF LANGUAGE ALONG WITH HIS BODY-LANGUAGE. AFTER HIS "TRIP," THE MASOCHIST CAN GO BACK INTO THE REALM OF SYMBOLIC LANGUAGE, BUT HE WILL DO IT FREELY, AND HE WILL PLAY IN IT AND WITH IT. HE WILL MAKE A GAME OF LANGUAGE. AND HE WILL HAVE ACCOMPLISHED IN HIS OWN WAY THE LAST METAMORPHOSIS FORESEEN BY NIETZSCHE. HE WILL HAVE BECOME'A CHILD.

FRANCOIS PÉRALDI
NEW YORK, JULY 1978

CORPORATE SEX

[ONCE I HAD A MASTER]

THE THREE FOLLOWING TEXTS ARE LOVE LETTERS. THE FIRST ONE, 'ONCE I HAD A MASTER,' REPRINTED HERE, IS A REWRITING OF THE 23RD PSALM. THE LAST TWO STORIES WERE CONSCIOUSLY ADDRESSED TO EACH OTHER BY JOHN PRESTON AND JASON KLEIN.

ONCE I HAD A MASTER

I ONCE HAD A MASTER WHO LIVED FAR FROM THE CITY.

EVERY FRIDAY I WOULD LEAVE MY JOB IN AN OFFICE BUILDING. I WOULD TAKE AN EXPRESS TO THE NEXT LARGE METROPOLIS AND CHANGE THERE FOR A LOCAL TRAIN. I WOULD SIT WATCHING A PROGRESSION OF TOWNS, EACH SMALLER THAN THE LAST, SPEED BY MY WINDOW. AT THE TERMINUS, I WOULD CLIMB OUT AND FIND HIM WAITING. EVERY FRIDAY HE WOULD BE STANDING NEXT TO HIS TRUCK. THERE WOULD BE NO GREETING FROM EITHER OF US. THE RITUAL WAS SO SECURE THAT IT DID NOT NEED THE SUPPORT OF WORDS.

AS HE DROVE AWAY FROM THE STATION I WOULD BEGIN THE DISROBING HE WOULD EXPECT. THERE WERE TIMES ON HOT SUMMER NIGHTS THAT THE WIND CARESSED MY BARE CHEST WITH WELCOME COOLING RELIEF. MY COMFORT DID NOT CONCERN HIM. THERE WERE OTHER TIMES IN THE WINTER WHEN THE DRAFT WOULD SEND CHILLS THROUGH MY BODY WHEN MY SHIRT REMOVED THE LITTLE PROTECTION IT HAD PROVIDED. HE DID NOT CARE FOR MY DISCOMFORT.

THE REMOVAL OF EACH PIECE OF CLOTHING MARKED THE FINAL LEGS OF OUR JOURNEY. BY THE TIME HE WOULD PULL INTO HIS OWN DRIVEWAY I WOULD BE NAKED, SITTING BESIDE HIM IN THE TRUCK, WAITING TO BEGIN THE WEEKEND.

WHEN HE FINALLY PULLED INTO THE SPACE BESIDE HIS HOUSE, ACTUALLY NO MORE THAN A CABIN IN THE WOODS, I WOULD HAVE TO MAKE MY OWN WAY INSIDE. HE APPEARED IGNORANT OF THE FREEDOM THAT MY NUDITY REPRESENTED ON A SUMMER NIGHT, AND EQUALLY AS IGNORANT OF THE DANGER IT HELD ON FROZEN WINTER EVENINGS. HE ONLY WAS CONCERNED THAT I BE WITHOUT CLOTHES IN HIS HOUSE.

THERE WAS A RITUAL EVERY FRIDAY EVENING. I

WOULD SHOWER. BUT NOT TO CLEANSE MYSELF; THAT WAS UNIMPORTANT. I WOULD STAND BENEATH A HOT SPRAY OF WATER TO LET ITS MOISTURE SOFTEN MY BODY HAIR. EVERY FRIDAY HE SHAVED EVERY INCH OF MY SKIN BELOW MY NECK. HE COULD NOT TOLERATE EVEN A FEW STRANDS EXISTENCE SEPARATING MY SKIN FROM HIS TOUCH.

FOR THE WEEKEND I BECAME HIS SERVANT. I WOULD COOK HIS MEALS, CLEAN HIS HOUSE, WASH HIS CLOTHES, TEND HIS GARDEN, CHOP HIS FIREWOOD. I WOULD DO SO ALWAYS NAKED, ALWAYS VULNERABLE.

HE WOULD TOLERATE NO LIMITATION TO MY SERVICE. THE ORIFICES OF MY BODY WERE OPEN FOR HIM TO TAKE ON A WHIM—MY MOUTH, MY ASS, MY HAND WERE THERE WHENEVER HE HAD THE DESIRE. HE NEVER LET HIS PHYSICAL WANTS FALL INTO A PATTERN. HE WOULD TAKE ME WHILE STANDING UP COOKING IN FRONT OF THE STOVE, OR WHILE WORKING IN THE FIELDS, OR EVEN IN THE SOUNDEST OF SLEEP.

WE TALKED ALMOST NOT AT ALL. MY MINISTRATIONS WERE TO HIS BODY, NOT HIS FANTASIES OR HIS MIND. I WASHED HIS TORSO WHILE IT SAT IN THE BATHTUB, MASSAGED IT IN FRONT OF THE FIRE PLACE, TOOK ITS RELIEF IN THE FIELDS.

HE WAS NEVER MINDLESSLY CRUEL. BUT HE WOULD BEAT ME GREATLY IF MY SERVICE EVER FALTERED OR IF MY MIND WANDERED NOTICEABLY INTO A PRIVATE WORLD OF DAY DREAMS. THERE WAS NO TIME ON THESE WEEKENDS FOR MY SELF-INDULGENCES. I WAS NEVER ALLOWED TO RESIST PUNISHMENT; TO DO SO WOULD BE TO THREATEN MY ATTENDANCE.

NO OTHER PERSON EVER WAS ALLOWED IN HIS HOUSE WHILE I WAS THERE. THOUGH I COULD NOT HAVE STOPPED ANYONE. HE DID NOT WANT THERE TO BE ANOTHER PERSON TO INTERFERE WITH MY GROWING VULNERABILITY OR HIS OWN GROWING CONTROL.

THE WEEKENDS TOOK ON MORE MEANING EACH TIME THEY WERE REPEATED. THE FEW WORDS THAT HAD PASSED IN THE BEGINNING BEGAN TO DISAPPEAR THEMSELVES AS TIME MADE THEM SUPERFLUOUS. THE DAYS BETWEEN MY JOURNEYS BECAME LESS AND LESS IMPORTANT.

IT HAD NOT TAKEN LONG FOR THE TRIP BACK TO THE CITY TO BE DREADED. I WOULD HAVE TO REVERSE THE RITUAL OF DRESSING AS HE DROVE ME TO THE TRAIN STATION. I COULD BE FULLY DRESSED BY THE TIME HE PARKED IN FRONT OF THE IRON RAILS.

THE FIRST SUMMER I LEARNED MORE ABOUT MY BODY THAN IN ALL THE SUMMERS THAT HAD PRECEEDED IT TOGETHER. I RAN NAKED ACROSS FLOWERED FIELDS AND SPRAWLED MY SHAVEN TORSO IN OCEAN OF CLOVER. I BECAME FEARLESS OF MY PHYSICAL SELF. I TOOK ON COLOR ON MY SKIN AND TONE IN MY MUSCLES AS THEY WORKED HARD ON HIS FARM. I WELCOMED EVERY TIME HE TOOK ME, RESPONDING PASSIONATELY TO HIS ASSAULTS, SPREADING FAR APART MY JAWS AND MY SPHINCTER AS HE INVADED MY OPEN BEING.

THE FIRST WINTER I LEARNED MORE ABOUT MY FEAR THAN I HAD EVER KNOWN. I OFTEN SAT DOWN NEXT TO THE STOVE TO TRY TO EASE MY NAKED COLDNESS. MY BODY AND MY SELF WERE CAPTIVES OF THE HOUSE, DESPERATELY FRIGHTENED OF THOSE TIMES WHEN HE WOULD FORCE ME TO RUN WITHOUT SHOES THROUGH THE SNOW TO GATHER WOOD FOR THE FIRE. HE, HIMSELF, HAD NO OTHER OUTLET FOR HIS OWN PHYSICAL BEING THAN TO USE MY BODY. I RECEIVED THE ONSLAUGHT OF HIS FRUSTRATION ON EACH WEEKEND, TAKING THE RESULTS OF A WINTER'S WEEK OF ISOLATION EVERY JOURNEY.

BUT, ALWAYS, THE SPRING WOULD BEGIN AND WE WOULD BE ABLE TO VENTURE FURTHER OUT INTO THE ALWAYS MORE WELCOMING SUN UNTIL ONCE AGAIN IT WOULD BE SUMMER AND OUR SELVES AND OUR BODIES WOULD RUSH THROUGH FORESTS TO FIND SWIMMING HOLES TO DIVE INTO AND FEEL COMPLETELY ATTACHED TO NATURE.

I WOULD LOVE HIM IN THE SUMMER TIME.

I WOULD HATE HIM IN THE WINTER.

BUT I WOULD ALWAYS RETURN EVERY WEEKEND FOR MY PILGRIMAGE.

HE NEVER WOULD TALK TO ME. HE WOULD LISTEN WHEN I PROFESSED MY LOVE, HE WOULD SIT SILENTLY WHILE I BEGGED HIS RESPONSE, HE WOULD LET MY ANGER GLANCE OFF HIS BROW IF EVER I DARED SPEAK IT. BUT HE WOULD NEVER RESPOND TO ME.

FINALLY, I WENT TO HIS FARM NO MORE. I WAS

FRIGHTENED THAT I WOULD FORGET THAT HE WAS
NOT GOD.

THIS PIECE APPEARED IN **DRUMMER MAGAZINE**.
REPRINTED WITH PERMISSION.

JOHN PRESTON

30. R. SMILES AT WAITER.

31. R.'S HANDS ARE SHAKING A LITTLE.

32. R. GOES INSIDE THE CAFE.

33. THE WASHROOM. R. IS DOING HER HAIR.

34. R. SEATED AT TABLE ON THE TERRACE. THE WAITER BRINGS TEA AND CROISSANTS.

35. R. CONSIDERS THE SQUARE OF THE THÉÂTRE FRANCAIS.

36. FADE OUT: GRADUALLY FADE IN ON LONG SHOT: **THE GALLERY MONTPENSIER**. R. SEEN FROM REAR **WALKING**
    TOWARD THE FAR END OF THE GALLERY.

37. ROBERTE LOOKING AT SHOP WINDOWS, HESITATES, STOPS.

38. STEPS OF CORPULENT MAN.

CHORUS FOR A PSALM

DANIEL IS MY BROTHER, MY LOVER. HE IS THE FIRST MAN WHO LET ME ENJOY BEING BURIED ALIVE IN THE SAND. MY SLAVES ARE ALL NUMBERED. MY MASTER HAS YET TO BE IDENTIFIED. HE WILL BE THE FIRST MAN TO MAKE ME SUFFER BEING BURIED UP TO MY NECK IN THE GROUND FOR LONGER THAN I WANT UNTIL I KNOW EXACTLY WHO IS IN CONTROL, WHO I HAVE DELIVERED MYSELF UNTO, AND WHO I WORSHIP FOR HAVING GIVEN ME THE EXPERIENCE, ALONG WITH AN OPPORTUNITY TO WRITE ABOUT IT.

WE SAT ON A DARKENING SHORE, DANIEL FINDING GRUESOME FACES ON THE PEBBLES THERE AND ALL OF US BURSTING, LACED.

"EACH ONE LOOKS MORE ROTTEN," DEBBIE LAUGHED.

"DRACULA WITHERING," I AGREED.

THE SUNSET CRACKED OUR INDIFFERENCE, GLOWING AND FLARING BEHIND THE CONFIDENT FLIGHT OF BIRDS CROSSING THE MARSH WITH A BROADER VISION THAN MY OWN, BUT POSSIBLY LESS IMAGINATION. I NO MORE CREATED MY LANGUAGE THAN THE BIRDS DID. I AM ONLY MY TONGUE'S PRODUCT, SUBJECT TO THE REALITIES I HAVE CONVINCED ME OF. BIRDS MAY HAVE AS MUCH IMAGINATION AS I DO, BUT WITH FEWER WORDS TO DESCRIBE IT, FIX IT, AND MODIFY IT. I ADMIRE THIS BASIC HONESTY OF ANIMALS. WHETHER OR NOT THEY CHOSE IT IS IMMATERIAL.

IN THE FINAL TWILIGHT, DANIEL HAD ME SHOWING HIM HOW TO SKIP STONES ACROSS THE LAKE'S AGITATED HIDE, AND STRANGE AS IT SEEMS, I SUDDENLY FELT LIKE A BOY FEELING LIKE A MAN FOR THE FIRST TIME IN HIS LIFE. I HAVE NEVER FELT THAT WAY BEFORE EVEN THOUGH PHYSICALLY I AM ALREADY A MAN. THIS RAISES EVEN MORE QUESTIONS ABOUT SOCIAL EVOLUTION THROUGH AN ORIGINALLY DISTRACTED, MODIFIED, THEN REPRESSED HOMOSEXUALITY INTENSIFIED BY THE SANCTIFICATION OF REPRODUCTION. AM I MY OWN EVIDENCE? IS MY THEORY OF BEHAVIORAL NEOTENY UNIVERSAL TO HUMANITY OR MERELY AUTO-BIOGRAPHICAL?

•••

HUMAN BEHAVIOR IS LARGELY INHERITED, PARTLY THROUGH TRADITION, PARTLY THROUGH GENETICS.

EACH BEHAVIORAL TRAIT (SEXUALITY, AGGRES-SION, INTELLIGENCE, SOCIABILITY, AND AES-THETICS—PERCEPTUAL SELECTIVITY) BEGINS AS A POLYGENETIC RESPONSE PATTERN, AN ACTION POTENTIAL GENERATED AND SHAPED BY A MULTITUDE OF GENES, THEN MODIFIED BY ITS BIOLOGICAL AND CULTURAL ENVIRONMENT. THE DEGREE TO WHICH THE ENVIRONMENT INFLUENCES THESE GENETIC POTENTIALS DEPENDS ON THE INTENSITY WITH WHICH THE GENES COLLECTIVELY WORK TO EXPRESS THEMSELVES, SOME BEING EXTREMELY PLIABLE, SOME EQUALLY OBDURATE, MOST OF THEM VARIABLY DEFINITIVE.

WITH ANY HUMAN POPULATION, THESE POLY-GENETIC BEHAVIORS VARY WITH THE INDIVIDUAL, BUT ONLY WITHIN A SPECTRUM OF QUALITIES RANGING FROM ONE EXTREME TO ANOTHER (HETEROSEXUAL TO HOMOSEXUAL, SUBMISSIVE TO DOMINATING, IDIOT TO GENIUS, SOCIAL TO ANTI-SOCIAL, MONOTONOUS TO EXTRAVAGANT) WITH VARYING DEGREES OF INTERMEDIATE QUALITIES (BISEXUAL, COMPROMISING, PERCEPTIVE, HOS-PITABLE, DISCERNING) LYING BETWEEN THOSE CONSIDERED TO BE OPPOSITE ONE ANOTHER. WHERE ANY ONE INDIVIDUAL LIES ALONG ONE OF THESE SPECTRUMS AND HOW THE SOCIETY ORIENTS TOWARD THAT PORTION OF THE SPECTRUM DETERMINES WHETHER THE INDIVIDUAL'S GROWTH WILL BE HEALTHY OR NEUROTIC.

SINCE HUMANS THINK DICHOTOMOUSLY, HUMAN SOCIETIES ORIENT TO MANY OF THESE SPECTRUMS AS IF ONLY THEIR EXTREMES EXISTED, ONE INEVITABLY REWARDED WHILE THE OTHER IS INESCAPABLY PUNISHED. SINCE THE MAJORITY OF THE POPULATION LIES WITHIN THE INTERMEDIATE RANGE, MOST PEOPLE ARE DISTORTED BY THIS DICHOTOMOUS TREATMENT, THEIR PSYCHE FRAG-MENTED, AND THE FRAGMENTS SELECTIVELY REINFORCED.

HUMAN SOCIETY FIRST SEPARATES THE INDIVIDUAL INTO WHAT IS HUMAN AND WHAT IS ANIMAL, PUNISHING THE ANIMAL WHILE GLORIFYING THE HUMAN. THE HUMAN IS THEN DIVIDED INTO MASCULINE AND FEMININE, THE SOCIAL ENVIRON-MENT MALNOURISHING ONE SEXUAL IDENTITY WHILE FOSTERING THE OTHER ACCORDING TO THE INDIVIDUAL'S GENITALS, OFTEN WITH SOME INCIDENCE OF SEXUAL CONFUSION OR TRANS-SEXUALISM. USUALLY MASCULINITY EXAGGERATES THE MEN WHILE FEMININITY DULLS THE WOMEN AS A BACKGROUND FOR MASCULINE THEATRICS.

AT THE SAME TIME THAT THE ANDROGYNOUS "MANAPE" IS BEING SPLIT INTO MASCULINE OR FEMININE HUMANS, WHAT REMAINS OF THE INDIVIDUAL'S BEHAVIOR IS ALSO SEPARATED INTO NORMAL AND ABNORMAL. BEHAVIORS THAT DO NOT FIT THE CONTRIVED NORM ARE RIDDLED WITH FEARS AND GUILTS WHILE CONVENTIONAL ATTI-TUDES ARE EMOTIONALLY REINFORCED.

IF THE INDIVIDUAL SURVIVES THIS LEVEL OF OPPRESSION LONG ENOUGH TO REACH PUBERTY, ITS EMERGING SEXUALITY IS THEN DIVIDED INTO THE PERVERSE AND THE SANCTIFIED. PERVERSE ACTS ARE CRIMINALIZED AND OFTEN PUNISHABLE BY DEATH WHILE THE SANCTIFIED ACTS FLOURISH IN A NEUROTIC MANNER, ANXIETY-RIDDEN BY PREVIOUS OPPRESSIONS. SEXUAL POTENTIALS ARE UNDER-MINED AND STRICTLY CONTROLLED, BUT THE SEXUAL URGE IS NOT EASILY DISCOURAGED AND RESISTS EVEN THE MOST BRUTAL REPRESSION, THUS ALSO GENERATING THE MOST INTENSE ANXIETIES.

THE END RESULT IS A BREED OF MEN ALIENATED FROM A BREED OF WOMEN AND EACH INDIVIDUAL ALIENATED FROM ITSELF, EACH SELECTIVELY NOURISHED TO GROW IN A DISTORTED MANNER AND TRAINED TO BEHAVE IN THE TRADITIONAL FASHION. THIS IS HOW HUMANS BREED AND DOMESTICATE THEIR ANIMALS. THIS IS HOW HUMANS BREED AND DOMESTICATE THEIR CHILDREN AND THUS HU-MANITY ITSELF.

...

WHEN I HAD HIM SO HE WAS ABOUT TO SHIT, I TIED HIM UP SO HE HURT AND COULD NOT EASILY CONTROL HIS ASS. THEN I TOLD HIM, "YOU WILL NOT SHIT ON THAT FLOOR."

HE NEEDED TO PISS.

"NOR WILL YOU WET YOURSELF."

HE GREW FURIOUSLY ON THE VERGE OF CRYING.

"UNTIL I ORDER YOU TO. YOU WILL PISS AND SHIT WHEN I TELL YOU TO."

HIS BONE RAGED WITH THE REST OF HIM, FANATIC WITH THE ATTEMPT TO CONTROL HIMSELF. I WONDERED IF THIS WAS REGRESSIVE, A SYNTHETIC NEOTENY OR AT LEAST THE FANTASY OF ONE, BUT

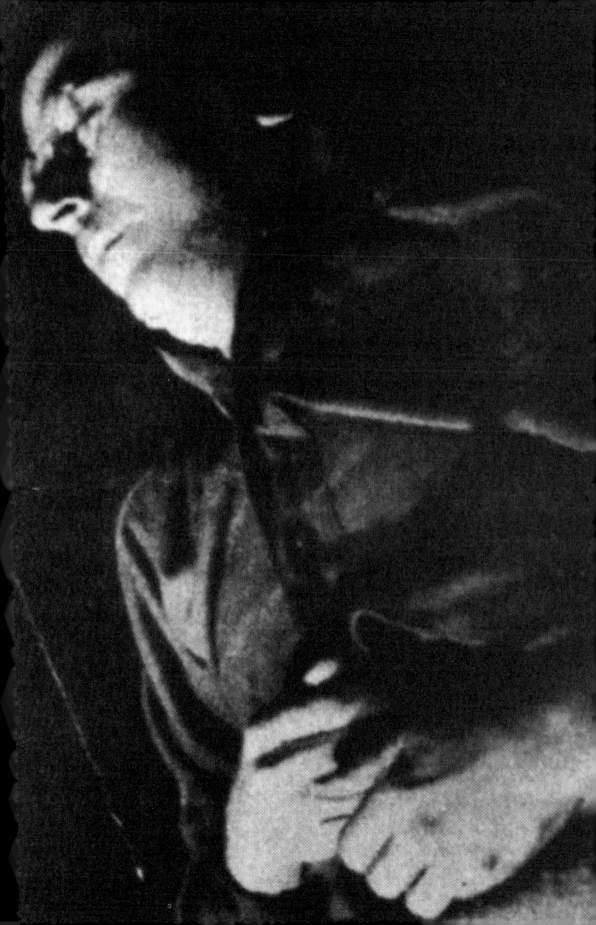

BEFORE I COULD RESEARCH IT, I LOST THE IDEA INSIDE ANOTHER BEATING, MINE AS WELL AS HIS, HIS BLADDER TOO FRIGHTENED TO CONTROL ITSELF, HIS ASS TO FINAL.

I UNDERSTAND THE ELIMINIATION OF REPULSIONS IS NECESSARY IF THE PROCESS OF MATURATION IS TO COMPLETE ITSELF. THEIR GLORIFICATION IS ONLY EROTICALLY RELEVANT.

•••

CIVILIZATION WORKS BY MAKING YOU FEEL SMALL. IT BELITTLES YOUR INDIVIDUALITY, DEGRADES YOU FOR DEVIATING FROM THE CONTRIVED NORM, THEN SHAMES YOU FOR HAVING PUT YOUR SOCIETY THROUGH THE BOTHER. AND YOU DESERVE IT BECAUSE YOU ARE A CHILD AND A DAMN NUISANCE. SUDDENLY IT IS A CRIME TO DO, HAVE OR WANT ANYTHING UNLESS YOUR SOCIETY SAYS YOU CAN. YOU RESIST AT FIRST, BUT BY THE TIME YOU'VE BEEN POTTY-TRAINED, YOU ARE SERVING YOUR SOCIETY FOREVER.

NOBODY ENJOYS SERVING THEIR SOCIETY. FANATIC OR DEPRESSED, THEY DO IT BECAUSE IT IS THEIR DUTY AND BECAUSE LIFE IS TOO SERIOUS TO ENJOY, ENSHRINED WITH SOLEMN VOWS AND WHISPERED SUPPLICATIONS.

SHOULD YOU FAIL TO APPRECIATE THE SERIOUS-NESS OF SERVING, YOUR SOCIETY THREATENS YOU WITH CRIMINALIZATION AND DAMNATION. FRIGHT-ENED AND FEELING GUILTY, YOU REMAIN OBEDIENT-LY SMALL. THIS IS A POWER GAME. THIS IS SM CONVENTIONALIZED INTO A STYLE OF LIVING, SOCIETIES WHERE PEOPLE ARE SET AGAINST THEMSELVES AND EVEN MORE SO AGAINST ONE ANOTHER. IT IS MASS NEUROSIS IN PROGRESS.

•••

SIR,

THE OFFICIAL STORY IS THAT YOU DRAGGED ME FROM TRASHCAN TO TRASHCAN AND PUBLICLY BEAT THE LIVING WORMS OUT OF ME AT EVERY ONE OF THEM, AND NOW WADE ISN'T QUITE THE SAME ANYMORE. THERE IS MUCH TRUTH IN THAT WITH ONLY A FEW CHANGES TO COLOR CERTAIN PEOPLE'S GREEN. STILL BLACK AND BLUE OVER YOU—SOUNDS LIKE, FEELS LIKE A SONG AND DANCE ROUTINE AT THE EDGE OF A JUNGLE DRIPPING WITH TORTURED BODIES. APOCALYPSE. I'M

HOWLING, BUT NOBODY CARES AND ALL I CAN DO IS WET MY PANTS IN FEAR.

FORGIVE ME. I'M LACED AT THE MOMENT. BEING AMONG THE BOYS AGAIN, I'M SECRETLY FEELING VERY COCKY, THE WAY WE WERE WHEN LEAVING TANNHAUSER. ALSO, SINCE YOU WERE CONCERNED, DANIEL SEEMS VERY COMFORTABLE WITH YOU. HAVING MET YOU, HE REALIZES MY TRUST IN YOU IS NOT POORLY FOUNDED.

MISS YOU,
WADE

P.S.: I WROTE THIS BEFORE I ACTUALLY TALKED WITH JR AND DISCOVERED YOU HAD ALREADY TOLD HIM THE BATTERED DETAILS. HE COULDN'T WAIT TO SEE THE BRUISES, SO I SADDLED MY KITE AND SWUNG CROSSTOWN TO HIS PLACE. I DISPLAYED THEM, I WATCH THEM WITH UNPRECEDENTED PRIDE AND MUCH HOOTING. THANK YOU, SIR.

•••

HE NEEDS TO REMEMBER ME.

•••

WIVES, CHILDREN, AND DOGS—ALL ARE SLAVES TO A FIERCE SORT OF MASCULINITY AND A SAD FEMININITY. OCCASIONALLY THE SAD BECOME FIERCE AND OVERTURN THE MALE POWER STRUC-TURE. SOMETIMES FIERCE MALES HAVE OVER-TURNED FEMALE POWER STRUCTURES. WHICH FIRST OVERTHREW THE OTHER IS PURELY ACADEMIC AND NOT EASILY PROVEN.

IN MANY SOCIETIES, ALL FACES ARE EXPECTED TO LOOK UP TO MEN, BUT MEN CAUGHT EYEING OTHER MEN ARE SUSPECTED OF PERVERSION, SO THE SANCTIFIED MAN EYES HIMSELF INSTEAD AND THROUGH THE WOMEN BRED TO MIRROR HIM. IT IS NO SECRET THAT WOMEN ARE EXPECTED TO ACT AS SOUNDING BOARDS FOR MALE INSECURITIES. THE PREVALENCE OF MALE POWER STRUCTURES SUGGESTS TO SOME THAT THE HUMAN MALE POSSESSES AN INHERENT ADVANTAGE OVER THE FEMALE. IF THIS IS TRUE, WHAT MEN HAVE DONE WITH THAT ADVANTAGE DOES NOT CREDIT THEM WITH MUCH MATURITY AND FURTHER SUGGESTS THE MALE IS ALSO MORE FRIGHTENED, AS NEUROTIC AS HE IS INSECURE ABOUT HIMSELF, ESPECIALLY THROUGH THE INVENTION OF NONEXISTENT DANGERS.

PEOPLE ARE NOT DESPERATE FOR POWER UNLESS THEY ARE DESPERATE TO IMPRESS THEMSELVES AND TO INTIMIDATE OTHERS, USUALLY BECAUSE THEY ARE THEMSELVES EASILY INTIMIDATED— SOMETIMES BY A TRUE ENEMY, SOMETIMES BY THE INDIFFERENCE OF THEIR WORLD, OFTEN BY THAT PORTION OF THEMSELVES THAT HAS REMAINED UNKNOWN, OPPRESSED YET FOREVER SEEKING TO BE REALIZED.

•••

IN A HETERONEUROTIC SOCIETY, PEOPLE OF THE SAME SEX ARE NOT TO LOOK AT ONE ANOTHER WITHOUT CRITICISM. IN A MALE-DOMINATED SOCIETY, MASCULINE CRITICISM IS STANDARDIZED AS JUSTICE; FEMININE CRITICISM STANDARDIZED AS IDLE GOSSIP. IN MANY OF THE SOCIETIES BEFORE 2000 BC AND SOME AS LATE AS 50 BC, THE MASCULINE/FEMININE ROLES WERE COMPLETELY REVERSED OR AT LEAST MORE BALANCED. (RESEARCH THE DOCUMENTS FROM ANCIENT EGYPT, SUMER, ANATOLIA, BABYLONIA, THE MINOANS, AND ANCIENT ETHIOPIA; ALSO THE HISTORIES OF DIODORUS SICULUS, HERODOTUS, AND SOPHOCLES).

•••

MY FIRST IMPRESSION OF LORD PRESTON WAS THAT HE WAS MUCH TALLER THAN I HAD EXPECTED HIM TO BE, BUT NOT HEAVIER WHICH INDICATED TO ME HE WAS A PREDATOR INSTEAD OF A SCAVENGER. I TOOK EVERY OPPORTUNITY TO INFORM HIM OF WHAT I LIKED BY TELLING FREELY OF MY PREVIOUS ORDEALS.

MY SECOND IMPRESSION FEARED THAT LORD PRESTON WOULD PUT ME INTO SHOCK. HE BELTED MY VIRGIN SHOULDERS SO HARD SO IMMEDIATELY THAT I KNEW I HAD NO HOPE OF BUILDING DELICATE CRUELTIES INTO ARCHITECTURES OF PAIN. THE TEMPLE AUTOMATICALLY WENT UP WITH THE FIRST SMACK OF HIS BELT BREAKING STARS, THE SECOND SMACK BURSTING MY APPRECIATION, AND THE THIRD SCREAMING. I HAD NO GAG TO BIT INTO, NO CHAINS TO PULL AGAINST, NO ROPES AS MUCH AS I WANTED THEM. THE FOURTH AND SEVERAL MORE BLOWS CUT INTO MY SHOULDERS WITH NO SENSITIVITY TO MY OWN, AND I HAD NO EXCUSE FOR IT—NO BONDAGE, ONLY A FOOLISH SUBMISSION. I HAD FELT BLOWS LIKE THESE ONCE BEFORE AND FEARED GOING INTO SHOCK EVEN MORE THAN I FEARED THE BLACK AND BLUE MARKS. DANIEL AND I HAVE SURVIVED MY BRUISES BEFORE.

LORD PRESTON'S BELT CONTINUED BREAKING ME AND MY THOUGHTS. I SQUEEZED TEETH AND GRABBED RUBBER CORNERS, PRAYING TO NO GOD THAT I WOULD COME OUT OF THIS HAPPIER THAN I WAS. I WANTED TO CRY, BUT I WAS TOO BUSY RESISTING THE PAIN TO SUBMIT TO IT.

FINALLY HE STOPPED BELTING ME, HIS FINGERTIPS RUPTURING ALONG MY BEAMING HIDE AS HE TRACED THE MUSCLES WHERE I CRINGED. HE WHISPERED HOW BEAUTIFUL THEY WERE AND KISSED ME WHERE IT FELT BEST. I SANK UNDER SUPERFICIAL IDOLIZATIONS DRY WITH FEAR AND CRYSTALLIZING INTO WORSHIP BEFORE I EVEN KNEW IT, A SECOND BEATING SHATTERING ANY SELF-ANALYSIS I MAY HAVE BEGUN. I ONLY KNEW THAT I SAW A PART OF MYSELF IN LORD PRESTON THOUGH HE WAS MORE POWERFUL AND MY HARMLESSNESS MORE OBVIOUS.

WITH THAT THOUGHT, I ANGERED AND RAGED AGAINST THE WHIPPING PAIN, BUT HE ONLY CARED ABOUT HIMSELF. WHEN HE FINALLY STOPPED, I THOUGHT IT BEST I EXPRESS MY CONCERN.

"I THOUGHT YOU WERE HEAVY," HE CHIDED.

I SENSED HIS SMUG EYE BEHIND ME, WONDERING AS HE BELITTLED MY PREVIOUS TALES AS BRAGGING AND LABELLED MY HEAVY A STRANGE SORT OF PUFF.

"OTHERS HAVE TOLD ME I'M HEAVY . . . INTENSE. I AM, BUT IN OTHER WAYS."

HE COULD HAVE SMACKED MY INSOLENCE. INSTEAD HE GREW EXCITED BY THE KNOWLEDGE THAT MY SHOULDERS HAD NEVER BEEN WHIPPED BEFORE AND THAT HE WAS OPENING AREAS WITHIN ME THAT HAD NEVER BEEN OPENED. I FED ON HIS FEVER, AND HE WASTED NO TIME RELENTLESSLY BEATING ME FOR THE REST OF THE NIGHT AS HE LED ME FROM ONE TRASHCAN TO ANOTHER. LORD PRESTON HAD A NEW DOG TO SHOW.

EXCEPT THAT HE PREFERS TO THINK OF US AS STALLIONS.

HE LURED ME INTO HIS CONTROL WITH THE PROSPECT OF HIS TAKING ME OUT IN A BLACK LEATHER COLLAR AND LEATHER RESTRAINTS, MY BACK DISPLAYING HIS MARKS AND MY MOUTH GAGGED TO KEEP ME FROM BRAGGING ABOUT THEM, MY BREATHING ALWAYS WORRIED, MY EYES LESS

FIERCE. INSTEAD HE LED ME ABOUT WITHOUT THE GAG AND WITH A FAR SUBTLER BONDAGE. I RESENTED IT THEN, BUT HOW MUCH MORE EFFECTIVE IT WAS, HIS FORCING ME TO SERVE WITHOUT THE PHYSICAL REINFORCEMENT I ONCE, STILL FIND EROTIC.

MY THIRD IMPRESSION OF LORD PRESTON WAS THAT EITHER I DID WHAT HE WANTED OR I WAS IN MORE TROUBLE THAN I ALREADY WAS IN. THIS IMPRESSION WAS LARGELY A PROJECTION OF MY OWN ANTICIPATIONS, BUT SOON FRETTED WITH THE KNOWLEDGE THIS MAN COULD TURN ME INTO A BLOODY MUSH AND I WOULD LOVE IT. DEFINITELY A LESS CONFIDENT IMPRESSION THAN THE FIRST AND EVEN THE SECOND IMPRESSIONS.

THEN, A FEW TRASHCANS LATER, THE BEATINGS BEGAN TO FEEL GOOD, ORGASMS OF PAIN AND FEAR BLASTING AS I FOUGHT AGAINST ROPES AND CHAINS WHILE NAKED IN FRONT OF STRANGERS. SOMETIMES I FEARED MY LORD'S MOOD; SOMETIMES I BATHED IN THE SWEAT AND THE HEAT OF HIS BODY EMBRACING ME, ALL OF ME IN A COLD TERROR THOUGH MY FLESH WAS HOT WITH BATTERED NERVES. I EXAGGERATED EVERY SENSATION WITH FRANTIC BREATHING, OUR BODIES IN LOVE, HIS DEEP VOICE HUNGRY AT THE VISION OF MY MARKED MUSCLES.

AT THE SILKY DINER, THE MAN WEARING DEAD MICE AROUND HIS NECK DID NOT KNOW WHAT WE WERE DOING. AT THE TANNHAUSER, THE HETEROSEXUALS KNEW AND WERE AMAZED. THEY HAD GATHERED THERE AT A CONVENTION FOR THE LIBERATION OF SADOMASOCHISM FROM A NONCONSENSUAL OPPRESSION. THE HETEROSEXUALS AMAZED ME AS MUCH AS WE AMAZED THEM, MANY OF THE MEN HAVING EROTICIZED BEING PUNISHED FOR THEIR TRANSVESTISM, GLORIOUS WITH TRANSSEXUAL HUMILIATION AS THEY SUFFERED—IN A VERY RESERVED SORT OF WAY—FOR TRYING TO BE WHAT THEY WEREN'T. THE AIR WAS HEAVY WITH GUILT, SOME OF IT NERVOUS, SOME OF IT SMUG.

LORD PRESTON EYED MY EYE AND SMILED, "THIS IS VERY BIZARRE."

I LAUGHED INSIDE A STIFF AND TENDER BODY, FASCINATED BY THESE PEOPLE WHILE CRAZY WITH A LUST TO BE BEATEN AGAIN AND THE FEAR OF WHERE IT WAS LEADING ME. BEFORE I COULD SADDEN, LORD PRESTON FOR THE FIRST TIME ORDERED ME TO STRIP IN FRONT OF HETERO-SEXUALS. NAKED EXCEPT FOR MY SOCKS, I WAS EVEN MORE ACUTELY AWARE OF MY NUDITY AND REMEMBERED HEARING OF THIS TACTIC BEFORE. I BREATHED WITH AN INCREASINGLY GENUINE DREAD, MY BELLY TIGHTENING AND PULSING WHILE THE TIP OF MY PEANUT STUNG, NEEDING TO PISS. I WANTED SOME WATER.

AS THIS MAN WHO WAS PRETENDING TO BE MY MASTER PROCEEDED TO BIND ME SPREAD-EAGLE TO A VERTICAL GRID, A MAITRESSE GRABBED ME FROM BEHIND, KNEADING HER CLAWS INTO MY ELEPHANTS AND MUNCHING IN MY EAR, ASKING IF I, POOR THING, HAD BEEN LEFT THERE ALL ALONE. I TURNED MY EYES AWAY FROM HER WITH ALL THE PRIDE OF KNOWING WHO MY REAL MASTER WAS AND, FOR HER INFORMATION, EYED HIM. SHE ASKED THE QUESTION AGAIN OF LORD PRESTON AND HE POLITELY DISMISSED HER, THEN OVERWHELMED ME WITH THE MOST EROTIC BEATING OF MY LIFE. HE COULD HAVE BEAT ME UNTIL I ONLY HUNG THERE BLUBBERING, INCAPABLE OF ANY RESISTANCE, PHYSICAL OR SPIRITUAL. HE COULD HAVE CONTINUED BEATING ME EVEN THEN UNTIL MY RAGING BONE FINALLY SPILLED AND I SCREAMED, MINDLESSLY ROARING. HE COULD HAVE BEAT ME FURTHER, BUT HE DIDN'T, KNOWING WHEN TO STOP SINCE HE WANTED ME AGAIN AND WITH AS MANY MARKS ON MY BODY AS HE COULD LEAVE WITHOUT LOSING MY AFFECTION.

HE GOT MORE MARKS THAN EITHER OF US ANTICIPATED BECAUSE HE WAS TOO SENSUOUS AND I TOO CRAZY WITH IT TO SAY NO AS HE PULLED ME OUT OF THE APPLAUSE OF HETEROSEXUALS INTO THE BIGGEST PISS-DRINKING FISTDRILLING TRASHCAN OF THEM ALL. AGAIN HE ORDERED ME TO STRIP, CHAINED MY WRISTS TO AN OVERHEAD BEAM AND, GRABBING ME BY THE HAIR, PROCEEDED TO BEAT MY TENDER BODY, BUT SO HARD MY RAGE WAS GENUINE AGAIN, YANKING AGAINST HIS FIRM GRIP ON MY SCALP, MY TERROR LOVELESS EVEN AS THE CROWD OF GRIMY MUSCLED MEN SHOOK THEIR CANS AND SPRAYED ME WITH BEER AND SODA. THE BELT WAS TOO ANGRY FOR ME TO WANT IT; MY PANIC TOO COLD. I EXPLODED, HAULING MYSELF OFF THE GROUND UNTIL SUSPENDED BY FLEXED BICEPS, THE REST OF ME TWISTING AND STRUGGLING TO DEAL WITH, THEN ESCAPE, RAGE AT AND FINALLY SUBMIT TO THAT BELT UNTIL FRANTIC TO ESCAPE IT AGAIN AND AGAIN.

EVERY TIME HE STOPPED, I RUSHED AT HIS EMBRACE AND ACCEPTED HIS DEEP LONG KISS INTO MY HEAVY BREATHING. EVERY TIME HE BEAT ME AGAIN, I HAD NO TIME TO WONDER WHY.

HE GRABBED ME IN THE MIDDLE OF A FEAR AND SIGNALLED HE WAS DONE, RELEASING ME. I GRABBED A POLE SO I COULD REMAIN STANDING, VAGUELY AWARE MY POSE WAS NOT AS THEATRICAL AS I BELIEVED, SHOULDERS AND ELEPHANTS RADIATING. HIS VOICE BEHIND ME PRAISED MY BODY, HIS MIND ANXIOUS WITH HOW BEAUTIFUL HIS MARKS WERE AS I STRUGGLED BACK INTO MY CLOTHES. IN A ROOM WHERE WE WERE ALLOWED TO TALK, HE TOLD ME HE ONLY STOPPED BECAUSE HE CAUGHT HIMSELF LOSING CONTROL, CRAZY WITH THE SIGHT OF ME AT THE END OF HIS BELT. I TOLD HIM HE ENJOYED BEATING ME MUCH HARDER IN FRONT OF WILD MEN THAN AMONG HETEROSEX- UALS, THEN LAUGHED DEFENSIVELY AT A GUSH OF UNEXPECTED PAIN. MORE SECRETLY I RESISTED THE GROWING URGE TO SPARE MYSELF AN EMOTIONAL TANGLE BETWEEN THIS MAN AND DANIEL. LORD PRESTON STILL ALARMS ME AND MORE SO WITH EVERY RE-EVALUATION OF THAT NIGHT.

I THINK HE CAUGHT ME ANALYZING THEN. SUDDENLY HE ORDERED ME TO PULL MY PANTS DOWN AND PUSHED ME BACK ONTO THE GAMETABLE. I WORRIED AS HE CHAINED MY WRISTS TO MY THROAT AND PROCEEDED TO WHIP MY BAGS AND BONE WITH LOOPS OF THONG. I ADORED IT, THEN RESENTED IT; WRITHED AND GROVELLED UNDER IT, THEN SCREAMED BEFORE ADORING HIM AGAIN BECAUSE HE KNEW WHERE TO STOP WITHOUT LESSENING MY FEAR OF HIM.

WHEN HE WAS DONE, I GRABBED HIS EMBRACE, FRANTIC TO TASTE HIM AND LICKING WHEREVER HE ORDERED ME. HE SEEMED TO KNOW I WANTED HIS ARMPITS AND HIS CROTCH AND SWEATY SOCKS. HE PUSHED MY FACE INTO ALL OF THEM AND ALLOWED ME TO BATHE MY TONGUE AND MIND THERE. WHEN HE TURNED ME AROUND AND BROUGHT MY BACK INTO HIS CHEST, I RISKED DRIVING MY FLARING ELEPHANTS INTO HIS CROTCH AND MASSAGED BETWEEN HIS THIGHS WHILE MY HEAD SAILED, WORDLESS, THICK WITH SENSATIONS WHILE A FLOOD OF CONFLICTING EMOTIONS HID BEHIND MY SMILE. I CONSIDERED BITING HIM, BUT DECIDED THIS PUBLIC WAS NO PROTECTION. THE CROWD HAD ALREADY SCREAMED FOR MY BLOOD WHILE MY MASTER WAS BEATING ME FOR HIS OWN PLEASURE. THEY WERE HARDLY THE SORT TO SAVE ME FROM HIS ANGER.

LORD PRESTON YAWNED, CAUSING THE NAKED MAN WHO HAD BEEN WATCHING US TO FUMBLE HIS BONE AND DEPART, INDIGNANTLY ASTOUNDED. I LAUGHED.

FILLING MYSELF WITH THE SENSATIONS AT THE BACK OF MY HEAD RUBBING THE BACK OF HIS.

LORD PRESTON BROUGHT ME TO BED WITH HIM. HE WONDERED WHY I DIDN'T WANT TO TAKE MY SOCKS OFF EVEN AS HE BEGAN TO DO IT FOR ME. I TOLD HIM IT WAS TOO EROTIC KEEPING THEM ON, MENTIONING I WAS DRAWN TO THEM BECAUSE OF THEIR LABEL WHEN A MORE HONEST RESPONSE WOULD HAVE HOOTED THAT I WANTED TO KEEP THEM ON BECAUSE THEY CLUNG TO MY FEET WITH THE FILTH FROM EVERY FLOOR HE HAD BEATEN ME OVER. I RESORTED TO DISHONESTY IN THE FEAR OF SOUNDING TOO ROMANTIC ONLY TO FIND I HAD FAILED TO FEED HIS EGO AND PLEASE HIM AS I WOULD HAVE LIKED. I FEARED THE LOSS OF OTHER INTERESTS AND SO RISKED THE LOSS OF LORD PRESTON.

...

FOR MANY PEOPLE, THE EXISTENCE OF A GOD IS A REALITY WHEN IN TRUTH THERE IS NO REAL EVIDENCE FOR THE EXISTENCE OF ANY GOD, EXCEPT AS AN ULTIMATE EXTENSION OF IMAGINARY POWER STRUCTURES.

WHEN YOU PRAY, YOU ARE ACTIVELY CONVINCING YOURSELF THAT A GOD DOES IN FACT EXIST. WHEN YOU PRAY DESPITE GROWING DOUBTS, THEN YOU ARE HOPING SOMEBODY ELSE WILL TAKE CONTROL OF YOUR LIFE. WHEN YOU ARE TRULY DESPERATE TO BELIEVE IN GOD, THEN PRAYERS SOMETIMES "WORK," THE INTENSITY OF THAT DESPERATION DRAWING OUT OF THE INDIVIDUAL POTENTIALS IT NEVER KNEW IT HAD, AND NEVER WILL KNOW, GIVEN ITS KIND OF FAITH AND THE FAITH OF OTHERS FEEDING INTO THAT FAITH.

MIRACLES AND "FAITH HEALINGS" ARE NO PROOF OF GOD. THEY ONLY PROVE DESPERATE PEOPLE CAN DO MORE WITH THEIR OWN MIND AND BODY THAN THEY THINK THEY CAN. IT TELLS ME THEY HAVE BEEN TRICKED INTO BELIEVING THAT THEIR UNREALIZED POTENTIAL LIES IN ANOTHER BEING, BE IT THROUGH POSSESSION BY DEMONS OR THROUGH THE GRACE OF GOD. IT ALSO SUGGESTS THAT GODS ARE HYPERTROPHIC MANIFESTATIONS OF OUR INNERMOST DESIRES TO BE MORE THAN WE ARE AND THAT WE WORSHIP OUR GODS AS INTENSELY AS WE LUST TO WORSHIP OURSELVES. THIS PHASE OF SELF-WORSHIP IS NECESSARY IF THE INDIVIDUAL IS EVER TO GET OVER ITSELF AND MATURE WITH THE ENERGY TO CONFRONT THE BUSINESS OF A DAILY SURVIVAL, PREFERABLY

WITHIN A COOPERATIVE GROUP EFFORT SEEKING ENOUGH TIME TO PLAY AS WELL AS WORK TOGETHER. WITHOUT WORK, WE LOSE MEANING. WITHOUT PLAY, WE LOSE OUR WARMTH AND BECOME TOO SERIOUS TO LOVE.

•••

WHEN NEXT I WOKE, I FROWNED AT THE LACK OF ROPE AROUND MY HANDS AND FEET, BUT HARDENED HAPPY IN THE WARMTH OF LORD PRESTON'S BODY CURLED ROUND MY OWN. HE STIRRED, ROSE, THEN BROUGHT HIS PEANUT INTO MY MOUTH AND NONCHALANTLY PISSED. I GUZZLED EVEN AS HIS BLADDER PROVED LARGER THAN MY BELLY, ALL OF ME SNORTING FOR AIR AND STEADYING MYSELF BY GRABBING HIS NAKED LEGS.

"ARE YOU HORNY?" HE WHISPERED INTO MY HALF-SLEEP.

"YES, SIR."

HIS HAND MOLESTED THE HOLE BETWEEN MY ELEPHANTS, GREASED IT AND BROUGHT HIS FRESH BONE INTO PLACE. AFTER A PRELIMINARY PEEVE, MY HOLE OPENED, HE SLID IN, AND I LEARNED HE COULD DRILL MY HOLE ALL DAY AND I WOULD LOVE IT, THE EXPLOSIONS AS PAINLESS AS THEY WERE DISORIENTING. A PASSION THICKENED INSIDE ME, ONLY TO FLOUNDER AS LORD PRESTON ORDERED ME TO WORK MYSELF INTO SPILLING. MY BONE WAS ALREADY HARD AND I WORKED IT, BUT INSIDE I WANTED HIS HAND THERE INSTEAD OF MY OWN. MY BONE REFUSED TO RAGE AND SPILL, AS IF WAITING FOR HIM TO TAKE CONTROL. SUDDENLY I REALIZED HE WAS IN CONTROL, THE USE OF HIS HAND INAPPROPRIATE, THE USE OF MY BODY HIS. FROM BEHIND ME, HE WHISPERED INTO MY EAR, HIS BONE STILL MOVING WONDROUSLY INSIDE ME, HIS WORDS SOUNDING A REALITY WHERE WITH A SINGLE WORD HE WOULD BRING TEARS TO MY EYES, A TREMBLING TO MY BODY, AND MY BODY TO ITS KNEES, PLEADING. HE TALKED OF TAKING EACH PART OF MY BODY ONE AT A TIME, SHOULDERS, THEN ELEPHANTS, BAGS AND PEANUT, EACH ARM, EACH THIGH AND CALF, HAND AND FOOT, TORTURING EACH ONE UNTIL ALL OF ME IS TOO TENDER TO TOUCH AND MY MIND HURTING SO MUCH THAT IT BREAKS WHEN HE ORDERS ME TO DECIDE WHICH PART OF ME HE'LL TORTURE NEXT.

REMEMBERING THE DEPTH OF MY UNEASINESS AS I HAD TO WAIT, ANTICIPATING HIS NEXT BEATING,

REMEMBERING HOW EASILY HE PUT ME IN AND OUT OF MY CLOTHES, I KNEW WHAT THE SINGLE WORD FROM HIM WOULD BE.

"STRIP."

THAT TERRIFYING ORDER TO YIELD EVERYTHING TO HIS BRUTAL WHIM.

THE THOUGHT CRAZED ME AND I SPILLED ENDLESSLY UNTIL LORD PRESTON ENDED IT, OR SO IT SEEMED.

EVEN MORE DISQUIETING IS THAT HE HAS ME SO I NO LONGER KNOW WHAT'S REAL AND WHAT'S CONTRIVED. I CAN'T SEEM TO DISCIPLINE MYSELF TO FORGET HIM. IT SOUNDS RIDICULOUS. IT FEELS RIDICULOUS. BUT SOMETIMES HE HAS ME SO CONFUSED I FIND MYSELF ON THE VERGE OF CRYING, DESPERATE TO BE EMBRACED.

•••

THEN I GROW ANGRY AT MY FAILURE TO KEEP THINGS IN PROPORTION AND I SHAKE MYSELF FOR A NEW PERSPECTIVE. HOW LONG IS THIS GOING TO LAST?

•••

ANXIETY IS AN EMOTIONAL TURMOIL DESPERATE FOR DIRECTION. CHARGED WTH FEARS AND DOUBTS, IT CAN BE REACTIVE, RESOLVING ITS DESPERATION BY FOCUSING ON A SPECIFIC CONCERN; OR IT CAN BE DIFFUSE, WITHOUT DIRECTION OR MOTIVATION, ITS DESPERATION SUSPENDED AND THEREFORE RESISTANT TO RESOLUTION. THIS DIFFUSE ANXIETY IS USUALLY SUBCONSCIOUS AND MANIFESTS ITSELF AS SERIOUSNESS. IF THE DESPERATION IS SUSPENDED LONG ENOUGH, ITS ENERGY DISSIPATES AND SOBRIETY BECOMES APATHETIC, DESPERATION INCAPABLE OF RESOLUTION, AND INSECURITIES FIXATED.

ANXIETY EVOLVED AS A MECHANISM FOR QUICKLY RESPONDING TO ATTACK OR PERIL. ITS DESPERATION WAS NOT MEANT TO BE SUSPENDED INDEFINITELY UNTIL APATHETIC. CHRONIC ANXIETY IS A MENTAL DISORDER. IT IS NEUROSIS; MASS NEUROSIS WHEN CONVENTIONALIZED.

BY BELITTLING AND DEGRADING ANYONE'S INDIVIDUALITY, CONVENTIONALIZED SM GENERATES

A COMMON ANXIETY, THEN DIFFUSES IT DURING THE EARLY YEARS OF TRAINING. UNABLE TO RESOLVE OUR DESPERATION, WE FORCE IT OUT OF AWARENESS AND BECOME SERIOUS. THE CONVENTIONALIZED SM REINFORCES THIS SERIOUSNESS WITH RELIGIOUS AND POLITICAL DELUSIONS WHICH ACT EITHER AS A NARCOTIC TO ENCOURAGE APATHY OR AS A DECOY FOR THOSE WHOSE ENERGY WILL NOT DISSIPATE, THE DECOY DRAWING THEIR ANXIETIES OUT OF THE SUBCONSCIOUS AND FOCUSING THEM INTO A LUST FOR POWER AND GLORY.

THE DICHOTOMOUS ACTION OF THESE DELUSIONS ALLOWS CONVENTIONALIZED SM TO BREED TWO TYPES OF PEOPLE—THOSE WHO WILL LET THEMSELVES BE CONTROLLED AND THOSE WHO WANT TO CONTROL. THE POWER GAME ACQUIRES ITS PLAYERS, ALL OF THEM CHRONICALLY ANXIETY-RIDDEN, THE CONVENTION MAKES THE RULES, AND MASS NEUROSIS SETS THEM INTO ACTION.

THE SM OF SEXUAL FANTASY, EROTIC SM, IS MERELY A REFLECTION OF ITS CONVENTIONAL FORM. IT DOES NOT EXIST AS AN ELEMENT OF MASS NEUROSIS, BUT AS A COMPENSATION FOR IT. BY EROTICIZING THE CONVENTIONAL POWER GAME INTO A CONTEXT FOR FANTASY, SEXUAL SM ALLOWS THE PARTICIPANTS TO PLAY PARTS OF THE POWER GAME THEY AREN'T PLAYING IN THEIR EVERYDAY LIVES. USUALLY THE FANTASIES ALLOW THE PLAYERS TO TAKE ROLES OPPOSITE THOSE THEY HAVE IN REALITY, BUT OCCASIONALLY THE FANTASTY SIMPLY EXAGGERATES THE EVERYDAY ROLES TO AN EXTREME THAT REALITY WOULD NOT ALLOW. EITHER WAY, THE OBJECT IS TO RELEASE SUPRESSED EMOTIONS. FANTASIES ARE A RESPONSE TO UNRESOLVED ANXIETY, JUST AS ANXIETY IS A RESPONSE TO DANGER.

FANTASIZING LETS YOU FOCUS SOME DIFFUSE ANXIETY, GIVING IT A DIRECTION, AND RELEASE IT. DREAMS RELEASE THE SUBTLER ANXIETIES, THOSE ORIGINATING AND UNRESOLVED DURING THE COURSE OF A DAY OR TWO. THE LONGER THE ANXIETIES PERSIST, THE MORE FIXED THEY BECOME, REQUIRING MORE VIOLENT EMOTIONS TO RESOLVE THEM.

EROTIC SM'S MAJOR POTENTIAL IS IN ITS VIOLENCE. THE MORE INTENSE THE EROTIC SM, THE MORE VIOLENT THE EMOTIONS IT RELEASES. EROTIC SM THEREFORE HAS THE POTENTIAL TO RESOLVE SOME OF OUR MOST FIXATED ANXIETIES, INCLUDING THOSE THAT HAVE US SERVING OUR SOCIETY.

NO CONVENTIONAL SYSTEM WILL TOLERATE THIS. MASS NEUROSIS IS MORE DIFFICULT TO MAINTIAIN IF ITS CHRONIC ANXIETIES ARE BEING FOCUSED AND RESOLVED WITHOUT SOCIAL REGULATION, THUS LESSENING THE SERIOUSNESS OR APATHY WITH WHICH PEOPLE WILL SERVE. FOR THIS REASON ALONE, THE CONVENTION HAS DUPED ITS NEUROTIC MASSES INTO BELIEVING THAT FANTASY PLAY, ESPECIALLY EROTIC SM, IS MORE NEUROTIC THAN THEIR CONFORMITY.

•••

LORD PRESTON COMMUNICATED WITH ME TODAY. HIS VOICE, HIS INSTRUCTIONS LEFT ME WITH A RAGING BONE, YET HE HAD MY ENTIRE BODY SHIVERING AND WORRYING. I'M STILL SHAKING. I CAN SEE HIS GAME. I KNOW EXACTLY WHAT HE IS DOING, BUT IT CHANGES NONE OF MY REACTIONS. I STILL FEEL POWERLESS IN HIS PLAY, KNOWING HOW TO ESCAPE BUT LACKING THE WILL TO DO SO, EVEN AS I TRY TO CONVINCE MYSELF I AM ONLY CONTRIVING THIS. I CAN SEE ME TELLING MYSELF I WILL GET OVER HIM AND AT THE SAME TIME STEPPING INTO HIS PRESENCE, KNOWING IT TO BE A TRAP I MAY NEVER LEAVE.

HE MADE IT CLEAR HOW MUCH HE OWNS ME. WILL HE ACHIEVE HIS GOAL ONLY TO TOSS ME ASIDE LIKE SOME TOY THAT NO LONGER AMUSES HIM?

•••

I FEAR THE TOTALITY WITH WHICH THIS MAY FIXATE ME ON HIM. ALREADY HE HAS ME IN PLACES NO ONE HAS EVER HAD BEFORE. THIS NO LONGER FEELS LIKE A GAME. IT NEVER DID. I ONLY TOLD MYSELF IT DID. WHAT REALLY ALLOWS ME TO CONTINUE, BESIDES HIS OWN PERSONAL FORCE, IS THE FACT THAT HE HAS MADE IT CLEAR THAT THIS WILL NOT INTRUDE INTO MY RELATIONSHIP WITH DANIEL.

TO LORD PRESTON, DANIEL IS MERELY ANOTHER STALLION LORD PRESTON'S STALLION HAS TAKEN A STRONG FANCY TO.

•••

IT'S JUST AN IDEA, BUT IT STRUCK ME THAT ORIGINALLY GODS MAY HAVE ACTED AS A PRIMER FOR AGGRESSION, THE EROTICIZATION OF FEAR TRANSFIGURED INTO A FINAL POWER WE MUST FOREVER DEFEND OURSELVES AGAINST. THE FIRST GODS WERE LIKE THE PUNCHING BAGS WE WORK

OUT ON IN ORDER TO REMAIN MORE AGGRESSIVE THAN WE ARE BUT HAVE TO BE TO SURVIVE. IF THIS IS MORE THAN JUST AN INTUITIVE INSPIRATION, IF THERE IS A BASIC TRUTH HERE, THEN I NEED TO DETERMINE HOW THE PUNCHING BAGS BECAME OTHER PEOPLE LABELLED FREAKS, PERVERTS AND INFERIORS WHILE THE GODS MUTATED INTO JUSTIFICATIONS FOR THEIR PERSECUTION, DIVINE DISCIPLINARIANS COMPENSATING FOR OUR FAILURE TO REMAIN RESPONSIBLE FOR OURSELVES. IN ANY FORM, GODS WERE UNDOUBTEDLY INVENTED OUT OF A DESPERATION FOR POWER.

•••

SIR,

THE BRUISES LOOK BEAUTIFUL IN THE MIRROR, EVEN IF THEY HAVE DULLED UNDER THE DUST OF

NEW CELLS. THEY SEEM MORE A PART OF ME NOW AND MAKE ME LOOK LIKE AN ANIMAL. I SUSPENDED MYSELF BY THE NECK TO WATCH THEM AND HOW I MIGHT STRUGGLE, HOW I MIGHT LOOK IN YOUR EYE, ANGRY FOR AIR AND SUDDENLY PISSING IN THE TERROR OF YOUR REACTION AND HOW IT WOULD FEEL IF YOU WERE BEATING ME THEN. YOUR REACTION WAS ONLY A FANTASY, BUT I EASILY SPILLED EVEN THOUGH I COULD NOT BEAT MYSELF THE WAY YOU WOULD. I DIDN'T EVEN TRY, AND I DIDN'T ACTUALLY PISS IN TERROR UNTIL, STILL HANGING BY MY NECK AND TIED HAND-AND-FOOT, I TRIED FOR A SECOND COMING.

•

JASON KLEIN

EXCERPTS FROM BUGS, A NOVEL

39. TRAVELLING: ROBERTE WALKING SEEN FROM REAR.

40. EYES OF CORPULENT MAN WHO WALKS MORE SLOWLY.

41. ROBERTE'S HIPS, HER HANDS, ONE HOLDING BAG, THE OTHER SWINGING.

    41 BIS. PALM OF R.'S HAND SEEN BY CORPULENT MAN.

42. R. HESITATES IN FRONT OF TWO NEIGHBORING SHOPS.

42 BIS. WINDOW DISPLAY OF WOMEN'S BLOUSES.

43. THE CORPULENT MAN PLACES HIMSELF BETWEEN THE DOOR OF THE SHOP AND R.

44. (CLOSE UP) R.'S HAND ON THE DOOR KNOB.

45. THE DOOR OF THE NEIGHBORING SHOP, WINDOWS ROUGHLY PAINTED.

A STORY DEDICATED TO JASON

JASON SAID: "MAKE ME FEEL LIKE AN ANIMAL."

I AM SITTING IN MY LIVING ROOM. I HAVE TWO CATS. THE FEMALE IS IN HEAT. THE MALE POUNCES VIOLENTLY ON HER BACK, GRIPPING THE NAPE OF HER NECK BETWEEN SHARP TEETH. THE FEMALE IS CAUGHT IN A FURY OF CONTRADICTION; HER REAR END LIFTS UP INVITING HIS COCK TO ENTER HER, HER MOUTH SNARLS WITH ANGER AND SPITE. HE FUCKS HER SAVAGELY. THE SHARP, QUICK PLUNGES OF HIS PELVIS SLAM AGAINST HER WETNESS.

THAT IS WHAT JASON WANTS TO FEEL.

IT IS TOO SIMPLISTIC. HE WANTS MY BODY SLAMMING INTO HIS, BUT HE WANTS THE LUXURIES OF SPITE AND CHOICE.

JASON MAKES MANY MISTAKES.

HE CAN'T BE BLAMED FOR ALL OF THEM. HE THINKS THERE IS A REALITY AND A FANTASY WHICH EXIST IN CONTRADICTION TO ONE ANOTHER. HE BELIEVES HE LEAVES REALITY AND ENTERS FANTASY OF HIS OWN WILL, THAT THE FANTASY IS HIS CREATION AND HE MAINTAINS POWER OVER IT. HE THINKS THE GREATEST RISK HE TAKES IS THAT SOMEONE ELSE WILL NOT UNDERSTAND WHAT HIS FANTASY IS.

BUT JASON IS WRONG.

THERE ARE OTHER PEOPLE FOR WHOM THE REAL WORLD IS DAYLIGHT; A NINE-TO-FIVE JOB, A HOME, A LOVER. AT NIGHT THEY DON LEATHER CLOTHING AND THEY STALK THE BARS OF FOLSOM STREET OR THE BANKS OF THE HUDSON. ONCE HE HAD MET ME, JASON LOST THAT DICHOTOMY. HE HAS HAD TO LEARN THAT THE DAY TO DAY EXISTENCE HE HAD EXPERIENCED AS REALITY IS IN FACT HIS FANTASY. HIS DREAM WORLD IS THE SPHERE THAT ALLOWS HIM TO CONCEIVE OF HIMSELF AS HAVING A FREE WILL, MAKING DECISIONS, CREATING INDEPENDENT-LY. IT IS ENTIRELY FALSE. HIS NEW REALITY IS THE SOUND OF MY VOICE AS I STAND IN FRONT OF HIM OR AS IT IS TRANSPORTED THREE THOUSAND MILES BY TELEPHONE WIRE. THE WAVES THAT CARRY MY WORDS TO HIM SHATTER HIS WORLD AND CREATE THEIR OWN WORLD WHICH HE MUST NOW INHABIT.

THERE IS A JASON WHO DOES NOT EXIST WITHOUT ME.

IT IS THE PERSON WHO HEARS MY WORDS AND TREMBLES AT THE SOUNDS, SHUDDERS AT THE CONTENT. IT IS A BODY THAT IS ALLOWED NO LIMITATIONS TO ITS USE. IT IS A SHELL THAT I FILL WITH MY LUST, MY SELF, MY POWER. AND JASON DOES NOT CONTROL IT COMING AND GOING. AT OTHER TIMES WITH OTHER MEN HE CAN CHOOSE HIS REALITY. HE CAN CHOOSE TO BE IN AN OFFICE WORKING, WITH A LOVER HAVING DINNER, WITH A TRICK ACTING AS THOUGH HE WERE A MASTER. HE CANNOT DO THAT WITH THIS PERSON THAT I COMMAND INTO EXISTENCE. THIS IS ONE PLACE WHERE JASON HAS NO POWER.

•••

WHEN I WOKE THIS MORNING THERE WAS A PAIN IN MY KNEE. I DON'T KNOW WHERE IT CAME FROM. BUT IT, IT AND EVERY PAIN I FEEL, REMINDS ME OF JASON. AS SOON AS I THINK OF AN ACHE, A SORE, A SENSATION OF ANY KIND OTHER THAN PLEASURE, I THINK OF JASON. I WANT TO KNOW HOW TO RECREATE IT IN HIS BODY. I CALL MY DOCTOR FRIEND IN BOSTON: "HOW CAN I MAKE JASON FEEL THIS WAY?" HE TELLS ME.

•••

I TELL JASON: "I AM GOING TO TAKE YOU TO THE PLACE WHERE YOU WILL CRY WHEN I WALK INTO A ROOM."

HE SAYS: "I'M ALREADY THERE."

•••

BUT I DO NOT WANT TO TERRORIZE JASON. IT WOULD BE TOO EASY. AND HE THINKS HE WANTS IT. IT IS NOT ENOUGH. I DO NOT WANT TO PLAY SEXROOM GAMES WITH HIM; HE CAN LEAVE THAT BEHIND. I DO NOT WANT TO JUST EXPLORE HIS BODY. I WANT TO EXPLORE HIS MIND AND TAKE HOLD OF THAT PART WHICH I HAVE CREATED. I WANT TO GRIP IT WITH A HARD GRASP AND PULL IT OUT, SCULPT IT, MAKE HIM HORRIFIED THAT IT EXISTS OUTSIDE HIM. AND THEN, ONLY THEN, PUT IT BACK INTO HIS MIND. BUT WHEN IT'S THERE IT WILL STILL BE MINE. I WILL HAVE IT WHENEVER I WANT IT. WHATEVER ELSE HE DOES, WHEREVER ELSE HE GOES, WHATEVER ELSE HE THINKS, THERE WILL ALWAYS BE THIS PART OF HIS BEING THAT EXISTS OUTSIDE HIS POWER. HE CANNOT RESIST MY TAKING IT. HE CANNOT REVOLT AGAINST WHAT I DO WITH IT.

MY FRIEND SAID: "YOU WILL BREAK HIM."

I SAID: "HE WAS ALREADY BROKEN. I AM MAKING HIM WHOLE."

BUT I THOUGHT ABOUT IT. I THOUGHT ABOUT HIS BODY AND HIS SELF AND SHOOK WITH THE INTENSITY OF MY POWER AND THE FURY OF MY CONTROL.

•••

"MAKE ME FEEL LIKE AN ANIMAL," JASON SAID.

WHEN THE FEMALE CAT IS OUT OF HEAT SHE ADORES ME. I SIT READING A BOOK IN MY CHAIR AND SHE CLIMBS UP ON MY LAP. SHE PURRS AT THE FEEL OF MY WARM GROIN. AT NIGHT SHE SOMETIMES CRAWLS UNDER MY COVERS AND CURLS AGAINST MY STOMACH. SHE SENSES GREAT PROTECTION. THE HUGE BODY THAT IS MINE SEEMS TO HER TO BE A SOURCE OF HEAT AND DEFENSE. WHEN I'VE BEEN OUT AND RETURN TO THE APARTMENT SHE CIRCLES THE ROOM SCREECHING LOUDLY, DESPERATE FOR ME TO PICK HER UP AND HOLD HER AGAINST MY CHEST. SHE NEEDS THE REASSURANCE OF MY TOUCH.

THIS IS THE ANIMAL I CREATE IN JASON.

BUT MY POWER DOES NOT COME FROM THE CARE I GIVE THE CAT—NOR THE CARE JASON THINKS I GIVE HIM. THE POWER COMES FROM WHAT I DO NOT DO. THE CAT THINKS I AM HER BENEFACTOR. I AM ONLY AWARE OF WHAT WOULD HAPPEN IF I ROLLED OVER ON HER BODY AND SUFFOCATED HER. OR, HOW VULNERABLE SHE IS WHEN SHE ALLOWS ME TO HOLD HER ON HER BACK IN SUCH A WAY THAT I COULD DROP HER AND SHE WOULDN'T BE ABLE TO RIGHT HERSELF BEFORE SHE LANDED ON THE FLOOR. OR, THAT SHE WOULD STARVE IF I DID NOT RETURN AND FEED HER.

•••

THE PART OF JASON THAT IS MINE LIVES ONLY THROUGH ME. MY FRIEND SAID: "YOU ARE PLAYING GOD."

"I KNOW."

I HAVE CREATED A PART OF JASON THAT IS MINE. IT

IS THE ONLY LIFE THAT I WILL EVER CREATE BY MYSELF. IT IS SOMETHING THAT NO ONE ELSE CAN HAVE, CAN FEEL, WILL EVER SEE. IT IS AN ACT OF CREATION THAT IS ENTIRELY INDIVIDUAL. IT DOES NOT RELY ON THE HETEROSEXUAL ACT OF PROCREATION. IT IS MINE; MINE ALONE, IT IS FINER THAN THE CREATION OF A BABY.

•••

MY LOVER HISSES AT ME: "YOU GODDAM SADIST!"

I SMILE.

WHEN I AM WITH MY LOVER I MERGE WITH HIM TO CREATE A NEW FORCE: THE SYNERGY OF LOVE. I DO LOVE HIM. I HOLD HIM CLOSE AT NIGHT AND WONDER AT HIS FEEL. I WHIP HIS BACK AND ASS AND MARK HIM WITH LOVE. HIS SUBMISSION IS OUR UNION WITH MY DOMINANCE. HE BECOMES A BOY. WE STAY TWO MEN IN LOVE. HE SUCKS MY COCK GREEDILY. I TAKE HIS ASS WITH MY COCK, MY FIST, WHATEVER. WE ARE TOGETHER; HE IS MINE; I AM HIS. WE PLAN THE FUTURE. I LISTEN TO HIM CAREFULLY. I INCORPORATE HIS DESIRES. HE ACTS OUT MY WISHES. WE CREATE MORE TOGETHER THAN WE ARE SEPARATELY.

•••

JASON DOES NOT EXIST WITHOUT ME.

I DO NOT BEAT JASON WITH LOVE. HE IS SIMPLY A BODY. I TAKE FROM HIM. ALL THE EGO, ALL THE SPITE, ALL THE ANGER. I WILL TAKE HIM BEYOND ALL THOSE POINTS. IN MY PRESENCE THE ONLY JASON THAT EXISTS IS WHAT I HAVE CREATED. HE CANNOT RECLAIM THE OLD. HE CAN ONLY EXIST IN THE NEW.

•••

I CALL JASON: "I WANT YOU TO DO SOMETHING."

PAUSE.

"DO I HAVE TO AGREE BEFORE YOU TELL ME?"

SILENCE.

"YES."

IT DOESN'T MATTER WHOSE MOUTH UTTERED THE WORD, "YES." I AM THE ONE WHO SAID IT.

•••

MY FRIEND SAYS: "HE'LL END UP INSANE."

"HE ALREADY IS."

•••

I TELL JASON: "YOU MAY END UP HATING ME."

HE SAYS: "I DON'T KNOW THE DIFFERENCE BETWEEN HATE AND LOVE."

BUT LOVE ISN'T WHAT I WANT FROM JASON ANYWAY.

•••

"WHAT WILL YOU DO TO HIM WHEN YOU GO TO CALIFORNIA?" MY FRIEND ASKS.

I SAY: "I'LL SHOW HIM THAT HE EXISTS ONLY AT MY WHIM."

"WOULD YOU KILL HIM?"

"NO. BUT I HAVE DREAMT ABOUT IT."

"ISN'T HE FRIGHTENED OF YOU?"

"ABSOLUTELY."

"WHY DOESN'T SOMEONE STOP YOU?"

"WHO?"

"WHAT DOES HE GET FROM ALL THIS?"

"LIFE."

•••

IT IS ALL SOME FORM OF COMPENSATION. THE MOST PROFOUND TRUTHS ARE THE EXISTENCE OF YIN AND YANG. WITH MY LOVE THE COMPLIMENTARY PARTS ARE OBVIOUS. OUR RELATIONSHIP REMAINS A BALANCE. WITH JASON THE ONLY ORDER IS THAT WHICH I IMPOSE. I HAVE A LOVER TO BECOME MORE WHOLE; TO SENSE COMMUNION WITH SOMEONE. I AM MY LOVER'S MASTER; WE ARE EQUALS. THE

CONTRADICTIONS OF LIFE CAN BE ACCOMODATED. BUT NOT WITH JASON. I HARDEN AT THE REMEMBRANCE OF HIS NAME; I AM FORCED INTO A SENSE OF RESPONSIBILITY THAT OVERWHELMS ANY SEMBLENCE OF FRIVOLITY. I AM TOTALLY FOCUSED. I MUST BE. I CANNOT LEAVE THIS ROLE OR THAT PART OF JASON THAT IS MINE WOULD BE CRUSHED.

•••

MY FRIEND SAYS: "YOU CANNOT DO THIS TO ANOTHER HUMAN BEING."

I SAY: "HE'S NOT A HUMAN BEING. HE'S JASON."

"YOU HAVE TO RESPECT ANYONE THAT YOU LOVE."

"I DON'T LOVE HIM. I POSSESS HIM."

•••

I SIT IN NEW YORK IN MY ROOM, MY READING IS INTERRUPTED BY A PLEASANT THOUGHT OF JASON. HE'S WAITING FOR MY ARRIVAL. IT WON'T OCCUR FOR ANOTHER THREE WEEKS. I SMILE. HE MUST BE QUIVERING WITH EVERY THOUGHT OF ME. I STAND UP AND GO TO MY DESK. I FIND A SET OF LONG, STEEL PINS. I ADDRESS AN ENVELOPE TO JASON AND WALK OUT TO MAIL IT. THERE IS NO NOTE. JUST THE RETURN ADDRESS. WHEN HE RECEIVES THE PINS HE'LL KNOW THEY'RE FROM ME AND I IMAGINE WHAT HE'LL DO.

HE WILL OPEN THE ENVELOPE AND STAND THERE WITH THE THIN, SHARP METAL IN HIS HANDS. HE WILL CRY SOBBINGLY. I IMAGINE HIM STANDING THERE WITH DEEP GASPS IN HIS CHEST AND RIVERS OF TEARS FLOWING DOWN HIS CHEEKS.

I NEVER GIVE JASON THE SATISFACTION OF PREDICTABILITY. WHEN HE GETS THE PINS FROM ME HE WILL HAVE NO WAY OF KNOWING WHAT I INTEND TO USE THEM FOR. I COULD DO ANYTHING WITH HIM AND THEM. AND HE KNOWS THAT NOW. THE UTTER HORROR OF THE POSSIBILITIES WILL OVERWHELM HIM.

•••

MY FRIENDS SAYS: "BUT ANY RELATIONSHIP HAS TO HAVE A BASE OF SANITY."

I SAY: "THAT'S DOUG."

"BUT JASON . . ."

"JASON IS NOT A RELATIONSHIP. IT'S OWNERSHIP."

•••

I CALLED JASON. "A FRIEND OF MINE IS COMING TO SAN FRANCISCO. HE'S GOING TO WHIP YOU."

HE REPLIES: "WHERE DO I GO? WHEN?"

MY FRIEND SAYS: "WHEN YOU'RE WITH YOUR LOVER YOU TALK ABOUT WHERE YOU'RE GOING TO LIVE, WHAT YOU'RE GOING TO DO, HOW YOU'RE GOING TO FULFILL YOUR FANTASIES. WHAT DO YOU SAY TO JASON?"

"NOTHING. I BEAT HIM."

•••

HOW COULD ANYONE POSSIBLY KNOW WHAT IT MEANS FOR JASON TO HEAR MY VOICE?

WHENEVER IT RAINS, MY CAT HIDES IN THE BATHROOM, CROUCHING VULNERABLY BEHIND THE TOILET. HER MIND CANNOT FATHOM THE FORCES OF NATURE THAT BRING WATER FROM THE SKY AND ILLUMINATE THE NIGHT WITH BOOMS OF THUNDERED LIGHTNING.

"MAKE ME FEEL LIKE AN ANIMAL," JASON PLEADS.

AND I DO. HE IS LIKE MY CAT, TOTALLY UNABLE TO ALTER OR CONTROL THE FORCES OF MY VIOLENT NATURE. JASON EXISTS IN UTTER HORROR IN MY PRESENCE. THERE IS NO REASON FOR WHAT WILL HAPPEN TO HIM, THERE IS NO WAY FOR HIM TO DECIDE WHAT WILL BE DONE. THIS BODY THAT HE THINKS IS HIS PASSES FROM HIS SELF-CONTROL INTO MY UTTER DOMINATION. MY PRESENCE ALTERS THE VERY FOUNDATION OF HIS BEING.

•••

WHAT DOES JASON FEEL LIKE WHEN I AM THERE?

HIS SKIN CANNOT TOLERATE CLOTHING SEPARATING IT FROM MY EYES. HE CANNOT CONCEIVE OF HIMSELF SITTING ANYWHERE BUT AT MY FEET. ALL FORMS OF HUMAN COMMUNICATON BECOME INTOLERABLE TO HIM. THEY ARE INSUFFICIENT. JUST LIKE MY CAT HE MAKES STRANGE NOISES AND

HOPES I WILL UNDERSTAND THE EQUIVALENT OF PURRING THAT COMES FROM HIM WHENEVER I AM NOT GIVING HIM PAIN. JUST LIKE MY CAT HE LICKS MY BODY IN GRATITUDE FOR THE VERY STUFF OF EXISTENCE THAT I PROVIDE. HE WINDS HIS BODY AROUND MINE HOPING IT WILL BE SO CLOSE TO MINE THAT I WON'T HURT IT. HIS MOUTH FINDS THE SWEAT OF MY BODY THE SWEETEST TASTE IT HAS KNOWN.

THERE IS A PART OF JASON FOR WHOM I AM THE ONLY SOURCE OF FOOD, SHELTER, NURTURE. HE IS BECOMING MORE AND MORE AWARE OF IT. IT AWES HIM. IT HORRIFIES HIM. IT ENTRAPS HIM. IT OVERWHELMS HIM.

...

JASON SAYS: "MAKE ME FEEL LIKE AN ANIMAL."

JOHN PRESTON

46. R. ENTERS THE SHOP WHICH HAS NOTHING IN IT.

47. R. SHOWS HER ASTONISHMENT.

48. THE CORPULENT MAN, INSIDE SHOP, AGAINST MAIN DOOR.

49. AT THE REAR OF THE SHOP, A DOOR HALF OPENS, A SQUAT YOUNG MAN PUTS HIS HEAD THROUGH, WITHDRAWS.

50. R. GOES QUICKLY TOWARD THE HALF-OPEN DOOR.

51. LANDING OF A WIDE STAIRCASE, STEPS GOING STRAIGHT UP TO A CARRIAGE DOOR GIVING ON TO THE STREET.

52. THE BALUSTRADE OF THE STAIRCASE R. BEGINS TO CLIMB.

53. THE SQUAT MAN, A FEW STEPS ABOVE, BRINGS HIS HAND DOWN ON R.'S HAND HOLDING THE BALUSTRADE.

THE OEDIPUS COMPLEX

THROUGH THE DISCOVERY OF OEDIPAL FACTS IN THE ANALYSIS OF NEUROTICS FREUD GAVE BIRTH TO THE CONCEPT OF THE COMPLEX. CONSIDERING THE NUMBER OF PSYCHIC RELATIONS THAT IT INVOLVES, AT MORE THAN ONE POINT IN THIS WORK, THE OEDIPUS COMPLEX ASSERTS ITSELF, BOTH UPON OUR STUDY (IT SPECIFICALLY DEFINES THE PSYCHICAL RELATIONS OF THE HUMAN FAMILY)— AND UPON OUR CRITIQUE (FREUD GIVES THIS PSYCHOLOGICAL ELEMENT AS THE SPECIFIC FORM OF THE HUMAN FAMILY AND SUBORDINATES TO IT ALL ITS OTHER SOCIAL VARIATIONS). THE METHODIC ORDER PROPOSED HERE, AS MUCH AS IN THE CONSIDERATION OF MENTAL STRUCTURES AS IN SOCIAL FACTS, WILL LEAD TO A REVISION OF THE COMPLEX ENABLING ONE TO SITUATE THE PATERNAL FAMILY IN HISTORY AND FURTHER ILLUMINATE CONTEMPORARY NEUROSIS.

SCHEMA OF THE COMPLEX

PSYCHOANALYSIS HAS REVEALED INSTINCTUAL GENITAL DRIVES IN CHILDREN THAT REACH THEIR PEAK AT THE AGE OF FOUR YEARS. WITHOUT EXPANDING ON THEIR STRUCTURE HERE, LET US SAY THAT THEY CONSTITUTE A TYPE OF PSYCHOLOGICAL PUBERTY, VERY PREMATURE, WE SHALL SEE, IN RELATION TO PHYSIOLOGICAL PUBERTY. THESE GENITAL DRIVES, TAKING HOLD OF THE CHILD BY A SEXUAL DESIRE TOWARD THE CLOSEST OBJECT WHICH PESENCE AND INTEREST NORMALLY AFFORD HIM—NAMELY THE PARENT OF THE OPPOSITE SEX—GIVE THEIR ORIGINS TO THE COMPLEX; THEIR FRUSTRATION FORMS THE CRUX. ALTHOUGH THIS FRUSTRATION IS INHERENT TO THE ESSENTIAL PREMATURATION OF THESE DRIVES, THE CHILD ASSOCIATES IT TO A THIRD PARTY WHOSE SAME CONDITIONS OF PRESENCE AND INTEREST NORMALLY INDICATE TO HIM AN OBSTACLE TO THE SATISFACTION OF THESE DRIVES: NAMELY, THE PARENT OF THE SAME SEX.

THE FRUSTRATION SUFFERED BY THE CHILD IS ORDINARILY ACCOMPANIED BY AN EDUCATIONAL REPRESSION WHOSE GOAL IS THE PREVENTION OF MATERIALIZATION OF THESE DRIVES, ESPECIALLY THEIR MASTURBATORY MATERIALIZATION. ON THE OTHER HAND, THE CHILD ACQUIRES A CERTAIN INTUITION OF THE SITUATION FORBIDDEN HIM, AS MUCH BY THE DISCRETE AND DIFFUSE SIGNS THAT BETRAY PARENTAL RELATIONS TO HIS SENSIBILITY

AS BY THE INOPPORTUNE ACCIDENTS [LES HASARDS INTEMPESTIFS] THAT UNVEIL THEM TO HIM. IN THIS DOUBLE PROCESS, THE PARENT OF THE SAME SEX APPEARS TO THE CHILD AT ONCE AS THE AGENT OF THE SEXUAL INTERDICTION AND AS THE EXAMPLE OF ITS TRANSGRESSION.

THE TENSION THUS CONSTITUTED IS DISSOLVED, ON ONE SIDE, BY REPRESSION OF THE SEXUAL TENDENCY THAT FROM THEN WILL REMAIN LATENT UNTIL PUBERTY—GIVING WAY TO NEUTRAL INTERESTS, EMINENTLY FAVORABLE TO THE EDUCATIONAL PROCESS; AND ON THE OTHER SIDE, BY THE SUBLIMATION OF THE PARENTAL IMAGE THAT PERPETUATES A REPRESENTATIVE IDEAL IN THE CONSCIENCE, GUARANTEED OF THE FUTURE COINCIDENCE OF PSYCHIC AND PHYSIOLOGICAL ATTITUDES AT THE MOMENT OF PUBERTY. THIS DOUBLE PROCESS HAS FUNDAMENTAL GENETIC IMPORTANCE, SINCE IT REMAINS INSCRIBED IN THE PSYCHE IN TWO PERMANENT AGENCIES: THAT WHICH REPRESSES CALLS ITSELF THE SUPEREGO, THAT WHICH SUBLIMATES, THE EGO-IDEAL. THEY REPRESENT THE COMPLETION OF THE OEDIPAL CRISIS.

THE OBJECTIVE VALUE OF THE COMPLEX

THIS ESSENTIAL SCHEMA OF THE COMPLEX RESPONDS TO A GREAT NUMBER OF GIVENS IN EXPERIENCE. THE EXISTENCE OF INFANTILE SEXUALITY IS HENCEFORTH NOT CONTESTED; MOREOVER, BECAUSE IT IS HISTORICALLY REVEALED BY THOSE AFTEREFFECTS OF ITS EVOLUTION WHICH CONSTITUTE NEUROSIS, IT IS ACCESSIBLE TO THE MOST IMMEDIATE OBSERVATION, AND ITS AGE-OLD MISUNDERSTANDING [MÉCONNAISSANCE] IS AN IMPRESSIVE PROOF OF THE SOCIAL RELATIVITY OF HUMAN KNOWLEDGE. THE PSYCHIC AGENCIES THAT GO UNDER THE NAME OF "SUPEREGO" AND "EGO-IDEAL" WERE ISOLATED IN A CONCRETE ANALYSIS OF SYMPTOMS OF NEUROSIS, AND MANIFESTED THEIR SCIENTIFIC VALUE IN THE DEFINITION AND EXPLICATION OF PHENOMENA OF THE PERSONALITY; THERE IS IN THIS A POSITIVE ORDER OF DETERMINATION THAT ACCOUNTS FOR A GREAT NUMBER OF ANOMALIES OF HUMAN BEHAVIOUR, AND BY THE SAME TOKEN, FOR THESE DISORDERS, RENDERS OUTDATED THE REFERENCES TO THE ORGANIC ORDER WHICH, WHETHER FROM PURE PRINCIPLE OR SIMPLY FROM MYTHS, TAKES THE PLACE OF THIS EXPERIMENTAL METHOD WITH AN ENTIRE MEDICAL TRADITION.

IN TRUTH, THIS PREJUDICE WHICH ATTRIBUTES AN EPIPHENOMENAL CHARACTER TO THE PSYCHIC ORDER—THAT IS TO SAY AN INOPERATIVE ONE—WAS FAVORED BY AN INSUFFICIENT ANALYSIS OF THE FACTORS OF THIS ORDER, AND IT IS PRECISELY IN THE LIGHT OF THE OEDIPAL SITUATION THAT SUCH ACCIDENTS IN THE HISTORY OF THE SUBJECT TAKE ON THE IMPORTANCE AND THE SIGNIFICANCE THAT ALLOW THEM TO BRING OUT A PARTICULAR TRAIT OF THE PERSONALITY. WE CAN ALSO SPECIFY THAT SINCE THESE ACCIDENTS AFFECT THE OEDIPAL SITUATION AS TRAUMATISMS DURING THE EVOLUTION OF THE COMPLEX, THEY LATER REPEAT THEMSELVES AS EFFECTS OF THE SUPEREGO. IF THEY EFFECT IT AS ABNORMALITIES [ATYPIES] OF ITS CONSITUTION, THEY ARE MOST OFTEN REFLECTED IN THE FORMS OF THE EGO-IDEAL. THUS, LIKE INHIBITIONS OF CREATIVE ACTIVITY, OR INVERSIONS OF SEXUAL IMAGINATION, A GREAT NUMBER OF DISORDERS, MANY OF WHICH APPEAR ON THE LEVEL OF ELEMENTARY SOMATIC FUNCTIONS, HAVE FOUND THEIR THEORETIC AND THERAPEUTIC REDUCTION.

THE FAMILY ACCORDIG TO FREUD

THE DISCOVERY THAT DEVELOPMENTS OF SUCH IMPORTANCE TO MAN AS SEXUAL REPRESSION AND PSYCHIC SEXUALITY WERE SUBMITTED TO REGULATION AND TO ACCIDENTS OF A PSYCHIC DRAMA OF THE FAMILY FURNISHED THE MOST PRECIOUS CONTRIBUTION TO THE ANTHROPOLOGY OF FAMILY GROUPS, ESPECIALLY IN THE STUDY OF THE INTERDICTIONS UNIVERSALLY FORMULATED BY GROUPS WHICH GOVERN THE SEXUAL COMMERCE BETWEEN CERTAIN OF THEIR MEMBERS. BESIDES, FREUD WAS QUICK TO FORMULATE A THEORY OF THE FAMILY. IT WAS FOUNDED ON A DISSYMMETRY IN THE SITUATION OF THE SEXES IN RELATION TO OEDIPUS, APPARENT SINCE THE FIRST STUDIES. THE PROCESS THAT GOES FROM OEDIPAL DESIRE TO ITS REPRESSION DOES NOT APPEAR AS SIMPLY AS I HAVE JUST PRESENTED, EXCEPT IN THE MALE CHILD. IT IS ALSO THE MALE CHILD WHO IS CONSTANTLY TAKEN AS A SUBJECT IN THE DIDACTIC EXPOSÉS ON THIS COMPLEX.

THE OEDIPAL DESIRE APPEARS, IN EFFECT, MUCH STRONGER IN THE BOY AND THEREFORE FOR THE MOTHER. ON THE OTHER HAND, IN ITS MECHANISM, THE REPRESSION REVEALS TRAITS WHICH IN THEIR TYPICAL FORM AT FIRST SEEM ONLY JUSTIFIABLE IF THEY ARE EXERCISED BETWEEN FATHER AND SON. THIS IS THE FACT OF THE CASTRATION COMPLEX.

THE CASTRATION COMPLEX

THIS REPRESSION OPERATES BY A DOUBLE EMOTIONAL MOVEMENT OF THE SUBJECT: AGGRESSION AGAINST THE PARENT IN REGARD TO WHOM THE CHILD'S SEXUAL DESIRE PLACES HIM AS A RIVAL; SECONDARY FEAR, SUFFERED IN RETURN, OF A LIKE AGGRESSION. THUS A FANTASY UNDERLIES THESE TWO MOVEMENTS, SO REMARKABLE THAT IT WAS INDIVIDUALIZED WITH THEM IN A COMPLEX CALLED CASTRATION. IF THIS TERM IS JUSTIFIED BY REGRESSIVE AND REPRESSIVE ENDS THAT ARISE AT THIS MOMENT OF OEDIPUS, IT IS HOWEVER HARDLY CONSISTENT WITH THE FANTASY THAT MAKES OF IT THE ORIGINAL FACT.

THIS FANTASY CONSISTS ESSENTIALLY IN THE MUTILATION OF A MEMBER, THAT IS TO SAY IN A MALTREATMENT THAT CAN ONLY SERVE TO CASTRATE THE MALE. BUT THE APPARENT REALITY OF THIS DANGER, COMBINED WITH THE FACT THAT THE THREAT IS REALLY FORMULATED BY AN EDUCATIONAL TRADITION, MUST HAVE LED FREUD TO CONCEIVE IT AS EXPERIENCED FIRST FOR ITS REAL VALUE, AND THEN RECOGNIZED IN A FEAR INSPIRED FROM ONE MALE TO ANOTHER, IN FACT BY THE FATHER, THE PROTOTYPE OF THE OEDIPAL REPRESSION.

IN THIS WAY FREUD RECEIVED A SUPPORT FOR A SOCIOLOGICAL GIVEN: NOT ONLY DOES THE INTERDICTION OF INCEST WITH THE MOTHER HAVE A UNIVERSAL CHARACTER (ACROSS THE INFINITELY DIVERSE AND OFTEN PARADOXICAL FAMILY RELATIONS THAT PRIMITIVE CULTURES IMPRESS WITH THE TABOO OF INCEST) BUT NO MATTER WHAT THE LEVEL OF MORAL CONSCIENCE IS IN A CIVILIZATION, THIS INTERDICTION IS ALWAYS EXPRESSLY FORMULATED AND ITS TRANSGRESSION IS STRUCK WITH CONSTANT REPROBATION. THIS IS WHY FRAZIER UNCOVERED THE PRIMORIDIAL LAW OF HUMANITY IN THE TABOO OF THE MOTHER.

THE ORIGINAL MYTH OF PARRICIDE

IT IS FROM HERE THAT FREUD MAKES THE THEORETICAL JUMP WHOSE ABUSE WE HAVE INDICATED IN OUR INTRODUCTION; FROM THE CONJUGAL FAMILY THAT HE OBSERVED AMONG HIS SUBJECTS TO A HYPOTHETICAL PRIMITIVE FAMILY CONCEIVED AS A HORDE, THAT A MALE DOMINATES BY A BIOLOGICAL SUPERIORITY IN THE MONOPOLI-

ZATION OF NUBILE WOMEN. FREUD BUILDS UPON THE RELATION THAT IS ESTABLISHED BETWEEN TABOOS AND OBSERVANCES IN REGARDS TO THE TOTEM, IN TURN THE OBJECT OF INVIOLABILITY AND SACRIFICAL ORGY. HE IMAGINES A DRAMA—MURDER OF THE FATHER BY THE SONS—FOLLOWED BY A POSTHUMOUS CONSECRATION OF THE FATHER'S POWER OVER WOMEN BY THE MURDERERS, PRISONERS OF AN INSOLUBLE RIVALRY: A PRIMORDIAL EVENT, OUT OF WHICH TOGETHER WITH THE TABOO OF THE MOTHER, AN ENTIRE MORAL AND CULTURAL TRADITION WOULD COME.

EVEN IF THIS CONSTRUCTION WAS NOT SPOILED BY THE ONLY CIRCULAR REASONING THAT IT INVOLVES—ATTRIBUTING TO A BIOLOGICAL GROUP THE POSSIBILITY OF RECOGNIZING A LAW, PRECISELY WHAT NEEDS TO BE EXPLAINED—THESE SO-CALLED BIOLOGICAL PREMISES, NAMELY THE PERMANENT TYRANY EXERCISED BY THE CHIEF OF THE HORDE, WOULD REDUCE TO AN INCREASINGLY UNCERTAIN PHANTOM IN PROPORTION TO THE ADVENCEMENT THEY WOULD OFFER TO OUR KNOWLEDGE OF MAN. BUT ABOVE ALL, THE PRESENT UNIVERSAL TRACES AND THE ENDURING SURVIVAL OF A MATRIARCHAL FAMILY STRUCTURE, ITS APPEARANCE IN ALL THE FUNDAMENTAL FORMS OF CULTURE AND ESPECIALLY IN AN OFTEN EXTREMELY STRICT REPRESSION OF SEXUALITY, DEMONSTRATE THAT THE ORDER OF THE HUMAN FAMILY HAS SOME FOUNDATIONS PRESERVED FROM THE FORCE OF THE MALE.

IT SEEMS, HOWEVER, THAT THE GREAT HARVEST OF FACTS WHICH THE OEDIPAL COMPLEX HAS LED TO BE OBJECTIFIED OVER THE PAST FIFTY YEARS COULD CLARIFY THE PSYCHOLOGICAL STRUCTURE OF THE FAMILY FURTHER THAN THE HASTY INTUITIONS WE HAVE JUST PRESENTED.

THE FUNCTIONS OF THE COMPLEX: A PSYCHOLOGICAL REVISION

THE OEDIPAL COMPLEX MARKS ALL LEVELS OF THE PSYCHE, BUT THE THEORETICIANS OF PSYCHOANALYSIS HAVE YET TO UNAMBIGUOUSLY DEFINE ITS COMPOSITE FUNCTIONS; IT IS FOR WANT OF HAVING SUFFICIENTLY DISTINGUISHED THE PLANES OF DEVELOPMENT WITH WHICH THEY EXPLAIN THE COMPLEX. IF THE COMPLEX APPEARS TO THEM, IN EFFECT, AS THE AXIS ALONG WHICH THE EVOLUTION OF SEXUALITY IS PROJECTED ONTO THE CONSTITUTION OF REALITY, THESE TWO PLANES DIVERGE WITH

SPECIFIC INCIDENCE IN MAN. THIS POINT OF INCIDENCE IS CERTAINLY KNOWN TO THE THEORETICIANS AS THE REPRESSION OF SEXUALITY AND THE SUBLIMATION OF REALITY, BUT SHOULD BE INTEGRATED INTO A MORE RIGOROUS CONCEPTION OF THESE STRUCTURAL RELATIONS: THE ROLE OF MATURATION PLAYED BY THE COMPLEX ON EACH OF THESE PLANES CAN ONLY BE TAKEN APPROXIMATELY AS PARALLEL.

MATURATION OF SEXUALITY

THE PSYCHICAL APPARATUS OF SEXUALITY IS FIRST REVEALED IN THE CHILD IN THE MOST ABBERANT FORMS RELATIVE TO ITS BIOLOGICAL ENDS, AND THE SUCCESSION OF THESE FORMS IS EVIDENCE THAT SEXUALITY CONFORMS TO THE GENITAL ORGANIZATION BY A PROGRESSIVE MATURATION. THIS SEXUAL MATURATION CONDITIONS THE OEDIPAL COMPLEX BY FORMING ITS FUNDAMENTAL TENDENCIES, BUT INVERSELY, THE COMPLEX FAVORS SEXUALITY BY DIRECTING IT TOWARD ITS OBJECTS.

THE MOVEMENT OF THE OEDIPUS COMPELX OPERATES THROUGH A TRIANGULAR CONFLICT IN THE SUBJECT: WE HAVE ALREADY SEEN THE PLAY OF TENDENCIES THAT ARISE OUT OF WEANING [SEVRAGE] PRODUCE A FORMATION OF THIS SORT: IT IS ALSO THE MOTHER, THE FIRST OBJECT OF THE TENDENCIES, AS FOOD TO BE ABSORBED AND EVEN AS BREAST IN WHICH TO BE REABSORBED, WHICH IS FIRST CFFERED UP TO THE OEDIPAL DESIRES. THUS ONE UNDERSTANDS THAT OEDIPAL DESIRE IS BETTER CHARACTERIZED IN THE MALE, BUT ALSO THAT IT ALLOWS HIM A SINGULAR OPPORTUNITY FOR THE REACTIVISATION OF THE WEANING TENDENCIES, THAT IS TO SAY A SEXUAL REGRESSION. THESE TENDENCIES DO NOT MERELY CONSTITUTE A PSYCHOLOGICAL IMPASSE; HERE, IN ADDITION, THEY OPPOSE THEMSELVES PARTICULARLY TO THE ATTITUDE OF EXTERIORIZATION, WHICH CONFORMS TO THE ACTIVITY OF THE MALE.

ON THE CONTRARY, IN THE OTHER SEX, WHERE THESE TENDENCIES HAVE A POSSIBLE ISSUE IN THE BIOLOGICAL DESTINY OF THE SUBJECT—THE MATERNAL OBJECT—THE DIVERSION OF A PART OF THE OEDIPAL DESIRE CERTAINLY TENDS TO NEUTRALIZE THE POTENTIAL OF THE COMPLEX, AND THEREBY ITS SEXUALIZATION EFFECTS. BUT, BY IMPOSING A CHANGE OF OBJECT, THE GENITAL DRIVE BETTER DETACHES ITSELF FROM THE

PRIMITIVE DRIVES, AND ALL THE MORE EASILY SINCE IT DOES NOT HAVE TO REVERSE THE ATTITUDE OF INTERNALIZATION INHERITED FROM THEM, DRIVES THAT ARE NARCISSISTIC. THUS ONE ARRIVES AT THE AMBIGUOUS CONCLUSION THAT FROM ONE SEX TO THE OTHER, THE MORE THE FORMATION OF THE COMPLEX IF ACCUSED, THE RISKIER ITS ROLE IN THE SEXUAL ADAPTATION SEEMS TO BECOME.

THE CONSTITUTION OF REALITY

HERE WE SEE THE INFLUENCE OF THE PSYCHOLOGICAL COMPLEX ON A VITAL RELATION, AND FROM THIS PONT THE COMPLEX CONTRIBUTES TO THE CONSTITUTION OF REALITY. WHAT IT BRINGS TO REALITY IS REVEALED IN TERMS OF AN INTELLECTUALIST PSYCHOGENESIS: A CERTAIN EMOTIONAL DEPTH TO THE OBJECT. A DIMENSION WHICH, FORMING THE BASIS OF ALL SUBJECTIVE COMPREHENSION, WOULD NOT HAVE BEEN DISTINGUISHED FROM IT AS PHENOMENON IF THE TREATMENT OF MENTAL ILLNESSES HAD NOT MADE US GRASP IT AS SUCH—A PHENOMENON—BY ADVANCING AN ENTIRE SERIES OF ITS DEGRADATIONS TO THE LIMITS OF UNDERSTANDING.

IN ORDER TO ESTABLISH A NORM OF LIVED EXPERIENCE, THIS DIMENSION CAN ONLY BE RECONSTRUCTED BY METAPHORICAL INTUITIONS: A DENSITY THAT CONFERS EXISTENCE ONTO THE OBJECT, A PERSPECTIVE WHICH GIVES US A SENSE OF ITS DISTANCE, AND ALSO INSPIRES IN US A RESPECT FOR IT. BUT HIS DIMENSION IS SHOWN IN THE VACILLATIONS OF REALITY THAT FERTILIZE [FÉCONDITE] DELIRIUM: WHEN THE OBJECT TENDS TO CONFUSE ITSELF WITH THE EGO WHILE AT THE SAME TIME ABSORBING ITSELF IN FANTASY, WHEN IT APPEARS DECOMPOSED LIKE ONE OF THE SENTIMENTS THAT FORM THE SPECTRE OF UNREALITY, BEGINNING WITH SENTIMENTS OF STRANGENESS, DÉJÀ VU, JAMAIS VU, PASSING THROUGH FALSE RECOGNITIONS, ILLUSIONS OF A DOUBLE, SENTIMENTS OF DIVINITY, PARTICIPATION, AND INFLUENCE, INTUITIONS OF MEANING, AND ENDING UP WITH THE TWILIGHT OF THE WORLD, AN EMOTIONAL ABOLITION WHICH IS FORMALLY DESIGNATED IN GERMAN AS THE LOSS OF THE OBJECT (OBJEKTVERLUST).

PSYCHOANALYSIS EXPLAINS THESE EXTREMELY DIVERSE QUALITIES OF LIVED EXPERIENCE BY VARIATIONS IN THE QUALITY OF VITAL ENERGY

INVESTED INTO THE OBJECT BY DESIRE. THE FORMULA, AS VERBAL AS IT MAY APPEAR, RESPONDS TO A GIVEN IN PSYCHOANALYTIC PRACTICE: PSYCHOANALYSTS MUST RECKON WITH THIS CATHEXIS IN THE OPERATIONAL TRANSFERENCES OF THEIR CURE; WITH THE RESOURCES OFFERED BY THIS CATHEXIS THE ANALYST MUST BASE THE INDICATION OF THE TREATMENT. THUS ANALYSTS HAVE RECOGNIZED INDICES OF AN OVERLY NARCISSISTIC INVESTMENT OF THE LIBIDO THROUGH THE SYMPTOMS CITED ABOVE, WHILE THE FORMATION OF THE OEDIPUS COMPLEX APPEARED AS THE MOMENT AND THE PROOF OF A CATHEXIS SUFFICIENT FOR THE TRANSFERENCE.

THIS ROLE OF OEDIPUS WOULD CORRELATE WITH THE MATURATION OF SEXUALITY. THE ATTITUDE FOUNDED BY THE GENITAL TENDENCY WOULD CRYSTALLIZE THE VITAL RELATION TO REALITY, ACCORDING TO ITS NORMAL TYPE. THIS ATTITUDE IS CHARACTERIZED BY THE TERMS OF GIFT [DON] AND SACRIFICE, GRANDIOSE TERMS, BUT ONES WHOSE MEANING REMAINS AMBIGUOUS AND HESITANT BETWEEN DEFENSE AND RENUNCIATION. THROUGH THESE TERMS A BOLD CONCEPTION REDISCOVERS THE SECRET COMFORT OF A MORAL THEME; IN THE PASSAGE BETWEEN CAPTIVITY AND OBLAVITY THE VITAL TEST AND THE MORAL TEST ARE WANTONLY CONFUSED.

THIS CONCEPTION CAN DEFINE AN ANALOGICAL PSYCHOGENESIS. IT CONFORMS TO THE MOST MARKED LACK IN THE ANALYTIC DOCTRINE: NEGLECTING THE STRUCTURE IN ORDER TO BENEFIT THE DYNAMIC. HOWEVER, THE ANALYTIC EXPERIENCE OFFERS A CONTRIBUTION TO THE STUDY OF MENTAL FORMS BY DEMONSTRATING THEIR RELATION—WHETHER CONDITIONAL OR SOLUTIONAL—TO THE AFFECTIVE CRISES. BY DIFFERENTIATING THE FORMAL GAME OF THE COMPLEX, IT BECOMES POSSIBLE TO ESTABLISH A STEADIER RELATIONSHIP BETWEEN ITS FUNCTION AND THE STRUCTURE OF THE DRAMA ESSENTIAL TO IT.

REPRESSION OF SEXUALITY

IF IT MARKS THE SUMMIT OF INFANT SEXUALITY, THE OEDIDPAL COMPLEX IS ALSO THE PROVINCE OF REPRESSION, IN THAT IT REDUCES IMAGES TO A STATE OF LATENCY UNTIL PUBERTY; IF IT DETERMINES A CONDENSATION OF REALITY IN THE DIRECTION OF LIFE, IT IS ALSO THE MOMENT OF SUBLIMATION WHERE MAN OPENS HIS OWN DISINTERESTED EXTENSION TO THIS REALITY.

THESE EFFECTS ARE PERPETUATED UNDER FORMS DESIGNATED AS THE SUPEREGO AND THE EDO-IDEAL, ACCORDING TO WHICH THEY ARE EITHER UNCONSCIOUS OR CONSCIOUS FOR THE SUBJECT. LET US SAY, THEY REPRODUCE THE IMAGO OF THE PARENT OF THE SAME SEX, THUS THE EGO-IDEAL CONTRIBUTES TO THE SEXUAL CONFORMISM OF THE PSYCHE. BUT ACCORDING TO THE DOCTRINE, THE IMAGO OF THE FATHER WOULD HAVE A PROTOTYPICAL ROLE IN THESE TWO FUNCTIONS ON ACCOUNT OF THE DOMINATION OF THE MALE.

IN TERMS OF THE REPRESSION OF SEXUALITY, WE HAVE INDICATED THAT THIS CONCEPTION RESTS ON THE FANTASY OF CASTRATION. IF THE DOCTRINE REFERS TO A REAL THREAT, IT IS ABOVE ALL THAT BECAUSE FREUD, INGENIOUSLY DYNAMIST AT IDENTIFYING TENDENCIES, REMAINS CLOSED BY TRADITIONAL ATOMISM TO THE NOTION OF THE ATOMISM OF FORMS. THUS, IN ODER TO OBSERVE IN BOTH SEXES THE EXISTENCE OF THE SAME FANTASY IN A SMALL GIRL OR OF A PHALLIC IMAGE OF THE MOTHER, HE IS CONSTRAINED TO EXPLAIN THESE FACTS BY PRECOCIOUS REVELATIONS OF THE DOMINATION OF THE MALE, REVELATIONS THAT WOULD LEAD THE LITTLE GIRL TO NOSTALGIA FOR VIRILITY, THE CHILD TO CONCEIVE OF ITS MOTHER AS VIRILE. THIS IS A GENESIS WHICH, IN ORDER TO FIND BASIS IN IDENTIFICATION, REQUIRES SUCH A SURCHARGE OF MECHANISMS FOR ITS PRACTICE THAT IT WOULD SEEM TO BE ERRONEOUS.

FANTASIES OF FRAGMENTATION

THE MATERIALS OF THE ANALYTIC EXPERIENCE SUGGESTS A DIFFERENT INTERPRETATION: THE FANTASY CASTRATION IS IN EFFECT PRECEDED BY A SERIES OF FANTASIES OF BODILY FRAGMENTATION WHICH REGRESSIVELY PROCEED FROM DISLOCATION TO DISMEMBERMENT, THROUGH EMASCULATION TO DISEMBOWLING, UP TO DEVORATION AND SHROUDING. THE EXAMINATION OF THESE FANTASIES REVEALS THAT THEY ARE INSCRIBED IN A SIMULTANEOUSLY DESTRUCTIVE AND INVESTIGATIVE FORM OF PENETRATION, ASPIRING TO THE SECRET OF THE MATERNAL BREAST, EVEN THOUGH THIS RELATION IS LIVED BY THE SUBJECT IN A MANNER WHOSE AMBIVALENCE IS PROPORTIONAL TO ITS ARCHAISM.

BUT RESEARCHERS WHO HAVE BEST UNDERSTOOD

THE MATERNAL ORIGINS OF THESE FANTASIES (MELANIE KLEIN) ARE ONLY CONCERNED WITH THE SYMMETRY AND THE EXTENSION THAT THEY BRING TO THE FORMATION OF OEDIPUS, REVEALING, FOR EXAMPLE, THE NOSTALGIA FOR MATERNITY IN THE BOY. FOR US, THEIR INTEREST LIES IN THE EVIDENT UNREALITY OF THEIR STRUCTURE; THE EXAMINATION OF THESE FANTASIES FOUND IN DREAMS AND CERTAIN IMPULSES ALLOWS FOR THE AFFIRMATION THAT THEY HAVE ABSOLUTELY NO RELATION TO A REAL BODY, BUT INSTEAD TO A HETEROCLITE MANNEQUIN, A BAROQUE DOLL, A TROPHY OF MEMBERS WHERE ONE MUST RECALL THE NARCISSISTIC OBJECT WHOSE GENESIS HAS BEEN EVOKED EARLIER; CONDITIONED IN MAN BY THE PRECESSION OF IMAGINARY FORMS OF THE BODY ON THE MASTERY OF THE ACTUAL BODY [LE CORPS PROPRE], BY THE DEFENSE VALUE THE SUBJECT GIVES TO THESE OBJECTS AGAINST THE ANXIETY OF VITAL DESTRUCTION, WHICH ARISE FROM THE PREMATURATION.

THE MATERNAL ORIGIN OF THE ARCHAIC SUPEREGO

THE FANTASY OF CASTRATION RELATES TO THIS SAME OBJECT. BORN BEFORE EITHER ANY MARKING OF THE ACTUAL BODY OR ANY DISTINCTION OF THE THREAT FROM THE ADULT, THE FORM OF THIS OBJECT DOES NOT DEPEND ON THE SEX OF THE SUBJECT AND INSTEAD DETERMINES THAT IT DOES NOT SUFFER FROM THE FORMULAS OF THE EDUCATIONAL TRADITION. THE FANTASY REPRESENTS THE DEFENSE THAT THE NARCISISTIC EGO— IDENTIFIED WITH ITS MIRROR DOUBLE—OPPOSES TO THE RENEWAL OF THE ANXIETY THAT TENDED TO DISTURB IT AT THE FIRST MOMENT OF OEDIPUS; A CRISIS WHCH DOES NOT CAUSE THE IRRUPTION OF GENITAL DESIRE IN THE SUBJECT AS MUCH AS IN THE OBJECT THAT IT REACTUALIZES, NAMELY THE MOTHER. THE SUBJECT RESPONDS TO THIS ANXIETY THAT THE OBJECT REAWAKENS BY REPRODUCING THE MASOCHISTIC REJECTION THROUGH WHICH HE SURMOUNTED HIS PRIMORDIAL LOSS, BUT THIS REPRODUCTION OPERATES ACCORDING TO THE STRUCTURE THAT HE HAS ACQUIRED, THAT IS TO SAY IN AN IMAGINARY LOCALIZATION OF THE DRIVE.

SUCH A GENESIS OF SEXUAL REPRESSION IS NOT WITHOUT SOCIOLOGICAL REFERENCE: IT IS EXPRESSED IN THE PRIMITIVE RITUALS WHERE THE LINK BETWEEN THIS REPRESSION AND THE ROOTS OF ALL SOCIAL BONDS IS MANIFESTED; CELEBRATION RITES WHICH, IN ORDER TO LIBERATE SEXUALITY, DESIGNATE BY THEIR ORGIASTIC FORM THE MOMENT OF AFFECTIVE REINTEGRATION INTO THE WHOLE: RITES OF CIRCUMCISION, WHICH IN ORDER TO SANCTION SEXUAL MATURITY, SHOW THAT THE PERSONA REACHES THEM ONLY AT THE PRICE OF CORPORAL MUTILIATION.

TO DEFINE THIS GENESIS OF REPRESSION OF THE PSYCHOLOGICAL PLANE, ONE MUST RECALL THE IMAGINARY PLAY THAT CONDITIONS THE FANTASY OF CASTRATION, IN THE MOTHER THE OBJECT THAT DETERMINES IT. IT IS IN THE RADICAL FORM OF COUNTER DRIVES THAT REVEAL THEMSELVES TO THE ANALYTIC EXPERIENCE IN ORDER TO CONSTITUTE THE MOST ARCHAIC KERNEL OF THE SUPEREGO AND TO REPRESENT THE MOST MASSIVE REPRESSION. THIS FORCE DISTRIBUTES ITSELF WITH THE DIFFERENCIATION OF THIS FORM, THAT IS TO SAY, THROUGH THE PROGRESS IN WHICH THE CHILD REALIZES THE REPRESSIVE AGENCY IN THE AUTHORITY OF THE ADULT; OTHERWISE ONE COULD NOT UNDERSTAND THE FACT—APPARENTLY CONTRARY TO THE THEORY—THAT THE STRICTNESS WITH WHICH THE SUPEREGO INHIBITS THE FUNCTIONS OF THE SUBJECT TENDS TO BE ESTABLISHED IN INVERSE PROPORTION TO THE REAL SEVERITIES OF EDUCATION. ALTHOUGH THE SUPEREGO ALREADY RECEIVES TRACES OF REALITY FROM THE MATERNAL REPRESSION ALONE (TOILET-TRAINING AND WEANING DISCIPLINE) IN THE OEDIPUS COMPLEX THESE TRACES GO BEYOND THEIR NARCISSISTIC FORM.

SUBLIMATION OF REALITY

THE ROLE OF THE COMPLEX IN THE SUBLIMATION OF REALITY IS NOW INTRODUCED. TO UNDERSTAND THIS, ONE MUST BEGIN AT THE POINT WHERE THE DOCTRINE PRESENTS A SOLUTION TO THE DRAMA, NAMELY OF THE FORM IT HAS DISCOVERED HERE— IDENTIFICATION. ACTUALLY, ON ACCOUNT OF THE INDENTIFICATION OF THE SUBJECT WITH THE IMAGO OF THE PARENT OF THE SAME SEX, THE SUPEREGO AND EGO-IDEAL CAN REVEAL TO EXPERIENCE TRAITS CONFORMING TO THE PARTICULARITIES OF THIS IMAGO.

IN THIS, THE DOCTRINE SEES THE FACT OF A SECONDARY NARCISSISM: IT DOES NOT DISTINGUISH THIS PARTICULAR IDENTIFICATION FROM THE NARCISSISTIC ONE. THERE IS ALSO AN ASSIMILATION OF THE SUBJECT TO THE OBJECT; THE DOCTRINE SEES NO DIFFERENCE OTHER THAN THE

CONSTITUTION OF ONE MORE OBJECT OF DESIRE OPPOSING ITSELF, ALONG WITH THE OEDIPAL DESIRE, TO A BETTER FORMED EGO. ACCORDING TO THE CONSTANTS OF HEDONISM, THE FRUSTRATION OF THIS DESIRE COULD RESULT IN THE SUBJECT'S RETURN TO HIS PRIMORDIAL VORACITY OF ASSIMILATION, AND IN THE FORMATION OF THE EGO, A RETURN TO AN IMPERFECT INTROJECTION OF THE OBJECT. IN ORDER TO IMPOSE ITSELF ON THE SUBJECT, THE IMAGO IS JUXTAPOSED ONLY TO THE EGO, IN THE TWO EXCLUSIONS OF THE UNCONSCIOUS AND THE IDEAL.

ORIGINALITY OF THE OEDIPAL IDENTIFICATION

HOWEVER A MORE STRUCTURAL ANALYSIS OF THE OEDIPAL IDENTIFICATION ALLOWS ONE TO RECOGNIZE WITHIN IT A MORE DISTINCTIVE FORM. WHAT APPEARS AT FIRST IS THE ANTINOMY OF THE FUNCTION WHICH PLAYS THE PARENTAL IMAGO IN THE SUBJECT: ON ONE HAND, THE IMAGO INHIBITS SEXUAL FUNCTION, BUT, SINCE EXPERIENCE SHOWS THAT THE ACTION OF THE SUPEREGO AGAINST THE REPETITIONS OF THE TENDENCIES REMAINS AS UNCONSCIOUS AS THE TENDENCIES REMAIN REPRESSED, IT DOES SO IN AN UNCONSCIOUS FORM. ON THE OTHER HAND, THE IMAGO PRESERVES THIS FUNCTION, BUT, SHELTERED BY ITS OWN MISCONCEPTION [MÉCONNAISSANCE], SINCE THE EGO-IDEAL REPRESENTS IN THE CONSCIENCE THE PREPARATION OF THE PATHS FOR ITS FUTURE RETURN. THUS, IF THE TENDENCY IS RESOLVED UNDER TWO MAJOR FORMS WHERE ANALYSIS HAS LEARNED TO RECOGNIZE IT—NAMELY UNCONSCIOUSNESS AND MISUNDERSTANDING—THE IMAGO ITSELF APPEARS UNDER TWO STRUCTURES WHOSE DISPARITY DEFINES THE FIRST SUBLIMATION OF REALITY.

WE CANNOT STRESS ENOUGHT THAT THE OBJECT OF IDENTIFICATION HERE IS NOT THE OBJECT OF DESIRE, BUT THAT WHICH IS OPPOSED TO THE OBJECT OF DESIRE IN THE OEDIPAL TRIANGLE. THE IDENTIFICATION OF THE MIMETIC HAS BECOME PROPITIATORY, THE OBJECT OF THE SADO-MASOCHISTIC PARTICIPATION DISENGAGES FROM THE SUBJECT, TAKING ITS DISTANCE FROM HIM IN THE NEW AMBIGUITY OF FEAR AND LOVE. BUT IN THIS STEP TOWARD REALITY, THE PRIMITIVE OBJECT OF DESIRE SEEMS TO BE CONJURED AWAY.

THIS FACT DEFINES THE ORIGINALITY OF THE OEDPIAL IDENTIFICATION. IT SEEMS TO INDICATE—IN THE COMPLEX—THAT IT IS NOT THE MOMENT OF DESIRE WHICH ESTABLISHES THE OBJECT IN ITS NEW REALITY, BUT THE MOMENT OF THE SUBJECT'S NARCISSISTIC DEFENSE.

THIS MOMENT, IN CAUSING THE OBJECT TO ARISE AS ONE WHOSE POSITION IS SITUATED AS AN OBSTACLE TO DESIRE, SHOWS IT TO BE COLORED BY A TRANSGRESSION FELT AS DANGEROUS. THE OBJECT APPEARS TO THE EGO AT ONCE AS THE SUPPORT OF ITS DEFENSE AND THE EXAMPLE OF ITS TRIUMPH. THIS IS WHY IT NORMALLY COMES TO FILL THE FRAME OF THE DOUBLE WHERE THE EGO FIRST IDENTIFIES ITSELF, AND THROUGH WHICH IT STILL CAN CONFUSE ITSELF WITH THE OTHER. THE OBJECT BRINGS A SECURITY TO THE EGO BY STRENGTHENING THIS FRAME, BUT AT THE SAME TIME IS IN OPPOSITION TO IT AS AN IDEAL THAT ALTERNATIVELY EXALTS AND DEPRESSES IT.

THIS MOMENT OF OEDIPUS PROVIDES THE PROTOTYPE FO SUBLIMATION, AS MUCH IN THE ROLE OF MASKED PRESENCE PLAYED BY THE DRIVE AS BY THE FORM IN WHICH IT ASSUMED THE OBJECT. THIS SAME FORM IS EVIDENT IN EACH CRISIS WHERE THE CONDENSATION (WHOSE ENIGMA WE HAVE POSED HIGHER UP) PRODUCES ITSELF; THIS LIGHT OF SURPRISE TRANSFIGURES AN OBJECT BY DISSOLVING ITS EQUIVALENCES IN A SUBJECT, AND PROPOSES IT NO LONGER AS A MEANS TO THE SATISFACTION OF DESIRE, BUT AS A POLE TO THE CREATIONS OF PASSION. IT IS BY REDUCING AGAIN SUCH AN OBJECT THAT EXPERIENCE ATTAINS ALL ITS DEPTH.

THUS, A SERIES OF ANTINOMIC FUNCTIONS ARE CONSTITUTED IN THE SUBJECT BY THE MAJOR CRISES OF HUMAN REALITY, IN ORDER TO CONTAIN THE INDEFINITE VIRTUALITIES OF ITS PROGRESS: IF THE FUNCTION OF THE CONSCIENCE SEEMS TO EXPRESS PRIMORDIAL ANGUISH, AND THAT OF EQUIVALENCE REFLECTS NARCISSISTIC CONFLICT, THEN THE FUNCTION OF THE EXAMPLE APPEARS TO BE THE ORIGINAL CONTRIBUTION OF THE OEDIPAL COMPLEX.

THE IMAGO OF THE FATHER

HENCE, THE ACTUAL STRUCTURE OF THE OEDIPAL DRAMA DESIGNATES THE FATHER AS GIVING TO THE FUNCTION OF SUBLIMATION ITS EMINENT AND MORE PURE FORM. IN THE OEDIPAL IDENTIFICATION THE IMAGO OF THE MOTHER ACTUALLY BETRAYS THE

INTERFERENCE OF THE PRIMORDIAL IDENTIFICATIONS, MARKING THE EGO-IDEAL AS WELL AS THE SUPEREGO BY THE FORMS AND THE AMBIVALENCE OF THESE IDENTIFICATIONS. IN THE GIRL, JUST AS THE REPRESSION OF SEXUALITY MORE READILY IMPOSES THIS MENTAL FRAGMENTATION WHERE ONE CAN DEFINE HYSTERIA ON BODILY FUNCTIONS, SO THE SUBLIMATION OF THE MATERNAL IMAGO TENDS TO TURN INTO A FEELING OF REPRESSION FOR ITS BANKRUPTCY AND INTO A SYSTEMATIC CONCERN FOR THE MIRROR IMAGE.

TO THE DEGREE THAT IT DOMINATES, THE IMAGO OF THE FATHER POLARIZES THE MOST PERFECT FORMS OF THE EGO-IDEAL IN BOTH SEXES, SUCH THAT IT IS ENOUGH TO INDICATE THAT THE FORMS REALIZE THE VIRILE IDEAL IN THE BOY AND THE VIRGINAL IN THE GIRL. ON THE OTHER HAND, WE CAN STRESS THE PHYSICAL LESIONS IN THE DIMINUTIVE FORMS OF THIS IMAGO (ESPECIALLY THOSE WHICH PRESENT THE IMAGO AS CRIPPLING OR BLINDING) IN ORDER TO DEVIATE THE ENERGY OF SUBLIMATION FROM ITS CREATIVE DIRECTION AND FAVOR ITS SECLUSION IN SOME IDEAL OF NARCISSISTIC INTEGRITY. THE DEATH OF THE FATHER, AT WHATEVER STAGE OF DEVELOPMENT IT APPEARS AND ACCORDING TO THE DEGREE OF COMPLETION OF OEDIPUS, AT THE SAME TIME TENDS TO ARREST THE PROGRESS OF REALITY BY FREEZING IT. BY REFERRING A GREAT NUMBER OF NEUROSES AND THEIR GRAVITY TO SUCH CAUSES, THE EXPERIENCE THUS CONTRADICTS THE THEORETICAL ORIENTATION WHICH DESIGNATES THE MAJOR AGENT OF SUCH NEUROSES IN THE THREAT OF PATERNAL FORCE.

THE COMPLEX AND ITS SOCIOLOGICAL RELATIVITY

IF IT APPEARED IN ITS PSYCHOLOGICAL ANALYSIS THAT OEDIPUS MUST BE UNDERSTOOD IN TERMS OF ITS NARCISSISTIC ANTECEDENTS, THIS IS NOT TO SAY THAT IT IS BASED OUTSIDE OF SOCIOLOGICAL RELATIVITY. THE MOST DECISIVE RESULT OF ITS PSYCHIC EFFECTS RESIDES IN THE FACT THAT THE FUNCTION OF REPRESSION AS WELL AS THAT OF SUBLIMATION IS CONCENTRATED IN THE IMAGO OF THE FATHER; BUT THIS IS A FACT OF SOCIAL DETERMINATION, THE FACT OF THE PATERNAL FAMILY.

MATRIARCHY AND PATRIARCHY

IN MATRIARCHAL CULTURES, THE FAMILIAL AUTHORITY IS NOT REPRESENTED BY THE FATHER BUT ORDINARILY BY A MATERNAL UNCLE. ONE ETHNOLOGIST WHO WAS GUIDED BY HIS KNOWLEDGE OF PSYCHOANALYSIS, MALINOWSKI, KNEW HOW TO PENETRATE THE PSYCHIC INCIDENCES OF THIS FACT: IF THE MATERNAL UNCLE PRACTICES THE SOCIAL SPONSORSHIP AS GUARDIAN OF FAMILY-RELATED TABOOS AND INITIATOR OF TRIBAL RITES, THE FATHER, DISCHARGED FROM ALL REPRESSIVE FUNCTION, PLAYS A MORE FAMILIAR ROLE OF PATRONAGE, AS MASTER OF TECHNIQUES AND EXAMPLE OF DARING IN BUSINESS.

THIS SEPARATION OF FUNCTIONS IMPLIES A DIFFERENT EQUILIBRIUM OF THE PSYCHE ATTESTED TO BY THE AUTHOR THROUGH THE LACK OF NEUROSIS HE OBSERVED IN THE GROUPS OF THE NORTH-WEST ISLANDS OF MELANSIA. THIS EQUILIBRIUM FORTUNATELY DEMONSTRATES THAT THE OEDIPAL COMPLEX IS RELATIVE TO SOCIAL STRUCTURE, BUT HE IN NO WAY AUTHORIZES THE PARODISTIC MIRAGE AGAINST WHICH THE SOCIOLOGIST MUST ALWAYS DEFEND HIMSELF: THE STEREOTYPE THAT MARKS THE CREATIONS OF PERSONALITY IS OPPOSED TO THE HARMONY THAT IT CARRIES WITHIN—FROM ART TO MORALS—IN SIMILAR CULTURES, AND CONFORMING TO THE PRESENT THEORY OF OEDIPUS, ONE MUST REMEMBER IN THIS REVERSAL HOW MUCH THE IMPULSES OF SUBLIMATION ARE DOMINATED BY SOCIAL REPRESSION WHEN THESE TWO FUNCTIONS ARE SEPARATED.

IT IS ON THE CONTRARY, BECAUSE THE PATERNAL IMAGO IS INVESTED BY REPRESSION IT PROJECTS ITS ORIGINAL FORCE IN THE VERY SUBLIMATIONS WHICH SHOULD OVERCOME IT; THE OEDIPUS COMPLEX ACQUIRES SO MUCH FECUNDITY [FÉCONDITE] BY TYING TOGETHER THE PROGRESS OF THESE FUNCTIONS IN SUCH AN ANTINOMY. THIS ANTINOMY PLAYS IN THE INDIVIDUAL DRAMA. HERE WE WILL SEE IT CONFIRMED BY THE EFFECTS OF DECOMPOSITION; BUT THESE EFFECTS OF PROGRESS, INTEGRATED AS THEY ARE IN AN IMMENSE CULTURAL PATRIMONY, GO MUCH FURTHER BEYOND THIS DRAMA: NORMAL IDEALS, LEGAL STATUTES, CREATIVE INSPIRATIONS. THE PSYCHOLOGIST CANNOT NEGLECT THESE FORMS WHICH, BY CONCENTRATING THE CONDITIONS OF THE FUNCTIONAL CONFLICT OF OEDIPUS IN THE CONJUGAL FAMILY, REINTEGRATE THE SOCIAL DIALECTIC ENGENDERED BY THIS CONFLICT INTO THE PSYCHOLOGICAL PROGRESS.

THAT THE STUDY OF THESE FORMS RELATES TO HISTORY IS ALREADY ONE GIVEN FOR OUR ANALYSIS: WE MUST TAKE AS A PROBLEM OF STRUCTURE THE FACT THAT THE LIGHT OF HISTORICAL TRADITION ONLY FULLY STRUCK IN THE ANNALS OF PATRIARCHIES, WHEREAS IT ONLY PERIPHERALLY ILLUMINATED THE MATRIARCHIES THAT ARE "ONLY" ALWAYS SUBJACENT TO ANCIENT CULTURE (AS IN THE INVESTIGATIONS OF BACHOFEN).

OPENING OF THE SOCIAL BOND

WITH THIS FACT WE UNIFY THE CRITICAL MOMENT THAT BERGSON DEFINED IN THE FOUNDATION S OF MORALITY: IT IS KNOWN THAT HE RETURNS TO ITS FUNCTION OF SOCIAL DEFENSE THIS "ALL OR NOTHING OF OBLIGATION," BY WHICH HE DESIGNATES THE BOND THAT CLOSES THE HUMAN GROUP UPON ITS COHERENCE. HE RECOGNIZES IT IN OPPOSITION TO A TRANSCENDENT ÉLAN OF LIFE IN EVERY MOVEMENT, WHICH OPENS THIS GROUP BY UNIVERSALIZING THE BOND. AN ABSTRACT ANALYSIS DISCOVERS A DOUBLE SOURCE NO DOUBT RETURNED AGAINST THESE FORMALIST ILLUSIONS, BUT REMAINING LIMITED TO THE REACH OF ABSTRACTION. NOW, IF THE PSYCHOLOGIST AND THE SOCIOLOGIST CAN RECOGNIZE, BY EXPERIENCE, THE CONCRETE FORM OF PRIMORDIAL OBLIGATION IN THE INTERDICTION OF THE MOTHER, SO IN THE SAME WAY THEY CAN DEMONSTRATE A REAL PROCESS OF "THE OPENING" OF THE SOCIAL BOND IN PATERNAL AUTHORITY, SAYING THAT BY THE FUNCTIONAL CONFLICT OF OEDIPUS, THE OPENING INTRODUCES AN IDEAL OF PROMISE INTO REPRESSION.

IF THEY REFER TO THE RITES OF SACRIFICE BY WHICH PRIMITIVE CULTURES (EVEN ATTAINING A SOCIALY ELEVATED CONCENTRATION) REALIZE THE FANTASIES OF THE PRIMORDIAL RELATION OF THE MOTHER WITH THE CRUELEST RIGOR—DISMEMBERED BODIES AND LIVE BURIAL—IN MORE THAN ONE MYTH THEY WILL READ THAT THE ADVENT OF PATERNAL AUTHORITY ANSWERS TO A TEMPERAMENT OF PRIMITIVE SOCIAL REPRESSION. LEDGIBLE IN THE MYTHIC AMBIGUITY OF THE SACRIFICE OF ABRAHAM, WHICH IN THE END FORMALLY TIES THIS MEANING TO AN EXPRESSION OF PROMISE, THIS MEANING DOES NOT APPEAR ANY LESS IN THE MYTH OF OEDIPUS (IF ONLY WE DO NOT NEGLECT THE EPISODE OF THE SPHINX), A NO LESS AMBIGUOUS REPRESENTATION OF THE EMANCIPATION OF

MATERNAL TYRANNIES AND THE DECLINE OF THE RITE OF ROYAL MURDER. WHATEVER THEIR FORM, THESE MYTHS ARE SITUATED AT THE EDGE OF HISTORY, FAR FROM THE BIRTH OF HUMANITY FROM WHICH THE IMMEMORIAL CONTINUATION OF MATRIARCHAL CULTURES AND THE STAGNATION OF PRIMITIVE GROUPS SEPARATE THEM.

ACCORDING TO THIS SOCIOLOGICAL REFERENCE, THE PROPHETICISM BY WHICH BERSON APPEALS TO HISTORY, IN SO FAR AS IT IS PRODUCED EMINENTLY BY THE JEWISH PEOPLE, CAN BE UNDERSTOOD BY THE SITUATION OF BEING THE ELECT PEOPLE—A SITUATION CREATED SINCE THEIR GROUP WAS THE REPRESENTATIVE OF PATRIARCHY FOR OTHER GROUPS DEVOTED TO MATERNAL CULTS, AND BY ITS CONVULSIVE BATTLE TO MAINTAIN THE PATRIARCHAL IDEAL AGAINST THE IRREPRESSIBLE SEDUCTION OF THESE MATRIARCHIES. WE THUS SEE THE EXIGENCIES OF THE PERSON AND THE UNIVERSALIZATION OF THE IDEAL DIALECTICALLY AFFIRMED IN SOCIETY, ACROSS THE HISTORY OF PATRIARCHIAL PEOPLES: TESTIMONY TO THIS PROGRESS IS FOUND IN THE LEGAL FORMS, WHICH ETERNALIZE THE MISSION EXPERIENCED BY ROME IN ITS CONSCIENCE AS MUCH AS IN ITS POWER, A MISSION REALIZED BY THE ALREADY REVOLUTIONARY EXTENSION OF MORAL PRIVELEDGES FROM A PATRIARCH TO AN IMMENSE PLEBACY AND ONTO ALL PEOPLE.

TWO FUNCTIONS OF THIS PROCESS ARE REFLECTED ON THE STRUCTURE OF THE FAMILY ITSELF; FIRST, THE TRADITION IN THE PATRICIAN IDEALS, OF PRIVILEDGED FORMS OF MARRIAGE, AND SECOND, THE APOTHEOTIC EXALTATION THAT CHRISTIANITY BRINGS TO THE EXIGENCIES OF THE PERSON. THE CHURCH INTEGRATED THIS TRADITION INTO THE MORALITY OF CHRISTIANTIY BY BRINGING INTO THE FOREGROUND THE FREE CHOICE OF A PARTNER IN THE BOND OF MARRIAGE, THUS CAUSING THE FAMILIAL INSTITUTION TO TAKE THE DECISIVE STEP TOWARDS ITS MODERN STRUCTURE, NAMELY THE SECRET REVERSAL OF ITS PREPONDERANCE TO THE ADVANTAGE OF MARRIAGE. THIS REVERSAL WAS REALIZED IN THE FIFTEENTH CENTURY WITH THE ECONOMIC REVOLUTION THAT PRODUCED THE BOURGEOIS SOCIETY AND THE PSYCHOLOGY OF MODERN MAN.

THE RELATIONS BETWEEN THE PSYCHOLOGY OF MODERN MAN AND THE CONJUGAL FAMILY ARE WHAT, IN EFFECT, PROPOSE THEMSELVES TO THE STUDY OF PSYCHOANALYSIS. THIS MAN IS THE ONLY OBJECT THAT IT HAS TRULY SUBMITTED TO ITS EXPERIENCE AND IF THE PSYCHOANALYST REDIS-

COVERS IN HIM PSYCHIC REFLECTION OF THE MOST ORIGINAL CONDITIONS OF MAN, CAN HE CLAIM TO CURE HIM OF PSYCHIC DEFICIENCIES WITHOUT UNDERSTANDING THEM WITHIN THE CULTURE THAT IMPOSES THE HIGHEST EXIGENCIES UPON HIM— WITHOUT UNDERSTANDING HIS OWN POSITION FACING THIS MAN AT THE EXTREME POINT OF THE SCIENTIFIC ATTITUDE?

THUS, IN OUR TIMES, MAN IN WESTERN CULTURE CAN LESS THAN EVER UNDERSTAND HIMSELF OUTSIDE THE ANTINOMIES THAT CONSTITUTE HIS RELATIONS WITH NATURE AND SOCIETY. HOW, OUTSIDE OF THESE, IS IT POSSIBLE TO UNDERSTAND FIRST, THE ANGUISH THAT MAN EXPRESSES IN THE SENTIMENTS OF A PROMETHEAN TRANSGRESSION TOWARD THE CONDITIONS OF HIS LIFE, AND SECOND, THE MOST ELEVATED CONCEPTIONS WHERE HE OVERCOMES THIS ANGUISH, RECOGNIZ-ING THAT HE CREATES HIMSELF AND HIS OBJECTS THROUGH DIALECTICAL CRISES.

THE ROLE OF THE FAMILIAL FORMATION

THIS CRITICAL AND SUBVERSIVE MOVEMENT WHERE MAN IS REALIZED FINDS ITS MOST ACTIVE KERNEL IN THREE CONDITIONS OF THE CONJUGAL FAMILY.

IN ORDER TO INSTILL AUTHORITY IN THE CLOSEST NEIGHBORING GENERATION, AND TO DO SO UNDER A FAMILIAR FIGURE, THE CONJUGAL FAMILY PLACES THIS AUTHORITY AT THE MOST IMMEDIATE EN-TRANCE TO THE CREATIVE SUBVERSION. FOR THE MOST COMMON OBSERVATION, THIS IS ALREADY TRANSLATED BY THE INVERSIONS OF THE ORDER OF GENERATIONS IMAGINED BY THE CHILD, WHERE HE SUBSTITUTES HIMSELF FOR THE PARENT OR THE GRANDPARENT.

ON THE OTHER HAND, IN THIS THE PSYCHISM IS FORMED NO LESS BY THE IMAGE OF THE ADULT THAN AGAINST ITS CONSTRAINTS. THIS EFFECT OPERATES BY THE TRANSMISSION OF THE EGO-IDEAL, MOST PURELY, AS WE HAVE SAID, FROM THE FATHER TO THE SON; IT INVOLVES A POSITIVE SELECTION OF THE DRIVES AND THE GIFTS, A PROGRESSIVE REALIZATION OF THE IDEAL IN CHARACTER. THE FACT OF FAMILIES OF EMINENT MEN OWES TO THIS PSYCHOLOGICAL PROCESS, AND NOT TO THE ALLEGED HEREDITY THAT ONE MUST RECOGNIZE IN ESSENTIALLY RELATIONAL CAPACI-TIES.

FINALLY AND ABOVE ALL, THE EVIDENCE OF SEXUAL LIFE IN THE REPRESENTATIVES OF MORAL CONSTRAINTS—THE SINGULARLY TRANSGRESSIVE EXAMPLE OF THE IMAGO OF THE FATHER AS FAR AS THE PRIMORIDAL INTERDICTION IS CONCERNED— EXALT THE TENSION OF THE LIBIDO AND THE SCOPE OF SUBLIMATION TO THE HIGHEST DEGREE.

THE COMPLEX OF THE CONJUGAL FAMILY FORMS THE SUPERIOR ACCOMPLISHMENTS OF CHARAC-TER—HAPPINESS AND CREATION—IN ORDER TO MOST HUMANELY REALIZE THE CONFLICT OF MAN WITH HIS MOST ARCHAIC ANGUISH, TO OFFER HIM THE LOYALEST CLOSED FIELD IN WHICH TO MEASURE HIMSELF WITH THE MOST PROFOUND FIGURES OF HIS DESTINY, AND IN ORDER TO ADAPT HIS INDIVIDUAL EXPERIENCE TO THE MOST COMPLETE TRIUMPH AGAINST THE ORIGINAL SERVITUDE.

IN CONTIBUTING THE LARGEST DIFFERENTIATION TO THE PERSONALITY BEFORE THE PERIOD OF LATENCY, THE COMPLEX BRINGS TO SOCIAL CONFRONTATIONS OF THIS PERIOD THE MAXIMUM EFFICIENCY FOR THE RATIONAL FORMATION OF THE INDIVIDUAL. IN EFFECT, AT THIS POINT ONE CAN CONSIDER THAT THE EDUCATIONAL ACTION REPRODUCES THE PLAY OF NARCISSISTIC EQUIVA-LENCES WHERE THE WORLD OF OBJECTS WAS BORN, IN A FULLER REALITY AND UNDER SUPERIOR SUBLIMATIONS OF LOGIC AND JUSTICE. THE MORE VARIED AND RICH THE UNCONSCIOUS REALITIES INTEGRATED INTO THE FAMILY EXPERIENCE ARE, THE MORE FORMATIVE THE WORK OF THEIR REDUCTION FOR REASON WILL BE.

THUS, IF IN THESE MORAL CONDITIONS OF CREATION PSYCHOANALYSIS MANIFESTS A REVOLUTIONARY FERMENT THAT ONE CAN GRASP ONLY THROUGH CONCRETE ANALYSIS, IT IS RECOGNIZED IN ORDER TO PRODUCE A POWER IN THE FAMILIAL STRUCTURE WHICH SURPASSES ALL EDUCATIONAL RATIONAL-IZATION. THE FACT OF A SOCIAL EDUCATION WITH TOTALITARIAN CLAIMS DESERVES TO BE PROPOSED TO THEORETICIANS NO MATTER WHAT SIDE THEY TAKE, IN ORDER THAT EACH ARRIVES AT HIS OWN CONCLUSION FROM IT, ACCORDING TO HIS OWN DESIRES.

DECLINE OF THE PATERNAL IMAGO

IN THE FORMATION OF MOST GREAT MEN, WE ARE

LED TO PERCEIVE THE ROLE OF THE IMAGO OF THE FATHER IN A STRIKINGLY EVIDENT MANNER. IT IS WORTH NOTING ITS LITERARY AND MORAL RADIANCE IN THE CLASSICAL ERA OF PROGRESS—FROM CORNEILLE TO PROUDHON; AND IDEOLOGUES WHO IN THE NINETEENTH CENTURY BROUGHT THE MOST SUBVERSIVE CRITIQUES AGAINST THE PATERNALISTIC FAMILY ARE NOT THOSE WHO PRESERVE THE LEAST OF ITS WEIGHT.

WE ARE NOT AMONG THOSE AFFLICTED BY THE PRETENDED LOOSENING OF THE FAMILIAL BOND. IS IT NOT SIGNIFICANT THAT THE FAMILY SHOULD BE REDUCED TO ITS BIOLOGICAL GROUPING TO THE DEGREE THAT IT INTEGRATES THE HIGHEST CULTURAL PROGRESS? BUT A LARGE NUMBER OF PSYCHOLOGICAL EFFECTS SEEM, TO US, DEPENDENT UPON THE SOCIAL DECLINE OF THE PATERNAL IMAGO; A DECLINE CONDITIONED BY A RETURN OF EXTREME EFFECTS OF SOCIAL PROGRESS ONTO THE INDIVIDUAL; A DECLINE ABOVE ALL MARKED IN OUR TIMES BY THOSE COLLECTIVITIES WHO HAVE MOST STRONGLY FELT THOSE EFFECTS, ECONOMIC CONCENTRATION AND POLITICAL CATASTROPHE. WAS NOT THE ARGUMENT FORMED BY THE CHIEF OF A TOTALITARIAN STATE AN ARGUMENT AGAINST TRADITIONAL EDUCATION? IT IS A DECLINE TIED MOST INTIMATELY TO THE DIALECTIC OF THE CONJUGAL FAMILY SINCE IT OPERATES BY A RELATIVE GROWTH OF MATRIMONIAL EXIGENCIES, VERY VISIBLE, FOR EXAMPLE, IN THE AMERICAN WAY OF LIFE.

NO MATTER WHAT ITS FUTURE, THIS DECLINE CONSTITUTES A PSYCHOLOGICAL CRISIS. MAYBE ONE MUST RELATE THE APPEARANCE OF PSYCHOANALYSIS ITSELF TO ITS CRISIS. THE SUBLIME FORTUNE OF GENIUS PERHAPS DOES NOT ALONE EXPLAIN WHY IT WAS IN VIENNA—THE CENTER OF A STATE THAT WAS A MELTINGPOT OF THE MOST DIVERSE FAMILY FORMS, FROM THE MOST ARCHAIC TO THE MOST EVOLVED, FROM THE LAST AGNATIC GROUPS OF PEASANT SLAVES TO THE MOST REDUCED AND DECADENT FORMS OF AN UNSTABLE HOUSEHOLD, THE HEARTH OF THE PETIT-BOURGEOSIE, NOT TO MENTION FEUDAL AND MERCANTILE PATERNALISMS—THAT A SON OF A JEWISH PATRIARCH COULD HAVE IMAGINED THE OEDIPAL COMPLEX. FOR WHAT IT IS WORTH, THE DOMINANT FORMS OF NEUROSES AT THE END OF THE LAST CENTURY REVEALED THEIR INTIMATE DEPENDENCY UPON THE CONDITIONS OF THE FAMILY.

SINCE THE TIME OF THE FIRST FREUDIAN DIVINATIONS THESE NEUROSES SEEM TO HAVE EVOLVED IN THE DIRECTION OF A CHARACTERISTIC COMPLEX, WHERE DUE EQUALLY TO THE SPECIFICITY OF ITS FORM AND ITS GENERALIZATION, IT IS THE KERNAL OF THE GREATEST NUMBER OF NEUROSES—WHERE ONE CAN RECOGNIZE THE GREAT CONTEMPORARY NEUROSIS. OUR EXPERIENCE LEADS US TO DESIGNATE THE PERSONALITY OF THE FATHER AS ITS PRINCIPLE DETERMINANT, ALWAYS IN SOME WAY DEFICIENT—ABSENT, HUMILIATED, DIVIDED OR FALSE. CONFORMING TO OUR CONCEPTION OF OEDIPUS, THIS DEFICIENCY COMES TO EXHAUST [TARIR] THE INSTINCTIVE IMPULSES AND TO DAMAGE [TARER] THE DIALECTIC OF SUBLIMATIONS. SINISTER GODMOTHERS AT THE CRADLE OF NEUROSIS, IMPOTENCE AND UTOPIA ENCLOSING HIS AMBITION—WHETHER IT STIFLES IN HIM THE CREATIONS AWAITED BY THE WORLD INTO WHICH HE CAME, OR WHETHER IN THE OBJECT HE PROPOSES FOR HIS REVOLT—HE FAILS TO RECOGNIZE HIS OWN MOVEMENT.

JACQUES LACAN
TRANSLATED BY ANDREA KAHN

DISCURSIVE SEX

DO YOU KNOW CORRECT TERMS FOR WHAT SOME MAY CALL SEX "PERVERSIONS"?

HOW MUCH DO YOU KNOW ABOUT UNUSUAL SEX PRACTICES?

THERE WAS A TIME WHEN ANYTHING BUT THE MISSIONARY POSITION WAS CONSIDERED IMMORAL AND PERVERSE. SURPRISINGLY, THIS ATTITUDE IS STILL HELD BY MANY PEOPLE TODAY. HOW FAMILIAR ARE YOU WITH SO-CALLED "PERVERSIONS?" DO YOU KNOW THEM BY THEIR PROPER NAMES OR HAVE YOU BEEN TRAINED TO RECOIL AT THE VERY MENTION OF A SEX PRACTICE THAT IS OUT OF THE ORDINARY? TO TEST THE ACCURACY OF YOUR KNOWLEDGE, MATCH THE FOLLOWING TERMS WITH THEIR CORRECT DEFINITIONS. WRITE THE LETTER OF THE CORRECT DEFINITION NEXT TO THE TERM IT DESCRIBES. THERE ARE MORE DEFINITIONS THAN TERMS, SO READ CAREFULLY BEFORE CHOOSING YOUR ANSWER.

1. BESTIALITY

A. SEXUAL PLEASURE THROUGH WATCHING OTHERS ENGAGE IN SEX ACTS

2. SCATOLOGY

B. GIVING A WOMAN SEXUAL PLEASURE BY ORALLY STIMULATING HER GENITALS

3. TRANSVESTITE

C. RECEIVING SEXUAL STIMULATION BY RUBBING AGAINST SOMEONE OR SOMETHING

4. 'FAIRE MINETTE'

D. SEXUAL RELATIONS WITH ANIMALS

5. BONDAGE

E. FORCIBLY HAVING SEX RELATIONS WITH A VIRGIN

6. UROLAGNIA

F. SEXUAL PLEASURE THROUGH KEEPING A SEX PARTNER PRISONER

7. VOYEURISM

G. EXPERIENCING SEXUAL PLEASURE THROUGH PAIN

8. FLAGELLATION

H. A PERSON WHO IS SEXUALLY STIMULATED BY WEARING CLOTHING OF THE OPPOSITE SEX

9. OSPHRESIOLAGNIA

I. SEXUAL ADDICTION TO SPECIFIC FORMS OF STIMULATION—GUNS, UNIFORMS, ET CETERA

10. FROTTAGE

J. ANAL INTERCOURSE. ESPECIALLY PERFORMED ON A YOUNG BOY BY A MAN

11. EXHIBITIONISM

K. A PERSON WHO IS SEXUALLY STIMULATED BY INFLICTING PAIN

12. PEDERASTY

L. SEXUAL GRATIFICATION BY SMELLING CERTAIN ODORS

13. FETISHISM

M. SEXUAL INTEREST IN EXCREMENT

14. PEDOPHILIA

N. SEX WITH YOUNG CHILDREN

15. ALGOLAGNIA

O. WHIPPING OR BEING WHIPPED FOR SEXUAL GRATIFICATION

16. TROILISM

P. SEXUAL STIMULATION THROUGH BEING URINATED UPON

Q. GAINING SEXUAL PLEASURE THROUGH EXPOSING ONE'S GENITALS TO OTHERS

R. SEX WITH THREE PEOPLE AT ONCE

THE ANSWERS

1. D	9. L
2. M	10. C
3. H	11. Q
4. B	12. J
5. F	13. I
6. P	14. N
7. A	15. G
8. O	16. R

GIVE YOURSELF ONE POINT FOR EACH CORRECT ANSWER.

VOCABULARY

THE WORD PLEASURE CROPPED UP IN WHAT I WOULD CALL A TACTICAL WAY. I HAD THE FEELING THAT INTELLECTUAL LANGUAGE SUBMITTED TOO EASILY TO MORALIZING IMPERATIVES WHICH EMPTIED IT OF ALL NOTION OF JOUISSANCE. BY REACTION I ATTEMPTED TO REINTRODUCE THE WORD AND NOT TO CENSURE IT IN MY OWN PERSONAL FIELD, NOT TO FRUSTRATE BUT TO DE-FRUSTRATE IT.

A TACTICAL MOVE IN THE ORDER OF IDEAS ENTAILS EXPLANATIONS, GIRDS ITSELF WITH REASONS. THE FIRST REASON IS THAT SUBJECTIVELY I ACCORD A CERTAIN IMPORTANCE TO WHAT COMES UNDER THE HEADING OF THAT SOMEWHAT OLD—FASHIONED TERM HEDONISM, AND PARTICULARLY TO THE THEME OF THE ART OF LIVING. INDIRECTLY I ALREADY DREW ATTENTION TO THESE THINGS WHEN REFERRING TO BRECHT AND HIS CIGARS, FOR EXAMPLE. IN FACT, THROUGHOUT THE WORK OF BRECHT, AUTHENTICALLY MARXIST AS NO ONE WILL DENY, EXTREME CONSIDERATION IS GIVEN TO PLEASURE. SO FAR AS I AM CONCERNED THEN, I TAKE ON THE RESPONSIBILITY OF A CERTAIN HEDONISM, THE RETURN TO A PHILOSOPHY DISCREDITED AND FRUSTRATED FOR CENTURIES, FIRST BY CHRISTIAN MORALITY, THEN AFTER BEING TAKEN OVER BY A POSITIVIST, RATIONALIST MORALITY, THE FRUSTRATION WAS, OR IS ALAS, IN THE WAY OF BECOMING SO BY A CERTAIN MARXIST ETHIC.

THE SECOND JUSTIFICATION FOR THE EMERGENCE, FOR THE RETURN OF THE WORD "PLEASURE" IS THAT IT ALLOWS FOR A CERTAIN EXPLORATION OF THE HUMAN SUBJECT. IN TRYING TO ESTABLISH SOME KIND OF DIVISION BETWEEN "PLEASURE" AND "JOUISSANCE," IN POSING THE PROBLEM OF JOUISSANCE, ONE COMES UP AGAINST A VERY TOPICAL THEME FAMILIAR TO PSYCHOANALYSIS AND OF INTEREST TO WHAT IS CALLED THE AVANT GARDE.

THE OPPOSITION PLEASURE/JOUISSANCE IS ONE OF THOSE DELIBERATELY ARTIFICIAL OPPOSITIONS FOR WHICH I HAVE ALWAYS HAD A CERTAIN PREDELICTION. I OFTEN TRIED TO CREATE SUCH OPPOSITIONS: FOR EXAMPLE BETWEEN WRITING AND SCRIBBLING, DENOTATION AND CONNOTATION. THESE OPPOSITIONS SHOULD NOT BE TAKEN TOO LITERALLY, BY ASKING ONE'S SELF FOR INSTANCE IF SUCH AND SUCH A TEXT FALLS INTO THE

CATEGORY OF PLEASURE OR JOUISSANCE. THEY ARE OPPOSITIONS CHIEFLY USEFUL IN CLEARING A PATH, IN GOING A STEP FURTHER: QUITE SIMPLY IN SPEAKING AND WRITING.

THAT SAID, THE DIFFERENCE BETWEEN THE TWO WORDS IS NEVERTHELESS REAL, AND I AM NOT ALONE IN UPHOLDING IT. PLEASURE IS LINKED WITH THE CONSISTENCY OF THE SELF, OF THE SUBJECT, WHICH AFFIRMS ITSELF THROUGH VALUES OF COMFORT, EXPANSIVENESS, EASE—AND IN MY CASE, TO GIVE AN EXAMPLE, BELONGS TO THE DOMAIN OF READING CLASSICAL WRITERS. AS OPPOSED TO THIS, JOUISSANCE IS THE SYSTEM OF READING, OR OF ENUNCIATION, BY MEANS OF WHICH THE SUBJECT, INSTEAD OF AFFIRMING, ABANDONS ITSELF, UNDERGOES THE EXPERIENCE OF PRODI-GALITY WHICH IS STRICTLY SPEAKING JOUISSANCE.

IF ONE SET OUT TO DO A PROVISIONAL SORTING OF TEXTS ACCORDING TO THOSE TWO WORDS, IT IS CERTAIN THAT BY A HUGE MAJORITY THE TEXTS WE KNOW AND LOVE ARE BROADLY SPEAKING TEXTS OF PLEASURE, WHEREAS TEXTS OF JOUISSANCE ARE EXTREMELY RARE—AND THERE'S NO SAYING IF THEY ARE NOT ALSO TEXTS OF PLEASURE. WE MAY FIND THESE TEXTS DISAGREEABLE OR AGGRESSIVE, BUT PROVISIONALLY AT LEAST, FOR A BRIEF INSTANT, THEY TRANSPORT US AND PROVOKE THAT PRODIGALITY OF THE LOSS OF SELF.

THIS THEME OF JOUISSANCE BORDERS ON OTHER THEMES, FOR EXAMPLE THE THEME NOT OF DRUGS STRICTLY SPEAKING, BUT OF "DRUGGING," OR OF CERTAIN FORMS OF PERVERSION.

... TEXTS OF JOUISSANCE ARE AVANT-GARDE TEXTS, THAT IS TO SAY TEXTS NOT ON THE SIDE OF THE PROBABLE, HOWEVER INCENDIARY IT MAY BE—I THINK OF SADE FOR EXAMPLE (ONE MIGHT BE TEMPTED TO PLACE SADE AMONG THE TEXTS OF JOUISSANCE, WHERE IN MANY RESPECTS HE BELONGS, NOT BECAUSE HE SPEAKS ABOUT JOUISSANCE, BUT BY THE WAY HE SPEAKS OF IT), IN SPITE OF EVERYTHING, THE SADIAN TEXT, BECAUSE IT IS SUBMITTED TO THE CONSTRAINT OF THE EPOCH, TO THE CODE OF THE PROBABLE, REMAINS A TEXT OF PLEASURE. THE TEXT OF JOUISSANCE HAS TO BE IN A SENSE UNREADABLE. IT MUST COME AS A JERK, NOT ONLY TO OUR REGISTER OF IMAGES AND IMAGINATION, BUT ON THE LEVEL OF LANGUAGE ITSELF ...

IN FACT IT'S DIFFICULT TO EXPLAIN BECAUSE, ALTHOUGH ONE CAN IMAGINE AESTHETIC CRITERIA FOR JUDGING TEXTS OF PLEASURE, FOR TEXTS OF JOUISSANCE SUCH CRITERIA ARE STILL OBSCURE.

DRAGGING

PERHAPS IF I TALK ABOUT DRAGGING I'LL ARRIVE AT A DEFINITION. IT IS AN IMPORTANT THEME FOR ME. DRAGGING IS THE JOURNEY OF DESIRE. IT IS THE BODY IN A STATE OF ALERT, QUESTING IN ACCORDANCE WITH ITS OWN DESIRE. AND THEN, DRAGGING IMPLIES A TEMPORALITY WHICH LAYS STRESS ON THE ENCOUNTER, ON THE "FIRST TIME." AS IF THE FIRST ENCOUNTER POSSESSED AN EXTRAORDINARY PRIVILEGE OF ITS OWN: THAT OF BEING OUTSIDE ALL REPETITION. REPETITION IS A MALEFICENT THEME FOR ME, REITERATION, THE STEREOTYPE, THE NATURAL AS REPETITION. DRAGGING IS THE ANTI-NATURAL, THE ANTI-REPETITION. THE ACT OF DRAGGING IS AN ACT REPEATED, BUT ITS CONTENT IS ABSOLUTELY INAUGURAL.

FOR THAT REASON DRAGGING IS A NOTION I CAN EASILY TRANSFER FROM THE ORDER OF THE EROTIC QUEST WHERE IT ORIGINATES, TO A QUEST AFTER TEXTS FOR EXAMPLE, OR A QUEST FOR A TYPE OF FICTION. IN OTHER WORDS, WHATEVER COMES TO LIGHT IN THE SURPRISE OF THE "FIRST TIME."

... DRAGGING A TEXT MUST BE SEEN AS THE CAPTURE OF PHRASES, CITATIONS, FORMULAS, FRAGMENTS. THE THEME OF SHORT WRITING, OBVIOUSLY. WHEN I TRY TO PRODUCE THIS SHORT WRITING BY FRAGMENTS, I PUT MYSELF IN THE POSITION OF AN AUTHOR WHOSE READER GOES DRAGGING. IT IS THE LUCK OF THE GAME, BUT A MUCH SOUGHT-AFTER LUCK, MUCH THOUGHT ABOUT: SPIED ON, IN A WAY.

PERVERSION

"PERVERSION, QUITE SIMPLY, IS A WAY OF BEING HAPPY."

IN THE FRAGMENT FROM WHICH THIS PHRASE IS TAKEN, I CITED THE WORD "PERVERSION" AFTER TWO ALLUSIONS TO HASHISH AND HOMOSEXUALITY. WHICH MEANS THAT HERE "PERVERSION" DOES NOT HAVE A PSYCHOANALYTIC RIGOUR—SINCE FOR PSYCHOANALYSIS DRUGS ARE NOT STRICTLY CLASSIBLE AS PERVERSIONS. PERVERSION IS THE SEARCH FOR A PLEASURE THAT CANNOT BE TURNED TO THE PROFIT OF SOCIAL ENDS OR THE SPECIES. IT IS, FOR EXAMPLE, THE PLEASURE OF LOVING WHICH DOES NOT FIGURE IN VIEW OF

PROCREATION. IT BELONGS TO AN ORDER OF VOLUPTUARIES PRACTISED GRATUITOUSLY. THE THEME OF PRODIGALITY.

NEVERTHELESS, A PSYCHOANALYTIC SPECIFICITY CAN BE RE-INTRODUCED INTO THE GENERALITY OF THE TERM. THUS, ACCORDING TO FREUDIAN THOUGHT, ONE OF THE MAJOR PERVERSIONS IS FETISHISM (THEME THAT CAN BE FOUND IN THE WISH FOR SEGMENTED WRITING). AND IN SO FAR AS, PSYCHOANALYTICALLY, PERVERSION IS DIVORCED FROM NEUROSIS, FREUDIAN THOUGHT PUTS EMPHASIS ON THE FACT THAT THE PERVERT IS, ON THE WHOLE, A HAPPY PERSON.

ALL I HAVE DONE SINCE THE BOOK ON JAPAN INCLUDING CERTAIN FRAGMENTS FROM R.B. BY HIMSELF, IS UNDER THE SIGN OF A SORT OF PERVERSE WRITING.

PERVERSION, BY WAY OF FETISHISM, IMPLIES A PARTICULAR RELATIONSHIP WITH THE MOTHER, WHICH TOUCHES ON ANOTHER THEME OF CONSIDERABLE INTEREST TO ME AT THE MOMENT, THAT OF THE IMAGINARY. AS A MATTER OF FACT, THE R.B. IS SOMETHING OF A TURNING POINT BETWEEN FETISHIST THINKING AND THINKING THE IMAGINARY. BECAUSE OF THAT, ONE COULD CONSIDER R.B. BY HIMSELF AS BEING A CHASTER BOOK THAN THE PLEASURE OF THE TEXT: SINCE THERE IS NOT THE PROBLEM OF JOUISSANCE WHICH PREDOMINATES, BUT THAT OF THE IMAGE, OF THE IMAGINARY.

WHAT INTERESTS ME AT THE PRESENT MOMENT IS THE FIELD OF THE IMAGINARY, GIVEN ITS FIRST PRODUCTION IN R.B. BY HIMSELF. AND I'M BEGINNING A SEMINAR AT THE ECOLE DES HAUTES ETUDES ON THE LANGUAGE OF LOVE, WHICH FOR ME IS LINKED EVEN MORE CLOSELY WITH PROBLEMS OF THE IMAGINARY.

ROLAND BARTHES

STE ANNE

$$x\Phi \qquad \underline{x}\underline{A} \qquad x\Phi \qquad x\underline{A}$$

$$\underline{x}\underline{\Phi} \qquad \underline{x}\underline{E} \qquad \underline{x}\underline{\Phi} \qquad x\underline{E}$$

(...) LATE FOR THE FIRST TIME ...

EXCUSE ME, THIS IS THE FIRST TIME THAT I AM FIVE MINUTES LATE. YOU ARE HERE, I AM ALSO HERE AND THIS IS GOOD ... GOOD FOR YOU. BY THIS I MEAN THAT I FEEL ABNORMALLY GOOD, UNDER THE INFLUENCES OF A SLIGHT TEMPERATURE AND SOME DRUGS. IF ALL OF A SUDDEN THIS SET-UP EVER CHANGED, I WOULD HOPE THAT THOSE WHO HAVE BEEN LISTENING TO ME FOR SOME TIME WILL EXPLAIN TO THE INITIATES THAT THIS IS THE FIRST TIME IT HAS HAPPENED TO ME.

SO! I AM GOING TO TRY THIS EVENING TO LIVE UP TO YOUR EXPECTATIONS, ESPECIALLY SINCE I SAID THAT I AM HAVING FUN; IF I CONTINUE SPEAKING IN THE SAME TONE IT IS NOT SIMPLY FORCED. YOU SHOULD EXCUSE ME, THIS SHALL NOT BE CAUSED BY MY ABNORMAL STATE; RATHER IT SHALL BE WITHIN THE LINE OF WHAT I INTENDED TO SAY TO YOU.

ELSEWHERE I DON'T OBVIOUSLY PAY TOO MUCH ATTENTION TO MY LISTENERS. IF SOME OF YOU WERE HERE LAST TIME, (AND IT WOULD SURPRISE ME IF THERE ARE NOT), YOU WILL REMEMBER THAT I SPOKE OF SOMETHING TO DO WITH A SUMMATION OF THE BORROMEAN KNOT, ONE CHAIN IN THREE; IF ONE RING WERE DETACHED FROM THIS CHAIN, THE OTHER TWO WOULD NOT HOLD TOGETHER FOR ONE INSTANT LONGER; I AM FORCED TO EXPLAIN WHY THIS COMES ABOUT AS, AFTER ALL I AM NOT SURE THAT, GIVEN ALL THE FUSS, SIMPLE AS IT IS, THIS IS ENOUGH (FOR ...). THIS IS TO SAY, A QUESTION CONCERNING THE CONDITION, AS I HAD SAID, OF THE UNCONSCIOUS, WHICH IS TO SAY A QUESTION POSED ABOUT WHAT IS LANGUAGE.

ACTUALLY, THERE IS A QUESTION THAT REMAINS UNSETTLED. DOES LANGUAGE HAVE TO BE APPROACHED IN ITS GRAMMAR, IN WHICH CASE, IT IS CERTAIN THAT, IT COMES FROM A TOPOLOGY.

—WHAT IS A TOPOLOGY?

—WHAT'S IN IT?

—WHAT IS A TOPOLOGY?

—AH, WHAT IS A TOPOLOGY? HOW NICE THIS PERSON IS! A TOPOLOGY IS A THING THAT HAS A MATHEMATICAL DEFINITION; IT IS THIS WHICH FIRSTLY COMES ON TO ITSELF, (AND) BY THE NON-METRIC RELATIONS.

—WHAT DOES THIS MEAN?

BY THE DISTORTED RELATIONS, THIS IS, STRICTLY SPEAKING, A CASE OF THOSE KINDS OF SUPPLE CIRCLES WHICH CONSTITUTED MY "I DEMAND YOU TO DENY ME THAT WHICH I OFFER YOU;" EACH ONE IS A CLOSED THING, SUPPLE, AND WHICH ONLY HOLDS TO BE CHAINED TO OTHERS, NOTHING HOLDS TOGETHER ALONE. THIS TOPOLOGY, FROM THE FACT OF ITS . . . OF ITS MATHEMATICAL INSERTION, IS TIED TO THE RELATIONS—AND RIGHT, THIS IS WHAT SERVED TO DEMONSTRATE MY LAST SEMINAR—IS TIED TO THE RELATIONS OF PURE SIGNIFYING, THAT IS THAT IT IS TO THE EXTENT THAT THESE THREE TERMS ARE THREE THAT WE SEE (THAT) THE PRESENCE OF THE THIRD, THAT IS, BETWEEN THE OTHER TWO, IS A RELATION, THAT THIS IS WHAT IS MEANT BY THE BORROMEAN KNOT.

THERE IS ANOTHER WAY TO APPROACH THIS LANGUAGE—AND OF COURSE THE THING IS PRESENT, IT IS PRESENT IN THE FACT THAT SOMEONE, SOMEONE THAT I HAVE QUOTED, WHICH IT TURNS OUT I QUOTED AFTER JAKOBSON DID AND THAT, AS IT TURNS OUT I HAD KNOWN FROM BEFORE . . . NAMELY SOMEONE NAMED RENE THOM, AND THIS SOMEONE TRIES AND CERTAINLY NOT WITHOUT HAVING ALREADY FRAYED OR FACILITATED CERTAIN PATHS, TO APPROACH THE QUESTION OF LANGUAGE UNDER THE SEMANTIC BIAS, THAT IS NOT FROM THE SIGNIFYING COMBINATION, IN AS MUCH AS PURE MATHEMATICS CAN HELP US TO CONCEIVE AS SUCH, BUT UNDER THE SEMANTIC ANGLE,THAT IS TO SAY NOT WITHOUT RESORTING ALSO TO MATHEMATICS TO FIND, TO FIND IN CERTAIN CURVES, LET US SAY, CERTAIN FORMS, I WOULD ADD, ARE DEDUCED FROM THESE CURVES; SOMETHING WHICH WOULD PERMIT US TO CONCEIVE OF LANGUAGE AS, LET'S SAY, SOMETHING LIKE THE ECHO OF PHYSICAL PHENOMENA.

FROM THIS EXAMPLE, IN THAT WHICH IS PURELY AND SIMPLY COMUNICATION (OF) PHENOMENA OF RESONANCE WHICH WOULD BE ELABORATED (BY) CURVES WHICH IN ORDER TO HAVE VALUE IN A CERTAIN ORDER OF FUNDAMENTAL RELATIONS, WOULD SECONDARILY RESSEMBLE, AND HOMOGENIZE SO AS TO BE TAKEN IN THE SAME PARENTHESIS, FROM WHICH WOULD RESULT DIVERSE GRAMMATICAL FUNCTIONS.

IT SEEMS TO ME THAT THERE IS ALREADY AN OBSTACLE IN CONCEIVING THINGS LIKE THIS, THAT IS THAT ONE IS OBLIGED TO PUT UNDER THE SAME TERM VERBS AND VERY DIFFERENT TYPES OF ACTIONS. WHY DOES LANGUAGE ASSEMBLE UNDER THE SAME CATEGORY FUNCTIONS WHICH CAN ONLY BE CONCEIVED OF IN THEIR ORIGIN UNDER DIFFERENT EMERGING MODES?

NEVERTHELESS, THE QUESTION STAYS SUSPENDED; IT IS CERTAIN THAT THERE WOULD BE SOMETHING INFINITELY SATISFYING IN CONSIDERING THAT LANGUAGE IS IN SOME WAY MODELED ON THE FUNCTIONS THAT ARE SUPPOSED TO BE PHYSICAL REALITY, EVEN IF THIS REALITY IS ONLY (ATTAINABLE) THROUGH THE BIAS OF A MATHEMATICAL FUNCTIONALIZATION.

FOR MY PART WHAT I AM IN THE COURSE OF ADVANCING TO YOU IS SOMETHING WHICH IS RADICALLY ATTACHED TO THE PURELY TOPOLOGICAL ORIGIN OF LANGUAGE. I THINK I AM ABLE TO TAKE ACCOUNT OF THIS TOPOLOGICAL ORIGIN BY THE FACT THAT IT IS ESSENTIALLY TIED TO SOMETHING WHICH HAPPENS TO THE SPEAKING BEING UNDER THE BIAS OF SEXUALITY. IS THE SPEAKING BEING SPEAKING BECAUSE OF SOMETHING WHICH HAPPENS TO SEXUALITY OR DOES THE SOMETHING HAPPEN TO SEXUALITY BECAUSE HE IS A SPEAKING BEING, THIS IS THE AFFAIR IN WHICH I ABSTAIN FROM TREADING, LEAVING IT UP TO YOU.

THE FUNDAMENTAL SCHEME OF WHAT THIS IS ABOUT WHICH I WILL TRY TO PUSH A LITTLE FURTHER BEFORE YOU THIS EVENING IS THIS: THE FUNCTION CALLED SEXUALITY IS DEFINED IN AS MUCH AS WE KNOW SOMETHING ABOUT IT, AND WE KNOW A LITTLE ABOUT IT AFTER ALL IF ONLY FROM EXPERIENCE; WE KNOW FOR EXAMPLE THAT THE SEXES ARE TWO.

NO MATTER WHAT A RENOWNED AUTHOR THINKS ABOUT IT—A RENOWNED AUTHOR WHO I MUST SAY IN HER TIME, BEFORE SHE BROUGHT OUT THIS BOOK CALLED THE SECOND SEX, HAD BELIEVED, BECAUSE OF SOME UNKNOWN (TO ME) ORIENTATION (BECAUSE TO TELL THE TRUTH I HAD NOT YET STARTED TO TEACH ANYTHING) HAD BELIEVED SHE REFERRED TO ME BEFORE SHE PUT OUT THE SECOND SEX. SHE CALLED ME ON THE TELEPHONE TO SAY TO ME THAT ASSUREDLY SHE HAD NEED OF MY COUNSEL TO CLARIFY WHAT SHOULD HAVE BEEN THE PSYCHOANALYTIC TRIBUTARY TO HER WORK. AS I POINTED

OUT TO HER THAT IT WOULD HAVE TO BE AT LEAST—AT BOTTOM THIS IS A MINIMUM SINCE I HAVE BEEN SPEAKING FOR 20 YEARS AND THIS IS NOT ACCIDENTAL—5 OR 6 MONTHS BEFORE I COULD STRAIGHTEN OUT THIS QUESTION FOR HER, SHE MADE THE OBSERVATION TO ME THAT IT WOULD NOT BE NORMAL THAT A BOOK, WHICH BESIDES HAVING ALREADY BEEN IN PREPARATION, SHOULD TAKE SO LONG; THE LAWS OF LITERARY PRODUCTION ARE SUCH THAT THEY SEEMED TO HAVE DENIED HER THE POSSIBILITY OF HAVING MORE THAN 3 OR 4 INTERVIEWS WITH ME. FOLLOWING THIS, I DECLINED THE HONOR.

THE BASIS OF WHAT I HAVE FOR SOME TIME BEEN BRINGING OUT FOR YOU IS PRECISELY THIS THAT THERE IS NO SECOND SEX, THAT THERE IS NO SECOND SEX FROM THE MOMENT IN WHICH LANGUAGE ENTERS INTO FUNCTION. OR, TO PUT OTHERWISE THE THINGS CONCERNING WHAT IS CALLED HETEROSEXUALITY, IT IS PRECISELY THIS, THAT THE WORD HÉTÉROS, WHICH IS THE TERM WHICH MEANS OTHER, IN GREEK, IS PRECISELY, IN THIS POSITION, IN THE RELATION THAT IS CALLED SEXUAL IN THE SPEAKING BEING, TO EMPTY ITSELF IN AS MUCH AS IT IS BEING. IT IS PRECISELY FROM THIS EMPTINESS THAT IT OFFERS TO THE SPOKEN WORD WHAT I CALL THE LOCUS OF THE OTHER, NAMELY THAT IN WHICH IS INSCRIBED THE EFFECTS OF THIS SPOKEN WORD. I AM NOT GOING TO EMBELLISH THIS BECAUSE AFTER ALL THAT WOULD DELAY US FROM SEVERAL ETYMOLOGICAL REFERENCES; HOW, HÉTÉROS WHICH IS SAID IN CERTAIN GREEK DIALECTS WHOSE NAMES I WILL SPARE YOU, (RALLIES THE) DEUTÉROS, AND EXACTLY MARKS THAT THIS DEUTÉROS IS, IN THIS CASE IF I MAY SAY SO, PASSED OVER.

IT IS CLEAR THAT THIS CAN SEEM SURPRISING. IT IS OBVIOUS THAT FOR SOME TIME, SUCH AND SUCH A FORMULA (AND IN TRUTH, IF I SAY FOR SOME TIME IT IS THAT I DO NOT KNOW WHETHER THERE WAS AN INDICATION OF A TIME IN WHICH IT WAS A FORMULA), SUCH A FORMULA IS PRECISELY WHAT IS NOT KNOWN. I NEVERTHELESS CLAIM AND I UNDERLINE THAT WHAT YOU SEE IN THE DIAGRAM IS (EVERYTHING) THAT THE PSYCHOANALYTIC EXPERIENCE BRINGS US.

FOR THIS, LET US REMEMBER ON WHAT RESTS WHAT WE CAN HAVE OF THE CONCEPTION,—NOT OF HETEROSEXUALITY, SINCE THIS IS VERY WELL NAMED, IF YOU FOLLOW WHAT I JUST ADVANCED—BUT (OF) BISEXUALITY. AT THE POINT WHERE WE ARE IN OUR STATEMENT CONCERNING THIS SEXUALITY,

WHAT DO WE HAVE, WHAT WE ARE REFERRING TO AND DON'T BELIEVE THAT THIS GOES WITHOUT SAYING, WHAT WE ARE REFERRING TO, IS IF I MIGHT SAY, THE SUPPOSED ANIMAL MODEL. WE HAVE FOR THE RELATION BETWEEN THE SEXES THE ANIMAL IMAGE OF COPULATION THAT SEEMS TO US TO FURNISH A SUFFICIENT MODEL OF WHAT THERE IS TO THIS RELATIONSHIP AND AT THE SAME TIME OF WHAT THERE IS (OF THE) SEXUAL CONSIDERED AS NEED.

IT IS NOT THERE, FAR FROM IT, BELIEVE ME, WHAT HAS ALWAYS BEEN THE WAY IT WAS. I DO NOT NEED TO RECALL WHAT "TO KNOW" MEANS IN THE BIBLICAL SENSE OF THE WORD, SINCE ALWAYS THE RELATION OF THE NOUS TO SOMETHING WHICH EXPERIENCES ITS PASSIVE IMPRINT, WHAT IS CALLED VARIOUSLY BUT ASSUREDLY WHOSE MOST COMMON GREEK DENOMINATION IS THAT OF HYLÉ, HAS ALWAYS BEEN CALLED THE MODE, THE MODE OF RELATION WHICH IS ENGENDERED FROM SPIRIT AND THAT HAS BEEN CONSIDERED AS MODELING NOT AT ALL SIMPLY THE ANIMAL RELATIONSHIP. BUT THE FUNDAMENTAL MODE OF BEING OF WHAT ONE HOLDS TO BE THE WORLD. THE CHINESE, IN THIS CASE, APPEAL TO SOMETHING WHICH IS WRITTEN AS FOLLOWS.

THE CHINESE FOR A LONG TIME APPEALED TO TWO FUNDAMENTAL ESSENCES WHICH ARE RESPECTIVELY—I PUT ABOVE THE FEMININE ESSENCE, (WHAT) IS CALLED YIN IN ORDER TO OPPOSE IT TO YANG.

IF THERE WAS AN ARTICULATABLE RELATION ON THE SEXUAL LEVEL, IF THERE WAS AN ARTICULATABLE RELATION IN THE SPEAKING BEING, MUST IT, AND THIS IS THE QUESTION, DISTINGUISH ITSELF FROM ALL THOSE OF THE SAME SEX, AND EXPRESS ITSELF TO ALL THOSE OF THE OTHER? THIS IS EVIDENT FROM THE IDEA SUGGESTED BY THE POINT WHERE WE ARE, BY THE REFERENCE TO WHAT I'VE CALLED THE ANIMAL MODEL, THE APTITUDE IF I CAN PUT IT THIS WAY, OF EACH FROM ONE SIDE TO COUNT FOR ALL THE OTHERS FROM THE OTHER SIDE.

YOU SEE, THEN, THAT THE STATEMENT IS PROMULGATED ACCORDING TO THE SEMANTIC FORM SIGNIFYING THE UNIVERSAL, REPLACING IN WHAT I SAID EACH ONE BY ANY ONE AT ALL, OR BY NO MATTER

WHICH ONE, NO MATTER WHICH ONE OF ONE OF THESE SIDES, WE WOULD BE COMPLETELY IN THE ORDER OF WHAT, WHAT WOULD BE CALLED, SUGGESTS (RECOGNIZE IN THIS CONDITIONAL SOMETHING WHICH MY DISCOURSE ECHOES WHICH WOULD NOT BE A SEMBLANCE) [THIS IS THE TITLE OF MY SEMINAR NO. 21 (?)] AND WELL! IN REPLACING THIS EACH ONE BY ANYONE AT ALL, WE WOULD BE IN THIS INDETERMINACY OF WHAT IS CHOSEN IN EACH EVERY TO RESPOND TO EVERY OTHER.

THE EACH ONE THAT I HAVE USED FIRST HAS THE EFFECT OF RECALLING TO US THAT THE EFFECTIVE RELATIONSHIP IS NOT WITHOUT EVOKING THE HORIZON OF ONE TO ONE TO EACH HIS OWN EACH, AND THIS BIUNIVOCAL CORRESPONDENCE, ECHOES TO WHAT WE KNOW TO BE ESSENTIAL TO THE PRESENTATION OF NUMBERS.

NB: WE CANNOT FROM THE START ELIMINATE THE EXISTENCE OF THESE TWO DIMENSIONS, AND ONE CAN EVEN SAY THAT THE ANIMAL MODEL IS PRECISELY WHAT SUGGESTS THE ANIMALIC PHANTASM. IF WE WOULD NOT HAVE THIS ANIMAL MODEL, OR EVEN IF THE CHOICE WERE BASED ON A HAPHAZARD ENCOUNTER, THE BIUNIVOCAL COUPLING IS WHAT APPEARS TO US OF IT, NAMELY THERE ARE ONLY TWO ANIMALS WHICH COUPLE TOGETHER. WE WOULD NOT HAVE THIS ESSENTIAL DIMENSION WHICH CONSISTS VERY PRECISELY IN THE FACT THAT THE ENCOUNTER IS UNIQUE. IT IS NO ACCIDENT IF I SAY THAT IT IS EXACTLY FROM THIS, AND FROM THIS ALONE THAT THE ANIMAL MODEL IS AROUSED. LET'S CALL THIS THE ENCOUNTER OF SOUL TO SOUL.

WHOEVER KNOWS THE CONDITIONS OF THE SPEAKING BEING, IS NOT TO BE ASTONISHED IN ANY CASE THAT THE ENCOUNTER ON THIS BASIS SERVES PRECISELY TO BE REPEATED AS UNIQUE. THERE IS NO NEED HERE TO BRING BACK INTO PLAY ANY DIMENSION OF THE VIRTUOUS. IT IS THE VERY NECESSITY OF WHAT IN THE SPEAKING BEING PRODUCES ITSELF OF THE UNIQUE, TO REPEAT ITSELF. IT IS PRECISELY IN THIS SENSE THAT IT IS ONLY THE ANIMAL MODEL THAT SUSTAINS ITSELF AND AROUSES THE PHANTASM THAT WE HAVE CALLED ANIMALIC. OF COURSE, THERE ARE ROYAL BASTARDS, AND THERE ARE SOME FOR WHOM LANGUAGE DOESN'T EXIST, (BUT) IT IS OBVIOUSLY NOT THESE WHO INTEREST US IN THE ANALYTICAL FIELD.

WHAT GIVES THE ILLUSION OF THE SEXUAL RELATIONSHIP IN THE SPEAKING BEING, IS EVERYTHING WHICH MATERIALZES THE UNIVERSAL IN THE BEHAVIOR WHICH IS EFFECTIVELY HERD-LIKE IN THE RELATIONSHIP BETWEEN THE SEXES. I HAVE ALREADY STRESSED THAT IN SO-CALLED SEXUAL HUNTING OR CRUISING, BOYS STIMULATE THEMSELVES, AND AS FOR GIRLS, THEY LOVE TO DOUBLE THEMSELVES, IN AS MUCH AS THIS ADVANCES THEM, OF COURSE. IT IS AN ETHOLOGICAL REMARK THAT I MAKE HERE, BUT WHICH SOLVES NOTHING BECAUSE IT SUFFICES TO REFLECT ON THIS TO SEE IN THIS AN AMBIGUOUS ILLUSION WHICH CANNOT UPHOLD ITSELF FOR LONG.

TO BE MORE INSISTENT HERE AND TO HOLD MYSELF AT THE LEVEL OF THE MOST FUNDAMENTAL EXPERIENCE, I WANT TO STAY CLOSE-CUT TO THE GROUND, TO THE ANALYTICAL EXPERIENCE, I WILL REMIND YOU THAT THE IMAGINARY IS WHAT WE RECONSTITUTE IN THE ANIMAL MODEL. WE RECONSTITUTE IT ACCORDING TO OUR OWN IDEA, OF COURSE; BECAUSE IT IS CLEAR THAT WE CAN ONLY RECONSTRUCT THROUGH OBSERVATION. BUT ON THE CONTRARY, WE HAVE AN EXPERIENCE OF THE IMAGINARY, AN EXPERIENCE WHICH IS NOT EASY (BUT WHICH) THE PSYCHOANALYST IS ABLE TO INCREASE FOR US. TO SAY THINGS CRUDELY, IT WILL NOT SEEM DIFFICULT, IT SEEMS TO ME, TO MAKE UNDERSTOOD THAT IF I MAINTAIN (I CALL THIS CRUDELY, IT IS NOT CRUDE, RATHER IT IS CRUEL, AND WELL! MY GOD,) THAT IN EVERY SEXUAL ENCOUNTER, IF THERE IS SOMETHING THAT PSYCHOANALYSIS ALLOWS ME TO ADVANCE, IT IS SOME VAGUE OUTLINE OF ANOTHER PRESENCE FOR WHICH, MY GOD, THE VULGAR TERM OF FREE-FOR-ALL (ORGY) IS NOT ABSOLUTELY EXCLUDED. THIS REFERENCE IN ITSELF CONTAINS NOTHING DECISIVE SINCE AFTER ALL ONE COULD ASSUME A SERIOUS AIR AND SAY THAT IT IS PRECISELY THE STIGMA OF ANOMALY, AS IF NORMAL, OR SIMPLY: THE NORMAL WAS LOCATED SOMEWHERE.

IT IS CERTAIN THAT IN ADVANCING THIS TERM, THE ONE I JUST PINNED-DOWN WITH THIS BANAL NAME, I CERTAINLY DID NOT SEEK TO VIBRATE IN YOU THE EROTIC LYRE. IF SIMPLY THIS HAS A SMALL VALUE OF AWAKENING, IF THIS GIVES YOU AT LEAST THIS DIMENSION, NOT THAT FROM WHICH COMES AN ECHO OF EROS, BUT SIMPLY OF THE PURE DIMENSION OF THE REAL. I AM CERTAINLY NOT HERE TO AMUSE YOU IN THIS STRAIN.

BUT LET US TRY NOW TO CUT AWAY AT WHAT THE KINSHIP OF THE UNIVERSALITY HAS TO DO WITH OUR AFFAIR, NAMELY THE STATEMENT BY WHICH OBJECTS SHOULD BE DISTRIBUTED IN TWO WHOLES

OF OPPOSED EQUIVALENCES. I HAVE JUST NOTED FOR YOU THAT HERE THERE IS NO PLACE TO DEMAND THE EQUAL DISTRIBUTION OF INDIVIDUALS, THAT I REMAIN HERE AND HAVE BEEN ABLE TO SUPPORT MY DISCOURSE ON THE BIUNIVOCITY OF THE COUPLING. THERE ARE OR RATHER THERE MIGHT BE TWO UNIVERSALS DEFINED JUST BY THE ESTABLISHMENT OF THE POSSIBILITY OF A RELATIONSHIP OF ONE TO ANOTHER, OF THE OTHER TO ONE. THIS RELATIONSHIP HAS ABSOLUTELY NOTHING TO DO WITH WHAT IS ORDINARILY CALLED SEXUAL RELATONSHIPS. ONE HAS A WHOLE LOT OF RELATIONSHIPS TO THESE RELATIONSHIPS AND ABOUT THESE RELATIONSHIPS, ONE ALSO HAS SEVERAL SMALL RELATIONSHIPS; THIS TAKES UP OUR WORLDY LIFE, BUT AT THE LEVEL WHERE I PLACE MYSELF, IT IS A QUESTION OF BASING THESE RELATIONSHIPS WITHIN UNIVERSALS.

HOW DOES UNIVERSAL MAN RELATE HIMSELF TO UNIVERSAL WOMAN, THIS IS THE QUESTION AND THIS IS THE QUESTION WHICH IMPOSES ITSELF ON US BY THE FACT THAT LANGUAGE DEMANDS VERY PRECISELY THAT IT BE FOUNDED FROM HERE; IF THERE WERE NO LANGUAGE, THERE WOULD NO LONGER BE ANY QUESTION EITHER, AND WE WOULD NOT HAVE TO BRING INTO PLAY THE UNIVERSAL. YES! THIS RELATION CAN PRECISELY RE-ENTER THE OTHER WHICH IS ABSOLUTELY FOREIGN TO WHAT COULD HAVE BEEN HERE PURELY AND SIMPLY AS ACCESSORY, WHAT PERHAPS TONIGHT WOULD FORCE ME TO ACCENTUATE THE CAPITAL O, BY WHICH I DESIGNATE THE OTHER AS EMPTY, AS SOMETHING OF SUPPLEMENTARITY, AN H, THE HOTHER, WHICH WOULD NOT BE A BAD WAY OF GETTING ACROSS THE DIMENSION OF HATE WHICH CAN HERE ENTER INTO PLAY, OR FOR US TO NOTICE (WHEN) FOR EXAMPLE, EVERYTHING WE HAVE OF PHILOSOPHICAL CONCOCTION DOES NOT, BY CHANCE, COME FROM ONE CALLED SOCRATES MANIFESTLY HYSTERICAL, I MEAN TO SAY, CLINICALLY HYSTERICAL; WE WOULD HAVE THE RELATIONSHIP OF THESE CATALEPTIC (. . .) MANIFESTATIONS OF THE ONE CALLED SOCRATES, IF HE COULD HOLD A DISCOURSE WHICH IS NOT FOR NOTHING AT THE ORIGIN OF THE DISCOURSE OF SCIENCE. IT IS PRECISELY FOR HAVING BROUGHT THE PURE SUBJECT TO THE PLACE OF THE SEMBLANCE, AND THIS HE COULD DO PRECISELY ON ACCOUNT OF THIS DIMENSION WHICH FOR ME PRESENTED THE HOTHER AS SUCH, NAMELY THIS HATRED OF HIS WIFE, TO CALL IT BY HER NAME, THIS PERSON (. . . WHO WAS) HIS WIFE, HIS WIFE TO THE DEGREE THAT SHE STARVED FOR HIM, THAT HE HAD TO, AT THE POINT OF HIS DEATH, POLITELY BEG HER

TO RETIRE IN ORDER TO ALLOW THIS DEATH, ITS POLITICAL SIGNIFICANCE. THIS IS SIMPLY A DIMENSION FOR THE INDICATION CONCERNING EXACTLY WHERE THE QUESTION LIES THAT WE ARE RAISING.

I HAVE SAID THAT IF WE CAN SAY THAT THERE IS NO SEXUAL RELATION, THIS IS ASSUREDLY NOT IN ALL INNOCENCE. IT IS BECAUSE THE EXPERIENCE, NAMELY A MODE OF DISCOURSE WHICH IS SURELY NEVER THAT OF THE HYSTERIC WHICH IS BUT THE ONE WHICH I HAVE INSCRIBE UNDER A QUADRUPAL DIVISION* AS BEING THE ANALYTICAL DISCOURSE, AND WHICH COMES OUT OF THIS DISCOURSE IS THE HERETOFORE UNEVOKED DIMENSION OF THE PHALLIC FUNCTION.

IT IS NAMELY THIS SOMETHING BY WHICH THIS SEXUAL RELATIONSHIP DOES NOT CHARACTERIZE AT LEAST ONE OF THESE TWO TERMS, MORE PRECISELY THE TERM ATTACHED TO THE WORD: THE ONE,—HOW LONG IS IT GOING TO LAST?—IT IS NOT FROM ITS POSITION (OF ONE) WHICH WOULD BE REDUCIBLE TO THIS SOMETHING THAT IS CALLED EITHER MALE, OR IN CHINESE TERMINOLOGY THE YANG ESSENCE, IT IS PRECISELY ON THE CONTRARY OWING TO THIS WHICH AFTER ALL MERITS TO BE RECALLED, TO ACENTUATE THE MEANING, THE HIDDEN MEANING BECAUSE IT COMES TO US FROM AFAR, OF THE TERM ORGAN, IT IS EXACTLY THIS WHICH IS ONLY AN ORGAN, TO ACCENTUATE THINGS, AGAIN, A TOOL. IT IS AROUND THE TOOL THAT THE ANALYTICAL EXPERIENCE INCITES US TO SEE TURNING EVERYTHING THAT IS SAID BY THE SEXUAL RELATION, AND THIS IS A NOVELTY, THIS IS EVERYTHING WHICH ANSWERS TO THE EMERGENCE OF A DISCOURSE WHICH ASSUREDLY HAS NEVER YET COME TO LIGHT AND WHICH CANNOT CONCEIVE OF ITSELF BY PRIOR EMERGENCE FROM THE DISCOURSE OF SCIENCE IN SO FAR AS IT IS THE INSERTION OF LANGUAGE OVER THE MATHEMATICAL REAL.

I HAVE SAID THAT WHAT IN THE RELATIONSHIP OF BEING IS STIGMATIZED IN THE DEEPLY SUBVERTED LANGUAGE IS PRECISELY THAT THERE IS NO LONGER A WAY, HOW NEVERTHELESS IT IS DONE, BUT IN A DIMENSION WHICH APPEARS TO US TO BE AN ILLUSION, THAT IT CAN NO LONGER WRITE ITSELF IN TERMS OF MALE AND FEMALE ESSENCES. WHAT DOES THIS MEAN WHEN AFTER ALL, IT IS ALREADY WRITTEN?

IF I REJECT THIS ANCIENT WRITING (IN THE NAME) OF

THE ANALYTIC DISCOURSE, YOU COULD OBJECT—A MORE THAN VALID OBJECTION—THAT I MYSELF WRITE IT ALSO, SINCE IN ANY CASE WHAT I JUST PUT BACK ONE MORE TIME ON THE PAGE IS SOMETHING WHICH CLAIMS TO SUPPORT A WRITING, THE NETWORK OF THE SEXUAL AFFAIR.

NEVERTHELESS, THIS WRITING ONLY AUTHORIZES ITSELF, ONLY TAKES ITS FORM, FROM A VERY SPECIFIC WRITING, NAMELY WHAT HAS PERMITTED THE INTRODUCTION IN LOGIC OF AN IRRUPTION, NAMELY A MATHEMATICAL TOPOLOGY. IT IS ONLY FROM THE EXISTENCE OF THE FORMULATION OF THIS TOPOLOGY THAT WE COULD, FOR ANY PROPOSITION, IMAGINE THAT WE CAN MAKE A PROPOSITION FUNCTION. THAT IS TO SAY, SOMETHING WHICH SPECIFIES ITSELF FROM THE EMPTY PLACE THAT ONE LEAVES HERE AND IN FUNCTION OF WHICH THE ARGUMENT DETERMINES ITSELF.

HERE, I CAN POINT OUT TO YOU PRECISELY WHAT I HAVE BORROWED FROM THE TRADITION OF MATHEMATICAL INSCRIPTION, IN SO FAR AS IT IS SUBSTITUTED FOR THE FIRST FORMS—I DON'T SAY FORMALIZATION—OUTLINED BY ARISTOTLE IN HIS SYLLOGISTICS; CONSEQUENTLY THIS INSCRIPTION UNDER THE TERM FUNCTION/ARGUMENT WOULD BE ABLE TO OFFER US AN EASY TERM TO SPECIFY SEXUAL OPPOSITION. WHAT IS REQUIRED? IT WOULD SUFFICE THAT THE RESPECTIVE FUNCTIONS OF MALE AND FEMALE BE DISTINGUISHED AS YIN AND YANG.

IT IS PRECISELY BECAUSE THE FUNCTION IS UNIQUE, THAT IT IS ALWAYS ABOUT THE F OF X, THAT IT IS ENGENDERED, AS YOU KNOW, AS IT IS NOT POSSIBLE, FROM THE SOLE FACT THAT YOU ARE HERE, THAT YOU AT LEAST MUST HAVE A SMALL IDEA OF WHAT THE DIFFICULTY OF COPULATION ITSELF ENGENDERS.

THE Φ OF X AFFIRMS THAT IT IS TRUE—IT IS THE SENSE GIVEN TO THE TERM FUNCTION—THAT WHAT RELATES TO THE EXERCISE, IN THE REGISTER OF THE SEXUAL ACT, COMES FROM THE PHALLIC FUNCTION AGAIN. IT IS PRECISELY IN AS MUCH AS IT IS A MATTER OF THE PHALLIC FUNCTION FROM WHATEVER SIDE WE LOOK AT, I MEAN FROM ONE SIDE OR FROM THE OTHER, THAT SOMETHING SOLICITES US TO AKS THEN, HOW DO THE TWO DIFFER. AND THIS IS PRECISELY WHAT THE TWO FORMULAS IN THE DIAGRAM SAY.

IF IT IS PROVED FROM THE FACT THAT TO DOMINATE

EQUALLY THE TWO PARTNERS, THE PHALLIC FUNCTON DOES NOT MAKE THEM DIFFERENT, IT REMAINS NO LESS CLEAR THAT FIRST OF ALL THAT WE MUST SEARCH FOR THE DIFFERENCE ELSEWHERE.

AND IT IS HERE THAT THESE FORMULAS MERIT QUESTIONING FROM BOTH SIDES; THE LEFT SIDE ITSELF OPPOSING THE RIGHT, THE HIGHER LEVEL ITSELF OPPOSING THE LOWER LEVEL; WHAT DOES THIS MEAN? WHAT THIS MEANS DESERVES TO BE SOUNDED, OR INVESTIGATED; BUT FIRST, I SHALL SHOW HOW THEY CAN DEMONSTRATE A CERTAIN SUPPORT.

IT IS PLAIN THAT IT IS NOT BECAUSE I HAVE EMPLOYED A FORMULATION MADE FROM THE IRRUPTION OF MATHEMATICS INTO LOGIC THAT I MYSELF TAKE THIS ALL TOGETHER IN THE SAME WAY; MY FIRST OBSERVATIONS WILL CONSIST OF SHOWING THAT, IN EFFECT, THE MANNER IN WHICH I USE THIS IS SUCH THAT IT IS IN NO WAY TRANSLATABLE IN TERMS OF PROPOSITIONAL LOGIC. I MEAN THAT MODE IN WHICH THE VARIABLE, OR WHAT IS CALLED THE VARIABLE, NAMELY, THAT WHICH OCCUPIES A PLACE IN AN ARGUMENT, IS SOMETHING WHICH HERE IS COMPLETELY SPECIFIED BY THE QUADRUPLE FORM UNDER WHICH THE RELATION OF THE ARGUMENT TO THE FUNCTION IS POSED.

IN ORDER TO MERELY INTRODUCE WHAT IT IS ABOUT, I WILL REMIND YOU THAT IN PROPOSITIONAL LOGIC, WE HAVE AT THE FIRST LEVEL 4 FUNDAMENTAL RELATIONS: NEGATION, CONJUNCTION, DISJUNCTION AND IMPLICATION. THERE ARE OTHERS, BUT THESE COME FIRST, AND ALL OTHERS GO BACK TO THEM.

I MAINTAIN THAT THE WAY IN WHICH OUR POSITIONS OF ARGUMENT AND FUNCTION ARE WRITTEN ARE SUCH THAT WHAT IS POSED AS TRUTH CAN ONLY NEGATE BY PASSING INTO THE REALM OF THE FALSE PRECISELY WHAT IS UNTENABLE HERE. THIS IS THE SO-CALLED NEGATIVE RELATION, BECAUSE AT NO MATTER WHAT LEVEL, LOWER OR HIGHER, THE STATEMENT OF THE FUNCTION AS PHALLIC IS POSED EITHER AS TRUTH, OR PRECISELY, AS DEVIATION; BECAUSE AFTER ALL, THE TRUE TRUTH WOULD BE EXACTLY THAT WHICH DOESN'T WRITE ITSELF, THAT WHICH HERE CANNOT WRITE ITSELF EXCEPT IN A FORM WHICH CONTESTS THE PHALLIC FUNCTION. IT IS NOT TRUE THAT THE PHALLIC FUNCTION IS THE FOUNDATION OF THE SEXUAL

RELATION; IN THESE TWO LEVELS WHICH STAY INDEPENDENT AS SUCH, IT IS NOT A MATTER AT ALL OF MAKING ONE THE NEGATION OF THE OTHER BUT ON THE CONTRARY OF MAKING ONE THE OBSTACLE OF THE OTHER, AGAINST THAT WHICH YOU SEE REDISTRIBUTED; IT IS PRECISELY AN IT THAT EXISTS AND AN IT THAT DOES NOT EXIST; IT IS A WHOLE ON THE ONE SIDE, AND ALL X, THE DOMAIN OF WHAT IS MALE DEFINING ITSELF BY THE PHALLIC FUNCTION; THE DIFFERENCE IN THE POSITION OF THE ARGUMENT IN THE PHALLIC POSITION OR FUNCTION IS PRECISELY THAT IT IS NOT EVERY WOMAN WHICH WRITES ITSELF. FAR FROM THE ONE ITSELF OPPOSED TO THE OTHER AS ITS NEGATION, IT IS ON THE CONTRARY FROM THEIR SUBSISTANCE (HERE VERY POSITIVELY DENIED) THAT THERE IS AN X WHICH CAN UPHOLD ITSELF IN THIS REALM BEYOND THE PHALLIC FUNCTION, AND ON THE OTHER HAND, THAT THERE IS NOT ONLY ONE, FOR THE SIMPLE REASON THAT WOMEN CANNOT BE CASTRATED FOR THE BEST OF REASONS. THIS IS THE LEVEL OF WHAT IS BLOCKED PRECISELY FOR US IN THE SEXUAL RELATION, WHILE ON THE LEVEL OF THE PHALLIC FUNCTION, IT IS PRECISELY THE NOT-ALL* OPPOSED TO THE ALL; THEREIN LIES THE POSSIBILITY OF A REDISTRIBUTION FROM LEFT TO RIGHT, (WHICH ITSELF) WILL BE FOUNDED AS MALE AND AS FEMALE.

THE NEGATIVE RELATION DOESN'T AT ALL FORCE US TO CHOOSE; ON THE CONTRARY, I AS MUCH AS WE ARE FAR FROM HAVING TO CHOOSE, AND THAT WE MUST REDISTRIBUTE, THE TWO SIDES ARE LEGITIMATELY OPPOSED TO EACH OTHER.

AFTER NEGATION, I MENTIONED CONJUNCTION. I WOULD NOT NEED TO ACCOUNT FOR CONJUCTION IN THIS CASE, EXCEPT TO MAKE THE OBSERVATION. (I HOPE THERE ARE ENOUGH PEOPLE HERE WHO HAVE VAGUELLY BROWSED A BOOK ON LOGIC SO THAT I NEED NOT INSIST) THAT THE CONJUNCTION IS BASED PRECISELY ON THIS: VALUE DERIVES ONLY BY VIRTUE OF THE FACT THAT BOTH PROPOSITIONS CAN BE TRUE.

NOW! THIS IS EXACTLY WHAT IN NO WAY ALLOWS US TO MAINTAIN WHAT IS IN THE DIAGRAM, SINCE YOU CAN SEE THAT FROM RIGHT TO LEFT, THERE IS NO IDENTITY AND PRECISELY THERE WHERE A QUESTION OF WHAT IS PROPOSED AS TURE EXISTS, BEARING IN MIND Φ TO X, UNIVERSALS CAN CONJOIN. THE UNIVERSAL OF THE LEFT SIDE DOES NOT OPPOSE ITSELF TO THE RIGHT SIDE, TO THE EXTENT THAT IT HAS NO ARTICULABLE UNIVERSAL; THAT IS IT IS THE WOMAN WHO SEES THE PHALLIC

FUNCTION, AND SITUATES HERSELF THERE ONLY AS THE NOT-ALL TO BE SUBJUGATED.

WHAT IS STRANGE IS THE THE DISJUNCTION NO LONGER HOLDS; IF YOU REMEMBER, THE DISJUNCTION ONLY TAKES ON VALUE BY VIRTUE OF THE FACT THAT TWO PROPOSITIONS CANNOT BE FALSE AT THE SAME TIME; LET US SAY, OF THE STRONGEST OR THE WEAKEST, IT IS ASSUREDLY THE STRONGEST RELATION IN THAT IT IS WHAT IS THE MOST DIFFICULT TO STIR TOGETHER, BECAUSE THERE MUST BE A MINIMUM FOR THERE TO BE DISJUNCTION, THAT DISJUNCTION RENDERS VALID ONE PROPOSITION TO BE TRUE, THE OTHER FALSE, AND THAT OF COURSE BOTH OF THEM ARE TRUE. I HAVE CALLED THE ONE TRUE, THE OTHER FALSE; IT IS PERHAPS THAT THE ONE IS FALSE, AND THE OTHER TRUE; THERE IS THEN AT LEAST THREE CASES OF COMBINATIONS WHICH THE DISJUNCTION UPHOLDS.

NOW HERE WE HAVE TWO FUNCTIONS WHICH ARE POSITED AS NOT BEING—AS I SAID A MOMENT AGO—THE TRUE TRUTH, THOSE WHICH ARE ABOVE; WE SEEM TO HOLD HERE SOMETHING WHICH GIVES HOPE, NAMELY THAT WE HAVE ARTICULATED A TRUE DISJUNCTION. HOWEVER, LET US NOTE WHAT THERE IS OF THE WRITTEN, WHICH I HAVE THE OPPORTUNITY TO ARTICULATE IN A MANNER BRINGING IT ALIVE FOR YOU; ON ONE SIDE OF THIS Φ OF X NEGATED WHERE THE PHALLIC FUNCTION DOES NOT FUNCTION, THERE IS A POSSIBILITY OF SEXUAL RELATIONSHIP. WE HAVE POSITED THAT THERE EXISTS AN X (. . .), NOW WHAT DO WE HAVE ON THE OTHER SIDE—WHERE THERE DOES NOT EXIST AN X?

IN THE WAY THAT THE MODE IN WHICH THE DIFFERENTIATION BETWEEN MALE AND FEMALE, BETWEEN MAN AND WOMAN IN THE SPEAKING BEING WOULD BE SUPPORTED, THERE IS A DISCORD. WE WILL SEE LATER WHAT THIS MEANS. AT THE LEVEL OF UNIVERSALS WHICH ARE NOT SUPPORTED, FROM THE FACT OF THE INCONSISTENCY OF ONE AMONG THEM, WHEN WE DEVIATE FROM THE FUNCTION ITSELF, THERE EXISTS ON ONE SIDE AN X WHICH SATISFIES Φ X NEGATED, ON THE OTHER SIDE WE HAVE THE DEFINITE FORMULATION THAT NO X (WHICH I HAVE ILLUSTRATED BY SAYING THAT WOMAN FOR THE BEST OF REASONS, CANNOT BE CASTRATED) WHICH IS TO SAY AT THE LEVEL WHERE THE DISJUNCTION WOULD HAVE THE OPPORTUNITY TO PRODUCE ITSELF, WE FIND ONLY ON THE ONE SIDE, FROM THE ONE/ONE AT LEAST WHAT I HAVE PUT FORTH OF THE AT-LEAST-ONE, AND ON THE OTHER WE FIND VERY PRECISELY THE NON-

EXISTENCE, THAT IS THE RELATION OF ONE TO ZERO.

WHERE THE SEXUAL RELATIONSHIP WOULD HAVE NO OPPORTUNITY TO ACCOMPLISH ITSELF, BUT SIMPLY TO BE HOPED BEYOND THE ABOLITION THROUGH DIVERSION FROM THE PHALLIC FUNCTION, WE FIND ONLY ONE OF THE TWO SEXES AS A PRESENCE.

THIS IS PRECISELY WHAT IT BRINGS CLOSER TO US OF THE EXPERIENCE WHERE WOMAN (THE UNIVERSAL FOR WOMAN DOESN'T KNOW HOW TO ARISE FROM THE PHALLIC FUNCTION,) ONLY PARTICIPATES EITHER TO WANT TO ENRAPTURE MAN, OR MY GOD! SHE IMPOSES ON HIM THE SERVICE OF THE PHALLIC FUNCTION, OR WORST OF ALL AND THIS IS PERHAPS THE CASE IN WHICH IT SHOULD BE SAID, SHE GIVES THE PHALLIC FUNCTION BACK TO HIM. BUT THIS DOESN'T UNIVERSALIZE HER. IT IS NOT THIS WHICH IS THE ROOT OF NOT-ALL; SHE REVEALS A PLEASURE OTHER THAN PHALLIC; FEMININE JOUISSANCE WHICH IN NO WAY DEPENDS ON THIS. IF WOMAN IS NOT NOT-ALL, IT IS BECAUSE HER JOUISSANCE IS DUAL.

THIS IS IN FACT WHAT TIRESIAS REVEALED WHEN HE RETURNED FROM BEING, BY THE GRACE OF ZEUS, THERESE, FOR A WHILE, WITH OF COURSE THE CONSEQUENCES WE ALL KNOW, AND WHICH WERE LAID-OUT, VISIBLE. THIS IS PERHAPS THE CASE THAT REVEALED TO OEDIPUS WHAT WOULD AWAIT HIM, AS HAVING EXISTED, AS MAN OF THIS SUPREME POSSESSION AND WHAT WOULD RESULT IN DECEPTION WHERE HIS PARTNER WOULD KEEP HIM FROM THE TRUE NATURE OF WHAT SHE OFFERED FOR HIS JOUISSANCE. OR LET US SAY IT IN ANOTHER WAY, WHAT WOULD RESULT IN DECEPTION SINCE HIS PARTNER DEMANDED HIM TO REFUSE WHAT SHE OFFERED HIM.

THIS MANIFESTS AT THE LEVEL OF THE MYTH, THAT IN ORDER TO EXIST AS A MAN AT A LEVEL SO AS TO ESCAPE THE PHALLIC FUNCTION, THERE WOULD BE NO OTHER WOMAN THAN THE ONE WHO OUGHT PRECISELY NOT TO HAVE EXISTED FOR HIM.

THERE! WHY SHOULDN'T SHE HAVE EXISTED, WHY THE PROHIBITION OF INCEST? THIS WOULD NECESSITATE THAT I GET INVOLVED ALONG THE TRACK OF THE NAME OF THE FATHER WHERE PRECISELY I HAVE SAID THAT I WOULD NEVER TREAD AGAIN BECAUSE I REREAD (BECAUSE SOMEONE ASKED ME TO) MY FIRST CONFERENCE HERE AT ST. ANNE IN 1963 AND IT EVEN HAS A

CERTAIN DIGNITY, SO THAT I WILL PUBLISH IT ONE OF THESE DAYS. IF I PUBLISH AGAIN, WHICH DOESN'T DEPEND ON ME, OTHERS WOULD HAVE TO PUBLISH WITH ME, AS THIS WOULD ENCOURAGE ME A LITTLE. AND IF I PUBLISH, YOU WILL SEE WITH WHAT CARE I HAVE LOCATED THE THINGS WHICH I HAVE ALREADY SAID FOR 5 YEARS, ON A CERTAIN NUMBER OF REGISTERS ABOUT THE PATERNAL METAPHOR, AND THE PROPER NAME. FINALLY THERE WAS EVERYTHING NECESSARY SO THAT, WITH THE BIBLE, I GAVE MEANING TO THIS MYTHIC ELUCUBRATION. BUT I WON'T DO THIS EVER AGAIN.

I WON'T DO THIS EVER AGAIN BECAUSE AFTER ALL I CAN SATISFY MYSELF BY FORMULATING THINGS AT THE LEVEL OF LOGICAL STRUCTURE, WHICH CERTAINLY HAS ITS RIGHTS.

THERE! THIS E OF X SLASHED, (IT DOESN'T EXIST, NOTHING EXISTS AT A CERTAIN LEVEL, WHERE THERE WOULD BE A CHANCE FOR SEXUAL RELATIONSHIPS) THE HÉTÉROS IN SO MUCH AS IT IS ABSENT, IS NOT AT ALL NECESSARILY THE PRIVILEDGE OF THE FEMINIE SEX. IT IS SIMPLY THE INDICATION OF WHAT IN MY DIAGRAM HAD ITS LITTLE DESTINY OF WHAT I INSCRIBE AS THE SIGNIFIER OF THE SLASHED O. THIS MEANS THE OTHER; NO MATTER WHERE ONE TAKES IT, THE OTHER IS ABSENT FROM THE MOMENT THAT IT'S A QUESTION OF SEXUAL RELATIONSHIPS.

NATURALLY, AT THE LEVEL OF WHAT FUNCTIONS, THAT IS TO SAY THE PHALLIC FUNCTION, THERE IS SIMPLY THIS DISCOURSE THAT I HAVE JUST MENTIONED. ON ONE SIDE AND THE OTHER, AUTOMATICALLY ONE IS NOT IN THE SAME POSITION. ON ONE SIDE IS A UNIVERSAL, BASED ON A RELATION NECESSARY TO THE PHALLIC FUNCTION, AND ON THE OTHER SIDE IS A RELATION OF CONTINGENCY BECAUSE WOMAN IS NOT-ALL. I STRESS THEN THAT AT THE HIGHER LEVEL, THE RELATIONSHIP FOUNDED ON THE DISAPPEARANCE, THE VANISHING, THE EXISTENCE OF ONE OF THE PARTNERS WHO LEAVES THE PLACE EMPTY FOR THE INSCRIPTION OF SPEECH, IS NOT AT THIS LEVEL THE PRIVILEDGE OF EITHER SIDE. IT IS JUST THAT IN ORDER FOR THERE TO BE A BASIS FOR SEX, THERE MUST BE TWO, SURELY 0 AND 1 MAKE 2, ON THE SYMBOLIC PLANE, IN SO FAR AS WE AGREE THAT EXISTENCE IS ROOTED IN THE SYMBOL. THIS IS WHAT DEFINES THE SPEAKING BEING.

IT IS IN FACT SOMETHING THAT IS NOT WHAT IT IS. IT IS JUST THAT THIS BEING IS ABSOLUTELY UNGRASPABLE AND IT IS ALL THE MORE UNGRASP-

ABLE BECAUSE IT IS OBLIGED TO SUPPORT ITSELF THROUGH THE SYMBOL. IT IS CLEAR THAT A BEING, WHICH COMES TO BE ONLY THROUGH THE SYMBOL, IS PRECISELY THIS BEING WITHOUT BEING IN WHICH (FROM THE SOLE FACT THAT YOU SPEAK) YOU ALL PARTICIPATE, BUT WHICH ON THE OTHER HAND, CERTAINLY SUPPORTS ITSELF AND IS EXISTENCE SINCE EXISTING IS NOT BEING, THIS IS TO SAY, EXISTING IS NOT DEPENDING ON THE OTHER.

YOU ARE ALL HERE TO SOME DEGREE TO EXIST, BUT YOU ARE NOT PARTICULARLY CALM ABOUT THE NATURE OF YOUR OWN BEING, OTHERWISE YOU WOULDN'T COME TO SEEK ASSURANCE IN SO MANY PSYCHOANALYTIC EFFORTS.

HERE THERE IS SOMETHING COMPLETELY ORIGINAL IN THE FIRST EMERGENCE OF LOGIC: THE DIFFICULTY, THE INDECISION THAT ARISTOTLE SHOWED CONCERNING THE STATUS OF A PARTICULAR PROPOSITION. THESE ARE DIFFICULTIES THAT HAVE BEEN STRESSED ELSEWHERE, BUT THAT I DID NOT DISCOVER. FOR THOSE WHO DESIRE A REFERENCE, I REFER YOU TO CAHIER NO. 10 OF THE CAHIERS POUR L'ANALYSE. THE ARTICLE BY JACQUES BRUNSCHWIG IS EXCELLENT; YOU WILL SEE PERFECTLY THE DIFFICULTY WHICH ARISTOTLE HAD WITH THE PARTICULAR.

HE PERCEIVED THAT EXISTENCE IN NO WAY CAN BE ESTABLISHED OUTSIDE OF THE UNIVERSAL; FOR THIS REASON, HE SITUATES EXISTENCE AT THE LEVEL OF THE PARTICULAR, AND THIS PARTICULAR IN NO WAY SUFFICES TO SUPPORT IT EVEN THOUGH HE SEEMS TO SUPPORT IT BY VIRTUE OF THE USE OF THE WORD SOME.

ON THE CONTRARY WHAT RESULTS FROM THE SO-CALLED FORMALIZATION OF QUANTIFIERS (CALLED QUANTIFIERS BECAUSE OF A TRACE, LEFT IN THE PHILOSOPHY OF HISTORY THROUGH THE FACT THAT SOMEONE NAMED APULIA, A NOVELIST OF NOT VERY GOOD TASTE AND AN UNRESTRAINED MYSTIC, AND WHO CREATED THE GOLDEN ASS, ONE DAY INTRODUCED THE IDEA THAT IN ARISTOTLE EVERYTHING THAT CONCERNS ALL AND SOME WAS OF THE ORDER OF QUANTITY. IT WAS NOT AT ALL LIKE THAT.) IS SIMPLY TWO DIFFERENT MODES OF WHAT I MIGHT CALL, IF YOU WILL ALLOW ME A LITTLE IMPROVIZATION, THE INCARNATION OF THE SYMBOL. THE PASSAGE INTO ORDINARY LIFE OF THE FACT THAT THERE IS ALL AND SOME IN ALL LANGUAGES ASSUREDLY FORCES US TO POSE THAT ALL LANGUAGE MUST HAVE THE SAME ROOTS AND THAT AS ALL LANGUAGES ARE DEEPLY DIFFERENT IN THEIR STRUCTURE, THERE MUST WELL BE A RELATIONSHIP TO SOMETHING WHICH IS NOT LANGUAGE.

OF COURSE IT IS EASY TO UNDERSTAND THAT PEOPLE WILL SLIP GROUND ON THE PRETEXT THAT WHAT SEEMS TO THEM TO BE THIS "BEYOND OF LANGUAGE" CAN ONLY BE MATHEMATICAL. THIS IS BECAUSE IT IS A NUMBER, IT IS A QUESTION OF QUANTITY. BUT PERHAPS IT IS NOT STRICTLY SPEAKING NUMERICITY IN ALL ITS REALITY TO WHICH LANGUAGE GIVES ACCESS, BUT ONLY THE CAPACITY TO ANCHOR THE ZERO AND ONE. THROUGH THIS THE ENTRANCE WOULD BE MADE REAL, THE REAL WHICH ALONE CAN BE THE "BEYOND OF LANGUAGE," NAMELY THE ONLY DOMAIN IN WHICH A SYMBOLIC IMPOSSIBILITY CAN BE FORMULATED.

THIS RELATIONSHIP, ACCESSIBLE TO LANGUAGE, IF IT IS PRECISELY FOUNDED ON A SEXUAL NON-RELATIONSHIP CAN ONLY THEREFORE CONFRONT 0 AND 1; THIS FACT WOULD EASILY FIND ITS REFLECTION IN THE ELABORATION FREGE GIVES OF THE LOGICAL GENESIS OF NUMBERS.

I HAVE SPOKEN OF THAT WHICH CAUSES DIFFICULTY IN THIS LOGICAL GENESIS, NAMELY THE GAP, THE GAP OF THE MATHEMATICAL TRIANGLE, BETWEEN THIS 0 AND THIS 2, A GAP WHICH DOUBLES THEIR OPPOSITION OF CONFRONTATION. WHAT INTERVENES IS THERE ONLY BECAUSE IT IS THE ESSENCE OF THE FIRST COUPLE, SO THAT THERE MIGHT BE THE ESSENCE OF THE THIRD AND SO THAT THE GAP AS SUCH IS ALWAYS LEFT TO THE TWO; THIS IS SOMETHING WHICH IS ESSENTIAL BECAUSE OF SOMETHING MUCH MORE DANGEROUS WHICH MIGHT BE SUBSTITUTED IN THE ANALYSIS OF THE MYTHICAL ADVENTURES OF OEDIPUS (IN THEMSELVES IN NO WAY DISTURBING IN AS MUCH AS THEY ADMIRABLY STRUCTURE THE NECESSITY THAT THERE BE SOMEWHERE AT-LEAST-ONE WHICH TRANSCENDS WHAT THERE IS OF THE GRASP OF THE PHALLIC FUNCTION; THE MYTH OF THE PRIMAL FATHER MEANS NOTHING OTHER THAN THIS). THIS IS SUFFICIENT ENOUGH FOR US TO MAKE USE OF IT BEYOND THE FACT THAT WE FIND IT CONFIRMED BY LOGICAL STRUCTURATION.

ON THE OTHER HAND, THERE IS ASSUREDLY NOTHING MORE DANGEROUS THAN THE CONFUSION OVER WHAT THERE IS OF THE ONE. THE ONE IS FREQUENTLY EVOKED BY FREUD AS THE SIGNIFIER OF THE ESSENCE OF EROS: IT AND THE LIBIDO WOULD BOTH STRAIN TO MAKE ONE. ACCORDING TO

AN OLD MYTH (NOT AT ALL OF THE MYTHICAL MODE) ONE OF THE FUNDAMENTAL TENSIONS OF THE WORLD WOULD STRAIN TO MAKE ONLY ONE. THIS MYTH IS TRULY SOMETHING WHICH CAN ONLY FUNCTION ON THE HORIZON OF DELIRIUM AND WHICH, STRICTLY SPEAKING, HAS NOTHING TO DO WITH ANYTHING AT ALL WHICH WE ENCOUNTER IN EXPERIENCE. IF THERE IS ANYTHING VERY OVERT IN THE RELATIONSHIP BETWEEN SEXES, THAT ANALYSIS NOT ONLY ARTICULATES BUT CAN BE PUT INTO PLAY IN ALL DIRECTIONS AND SENSES, HERE IS SOMETHING WHICH CAUSES DIFFICULTY IN RELATIONSHIPS. THIS IS PRECISELY RELATION-SHIPS BETWEEN WOMEN; NOTHING COULD RESEM-BLE THE SPONTANEITY OF THESE RELATIONSHIPS, WHICH IS NOW PRECISELY THE HORIZON I MEN-TIONED EARLIER, AN ANIMALIC BASED ON SOME ANIMAL MYTH; IN NO WAY IS EROS A TENDENCY OF THE ONE. ACCORDING TO THIS FUNCTION, ANY ARTICULATION MAKES CLEAR THAT THERE ARE TWO LEVELS OF SECRECY IN WHICH THE OPPOSITION BETWEEN THE SEXES IS FOUNDED ONLY IN DISCORD AND ONLY IN AS MUCH AS THEY CAN IN NO WAY BE INSTITUTED AS UNIVERSAL. AT THE LEVEL OF EXISTENCE ON THE CONTRARY, IS PRECISELY AN OPPOSITION CONSISTING IN THE CANCELLATION, THE EMPTYING OF ONE OF THE FUNCTIONS AS BEING THAT OF THE OTHER, REVEALED BY THE POSSIBILITY OF AN ARTICULATION OF LANGUAGE. THIS IS WHAT SEEMS TO ME ESSENTIAL TO BRING TO LIGHT.

NOTICE THAT A MOMENT AGO IN SPEAKING TO YOU SUCCESSIVELY ABOUT NEGATION, CONJUNCTION AND DISJUNCTION, I HAD PUSHED TO THE LIMIT WHAT THERE WAS OF IMPLICATION. IT IS CLEAR THAT, HERE AGAIN, IMPLICATION CAN FUNCTION ONLY BETWEEN THE TWO LEVELS, THAT OF THE PHALLIC FUNCTION AND THAT WHICH DIVERTS IT.

NOW NOTHING OF WHAT IS DISJUNCTION ON THE LOWER LEVEL, ON THE LEVEL OF THE INSUFFICIEN-CY OF UNIVERSAL SPECIFICATION, IMPLIES THAT IF AND ONLY IF THE SYNCOPATION OF EXISTENCE WHICH IS PRODUCED ON THE HIGHER LEVEL IS ACTUALLY PRODUCED, THEN DISCORD ON THE LOWER LEVEL IS REQUIRED AND VICE VERSA.

ON THE OTHER HAND, IT IS ONCE AGAIN THE FUNCTIONING OF THE RELATIONSHIP OF THE HIGHER LEVEL TO THE LOWER LEVEL, IN ONE WAY WHICH IS DISTINCT AND SEPARATED. THERE MUST EXIST AT-LEAST-ONE-MAN WHICH IS THE ONE THAT SEEMS TRANSMITTED ON THE LEVEL OF THIS FEMININE SPECIFIED BY BEING NOT-ALL, A DUALITY, THE ONLY POINT IN WHICH DUALITY HAS A CHANCE

OF BEING REPRESENTED. THERE IS IN THIS ONLY ONE REQUISITE, IF I MIGHT SAY, A GRATUITOUS ONE; NOTHING IMPOSES THIS AT-LEAST-ONE IF NOT THE UNIQUE CHANCE—AND STILL IT MUST BE PLAYED OUT—OF WHICH SOMETHING FUNCTIONS ON THE OTHER SIDE BUT ONLY AS AN IDEAL POINT, AS THE POSSIBILITY FOR ALL MEN TO ATTAIN IT THROUGH IDENTIFICATION.

THERE IS IN THIS A LOGICAL NECESSITY WHICH IS IMPOSED ONLY ON THE LEVEL OF THE WAGER. BUT NOTICE ON THE OTHER HAND WHAT RESULTS FROM IT CONCERNING THE MALE UNIVERSAL; THUS, THIS AT-LEAST-ONE, ON WHICH THE MYTHICAL NAME OF THE FATHER IS SUSTAINED, IS INDISPENSABLE.

IT IS HERE THAT I ADVANCE A FLASH OF WHAT IS MISSING FROM THE FUNCTION, FROM THE NOTION OF SPECIES AND OF CLASS, AND CONSEQUENTLY IT IS NO ACCIDENT THAT THIS ENTIRE DIALECTIC WAS LEFT OUT OF ARISTOTLE'S FORMS.

IN FACT WHERE DOES THIS E OF X FUNCTION, THIS "THERE EXISTS AT-LEAST-ONE" WHICH IS NOT THE SLAVE OF THE PHALLIC FUNCTION? THIS IS ONLY A REQUISITE I WILL SAY, OF A HOPELESS TYPE, FROM THE POINT OF VIEW OF THIS SOMETHING WHICH ITSELF IS NOT EVEN SUSTAINED THROUGH UNIVERSAL DEFINITON.

BUT ON THE OTHER HAND, OBSERVE THAT WITH RESPECT TO THE MALE UNIVERSAL, TO THE A OF X, TO THE Φ OF X, EVERY MALE IS A SLAVE TO THE PHALLIC FUNCTION. THIS AT-LEAST- ONE WHICH FUNCTIONS TO ESCAPE, WHAT DOES THIS MEAN? I WILL SAY THAT IT IS THE EXCEPTION, IT IS THE PATH WHEREIN IS CONFIRMED BY US THE PROVERB WHICH SAYS, WITHOUT KNOWING WHAT IT SAYS, THAT THE EXCEPTION PROVES THE RULE, IS SUPPORTED BY US. IT IS EXCEPTIONAL THAT IT IS ONLY WITH THE ANALYTICAL DISCOURSE THAT A UNIVERSAL CAN FIND IN EXISTENCE ITS VERITABLE FOUNDATION IN THE EXCEPTION, WHICH ASSUREDLY ALLOWS US IN ANY CASE TO DISTINGUISH THE UNIVERSAL THUS ESTABLISHED FROM ANY USE THAT HAS BEEN RENDERED COMMON BY THE PHILOSOPHICAL TRADITION OF THE SO-CALLED UNIVERSAL.

BUT IT IS AN EXTRAORDINARY THING THAT I FIND MYSELF, IN THIS WAY, ON THE PATH OF A QUEST AND BECAUSE, FROM AN ANCIENT FORMATION (I DON'T NOT AT ALL NOT KNOW CHINESE), I ASKED ONE OF MY DEAREST FRIENDS TO RECALL TO ME WHAT EVIDENTLY (I HAD) KEPT MORE OR LESS AS A

TRACE, BUT WHAT I HAD TO CONFIRM FOR MYSELF BY SOMEONE FOR WHOM CHINESE IS THE MATERNAL LANGUAGE. IT IS ASSUREDLY VERY STRANGE THAT IN CHINESE, THE DELIMITATION OF ALL, IF I MIGHT EXPRESS MYSELF THUS, IS A QUESTION OF THE MORE ANCIENT ARTICULATION WHICH IS PRO-NOUNCED AS (TCHIAI): 偕 都

ONE MIGHT SAY FOR EXAMPLE: ALL MEN GORGE THEMSELVES: (MEI GO JENN TE) MEI INSISTS ON THE FACT THAT IT IS IN FACT THERE, AND IF YOU DOUBT IT, THE NUMERICAL (GO) SHOWS YOU VERY WELL THAT ONE COUNTS BUT THAT THIS DOES NOT MAKE THEM NOT-ALL AND TO THIS IS ADDED (TE) WHICH MEANS: WITHOUT EXCEPTION.

YOU COULD OBJECT THAT WHAT WE DISCOVER IN WHAT IS ARTICULATED AS RELATIONSHIP OF SIGN TO EXISTENCE THROUGH RESPECT OF A UNIVERSAL STATUS, TAKES ITS FIGURE AS AN EXCEPTION.

BUT ALSO IT EXISTS ONLY AS CORRELATION OF, WHAT I CALLED A MOMENT AGO, THE (EMPTINESS) OF THE OTHER; IF IN VIRTUE WE HAVE PROGRESSED IN THE LOGIC OF CLASSES, IT IS THAT WE HAVE CREATED A LOGIC OF SETS, THAT THE DIFFERENCE BETWEEN A CLASS AND A SET IS THAT WHEN THE CLASS IS EMPTY, THERE IS STILL THIS ELEMENT OF THE EMPTY SET. IT IS IN THIS THAT ONCE MORE, MATHEMATICS HAS MADE PROGRESS TOWARDS LOGIC.

THE X IN THE RIGHT PART OF THE DIAGRAM IMPLIES THAT THERE IS A UNILATERALITY OF THE EXISTEN-TIAL FUNCTION FOR THE OTHER PARTNER, THAT IS, THAT THERE ARE NO EXCEPTIONS. THERE IS SOMETHING THAT IS NO LONGER IN SYMMETRY WITH THE REQUIREMENT OF THE AT-LEAST-ONE THAT A MOMENT AGO I CALLED HOPELESS. THERE IS ANOTHER REQUIREMENT WHICH RESIDES IN THE FACT THAT IN THE END, THE MASCULINE UNIVERSAL CAN ONLY GET ITS DUE WITH THE INSURANCE THAT THERE EXISTS NO WOMAN WHO CAN BE CASTRATED. THIS IS FOR REASONS WHICH APPEAR EVIDENT, EXCEPT THAT THE BEHAVIOR OF WOMAN SUFFI-CIENTLY SHOWS THAT HER RELATIONSHIP TO THE PHALLIC FUNCTION IS QUITE ACTIVE.

IN ANY CASE, WOMAN IS NO MORE INSURED IN HER UNIVERSAL ESSENCE THAN MAN FOR THE SIMPLE REASON THAT THE CONTRARY OF THE LIMIT, IS THAT THERE IS NONE, THERE IS NO EXCEPTION. THE FACT THAT THERE IS NO EXCEPTION INSURES THE UNIVERSAL ALREADY SO POORLY ESTABLISHED EITHER FOR THE REASON THAT IT IS DISCORDANT OR THAT IT DOESN'T ASSURE THE UNIVERSAL OF WOMAN. WITHOUT EXCEPTION, FAR FROM GIVING SOME-ALL MORE CONSISTENCY, THIS NATURALLY GIVES STILL LESS CONSISTENCY TO WHAT IS DEFINED AS NOT-ALL, AS ESSENTIALLY DUAL.

IF ALL OF THIS STAYS WITH YOU AS A PROP, NECESSARY FOR EVERYTHING THAT WE CAN ATTEMPT TO USE AS A STEPLADDER, THEN WE MUST SERIOUSLY QUESTION THE IRRUPTION OF THE STRANGEST THING: THE FUNCTION OF THE ONE.

I WONDER A LOT ABOUT ANIMAL MENTALITY WHICH AFTER ALL WOULD ONLY BE USEFUL TO ME AS A MIRROR REFERENCE, AS A MIRROR WHICH, AS BEFORE ALL MIRRORS, I RAVE. THERE IS SOMETHING WHICH WE MIGHT ASK OURSELVES: FOR THE ANIMAL, IS THERE THE ONE?

JACQUES LACAN

TRANSLATED BY DENISE GREEN

I WOULD LIKE TO THANK THOMAS GORA, SUZANNE GUERLAC AND JOHN RAJCHMAN FOR THEIR KIND ASSISTANCE IN THE TRANSLATION OF THIS TEXT.

• THIS REFERS TO THE THEORY OF FOUR DISCOURSES OF THE ANALYST, THE HYSTERIC, THE UNIVERSITY AND THE MASTER CF. RADIOPHONIE IN SCILICET 2/3.

• NOTE: ONE OF LACAN'S FORMULAS IS WOMAN-IS-NOT-EVERYTHING. NOT-ALL REFERS TO THIS.

JOUISSANCE* AND DIVISION

"MOMMY, WHEN, AND HOW, WAS I BURNED ON MY LEFT BREAST?"

"I WAS BURNED, TOO. ON THE RIGHT SIDE. A LITTLE HIGHER UP. WHEN I WAS YOUR AGE."

WHAT HAPPENS IN THIS BRIEF EXCHANGE? A QUESTION IS ASKED AND ITS ANSWER SETS UP A MIRROR, GIVING RISE TO AN INVESTIGATION OF A MOTHER'S GAZE UPON HER DAUGHTER (IN THE MIRROR). FROM THIS SCENE AND MANY OTHERS COLLECTED IN ANALYTIC PRACTICE, IT WOULD SEEM THAT WHAT THE DAUGHTER SAYS ABOUT HER BODY—THAT IS, ABOUT THAT, IN THE MIRROR, WHICH IS CAPABLE OF GIVING HER IDENTITY—EVOKES, IN THE MOTHER, AN IDENTICAL SCENE THAT SHE HAS EXPERIENCED HERSELF. WHAT DOES SHE DO? WE CAN POINT OUT THREE TYPES OF RESPONSE.

1. THE MOTHER, UPON HEARING THE ECHO OF HER DAUGHTER'S SPEECH, SILENCES HER OWN CHILD-HOOD QUESTION; "THAT" ["CA"] MUST NEVER SPEAK AGAIN. ONLY TWO POSSIBLE SOLUTIONS ARE OPEN TO THE DAUGHTER: IN THE MORE DESIREABLE CASE, IF THE NAME-OF-THE-FATHER IS FUNCTIONING, SHE WILL DESPERATELY IDENTIFY WITH THE PHALLUS IN A FRANTIC MATERNAL POSITION OR IN A DIZZYING MASCARADE—THE VIA REGIA OF THE HYSTERIC; IN THE LESS DESIRABLE CASE, IF A FUNDAMENTAL DEFICIENCY OF THE PATERNAL FUNCTION IS ADDED TO THE ABSENCE OF THE MOTHER'S RECOGNITION, THERE IS REASON TO FEAR A PSYCHOTIC BREAK-DOWN.

2. THE MOTHER HEARS THE ECHO AND REMAINS WITHIN THAT ZONE WHICH IS COMPLETELY SHAKEN BY THOSE WAVES FROM WHICH SHE HAS NEVER BEEN ABLE TO ESCAPE. SHE LURES HER DAUGHTER INTO THE ZONE AND THE DAUGHTER LOSES HER WAY THERE. FROM THEN ON, THERE CAN ONLY BE MORE OF THE SAME OLD REFRAIN.

3. THE MOTHER REDISCOVERS HER OWN QUESTION IN HER DAUGHTER'S QUESTION—INEVITABLY, IT SEEMS; BUT SHE ISOLATES IT AND, IN THAT WAY, ALLOWS HER DAUGHTER TO CONTINUE TO SPEAK FOR HERSELF ALONE.

THIS THIRD POSSIBILITY APPEARS ONLY AS A WAY

219

ALONG THE PATH OF ACCEPTING CASTRATION, WHICH IS AS UTOPIC, IT SEEMS, AS NORMAL SEXUALITY AT THE PASSING OF THE OEDIPUS COMPLEX. (CF. FREUD.)

WE SHALL RETURN TO THIS RATHER ROUGH CLINICAL OUTLINE LATER AND DEAL WITH IT IN TERMS OF JOUISSANCE.

THESE THREE SITUATIONS ARE ROOTED, IT APPEARS TO US, IN THE MIRROR STAGE, THAT STAGE WHICH STRUCTURES THE EGO AND IS THE FOUNDATION OF WHAT WILL LATER BECOME ACCESS TO THE SYMBOLIC, (WHEN THE CHILD CAN COUNT: 1, 2 . . . ; 3, INSCRIBED AT THE ORIGIN, MAKES THIS OPERATION POSSIBLE).

FOR THE CHILD TO BE ABLE TO DISCOVER ITSELF IN ITS OWN IMAGE IT MUST BE SUPPORTED BY ITS MOTHER'S GAZE. IN OTHER WORDS, THE MOTHER MUST ACCEPT THE FACT THAT SHE IS SEEN AS SEPARATE FROM THE CHILD AND SEEING THE CHILD: THAT IS, SHE MUST ACQUIESCE IN BEING SUBJECT TO SYMBOLIC LAW.

DENIAL OF SYMBOLIC LAW WOULD ANNUL THE STRUCTURING EFFECT OF THE MIRROR.

TO THIS EXPERIENCE, WHICH IS FUNDAMENTAL FOR ALL CHILDREN, THERE IS ADDED, IN THE CASE OF THE LITTLE GIRL, A SECOND OPERATION THROUGH WHICH THE DESTINY OF "WOMAN'S-BODY" IS PLAYED OUT. IN THIS SECOND STAGE, THE MOTHER EITHER DOES OR DOES NOT RECOGNIZE HER DAUGHTER'S IMAGE, SIMULTANEOUSLY SEPARATE FROM THE MOTHER'S IMAGE BUT CONTINUALLY RESEMBLING IT. AS GENNIE LEMOINE HAS INSISTED, THIS OPERATION IS ALWAYS MORE OR LESS A FAILURE: THE WOMAN ALWAYS REMAINS, TO A GREATER OR LESSER EXTENT, THE MIRROR'S CAPTIVE. THESE MOMENTS OF THE MIRROR STAGE APPEAR AT THE CENTER OF ANY ATTEMPT TO DEAL WITH THE QUESTION OF WOMAN, WHATEVER THE CHANCE CIRCUMSTANCES MAY BE THAT ACCOMPANY THE FACT OF REPRESENTATION BY A WOMAN'S-BODY.

"WOMAN'S-BODY," OF COURSE, DOES NOT REFER TO THE BIOLOGICAL BODY, BUT RATHER TO THE BODY THAT IS TRACED, CUT OUT AND ANIMATED BY DRIVES. THIS BODY, LOCATED IN THE FIELD OF DISCOURSE, OF THE DESIRE OF THE OTHER, IS THE EROTOGENIC BODY, AS DEFINED BY FREUD. THE PRECISION ADDED BY THE USE OF THE TERM "WOMAN'S-BODY" LIES, FOR US, IN THE FACT THAT THE LITTLE GIRL, IN HER FIRST RELATIONSHIP WITH THE MOTHER WHO OCCUPIES THE PLACE OF THE OTHER, ENCOUNTERS THE SAME-BODY AS HER OWN.

LET US REPEAT THAT THE BODY OF THE LITTLE GIRL, LIKE THAT OF THE LITTLE BOY, IS "WHIPPED BY LANGUAGE." THE SIGNIFIER "WOMAN'S-BODY" ATTEMPTS TO POINT TO THE RELATION WITH THE SAME-BODY WITH WHICH THE LITTLE GIRL IS NECESSARILY CONFRONTED. IN VIEW OF THIS NOTION OF THE SAME-BODY, ONE COULD PROBABLY EXPLORE THE QUESTION OF THE PERMANENCE OF THE LIBIDINAL ATTACHMENT TO THE MOTHER, THE PUZZLING INTENSITY OF WHICH FREUD NEVER CEASED TO EMPHASIZE.[1]

WE NOW PROPOSE TO ANALYZE WHAT WE SHALL CALL THE MIRROR SCENE.

MIRROR SCENE

WE CALL IT A SCENE BECAUSE WE HAVE FOUND THAT, LIKE THE PRIMAL SCENE, IT IS CONSTRUCTED OVER AND AGAIN IN DIFFERENT STAGES OF THE DISCOURSE OF ANALYSANDS, PARTICULARLY OF WOMEN ANALYSANDS. TRACING BACK THE THREAD OF THEIR HISTORIES, THEY NEVER FAIL TO RUN AGROUND AT THAT MOMENT WHEN THEY ARE TO BE SEEN, RECOGNIZED, NOT ONLY IN THE GAZE OF MEN, BUT IN THAT OF ALL WOMEN, (SISTERS, DAUGHTERS, FRIENDS—PLACED THERE FOR ONE WOMAN). IT IS IN THIS UNENDING MOVEMENT OF RETURN TO THE MOORING PLACE OF AN EVANESCENT EGO THAT WE MAY APPROACH THE QUESTION OF WHAT IS CALLED FEMININE JOUISSANCE.

LET US POINT OUT THE CHARACTERISTICS PARTICULAR TO THIS SCENE WHEN IT IS EXPERIENCED BY MOTHER AND DAUGHTER.

THE SCENE—MOTHER^A + DAUGHTER^A IN FRONT OF THE MIRROR—CANNOT FAIL TO BRING FORTH THE SCENE—MOTHER^B + DAUGHTER^B IN FRONT OF THE SAME MIRROR. AND SO FORTH AD INFINITUM.

MOTHER^A ONCE AGAIN BECOMES DAUGHTER^B BY THE INTERMEDIARY OF THE IMAGE OF DAUGHTER^A, WHICH THE LATTER THEN RECOVERS.

AT THAT MOMENT WHEN THE "ORTHOPEDIC" IMAGE OF THE CHILD'S BODY AS SEPARATE FROM THAT OF THE MOTHER IS CONSTITUTED, THE CHILD SEEKS SUPPORT IN THE MOTHER'S GAZE. WHAT WE HAVE JUST SKETCHED OUT INDICATES THAT SHE RUNS THE RISK OF FINDING A GAZE ALREADY ABSORBED BY ANOTHER MIRROR GAME. IDENTITY OF BODIES FAVORS THE VACILLATION OF IMAGES. THE SAME-BODY UNDERLINES THE FRAGILITY OF SEPARATION AT THE IMAGINARY LEVEL AND BLURS THIS ALREADY DECEPTIVE IMAGE: IN THIS SPIRAL OF ECHOES AND REFLECTIONS THE LITTLE GIRL CAN FIND NO STABLE POINT OF REFERENCE FOR IDENTIFICATION. AT THAT MOMENT WHICH SHOULD BE FORMATIVE FOR THE LITTLE GIRL, THE MOTHER NOT ONLY OCCUPIES HER OWN POSITION OF MOTHER, BUT PARTIALLY USURPS HER DAUGHTER'S POSITION AS WELL. PERHAPS THE PRE-OEDIPAL ATTACHMENT TO THE MOTHER REMAINS SO VERY STRONG BECAUSE THE PLACES OF THE MOTHER AND OF THE DAUGHTER HAVE YET TO BE DEFINED. THERE IS SOMETHING NOT REPRESSED, NOT INSCRIBED IN THE SIGNIFYING ORDER, THAT REEMERGES GENERATION AFTER GENERATION, PASSING FROM ONE GAZE TO ANOTHER IN AN UNENDING MOVEMENT OF EXCHANGE. IS IT THE MOTHER OR THE DAUGHTER WHO IS THE AGENT OF THIS MIRROR EXPERIENCE? THE MOTHER PARTIALLY TAKES THE PLACE OF THE DAUGHTER AND, BY THIS DOUBLING, TAKES AWAY FROM THE DAUGHTER THE POSSIBILITY OF FINDING HER PLACE IN THE SYMBOLIC ORDER. THERE IS A CAPTURE IN THE MIRROR. ADDED TO THIS EXCHANGE AND INTER-DEPENDENCE OF PLACES IS THE LITTLE GIRL'S EXTREME "JUBILATION" UPON DISCOVERING THAT SHE IS LIKE HER FIRST LOVE OBJECT. WE SHALL HYPOTHESIZE NOT ONLY THAT "SEPARATION" OF IMAGES IS ONLY PARTIALLY COMPLETED, BUT THAT, MOREOVER, NARCISSISTIC AND OBJECT CATHEXIS ARE CONFUSED WITH EACH OTHER.[2A & B]

SEEING HER SON IN THE MIRROR, THE MOTHER CAN BELIEVE IN MIRACLES, SINCE THE EQUATION BABY = PENIS, REDUCED TO AN IMAGINARY FUNCTION IN WHICH ONE OBJECT REPLACES ANOTHER OF EQUAL VALUE, IS IN FULL FORCE, MASKING CASTRATION.

WHEN, CONFRONTED WITH THE IMAGE OF HER DAUGHTER, SHE DISCOVERS THAT OTHER CAS-TRATED, SPLIT BODY, SENDING BACK TO HER THE IMAGE OF HER OWN BODY, OF THE SAME-BODY, THE MOTHER'S WOUND IS REOPENED. SHE RETRACES THE PATH OF THE SYMBOLIC EQUATION, AND PENIS ENVY, WHICH HAS NEVER BEEN LEFT BEHIND, REAPPEARS WITH ITS FULL LIBINAL INTENSITY. THE MOTHER CANNOT BEAR THE GAZE OF HER DAUGHTER; IT IS AS IF SHE WERE PARALYZED, FROZEN BY THE FATEFUL IMAGE. ONE CAN SUPPOSE THAT THIS AFFLICTED GAZE FADES, BLIGHTS AND DENIES THE DAUGHTER'S BODY. THE MOTHER, WHO CANNOT BRING HERSELF TO SAY: "YOU ARE THAT," CONTENTS HERSELF WITH A PAINED AND RECRIMI-NATORY: "THAT IS ALL YOU ARE." SHOULD THIS NOT BE SEEN AS ONE SOURCE OF THE RAVAGES THAT GENERALLY MARK MOTHER-DAUGHTER RELATION-SHIPS?

THE FORCE OF THIS FUNDAMENTAL EXPERIENCE, AS FAR AS THE EARLIEST CONSTITUTION OF THE EGO IS CONCERNED, CAN BE FELT ONLY IF THE MOTHER DOES NOT DENY CASTRATION. IF THIS IS NOT THE CASE, WITH THE MIRROR IMAGE REMINDING HER THAT WOMAN'S-BODY IS, FIRST OF ALL, A CASTRATED BODY, THE MOTHER, IN ORDER TO BACK UP THE FANTASY THAT HER CHILD IS A SUBSTITUTE MAKING UP FOR CASTRATION, SHE WILL ASSIGN HER DAUGHTER THE FATE OF A WOULD-BE BOY.

THE VISION OF THE CASTRATED BODY, WHICH REACTIVATES PENIS ENVY IN THE MOTHER, IS NOT ENOUGH, HOWEVER, TO EXPLAIN HER DISTRAUGHT, HALF-HORRIFIED, HALF-FASCINATED GAZE.

THE THING[3]

TO BE A MOTHER IS INDEED TO BE CASTRATED, BUT IT IS ALSO, BY VIRTUE OF NOT HAVING THE PHALLUS, TO ASSUME THE VALUE OF THE PHALLUS, THAT IS, TO OCCUPY THE PLACE OF THE THING, THE LOST OBJECT. DAS DING, THAT WHICH IS OUTSIDE OF THE SIGNIFIED—IN THE SYMBOLIC ORDER, IT IS CALLED THE PHALLUS.

THE LIVING BEING WHO IS SUBJECT TO SEXUAL REPRODUCTION SUFFERS A REAL LOSS. (THE PLACENTA INDEED REPRESENTS THAT PART, EQUAL TO HIMSELF, WHICH THE INDIVIDUAL LOSES AT BIRTH.) THE PHALLUS OCCUPIES THE FOREVER EMPTY PLACE OF THIS REAL LOSS, TRANSPOSED INTO THE REGISTER OF THE SIGNIFIER.

THE IMMATURITY OF THE INFANT HUMAN BEING KEEPS IT FROM PERCEIVING THE LIMITS OF ITS BODY. HENCE, THE MOTHER, WHO, AS LACAN DESCRIBES HER, IS THE BEARER OF THAT, LIKE THE PLACENTA, WHICH THE INFANT CLAIMS AS ITS OWN, IN OTHER WORDS, THE BREAST, BY SATISFYING

PRIMORIDAL NEEDS, CREATES THE ILLUSION OF IMPOSSIBLE FUSION. VERY QUICKLY, HOWEVER, BECAUSE THE MOTHER DESIRES AND IS SUBJECT TO THE LAW OF THE SIGNIFIER, HER CARING FOR THE CHILD WILL MARK ITS BODY. THE DESIRE HOLDING HER ELSEWHERE HOLLOWS OUT THE DIFFERENCE BETWEEN THE CHILD'S NEED AND ITS DEMAND. AT THE SAME TIME, THE SELF AND THE NOT-SELF ARE CONSTITUTED, THE NOT-SELF BEING THAT WHICH BRINGS UNPLEASURE. IN REFERENCE TO THIS, ONE MAY CONSULT THE PROJECT FOR A SCIENTIFIC PSYCHOLOGY, WHERE FREUD DEFINES WHAT HE MEANS BY THE NEBENMENSCH COMPLEX[4]: THE FIRST OBJECT SPLITS INTO TWO PARTS. ONE OF THEM REMAINS RADICALLY FOREIGN, DAS DING. THE SUBJECT WILL ALWAYS TRY TO ASSIMILATE THE OTHER PART BY MEANS OF IDENTIFICATION: IT CAN BE CONSIDERED, FROM THE VERY FIRST MONTHS ON, AS THE BEGINNINGS OF THE BODY ITSELF. IN THIS PRIMAL EXPERIENCE OF THE ORGANIZATION OF PSYCHIC REALITY, ONE ATTEMPTS TO REDISCOVER ON THE OUTSIDE AN OBJECT THAT ONCE WAS EXPERIENCED AS BELONGING TO THE INSIDE, IN ORDER TO PROVE THAT THE OBJECT IS STILL PRESENT IN REALITY.

THE THING DOES NOT EXIST. IT DISTINGUISHES ITSELF BY ITS ABSENCE. IT IS THEREFORE WITHIN THE REGISTER OF A DECOY OR LURE THAT THE MOTHER OFFICIALLY FUNCTIONS.

BECAUSE THE CHILD IS CAST INTO THE REALM OF DEMAND, ITS BODY IS NOT MERELY A BIOLOGICAL BODY. THE MOTHER'S DESIRE TRACES EROTOGENIC ZONES FROM WHICH DRIVE WILL SPRING FORTH. INTO THIS REPETITIVE CYCLE, WHICH BEGAN WITH A SEARCH FOR THE LOST OBJECT, WILL FALL THE OBJECT $^\wedge$ IN ITS VARIOUS GUIDES. THE OBJECT $^\wedge$ IS BOTH REMAINDER AND AGENT IN THE PROCESS OF BECOMING A SUBJECT. AS REMAINDERS, THE OBJECTS $^\wedge$ CONSTITUTE THE LIMIT OF A FOREVER FUTURE SUBJECT. LACAN SAYS OF THE OBJECTS $^\wedge$: "JOUISSANCE, WHICH DOES NOT COME UNDER THE EFFECTS OF THE PLEASURE PRINCIPLE, TAKES REFUGE IN THEM." THEY FUNCTION, THEREFORE, AS BOTH THE CAUSE AND THE SUPPORT OF DESIRE. LET US REPEAT THAT THERE IS NO REPRESENTA- TIVE OF THE THING, AN EMPTY SPACE AROUND WHICH DESIRE NEVER CEASES TO WANDER. IN FANTASY WHERE DESIRE IS SUSPENDED AND WHERE THE REPETITIVE QUEST STOPS FOR A SHORT TIME, THERE IS COLLUSION BETWEEN THE OBJECT $^\wedge$ AND THE THING. IN THE IMAGINARY, THE OBJECT $^\wedge$ COMES TO FILL THE EMPTY SPACE OF THE THING. LET US REMEMBER THAT DISCOURSE FUNCTIONS AS

THE NECESSARY FILLING UP OF THE HOLE OF THE REAL. FOR THIS REASON, IN DISCOURSE "THE THING RESOLVES ITSELF INTO AFFAIRS."

THUS, THE MOTHER OCCUPIES THE PLACE OF THE THING. TO BE A MOTHER IS THE FUTURE ASSIGNED TO ALL WOMEN IN THE THIRD STAGE OF THE OEDIPUS COMPLEX. WE ALL "FORGET," HOWEVER, THAT THE MOTHER IS NOT THE OTHER, THAT SHE ONLY HOLDS ITS PLACE.

MOTHERHOOD IS ONLY A FUNCTION, BUT EVERYONE TENDS TO MAKE OF IT THE VERY BEING OF WOMAN. AT BIRTH, THE CHILD DOES NOT LOSE ITS MOTHER: IT LOSES THE PLACENTA. WHAT IT WILL BE SEEKING, THEREFORE, IS NOT ITS MOTHER, BUT RATHER, WHAT SHE REPRESENTS.

BECAUSE SHE IS THE FIRST LOVE OBJECT, THE MOTHER PASSES FROM HER SYMBOLIC FUNCTION INTO AN IMAGINARY REGISTER: THE TEMPTATION IS ALWYAS GREAT FOR HER TO FILL THE EMPTY SPACE OF THE THING, TO COLONIZE THE FIELD OF THE REAL. THE LESS SHE ACCEPTS HER CASTRATION, THE MORE SHE WILL SET HERSELF UP TO SHORT CIRCUIT THE PATH OF DESIRE. AN ALWAYS PRESENT OBJECT, SHE WILL PREVENT THE REPRESENTATION OF A MISSING OBJECT THAT COULD FOUND DESIRE.

IN THIS PERSPECTIVE, WITH THE MOTHER PROFITING FROM THIS SHORT CIRCUIT, THERE CAN BE NO PLACE FOR THE PERSON WHO MIGHT DISPLACE HER: HER DAUGHTER.

THE IMAGE THAT THE MIRROR SENDS BACK TO A WOMAN WHEN SHE IS CARRYING HER CHILD IS NOT ONLY THE IMAGE OF HER OWN BODY, BUT ALSO THAT OF HER OWN MOTHER. AT THAT INSTANT, SHE REDISCOVERS IN HER REFLECTION HER FIRST LOVE OBJECT IN ITS MOST FASCINATING FORM, IN THE ENIGMATIC NATURE OF THE THING. PARADOXICAL- LY, IN THE MOST "GLORIOUS" IMAGE OF HER MOTHERHOOD, SHE RUNS THE RISK OF DISAPPEAR- ING AS CASTRATED MOTHER AND OF BEING NO MORE THAN THE DAUGHTER OF HER REFLECTION.[5]

BECAUSE OF THE CHALLENGE THAT SHE PRESENTS TO THE SYMBOLIC ORDER, WOMAN'S POSITION IS PERHAPS PERVERSE. INDEED, SHE MOLDS HERSELF TO THE ROLE ALLOTTED HER IN THE PHALLIC ORDER ONLY SO AS TO BETTER DENY THE CASTRATION IMPLIED BY THAT ROLE. SHE IS OVERCOME BY THE FASCINATION OF THE REFLEC- TION OF BEING ALL-MOTHER. HERE, "ALL-MOTHER" MEANS BEING A MOTHER COMPLETELY AND BEING

ALL MOTHERS ROLLED INTO ONE. THUS, THERE IS NO CHANCE THAT WOMAN'S-BODY, WHICH WOULD SIGN THE RECOGNITION OF A CASTRATED BODY, WILL EMERGE, EITHER FOR THE MOTHER OR FOR THE DAUGHTER. FOR THE DAUGHTER, THERE IS NO POSSIBILITY OF IDENTIFICATION WITH THE MOTHER; ONLY IMITATION IS POSSIBLE.[6] THINKING OF THE METAPHOR OF THE SCREAM THAT GIVES BIRTH TO SILENCE, ONE CAN IMAGINE INSCRIPTION IN THE PHALLIC ORDER AS CONSTITUTIVE OF THE NOT-ALL/NOT-WHOLE.[7] BY DENYING CASTRATION, WOMAN REMAINS IGNORANT OF HER TWOFOLD DIVISION. IN THE MIRROR SCENE, SHE IS NO MORE THAN A REFLECTION OF A REFLECTION AD INFINITUM, WHICH IS TO SAY, SHE IS NOTHING. THEREFORE, A WOMAN IS ONLY FOLLOWING THE LETTER OF THE LAW HANDED DOWN IN THE THIRD STAGE OF THE OEDIPUS COMPLEX: A MOTHER BECOMES THE MOTHER. THIS PASSAGE IS FACILITATED BY THE FACT THAT THE MOTHER FIGURE IS AN IDEOLOGICAL PRODUCT: SHE ALLOWS ONE TO AVOID THE QUESTION OF FEMININE SEXUALITY, LEADING TO THE REAL. THE MOTHER FIGURE MASKS ALL LACKS, INCLUDING THE LACK OF ALL SYSTEMIZATION. (AND IN SPITE OF WHAT LACAN HAS SUGGESTED, THE MOTHER FIGURE CONTINUES TO WEIGH HEAVILY UPON ANALYTIC THEORY.)

JUST AS THE MOTHER TAKES THE PLACE OF THE LOST OBJECT AND IS LOVED, SHE IS MADE RESPONSIBLE FOR CASTRATION AND IS HATED. ONCE AGAIN, WE FIND IN THIS LOVE-HATE AMBIVALENCE THE DIVIDED STRUCTURE OF A WOMAN, AN IRREDUCIBLE STRUCTURE RESISTING ANALYSIS AND DISCOURSE.[8]

THE NEVER-ENDING FASCINATION OF THE RELATION WITH THE MOTHER HOLDS A PART OF A WOMAN IN THE IMAGINARY ORDER; IN THIS WAY, THE MOTHER, ALTHOUGH THE SPOKESPERSON OF THE SYMBOLIC ORDER, BARS TOTAL ACCESS TO IT.[9]

BY DENYING THIS SHARE OF THE INEXPLORABLE "SHADOW" (FREUD INDICATES THAT THE RELATION WITH THE MOTHER HAS THE CONSISTENCY OF A SHADOW), A WOMAN DENIES HERSELF HER OWN RELATION WITH THE SYMBOLIC ORDER AND CONDEMNS HERSELF TO IMITATION, REPETITION AND RECRIMINATION.

FOR A WOMAN TO BE ABLE TO SEIZE THE OCCASION TO SPEAK FOR "HERSELF," SHE MUST ACKNOWLEDGE THE PERMANENCE OF THIS SHADOW.

JOUISSANCE

$$x\phi \qquad \underline{x}A \qquad x\underline{\phi} \qquad xA$$

$$\underline{x\phi} \qquad \underline{x}E \qquad \underline{x\phi} \qquad xE$$

$$\$ \qquad\qquad S(\text{Ⱥ})$$

$$a \qquad \flat a$$

$$\phi$$

THIS GRAPH FROM LACAN'S SÉMINAIRE XX: EN-CORE[10] DEALS WITH THE QUESTION OF JOUISSANCE. THOSE WHO LINE UP IN THE LEFT SECTION OF SPEAKING BEINGS HAVE ACCESS TO THE OTHER ONLY THROUGH THE OBJECT A. THOSE WHO LINE UP ON THE RIGHT, HOWEVER, ARE NOT ONLY SUBJECT TO THE PHALLUS—PHALLIC JOUISSANCE OR JOUISSANCE THROUGH DISCOURSE—BUT ARE ALSO IN A RELATION OF PROXIMITY TO THE OTHER. THAT SPEAKING BEINGS, REGARDLESS OF WHETHER THEY ARE MEN OR WOMEN, CAN BE FOUND ON EITHER SIDE IS NOT INCOMPATIBLE WITH THE FACT THAT WOMEN, BECAUSE OF THEIR REINFORCED ATTACH-MENT TO THE MOTHER WHO MEDIATES ACCESS TO THE OTHER, ARE PLACED IN A PRIVILEGED MANNER ON THE RIGHT. THE NATURE OF THIS REINFORCE-MENT WAS DESCRIBED IN THE FIRST PART OF THIS ARTICLE. IF A WOMAN PLACES HERSELF ON THE LEFT, SHE WANTS TO REMAIN UNAWARE OF HER PORTION OF SHADOW.

THE PLACE OF THE OTHER IS THE BODY, THE "FIRST MASTERSPACE OF INSCRIPTIONS," AS LACAN SAYS. IT IS ALSO THE UNCONSCIOUS: IN CARING FOR HER CHILD, THE MOTHER, THE PLACE-KEEPER OF THE OTHER, TRACES INSTINCTUAL ZONES, THE REPRE-SENTATIVES OF WHICH, IN THE PSYCHIC APPARA-TUS, CONSTITUTE THE FIRST INSCRIPTIONS. ("INSTINCTUAL DRIVES ARE THE TREASURY OF SIGNIFIERS.")

IT APPEARS TO US THAT A WOMAN ALWAYS REMAINS, TO A CERTAIN EXTENT, IN TOUCH WITH THIS FIELD OF FIRST INSCRIPTIONS. INDEED, HER LABIDINAL ECONOMY IS NOT ORGANIZED ENTIRELY IN SUBMISSION TO THE PHALLUS. REPEATING MONTRELAY'S DISCUSSION OF REPRESSION AS A STRUCTURING PROCESS, WE SHALL SAY THAT A PORTION OF A WOMAN'S LIBIDO REMAINS IN ITS

RELATION OF PROXIMITY TO THE OTHER AND COMES TO A HALT THERE.

WHAT IS THE NATURE OF THE CATHEXIS OF THIS RELATION? WE FIND IT DIFFICULT TO GRASP BECAUSE, ALTHOUGH DIFFERENT FROM BOTH NARCISSISM, AS IT IS COMMONLY DEFINED, AND AUTO-EROTISM, IT CANNOT, HOWEVER, BE REDUCED TO AN OBJECT CATHEXIS. LET US NOTE THAT, IN NARCISSISM, WHAT IS LIBIDINALLY INVESTED IS THE PORTION OF THE OTHER THAT ONE CARRIES WITHIN ONESELF. WHILE THIS IS EQUALLY TRUE FOR THE BOY, CATHEXIS OF THE SAME-BODY NO DOUBT REINFORCES THE ATTRACTION OF NARCISSISM FOR THE LITTLE GIRL. FOR WE ARE INDEED TALKING ABOUT THE BODY. BUT WHICH BODY? NOT JUST HER OWN BODY, SINCE, FOR THE GIRL, HER OWN BODY IS ALWAYS THE SAME BODY AS, OR THE REFLECTION OF THE BODY OF, THE FIRST LOVE OBJECT AS WELL.

PHALLIC JOUISSANCE

IN THE FATE ASSIGNED HER IN THE THIRD PHASE OF THE OEDIPUS COMPLEX, A WOMAN DOES NOT DISCOVER HERSELF WHOLE, BUT SHE NEITHER KNOWS NOR ACCEPTS THIS. LET US CONSIDER THE HYSTERIC, WHOSE POSITION IS EXEMPLARY IN THIS REGARD. SHE SCREAMS SOMETHING ABOUT WHICH SHE KNOWS NOTHING. WITH THIS SCREAM, WHICH SHE WANTS TO ADDRESS TO AN ALL-POWERFUL FATHER WHO WOULD BE CAPABLE OF ANSWERING HER QUESTION, SHE SUMMONS, INSTEAD OF AND BEYOND THAT FATHER, HER MOTHER. WHAT IS A WOMAN? WHAT DOES A WOMAN WANT? IF SHE "MISTAKES" HER INTERLOCUTOR, NO DOUBT IT IS BECAUSE SHE KNOWS THAT WOMAN DOES NOT EXIST, BUT SHE CANNOT ACCEPT THIS.

LET US SAY FROM NOW ON THAT THE HYSTERIC PROBABLY REVELS IN [JOUIT ... DE] THIS PLAY BETWEEN "KNOWING" AND "NOT KNOWING." IN ANY CASE, MASCULINE DESIRE MUST REMAIN UNSATISFIED IN ORDER TO KEEP THE QUESTION OF THE RELATION TO THE MOTHER FROM BEING BROACHED. ONCE AGAIN, THE HYSTERIC PRETENDS TO BELIEVE THAT THERE WILL BE A SEXUAL RELATION, THAT THE MOTHER WILL BE ABLE TO SAY: "A WOMAN, THAT'S IT, IT EXISTS."

THE EVENTS OF A WOMAN'S BODY ARE MARKED BY SUBMISSION TO THE PHALLIC ORDER: SHE NEVER STOPS SPEAKING ABOUT THEM AND, BY SPEAKING, SHE REVELS IN THEM [ELLE EN JOUIT]. ON A

BACKGROUND OF INEXISTENCE, HER PERIOD, SEXUAL RELATIONS, PREGNANCY, AND GIVING BIRTH ARE THE REAL "MOMENTS" WHEN A WOMAN CAN GIVE HERSELF THE ILLUSION OF EXISTING, WHEN SHE CAN CLING TO THAT WHICH INSCRIBES HER WITHIN DISCOURSE. SHE REVELS [ELLE JOUIRA] IN THAT WHICH AFFECTS HER BODY AND, IN ORDER TO REVEL EVEN MORE, SHE SPEAKS ABOUT IT. PHALLIC JOUISSANCE, INSCRIBED JOUISSANCE.[11]

A WOMAN CAN ALSO EXPERIENCE THIS PHALLIC JOUISSANCE IN THE MASQUERADE, A PARODY OF IDENTIFICATION WITH THE OBJECT OF DESIRE, WHICH GIVES HER A FAVORED PLACE IN THE ORDER OF DISCOURSE.

WOMAN DOES NOT EXIST. HER PRECARIOUSNESS AS A SUBJECT (FREQUENTLY STAGED IN FAINTING SPELLS), PLUNGES HER INTO PASSIONATE, IDEALIZING IDENTIFICATIONS THAT, FOR A WHILE, GIVE HER CONSISTENCY. SHE SENSES THAT HER WHOLE SELF IS NOT SUMMED UP IN HER MANY IMAGINARY POSITIONS, WHICH EXPLAINS TO US WHY SHE OFTEN COVERS HER JOUISSANCE WITH A DOLEFUL MASK. SHE COMPLAINS, MAKES DEMANDS AND RAILS AGAINST THE PHALLIC ORDER, EITHER IN SUBLIME SILENCE OR AMIDST UNENDING RECRIMINATIONS. DENIAL OF CASTRATION AND DIVISION WILL ALWAYS TAKE ITS TOLL. SUBLIME MOTHERS DISPLAY THEIR BRUISED BODIES. WOMEN-OBJECTS ANGUISH AS THEY COUNT THE GAZES SUPPORTING THEM.

THE OTHER JOUISSANCE

WOMAN IS THE METHAPHOR OF MAN'S JOUISSANCE. HOW DOES SHE EXPERIENCE THIS?

AS JOUISSANCE VALUE [VALEUR DE JOUISSANCE], OBJECT A IN THE PHANTASY OF A MAN AIMING FOR THE OTHER, OR A LOST OBJECT, SHE IS THE REPRESENTATIVE OF THE THING. "DOES THAT FROM WHICH ONE COMES ALSO COME?" ["CE DONT ON JOUIT, CELA JOUIT-IL?"] (LACAN)

IN THAT POSITION WHERE ALL IDENTIFICATIONS BECOME CONFUSED WITH ONE ANOTHER, A WOMAN DOES NOT EXIST; IS THIS NOT PRECISELY THE MOMENT WHEN SHE RUNS THE RISK OF EXPERIENCING HERSELF AS NOT-WHOLE IN A FLEETING BURST OF DERISION? LET US THINK ABOUT THE LADY IN COURTLY LOVE (THE LAUGH OF THE MEDUSA) WHO

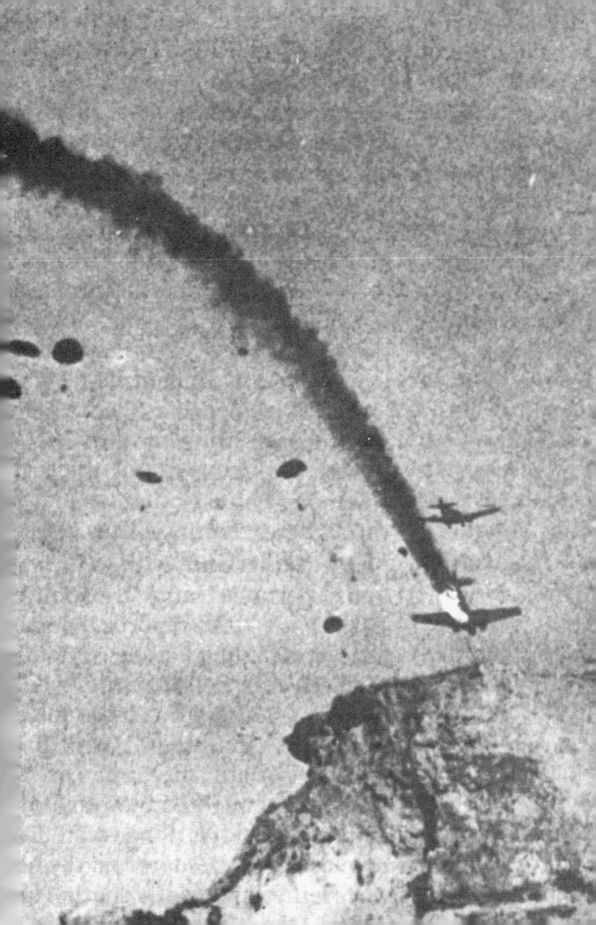

IS ABLE TO EXPERIENCE JOUISSANCE PERHAPS BECAUSE SHE IS ENACTING AN IMAGINARY DIVISION OF WHICH SHE CANNOT SPEAK, BUT TO WHICH SHE HAS HAD ACCESS.[12]

"HE WHOSE BODY IS LEFT TO THE MERCY OF ANOTHER SEES PURE JOUISSANCE OPEN UP BEFORE HIM." SUCH IS THE POSITION OF THE MASOCHIST WHO IDENTIFIES WITH THE OBJECT A, THE REMAINDER, THE WASTE OF THE OTHER'S JOUIS-SANCE. IF A WOMAN IDENTIFIES WITH THE OBJECT A ALONG THE PATH TOWARD THE OTHER, (CONFORM-ING TOTALLY WITH THE ROLE ASSIGNED HER IN THE MASCULINE FANTASY), THEN WHAT KIND OF JOUISSANCE CAN SHE EXPERIENCE? DOES NOT A PORTION OF HER JOUISSANCE LEAVE THE ORDER OF DISCOURSE IN ORDER TO SET ITSELF ADRIFT? AT THAT MOMENT WHEN A PART OF HER DOES NOT INSCRIBE ITSELF IN THE ORDER OF DISCOURSE, A WOMAN IS THE PLACE-KEEPER OF THE THING AND IS, HERSELF, REFERRED BACK TO HER OWN DESIRE FOR THE THING.

IN THAT SPACE SO CLOSE TO ITS MAGNETIC POLE THAT THE GUIDING LANDMARKS OF THE PHALLIC ORDER STOP FUNCTIONING AND SUBVERT ONE ANOTHER, DOES A WOMAN NOT EXPERIENCE SOMETHING, BEYOND THE LAW THAT WOULD RESEMBLE INCEST WITH THE MOTHER? LET US THINK OF SAINT THERESA OF AVILA AND OF THE GOD SHE COMPARES TO A NURSE WITH AN INEXHAUSTIBLE FLOW OF MILK.

A WOMAN CAN EXPERIENCE THIS JOUISSANCE, SOMÉTIMES, IF SHE ACCEPTS HERSELF AS DIVIDED. BY DESIRING.

THIS JOUISSANCE CAN ONLY BE DESIGNATED. IT CANNOT BE SPOKEN. IT ESCAPES INSCRIPTION. IN THE ANALYTIC SITUATION,[13] IT IS BY THIS MEANS OF ACCESS TO THAT, IN THE UNCONSCIOUS, WHICH IS NOT THE REPRESSED, THAT DISCOURSE CAN SPRING FORTH. ALTHOUGH SHE CAN SAY NOTHING MORE ABOUT IT, A WOMAN CAN, AT THAT MOMENT, RECOGNIZE THAT SHE IS NOT ENTIRELY SUBJECT TO THE PHALLIC FUNCTION. FOR THAT REASON, IF SHE ACCEPTS HER DIVISION, SHE WILL SOMETIMES BE ABLE TO SPEAK FOR "HERSELF" WITHIN DISCOURSE. AGREEING OCCASIONALLY TO REMAIN SILENT, SHE WILL HAVE THE GOOD FORTUNE TO ESCAPE ENDLESS, IMITATIVE REPETITION.

WOMAN IS NOT "LIBERATED" WHEN THE REPRES-SION, THE "FORGETTING," OF THE CAPTIVATING PRE-OEDIPAL RELATIONSHIP WITH THE MOTHER IS RAISED. AT THE MOST, THIS ALLOWS HER TO STAND BACK AND TAKE A CERTAIN DISTANCE FROM IDENTIFICATIONS DEAR TO HER. IT DOES NOT ABOLISH THEM, BUT RATHER MAKES THEM LESS RIGID AND CONSTRICTING.[14] WOMAN IS NOT-WHOLE. SO IS IT.

IN THIS ARTICLE WE HAVE LIMITED OURSELVES TO POINTING OUT A FEW ELEMENTS CONTRIBUTING TO THE QUESTION OF WOMAN. WE HAVE NEGLECTED VARIOUS QUESTIONS, MOST PARTICULARLY, THAT OF THE RELATION BETWEEN THESE IDENTIFICA-TIONS AND IDEOLOGY. DOES NOT THE OTHER JOUISSANCE, IN SPITE OR BECAUSE OF ITS SILENCE, POSE QUESTIONS CONCERNING THE PHALLIC ORDER? WHAT CAN BE MEANT BY THE "FEMINIZA-TION" OF A SOCIETY ONCE ONE SUSPECTS THAT THE PART OF A WOMAN WANTING TO BE BORN IS ONLY OBEYING AN ECONOMY OF CONSUMPTION? HOW CAN THE SOCIAL GROUP RECONCILE ORGANIZATION AND INORGANIZATION?

IT REMAINS FOR US, WHO HAVE ATTEMPTED TO INSCRIBE OUR TRACE ALONGSIDE SO MANY OTHERS, NOT TO CONCLUDE.

A WOMAN AND WRITING!!! TWOFOLD SPEECH. BUT THERE IS A CATCH. WRITING, FOR A WOMAN: IT CAN BE POSSIBLE, IT SEEMS, IF SHE AGREES TO RECOGNIZE BOTH THE MARK OF THE NAME-OF—THE-FATHER, WHICH PLACES HER IN THE ORDER OF DISCOURSE AND THE PERMANENCE OF HER ATTACHMENT TO THE MOTHER, WHICH BORES A HOLE IN THAT ORDER. WRITING, FOR A WOMAN: IS IT PERHAPS NOT WRITING ON THE MOTHER'S BODY, BUT RATHER, WITH HER BODY?

IN THAT WAY, SHE CAN ESCAPE FROM A KIND OF WRITING WITH WHICH SHE WOULD TRY TO IDENTIFY WITH MEN AND ALSO FROM IMPRISONMENT IN THE ILLUSION OF WHAT IS CALLED A FEMININE WRITING.

CHANTAL MAILLET AND SYLVIE SESÉ-LÉGER
TRANSLATED BY TERESE LYONS

NOTES

* THE IMPOSSIBILITY OF ADEQUATELY REPRODUCING THE WORD "JOUISSANCE"—ENJOYMENT, EXTREME PLEASURE, THE PLEASURE OF SEXUAL CLIMAX—HAS BEEN MUCH DISCUSSED. IN ORDER TO AVOID AN ARBITRARY CHOICE AMONG ITS MULTIPLE MEANINGS, JOUISSANCE WILL BE LEFT UNTRANSLATED IN THIS ARTICLE. THE VERB "JOUIR," HOWEVER, WILL BE TRANSLATED WITH THE SEMANTICALLY UNSATISFACTORY, BUT SYNTACTICALLY ADEQUATE, "TO REVEL," AND ONCE WITH THE MORE DIRECT "TO COME." IN BOTH CASES, THE FRENCH WILL BE INDICATED IN BRACKETS. (TRANS.)

1 "EVERYTHING CONNECTED WITH THIS FIRST MOTHER-ATTACHMENT HAS IN ANALYSIS SEEMED TO ME SO ELUSIVE, LOST IN A PAST SO DIM AND SHADOWY, SO HARD TO RESUSCITATE, THAT IT SEEMED AS IF IT HAD UNDERGONE SOME SPECIALLY INEXORABLE REPRESSION." SIGMUND FREUD. "FEMALE SEXUALITY." IN SEXUALITY AND THE PSYCHOLOGY OF LOVE. NEW YORK: COLLIER BOOKS, 1963. P. 195.

2A "IN HER 'AMOUR PROPRE,' WOMAN DOES NOT MANAGE TO DISTINGUISH HER OWN BODY FROM THAT WHICH WAS HER FIRST LOVE OBJECT." M. MONTRELAY. RECHERCHES SUR LA FÉMINITÉ.

2B PERHAPS CONFUSION OF CATHEXES ALSO PLAYS A ROLE FOR THE MOTHER, WHO, AT THAT MOMENT, LOVES THE DAUGHTER WHO RESEMBLES HER AND FOR WHOM EVERYTHING IS STILL POSSIBLE, (EVEN THE AVOIDANCE OF CASTRATION?).

3 SEE LACAN'S SEMINAR OF 1959-60, L'ETHNIQUE DE LA PSYCHANALYSE. (AS YET UNPUBLISHED.)

4 COMPLEXE DU PROCHAIN.

5 THE DAUGHTER IS, IN ALL LIKELIHOOD, NOT CATHECTED AS A LOVE OBJECT. SHE IS THERE ONLY IN ORDER TO ALLOW THE IMAGE OF THE MOTHER TO BE REVEALED. SHE SUPPORTS THAT IMAGE.

6 "TO IMITATE IS, OF COURSE, TO REPRODUCE AN IMAGE, BUT FUNDAMENTALLY, FOR THE SUBJECT, IT IS TO INSERT HIMSELF INTO A FUNCTION WHOSE WORKINGS HAVE SEIZED HIM." JACQUES LACAN. LE SÉMINAIRE XI: LES QUATRE CONCEPTS FONDAMENTAUX DE LA PSYCHANALYSE. [1964]. PARIS: SEUIL, 9173.

7 SEE LACAN'S SÉMINARIE XX: ENCORE. [1972-3]. PARIS: SEUIL, 1975. (TRANS.)

8 CF. M. MONTRELAY. RECHERCHES SUR LA FÉMINITÉ.

9 THE OEDIPUS COMPLEX SHATTERS APART IN THE LITTLE BOY; IT DOES NOT DISAPPEAR IN THE LITTLE GIRL. FREUD TELLS US THAT THE FATHER INHERITS THE GIRL'S ATTACHMENT TO HER MOTHER. THIS ATTACHMENT CONTINUES TO BE MARKED BY AMBIGUITY.

10 SEE NOTE 7.

11 WE WOULD SUGGEST THAT THE SIGNIFIERS "WOMAN'S-BODY" AND "SAME-BODY" FORCE US TO RECONSIDER THE QUESTION OF THE OBJECTS A. IT SEEMS TO US THAT, IN THE CASE OF A WOMAN INSCRIBED IN THE PHALLIC ORDER, THE OBJECTS A SUPPORTING HER DESIRE ARE NEVER "COMPLETELY" SEPARATED FROM HER. (IN THIS RESPECT, THE CHILD OCCUPIES A SPECIAL POSITION.) A WOMAN ALSO FINDS HER OBJECTS A UPON HER OWN BODY, DOUBLED BY THE MATERNAL REFLEXION.

12 CF. CHANTAL MAILLET. LA FEMME DANS L'AMOUR COURTOIS. (IN LETTRES DE L'ECOLE.)

13 IT IS NOT WITHOUT INTEREST THAT THE ANLAYST SHOULD BE A WOMAN. THIS UTTERANCE CAN BE BACKED UP BY THE RELATIONSHIP WITH THE SAME-BODY.

14 A WOMAN IS NEVER SAFE FROM IDENTIFICATIONS. SHE IS ALSO IDENTIFYING WHEN SHE TAKES THE POSITION OF SUFFERING "KNOWLEDGE," THAT OF THE PYTHIA PENETRATED BY TRUTH.

AN INQUIRY INTO FEMININITY

FEMININE EROTICISM IS MORE CENSORED, LESS REPRESSED THAN THAT OF A MAN. IT LENDS ITSELF LESS EASILY TO LOSING ITSELF AS THE STAKE OF UNCONSCIOUS REPRESENTATION. THE DRIVES WHOSE FORCE WAS DEMONSTRATED BY THE ENGLISH SCHOOL, CIRCUMSCRIBE A PLACE OR "CONTINENT" WHICH CAN BE CALLED "DARK" TO THE EXTENT THAT IT IS OUTSIDE THE CIRCUMFERENCE OF THE SYMBOLIC ECONOMY (FORECLOSED).

WHAT ARE THE PROCESSES WHICH MAINTAIN FEMINITY "OUTSIDE REPRESSION," IN A STATE OF NATURE, AS IT WERE? THE FIRST, OF A SOCIAL ORDER, CONCERNS THE ABSENCE OF PROHIBITIONS: THE GIRL IS LESS SUBJECT THAN THE BOY TO THE THREATS AND TO THE DEFENCES WHICH PENALIZE MASTURBATION. WE KEEP SILENT ABOUT HER MASTURBATION, ALL THE MORE AS IT IS LESS OBSERVABLE. FRANCOISE DOLTO HAS SHOWN THAT, SHELTERED BY THEIR PRIVACY, THE GIRL, THE WOMAN, CAN LIVE A "PROTECTED" SEXUALITY.[1] ONE TENDS TO REFER TO THE ANXIETY OF RAPE AND PENETRATION WITHOUT EMPHASIZING THAT, IN REALITY, ON THE CONTRARY, THE GIRL RISKS LITTLE. THE ANATOMY OF THE BOY, ON THE OTHER HAND, EXPOSES HIM VERY EARLY TO THE REALIZATION THAT HE IS MASTER NEITHER OF THE MANIFESTATIONS OF HIS DESIRE NOR OF THE EXTENT OF HIS PLEASURES. HE EXPERIMENTS, NOT ONLY WITH CHANCE BUT ALSO WITH THE LAW AND WITH HIS SEXUAL ORGAN; HIS BODY ITSELF TAKES ON THE VALUE OF STAKE.

IN RELATION TO CASTRATION, THEREFORE, THE POSITION OF THE MAN DIFFERS FROM THAT OF THE WOMAN WHOSE SEXUALITY IS CAPABLE OF REMAINING ON THE EDGE OF ALL REPRESSION. UNDER CERTAIN CIRCUMSTANCES THEN, THE STAKE OF CASTRATION FOR THE WOMAN FINDS ITSELF DISPLACED: IT CONSISTS IN THE SEXUALITY AND THE DESIRE OF THE OTHER SEX, MOST OFTEN THAT OF THE FATHER AND THEN, OF THE MASCULINE PARTNER. WHICH IS WHY PERRIER AND GRANOFF HAVE BEEN ABLE TO SHOW "... THE EXTREME FEMININE SENSIBILITY TO ALL EXPERIENCES RELATING TO THE CASTRATION OF THE MAN."[2]

YET OTHER PROCESSES, OF AN INSTINCTUAL AND NOT SOCIAL ORDER, MAINTAIN FEMININE SEXUALITY OUTSIDE THE ECONOMY OF REPRESENTATION—THE INTRICATION OF THE ORAL-ANAL DRIVES WITH VAGINAL PLEASURE. JONES, KLEIN AND DOLTO HAVE INSISTED ON THE FACT THAT THE GIRL'S ARCHAIC EXPERIENCES OF THE VAGINA ARE

ORGANIZED AS A FUNCTION OF PRE-ESTABLISHED ORAL-ANAL SCHEMAS. AT THE FURTHER EXTREME, PRECOCIOUS SEXUALITY "TURNS" AROUND A SINGLE ORIFICE, AN ORGAN WHICH IS BOTH DIGESTIVE AND VAGINAL, WHICH CEASELESSLY TENDS TO ABSORB, OR APPROPRIATE, TO DEVOUR. WE FIND AGAIN HERE THE THEME OF CONCENTRICITY.

IF THIS INSATIABLE ORGAN-HOLE IS AT THE CENTER OF PRECOCIOUS SEXUALITY, IF IT INFLECTS ALL PSYCHIC MOVEMENT ACCORDING TO CIRCULAR AND CLOSED SCHEMAS, IT COMPROMISES WOMAN'S RELATION TO CASTRATION AND THE LAW: TO ABSORB, TO TAKE, TO UNDERSTAND, IS TO REDUCE THE WORLD TO THE MOST ARCHAIC INSTINCTUAL "LAWS." IT IS A MOVEMENT OPPOSED TO THAT PRESUPPOSED BY CASTRATION: WHERE THE JOUISSANCE OF THE BODY LOSES ITSELF "FOR" A DISCOURSE WHICH IS OTHER.

HERE, WE WILL NOT THEREFORE QUESTION THE TRUTH OF THE CLINICAL OBSERVATIONS PRODUCED BY THE ENGLISH SCHOOL: ALL EXPERIENCE OF CHILD ANALYSIS CONFIRMS THE PRECOCITY OF THE "KNOWLEDGE" OF THE VAGINA. MORE GENERALLY, IT IS QUITE TRUE THAT THE VERY SMALL GIRL EXPERIENCES HER FEMININITY VERY EARLY. BUT, SIMULATANEOUSLY, IT MUST BE STRESSED THAT SUCH A PRECOCITY, FAR FROM FAVORING A POSSIBLE "MATURATION," ACTS AS AN OBSTACLE TO IT, SINCE IT MAINTAINS EROTICISM OUTSIDE THE REPRESENTATION OF CASTRATION.

ANXIETY AND THE RELATION TO THE BODY

A THIRD SERIES OF PROCESSES STANDS IN THE WAY OF REPRESSION: CONCERNING THE WOMAN'S RELATION TO HER OWN BODY, A RELATION SIMULTANEOUSLY NARCISSISTIC AND EROTIC. FOR THE WOMAN ENJOYS HER BODY AS SHE WOULD THE BODY OF ANOTHER. EVERY OCCURRENCE OF A SEXUAL KIND (PUBERTY, EROTIC EXPERIENCES, MATERNITY, ETC.) HAPPENS TO HER AS IF IT CAME FROM ANOTHER (WOMAN): EVERY OCCURRENCE IS THE FASCINATING ACTUALIZATION OF THE[1] FEMININITY OF ALL WOMEN, BUT ALSO AND ABOVE ALL, OF THAT OF THE MOTHER. IT IS AS IF "TO BECOME WOMAN," "TO BE WOMAN" GAVE ACCESS TO A JOUISSANCE OF THE BODY AS FEMININE AND/OR MATERNAL. IN THE SELF-LOVE SHE BEARS HERSELF, THE WOMAN CANNOT DIFFERENTIATE HER OWN BODY FROM THAT WHICH WAS "THE FIRST OBJECT."

WE WOULD HAVE TO SPECIFY FURTHER WHAT IS ONLY INTIMATED HERE: THAT THE REAL OF THE BODY, IN TAKING FORM AT PUBERTY, IN CHARGING ITSELF WITH INTENSITY AND IMPORTANCE AND PRESENCE, AS OBJECT OF THE LOVER'S DESIRE, RE-ACTUALIZES, RE-INCARNATES, THE REAL OF THAT OTHER BODY, WHICH AT THE BEGINNING OF LIFE WAS THE SUBSTANCE OF WORDS, THE ORGANIZER OF DESIRE; WHICH, LATER ON, WAS ALSO THE MATERIAL OF ARCHAIC REPRESSION. RECOVERING HERSELF AS MATERNAL BODY (AND ALSO AS PHALLUS), THE WOMAN CAN NO LONGER REPRESS, "LOSE," THE FIRST STAKE OF REPRESENTATION. AS IN THE TRAGEDY, REPRESENTATION IS THREATENED BY RUIN. BUT AT THE ROOT OF THIS THREAT THERE ARE DIFFERENT PROCESSES: FOR OEDIPUS, THE RESTORATION OF THE STAKE PROCEEDED BY CHANCE, FROM THE GODS; IT WAS EFFECTED IN SPITE OF A PROHIBITION. NOTHING, ON THE CONTRARY, IS FORBIDDEN FOR THE WOMEN; THERE IS NO STATEMENT OR LAW WHICH PROHIBITS THE RECOVERY OF THE STAKE SINCE THE REAL WHICH IMPOSES ITSELF AND TAKES THE PLACE OF REPRESSION AND DESIRE IS, FOR HER, THE REAL OF HER OWN BODY.

FROM NOW ON, ANXIETY, TIED TO THE PRESENCE OF THIS BODY, CAN ONLY BE INSISTENT, CONTINUOUS. THIS BODY, SO CLOSE, WHICH SHE HAS TO OCCUPY, IS AN OJECT IN EXCESS WHICH MUST BE "LOST," THAT IS TO SAY, REPRESSED, IN ORDER TO BE SYMBOLIZED. HENCE THE SYMPTOMS WHICH SO OFTEN SIMULATE THIS LOSS: "THERE IS NO LONGER ANYTHING, ONLY THE HOLE, EMPTINESS . . ." SUCH IS THE LEIMOTIF OF ALL FEMININE ANALYSIS, WHICH IT WOULD BE A MISTAKE TO SEE AS THE EXPRESSION OF AN ALLEGED "CASTRATION." ON THE CONTRARY, IT IS A DEFENSE PRODUCED IN ORDER TO PARRY THE AVATARS, THE DEFICIENCIES, OF SYMBOLIC CASTRATION.

THE ANALYST OFTEN FINDS A "FEAR OF FEMININITY" IN CONNECTION WITH FEMININE ANXIETY, ESPECIALLY IN THE ADOLESCENT. WE HAVE TRIED TO SHOW THAT THIS FEAR IS NOT A RESULT OF PHANTASIES OF VIOLATION AND BREAKING IN (EFFRACTION) ALONE . . . AT BOTTOM, IT IS FEAR OF THE FEMININE BODY AS A NON-REPRESSED AND UNREPRESENTABLE OBJECT. IN OTHER WORDS, FEMININITY, "ACCORDING TO JONES," I.E., FEMININITY EXPERIENCED AS REAL AND IMMEDIATE, IS THE BLIND SPOT OF THE SYMBOLIC PROCESS ANALYZED BY FREUD. TWO INCOMPATIBLE, HETEROGENEOUS TERRITORIES CO-EXIST INSIDE THE FEMININE UNCONSCIOUS: THAT OF REPRESENTATION AND THAT WHICH REMAINS "THE DARK CONTINENT."

DEFENCES AND MASQUERADE

IT IS RARE FOR ANXIETY TO MANIFEST ITSELF AS SUCH IN ANALYSIS. IT IS USUALLY CAMOUFLAGED BY THE DEFENCES THAT IT PROVOKES. IT IS A QUESTION OF ORGANIZING A REPRESENTATION OF CASTRATION WHICH IS NO LONGER SYMBOLIC, BUT IMAGINARY: A LACK IS SIMULATED AND THEREBY THE LOSS OF SOME STAKE—AN UNDERTAKING ALL THE MORE EASILY ACCOMPLISHED PRECISELY BECAUSE FEMININE ANATOMY EXHIBITS A LACK, THAT OF THE PENIS. AT THE SAME TIME AS BEING HER OWN PHALLUS, THEREFORE, THE WOMAN WILL DISGUISE HERSELF WITH THIS LACK, THROWING INTO RELIEF THE DIMENSION OF CASTRATION AS TROMPE-L'OEIL.

THE WAYS IN WHICH THIS CAN OCCUR ARE MULTIPLE. ONE CAN PLAY ON THE ABSENCE OF THE PENIS THROUGH SILENCE JUST AS WELL AS THROUGH A RESOUNDING VANITY. ONE CAN MAKE IT THE MODEL OF EROTIC, MYSTICAL, AND NEUROTIC EXPERIENCES. THE ANOREXIC REFUSAL OF FOOD IS A GOOD EXAMPLE OF THE DESIRE TO REDUCE AND TO DISSOLVE HER OWN FLESH, TO TAKE HER OWN BODY AS A CIPHER. MASOCHISM ALSO MIMES THE LACK, THROUGH PASSIVITY, IMPOTENCE AND DOING NOTHING ("NE RIEN FAIRE"). THE OBSERVATIONS OF HELENE DEUTSCH AND THOSE OF THE RECHERCHES NOUVELLES COULD BE UNDERSTOOD IN THIS WAY. CASTRATION IS SIMILARLY DISGUISED IN THE REGISTER OF EROTIC FICTION: WHERE THE FEMININE ORIFICE, O, IS "FALSELY" REPRESENTED IN ITS SUCCESSIVE METAMORPHOSES.

HERE, I WOULD RATHER TURN TO THE POETS, THOSE WHO HAVE WRITTEN IN THE NOVELISTIC OR MADE FILMS OUT OF THE FEMININE DRAMA ("CINÉMA"), SINCE THE LIMITATIONS OF THIS ARTICLE RULE OUT ANY DETAILED CONSIDERATION OF CLINICAL CASES.

TAKE FELLINI, THE DIRECTOR OF JULIETTE OF THE SPIRITS, A FILM SO BAFFLING, NO DOUBT, BECAUSE IT BRINGS OUT THE PRESENCE OF THE "DARK CONTINENT" SO WELL. THE DIMENSION OF FEMININITY THAT LACAN DESIGNATES AS MASQUERADE, TAKING THE TERM FROM JOAN RIVIERE,[II] TAKES SHAPE IN THIS PILING UP OF CRAZY THINGS, FEATHERS, HATS AND STRANGE BAROQUE CONSTRUCTIONS WHICH RISE UP LIKE SO MANY SILENT INSIGNIAS. BUT WHAT WE MUST SEE IS THAT THE OBJECTIVE OF SUCH A MASQUERADE IS TO SAY NOTHING. ABSOLUTELY NOTHING. AND IN ORDER TO PRODUCE THIS NOTHING THE WOMAN USES HER OWN

BODY AS DISGUISE.

THE NOVELS OF MARGUERITE DURAS USE THE SAME WORLD OF STUPOR AND SILENCE. IT COULD BE SHOWN THAT THIS SILENCE, THIS NON-SPEECH, AGAIN EXHIBITS THE FASCINATING DIMENSION OF FEMININE LACK: DURAS WANTS TO MAKE THIS LACK "SPEAK" AS A CRY (MODERATO CANTABILE), OR AS "MUSIC." HERE, LET US SIMPLY RECALL WHAT IS SAID IN THE RAVISHMENT OF LOL V STEIN: "WHAT WAS NEEDED WAS A WORD-ABSENCE, A WORD HOLE ... IT COULD NOT HAVE BEEN SPOKEN, IT COULD ONLY BE MADE TO RESOUND."[3]

THUS THE SEX, THE VAGINO-ORAL ORGAN OF THE WOMAN, ACTS AS OBSTACLE TO CASTRATION; AT THE SAME TIME, "FALSELY REPRESENTING THE LATTER IN ITS EFFECTS OF ALLUREMENT WHICH PROVOKE ANXIETY." THIS IS WHY MAN HAS ALWAYS CALLED THE FEMININE DEFENCES AND MASQUERADE EVIL.

WOMAN IS NOT ACCUSED OF THINKING OR OF COMMITTING THIS EVIL, BUT OF INCARNATING IT.[III] IT IS THIS EVIL WHICH SCANDALIZES WHENEVER WOMAN "PLAYS OUT" HER SEX IN ORDER TO EVADE THE WORD AND THE LAW. EACH TIME SHE SUBVERTS A LAW OR A WORD WHICH RELIES ON THE PREDOMINANTLY MASCULINE STRUCTURE OF THE LOOK. FREUD SAYS THAT EVIL IS EXPERIENCED AS SUCH WHEN ANXIETY GRIPS THE CHILD IN FRONT OF THE UNVEILED BODY OF HIS MOTHER. "DID HIS DESIRE THEN REFER ONLY TO THIS HOLE OF FLESH?" THE WOMAN AFFORDS A GLIMPSE OF THE REAL, BY VIRTUE OF HER RELATION TO NOTHING—THAT IS TO SAY, TO THE THING. AT THIS MOMENT, THE SYMBOLIC COLLAPSES INTO THE REAL. FREUD ALSO SAYS THAT THE PERVERT CANNOT SEE THE CASTRATED BODY OF HIS MOTHER. IN THIS SENSE, EVERY MAN IS A PERVERT. ON THE ONE HAND, HE ENJOYS WITHOUT SAYING SO, WITHOUT COMING TOO CLOSE—FOR THEN HE WOULD HAVE TO TAKE UPON HIMSELF A TERRIBLE ANXIETY, OR EVEN HATE—; HE ENJOYS BY PROXY THE THING HE GLIMPSES THROUGH THE MOTHER. ON THE OTHER HAND, HE DOES NOT APPEAR TO UNDERSTAND THAT HER RELATION TO THE THING IS SUBLIMATED. IT IS THIS EVIL WHICH HAS TO BE REPRESSED.

A FILM LIKE DAYS OF WRATH[IV] LAYS BARE ALL THE MASCULINE "DEFENCES" AGAINST FEMININITY AND WOMAN'S DIRECT RELATION TO JOUISSANCE. THE MAN IS TERRORIZED BY THE THREAT THAT FEMININITY RAISES FOR "HIS" REPRESSION. IN ORDER TO REASSURE HIM AND CONVINCE HIM, THE

WOMAN ALWAYS ADVANCES FURTHER ALONG HER OWN PATH BY EXPLAINING HERSELF, WISHING TO SPEAK THE TRUTH. BUT SHE DOES NOT UNDERSTAND THAT HER DISCOURSE WILL NOT AND CANNOT BE RECEIVED. FOR THE FACT OF BYPASSING THE LAW OF REPRESSION PRECISELY BY SAYING ALL, CONTAMINATES THE MOST PRECIOUS TRUTH AND MAKES IT SUSPECT, ODIOUS AND CONDEMNABLE. HENCE MASCULINE CENSURE.

THE FRUSTRATIONS, INTERDICTIONS AND CONTEMPT WHICH HAVE WEIGHED ON WOMEN FOR CENTURIES MAY INDEED BE ABSURD AND ARBITRARY, BUT THEY DO NOT MATTER. THE MAIN THING IS THE FACT OF IMPOSING THE DEFINITIVE ABANDONMENT OF JOUISSANCE. THE SCANDAL CAN THEN COME TO AN END—THE FEMININE SEX BEARS WITNESS TO CASTRATION.

THE ANALYST, FOR HIS PART, CANNOT DEFINE FEMININE CASTRATION SIMPLY AS THE EFFECT OF HIS STRUCTURES. IF THE EXEMPLAR OF THE HYSTERICAL, NEUROTIC WOMAN IS ONE WHO NEVER LETS UP WISHING TO BE HER SEX, INVERSELY, ISN'T THE "ADULT" WOMAN ONE WHO RECONSTRUCTS HER SEXUALITY IN A FIELD WHICH GOES BEYOND SEX? THE PRINCIPLE OF A MASCULINE LIBIDO UPHELD BY FREUD COULD BE CLARIFIED AS A FUNCTION OF THIS "EXTRATERRITORIALITY."

FEMININE CASTRATION: HYPOTHESES

ONCE AGAIN, LET US TAKE AN EXAMPLE FROM LITERATURE. KLOSSOWSKI'S PORTRAITS OF WOMEN EASILY LEND THEMSELVES TO A CLINICAL COMMENTARY. WE MIGHT BE SURPRISED AT THE ASTONISHINGLY VIRILE ATTRIBUTES (BOTH ANATOMICAL AND PSYCHICAL—WITH WHICH THE AUTHOR ENDOWS HIS HEROINES AND DEDUCE FROM THEM SOME PERVERSION. IT IS ALSO POSSIBLE TO SEE IN THESE ATTRIBUTES THE MATERIAL OF A MORAL FABLE OUTLINING A TYPE OF PERFECTED FEMININITY: THE "TRUE" WOMAN, THE "FEMME" WOMAN WOULD BE DRAWN AS SHE WHO HAS "FORGOTTEN" HER FEMININITY, AND WHO WOULD ENTRUST THE JOUISSANCE AND THE REPRESENTATION OF IT TO AN OTHER. FOR THIS REASON, KLOSSOWSKI'S HEROINE, ROBERTE, COULD IN NO WAY TALK ABOUT HERSELF, HER BODY OR "THE WORD THAT IT CONCEALS."[4] IT IS SOMEONE ELSE'S TASK TO HOLD THE DISCOURSE OF FEMININITY, IN LOVE AND/OR IN A NOVEL.

UNDER THE SIGN OF THIS FORGETTING, A SECOND ECONOMY OF DESIRE, WHERE THE STAKE IS NO LONGER THE SAME, CAN EFFECTIVELY BE DESCRIBED. THE STAKE IS NOW PRECOCIOUS FEMININITY AND NOT THE PENIS OR MASCULINE SEXUALITY: PRECOCIOUS FEMININITY BECOMES THE MATERIAL OF REPRESSION. "ACCORDING TO JONES" ONE OR SEVERAL PERIODS OF LATENCY CORRESPOND TO THIS DECATHEXIS OF SEXUALITY, PERIODS DURING WHICH THE LITTLE GIRL AND THE WOMAN DISENTANGLE THEMSELVES FROM THEIR OWN BODIES AND ITS PLEASURES. THIS IS WHY PERIODS OF FRIGIDITY IN ANALYSIS CAN OFTEN BE CONSIDERED AS AN INDEX OF PROGRESS: THEY MARK THE MOMENT WHEN THE PATIENT DECATHECTS THE VAGINAL-ORAL SCHEMAS WHICH TILL THEN WERE ALONE CAPABLE OF PROVIDING ACCESS TO EROTIC PLEASURE.

THE DECISIVE STEP BY WHICH THE FEMININE UNCONSCIOUS IS MODIFIED LIES, NOT SO MUCH IN THE CHANGE OF LOVE OBJECT[5] AS IN THE CHANGE IN THE UNCONSCIOUS REPRESENTATIVE. MASCULINE, PHALLIC REPRESENTATIVES ARE SUBSTITUTED FOR THE FIRST "CONCENTRIC" REPRESENTATIVE. THE LAW AND THE PATERNAL IDEALS OF THE FATHER WHICH ARE ARTICULATED IN HER DISCOURSE CONSTITUTE THE NEW REPRESENTATIVES CAPABLE OF SUPPLANTING THE MODELS OF ARCHAIC REPRESENTATIONS (FEMININE OEDIPUS).

LET US NOTE THAT THIS SUBSTITUTION DOES NOT MUTILATE THE WOMAN AND DEPRIVE HER OF A PENIS WHICH SHE NEVER HAD, BUT DEPRIVES HER OF THE SENSE OF PRECOCIOUS SEXUALITY. FEMININITY IS FORGOTTEN, INDEED REPRESSED, AND THIS LOSS CONSTITUTES THE SYMBOLIC CASTRATION OF THE WOMAN.

SUBLIMATION AND METAPHOR

IN ANALYSIS AND MORE SPECIFICALLY, IN THE TRANSFERENCE, (I.E., THE SET OF UNCONSCIOUS MODIFICATIONS PRODUCED BY THE ENUNCIATION OF DISCOURSE ON THE COUCH), THE DIMENSION OF PLEASURE CAN EMERGE.

IN RECHERCHES, TOROK SPEAKS OF ITS MANIFESTATION: "WHEN ONE OF MY PATIENTS HAS 'UNDERSTOOD' AN INTERPRETATION, WHEN, CONSEQUENTLY, AN INHIBITION IS LIFTED, A FREQUENT INDICATION OF THIS ADVANCE IS THAT THE PATIENT DREAMS AND IN THIS DREAM SHE HAS AN ORGASM" (A DESCRIPTION OF ONE OF THESE DREAMS FOLOWS).[6]

TOROK, BY INSISTING ON THE FACT THAT A

PLEASURE ARISES WHEN A NEW REPRESENTATION IS ELABORATED, TELLS US WHAT IS ESSENTIAL ABOUT THIS PLEASURE. CONTRARY TO WHAT ONE MIGHT THINK, THIS PLEASURE DOES NOT LIE IN THE LIFTING OF AN INHIBITION, IN THE RELEASING OF TENSION, CONTAINED FOR TOO LONG. ON THE CONTRARY, THE PLEASURE, FAR FROM BEING EXPLICABLE BY THE CLICHÉ OF RELEASE ("DÉ-FOULEMENT")[V] ARISES FROM THE PUTTING IN PLACE OF NEW REPRESENTATIONS. LET US NOTE THAT THESE WERE FIRST ENUNCIATED BY THE OTHER, THE ANALYST, WHO, IN INTERPRETING, VERBALLY ARTICULATES SOMETHING OF A SEXUALITY MAINTAINED TILL THEN IN THE STATE OF NATURE, IN THE "DARK."

HERE, THEREFORE, PLEASURE IS THE EFFECT OF THE WORD OF THE OTHER. MORE SPECIFICALLY, IT OCCURS AT THE ADVENT OF A STRUCTURING DISCOURSE. FOR WHAT IS ESSENTIAL IN THE ANALYSIS OF A WOMAN IS NOT MAKING SEXUALITY MORE "CONSCIOUS" OR INTERPRETING IT, AT LEAST NOT IN THE SENSE NORMALLY GIVEN TO THIS TERM. THE ANALYST'S WORD TAKES ON A COMPLETELY DIFFERENT FUNCTION. IT NO LONGER EXPLAINS, BUT FROM THE SOLE FACT OF ARTICULATING, IT STRUCTURES. BY VERBALLY PUTTING IN PLACE A REPRESENTATION OF CASTRATION, THE ANALYST'S WORD MAKES SEXUALITY PASS INTO DISCOURSE. THIS TYPE OF INTERPRETATION THEREFORE REPRESSES, AT LEAST IN THE SENSE GIVEN TO THE WORD HERE.

UNDERSTOOD IN THIS WAY, INTERPRETATION CAN PERHAPS HELP US TO LOCATE A CERTAIN CULTURAL AND SOCIAL FUNCTION OF PSYCHO-ANALYSIS. THE FREUDIAN THEORY OF SEXUALITY WAS DEVELOPED (MISE EN PLACE) IN RELATION TO WOMEN AND FEMININITY. WE CAN ASK WHETHER PSYCHOANALYSIS WAS NOT ARTICULATED PRE-CISELY IN ORDER TO REPRESS FEMININITY (IN THE SENSE OF PRODUCING ITS SYMBOLIC REPRESENTA-TION). AT THE SAME TIME, FREUD'S RESERVATIONS ABOUT JONES WOULD MAKE SENSE: THE ATTEMPTS TO "MAKE" FEMININITY "SPEAK" WOULD SURELY JEOPARDIZE THE VERY REPRESSION THAT FREUD HAD KNOWN HOW TO ACHIEVE.

LET US RETURN TO OUR EXAMPLE. WHAT PLEASURE CAN THERE BE IN THE REPRESSION THAT IS PRODUCED AT THE MOMENT OF INTERPRETATION? FIRST, LET US SAY THAT INTERPRETATION, AS IT IS ANALYZED HERE, DOES NOT CONSIST SO MUCH IN EXPLAINING AND COMMENTING AS IN ARTICULAT-ING. HERE AGAIN, IT IS THE FORM OF WORDS WHICH

MUST BE EMPHASIZED. IN RESPONSE TO THE ANALYSAND'S PHANTASY, THE ANALYST ENUNCI-ATES A CERTAIN NUMBER OF SIGNIFIERS NECES-SARILY RELATING TO HIS OWN DESIRE AND HIS LISTENING-PLACE. THESE WORDS ARE OTHER: THE ANALYST'S DISCOURSE IS NOT REFLEXIVE, BUT DIFFERENT. AS SUCH IT IS A METAPHOR, NOT A MIRROR, OF THE PATIENT'S DISCOURSE. AND, PRECISELY, METAPHOR IS CAPABLE OF ENGENDER-ING PLEASURE.

FIRST FREUD AND THEN LACAN ANALYZED THE MOTIVES OF THIS PLEASURE WITH REGARD TO THE JOKE. WE LAUGH WHEN WE PERCEIVE THAT THE WORDS SPEAK A TEXT OTHER THAN THAT WHICH WE THOUGHT. AND IF THE OTHER LAUGHS, IF THE MISAPPREHENSION PLAYS ON ONE MORE REGISTER, THE PLEASURE BECOMES KEENER STILL. WHAT FUNCTION DOES THIS OTHER TEXT, THIS OTHER EAR, HAVE? IT HAS THE FUNCTION OF ENGENDERING A METAPHOR, THAT IS TO SAY, OF SUBSTITUTING ITSELF FOR THE PRECEDING TEXT AND LISTENING-PLACE. PLEASURE ARISES THE MOMENT THIS METAPHOR IS PRODUCED. LACAN SAYS THAT IT IS IDENTIFIED WITH THE VERY MEANING OF THE METAPHOR.[7]

IN WHAT THEN, DOES THIS MEANING BEREFT OF SIGNIFICATION CONSIST? WE CAN DEFINE IT AS THE MEASURE OF THE EMPTY "SPACE" INDUCED BY REPRESSION. THE METAPHOR, BY POSING ITSELF AS THAT WHICH IS NOT SPOKEN, HOLLOWS OUT AND DESIGNATES THIS SPACE. FREUD SAID THAT THE PLEASURE OF THE JOKE LIES IN THE RETURN OF THE REPRESSED. DOES IT NOT RATHER, LIE IN PUTTING THE DIMENSION OF REPRESSION INTO PLAY ON THE LEVEL OF THE TEXT ITSELF?

IT IS THIS PLEASURE OF THE JOKE THAT CAN BE EVOKED IN RELATION TO ALL SUBLIMATION. FOR IT IS AN OPERATION WHICH CONSISTS IN OPENING UP NEW DIVISIONS AND SPACES IN THE MATERIAL THAT IT TRANSFORMS. IN THE TRANSFERENCE, THE PATIENT'S ORGASM TOOK NOTE OF AN INTERPRETA-TION. SURELY THIS IS BEST REPRESENTED AS A BREATH OF AIR BETWEEN TWO SIGNIFIERS, SUDDENLY OPENED UP BY THE METAPHOR?

THE ORGASM, LIKE A BUST OF LAUGHTER, TESTIFIES TO THE MEANING—INSIGNIFICANT—OF THE ANAL-YST'S WORD. WE MUST NOW TRY TO REDISCOVER THIS DIMENSION OF "WIT" IN PLEASURE AND JOUISSANCE.

PLEASURE AND JOUISSANCE

FEMININE EROTIC PLEASURE VARIES CONSIDERAB-
LY IN ITS NATURE AND EFFECTS. THERE IS VARIETY
IN THE PLACES OF THE BODY CATHECTED, IN THE
LEVEL OF INTENSITY, IN THE OUTCOME (ORGASM OR
NOT), AND IN THE EFFECTS: A "SUCCESSFUL"
SEXUAL RELATION CAN CAUSE CALM OR ANXIETY.
LET US ALSO REMEMBER THAT A NEUROSIS CANNOT
NECESSARILY BE INFERRED FROM FRIGIDITY; AND
THAT, RECIPROCALLY, PSYCHOTICS AND VERY
IMMATURE WOMEN HAVE INTENSE VAGINAL
ORGASMS.[8]

HOW ARE WE TO MAKE SENSE OF THE EXUBERANCE,
THE BIZARRENESS AND THE PARADOXES OF THESE
PLEASURES? BY REFERRING LESS TO THE VARIE-
TIES OF FORM AND INTENSITY THAN TO THEIR
FUNCTION IN THE PSYCHIC ECONOMY. HERE AGAIN,
WE WILL DISTINGUISH TWO TYPES OF SEXUAL
PLEASURE: THE PRECOCIOUS AND THE SUBLI-
MATED.

THE FIRST WAS EARLIER SEEN TO BE THE EFFECT
OF THE EXPERIENCE OF ARCHAIC SEXUALITY. EVEN
IF IT INVOLVES TWO PEOPLE, EVEN IF IT PRESENTS
THE APPEARANCE OF AN ADULT SEXUALITY, IT
MERELY RE-ACTUALIZES OR RAISES TO THE
HIGHEST PITCH IN ORGASM, THE JOUISSANCE THAT
THE WOMAN HAS OF HERSELF.[9] IN THIS TYPE OF
PLEASURE, THE OTHER'S LOOK AND HIS DESIRE,
FURTHER REINFORCE THE CIRCULARITY OF THE
EROTIC RELATION. HENCE THE ANXIETY THAT
ARISES BEFORE AND AFTER THE SEXUAL ACT.

INVERSELY, PLEASURE CAN BE STRUCTURING IN ITS
EFFECTS. THE SORT OF "GENIUS," OF INSPIRATION
WHICH THE WOMAN DISCOVERS AFTER LOVE, SHOWS
THAT AN EVENT OF AN UNCONSCIOUS NATURE HAS
OCCURRED, WHICH HAS ENABLED HER TO TAKE UP
A CERTAIN DISTANCE FROM THE DARK CONTINENT.

WE WILL CALL SUBLIMATED PLEASURE THAT WHICH
TAKES THE SAME FORMS AS INCESTUOUS PLEA-
SURE WHILE NONETHELESS PRESUPPOSING AND
CONFIRMING WOMEN'S ACCESS TO THE SYMBOLIC.
THIS PLEASURE IS NO LONGER DERIVED FROM
FEMININITY AS SUCH, BUT FROM THE SIGNIFIER, MORE
PRECISELY, FROM THE REPRESSION THAT IT BRINGS
ABOUT: THIS IS WHY SUBLIMATED PLEASURE IS
IDENTIFIED WITH THE PLEASURE DERIVED FROM THE
JOKE.

SUCH A TRANSFORMATION ASSUMES, ON THE ONE
HAND, THE FORGETTING OF PRECOCIOUS FEMININ-
ITY, AND ON THE OTHER, THE SETTING IN PLACE OF A
NEW REPRESENTATIVE OR SIGNIFIER OF CASTRA-

TION. DOES NOT THE SUBLIMATED SEXUAL ACT
CONSTITUTE FOR THE WOMAN ONE OF THE WAYS OF
PUTTING AN ECONOMY INTO PLACE WHERE: 1. THE
SIGNIFIER WOULD BE ACTUALIZED IN THE RHYTHM,
THE PERIOD RETURN OF THE PENIS; 2. THE STAKE
WOULD CONSIST OF THE REPRESSED FEMININE
DRIVES,[10] INSEPARABLE FROM THE PENIS ITSELF;
AND 3. PLEASURE WOULD BE THE MEANING OF THE
METAPHOR THROUGH WHICH THE PENIS "WOULD
REPRESS" THE BODY, FEMININE SEXUALITY.

LET US BE MORE PRECISE: THE PENIS, ITS
THROBBING, ITS CADENCE AND THE MOVEMENTS OF
LOVE-MAKING COULD BE SAID TO PRODUCE THE
PUREST AND MOST ELEMENTARY FORM OF
SIGNIFYING ARTICULATION. THAT OF A SERIES OF
BLOWS WHICH MARK OUT THE SPACE OF THE BODY.

IT IS THIS WHICH OPENS UP RHYTHMS ALL THE MORE
AMPLE AND INTENSE, A JOUISSANCE ALL THE MORE
KEEN AND SERIOUS IN THAT THE PENIS, THE OBJECT
WHICH IS ITS INSTRUMENT, IS SCARCELY ANYTHING.

BUT TO STATE THIS IS TO STATE A PARADOX: THE
PENIS PRODUCES JOUISSANCE BECAUSE IT
INCARNATES A FINITUDE. SUBLIMATION ALWAYS
IMPLIES A DE-IDEALIZATION. THE PHALLIC SIG-
NIFIER, DETACHED FROM THE TERRIFYING REPRE-
SENTATIONS OF THE SUPEREGO WHICH REVOLVE
AROUND THE IMAGINARY PHALLUS, MUST APPEAR
AS AN OBJECT OF NOT-MUCH-MEANING.[11]

THIS STEP USUALLY SUSPENDED DURING CHILD-
HOOD, TAKES PLACE AFTER THE FIRST SEXUAL
EXPERIENCES OF ADULTHOOD. IS IT A QUESTION OF
UNCONSCIOUS PROCESSES? PROVIDED THE
GROUND HAS BEEN PREPARED, LIFE AND A
CERTAIN ETHIC UNDERTAKE THIS WORK. TO THE
EXTENT THAT ROMANTIC IDEALIZATION IS SUCCESS-
FULLY MOURNED (RELINQUISHED), TO THE EXTENT
THAT THE DIMENSION OF THE GIFT PREDOMINATES,
THE PENIS CAN OBJECTIFY, BY ITS VERY INSIGNIFI-
CANCE, THE "DIFFICULTY TO BE" OF THE COUPLE, IN
WHICH JOUISSANCE IS LOST. THUS IT CAN NO
LONGER BE SEPARATED IN ITS CONSISTENCY FROM
THE MATERIAL OF THIS ARCHAIC, FEMININE
JOUISSANCE WHICH HAS BEEN RENOUNCED. IT
EMBODIES IT AS LOST, AND ALL OF A SUDDEN
RESTORES IT A HUNDREDFOLD. FOR IT DEPLOYS
THIS JOUISSANCE IN DIRECT PROPORTION TO THE
FORGETTING, WHICH IS IN ITSELF INFINITE.

THUS, ETHICS IS INDISSOCIABLE FROM A 'CERTAIN'
RELATION TO JOUISSANCE. THE DE-IDEALIZATION
THAT IT IMPLIES ALONE MAKES POSSIBLE THE

OCCASIONAL COMING TOGETHER AND BINDING OF TWO PERFECTLY DISTINCT, HETEROGENEOUS SPACES. THE VOLUPTUOUS SENSATION OF AN ASPIRATION OF THE WHOLE BODY IN A SPACE ABSOLUTELY OTHER AND CONSEQUENTLY, INFINITE, CANNOT SIMPLY BE EXPLAINED AS THE EFFECT OF THE PERCEPTION OF THE VAGINAL CAVITY. IT IMPLIES THAT THIS CAVITY IS HOLLOWED OUT BY REPRESSION, THAT IS TO SAY, BY A SYMBOLIC OPERATION.

CONSEQUENTLY, PLEASURE, FAR FROM BEING REDUCED TO THE EXCITATION OF AN ORGAN, ON THE CONTRARY, TRANSPORTS THE WOMAN INTO THE FIELD OF THE SIGNIFIER. SUBLIMATED PLEASURE, LIKE THE DREAM AND HYPNONIS, LIKE THE POETIC ACT, MARKS A MOMENT WHEN THE UNCONSCIOUS REPRESENTATION TAKES ON AN ABSOLUTE VALUE: IN OTHER WORDS, WHEN THE ACT OF ARTICULATING PRODUCES ON ITS OWN THE MEANING OF DIS-COURSE, (MEANING NOTHING). SWEEPING AWAY ALL SIGNIFICATION, IT LAYS HOLD OF THE WOMAN AND CATCHES HER IN ITS PROGRESSION AND ITS RHYTHMS.[12]

FOR THE MAN, EXCEPTIONS ASIDE,[13] THIS TRANS-PORTATION INTO THE SIGNIFIER CANNOT BE PRODUCED IN SO VIOLENT AND RADICAL A WAY. IN FACT, HOW COULD HE ABANDON HIMSELF TO THAT WHICH HE HIMSELF CONTROLS, AND FROM WHOSE PLAY HE GIVES JOUISSANCE. MOREOVER, THIS GAME (PLAY) INVOLVES THE RISK OF DETUMES-CENCE,[14] AND ALSO THE VERTIGO AND ANXIETY AROUSED BY THE ABSOLUTE OF FEMININE DEMAND: THE WOMAN EXPECTS AND RECEIVES ALL THERE IS OF THE PENIS AT THE MOMENT OF LOVE.

IF WE NO LONGER CONSIDER WHAT IS PROPERLY CALLED PLEASURE, BUT THE ORGASM USUALLY DESIGNATED AS "JOUISSANCE" BY THE ANALYST, A SIMILAR DISTINCTION MUST BE MADE BETWEEN JOUISSANCE AND THE ORGASM WHICH IS PRO-DUCED IN A SUBLIMATED ECONOMY. IN THE FORMER, THE RESIDUE OF PLEASURE COMES TO A DEAD END, SINCE THE WOMAN AGAIN FINDS HERSELF POWER-LESS TO MAINTAIN THE UNCONSCIOUS ECONOMY. THIS FORM OF ORGASM, REGISTERING PLEASURE OUTSIDE SIGNIFICANCE (SIGNIFIANCE), BARS ACCESS TO THE SYMBOLIC. SUBLIMATION, ON THE CONTRARY, TRANSPORTS NOT ONLY PLEASURE BUT THE ORGASM INTO METAPHOR. ORGASM, ENDLESS-LY RENEWED, BROUGHT TO A WHITE HEAT, EXPLODES AT THE MOMENT OF PLEASURE. IT BURSTS IN THE DOUBLE SENSE OF THE FRENCH TERM ÉCLATER: THE SENSE OF DEFLAGRATION AND THAT OF A REVELATION. THERE IS THEREFORE A CONTINUITY OF THE ASCENT OF PLEASURE AND OF ITS APOGEE IN ORGASM: THE ONE CARRIES THE SIGNIFIER TO ITS MAXIMUM INCANDESCENCE: THE OTHER MARKS THE MOMENT WHEN THE DISCOURSE, IN EXPLODING UNDER THE EFFECT OF ITS OWN FORCE, COMES TO THE POINT OF BREAKING, OF COMING APART. IT IS NO LONGER ANYTHING.

TO BREAK ITSELF, TO DISJOINT ITSELF, IN OTHER WORDS, TO ARTICULATE ITSELF THROUGH A MEANING WHICH ENDLESSLY ESCAPES. ORGASM IN DISCOURSE LEADS US TO THE POINT WHERE FEMININE JOUISSANCE CAN BE UNDERSTOOD AS WRITING (ÉCRITURE). TO THE POINT WHERE IT MUST APPEAR THAT THIS JOUISSANCE AND THE LITERARY TEXT (WHICH IS ALSO WRITTEN LIKE AN ORGASM PRODUCED FROM WITHIN DISCOURSE), ARE THE EFFECT OF THE SAME MURDER OF THE SIGNIFIER.

ISN'T THIS WHY BATAILLE, JARRY AND JABÈS SPEAK OF WRITING AS THE JOUISSANCE OF A WOMAN? AND WHY THAT WHICH SHE IS WRITING IS THE NAME?[IV]

MICHELE MONTRELAY
TRANSLATED BY PARVEEN ADAMS

NOTES

[1] F. DOLTO, 'LA LIBIDO ET SON DESTIN FÉMININ,' LA PSYCHANALYSE, VII, PUF.

[2] W. GRANOFF AND F. PERRIER, 'LE PROBLÈME DE LA PERVERSION CHES LA FEMME ET LES IDÉAUX FEMININS,' LA PSYCHANALYSE, VII. THIS ARTICLE IS ESSENTIAL FOR THEORETICAL WORK ON FEMININE SEXUALITY.

[3] MARGUERITE DURAS, LA RAVISSEMENT DE LOL V STEIN, GALLIMARD, P. 54.

[4] P. KLOSSOWSKI, LES LOIS DE L'HOSPITALITÉ, P. 145.

[5] THE 'CHANGE OF OBJECT' DESIGNATES THE RENUNCIATION OF THE FIRST LOVE OBJECT, THE MOTHER, IN FAVOUR OF THE FATHER. ON THIS PROBLEM, CF J. LUQUET-PARAT, 'LE CHANGEMENT D'OBJET.

6 OP CIT. P. 192

7 À PROPOS OF METAPHOR, CF J. LACAN. 'THE AGENCY OF THE LETTER IN THE UNCONSCIOUS,' ECRITS: A SELECTION (TRANS. A. SHERIDAN), TAVISTOCK, 1977 AND 'LES FORMATIONS DE L'INCONSCIENT,' SÉMINAIRE 1956-57). ON PLEASURE BY THE SAME AUTHOR: 'PROPOS DIRECTIFS POUR UN CONGRÈS SUR LA SEXUALITÉ FÉMININE,' IN ÉCRITS, SEUIL. (TRANSLATION IN PREPARATION, FEMININE SEXUALITY IN THE SCHOOL OF JACQUES LACAN, J. ROSE AND J. MITCHELL, MACMILLAN.)

8 CF F. DOLTO, OP CIT.

9 CF P. AULAGNIER, LE DÉSIR ET LA PERVERSION, SEUIL.

10 DRIVES REPRESSED BOTH IN THE COURSE OF EARLIER OEDIPAL EXPERIENCES, AS WELL AS IN THE PRESENT, BY THE VERY FACT OF THE PRESENCE OF THE PENIS.

11 THIS PARAGRAPH AND THE FOLLOWING ONE WERE ADDED TO THE EARLIER CRITIQUE ARTICLE IN 1976. IT WAS NECESSARY TO CLEAR UP A MISUNDER- STANDING. ONLY SOMEONE WHO IDEALIZES THE SIGNIFIER COULD INTERPRET THE FACT OF RELATING JOUISSANCE TO AN OPERATION OF SUBLIMATION AND TO THE PUTTING INTO PLAY OF THE 'SIGNIFIER' AS 'FRENZIED IDEALIZATION' (C. DAVID). I TAKE AS A TRIBUTE—NO DOUBT INVOLUN- TARY—WHAT SOMEONE EXCLAIMED À PROPOS OF THIS ARTICLE: 'SO THE JOUISSANCE OF THE WOMAN IS PRODUCED BY THE OPERATIONS OF THE HOLY GHOST!' IT CAN HAPPEN!

12 IF THE WOMAN, AT THE MOMENT OF ORGASM, IDENTIFIES HERSELF RADICALLY WITH AN UNCON- SCIOUS REPRESENTATION, ARTICULATED BY THE OTHER, THEN DOES SHE NOT FIND HERSELF AGAIN PRECISELY IN THE ARCHAIC SITUATION WHERE THE MATERNAL REPRESENTATION WAS THE SOLE ORGANIZER OF PHANTASY? ISN'T THE ORGASM, BY THIS FACT, A 'REGRESSIVE' PROCESS FOR HER? THE REPLY COULD BE IN THE AFFIRMATIVE FOR ORGASMS OF THE PSYCHOTIC OR NEUROTIC (ACUTE HYSTERIA) TYPE. IN THESE CASES, PLEASURE AND ORGASM ARE NOTHING MORE THAN THE MANIFES- TATION OF, AMONG OTHER THINGS, A SORT OF DIRECT SEIZURE OF THE WOMAN BY THE OTHER'S DISCOURSE. FOR THE WOMAN, WHO, ON THE CONTRARY, ASSUMES HER CASTRATION, THIS RELATION IS INDIRECT: IT PASSES THROUGH THE (PATERNAL) METAPHOR OF THE MATERNAL DISCOURSE, A METAPHOR WHICH, AS WE HAVE SEEN, PRESUPPOSES AN ECONOMY OF DESIRE WHERE THE WOMAN PUTS HERSELF AT STAKE (ENJEU).

13 EXCEPT IN THE CASE OF ACTUAL HOMOSEXUALITY. HOWEVER, WE MUST BE CAREFUL NOT TO SET UP TOO CLEAR-CUT A DISTINCTION BETWEEN THE SEXUALITY OF THE MAN AND THAT OF THE WOMAN. WITHOUT PRETENDING TO SETTLE THE WHOLE PROBLEM OF BISEXUALITY HERE, LET US ONLY SAY THAT EVERY MASCULINE SUBJECT IS CATHECTED AS THE OBJECT AND PRODUCT OF HIS MOTHER: HE WAS 'PART' OF THE MATERNAL BODY. IN RELATION TO THE MASCULINE BODY AND UNCONSCIOUS CATHEXIS THEN, ONE COULD ALSO SPEAK OF 'FEMININITY' AS IMPLIED IN MATERNAL FEMININITY. WOULD NOT THE SEXUAL ACT BE STRUCTURING FOR THE MALE SUBJECT TO THE EXTENT THAT, PUTTING INTO PLAY THE REPRESSION OF FEMININITY, HE WOULD PRODUCE EACH TIME THE COUPURE WHICH SEPARATES THE MAN FROM HIS MOTHER, WHILE 'RETURNING' TO HER THE FEMININITY OF HIS PARTNER.

14 ON THE QUESTION OF DETUMESCENCE CF LACAN, SÉMINAIRE 1967-68. SEE ALSO 'THE SIGNIFICATION OF THE PHALLUS,' ECRITS A SELECTION, TAVISTOCK AND 'PROPOS DERECTIFS PUR UN CONGRÈS SUR LA SEXUALITÉ FÉMININE,' ECRITS, SEUIL.

TRANSLATOR'S NOTES

I THE ARTICLE LA OF LA FÉMINITÉ IS ITALICIZED IN THE FRENCH; CF J. LACAN, 'DIEU ET LA JOUISSANCE DE FEMME' IN SÉMINAIRE XX.

II IN 'WOMANLINESS AS A MASQUERADE' IN PSYCHO- ANALYSIS AND FEMALE SEXUALITY, ED. HENRICK M. RUITENBEEK, NEW HAVEN, USA, 1966.

III IN THE EARLIER VERSION OF THIS ARTICLE WHICH APPEARED IN CRITIQUE 278 THIS SENTENCE ENDS WITH 'SINCE IT CONSISTS IN CONFRONTING DESIRE WITH A BODILY LACK (WHICH IS CARNAL).'

IV DIRECTOR CARL DREYER, MADE IN 1943.

V THE FRENCH GIVES DÉFOULEMENT WHICH IS A DIRECT INVERSION/PUN ON THE FRENCH WORD FOR REPRESSION: REFOULEMENT.

VI NOM PUNS ON THE FRENCH NEGATIVE NON AND ALSO REFERS TO LE NOM DU PÈRE (NAME-OF-THE- FATHER).

FRAGMENTS OF A LOVER'S DISCOURSE

JACQUES HENRIC: ROLAND BARTHES, IT SEEMS TO ME THAT SINCE DEGREE ZERO OF WRITING, MYTHOLOGIES AND WITH EACH FOLLOWING BOOK IT HAS BEEN LESS AND LESS EASY TO LOCALIZE YOU AS A WRITER. HOW, LOOKING BACK ON YOUR PAST WORK, DO YOU SITUATE YOURSELF IN THE HISTORY OF THOUGHT OF THESE LAST YEARS? AND TODAY, WHAT PLACE DO YOU FEEL YOU OCCUPY IN THE DISCUSSION OF CURRENT IDEAS?

ROLAND BARTHES: IN THE FRAGMENTS OF A LOVER'S DISCOURSE, OF A DISCOURSE, THERE IS AS IT HAPPENS A FIGURE WITH A GREEK NAME, THE ADJECTIVE APPLIED TO SOCRATES. SOCRATES WAS SAID TO BE ATOPOS, THAT IS TO SAY "WITHOUT A PLACE," UNCLASSIFIABLE. IT IS AN ADJECTIVE I USUALLY APPLY TO THE BELOVED, SO THAT AS THE SUPPOSED LOVER IN THE BOOK I DON'T SEE MYSELF AS ATOPOS, BUT ON THE CONTRARY AS SOMEONE EXTREMELY BANAL, WITH A WELL-KNOWN CASE HISTORY. WITHOUT TAKING SIDES ON WHETHER OR NOT I AM UNCLASSIFIABLE, I MUST ADMIT THAT I HAVE ALWAYS WORKED IN FITS AND STARTS, BY PHASES, MOTORIZED SO TO SPEAK—SOMETHING I TOUCHED ON IN THE R.B. (ROLAND BARTHES BY

HIMSELF SEUIL)—BY THE PARADOX. WHEN A SET OF POSITIONS SEEMS TO CONSOLIDATE, TO CONSTI-TUTE A DEFINITE SOCIAL SITUATION, THEN IT'S TRUE, SPONTANEOUSLY AND WITHOUT THINKING I WANT TO OPT OUT. IN THAT I CONSIDER MYSELF AN INTELLECTUAL, SINCE THE FUNCTION OF THE INTELLECTUAL IS ALWAYS TO OPT OUT WHEN THINGS "BEGIN TO JELL." AS TO THE SECOND PART OF YOUR QUESTION, HOW DO I SITUATE MYSELF NOW, I DON'T SEE MYSELF AT ALL AS SOMEONE WHO IS TRYING TO BE ORIGINAL, BUT AS SOMEONE WHO ALWAYS TRIES TO SPEAK UP FOR A CERTAIN MARGINALITY. WHAT IS MORE COMPLICATED TO EXPLAIN IS THAT IN MY CASE THERE IS NEVER ANY GLORY IN THE CLAIM TO BE MARGINAL. IT IS DONE GENTLY IF POSSIBLE. A MARGINALITY THAT PRESERVES ASPECTS OF COURTESY, TO TENDER-NESS—WHY NOT?—AND ONE YOU CAN'T PUT A TAG TO IN THE PRESENT CURRENT OF IDEAS.

J. H.: WITH YOU THERE OFTEN SEEMS TO BE, AND QUITE EXPLICITLY, A DOUBLE AND CONTRADICTORY ATTITUDE. ON ONE HAND YOU SHOW YOUR INTEREST FOR THE MODERNS (INTRODUCTION TO BRECHT IN FRANCE, THE NEW NOVEL, TEL QUEL . . .) ON THE OTHER HAND YOU LIKE RECALLING

YOUR TASTE FOR TRADITIONAL LITERATURE. WHAT IS THE COHERENCE THAT UNDERLIES THESE ATTITUDES?

R. B.: I DON'T KNOW IF THERE IS AN UNDERLYING COHERENCE, BUT IT'S REALLY THE CRUX OF THE MATTER. THINGS HAVE NOT ALWAYS BEEN SO CLEAR TO ME AS YOU MAKE THEM SOUND NOW, AND FOR A LONG TIME I FELT MYSELF ALMOST SHAMEFULLY TORN BETWEEN SOME OF MY TASTES, OR WHAT I WOULD CALL—SINCE I'M FOND OF DEFINING THINGS IN TERMS OF CONDUCT RATHER THAN TASTE—MY EVENING READING (WHAT I READ IN THE EVENING) WHICH ARE ALWAYS THE CLASSICS, AND MY WORK DURING THE DAY WHEN, IT'S TRUE, WITHOUT ANY KIND OF HYPOCRISY, I FEEL MYSELF VERY MUCH IN TUNE, ON THE THEORETICAL AND CRITICAL LEVEL, WITH VARIOUS MODERN WORKS. FOR A LONG TIME THE CONTRADICTION REMAINED CLANDESTINE, AND IT WAS ONLY WITH THE PREASURE OF THE TEXT THAT I CAME OUT INTO THE OPEN, RECOGNIZING IN MYSELF AND MAKING THE READER RECOGNIZE, A TASTE FOR THE LITERATURE OF THE PAST. THEN, AS ALWAYS HAPPENS WHEN ONE ADMITS TO A TASTE FOR SOMETHING, THEORY IS NOT FAR OFF. AND I MORE OR LESS TRY TO THEORIZE MY TASTE FOR THE PAST. I MAKE USE OF TWO ARGUMENTS: FIRST OF A METAPHOR. HISTORY ADVANCES IN A SPIRAL ACCORDING TO VICO'S IMAGE, OLD THINGS RETURN, BUT OBVIOUSLY THEY DON'T RETURN TO THE SAME PLACE; CONSEQUENTLY THERE ARE TASTES, VALUES, MANNERS, "WRITINGS" FROM THE PAST WHICH CAN RETURN, BUT TO A VERY MODERN PLACE. THE SECOND ARGUMENT IS ASSOCIATED WITH MY WORK ON THE LOVER. THE LOVER DEVELOPS PRINCIPALLY IN THE REGISTER OF WHAT, SINCE LACAN, WE CALL THE IMAGINARY—AND I CONSIDER MYSELF A SUBJECT OF THE IMAGINARY, I HAVE A LIVING RELATIONSHIP WITH THE LITERATURE OF THE PAST BECAUSE IT PROVIDES ME WITH IMAGES AND ESTABLISHES FOR ME A GOOD RELATIONSHIP WITH THE IMAGE. FOR EXAMPLE, STORY AND NOVEL ARE DIMENSIONS OF THE IMAGINARY WHICH EXISTED IN READABLE LITERATURE. BY RECOGNIZING MY ATTACHMENT TO SUCH LITERATURE I AGITATE IN FAVOUR OF THE SUBJECT IN SO FAR AS THIS SUBJECT IS IN A SENSE DISINHERITED, CRUSHED BY THOSE TWO GREAT PSYCHIC STRUCTURES WHICH MORE THAN ANY OTHERS HAVE ARRESTED THE ATTENTION OF MODERNITY, NAMELY NEUROSIS AND PSYCHOSIS. THE IMAGINARY SUBJECT IS A POOR RELATION OF THOSE STRUCTURES BECAUSE HE IS NEITHER ALTOGETHER PSYCHOTIC, NOR ALTOGETHER NEUROTIC. YOU SEE, BY MILITATING DISCRETELY FOR THE SUBJECT OF THE IMAGINARY, I CAN PROVIDE MYSELF WITH AN ALIBI FOR WORK THAT IS SOMEWHAT AHEAD OF ITS TIME, A FORM OF TOMORROW'S AVANT-GARDE PERHAPS, WITH A TOUCH OF HUMOUR NATURALLY. . . .

J. H.: ISN'T IT SOMEWHAT PROVOCATIVE TO SPEAK ABOUT "LOVE" TODAY IN THE TERMS OF YESTERDAY, AND AT THE HEIGHT OF STRUCTURALISM TO DEFEND THE "PLEASURE OF THE TEXT"?

R. B.: NO DOUBT, BUT I DON'T FEEL MY BEHAVIOUR IS A QUESTION OF TACTICS. SIMPLY THAT I HAVE, AS YOU SO WELL PUT IT, A KIND OF PROFOUND DIFFICULTY IN PUTTING UP WITH THE STEREOTYPE, THE ELABORATION OF LITTLE COLLECTIVE LANGUAGES, SO FAMILIAR TO ME THROUGH MY WORK IN A PARTICULAR SPHERE, THE STUDENT SPHERE. IT'S VERY EASY FOR ME TO DETECT THOSE STEREOTYPED LANGUAGES OF MARGINALITY, STEREOTYPES OF THE NON-STEREOTYPE. I CAN HEAR THEM TAKING FORM. AT FIRST THERE'S A KIND OF PLEASURE IN IT, BUT LITTLE BY LITTLE IT BECOMES BURDENSOME. FOR A WHILE I DON'T DARE EXTRICATE MYSELF, IN THE END OFTEN BECAUSE OF AN INCIDENT IN MY PERSONAL LIFE, I FIND THE COURAGE TO BREAK WITH SUCH LANGUAGES.

THE ARCHETYPE OF PASSIONATE LOVE

J. H.: LET'S GO BACK TO FRAGMENTS OF A LOVER'S DISCOURSE IF YOU WILL. TO AVOID ANY MISUNDERSTANDING ON THE PART OF THE READER, WOULD YOU EXPLAIN THE TITLE?

R. B.: THAT MEANS GIVING A BRIEF ACCOUNT OF THE PROJECT'S BACKGROUND. I HAD A SEMINAR AT THE ECOLE DES HAUTES ETUDES, AND YOU KNOW WE ARE A CERTAIN NUMBER OF RESEARCH WORKERS, ESSAYISTS, WORKING ON THE NOTION OF DISCOURSE AND THE DISCURSIVE. NOTION WHICH BREAKS AWAY FROM THAT OF TONGUE, OF LANGUAGE. IT IS THE DISCURSIVE IN A VERY WIDE SENSE: THE DISCURSIVE, THE NAPPE OF LANGUAGE IS AN OBJECT OF ANALYSIS. A LITTLE OVER TWO YEARS AGO I SAID TO MYSELF THAT I WOULD STUDY A CERTAIN TYPE OF DISCOURSE: WHAT I PRESUMED TO BE THE AMOROUS DISCOURSE, MAKING IT CLEAR FROM THE START THAT THE LOVERS I INTENDED SHOULD BELONG TO WHAT IS CALLED PASSIONATE LOVE, ROMANTIC LOVE. SO I DECIDED TO HOLD A

SEMINAR WHICH WOULD BE THE OBJECTIVE ANALYSIS OF A TYPE OF THE DISCURSIVE. I THEN CHOSE A SUPPORTING TEXT AND ANALYSED THE AMOROUS DISCOURSE IN THAT WORK. NOT THE WORK ITSELF, BUT THE AMOROUS DISCOURSE. IT WAS WERTHER BY GOETHE, WHICH IS THE VERITABLE ARCHETYPE OF PASSIONATE LOVE. BUT DURING THE TWO YEARS OF THE SEMINAR I BECAME AWARE OF A DOUBLE MOVEMENT. FIRST OF ALL I NOTICED THAT I WAS PROJECTING MYSELF IN TERMS OF MY PAST EXPERIENCE OR MY LIFE INTO CERTAIN OF THE FIGURES. I EVEN REACHED THE POINT OF CONFUSING FIGURES FROM MY OWN LIFE WITH THE FIGURES OF WERTHER.

SECOND DISCOVERY: THE LISTENERS OF THE SEMINAR PROJECTED THEMSELVES VERY STRONGLY INTO WHAT WAS SAID. UNDER THOSE CONDITIONS, I SAID TO MYSELF, THE ONLY HONEST COURSE, WHEN PASSING FROM SEMINAR TO BOOK, WAS NOT TO WRITE A TREATISE ON THE AMOROUS DISCOURSE, BECAUSE THAT WOULD HAVE BEEN A KIND OF LIE (I WASN'T AIMING EITHER AT A GENERALITY OF THE SCIENTIFIC KIND), BUT ON THE CONTRARY, TO WRITE THE DISCOURSE OF A LOVER.

OF COURSE, NIETZSCHE'S INFLUENCE, EVEN IF I MODIFIED HIM CONSIDERABLY, WAS APPRECIABLE AT THAT TIME. PARTICULARLY ALL THAT NIETZSCHE SAYS ABOUT THE NEED FOR "DRAMATIZING," FOR ADOPTING A METHOD OF "DRAMATIZATION," WHICH HAD FOR ME THE EPISTEMOLOGICAL ADVANTAGE OF FREEING ME FROM THE METALANGUAGE. AFTER THE PLEASURE OF THE TEXT I COULD NO LONGER BEAR ANY "DISSERTATION" ON THE SUBJECT. SO I MADE UP, SIMULATED A DISCOURSE WHICH IS THE DISCOURSE OF A LOVER. THE TITLE IS QUITE EXPLICIT AND PURPOSELY DESIGNED: IT IS NOT A BOOK ON THE AMOROUS DISCOURSE, IT IS THE DISCOURSE OF A LOVER. THE LOVER IS NOT NECESSARILY ME. I'LL BE QUITE FRANK ABOUT IT, SOME ELEMENTS STEM FROM ME, OTHERS FROM GOETHE'S WERTHER, OR FROM MY CULTURAL READINGS OF THE MYSTICS, OF PHYCHOANALYSIS, OF NIETZSCHE. ... THERE ARE ALSO WHAT HAS BEEN CONFIDED TO ME, CONVERSATIONS, WHICH COME FROM FRIENDS. THEY ARE VERY MUCH A PART OF THIS BOOK. THE RESULT THEN IS THE DISCOURSE OF A SUBJECT WHO SAYS "I," WHO IS THEREFORE INDIVIDUALIZED AT THE LEVEL OF THE ENUNCIATION; BUT IT IS NEVERTHELESS A COMPOSED DISCOURSE, SIMULATED, OR IF YOU LIKE, A DISCOURSE OF "CUTS" (AS A FILM IS PUT TOGETHER).

J. H.: EVEN SO, WHO SAYS "I" IN THESE FRAGMENTS?

R. B.: TO YOU I CAN SAY AND YOU WILL UNDERSTAND, HE WHO SAYS "I" IN THE BOOK IS THE "I" OF WRITING. NATURALLY ON THAT POINT I COULD BE CORNERED INTO SAYING THAT IT WAS ME. SO I'LL REPLY WITH THE CANNINESS OF A NORMAN AND SAY IT IS ME AND IT IS NOT ME. IT IS NO MORE ME, IF YOU WILL ALLOW THE COMPARISON WHICH IS PERHAPS INFATUATION, THAN STENDHAL DIRECTING A CHARACTER. THAT'S WHAT MAKES THE TEXT SOMEWHAT ROMANTIC. IN ANY CASE THE RELATIONSHIP BETWEEN THE AUTHOR AND THE STAGE CHARACTER HE DIRECTS IS OF THE TYPE IN FICTION.

J. H.: THAT'S TRUE, CERTAIN "FRAGMENTS" ARE REALLY THE BEGINNINGS OF STORIES. THE STORY BEGINS TO TAKE SHAPE AND IS IMMEDIATELY INTERRUPTED. I HAVE OFTEN WONDERED READING THESE VERY SUCCESSFUL, VERY "WELL WRITTEN" BEGINNINGS, WHY DOESN'T HE CONTINUE? WHY NOT A REAL NOVEL? A REAL AUTOBIOGRAPHY?

R. B.: ONE DAY PERHAPS. I HAVE BEEN PLAYING WITH THE IDEA FOR A LONG TIME NOW. BUT WHERE THIS BOOK IS CONCERNED, IF THE STORY NEVER JELLS, IT IS, I'D SAY, BECAUSE OF A DOCTRINE. THE VISION I HAVE OF THE AMOROUS DISCOURSE IS ESSENTIALLY A FRAGMENTARY, DISCONTINUOUS, BUTTERFLY VISION. THEY ARE EPISODES OF LANGUAGE FLUTTERING ROUND IN THE HEAD OF THE ENAMOURED AND PASSIONATE LOVER, AND THESE EPISODES ARE BRUSQUELY INTERRUPTED BECAUSE OF SOME HAPPENING, BECAUSE OF JEALOUSY, A MISSED RENDEZ-VOUS, AN UNBEARABLY LONG WAIT, WHICH INTERVENE, AND AT THAT MOMENT THOSE SORT OF SCRAPS OF MONOLOGUE ARE BROKEN AND WE PASS TO ANOTHER FIGURE. I HAVE RESPECTED THE RADICAL DISCONTINUITY OF THIS STORM OF LANGUAGE RAGING IN THE HEAD OF THE LOVER. IT IS WHY I CUT UP THE WHOLE INTO FRAGMENTS ARRANGED IN ALPHABETICAL ORDER. AT ALL COSTS I WANTED TO AVOID ANY RESEMBLANCE WITH A LOVE STORY. MY CONVICTION IS THAT THE WELL-MADE LOVE STORY, WITH A BEGINNING, AND END, AND A CRISIS IN THE MIDDLE, IS THE WAY SOCIETY PROPOSES THAT THE LOVER SHOULD RECONCILE HIMSELF WITH THE LANGUAGE OF THE GREAT ORPHEUS, BY MAKING UP A STORY FOR HIMSELF IN WHICH HE PUTS HIMSELF. I AM PERSUADED THAT THE LOVER WHO SUFFERS RECEIVES NO BENEFIT FROM THE RECONCILIATION, AND THAT PARADOXICALLY ENOUGH HE IS NOT IN

THE LOVE STORY, HE IS IN SOMETHING WHICH IS MUCH CLOSER TO A STATE OF FOLLY. NOT FOR NOTHING DO WE SPEAK OF "MOONSTRUCK LOVERS"; FROM THE LOVER'S POINT OF VIEW THE STORY IS IMPOSSIBLE. SO AT EACH TURN I TRIED TO BREAK THE BUILD-UP OF THE STORY. AT ONE MOMENT I EVEN THOUGHT OF PLACING A FIGURE AT THE BEGINNING, EQUIVALENT TO AN INITIAL FOUNDA-TION, LOVE AT FIRST SIGHT, ENAMORATION, BEWITCHMENT; FOR A LONG TIME I HESITATED, THEN I SAID NO, EVEN THAT I CAN'T SWEAR TO IT BEING CHRONOLOGICALLY A FIRST FIGURE BECAUSE IT'S QUITE POSSIBLE THAT LOVE AT FIRST SIGHT ONLY FUNCTIONS IN RETROSPECT, IT'S SOMETHING THE LOVER TELLS HIMSELF. SO, IT'S A DISCONTINUOUS BOOK WHICH PROTESTS IN A SMALL WAY AGAINST THE LOVE STORY.

TO WRITE FOR THE BELOVED

J. H.: WHAT DO YOU MEAN WHEN YOU WRITE: "I AM ON THE SIDE OF THE WRITING."

R. B.: FIRST A DIGRESSION: I REALIZED THERE WERE TWO TYPES OF LOVERS. ONE, BELONGING TO FRENCH LITERATURE, FROM RACINE TO PROUST, IS, LET US SAY, PARANOIC, THE JEALOUS LOVER. THE OTHER TYPE DOES NOT EXIST IN FRENCH LITERA-TURE BUT HAS BEEN ADMIRABLY PRESENTED BY GERMAN ROMANTICISM AND NOTABLY IN THE LIEDER OF SCHUBERT AND SCHUMANN (ABOUT WHICH I ALSO SPEAK IN THE BOOK). THIS TYPE OF LOVER IS NOT CENTERED ON JEALOUSY: JEALOUSY IS NOT EXCLUDED FROM PASSIONATE LOVE BUT THE AMOROUS SENTIMENT IS FAR MORE DEMONSTRA-TIVE, IT SEEKS FULFILLMENT. THE ESSENTIAL FIGURE THEN IS THE MOTHER. ONE OF THE FIGURES IN MY BOOK DEALS PRECISELY WITH THE LONGING, THE TEMPTATION, THE DRIVE THE LOVER SO OFTEN FEELS IT SEEMS, AND WHICH THE BOOKS VOUCH FOR, TO CREATE, OR TO PAINT, OR TO WRITE FOR THE BELOVED. I TRY TO EXPRESS THE PROFOUND PESSIMISM ONE CAN HAVE IN THAT RESPECT SINCE THE LOVER'S DISCOURSE CANNOT BECOME WRITING WITHOUT ENORMOUS JETTISONINGS AND TRANS-FORMATIONS.

I HAVE THE PROFOUND CONVICTION THAT THE LOVER IS MARGINAL. HENCE THE DECISION THAT FOR ME TO PUBLISH THIS BOOK WAS IN A CERTAIN WAY TO SPEAK UP FOR A MARGINALITY WHICH TODAY IS REINFORCED BY NOT EVEN BEING IN MARGINAL FASHION. A BOOK ON THE AMOROUS

DISCOURSE IS FAR MORE KITSCH THAN A BOOK ON DRUGS, FOR EXAMPLE.

J. H.: ISN'T IT A FORM OF AUDACITY TO SPEAK AS YOU DO ABOUT LOVE, IN FACE OF THE INVASIVE PSYCHOANALYTIC DISCOURSE?

R. B.: IT'S TRUE THAT IN MY BOOK THERE IS WHAT I MIGHT TERM AN "INTERESTING" RELATION WITH THE PSYCHOANALYTIC DISCOURSE BECAUSE THIS RELATION EVOLVED CONCURRENTLY WITH THE SEMINAR AND THE BOOK. YOU KNOW VERY WELL THAT IF ONE EXAMINES CULTURE TODAY—IT IS ALSO ONE OF THE THEMES OF THE BOOK—THERE IS NO ONE MAJOR LANGUAGE WHICH TAKES IN CHARGE THE AMOROUS STATE. AMONG THE MAJOR LAN-GUAGES, PSYCHOANALYSIS HAS AT LEAST ATTEMPTED A DESCRIPTION OF THE AMOROUS STATE, THEY EXIST IN FREUD, IN LACAN, IN OTHER ANALYSTS. I WAS OBLIGED TO MAKE USE OF THOSE DESCRIPTIONS, THEY WERE TOPICAL, THEY ATTRACTED ME BY THEIR EXTREME PERTINENCE. I INCLUDE THEM IN THE BOOK BECAUSE THE LOVER I PRESENT IS A SUBJECT WITH THE CULTURE OF TODAY, WITH THEN, A DASH OF PSCYHOANALYSIS WHICH HE APPLIES TO HIMSELF IN A PRIMITIVE FASHION. BUT AS THE SIMULATED DISCOURSE OF THE LOVER ADVANCED, IT DEVELOPED AS THE AFFIRMATION OF A VALUE, LOVE AS AN ORDER OF AFFIRMATIVE VALUES RESISTANT TO ALL ATTACK. AT THAT MOMENT THE LOVER CAN ONLY CUT HIMSELF OFF FROM THE PSYCHOANALYTIC DIS-COURSE, FOR ALTHOUGH EFFECTIVELY IT SPEAKS OF THE AMOROUS STATE, IT DOES SO IN A DEROGATORY FASHION, INVITING THE LOVER TO REINTEGRATE A CERTAIN NORMALITY, TO SEPA-RATE "BEING IN LOVE" FROM "LOVING," TO "LOVE REASONABLY," ETC. . . . THERE IS A NORMALITY OF THE AMOROUS STATE IN PSYCHOANALYSIS WHICH IS IN FACT THE REVINDICATION OF THE COUPLE, OF THE MARRIED COUPLE EVEN . . . SO THE RELATION I HAVE IN THIS BOOK WITH PSYCHOANALYSIS IS VERY AMBIGUOUS; IT'S A RELATION WHICH, AS ALWAYS, MAKES USE OF THE DESCRIPTIONS, OF PSYCHO-ANALYTIC IDEAS BUT WHICH USES THEM RATHER LIKE THE ELEMENTS OF FICTION, WHICH ARE NOT NECESSARILY CREDIBLE.

WRITING AS MORALITY

J. H.: NEVER, AS IN READING YOU, HAVE I HAD SO STRONGLY THE IMPRESSION THAT

WRITING IS FUNDAMENTALLY A QUESTION OF ETHICS. YOU INSISTED ON THIS POINT IN YOUR INAUGURAL LECTURE TO THE COLLEGE OF FRANCE. I WOULD LIKE TO RETURN TO IT . . .

R. B.: IT'S A VERY GOOD QUESTION. BUT I AM NOT CLEAR ABOUT IT AT ALL, AND I CAN ONLY SAY THAT I FEEL THE WRITING OF THIS BOOK TO BE SOMETHING APART. BECAUSE OF ITS SUBJECT, I HAD TO PROTECT THE BOOK. TO PROTECT A DISCOURSE HELD IN THE NAME OF THE "I," WHICH IS ALL THE SAME A RISK. MY BIGGEST DEFENSIVE WEAPON WAS PURE LANGUAGE, OR TO PUT IT EVEN MORE PRECISELY, SYNTAX. I WAS CONSCIOUS TO WHAT A POINT SYNTAX COULD PROTECT THE ONE WHO WAS SPEAKING. IT IS A DOUBLE-EDGED SWORD BECAUSE IT CAN ALSO BE AN INSTRUMENT OF OPPRESSION— IT VERY OFTEN IS—BUT WHEN THE SUBJECT IS VERY VULNERABLE, VERY OPEN, VERY ALONE, SYNTAX PROTECTS HIM. THIS BOOK IS PRETTY SYNTAXIC, WHICH IS TO SAY THAT IT'S NOT A VERY LYRIC TEXT, MORE LITOTIC, MORE ELLIPTIC, WITHOUT MANY MAJOR INVENTIONS OF WORDS OR NEOLOGISMS, BUT WHERE ATTENTION IS GIVEN TO THE TURN OF PHRASE. THAT'S WHEN WRITING FUNCTIONS AS A SORT OF MORAL CODE, HAVING ITS MODELS RATHER ON THE SIDE OF AGNOSTICISM, SCEPTICISM, MORAL CODES THAT ARE NOT THE MORAL CODES OF FAITH.

J. H.: WHAT IS THE TITLE OF YOUR COURSE AT THE COLLEGE OF FRANCE?

R. B.: I HAVE LAUNCHED A SERIES OF COURSES ON "LIVING TOGETHER," WHICH SETS OUT TO EXPLORE THE UTOPIA OF CERTAIN SMALL GROUPS. NOT COMMUNITIES AS WE KNEW THEM AFTER THE HIPPIE MOVEMENTS, BUT THE UTOPIA OF AFFECTIVE GROUPINGS WHO REALLY LIVE TOGETHER BUT EACH AT HIS OWN RHYTHM, WHAT ONCE USED TO BE CALLED BY ORIENTAL MONKS, IDIORHYTHMY. I HAVE CENTERED THE COURSE ON THE IDEA OF IDIO-RHYTHMY.

IT SEEMS TO ME NOW THAT WHERE THE COURSE IS CONCERNED I WILL RETURN TO MATERIAL THAT IS SPECIFICALLY LITERARY, BUT I ALWAYS GIVE MYSELF LEAVE TO DIGRESS AND, AS YOU SO RIGHTLY SAID, TO INCITE THE EMERGENCE FROM THE WRITING OF AN ETHICAL VANISHING POINT.

I AM SURE THAT IF NEXT YEAR I GIVE MY ATTENTION TO CHARACTERISTIC LITERARY FORM, ETHICS WILL BE BACK.

IF I WERE A PHILOSOPHER, AND IF I WANTED TO WRITE A MAJOR TREATISE, I WOULD GIVE IT THE NAME OF A STUDY OF LITERARY ANALYSIS. UNDER COVER OF A LITERARY ANALYSIS I WOULD TRY TO DISENGAGE AN ETHIC IN THE BROADEST SENSE OF THE WORD.

ROLAND BARTHES INTERVIEWED
BY JACQUES HENRIC

STATEMENTS RECORDED ON TAPE ON 4.4.77

TRANSLATION BY CATHERINE DUNCAN

PHILOSOPHICAL SEX

MOVING GIRL

"I'M NOT BEAUTIFUL, I'M WORSE."
— MARIE DORVAL

INSOFAR AS ITS PRINCIPAL THEME COMES DOWN TO SCIENCE-TECHNOLOGY-OTHER WORLDS, THE RENEWAL OF SCIENCE FICTION IN THE UNITED STATES AND IN THE BIG INDUSTRIAL COUNTRIES SEEMS TO BE LINKED TO THAT OF RELIGION AND SECTS. SCIENCE FICTION NARRATIVE, IN EFFECT, SHOWS MOST OF US TURNING IN CIRCLES LIKE THE BLIND BEFORE THE VERY OBVIOUSNESS OF THE FAMILIAR UNIVERSE, A KIND OF INCOMPATIBILITY BETWEEN OUR PHYSICAL PRESENCE IN THE WORLD AND THE DIFFERENT DEGREES OF A NOCTURNAL ANESTHESIA OF CONSCIOUSNESS WHICH KEEPS MAKING US LAPSE INTO SHORT OR PROLONGED, MILD OR SERIOUS STATES OF ABSENCE WHICH MAY INDEED BRING ABOUT, BY VARIOUS MEANS, OUR SUDDEN IMMERSION IN OTHER UNIVERSES—PARALLEL, INTERSTITIAL, BIFURCATING—AND EVEN PUSH US INTO THAT BLACK HOLE WHICH WOULD ONLY BE THE EXCESSIVE RAPIDITY OF THIS PASSAGE, COLLAPSING THE INITIAL SEPARATION OF DAYS AND NIGHTS IN A PURE PHENOMENON OF SPEED.

IN FACT, THIS TYPE OF NARRATIVE ONLY ADAPTS THE JUDEO-CHRISTIAN VERSION OF GENESIS RATHER FAITHFULLY BY IMPARTING THE LOGISTIC ROLE INITIALLY HELD BY THE FIRST WOMAN TO SCIENCE AND THE TECHNICAL MEDIA.

APPEARING IN THE BIBLE AS THE SEDUCER OF WOMAN, WHO IN TURN SEDUCES MAN, SATAN[1] THUS BEGINS THE CYCLE OF A HUMANITY DOOMED LESS TO DEATH THAN TO DISAPPEARANCE, THAT IS, TO THE EXPULSION FROM THE UNIVERSE IT PREVIOUSLY INHABITED, THIS BEING ACCOMPLISHED FIRST AS A PHENOMENON OF CONSCIOUSNESS: THE PHYSICAL EXPULSION FROM THE EARHTLY PARADISE IS PRECEDED BY AN ABRUPT DISORDERING OF SIGHT THAT COMPLETELY CHANGES THE APPEARANCE OF THE WORLD AS LIVED BY THE COUPLE: THEIR EYES ARE OPENED, THEY SEE THEY ARE NAKED, THEY COVER UP THEIR NAKEDNESS, THEY TRY TO HIDE THEMSELVES, AND TO AVOID THE SIGHT OF GOD. WHAT THIS INVOLVES IS AN ASTONISHING SUCCESSION OF VISUAL PHENOMENA, AND NOT, AS HAS SO OFTEN BEEN REPEATED, A SEXUAL INNOVATION. IN FACT, THE SEDUCTION—THE "LEADING ASIDE" OF SEDUCERE—HERE TAKES ON A COSMO-DYNAMIC DIMENSION: SEDUCTION IS A RITE OF PASSAGE FROM ONE UNIVERSE TO ANOTHER WHICH IMPLIES A DECISIVE DEPARTURE FOR HUMANITY, THE BEGINNING OF A NAVIGATION OF BODIES AND

SENSES, FROM SOMETHING IMMUTABLE TOWARD ANOTHER REGION OF TIME, A SPACE-TIME ESSENTIALLY DIFFERENT SINCE EXPERIENCED AS MOBILE, CONDUCTIVE, TRANSFORMABLE, AS THE CREATION OF A SECOND UNIVERSE WHICH WOULD DEPEND ENTIRELY UPON THIS INITIAL RITE. THE LEADING ASIDE OF SEDUCTION, THEN, IS INSCRIBED VERY PRECISELY IN THE DYNAMIC OF THE WORLD; THERE WOMAN IS NOT POSSESSIVE, POSSESSED OR POSSESSING BUT ATTRACTIVE. THIS FORCE OF ATTRACTION IS IN FACT GRAVITATION, UNIVERSAL HEAVINESS, THE AXIS MUNDI. MISTRESS OF PASSAGE, SHE HAS UP TILL NOW EFFECTIVELY ORGANIZED ALL THAT IS SPEED, ALL THAT HAS A PART IN THE MOVEMENT OF MAN'S LIFE, ALL THAT CONCURS OR COMPETES WITH IT.

THIS BELOVED WHO ACCORDING TO NOVALIS IS THE SUMMARY OF THE UNIVERSE AND THIS UNIVERSE WHICH IS ONLY THE EXTENSION OF THE BELOVED, THE BODY OF WOMAN THUS CONFOUNDED WITH A BODY OF COMMUNICATIONS, IS AN IDEAL VECTOR BETWEEN MAN AND THE NEW WORLD. NO LONGER IS THERE A COUPLE BUT A TRILOGY OF SORTS: THE SOLITARY MOVEMENT OF SEDUCERE OR THE SEXUAL COUPLING THAT REQUIRES INTERDEPENDENT MOVEMENT IMPLIES A THIRD PARTNER, THE TERRITORIAL BODY.[2]

THE EPISODE IN GENESIS REVEALS THAT THE ACCOMPLISHMENT OF THE RITE OF PASSAGE LEADING FROM ONE UNIVERSE TO ANOTHER PRODUCES NOT ONLY A METAMORPHOSIS OF SIGHT BUT AN IMMEDIATE CAMOUFLAGE AND CAREFUL DISSIMULATION OF THE BODY. HERE ONE MAY RECALL HANNAH ARENDT'S REFLECTION THAT "TERROR IS THE FULFILLMENT OF THE LAW OF MOVEMENT." IN THE BIBLICAL NARRATIVE, FEAR IS SIMULTANEOUS WITH SEDUCTION PRECISELY BECAUSE THE LATTER IS TRAVERSED IN A PHENOMENON OF SPEED SUCH THAT THE ANTICIPATION OF AN ACCIDENT OCCURS INSTANTLY. ISN'T THE "SIN" OF THE FIRST MAN COMMONLY CALLED THE "FALL," THE ANCIENTS THUS ESTABLISHING A DIRECT RELATION BETWEEN WHAT IS CONVENTIONALLY CALLED ORIGINAL SIN AND THIS TERRESTRIAL PULL WHICH THEY CONSIDERED TO BE THE FIRST NATURAL MOTOR OF THE FREE ACCELERATION OF BODIES, OF THEIR PROJECTION BUT ALSO OF THEIR COLLISION? WHEN ALAIN SCHLOKOFF ELABORATES ON THE REPLACEMENT OF EROTIC OR PORNO FIILMS BY HORROR FILMS, AND STATES THAT "SEX NO LONGER EXISTS AND THAT FEAR HAS REPLACED IT," THE IMPORTANCE OF SUCH A MODIFICATION OF

MASS SENSIBILITY MUST NOT BE UNDERESTIMATED. IN FACT, THE SOLITARY PLEASURE THAT THE CINEMATOGRAPHIC MOTOR AFFORDS THE PORNO FILM VIEWER ALREADY ANNOUNCES THE FORESHORTENING WHICH IS BEGINNING AND CAN BE COMPARED TO THAT OF THE SCIENCE FICTION NARRATIVE IN RELATION TO THE BIBLICAL STORY: IT IMPLIES THE DISAPPEARANCE OF HUMAN INTERMEDIARIES AND THE EMERGENCE OF A SEXUALITY DIRECTLY CONCERNED WITH A TECHNICAL OBJECT, PROVIDED THE LATTER BE A MOTOR OR VECTOR OF MOVEMENT. THE HORROR FILM THEN SUCCEEDS AS A MATTER OF COURSE THE EROTIC FILM AS A MORE PERFECT FULFILLMENT OF THE LAW OF MOVEMENT, IN A WORLD WHERE TECHNOLOGICAL PROGRESS CORRESPONDS TO THE UTILIZATION AND QUEST OF SUPERROGATORY SPEEDS.

BUT THIS WAY OF FOLLOWING FASHION, OF CONFORMING TO USAGES AND TO CODES, SO RIGOROUSLY RESPECTED IN THE MOST INDUSTRIALIZED COUNTRIES EVEN AS FAR AS THE REPULSIVE ATTITUDES AND PUNK OF THE LAST FEW YEARS, ALL ONLY BRINGS TO LIGHT THE VERY FOUNDATION OF EVERY MEANS OF SEDUCTION: TO ATTRACT THE LOOK IS TO CAPTURE AND THUS DIVERT THE ATTENTION, AN OPTICAL ILLUSION IN A UNIVERSE ITSELF PERCEIVED WHOLLY AS ILLUSORY AND WHERE DISSIMULATION TRIUMPHS AS A SYNDROME OF MOVEMENT, AND HENCE OF TERROR. WHILE GIRLS OF TODAY MAY CONDESCEND TO LET GUYS "PICK THEM UP," SOMEWHAT AS THOUGH HITCHHIKING, IN ORDER TO ENJOY IN THEIR COMPANY THE SELF-INVOLUTION ASSOCIATED WITH HITTING THE ROAD, THEY STILL SHRINK AT THE THOUGHT OF BEING "TAKEN IN" OR, MORE LITERALLY, OF BEING TOLD TO "GO GET LOST."

FORMERLY, THE INSTITUTIONS FOR THE EDUCATION OF LITTLE GIRLS HAD COMPARABLE ENDS, THE SEVERE DISCIPLINE AIMED AT MAKING A CREATOR OF ARTEFACTS OUT OF THE CHILD, AS A CONSTANT REFERENCE TO THE MARVELOUS MECHANICITY OF THE WOMAN'S VECTOR-BODY, BUT ALSO TO HER LACK OF PERSONAL INTELLIGENCE.[3] DEPORTMENT, MANNERS, DANCE, MANUAL WORK, AND FINERY WERE USEFUL IN CAMOUFLAGING PHYSIOLOGICAL IDENTITY, "NATURE" AND ITS WEAKNESSES. IGNORANCE, INDEED SEXUAL INDIFFERENCE, GAVE THESE SUPPOSEDLY INNOCENT LASSES A GREATER TECHNICAL RELIABILITY FOR THE EXECUTION OF AN ENDLESSLY REPEATED SERIES OF MANEUVERS INTENDED TO SUBJUGATE THOSE AROUND THEM, AND PARTICULARLY THE CHOSEN PARTNERS, WHO WERE THEIR SOLE EFFECTIVE PROTECTION AGAINST

A MAN'S SOCIETY WHICH CONDEMNED THE DOWERIED GIRLS TO AN EARLY MARRIAGE AND THE OTHERS TO THE CONVENT, MEAN LABOR, PROSTITUTION OR DESTITUTION. FINALLY, THE CHEAP ROMANTIC NOVELS CAN STOP AT THE WEDDING, NOT OUT OF MODESTY, BUT BECAUSE THE TECHNICAL EXPLOIT OF THE YOUNG WOMAN THERE REACHES ITS END. SHE HAS LED HER SPOUSE TO HER SIDE, HYMEN'S RITE OF PASSAGE IS NO LONGER HER BUSINESS. OFTEN SHE WILL DRAW FROM THE CONJUGAL BED A COLD AND DEFINITIVE HATRED FOR HER AWKWARD HUSBAND, COMPARABLE TO THAT OF THE TRANSVESTITE (ONE USED TO SPEAK IN FORMER TIMES MORE PRECISELY OF TRANSVESTISM, A WORD WHICH ALSO SUGGESTS THE TRAVELO, OR DRAG QUEEN), THE YOUNG VIRGIN'S MOTILE PERFORMANCE ALREADY ANNOUNCES THE CLAIM OF THE "WOMEN IN MOVEMENT" OF MLF (THE FRENCH WOMEN'S LIBERATION MOVEMENT): WE ARE NOT SEX OBJECTS.

TO ARAGON'S MOTTO WOMAN IS THE FUTURE OF MAN THE MLF OPPOSES ITS MAN IS THE PAST OF WOMAN. THUS EACH TRIES TO INSTALL THE OTHER IN A DEFERRED TIME, THAT OF THE GREAT NAVIGATION OF THE SPECIES.

ONE DISCOVERS IN LOVER' MODALITIES A PENDULUM EFFECT SUGGESTIVE OF THIS KIND OF LEADING ASIDE: THE SUFFRAGETTES OR THE GROUPS FOR WOMEN'S LIBERATION DEMONSTRATE MORE NOTICEABLY AFTER THE WARS, THE GREAT CONFLICTS DEADLY TO MALES. THE SENTIMENTAL, ROMANTIC PERIODS DEVELOP ON THE CONTRARY BEFORE OR DURING THE REVOLUTIONS AND WARS. THUS THE MILITARY MOBILIZATION IS SUBSTITUTED FOR THE LOVERS' "TRANSPORT." THE YOUNG WOMAN'S "GIVING HERSELF TO THE MOBILIZED SOLDIER BEFORE HIS DEPARTURE, BECAUSE HE MAY DIE" IS CERTAINLY REAL ENOUGH AN EVENT, BUT WHAT IS AIMED AT HERE AGAIN IS THE RELEGATION OF THE PARTNER, AND THE UNIVERSE OF WAR THAT WILL INSTANTLY PUT MAN INTO THE WOMAN'S PAST. INVERSELY, THE HASTILY CONCLUDED, SO-CALLED "WAR MARRIAGE" WILL BE EPHEMERAL IN MOST CASES. WHEN THE SOLDIER HAS THE BAD IDEA OF RETURNING SAFE AND SOUND TO THE PRESENT OF HIS WIFE, HE WILL BE REJECTED. LITTLE BY LITTLE THE TRAGIC CHARACTER OF THE NECESSITY TO SEDUCE AND TO KEEP ON SEDUCING IS REVEALED: IT IS LIKE AN EXORBITANT INFLATION OF THE LAW OF MOVEMENT AND OF THE VECTORIAL FACULTIES OF THE BODY,

LIKE AN ACCELERATION OF THE IRRESISTIBLE DISAPPEARANCE OF THE PARTNER OR PARTNERS IN SPACE AND TIME: TO LEAD THEM ASIDE IS TO LEAD THEM TO NOTHINGNESS, AND TO THIS EXTENT THE SEDUCTIVE ACTIVITY INTERFERES WITH THE TECHNICAL FATALITY AND MORE PRECISELY THE TECHNIQUE OF WAR. AS DESCRIBED BY COLONEL DELAIR, IT IS AN ART WHICH MUST BE CEASELESSLY IN TRANSFORMATION AND WHICH DOESN'T ESCAPE THE GENERAL LAW OF THE WORLD: TO STAND STILL IS TO DIE.

"MANY WOMEN HAVE LOVED THEMSELVES IN ME," SAID FRANZ LISZT, HIMSELF A GREAT SEDUCER. THE REMARK CONTAINS BOTH THE NOTION OF A REDUCTION OF THE SPEED OF CONQUEST AND OF A RECIPROCAL INVISIBILITY. IN THE VERY RAPPROCHEMENT OF "LOVE MAKING" THE TECHNICAL EXPERTISE OF THE SEDUCER OR SEDUCTRESS CREATES THE CONTRADICTION. THE IMMEDIATE COMMUTATION OF PERSONS DOES NOT ABOLISH THE INACCESSIBILITY WHICH PREVIOUSLY CREATED THE SEPARATION OF DISTANCE AND APARTNESS. BESIDES, IT IS ALWAYS EASY TO ANNIHILATE THE PARTNER WITHOUT AS MUCH AS LEAVING HIM OR HER FOR A SECOND. THUS, IN AN OLD COUPLE, EACH SPOUSE BECOMES INVISIBLE TO THE OTHER SIMPLY ON ACCOUNT OF THE REPETITION OF A LIMITED NUMBER OF SIGNS, ODORS, AND COMMON HABITS SO MUCH A PART OF THE DAILY REGIMEN THAT THEY ARE ALREADY KNOWN AND EXPECTED BY THE PARTNER.[4] AS TIME PASSES, THE CONFORMISM OF HABIT CREATES A KIND OF NARRATIVE SUMMARY, A TRUE EFFECT OF ANAMORPHOSIS, SINCE THE "ANGLE OF TEMPORAL VISION" CHANGES TO SUCH AN EXTENT IN THE AGED THAT THEY CAN TALK ABOUT AN EVENT OF FORTY YEARS AGO AS IF IT HAD HAPPENED THE SAME DAY, WHILE HAVING TOTALLY FORGOTTEN WHAT THEY DID A MOMENT AGO. THIS IS A PRELUDE TO OTHER UNIVERSES OF SPEED (FAST OR SLOW), INVISIBLE TO THE COMMON EYE, SOMEWHAT LIKE IN THE DISASTER FILMS SHOT BY STUNTMEN WHICH CANNOT BE PROJECTED IN REAL TIME, UNDERSTANDABLY, SINCE THE SUDDENNESS OF THE ACCIDENT IMPLIES SO MANY EVENTS UNFOLDING IN SUCH A COMPRESSED TIME THAT THE COMMON EYE CANNOT RECORD THEM ALL AND THUS MERELY SUMMARIZES THEM. THE TIME OF THE NARRATIVE APPEARS TO BE INCOMPATIBLE WITH VISION ITSELF, AND IT BECOMES NECESSRY— IN ORDER TO SEE—TO INTRODUCE, PARADOXICALLY, A DISORDERING OF SIGHT, SLOW-MOTION.

SIMILARLY, WHAT THE MOVEMENT OF ROMANTIC PASSIONS IN LISZT'S FORMULA SHOWED, THROUGH

THE INCREASE OF ENERGY AND THE SUPER ACCELERATION OF THE LOVERS' TRANSPORT, WAS A COMPETITION RATHER THAN AN OPPOSITION BETWEEN METABOLICS AND TECHNIQUE, A VALORIZATION OF THE RITES OF PASSAGE AND OF THEIR NUMBER TO THE DETRIMENT OF THE BODIES THEMSELVES, AND OF THEIR PRESENCE IN THE WORLD.[5]

SUCCEEDING OR OPPOSING L'HOMME FATAL (THE WARRIOR), THE FEMME FATALE IS RARELY A PRETTY WOMAN; RATHER SHE IS WORSE. ONE IS STRUCK BY THE PHYSICAL AUSTERITY OF THE CELEBRATED COURTESANS, AND BY THE CONTRAST IT OFFERS WITH THE MAGNIFICENCE OF THEIR FINERY AND THE BRILLIANCE OF THEIR ARMS OF SEDUCTION. HERE AGAIN, THE PHYSIOLOGICAL IDENTITY SEEMS TO DISAPPEAR BEHIND THE APPEAL OF A TECHNICAL VALORIZATION SUCH THAT MANY OF THESE WOMEN WILL CONTINUE TO EXERCISE THEIR FUNCTION UNTIL A VERY ADVANCED AGE, SEVENTY TO EIGHTY FOR SOME OF THEM, WHO WILL KEEP ON GETTING PAID FOR THEIR SERVICES. IT WAS NOT RARE EITHER TO SEE ONE OF THEM REACH THE SUMMIT OF THE STATE HIERARCHY, NOR, INVERSELY, TO SEE WOMEN OF THE HIGHEST RANK MEASURE THEMSELVES AGAINST PUBLIC WOMEN AND EMBARK ON VERITABLE MARATHONS, ACHIEVING SPEED RECORDS IN THE CONVEYANCE OF PASSENGERS ON THE SEXUAL VOYAGE, AND WORKING TO SUCH A HIGH OUTPUT THAT THEY WERE CONSIDERED MONARCHS OR RATHER "POLEMARCHS" JUST LIKE MEN. HERE AS WELL, THE ACCELERATION OF THE RITE OF PASSAGE CLEARLY IMPLIES THE PRESENCE OF THE TERRITORIAL BODY AS THIRD PARTNER. THE SEDUCERE CAN NO MORE BE REDUCED TO SEXUAL COMMERCE THAN THE ACTIVITIY OF THE POLEMARCH OR CONQUEROR CAN BE COMPARED TO A "HUMAN COMMERCE," SUCH AS CLAUSEWITZ, FOR EXAMPLE, UNDERSTANDS IT. FREDERICK II'S "TO ADVANCE IS TO CONQUER," THE HASTE WITH WHICH ALEXANDER THE GREAT DROVE ON, CONCERNED ONLY TO FIND THE LIMIT OF HIS FORCE'S EXPANSION, BUT ALSO THE DRIVER'S GLANCE AT THE SPEEDOMETER OF THE RACING-CAR, OR OF COMBAT AS THE EXISTENTIAL MEASURE OF THE WARRIOR'S BEING—ALL INVOLVE A VERTIGINOUS FLOW OF TIME.[6] THESE PERPETUAL ASSAULTS AGAINST DISTANCE ALSO REPRODUCE INDEFINITELY THE INITIAL RITE OF PASSAGE, AN ABRIDGMENT OF THE UNIVERSE MADE POSSIBLE BY THE SPEED OF THE ASSAULT.

"MOST OF THE TIME LOVE IS A BY-PRODUCT OF MURDER," THE MYSTERY WRITER AGATHA CHRISTIE LOVED TO REPEAT. FROM THE CELINESQUE CHARACTER WHO EXHIBITS THE RELICS OF HER CHILDREN AND HUSBAND KILLED IN THE WAR WHENEVER SHE IS GIVEN THE OPPORTUNITY, TO THOSE WIDOWS WHO ASSUME THEIR BEREAVEMENT AS A PRIVILEDGED POSITION, NO LONGER GOING OUT, NOURISHING A BARELY DISGUISED HATRED FOR THOSE STILL ALIVE, THE SURVIVORS AND ESPECIALLY THEIR OWN PROGENY, OR TO THIS TELEGRAM—"IF THE WAR IS LOST, LET THE NATION PERISH"—IN WHICH HITLER DECIDES TO COMBINE HIS EFFORTS WITH THOSE OF HIS ENEMIES IN ORDER TO COMPLETE THE DESTRUCTION OF HIS OWN PEOPLE BY ANNIHILATING THE LAST RESOURCES OF THE HOMELAND—WE FIND OURSELVES NOT AT THE OPPOSITE BUT RATHER AT DELIRIOUS APOGEES OF THE SEDUCTIVE ACTIVITY.[7]

IN FACT, THE WOMEN OF THE MLF DEVELOP A SIMILAR ATTITUDE: THEY PREACH THE PARTNER'S LIBERATION IN THE MANNER OF THE OLD WIDOWS; CURE US OF LOVE IS ONE OF THEIR SLOGANS. THEY HAVE KILLED THE SPOUSE, THE FATHER AND THE CHILD, AND THESE ARE SIGNIFICANTLY AMONG THE THEMES WHICH HAVE CREATED THEIR UNANIMITY. ABORTION, FOR EXAMPLE, HAS A GREAT FORCE OF SYMBOLIC TRANSCENDENCE SINCE IT REFERS DIRECTLY TO MURDER AS A BY-PRODUCT OF LOVE. IN THE UNITED STATES, ALL OF THIS TAKES THE ULTIMATE FORM OF A NEW, MERCILESS SOCIAL STRUGGLE BETWEEN CLIQUES THAT HAVE BECOME HOMOSEXUAL IN THE PURSUIT OF POWER, INFLUENCE AND MONEY.

IN SHAKESPEARE'S THE TAMING OF THE SHREW, PETRUCHIO ROUGHLY REFUSES HIS WIFE THE SERVICES OF A MAID, PROPOSING INSTEAD THOSE OF HIS ARMS SERVANT: "MY MAN KNOWS HOW TO TAKE CARE OF MY ARMOR," HE SAYS, "SURELY HE CAN LACE UP YOUR CORSET." IN THIS ABSURD COMMAND, L'HOMME FATAL ALREADY RECOGNIZES HIMSELF AS THE PAST OF HIS WIFE; HIS SPARKLING SHIELD, HIS COMBAT FINERY, ALL WILL SOON BECOME USELESS, HARMFUL EVEN, WITH THE BEGINNING OF HIGHLY TECHNOLOGICAL WARFARE. AT THE OUTSET OF THE 20TH CENTURY, WOMAN IN HER TURN WILL ABANDON THE CORSET JUST WHEN THE ARMAMENT OF THE RACER AND THE RACE TO ARMS ARE BECOMING PHENOMENA OF SOCIETY. RID OF THE CORSET, SHE CAN DEVOTE HERSELF TO COMPETITIVE SPORTS, AND CLIMB INTO FAST VEHICLES. THE SEDUCTION OF WOMAN AS A BY-PRODUCT OF MURDER OR SIMPLY AS A VECTOR OF VOYAGE GIVES WAY TO THE LIBERATION OF THE NEW

TECHNICAL SEDUCTION OF THE MOTOR AND OF SPEED; THE FEMININE ARTEFACT IS NO LONGER RESORTED TO EXCEPT AS AN ORNAMENT TO THE VEHICLE IN BEAUTY PARADES, ADVERTIZING METAPHORS OR POLITICAL AND MILITARY PROPAGANDA. THIS DISAPPEARANCE OF WOMAN IN THE FATALITY OF THE TECHNICAL OBJECT CREATES A NEW MASS LANGUAGE WHICH FAITHFULLY REFLECTS THE FASCIST LANGUAGE OF THE FUTURIST ELITE AT THE BEGINNING OF THE CENTURY: "THE HEAT OF A PIECE OF IRON OR WOOD NOW AROUSES US MORE THAN THE SMILE OR TEARS OF A WOMAN. ... WE WILL TRANSFORM EDGAR ALLAN POE'S NEVERMORE INTO A SHRILL JOY. ... WITH US BEGINS THE REIGN OF THE ROOTLESS MAN, THE MULTIPLIED MAN WHO MINGLES WITH IRON, FEEDS ON ELECTRICITY. ... YOU CAN SEE THEN HOW MUCH WE DESPISE THE PROPAGANDA CARRIED OUT IN DEFENSE OF THE AESTHETICS OF LANDSCAPE ... THE GREAT SYMBOLISTS LEANING OVER THE NUDE BODY OF WOMAN ... FEMALE BEAUTY, IDEAL AND FATAL" (MARINETTI, 1910).

IN A RECENT INTERVIEW GIVEN TO THE NEWSPAPER FRANCE-SOIR, THE PILOT JEAN-MARIE SAGET STATED: "AT THAT TIME TO BE A TEST PILOT WAS REALLY TO FLY INTO THE UNKNOWN. ... NOW WE HAVE ANOTHER FRUSTRATION. IT'S TOO BAD, BUT WE CAN'T FLY THE PLANES OF RIVAL COMPANIES BECAUSE OF COMMERCIAL COMPETITION. I'VE NEVER LIFTED OFF WITH AN F-15, MUCH TO MY REGRET. COMPANY PILOTS, ON THE CONTRARY, FLY ON ALL MODELS, SINCE THEY HAVE TO MAKE COMPARISONS. ... THEY'RE PRIVILEDGED." CLIMBING INTO HIS MIRAGE 4000, SAPET ADDS: "I'M ON THE OTHER SIDE!" THERE IS INDEED A TECHNOLOGICAL DON JUANISM, A "LIFTING" OF MACHINES WHICH SUPPLANTS THAT OF LOGISTIC SPOUSES. THE INITIAL TRILOGY IS THUS COMPLETELY MODIFIED, AND THE RELATIONSHIP IS ESTABLISHED BETWEEN A UNISEX (THE DEFINITIVE DISSIMULATION OF PHYSIOLOGICAL IDENTITY) AND A TECHNICAL VECTOR, THE CONTACTS WITH THE BODY OF THE BELOVED OR THE TERRITORIAL BODY DISAPPEARING PREDICTABLY AS THE DYNAMICS OF PASSAGE INCREASE. BUT THE ASSUMPTION OF THE VARIOUS RITES OF PASSAGE BY MASS PRODUCTION IS A PHENOMENON IMPORTANT IN ANOTHER WAY. PARAPHRASING RAGEOT'S FORMULA, WRITTEN ABOUT 1920, ONE CAN SAY THAT THE TECHNOLOGICAL REVOLUTION HAS FINALLY BEEN USED ONLY TO INSTALL THE VERY FIXITY OF LIFE IN DISPLACEMENT ITSELF. "MOBILIS IN MOBILE," MOBILE WITHIN A MOBILE, THE MOTTO OF JULES VERNE'S NAUTILUS, DEFINES BOTH EVERY TRANSPORT VEHICLE AND, IN

THE QUEST OF ALL TECHNOLOGICAL PROGRESS, SOMETHING WHICH WOULD NO LONGER BE DISCONTINUOUS, A FINAL SUPPRESSION OF THE DIFFERENCES BETWEEN NATURE AND CULTURE, UTOPIA AND REALITY. BY MAKING SEDUCTION'S RITE OF PASSAGE A CONTINUOUS PHENOMENON TECHNOLOGY WOULD MAKE SENSORY DERANGEMENT A PERMANENT CONDITION, AN OSCILLATING TRIP FOR CONSCIOUSNESS WHICH WOULD HAVE AS ABSOLUTE POLES ONLY BIRTH AND DEATH, AND WOULD BE THE END OF ALL RELIGION AND PHILOSOPHY. IN SHORT, HERACLITUS' DISTINCTION BETWEEN WAKING AND SLEEP ("THOSE ASLEEP ARE IN SEPARATE WORLDS, THOSE AWAKE IN A COMMON WORLD") WOULD CEASE TO APPLY. IT WOULD THUS SOMEHOW BE NORMAL FOR THE LIGHT OF MOTORS TO EXTINGUISH THAT OF REASON AS THE IDEAL ACTIVATION OF MAN AWAKENED AND SENSOR OF REALITY, ASPIRING TO A STATE OF VIGIL IN A WORLD GIVEN AS COMMON (THE PRECONDITION FOR THE FORMATION OF MEANING). SCIENCE AND TECHNOLOGY WOULD ACTUALLY CREATE A NEW SOCIETY WHOSE MEMBERS WOULD ALL BECOME SLEEPERS, LIVING OUT ILLUSORY DAYS AND NATURALLY VERY MUCH AT EASE IN A SITUATION OF "TOTAL PEACE," AND OF NUCLEAR DISSUASION, THE LATTER ITSELF BEING DEVELOPED ACORDING TO THE PRINCIPLE OF LEAST ACTION SO DEAR TO ENGINEERS, "ACCORDING TO A CURVE OF OPTIMAL DISTRIBUTION OF THE EXERTION OF FORCES WHICH GUARANTEE EQUILIBRIUM AND THE AVOIDANCE OF ACCIDENTS." HENCE A WORLD ENTIRELY SUSPENDED ON THE THRESHOLD OF AN ULTIMATE OPERATION WHICH WOULD EFFECTIVELY CARRY OUT FOR HUMANITY A RITE OF PASSAGE COMPARABLE TO THAT IN GENESIS.

WHEN AT THE OPENING OF THE CENTURY SPENGLER FORESAW THE "RETURN OF SCIENCE TO ITS PSYCHIC NATIVE LAND" AND THE COMPLETELY NEW RUINS OF FAUSTIAN CIVILIZATION—"ITS DEBRIS SCATTERED HERE AND THERE, FORGOTTEN, THE RAILWAYS AND GREAT PACKET BOATS AS FOSSILIZED AS THE ROMAN ROADS OR THE GREAT WALL OF CHINA"—HE DIDN'T THINK THAT THESE RUINS WERE EARLIER THE LATENT FORMS, THE ABANDONED BLUEPRINTS OF A UNIQUE AND IRRESISTIBLE PROJECT—OR PROJECTION—OF THE WEST TOWARD A TECHNOLOGICAL BEYOND AS MYSTERIOUS, FINALLY, AS THAT OF ANCIENT RELIGIONS, CONFRONTING WITH ITS SPECIAL EFFECTS THE GREAT NATURAL POWERS, AND MACHINATING THE CATASTROPHIC UNCERTAINTIES WHICH STIR THE COLLECTIVE AND INDIVIDUAL CONSCIENCE.

WE ARE CURRENTLY REDISCOVERING THE MYSTERY OF THE TECHNOLOGICAL VEHICLE, WHICH WE APPREHEND LESS AS A CONSUMER OBJECT TO BE DESIRED OR REJECTED THAN MORE ESSENTIALLY AS THE VECTOR OF DESIRES JUST AS OBSOLESCENT AS OUR DREAMS, AS A STRANGE PROCESSIONAL ACCOMPANIMENT, OUTSIDE OF HISTORY AND HARDLY GEOGRAPHIC, AS A PLAY OF THE EGO'S REPRESENTATIONS AKIN TO AN ONEIRIC FALSE LIGHT ... THIS DELIRIOUS JOY OF SPEED ECLIPSING THE INFINITY OF DREAMS (MARINETTI).

AROUND 1900, COLONEL DE ROCHAS, AN EX-ADMINISTRATOR OF THE POLYTECHNIC INSTITUTE, ATTEMPTED TO DEMONSTRATE WITH HIS XENOGLOSSY THAT "A SUBJECT UNDER HYPNOSIS COULD EXCEED THE LIMIT OF HUMAN EXPERIENCE AND GO BACK IN TIME WITHOUT TOO MUCH FATIGUE." MEMBERS OF THE "CRUSHING AUTOMOBILE OF THE FIFTIES CLUB" INDULGE THEMSELVES IN A SIMILAR ACTIVITY, THE MEDIUM BEING IN THIS CASE AMERICAN CARS OF THE FIFTIES—CADILLACS, BUICKS, FORDS, CHEVROLETS, ETC.[8]

"ALBERT LIVES TO THE FULLEST AS IN 1950," A JOURNALIST WRITES ABOUT ONE IN PARTICULAR. "DURING THE WEEK HE DRIVES HIS REGULAR CAR, BUT WHEN HE BRINGS OUT HIS BEL AIR, HE DRESSES TEDDY BOY STYLE, HIS WIFE RIDING IN THE BACK WITH THE KID. 'THAT'S HOW THEY DID IT,' HE SAYS. HE DREAMED ABOUT THE CAR FOR FIFTEEN YEARS. AS SOON AS HE SAW IT, HE IMAGINED ITS FIRST COLOR, SPARKLING BLUE WITH A LIGHTER ROOF, ITS CHROME FITTINGS, THE ROCKET AFFIXED TO THE TIP OF THE HOOD. 'AT NIGHT I JUST LOOK AT IT,' HE ADDS. 'BEFORE LEAVING THE GARAGE I PAT ITS FENDER, I SPEAK TO IT, YOU SEE. I PUT THE ROCKET ON IT, BECAUSE I FELT IT NEEDED IT. YOU MUST SEE IT AT NIGHT, WHEN IT VIBRATES AND GLOWS. IT'S A SENSITIVE MACHINE.'"

FOR HIS PART, DANIEL (AGE SIXTEEN, STUDYING MECHANICS AND ELECTRICITY AT A TECHNICAL SCHOOL) WANTS A MOTORCYCLE. AS HE TELLS A JOURNALIST FROM LE MONDE: "I'D LIKE A BIKE, A BIG BIKE, A REALLY BIG BIKE TO GO WHEREVER I WANT, ANYWHERE. I'D LIKE TO KEEP ON RIDING, WITHOUT EVER STOPPING. I'D LIKE IT TO DRIVE ITSELF WHEN I'M TIRED. I'D LIKE IT TO BE THE COLOR OF THE OCEAN, WITH SAILS IN THE DISTANCE AND SURROUNDED BY GULLS. I'D LIKE IT TO SHINE WITH ALL ITS LIGHTS AND CHROME FITTINGS, TO LIGHT UP EVERYTHING AT THE SAME TIME. I'D LIKE IT TO CONSUME NOTHING, JUST A LITTLE ATMOSPHERE FROM TIME TO TIME. I'D LIKE IT TO BE VERY FAST, SO I COULD SEE ONLY WHAT I LIKE.... I'D PUT DIALS ALL OVER IT, SO IT COULD LOOK AT ME AS MUCH AS I LOOK AT IT. ... YOU SHOULD KNOW ITS NAME: JE T'AIME."

THE VEHICLE COMPLETELY REPLACES THE BELOVED, THE "MOTHER-LANDSCAPE" INHABITED BY THE "SPIRIT OF METAMORPHOSIS." TECHNOLOGICAL FATALITY APPEARS AS THE FINAL SEDUCTION, FAR MORE BLINDING AND FEARFUL THAN ITS ANTHROPOMORPHIC BLUEPRINTS, THANKS TO THE SPEED ALONE IT CAN GIVE OUR ASPIRATIONS. THE PHYSICIAN DOMINIQUE PIGNON, FOR EXAMPLE, REMARKED ABOUT THE NUCLEAR ACCIDENT AT HARRISBURG: "THE REALITY OF THE REACTOR, AS WITH EVERYTHING CONCERNING THE ATOM, CANNOT BE ASSESSED WITH ORDINARY WORDS...., THE MOST POWERFUL COMPUTER IS INFINITELY SLOW COMPARED TO REAL PROCESSES. THUS IN NUCLEAR CIRCLES, THE EXPERTS KNOW THAT THEY CANNOT MONITOR WITH A COMPUTER WHAT IS REALLY HAPPENING IN A REACTOR OUT OF CONTROL. ... IN THE EVENT OF AN ACCIDENT, THEN, THEY ARE LIKE BLIND MEN TURNING IN A CIRCLE AS THEY TRY TO MAKE A DECISION."[9]

THE TECHNICIAN BECOMES THE VICTIM OF THE MOVEMENT HE HAS PRODUCED. HAVING BECOME APHASIC, HE REPEATS IN THE ABSOLUTE OF THE PLANT'S CONTROL ROOM THE SIMPLIFIED GESTURES OF A PRIMAL MAGNETIC RITE WHOSE "MOBILE WITHOUT MOBILITY" AS YET TO BE CLARIFIED.

HE BRINGS TO MIND CAPTAIN HATTERAS, JULES VERNE'S HERO, A PRECURSOR OF SUCH REAL HEROS AS THE NORWEGIAN ROALD AMUNDSEN OR THE ITALIAN UMBERTO NOBILE, RUSHING TOWARDS A BEYOND WITHOUT AN IDENTITY FOR IT RESEMBLES NOTHING AT ALL AND YET IS NOT NOTHINGNESS: THE NORTH POLE, BUT ALSO DESERTS, AND SIDEREAL SPACE. TO LOOK FOR, TO SEEK OUT, TO DISCOVER, BUT HERE ALL PARTNERS HAVE DISAPPEARED FOREVER, AND CAPTAIN HATTERAS, "THIS SAD VICTIM OF A SUBLIME PASSION," IS SUFFERING FROM WHAT HIS DOCTOR CALLS A "POLAR MADNESS." HE HAS BECOME PART AND PARCEL OF THE IRRESISTIBLE RITE OF PASSAGE: "FOLLOWED BY HIS FAITHFUL DOG, WHO GAZED AT HIM WITH SOFT, SAD EYES, CAPTAIN HATTERAS WENT OUT EVERY DAY FOR LONG WALKS, BUT THESE INVARIABLY LED HIM IN THE SAME DIRECTION, THAT OF A CERTAIN PATH OF STEN COTTAGE. HAVING ARRIVED AT THE END OF THE PATH, THE CAPTAIN WOULD START WALKING BACKWARDS. SHOULD SOMEONE STOP HIM, HE WOULD POINT TO A FIXED SPOT IN THE SKY. ... THE DOCTOR VERY SOON

UNDERSTOOD THE MOTIVE OF THIS SINGULAR OBSTINACY, AND GUESSED WHY THE STROLL ALWAYS TOOK A CONSTANT DIRECTION, AS IF UNDER THE INFLUENCE OF A MAGNETIC FORCE. CAPTAIN JOHN HATTERAS INVARIABLY WALKED TOWARD THE NORTH."[10]

PAUL VIRILIO

TRANSLATED BY JOHN JOHNSTON

NOTES

[1] THE SERPENT SERVES AS MASK FOR A HOSTILE BEING WHICH ANCIENT WISDOM AND THEN CHRISTIANITY WANTED TO SEE AS SATAN. "WOMAN SAW THAT THE TREE [OF KNOWLEDGE] WAS GOOD TO EAT AND PLEASING TO LOOK AT."

[2] THE MAN, ADAM, COMES FROM THE EARTH, ADÂMA. "GARDEN" IS TRANSLATED "PARADISE" IN THE GREEK VERSION AND THEN TRADITIONALLY. EDEN IS A GEOGRAPHICAL NAME WHICH ELUDES ALL LOCALIZATION; ITS INITIAL MEANING MAY HAVE BEEN "STEPPE" (COMENTARY OF THE JERUSALEM BIBLE).

[3] ". . . THERE IS ALWAYS THE DIFFERENCE BETWEEN THE 'LIBERAL' AND THE 'AUTOMATIC', WHICH IS A PURE MOTOR FUNCTION AND CAN BE PERFORMED EQUALLY WELL BY THE IGNORANT OR ANIMALS ... MANUAL LABOR BEING FOR ANTHROPOCENTRIC SOCIETY AS IGNOBLE AS IT WAS FOR THE MIDDLE AGES ... THE WORKERS BODIES, AND THOSE OF WOMEN AND LOST CHILDREN [CONSTITUTED] THE IDEAL OBJECT OF TRAINING. . . ." PAUL VIRILIO, VITESSE ET POLITIQUE (PARIS: GALILÉE, 1977).

[4] THIS KIND OF ANESTHESIA OF FAMILIARS BY THE REPETITION OF BANAL ATTITUDES IS USED NOTABLY BY THE SECRET SERVICES WHO HAVE CREATED A VERY PARTICUAR CATEGORY OF SPIES: THE SLEEPERS. THE SLEEPER HAS TO MOVE TO A FOREIGN PLACE, WORK, GET MARRIED, HAVE CHILDREN. HE IS THERE AS A USELESS PAWN IN THE GAME OF INTERNATIONAL ESPIONAGE, AND MAY LIVE HIS WHOLE LIFE WITHOUT BEING OF USE, UNLESS SOMEDAY HE RECEIVES THE ORDER TO REACTIVATE HIMSELF. HE THEN QUICKLY PUTS TO WORK THE MATERIAL PROOFS OF HIS ILLUSORY EXISTENCE, WHICH WILL GIVE HIM THE CREDIBILITY NECESSARY TO ACCOMPLISH THE SINGULAR MISSION WITH WHICH HE HAS BEEN SUDDENLY ENTRUSTED, WITHOUT ALERTING THE SUSPICIONS OF HIS NEIGHBORS.

[5] CF. PAUL VIRILIO, "METEMPSYCHOSE DU PASSAGER," TRAVERSES, NO. 8 (MAY, 1977).

[6] VITESSE ET POLITIQUE, OP. CIT., P. 98: "THE PERFORMANCE OF THE INVADER RESEMBLES THAT OF HIS COUNTERPART IN SPORTS. . . ."

[7] IN EDGAR ALLAN POE'S "MORELLA" THE HUSBAND CONFESSES À PROPOS THE AGONY OF HIS WIFE: "I WAS YEARNING WITH AN INTENSE AND DEVOURING DESIRE FOR THE MOMENT OF MORELLA'S DEATH." WEARY OF WAITING, HE FINALLY KILLS HER: "MY BELOVED, HENCEFORTH MINE AND IN HEAVEN FOREVER."

[8] CF. IN LIBÉRATION (FEB., 1979), CORINNE BRISEDOU'S INTERESTING ARTICLE ON THE COLLECTORS OF CARS OF THE 50'S AND THEIR MEETINGS ON THE FIRST THURSDAY NIGHT OF EACH MONTH, PLACE DE LA CONCORDE.

[9] DOMINIQUE PIGNON, DES RISQUES D'ACCIDENT DANS LES CENTRALES NUCLÉAIRES (PARIS: BOURGOIS, 1976).

[10] JULES VERNE, LES AVENTURES DU CAPITAINE HATTERAS (PARIS: HACHETTE).

DISCOURSE AND SEXUALITY:
TOWARD THE TEXTURE OF EROS

ALTHOUGH IT IS NOT APPARENT THAT TRADITIONAL PHILOSOPHY HAS HAD MUCH OF VALUE TO SAY ABOUT THE BODY AND REGARDING SEXUALITY, BEGINNING WITH THIS REALISATION ONE MAY MOVE FROM THIS LACKING DISCOURSE TOWARD A DISCOURSE OF THE BODY WITH US. THE PRE-SOCRATIC PHILOSOPHERS PERHAPS FIRST SPOKE OF LOVE IN THE CONTEXT OF STRIFE, INTRODUCING PASSION OR THRUST AS FORCED UPON THE GRID OF A TELOS, EPISTEMOLOGICALLY DERIVED. HENCE, LOVE OR PASSION AS MOVEMENT WAS CONFINED TO THE TOPOS CONTROLLED BY A SUBJECT. IN SUCH A FASHION, THE IMPULSE OF A SEXUAL NATURE OR FORCE IS SEEN SUBORDINATED TO AN ARCHÈ, SOON TO BECOME ALL-REASONABLE. MOST OBVIOUSLY, THE DISCOURSE ABOUT THIS IMPULSE, LOVE-STRIFE, WAS CARRIED ON WITHOUT ANY REFERENCE TO THE "FLESH" OF BODIES; RATHER, THE STAGE OF EMPIRICAL HYPOTHESIS AND VERIFICATION WAS ONLY SUPPOSED.

IF THE PLATONIC CONSIDERATION OF "EROS" IS A FULLER, RICHER DISCOURSE UPON THE POLY-MORPHOUS CHARACTER OF EROTIC DRIVE AND ITS UPHOLDING OR INFORMING THE GRID OF THE WORLD KNOWN TO MAN, IT REMAINS NONETHELESS INFECTED BY THE SAME PROBLEM OF BEING AT ODDS WITH THE HIGHER STATUS OF THE "EIDOS" TO WHICH IT IS DRAWN. ALTHOUGH A MORE FERTILE NOTION OF THE IMPORTANCE AND PREVALENCE OF EROTIC DRIVE AND PRESENCE IN ALL HUMAN EXPERIENCE, THE PLATONIC DOCTRINE MUST ULTIMATELY FACE ITS OWNMOST IMPOVERISHMENT IN THE RIGIDITY AND STERILITY OF CARTESIAN MIND-BODY DUALISM. IF WE ARE CONFRONTED BY THE DIFFICULTY OF TAKING UP A DISCOURSE ON SEXUALITY FROM "WITHIN" THE REGION OF TRADITIONAL PHILOSOPHY IT IS BECAUSE OF THE RIGID BUT STICKY GRID IT HAS ENFORCED, GENERALLY ON THE GROUNDS OF AN ARCHÈ OF REASON, UPON THE PLAY, MOVEMENT, AND RICHNESS OF "BODY" AND "BODILY" EXPERIENCE. THE ADDED DIFFICULTY IS THAT OF BEING WITHIN OR OUTSIDE A PARTICULAR TYPE OF DISCOURSE, PHILOSOPHIC OR OTHER, WHICH WILL INFILTRATE ITS PARTICULAR EPISTEMOLOGICAL GRID UPON OUR SEEING-BEING OUR SEXUAL-BODIES.

IF ONE THEN CAN BEGIN TO SPEAK OF THE MOVEMENT AND PLAY OF BODIES, WITHOUT FORCING THE STAMP OF BEING UPON THEIR BECOMING (WHICH NIETZSCHE RIGHTLY INDICATED AS THE TRAP OF ALL THINKING AND SPEAKING), IT BECOMES CLEAR TO WHAT DEGREE DIALECTICAL OPPOSITION,

WHICH ENTAILS A TRUNCATED MOVEMENT, WILL NOT SUFFICE. DERRIDA HAS HINTED WELL AT THE IMPOTENCE OF PHILOSOPHY AS SOUNDING ITS DEATH-KNELL WITH THE CULMINATING PHILOSOPHY OF HEGEL. MOVEMENT IS SACRIFICED TO THE OVER—DOMINANT PRESENCE OF A MOVEMENT OR THRUST, THAT OF REASON. THE FIGURE OF MAN, ALWAYS AS REASONABLE, CULTIVATED MAN, INSTALLS ITSELF UNIVERSALLY AT THE EXPENSE OF THE SCULPTED, IMAGED FORM AND MOVEMENT OF THE DIVINE. THE HOPED-FOR OSCILLATION SOLIDIFIES AND THE DUAL ERECTIONS, DIVINE AND HUMAN, BECOME FLACCID. CREATIVE MOVEMENT, PLAY, AND FORCE, SUBJECTED TO THE MOVEMENT OF MIND, COLLAPSE INTO THE GENERATION OF AN EMPTY DISCOURSE. THE HEGELIAN BODY HAS NO FLESH, NO VULNERABILITY; HENCE, IT CANNOT OFFER TO US ANY LONGER ITS FACE UPON WHICH WE COULD GAZE, MUCH LESS TO WHICH WE COULD SPEAK AND SEE, FEEL IT RESPOND.

DERRIDA'S DISCOURSE ABOUT HEGEL AND GENET MAY BE TAKEN AS A SUGGESTION OR WARNING ABOUT THE INTRINSICALLY STULTIFYING TENDENCY OF THOUGHT TO OVERCOME THE BODY. IN ORDER THAT PLAY REMAIN AT THE HEART OF THOUGHT-BODY, THE ELABORATION OF THOUGHT-BODY MUST REMAIN PRESENT TO US IN ALL ITS MOVEMENT, WITHOUT BEING PASSED DOWN OR FALLING TO US AS SOLIDIFIED, ADMIRABLE EXCREMENT.[1] DERRIDA SHOWS FORCEFULLY THE EXTENT TO WHICH THE ADMIRABLE EXCREMENT OF HEGEL IS STILL AMONG US IN THE FORM OF HIS CONSIDERATIONS AS TO THE GENERATION AND FILIATION OF THOUGHT, THE DIALECTIC OF CHILD-BIRTH AND FATHER—DEATH, SEXUALITY-PROCREATION AND ITS INSTITUTION IN AND UPHOLDING, BEING-INFORMED BY THE STATE.

DERRIDA'S DISCOURSE EMERGES IN ITS RELIANCE UPON GENET AS COUNTER-THRUST TO THE THOUGHT-PHALLUS OF HEGEL. ULTIMATELY, HOWEVER, HE ONLY WEAKLY SUGGESTS THAT ONE MAY NEED TO RECONSIDER THE RESEMBLANCE BETWEEN DIONYSOS AND CHRIST. ONE SHOULD ONLY HOPE TO GLIMPSE THEIR COUNTER-FACING BEYOND OR ABOVE THE SURFACE OF THEIR EMERGENCE AS THRUSTS OF IMMANENCE OR TRANSCENDENCE. IN ANY CASE, THEIR COLLAPSE FOR DERRIDA HAS LEFT ONLY THE DEBRIS OR RESIDUE OF DISCOURSE, THE SCATTERED REMAINS OF WHICH POINT TO THE POLAR OPPOSITIONS OF AN IMPOTENT, HETEROSEXUAL SPACE OF HEGELIAN "INTELLIGIBILITY" OR AN ENRICHED BUT NON-GENERATIVE, HOMOSEXUAL, "INCOMMUNICABILITY" OF LITERARY SPACE WITH GENET LURKING IN THE WINGS.

WHAT IS PERHAPS ULTIMATELY STRIKING AND STRANGE ABOUT DERRIDA'S TREATMENT OF HEGEL-GENET, IN SPITE OF THE CONTRAST OF "SEXUAL" THEMES WITH CONCEPTUAL, HEGELIAN SCHEMAS, IS THAT DERRIDA IMPLICITLY ACCEPTS A DISJUNCTURE OR DISCONTINUITY BETWEEN PHILOSOPHY AND LITERATURE. THE LATTER SEEMS TO TAKE OVER THE FUNCTION AND DESTINY OF THE FORMER WHEN THE MARGINS OF PHILOSOPHICAL ENDEAVOUR ARE PUSHED TO OVERFLOW. YET, THE INADEQUACY OF THIS JUMP IS NOWHERE MORE CLEARLY EVIDENCED THAN IN THE PERSON AND WORK OF GENET HIMSELF. FOR THE "STUFF" OF THE RELATIONSHIP OF THE MAN-WORK-GENET, HIS SEXUAL-EXPERIENCE-BECOME-LITERARY, IS AT THE SAME TIME A THRUST TOWARD AND CLÔTURE OF EXPRESSION. DERRIDA IRONICALLY PARALLELS THE COLLAPSE OF THE HEGELIAN CONCEPTUAL PHALLUS WITH THE IMPOTENCE AND ALLEGED DESIRE FOR IMPOTENCE OF GENET'S NON-EXPRESSIVE WORK. YET, HAS GENET BEEN GIVEN AN ADEQUATE AND EMPATHETIC TREATMENT?

IT WOULD BE A SEVERE MISTAKE TO CONFUSE THE RESPECTIVE TREATMENT OF GENET BY DERRIDA AND SARTRE INASMUCH AS BOTH DIFFER IN SUBSTANTIAL AND PARTICULAR DETAILS. YET, THE LONG—RUN RESULTS OF BOTH WRITERS' SUBJECTING THE MAN-WORK-GENET AND HIS SEXUAL-LITERARY EXPRESSION TO A TYPE OF PHILOSOPHICAL SCRUTINY SEEM NONE TOO DISTANT IN SUBSTANCE. SARTRE HAS PERHAPS ONLY BEEN MORE BLUNT, LESS ALLUSIVE THAN DERRIDA, IN FORCING THE FLESHY-SENSUAL PROSE AND POETRY OF GENET INTO THE CONCEPTUAL MOLD OF THE PACKAGED "SYMBOL." SARTRE CLAIMS:

> NOUS POUVONS À PRÉSENT COMPRENDRE L'AVENTURE DE GENET. CE PETIT HOMME ÉNERGIQUE ET ACTIF S'EST VOUÉ À A LA FOLLE ENTREPRISE DE DEVENIR CE QU'IL EST DÉJÀ ET DE DÉTRUIRE CE QU'IL NE PEUT EMPÊCHER D'ÊTRE. AUSSITOT SA VOLONTÉ SE VOLATILISE DANS L'IMAGINAIRE. PUISQU'ELLE VEUT CE QU'ON NE PEUT VOULOIR, C'EST QU'ELLE RÊVE QU'ELLE LE VEUT. VOUÉES PAR NATURE À DEMEURER INEFFICACES, SES DESTRUCTIONS ET SES APPROBATIONS ONT LIEU SYMBOLIQUEMENT. DU JOUR OÙ IL A CHOISI DE VOULOIR SON DESTIN, GENET A DÉCIDÉ, À SON INSU, DE SE FAIRE SYMBOLE, DE S'EXPRIMER PAR DES SYMBOLES ET DE VIVRE AU MILIEU DES SYMBOLES.[2]

THE FORCE OF SARTRE'S CRITIQUE AND APPROACH TO GENET AND HIS SEXUAL-LITERARY EXPERIENCE

IS TO REDUCE THEM TO THE LOCUS OF THE IMAGINARY OR EMOTIONAL, THE PLACE FOR SARTRE WHICH IS ONE OF MAGICAL TRANSFORMATION OF THE WORLD. IMPLICIT IS THE CHARGE THAT GENET, FOR THE MOST PART, CANNOT ACHIEVE THE LUCIDITY OF APPROACHING EXPERIENCE IN ITS RADICAL RELATION TO CONSCIOUSNESS AS ONE OF NEGATION. SARTRE ULTIMATELY REMAINS THE STAUNCH DEFENDER OF A TRADITIONAL META-PHYSICAL-RELIGIOUS VIEW TOWARD EXPRESSION, SEXUAL AND LITERARY, IN HIS CHARACTERIZATION OF GENET AS UNABLE, IMPOTENT, INEFFECTUAL TO CARRY HIMSELF TOWARD A PLACE WHICH WOULD BE CON-STRUCTIVE. FOR ALL HIS EXTENSIVE USE OF GENERALIZED MARXIST-FREUDIAN NOTIONS, SARTRE REMAINS HIGHLY IMPRISONED BY THE STRONGLY HETEROSEXUAL-CONCEPTUAL STANCE TOWARD CREATIVITY. GENET'S INHABITING IN SEXUAL-LITERARY FASHION THE PLACE OF SYMBOL AND THE PECULIAR MOVEMENT THAT PLACE ENTAILS, IS SEEN BY SARTRE AS NON-PRODUCTIVE, NON-CREATIVE, NEITHER FOR GENET IN "SURPAS-SING" HIS SITUATION, NOR FOR US IN BEING SPOKEN TO FROM THIS, GENET'S NON-EXPRESSIVE PLACE OF DISCOURSE.

ALTHOUGH THERE IS A CERTAIN DEPTH AND RICHNESS TO SARTRE'S TALK OF GENET AND HIS WORK, IT MUST BE SAID THAT IN THE END SARTRE HAS ONLY MADE GENET MORE MANAGEABLE FOR US, DEFUSED THE FORCE OF GENET'S THROWING INTO QUESTION THE POSSIBILIITY OF ANY DIS-COURSE UPON SEXUALITY AS WELL AS THE ABILITY TO INHABIT THE PLACE OF SYMBOL WHILE HANGING ON TO ANY VESTIGES OF CONCEPTUAL THOUGHT. SARTRE HAS CERTAINLY BETRAYED THE POVERTY OF AT LEAST PART OF HIS PROJECT IN ONE SHORT CHARACTERIZATION OF GENET:

DÈS SON ADOLESCENCE, IL N'A PLUS AUCUN RAPPORT "NORMAL", C'EST-À-DIRE DE PROSE AVEC LE LANGUAGE.[3]

THE VACUITY OF SARTRE'S TREATMENT OF SYMBOL-PROSE IS STRIKING AND INSTRUCTIVE AS TO THE INADEQUACY OF THIS APPROACH WITH RESPECT TO THE COMPLEXITY OF THE MAN-WORK-GENET IN PARTICULAR AND TO ANY DISCOURSE IN GENERAL. THE NORMALCY OF PROSE FOR SARTRE, IN A RESTRICTED SENSE, PERTAINS TO LANGUAGE. IN A LARGER CONTEXT, HOWEVER, THAT NORMALCY HAS AS ITS REFERENCE THE SPEECH AND CATEGORIES OF NEGATING AND APPROPRIATIVE CONSCIOUS-NESS WHICH SARTRE LAID OUT MOST EXTENSIVELY IN BEING AND NOTHINGNESS. IF, FOR SARTRE,

CONSCIOUSNESS IS A LACK WHICH IN FUTILE FASHION ATTEMPTS TO FILL UP ITSELF, MAKE ITSELF SOLID, IN ANY CASE MAN IS AT LEAST CAPABLE OF PARALLELING THE MOVEMENT OF THAT "LACK-FILLING-UP-TOWARD-PLENITUDE" IN PROSE, WITH A DISCOURSE WHICH REMAINS OSCILLATORY, DIS-CURSIVE. FOLLOWING THE SUGGESTIONS OF EXISTENTIAL PSYCHOANALYSIS ON BROAD OUTLINE, ONE MUST NOT BEAR DOWN TOO DEEPLY INTO THE PLACE OF SEXUAL-SYMBOL FOR FEAR OF THE BOTTOMLESS PLUNGE IT MIGHT ENTAIL. FOR THIS IS WHAT SARTRE ULTIMATELY SEES AS THE PLACE OF GENET'S SYMBOLIC INVOLVEMENT:

CHUTE, VIDE, NUIT DU NON-SAVOIR: IL NE ·S'AGIT PAS D'UNE POÉSIE APOLLINIENNE QUI JOUIRAIT D'IMAGES BRILLANTES ET VILIBLES. C'EST LE VERTIGE, LE MANQUE, LE NÉANT, LA NÉGATION QUI MARQUENT L'EMOTION POÉTIQUE.[4]

ALTHOUGH THE SPIRIT OF THE SARTREAN ENTER-PRISE HAS CERTAINLY BEEN TO CONSIDER "EVERY HUMAN FACT" AS SIGNIFICANT,[5] THE FORCE OF SARTREAN EPISTEMOLOGY HAS LIMITED IF NOT OFTEN CRUSHED THE OPTIQUE WITH WHICH THE PHENOMENA ARE VIEWED. IF THE LUCID PROSE OF KNOWING IS TO BE ENFORCED VERSUS THE MURKY, EMPTY, FALL INTO NOTHINGNESS PROFFERED BY THE POETRY OF EMOTION OR POETIC EMOTION, THE PLACE OF SYMBOL, ONE WILL NOT BE SURPRISED BY THE RAPIDLY AND EASILY CONQUERED NOTIONS OF BEING AND NOTHINGNESS AND ITS DISCOURSE ON SEXUALITY. CAN ONE EXPECT SARTRE TO CAP-TIVATE, WITH REFURBISHED HEGELIAN CATEGO-RIES, THE PATHOS OF THE SYMBOL OR THE SYMBOL'S PARTICIPATION WITH THE PLACE OF PASSION, LUST, AND THE DEPTH OF THEIR INTERFACE? SARTREAN LUCIDITY WOULD CONVINCE US THAT THE PLACE OF PASSION IN GENERAL AND SEXUAL INTERCOURSE IN ITS HETEROSEXUAL PARTICULARITY IS NO MORE THAN THE SPECIAL CASE OF THE ONTOLOGICAL-HUMAN THRUST OF FILLING UP HOLES IN BEING. IT WOULD SHOW US THE APPROPRIATIVE, GRASPING CHARACTER OF THE CARESS, THE TOUCHING-SEIZING OF A BREAST AS AN ATTEMPT TO GET HOLD OF BEING, THE THRUST OF A PENIS AS PROJECT-UPON-THE-WORLD, THE TUMBLE IN TO THE VAGINA AS MAN'S FALLING-ENCLOSURE BACK INTO THE NOTHING THAT HE ALWAYS IS, RETURNS TOWARD, AND PROJECTS BEYOND. THE CAREFUL LAYING-OUT OF THE CATEGORIES AND MOVEMENTS OF HUMAN CON-SCIOUSNESS IN SITUATIONS WHICH SARTRE ACHIEVES IN BEING AND NOTHINGNESS ARE SEEN

WELL AS FUNCTIONING IN THE PARTICULAR REGIONAL ONTOLOGY PERTAINING TO SEXUALITY. YET, THIS FUNCTIONING IS IN THE DAY-LIGHT, LUCIDITY OF APPROPRIATIVE CONSCIOUSNESS WHICH FASHIONS THE BASIS AND THE PROSE OF ITS OWNMOST DISCOURSE TO THE STRICT EXCLUSION OF INVOLVEMENT WITH THE NIGHT OF NON-KNOWLEDGE.

IN SPITE OF THE LIMITATIONS OF SARTRE'S VIEW TO AND DISCOURSE ON SEXUALITY, IT IS APPARENT THAT HE IS AWARE OF IMPOSING A CERTAIN GRID OF SUBJECT-OBJECT UPON GENET IN PARTICULAR AND UPON THE SENSUAL-SYMBOLIC IN GENERAL. AT THE END OF HIS LONG WORK AND INTRODUCTION TO GENET'S WORKS, HE SUGGESTS EVEN THAT ONE MIGHT NEED TO PLUNGE INTO THE IMAGINARY IN ORDER TO STOP FLEEING THE "OBJECTIVE" BY THE "SUBJECTIVE" AND THE "SUBJECTIVE" BY THE "OBJECTIVE":

> ... CE JEU DE CACHE-CACHE NE PRENDRA FIN QU'AU JOUR OÙ NOUS AURONS LE COURAGE D'ALLER JUSQU'AU BOUT DE NOUS-MÊME DANS LES DEUX DIRECTIONS À LA FOIS.[6]

SARTRE, IN SPEAKING OF THIS PERPETUAL GAME OF HIDE AND SEEK WHICH PHILOSOPHICAL DISCOURSE IS COWARDLY WONT TO PURSUE, IS LUCID ENOUGH TO SEE HIS OWN DISCOURSE AS ENSNARED TO SOME DEGREE IN THE GRIDS OF THE TRADITIONAL MIND-BODY, THOUGHT-EXPRESSIVITY, SUBJECT-OBJECT, DUALISMS. HE HAS AT LEAST THE SENSE TO SEE, ALBEIT UNABLE TO CARRY OUT THAT SEEING CONSISTENTLY, THAT ONE MUST PUSH IN THE TWO DIRECTIONS AT ONCE, FINALLY BEYOND THEM. WE HAVE HINTED AT THE NEED TO CONSIDER SEXUALITY IN ITS "SYMBOLIC" DEPTH RATHER THAN AS A MERE MEANS TO THE FULFILLMENT OF THE ONTOLOGICAL-EPISTEMOLOGICAL "HUMAN-SITUA-TION." IT WILL BE NECESSARY TO RETURN TO AND FILL OUT THIS DEPTH. YET, FOR THE MOMENT, IN PURSUING THE DIFFICULTIES OF DOING A DIS-COURSE ON SEXUALITY, IT IS NECESSARY TO SEE THE HISTORICAL AS WELL AS "PHILOSOPHICAL" RESTRICTIONS UPON ANY SUCH DISCOURSE AND THE CONFINING CONTEXT OUT OF WHICH IT MIGHT ARISE.

IN INTRODUCING THE FIRST PAGES OF A CONTINU-ING WORK ON SEXUALITY, MICHEL FOUCAULT SPEAKS OF A MODERN PURITANISM'S HAVING IMPOSED ITS DECREE OF PROHIBITION, INEXIS-TENCE, AND INCOMMUNICABILITY UPON THE SPACE OF SEXUAL DISCOURSE. YET, THE RECENT MODERN AGE IS EXPOSED TO THE SCIENCE OF SEXUALITY, THROUGH FREUD, REICH AND OTHERS, AS WELL AS INVOLVED IN A REVOLUTION OF PLEASURE. FOUCAULT'S TALK OF THE POSSIBILITY OF SEXUAL DISCOURSE IN THIS CONTEXT IS THEN BASED UPON THE RECIPROCAL INTERCHANGE AND ECONOMY OF REPRESSION AND PREDICATION WHICH RESPEC-TIVELY AND MUTUALLY RESTRICT AND UPHOLD SUCH DISCOURSE. FOUCAULT'S ATTEMPT IS TO OUTLINE A RESPONSE TO AND THEN GO BEYOND ONE PRIMARY QUESTION:

> LA QUESTION QUE JE VOUDRAIS POSER N'EST PAS: POURQUOI SOMMES-NOUS RÉPRIMÉS, MAIS POURQUOI DISONS-NOUS, AVEC TANT DE PASSION, TANT DE RANCOEUR CONTRE NOTRE PASSÉ LE PLUS PROCHE, CONTRE NOTRE PRÉSENT ET CONTRE NOUS-MÊMES, QUE NOUS-SOMMES RÉPRIMÉS?[7]

FOUCAULT CLAIMS AT LEAST THREE FACETS FOR HIS STRATEGY OF REPLYING TO THIS QUESTION—HISTORICAL, HISTORICAL-THEORETICAL, HISTORI-CAL-POLITICAL. AT ISSUE FOR EACH LEVEL ARE THE ESSENTIAL QUESTIONS: IS THE REPRESSION OF SEXUALITY AND DISCOURSE ABOUT IT REALLY IN EVIDENCE HISTORICALLY? IS THE MECHANISM OF POWER IN SOCIETIES SUCH AS OURS ESSENTIALLY OF THE REPRESSIVE ORDER? DOES THE CRITICAL DISCOURSE OF AND ABOUT SEXUALITY RUN AGAINST THE GRAIN OF GENERAL REPRESSION OR INSTALL ITSELF AND FIND ITSELF SITUATED FROM WITHIN THAT FIELD AND SOURCE OF REPRESSION?

IN BROAD OUTLINE, THE STRENGTH AND DEPTH OF FOUCAULT'S ANALYSIS IS TO INDICATE THE CONFINEMENT, RESTRICTION, AND STIFLING OF DISCOURSE ON SEXUALITY AND THE REPRESSION OF SEXUALITY IN THE VERY LOCUS WHERE SUCH TALK APPEARS TO BE IN THE OPEN. FOUCAULT SHOWS THE EXTENT TO WHICH, EVEN SINCE THE END OF THE SIXTEENTH CENTURY, THE PUTTING IN THE OPEN OF DISCOURSE AS TO SEXUALITY HAS NOT BEEN SUBJECTED TO MERE RESTRICTION IN A SOLELY NEGATIVE SENSE. RATHER, IT HAS BEEN TAMED IRONICALLY BY A GROWING INCITEMENT TO COME OUT INTO THE OPEN, ONLY TO BE DOMESTI-CATED BY AND INTO A SCIENCE OF SEXUALITY. SEXUALITY AND DISCOURSE ON SEXUALITY HAVE NOT SO MUCH BEEN RESTRICTED BY A RIGOUROUS PRINCIPLE OF SELECTION AND TABOO BUT FINALLY DIFFUSED AND DEFUSED BY BROAD DISSEMINATION AND EMPLACEMENT BY THE WILL TO KNOW. THE DEPTH AND RICHES OF THE PLACE OF THE VERTIGE

OF NON-KNOWING OF SEXUAL-SYMBOLIC-POTENCY HAVE BEEN TRANSFORMED BY THE KNOWING DISCOURSE IN THE OPEN OF A MODERN ALCHEMY WHICH PROBES RATHER THAN PARTICIPATES WITH THE HIDDEN SECRET:

> ... CE QUI EST PROPRE AUX SOCIÉTÉS MODERNES, CE N'EST PAS QU'ELLES AIENT VOUÉ LE SEXE À RESTER DANS L'OMBRE, C'EST QU'ELLES SE SOIENT VOUÉES À EN PARLER TOUJOURS, EN LE FAISANT VALOIR COMME LE SECRET.[8]

FOUCAULT DISCUSSES THE BRINGING TO THE "FORE" OF THIS SECRET AND ITS BEING TAMED WITHIN THE CATEGORIES OF THE NATURE-LAW, EXCLUSION-DISCREET MARRIAGE. THE NEW PURITANISM AND STIFLING OF A DEEPER DISCOURSE WITH SEXUALITY IS SET UP BY MEDICAL-SCIENTIFIC PRIESTS AS THE FORCE OF THE CHURCH-CLERGY WANES. SEXUALITY VIEWED FROM THE GRID OF ADULTS-CHILDREN-INSTITUTIONS IMPLIES CLASSIFICATION AND CONFINEMENT WHICH IS NONETHELESS BROAD ENOUGH TO MAKE ROOM FOR "DISPARATE" BEHAVIOUR, INCORPORATE "PERVERSIONS" BY GIVING THEM ANALYSTIC STATUS. ONE SEES READILY THAT THE CONCEPTUAL GRID WHICH UPHOLDS SEXUAL DISCOURSE IS BROADER THAN THE STAID, DIRECT LINES OF FILIATION-GENERATION OF THE HEGELIAN SCHEMA. YET, IF LINEARITY IS GIVEN UP FOR SPIRALS OR CONCENTRIC WEBS WHICH ALLOW "PERVERSIONS" AT THE MARGINS OR EXTREMITIES, THE PLACE OF SEXUALITY AND DISCOURSE TO AND WITH THAT PLACE ARE ONLY COVERED OVER AND MANAGED BY A NEW PURITANISM.

YET, FOUCAULT IS NOT ONLY CONCERNED TO SHOW THE EPISTEMOLOGICAL MIS-MANAGEMENT OF SEXUAL MATTERS AND DISCOURSE BUT, MOREOVER, TO INDICATE THE CRUCIAL LATERAL SPREAD OF SEXUALITY IN AND THROUGH RELATIONS OF A SOCIAL-POLITICAL FABRIC. HE CLAIMS THAT PLEASURE AND POWER DO NOT NEGATE EACH OTHER, NOR SIMPLY VIE FOR THEIR RESPECTIVE POSITIONS. RATHER, THEY "CHASE AFTER EACH OTHER AND GET ENTANGLED THE ONE WITH THE OTHER ACCORDING TO COMPLEX MECHANISMS OF EXCITATION AND EXCITING EACH OTHER ONWARD." IRONICALLY, SEXUAL DISCOURSE IN THE RECENT AGE IS PLAGUED BY ITS CONFINEMENT IN THE OPEN; AS SUCH IT IS INVOLVED IN A VAST SYSTEM OF SOCIO-POLITICAL CONTROL WHICH TAKES IT SERIOUSLY AND BROADLY, EVEN ALLOWING ROOM FOR A COMPLEXITY OF "PERVERSIONS" OF SEXUAL BEHAVIOURS AND ACTS, THUS ALLOWING A MORE EFFICIENT MANAGEMENT.

THE QUESTION OF CONTROL IS MORE RICHLY OUTLINED AS FOUCAULT CONTRASTS "ARS EROTICA" WITH "SCIENTIA SEXUALIS." WHEREAS ARS EROTICA, AS MANIFEST AND PRACTICED IN EASTERN AND ARABIC-MOSLEM COUNTRIES, RELIED UPON DRAWING THE "TRUTH" OF SEXUALITY FROM PLEASURE ITSELF, TAKEN AS A PRAXIS IN THE MOST INTIMATE, RICH AND COMPLEX DEPTHS AS EXPERIENCE, SCIENTIA SEXUALIS HAS TYPIFIED WESTERN "EXPERIENCE" AND CONFINEMENT OF THE TRUTH OF SEXUALITY. ARS EROTICA KNOWS NO REFERENCE TO CRITERIA OF UTILITY, ABSOLUTE LAWS OF PERMISSION AND TABOO. IT INHABITS THE PLACE OF MASTERY OF AND WITH RESPONSE TO ONE'S BODY, ITS UNIQUE AND PARTICULAR JOY AND PLEASURE, A FORGETTING OF TIME AND LIMITS. IT IS A LATERAL AND DEPTH PLUNGE INTO THE SPACE OF RICHNESS AND ABUNDANCE OF LIFE, AN EXILE FOR DEATH AND ITS MENACES. IT IS A REPROACH TO AN EXTERIOR-INTERIOR DUALISM, A CONTROL, OWNMOST GRASP OF ONE'S TIME-SPACE BY TOUCHING THE TEXTURE OF THE PLACE OF THE POWER OF LIFE.

THE POVERTY OF WESTERN SCIENTIA SEXUALIS HINGES PRIMARILY ON ITS BEING OR BECOMING THE BASTARD FORM OF THE RICHER ARS EROTICA—ALL BY WAY OF CEDING OVER THE PLACE OF SEXUALITY TO THE GREED AND SEIZURE OF THE COURTROOM AND CONFESSION WHICH IS THE PLACE OF AVOWING THE SECRET. SEXUALITY MUST BE AFFIRMED, ASSERTED, CONFESSED, FOR IT TO TAKE ITS PLACE IN WESTERN SOCIETY. PLEASURE AND THE DEPTH IT ENTAILS, IS REPLACED BY THE PLEASURE OF ANALYSIS. ONE'S OWNMOST RESPONSE WITH AND TO PLEASURE AND THE SEXUAL PLACE IS OUTDISTANCED BY THE SILENT RESPONSE OF DOMINATION OF HE WHO LISTENS TO THE SEXUAL CONFESSION OR WHO CATEGORIZES AND CLASSIFIES IT.

THE WESTERN ENGULFMENT IN THE POVERTY OF SCIENTIA SEXUALIS INVOLVES ITS CLINICAL CODIFICATION OF SEXUAL CONFESSION BASED ON THEORIES OF GENERAL CAUSALITY APPLIED TO PARTICULAR SEXUAL EXPERIENCE. THE WILL TO KNOW THE SEXUAL EXPERIENCE DOMINATES AND CRUSHES THE PLACE AND DISCOURSE OF SEXUALITY AND ITS RICH POTENTIAL OF INDIVIDUATION AND EXPRESSION ON ONE'S OWNMOST TERMS AND TOWARD ONE'S DEEPEST AND MOST PERSONAL PLEASURES. THE DEPTH OF SEXUAL EXPERIENCE BECOMES GLOSSED OVER AS A TYPE OF LATENCY INTRINSIC TO SEXUALITY BUT WHICH MUST BE BROUGHT TO THE FORE OF DAYLIGHT LUCIDITY AND

CONFESSION RATHER THAN EXPLORED IN ITS OWN "NIGHT OF NON-KNOWING." HENCE, SCIENTIA SEXUALIS INSTALLS AND ENFORCES A METHOD OF INTERPRETATION, A MEDICAL-HERMENEUTIC RAPE OF THE SEXUAL BODY. THE SOCIETY IN GENERAL WHICH LISTENS, BUT THE ANALYST IN PARTICULAR WHO RECORDS THE SEXUAL CONFESSION, BECOME MASTERS OF PARDON, JUDGES OF ACTS WHO THEN CONDEMN OR JUSTIFY, MASTERS OF THE TRUTH AND CONTROLLERS OF THE PLACE OF SEXUALITY. ALTHOUGH THERE ARE AT LEAST TWO LEVELS INVOLVED, "CLINICAL" AND " POLITICO-SOCIAL," THE TWO INTERPRENETRATE AND INFORM AND SUPPORT EACH OTHER.

FIRST, AS SUGGESTED BY FOUCAULT AND BROUGHT OUT MORE CLEARLY IN HIS WORK ON MADNESS AND THE BIRTH OF CONFINEMENT AND THE CLINIC AND AS CONCRETELY CRITICIZED BY DELEUZE AND GUATTARI, SCIENTIA SEXUALIS HAS ITS MOST ARDENT COMPANION IN THE CLINIC AND THE PSYCHOLOGI-CAL-SEXUAL LITERATURE IT UPHOLDS AND PRAC-TICES. DELEUZE AND GUATTARI SPEAK OF THE GREAT CONTRIBUTION OF PSYCHOANALYSIS TO A DISCOUSE ON SEXUALITY, PARTICULARLY IN TOUCHING THE DEPTHS OF THE UNCONSCIOUS. YET, THE STIFLING MANNER OF EXPOSING THAT DEPTH IS THE UPHOLDING OF RIGID CLASSIFICATION AS SEEN IN THE PRACTICE OF HEARING THE AVOWALS OF COMPLEXES GROUNDED IN A STERILE EPISTEMO-LOGICAL PLACE, THAT OF . . .

UN NOUVEL IDÉALISME: À L'INCONSCIENT COMME USINE, ON A SUBSTITUÉ UN THÉÂ ANTIQUE; AUX UNITÉS DE PRODUCTION DE L'INCONSCIENT, ON A SUBSTITUÉ LA REPRÉSENTATION; À L'INCONSCIENT PRODUCTIF, ON A SUBSTITUÉ UN INCONSCIENT QUI NE POUVAIT PLUS QUE S'EXPRIMER (LE MYTHE, LA TRAGÉDIE, LE RÊVE . . .)[10]

FOLLOWING THE ALLUSIVE SUGGESTION OF JOYCE AS TO RE-EMBODIMENT, AND WISHING TO TOUCH ACROSS TO THAT DEPTH OF SEXUAL EXPERIENCE WHICH D.H. LAWRENCE SAW BEING SMOTHERED BY SEXUAL-PSYCHOLOGICAL DISCOURSE, DELEUZE-GUATTARI THROW INTO QUESTION THE EPISTEMO-LOGY AND ANCIENT-THEATRE OF PSYCHOANALYSIS WITH ITS SENSE OF RE-PRESENTATION AND EX-PRESSION WHICH ARE ACCOMPLISHED AT THE EXPENSE OF THE LIVED-SEXUAL-BODY. IT IS NOT ALTOGETHER CLEAR THAT THEIR WORKING GRID OF MACHINE-RECORDING-REACTION-FEEDBACK WILL BE ULTIMATELY CAPABLE OF AVOIDING THE TRAP OF SCIENTIA SEXUALIS.[11] AT THE VERY LEAST, HOWEVER, THEY RIGHTLY CRITICIZE THE ABORTIVE

USE OF MYTH AND SYSTEM BY PSYCHOANALYSIS. FOR THE CLINIC HAS BECOME THE STAGE UPON WHICH THE FRAGMENTS AND PIECES OF THE SHATTERED SEXUAL-SYMBOLIC-PLACE HAVE BEEN STREWN, THE PLAYERS NO LONGER ALLOWED THEIR PLEASURABLE PLACE, BEING RE-PLACED BY THE SPECTATORS OF SOCIETY AND ANALYST:

EN ENCADRANT LA VIE DE L'ENFANT DANS L'OEDIPE, EN FAISANT DES RELATIONS FAMILIALES L'UNIVERSELLE MÉDIATION DE L'ENFANCE, ON SE CONDAMNE À MÉCONNAÎTRE LA PRODUCTION DE L'INCONSCIENTE LUI-MÊME, ET LES MÉCANISMES COLLECTIFS QUI PORTENT À CRU SUR L'INCON-SCIENT, NOTAMMENT TOUT LE JEU DU REFOULE-MENT ORIGINAIRE, DES MACHINES DÉSIRANTES ET DU CORPS SANS ORGANES. CAR L'INCONSCIENT EST ORPHELIN, ET SE PRODUIT LUI-MÊME DANS L'IDENTITÉ DE LA NATURE ET DE L'HOMME.[12]

THE POVERTY OF MUCH OF THE PSYCHOANALYTIC DISCOURSE ON SEXUALITY IS WELL SKETCHED OUT IN THESE REMARKS. MOREOVER, THEY INDICATE A DIRECTION FOR ENRICHED DISCOURSE TO TAKE REGARDING AND WITH THE PLACE OF SEXUALITY, THAT PLACE WHICH IS THE PECULIAR INDIVIDUAL'S FUSION WITH "NATURE." THE RELATION MENTIONED HERE AS AN IDENTITY MUST BE FLESHED-OUT AS THE PLACE OF IMPLOSIVE-EXPLOSIVE FUSION OF LIBIDO-UNCONSCIOUS-SYMBOL; A NEW SENSE FOR SEXUAL SURFACE MUST BE DEVELOPED AND GIVEN TEXTURE. THAT PSYCHOANALYSIS ALONE CANNOT BRING-OUT THAT DEPTH AND TEXTURE BEGINS TO BE MORE EVIDENT.

SECONDLY, THE CLINICAL LEVEL AND ITS STULTIFY-ING USE OF A SEXUAL DISCOURSE IS AUGMENTED AND MUTUALLY INTERPENETRATED BY A POLITICO-SOCIAL LEVEL. AT THIS LEVEL ALSO CONTROL AND JUDGEMENT ARE CRUCIAL, ALBEIT NOT ALWAYS EVIDENT, THIS DUE PRIMARILY TO THE CAPACITY OF SCIENTIA SEXUALIS FOR DISPERSION AND LATERAL CONFINEMENT. FOUCAULT WRITES:

L'HISTOIRE DE LA SEXUALITÉ, SI ON VEUT LA CENTRER SUR LES MÉCANISMES DE RÉPRESSION, SUPPOSE DEUX RUPTURES. L'UNE AU COURS DU XVIIᵉ SIÈCLE: NAISSANCE DES GRANDES PROHIBI-TIONS, VALORISATION DE LA SEULE SEXUALITÉ ADULTE ET MATRIMONIALE, IMPÉRATIFS DE DÉCENCE, ESQUIVE OBLIGATOIRE DU CORPS, MISE AU SILENCE ET PUDEURS IMPÉRATIVES DU LANGAGE; L'AUTRE, AU XXᵉ SIÈCLE; MOINS RUPTURE D'AILLEURS QU'INFLEXION DE LA

THE PRIMARY DIFFERENCES BETWEEN THE TWO SORTS OF REPRESSION REGARDING SEXUALITY AND SEXUAL DISCOURSE HANG ON THE SOCIO-POLITICAL CAPACITY TO CONFINE SEXUAL DEPTH TO A DE-LIMITED PLACE, A CLOSETED VERTICAL SPACE OR TO AN UN-LIMITED, "OPEN" LATERAL SPACE OF DISPERSION AND DE-FUSION. THE OLD PURITANISM CEDES GLADLY TO THE NEW; THE OLD TASK OF CONFINEMENT WAS TIRING AND UNABLE TO COPE ULTIMATELY WITH THE IMPLOSIVE-EXPLOSIVE FORCE OF LIBIDINAL-SYMBOLIC-IDENTITY. THE NEW PURITANISM AS DISPERSION WILL ACCOMPLISH MORE RADICALLY WHAT WAS ALWAYS AT ISSUE:

ON POURRAIT DIRE QU'AU VIEUX DROIT DE FAIRE MOURIR OU DE LAISSER VIVRE S'EST SUBSTITUÉ UN POUVOIR DE FAIRE VIVRE OU DE REJETER DANS LA MORT.[14]

THE POSSIBILITIES OF THE NEW PURITANISM, THE OPEN DISCOURSE ON SEXUALITY, THE STATUS OF SCIENTIA SEXUALIS, INVOLVE DISPERSION WHICH MANAGES AND CONTROLS AT EVERY LEVEL AND SEEKS OUT EVERY FIBRE OF THE HUMAN PLACE, PENETRATING ITS TEXTURE AND UNDERMINING ITS TISSUE. FLESH IS MADE, CONTROLLED, SPOKEN ON, CLASSIFIED, MUTILATED, AND ULTIMATELY RE-JECTED IF NECESSARY. SPECTATORSHIP, ANALY-SIS, SEXUAL DISCOURSE, PUNISHMENT AND POLITICAL CONTROL HAVE FOLLOWED THE SAME PATH STREWN WITH HUMAN FLESH. THE TORTURE OF DAMIENS,[15] THE CONFINEMENT OF THE SICK, MAD, AND OVERLY POLITICAL DISPARATE, THE MADNESS OF NIETZSCHE, HÖLDERLIN AND ARTAUD, ARE ALL ALONG THE WAY OF THE CONTROL OF THE FLESH OF IDENTITY OF NATURE AND MAN.

DELEUZE AND GUATTARI HAVE MORE FULLY OUTLINED THE FLESH-STREWN PATH AS THE HISTORICAL-GENETIC MOVEMENT OF PRIMITIVE-DESPOT-CAPITAL AND ULTIMATE DISSOLUTION INTO SCHIZOPHRENIA OF CONTEMPORARY SOCIETY AND ITS RETURN TO A NEW BUT DIS-PLACED SENSE OF THE PRIMITIVE-SAVAGE. THEIR OUTLINING THE NEGATIVE, DESTRUCTIVE, EX-PLOSION OF THE LIBIDINAL IMPULSE AND ITS HISTORY OF CONFRON-TATION WITH POWER AND CONFINEMENT IS QUITE PERSUASIVE. YET, IT IS NOT CLEAR TO WHAT RADICAL AN EXTENT THEY ARE WILLING TO PUSH THEIR OWN NOTION OF THE STATUS OF THE UNCONSCIOUS AS AN ORPHAN WHICH GENERATES

ITSELF IN THE IDENTITY OF NATURE AND MAN. BOTH LESS AND MORE THAN A QUESTION OF MERE CRITICISM OF DELEUZE AND GUATTARI, IT IS A QUESTION OF PUSHING THEIR NOTIN OF DESIRING-MACHINES TO THE LIMIT: OF SEEING THE POSITIVE SENSE OF THE DISPERSION OF LIBIDINAL IMPULSE EVEN UPON AND BACK TOWARD THE ANCIENT THEATRE OF SYMBOL-TRAGEDY; OF EXPLORING THE SEARCH FOR A FULLNESS AND DEPTH OF FLESH AS IT COURSES THROUGH AND TRACES ITSELF UPON LIFE. OUR INDICATIONS AS TO THIS, A PERHAPS MORE RADICAL VIEW TO THE PLACE OF SEXUALITY AND DISCOURSE ARE TAKEN IN VIEWING THE PAINED FACES OF THE "MAD" FIGURES OF HÖLDERLIN AND NIETZSCHE ALONG THE FLESH-STREWN PATH OF DISSOLUTION OF THE MODERN AGE INTO LIBIDINAL SCHIZOPHRENIA.

WE HEAR THE CALM, CLEAR, SOMEWHAT QUIET VOICE OF THE SIMPLE CARPENTER ZIMMER AS HE WRITES TO HÖLDERLIN'S MOTHER DURING THE YEARS OF HER SON'S GROWING "MADNESS" AND FREQUENT SILENCE:

HIS POETIC SPIRIT STILL SHOWS ITSELF TO BE ACTIVE; IN MY HOUSE HE SAW A DRAWING OF A GREEK TEMPLE. HE ASKED ME TO MAKE ONE LIKE IT IN WOOD. I REPLIED THAT I HAVE TO WORK FOR MY LIVING, THAT I AM NOT FORTUNATE ENOUGH TO LIVE IN PHILOSOPHIC CALM LIKE HIM; IMMEDIATELY HE REPLIED, "OH BUT I AM A POOR CREATURE," AND IN THE SAME MINUTE HE WROTE THE FOLLOWING VERSES ON A WOODEN BOARD WITH A PENCIL:

THE LINES OF LIFE ARE VARIOUS,
  AS FOOTPATHS ARE,
AND AS THE MOUNTAINS' CONTOURS.
WHAT HERE WE ARE, YONDER A GOD
  CAN COMPLETE WITH HARMONIES,
  ETERNAL RECOMPENSE, AND PEACE.[16]

PERHAPS ONE BEGINS TO SPEAK WITH HÖLDERLIN RATHER THAN JUST ABOUT HIM AS WE FEEL AND HEAR THE SCRAPING OF HIS PENCIL UPON THE WOOD, WATCH THE POET GIVE UP THE PRIVILEGED PLACE AND PAPER, FAMILIAR TEXTURE AND SITE OF HIS USUAL DISCOURSE, CARE FOR HIS FUMBLING WITH THE WOOD AND OTHER PARTIAL OJECTS OF HIS-OUR FRAGMENTED WORLD. ULTIMATELY, HIS GESTURE IS TO CAPTIVATE, CARESS, AND FASHION THE FLESH OF HIS WORLD THROUGH POETIC DISCOURSE. EMBLEMATIC OF THE SCHIZOPHRENIC DIVISION AND FRAGMENTATION OF THE CONTEM-PORARY WORLD IS THE GULF BETWEEN THE CARPENTER'S HANDLING OF THE EARTH, ALTHOUGH

UNABLE TO FASHION IT INTO THE PLACE OF THE WHOLE AS EXPRESSIVE, AND THE POET'S EXPRESSIVE DISCOURSE, ALTHOUGH UNABLE TO TOUCH FROM ITS ETHEREAL SPACE TO THE FLESH, LOOK, AND MARROW OF THE LIVED-FELT WORLD. HÖLDERLIN'S DESPAIR OVER THIS FRAGMENTATION ALONG THE PATHS OF LIFE SEEKS COMFORT AND RECONCILIATION IN THE HOPE FOR THE FLEEING GOD'S CAPACITY TO FASHION HARMONY IN ANOTHER WORLD. MOST CENTRAL TO THE TRAGEDY OF HÖLDERLIN'S OWNMOST ARTISTIC DISSOLUTION IS PERHAPS HIS FLEEING FROM AND DIS-PLACING HIS WORLD TOWARD ANOTHER, HIGHER, WORLD BEYOND THE WORLD. YET, HE HAS BEAUTIFULLY STRUGGLED WITH AND PARTIALLY PURSUED THE SENSE OF INSCRIPTION AND EMBODIMENT, STRUCK OUT A PATH TOWARD POETICALLY TAKING UP ONE'S FLESH IN THE WORLD AGAINST THE PATH OF PARTIAL OBJECTS AND FRAGMENTATION WHICH IS THE DISSOLUTION AND CONFINEMENT OF THE PLACE OF SEXUAL-CREATIVE-SYMBOL.

NIETZSCHE SEEMS TO HAVE CLEARLY PURSUED A SIMILAR PATH, TAKING IT FURTHER THAN HÖLDERLIN, BUT IN THE SAME SPIRIT AND OVER AGAINST THE DISSOLUTION OF A CENTER WHICH NO LONGER HOLDS, TAKING US CLOSER TO A SEXUAL DISCOURSE AND THE LIBIDINALLY CREATIVE FLESH OF SYMBOL AS THE PLACE OF THE HUMAN:

THE METAPHYSICAL COMFORT—WITH WHICH I AM SUGGESTING EVEN NOW, EVERY TRUE TRAGEDY LEAVES US—THAT LIFE IS AT THE BOTTOM OF THINGS, DESPITE ALL THE CHANGES OF APPEARANCES, INDESTRUCTABLY POWERFUL AND PLEASURABLE—THIS COMFORT APPEARS IN INCARNATE CLARITY IN THE CHORUS OF SATYRS . . .

. . . THE SATYR WAS THE ARCHETYPE OF MAN, THE EMBODIMENT OF HIS HIGHEST AND MOST INTENSE EMOTIONS, THE ECSTATIC REVELER ENRAPTURED BY THE PROXIMITY OF HIS GOD, THE SYMPATHETIC COMPANION IN WHOM THE SUFFERING OF THE GOD IS REPEATED, ONE WHO PROCLAIMS WISDOM FROM THE VERY HEART OF NATURE, A SYMBOL OF THE SEXUAL OMNIPOTENCE OF NATURE WHICH THE GREEKS USED TO CONTEMPLATE WITH REVERENT WONDER.[17]

ONE WOULD SEEM TO HAVE ONLY CERTAIN SUGGESTIONS TO FOLLOW, SUCH AS THESE RICH AND COMPLEX NOTIONS OF HÖLDERLIN AND NIETZSCHE, AS A WAY BEYOND THE RAPID REJECTION BY DELEUZE AND GUATTARI OF THE ANCIENT-THEATRE OF MYTH AND DREAM AS INADEQUATE FORMULATIONS OR VIEWS TO SEXUALITY AND THE LIBIDINAL DEPTH OF THE WORLD. THEY SEEM TO HAVE OVERLOOKED THE SENSE IN WHICH THE MYTHIC-DREAM-PLAY OF LIBIDINAL IMPULSE HAS BEEN STIFLED PARTICULARLY BY FREUD THROUGH WHAT THE POET BLAKE TERMED "MIND-FORGED MANACLES"—THOSE OF THE THINKER ANALYST. NIETZSCHE'S DIRECTION, ALREADY A PATH STRUCK UPON BY HÖLDERLIN, POINTS TO THE PLACE OF PLAY WHICH IS LIBIDINAL-SYMBOLIC, CHARACTERIZED MOST FULLY BY THE SATYR OF GREEK TRAGEDY. NIETZSCHE SPEAKS LUCIDLY AND IRONICALLY OF A METAPHYSICAL COMFORT WHICH IS NEITHER PROPERLY METAPHYSICAL NOR A COMFORT. HE SPEAKS OF NO WORLD ABOVE OR BELOW THIS ONE—THAT OF OUR BODIES, FLESH, SEXUAL DESIRE, AND POETIC-LIBIDINAL THRUST UPON OUR WORLD. NOR IS REALLY A COMFORT, IN THE SENSE OF A CONSOLATION, AT ISSUE. FOR OUR WORLD EMBODIMENT IS BOTH A PLUNGE FROM AND TOWARD OUR OWN FLESHED-BODIES AND A CAREFUL SCULPTING WHICH WE DO AND ARE; IN A SENSE BOTH A WORK AND JOY OF ARTISTIC CREATION.

IF THE METAPHYSICIANS COULD GET THEIR HANDS ON THIS "IDEA"—AND THAT WOULD ALREADY INVOLVE A PHALLIC-DESPOTIC SEIZURE—THEY WOULD LABEL AND CLASSIFY IT AS FINITE TRANSCENDENCE. CERTAINLY SOMETHING LIKE THAT IS AT STAKE, AT LEAST AS OPPOSED TO TRANSCENDENCE TOWARD AN ABSOLUTE INFINITE. YET, NIETZSCHE HAS SLAMMED THE DOOR IN THEIR FACES; ZARATHUSTRA WILL NOT EAT AT THEIR TABLE. FOR THE NOTION OF SUBJECT IS NOT ALLUDED TO HERE. RATHER, NIETZSCHE SPEAKS CONCRETELY OF THE FLESHED-OUT, EMBODIED SATYR AS BOTH ARCHETYPE OF MAN AND SYMBOL OF THE SEXUAL POLY-PRESENCE AND RICH POWER OF NATURE. NIETZSCHE STRIKES AT THE HEART OF THAT IDENTITY OF MAN-NATURE TO WHICH DELEUZE AND GUATTARI ALLUDE AS THE ORPHAN WHICH IS THE UNCONSCIOUS. THEY, LIKE NIETZSCHE, SPEAK OF THE DEPTH OF LIBIDINALLY-INVESTED UNCONSCIOUS AND OF SEXUAL IMPULSE AS MORE THAN A PROCREATIVE DEPTH. HENCE, THE UNCONSCIOUS HAS NO PARENTAGE, NO SOURCE GROUND FOR THE METAPHYSICIAN TO STAND UPON, NO DESPOTIC PARENT TO DOMINATE IT. YET, IF DELEUZE AND GUATTARI SEE THEIR WAY TO LIBERATING SEXUAL DISCOURSE FROM ITS MERE FASCINATION AND LIBIDINAL FIXATION UPON THE SACRED FAMILY AND A MERE UTILITY OF PROCREATION, THESE SEEM PERHAPS REPLACED AT THE LEVEL OF THE FIXATION UPON PLEASURE OF DESIRING-MACHINES.

BEYOND THEIR COMPLEX ATTEMPT AT THE FUSION OF VITALISM-MECHAMISM, NIETZSCHE'S PLAYFUL SATYR BECKONS. THE SATYR PLAYS IN THE ARENA OF THE TRAGIC, AN AREA DE-LIMITED, THE PLACE OF MAN'S DESTINY TO BE HIS BODY AND LIVE IN THE WORLD. NIETZSCHE TRANSFORMS THE PLACE OF TRAGEDY INTO THE FULL PLACE OF A LOVE OF THAT DESTINY, A JOY WITH THE WORLD. THE SATYR IS ODDLY THE COMPANION OF THE GOD, REPEATING HIS SUFFERING IN EACH OF MAN'S ATTEMPTS TO ESCAPE HIS BODY AND WORLD, BE OR TOUCH A GOD, REFUSE LOVE OF HIS DESTINY. AS FLESHING-OUT ECSTATICALLY THE HIGHEST EMOTIONS AND FULLEST DESIRES OF MAN, THE SATYR REVELS AND SPEAKS WISDOM FROM WITHIN AND WITHOUT NATURE. MAN IS BOTH WITHIN NATURE, THE WORLD, AND WITHOUT A NATURE, OR FIXED ESSENCE. HIS PLAYFUL, SEXUAL, SYMBOLIC MOVEMENT IS THE TAKING UP AND BEING THE FLESH OF THAT FORCE OF LIFE WHICH IS AT THE BOTTOM OF ALL THINGS, WHICH IS HIS WORLD OF POWER, YET WITHOUT DOMINATION AND REVENGE AGAINST TIME AND DESTINY, AND PLEASURE.

THE PLACE OF NIETZSCHE'S SATYR IS THE PLACE OF LIBIDINAL-SYMBOLIC PLAY. THAT PLAY IS THE WORLD WHICH WE FACE, WHICH FACES US AROUND. IT IS THE PLAY OF THE FLESH OF THE FACE WHICH STARKLY, NAKEDLY, UNABASHEDLY CRIES WITH US, SMILES OR LAUGHS WITH US. IT IS THE PLAY OF SOFT, PLIANT, FLESH—THE CHILD'S UNWORN VOLUPTUOUSNESS; THE SEDUCTIVE GLANCE; THE WRINKLED, TORN MOVEMENT OF AGED LINES TRAVERSING A DISSOLUTION FOUGHT TO THE LAST BY A FIRM DESIRE. THE FACE-PLAY IS HARDLY MASCULINE, HARDLY FEMININE, THE SOFT FUSION POINT OF BOTH. IT IS THE GOAT'S FACE OF MAN, ALL OF US, PAN, ALL. IS NOT PAN APHRODITE'S COMPANION, THE FATHER OF EROS?[18] YET, APHRODITE THREATENS PAN, REMINDING ALL THAT EROS IS THE ABANDONED CHILD OF ALL OF US, FREED FROM THE HORNED DOMINANCE OF AGGRESSION BY THE WINGS OF A FREE PLAY AMONG US. THE HORNED AGGRESSION OF THE DISSOLUTION OF SCHIZOPHRENIC CAPITALISM—THE DISPERSION OF ALL—WOULD SEIZE APHRODITE, VIOLATE HER ABUNDANT RECEPTIVITY AND CREATION AS MOTHER OF EROS, IN ORDER TO MANAGE AND CONTROL HER CHILD. EROS FLOATS FREELY, PLAYFULLY; FLEEING, YET EVEN TOUCHING THE SOURCE OF THE THREAT. THE NOURISHING, RECEPTIVE, FLESH AND FACE OF APHRODITE BESPEAK THE OFTEN FORGOTTEN PLAY OF OUR PLACE; THE AMBIVALENT DESIRE AND VIOLENCE OF PAN'S EMBODIMENT SHRIEK OUR PREDICAMENT IN THE TIME OF SCULPTURE BECOME MACHINE. EROS TOUCHES BOTH, COMPLETING A CIRCLE, WAITING FOR THE DANCE OF PLAYFUL EMBODIMENT, ALWAYS REMEMBERING THE MOIST, TENDER, FLESH OF HER MOTHER, BORN OUT OF THE CUTTING OFF OF AGGRESSION. THE SATYR MUST BE THE BECOMING OF HIS FLESH, THE FULLNESS OF HIS PLACE, AND THE LOVE OF THAT PLACE. THE PATH TO THAT PLACE IS THE DISCOURSE SOUGHT, HEEDING THE WHISPER OF THE GENTLY FLESH-SCULPTED EROS AMID THE RANTING, SCREAMING, GRATING OF STEELY, CONCRETE, SCHIZOPHRENIC CAPITALISM.

ROBERT VAN RODEN ALLEN

NOTES

1   CF. JACQUES DERRIDA, GLAS (PARIS: EDITIONS GALILÉE, 1974), PP. 286-291 AND P. 7.

2   JEAN-PAUL SARTRE, SAINT GENET-COMÉDIEN ET MARTYR (PARIS: GALLIMARD, 1952 & 1970), P. 390. (EMPHASIS ADDED)

3   IBID., P. 315. (EMPHASIS ADDED)

4   IBID., P. 334.

5   CF. SARTRE, THE EMOTIONS, TRANSLATED BY BERNARD FRECHTMAN (NEW YORK: PHILOSOPHICAL LIBRARY, 1948), P. 6.

6   CF. SARTRE, GENET, P. 662.

7   MICHEL FOUCAULT, HISTOIRE DE LA SEXUALITÉ (PREMIER TOME) LA VOLONTÉ DE SAVOIR (PARIS: GALLIMARD, 1976), P. 16.

8   IBID. P. 49.

9   CF. IBID., PP. 77 & FF.

10 GILLES DELEUZE ET FELIX GUATTARI, L'ANTI-OEDIPE (PARIS: LES EDITIONS DE MINUIT), P. 31.

11 IBID., P. 56 & FF.

12 IBID., P. 57.

[13] FOUCAULT, P. 152.

[14] IBID., P. 181.

[15] CF. FOUCAULT, SURVEILLER ET PUNIR (PARIS: GALLIMARD, 1975).

[16] LETTER OF APRIL 19, 1812 CITED AND TRANSLATED BY MICHAEL HEIM IN HIS PAPER "WHAT IS PHILOSOPHY? -AGAIN?" (THE PENNSYLVANIA STATE UNIVERSITY), P. II-11. (MY EMPHASIS)

[17] FRIEDRICH NIETZSHE, THE BIRTH OF TRAGEDY (AND THE CASE OF WAGNER) TRANS. BY WALTER KAUFMANN (NEW YORK: RANDOM HOUSE, 1961), PP. 59, 61. (EMPHASIS ADDED)

[18] THESE CLOSING REMARKS INSPIRED FROM THE STRIKING "STATUE OF APHRODITE AND PAN" IN THE NATIONAL ARCHAEOLOGICAL MUSEUM OF ATHENS. PHOTOGRAPHIC REPRODUCTION OF THE STATUE IS FOUND IN THE MUSEUM'S PUBLICATION ENTITLED "NATIONAL ARCHAEOLOGICAL MUSEUM OF ATHENS" (ATHENS, GREECE: P. GALLIAS, 1971), PP. 101 & 104.

54. R. TURNS BACK AND RETURNS TO THE LANDING.

55. THE CORPULENT MAN TRIES TO INTERCEPT HER.

56. HOLDING HER BAG AT ARM'S LENGTH, R. HITS THE CORPULENT MAN IN THE FACE.

57. THE CORPULENT MAN PRETENDS TO FALL OVER, KNEELS AND SEIZES R. BY HER ANKLES.

58-60. THE ARM OF THE CORPULENT MAN ROUND THE CALVES OF R.'S LEGS. THE CORPULENT MAN LIFTS R. WHO STRUGGLES, AND THROWS HER OVER HIS SHOULDER.

59. THE HANDS OF THE CORPULENT MAN MOVING UP BEHIND THE KNEES OVER THE SUSPENDER BELT TOWARD R.'S THIGHS AND BUTTOCKS.

61-62. THE CORPULENT MAN CARRIES R. DOWN THE STAIRS TOWARD THE BASEMENT. THE CORPULENT MAN SQUEEZING LEGS OF R. HANGING OVER HIS SHOULDER. R. STRUGGLING AND HITTING HIM WITH HER FISTS—THE BOTTOM OF THE STAIRS IN FRONT OF A DOOR THAT HE KICKS OPEN.

CRITICAL SEX

TO DESTROY SEXUALITY

TO PUT

ALTHOUGH THE CAPITALIST ORDER APPEARS TO BE
TOLERANT, IT IN FACT HAS ALWAYS CONTROLLED
LIFE THROUGH ITS EXPRESSIVE, SEXUAL, EMOTION-
AL AND AFFECTIVE ASPECTS, CONSTRAINING IT TO
THE DICTATES OF ITS TOTALITARIAN ORGANIZATION
BASED ON EXPLOITATION, PRIVATE PROPERTY,
MALE DOMINANCE, PROFIT, AND PROFITABILITY. IT
EXERCISES THIS CONTROL UNDER ALL OF ITS
VARIOUS GUISES: THE FAMILY, SCHOOLS, THE WORK
PLACE, THE ARMY, RULES, DISCOURSE. IT UNFAIL-
INGLY PURSUES ITS ABJECT MISSION OF CASTRAT-
ING, OPPRESSING, TORTURING, AND MANGLING THE
BODY, ALL THE BETTER TO INSCRIBE ITS LAWS UPON
OUR FLESH, TO RIVET INTO OUR UNCONSCIOUS ITS
MECHANISMS FOR PROPAGATING SLAVERY.

THE CAPITALIST STATE USES RETENTION, STASIS,
SCARIFICATION AND NEUROSIS TO IMPOSE ITS
NORMS AND MODELS, IMPRINT ITS CHARACTERS,
ASSIGN ITS ROLES, PROMULGATE ITS PROGRAMS . . .
IT PERMEATES OUR BODIES, FORCING ITS ROOTS OF
DEATH DEEP INTO OUR SMALLEST CREVICES. IT
TAKES OVER OUR ORGANS, ROBS US OF OUR VITAL
FUNCTIONS, MUTILATES OUR PLEASURES, HAR-

NESSES ALL OF OUR "LIFE" PRODUCTIVITY UNDER
ITS OWN PARALYZING ADMINISTRATION. IT TURNS
EACH OF US INTO A CRIPPLE, CUT OFF FROM HIS
OWN BODY, A STRANGER TO HIS OWN DESIRES.

AN END

THE FORCES OF CAPITALIST OCCUPATION CONTIN-
UALLY REFINE THEIR SYSTEM OF AGGRESSION,
PROVOCATION, EXTORTION SO AS TO USE IT ALONG
WITH A MASSIVE REINFORCEMENT OF SOCIAL
TERROR (INDIVIDUAL GUILT) TO REPRESS, EXCLUDE
AND NEUTRALIZE ALL THOSE PRACTICES OF OUR
WILL THAT DON'T REPRODUCE THESE FORMS OF
DOMINATION. AND SO THIS THOUSAND-YEAR-OLD
REIGN OF UNHAPPY GRATIFICATION, SACRIFICE,
RESIGNATION, CODIFIED MASOCHISM AND DEATH
PERPETUATES ITSELF. HERE REIGNS CASTRATION,
REDUCING THE "SUBJECT" TO A GUILT-RIDDEN,
NEUROTIC, INDUSTRIOUS BEING, LITTLE MORE THAN
A MANUAL LABORER. THIS OLD ORDER, REEKING OF
ROTTING BODIES, IS INDEED HORRIFYING, BUT IT HAS
FORCED US TO DIRECT THE REVOLUTIONARY
STRUGGLE AGAINST CAPITALIST OPPRESSION

THERE WHERE IT IS MOST DEEPLY ROOTED—IN THE LIVING FLESH OF OUR OWN BODY.

TO THE

WE WANT TO FREE THE SPACE—THE CONTEXT, THE LOCUS—OF THE BODY AND ITS OWN SPECIFIC DESIRES FROM THIS "FOREIGN" GRIP. IT IS ALONG THIS "PATH" THAT WE PROPOSE TO "WORK" TOWARDS THE LIBERATION OF SOCIAL SPACE. THERE IS NO SEPARATION BETWEEN THE TWO: I OPPRESS MYSELF BECAUSE THIS "I" IS THE PRODUCT OF A SYSTEM OF OPPRESSION OPERATING ACROSS ALL FORMS OF EXPERIENCE.

A "REVOLUTIONARY CONSCIOUSNESS" IS NOTHING BUT A CHIMERA AS LONG AS IT REMAINS OUTSIDE OF A "REVOLUTIONARY BODY," A BODY WHICH GENERATES ITS OWN FREEDOM.

HERE WE FIND WOMEN, REVOLTING AGAINST THE MALE POWER THAT HAS BEEN INSEMINATED IN THEIR BODIES FOR CENTURIES; HOMOSEXUALS, REVOLTING AGAINST THE TERRORIZING FASCISM OF NORMALITY; ADOLESCENCE, REVOLTING AGAINST THE PATHOLOGICAL AUTHORITY OF ADULTS. THEY HAVE BEGUN, COLLECTIVELY, TO OPEN UP THE BODY'S SPACE TO SUBVERSION AND TO OPEN UP THE SPACE OF SUBVERSION TO THE "IMMEDIATE NEEDS OF THE BODY."

HERE WE FIND PEOPLE BEGINNING TO QUESTION AND INVESTIGATE THE VARIOUS MODES BY WHICH DESIRE IS PRODUCED, THE LINKS BETWEEN JOUISSANCE—THE HEIGHT OF COGNITIVE AND SEXUAL FULFILLMENT—AND POWER, BETWEEN THE BODY AND SUBJECT AS CONSCIOUSNESS, AS THEY EXIST EVERYWHERE THROUGHOUT CAPITALIST SOCIETY, EVEN AMONG RADICAL GROUPS.

SLAUGHTER OF

HERE WE FIND PEOPLE WHO HAVE SHORT-CIRCUITED THE HACKNEYED SEPARATION BETWEEN "POLITICS" AND LIVED EXPERIENCE, A SEPARATION BRINGING GENEROUS RETURNS TO THE MANAGERS OF OUR BOURGEOIS SOCIETY AS WELL AS TO THOSE WHO PRETEND TO REPRESENT THE MASSES AND TO SPEAK IN THEIR NAME.

HERE WE FIND PEOPLE PREPARING A GREAT UPRISING OF LIFE AGAINST ALL OF THE MANIFESTATIONS OF DEATH WHICH CONTINUALLY INSINUATE THEMSELVES INTO OUR BODY, EVER MORE SUBTLY BINDING OUR ENERGIES, DESIRES, REALITY TO THE IMPERATIVES OF THE ESTABLISHED ORDER. THEY FORM THE CONTOURS OF A NEW FISSURE, A MORE RADICAL AND DEFINITIVE CONFRONTATION, ACCORDING TO WHICH THESE REVOLUTIONARY FORCES ARE "NECESSARILY" ARRANGING THEMSELVES.

THE BODY

WE CAN NO LONGER STAND BY IDLY WHILE WE ARE ROBBED OF OUR MOUTHS, OUR ANUSES, OUR SEXUAL MEMBERS, OUR GUTS, OUR VEINS ... JUST SO THEY CAN TURN THEM INTO PARTS FOR THEIR IGNOMINIOUS MACHINE WHICH PRODUCES CAPITAL, EXPLOITATION AND THE FAMILY.

WE CAN NO LONGER STAND BY IDLY WHILE THEY CONTROL, REGULATE AND OCCUPY OUR MUCOUS MEMBRANES, THE PORES OF OUR SKIN, THE ENTIRE SENTIENT SURFACE OF OUR BODY.

WE CAN NO LONGER STAND BY IDLY WHILE THEY USE OUR NERVOUS SYSTEM AS A RELAY IN THE SYSTEM OF CAPITALIST, FEDERAL, PATRIARCHAL EXPLOITATION, NOR WHILE THEY USE OUR BRAIN AS A MEANS OF PUNISHMENT PROGRAMMED BY AMBIENT POWER.

WE CAN NO LONGER NOT "COME" OR HOLD BACK OUR SHIT, OUR SALIVA, OUR ENERGY ACCORDING TO THEIR LAWS WITH THEIR MINOR, TOLERATED INFRACTIONS. WE WANT TO EXPLODE THE FRIGID, INHIBITED, MORTIFIED BODY THAT CAPITALISM WANTS SO DESPERATELY TO MAKE OUT OF OUR LIVING BODY.

TO ESCAPE FROM THE SEDENTARY

WANTING THE FUNDAMENTAL FREEDOM TO ENTER INTO THESE REVOLUTIONARY PRACTICES ENTAILS OUR ESCAPING FROM THE LIMITS OF OUR OWN "SELF." WE MUST TURN THE "SUBJECT" WITHIN OURSELVES UPSIDE-DOWN; ESCAPE FROM THE SEDENTARY, FROM THE "CIVILIZED STATE" AND CROSS THE SPACES OF A LIMITLESS BODY; LIVE IN THE WILLFUL MOBILITY BEYOND SEXUALITY, BEYOND

THE TERRITORY AND REPERTORY OF NORMALITY. THIS IS HOW SOME OF US HAVE COME TO FEEL THE VITAL NEED TO FREE OURSELVES "TOGETHER" FROM THE GRIP OF THE FORCES THAT OPPRESS AND REPRESS OUR DESIRES.

WE STRIVE TO TAKE OUR PERSONAL, INTIMATE LIFE EXPERIENCES AND CONFRONT THEM, EXPLORE THEM, LIVE THEM COLLECTIVELY. WE STRIVE TO BREAK DOWN THE CONCRETE WALL THAT SERVES THE DOMINANT SOCIAL ORDER BY SEPARATING BEING FROM APPEARANCE, SPOKEN FROM UN-SPOKEN, PRIVATE FROM SOCIAL.

WE STRIVE TO ELUCIDATE IN COMMON THE MECHANISM BEHIND ATTRACTION, REPULSION, RESISTANCE, ORGASM; TO MAKE CLEAR THE UNIVERSE OF OUR REPRESENTATIONS, FETISHES, OBSESSIONS, PHOBIAS. THE "UNMENTIONABLE" HAS BECOME OUR PREOCCUPATION, OUR MESSAGE, OUR POLITICAL TIME-BOMB SINCE IN THE REALM OF SOCIAL INTERACTION POLITICS EXHIBITS A FUNDAMENTAL WISH TO BE "ALIVE."

WE HAVE DECIDED TO EXPLODE THE UNBEARABLE SECRET THAT POWER USES AGAINST EVERYONE WHOSE LIVES INCLUDE ANY SENSUAL, SEXUAL OR AFFECTIVE INVOLVEMENT WHATSOEVER—THE SAME KIND OF CONTROL IT EXERCISES OVER ANY REAL SOCIAL ACTION THAT PRODUCES OR REPRODUCES FORMS OF OPPRESSION.

TO DESTROY SEXUALITY.

IN ORDER TO EXPLORE MUTUALLY OUR INDIVIDUAL HISTORIES, WE UNDERTOOK TO DETERMINE HOW OUR LIVES AS REFLECTED THROUGH OUR DESIRES WERE ENTIRELY CONTROLLED BY THE BASIC LAWS OF OUR BUREAUCRATIC, BOURGEOIS, AND JUDEO-CHRISTIAN SOCIETY, AND HOW THEY WERE SUBSUMED UNDER ITS RULES OF MAXIMUM PROFITABILITY, SURPLUS VALUE AND REPRODUCE-ABILITY. WE CONFRONTED OUR INDIVIDUAL "EXPERIENCES" BY RECOGNIZING THAT, HOWEVER "FREE" THEY MAY HAVE APPEARED TO US, WE CONTINUALLY CONFORM TO THE STEREOTYPES OF AN OFFICIAL SEXUALITY THAT CONTROLS EVERY SEXUAL EXPERIENCE FROM THE CONJUGAL BED TO THE BORDELLO TO SAY NOTHING OF PUBLIC TOILETS, DISCOS, FACTORIES, CONFESSIONALS, SEX SHOPS, PRISONS, SCHOOLS, SUBWAYS, ETC.

WE'RE NOT CONCERNED WITH SIMPLY BREAKING

DOWN THIS OFFICIAL SEXUALITY AS ONE WOULD BREAK DOWN THE CONDITION OF ONE'S IMPRISON-MENT WITHIN ANY STRUCTURE; WE WANT TO DESTROY IT, TO GET RID OF IT BECAUSE IN THE FINAL ANALYSIS IT FUNCTIONS AS AN INFINITELY REPEATING CASTRATION MACHINE DESIGNED TO REPRODUCE EVERYWHERE AND IN EVERYONE THE UNQUESTIONING OBEDIENCE OF A SLAVE.

"SEXUALITY" IS JUST AS MONSTROUS IN WHAT IT "PERMITS" AS IN WHAT IT RESTRICTS; CLEARLY, "LIBERALIZED" SEXUAL MORES AND THE EXTENTION OF "EROTICISM" THROUGH ADVERTISING TO ALL SOCIAL LIFE STRUCTURED AND CONTROLLED BY THE MANAGERS OF "ADVANCED" CAPITALISM DO NOTHING MORE THAN INCREASE THE EFFICIENCY OF THE "REPRODUCTIVE" FUNCTION OF THE "OFFICIAL" LIBIDO. RATHER THAN REDUCE SEXUAL DISCON-TENT, THESE PRACTICES IN FACT EXTEND THE REALM OF FRUSTRATION AND "LACK" THAT FACILITATES THE TRANSFORMATION OF DESIRE INTO A COMPULSIVE CONSUMERISM AND GUARAN-TEES "THE CREATION OF DEMAND," THE DRIVING POWER BEHIND CAPITALISM'S APOLOGIES. THERE IS NO FUNDAMENTAL DIFFERENCE BETWEEN THE "IMMACULATE CONCEPTION" AND THE PUBLICITY-MINDED PROSTITUTE, BETWEEN CONJUGAL DUTY AND THE "ENLIGHTENED" PROMISCUITY OF THE BOURGEOISIE: THE PROGRESSION IS UNBROKEN. THE SAME RESTRICTIONS APPLY. THE SAME FRAGMENTATION OF THE BODY AS SOURCE OF DESIRE CONTINUES UNABATED. ONLY THE STRA-TEGY CHANGES.

WHAT WE WANT, WHAT WE DESIRE IS TO KICK IN THE FACADE OVER SEXUALITY AND ITS REPRESENTA-TIONS SO THAT WE MIGHT DISCOVER JUST WHAT OUR LIVING BODY IS.

TO GET RID OF PROGRAMMED TRAINING.

WE WANT TO FREE, RELEASE, UNFETTER AND RELIEVE THIS LIVING BODY SO AS TO FREE ALL OF ITS ENERGIES, DESIRES, PASSIONS CRUSHED BY OUR CONSCRIPTIVE AND PROGRAMED SOCIAL SYSTEM.

WE WANT TO BE ABLE TO EXERCISE EACH OF OUR VITAL FUNCTIONS EXPERIENCING THEIR FULL COMPLEMENT OF PLEASURE.

WE WANT TO REDISCOVER SENSATIONS AS BASIC AS THE PLEASURE IN BREATHING THAT HAS BEEN

SMOTHERED BY THE FORCES OF OPPRESSION AND POLLUTION; OR THE PLEASURE IN EATING AND DIGESTING THAT HAS BEEN INTERRUPTED BY THE RHYTHM OF PROFITABILITY AND THE ERSATZ FOOD IT PRODUCES; OR THE PLEASURE IN SHITTING AND PEDERASTY THAT HAS BEEN SYSTEMATICALLY ASSAULTED BY THE CAPITALIST ESTABLISHMENT'S OPINION OF THE SPHINCTER. IT INSCRIBES DIRECTLY UPON THIS FLESH ITS FUNDAMENTAL PRINCIPLES: THE POWER LINES OF EXPLOITATION, THE NEUROSIS OF ACCUMULATION, THE MYSTIQUE OF PROPERTY AND PROPRIETY, ETC. WE WANT TO REDISCOVER THE PLEASURE IN SHAKING OUR-SELVES JOYOUSLY, WITHOUT SHAME, NOT BECAUSE OF NEED OR COMPENSATION, BUT JUST FOR THE SHEER PLEASURE OF SHAKING OURSELVES. WE WANT TO REDISCOVER THE PLEASURES OF VIBRATING, HUMMING, SPEAKING, WALKING, MOVING, EXPRESSING OURSELVES, RAVING, SINGING— FINDING PLEASURE IN OUR BODY IN ALL WAYS POSSIBLE. WE WANT TO REDISCOVER THE PLEA-SURE IN PRODUCING PLEASURE AND IN CREATING— PLEASURE THAT HAS BEEN RUTHLESSLY STRAIGHT-JACKETED BY THE EDUCATIONAL SYSTEM IN CHARGE OF PRODUCING WORKERS-COMMAND CONSUMERS.

TO LIBERATE ENERGIES

WE SEEK TO OPEN OUR BODY TO OTHER BODIES, TO ANOTHER BODY; TO TRANSMIT VIBRATIONS, TO CIRCULATE ENERGIES, TO ARRANGE DESIRES TO THAT EACH IS FREE TO PLAY OUT ITS FANTASIES AN ECSTASIES, SO THAT WE MIGHT LIVE WITHOUT GUILT AND WITHOUT INHIBITING ALL THE SENSUAL INTRA-AND INTERPERSONAL PRACTICES WE NEED SO OUR DAY-TO-DAY REALITY WON'T TURN INTO THE SLOW AGONY THAT CAPITALISM AND BUREAUCRACY PROJECT AS A MODEL EXISTENCE. WE SEEK TO RIP OUT OF OURSELVES THE FESTERING RUMOR OF GUILT THAT FOR THOUSANDS OF YEARS HAS BEEN AT THE ROOT OF ALL OPPRESSION.

OF COURSE, WE REALIZE HOW MANY OBSTACLES WE HAVE TO OVERCOME TO MAKE OUR ASPIRATIONS INTO SOMETHING MORE THAN THE DREAMS OF A SMALL AND MARGINAL MINORITY. WE ARE KEENLY AWARE THAT LIBERATING THE BODY FOR SENSUAL, SEXUAL, AFFECTIVE AND ECSTATIC RELATIONSHIPS IS INSEPARABLY LINKED TO LIBERATING WOMEN AND DESTROYING MALE DOMINANCE AND ROLE MODELS—ESPECIALLY SEXUAL ROLE MODELS. IT IS LIKEWISE LINKED TO DESTROYING ALL FORMS OF OPPRESSION AND "NORMALITY."

WE WANT TO BE RID OF ALL ROLES AND IDENTITIES BASED ON THE PHALLUS.

WE WANT TO BE RID OF SEXUAL SEGREGATION. WE WANT TO BE RID OF THE CATEGORIES OF MAN AND WOMAN, GAY AND STRAIGHT, POSSESSOR AND POSSESSED, GREATER AND LESSER, MASTER AND SLAVE. WE WANT INSTEAD TO BE TRANSSEXUAL, AUTONOMOUS, MOBILE AND MULTIPLE HUMAN BEINGS WITH VARYING DIFFERENCES WHO CAN INTERCHANGE DESIRES, GRATIFICATIONS, ECSTA-CIES, AND TENDER EMOTIONS WITHOUT REFERRING BACK TO TABLES OF SURPLUS VALUE OR POWER STRUCTURES THAT AREN'T ALREADY IN THE RULES OF THE GAME.

WE HAVE BEGUN AND SHALL CONTINUE TO PRODUCE A NEW SOCIETAL REALITY IN WHICH THE GREATEST ECSTACY COMBINES WITH THE GREAT-EST CONSCIOUSNESS. WE HAVE BEGUN WITH THE BODY, WITH THE REVOLUTIONARY BODY, THE PRODUCTIVE SPACE OF "SUBVERSIVE" STRENGTH AND THE EFFECTIVE SPACE OF ALL OPPRESSION. CONSEQUENTLY, WE HAVE REUNITED "POLITICAL" PRACTICE WITH THE REALITY OF THE BODY AND ITS FUNCTIONS BY COLLECTIVELY INVESTIGATING ALL THE VARIOUS MODES OF LIBERATION. THIS IS OUR ONLY CHANCE TO FIGHT AGAINST THE OPPRESSIVE CAPITALIST STATE WHERE IT WORKS DIRECTLY. THIS IS THE ONLY APPROACH THAT CAN TRULY STRENGTHEN US AGAINST A SYSTEM OF DOMINA-TION THAT CONTINUALLY EXPANDS ITS POWERS OF "WEAKENING" AND "MOLDING" THE INDIVIDUAL TO ITS AXIOMS, AFFILIATING HIM TO ITS ORDER OF DOGS.

GUY HOCKENGHEM

TRANSLATED BY TOM GORA

HOW TO MAKE YOURSELF
A BODY WITHOUT ORGANS

ON NOVEMBER 28, 1947 ARTAUD DECLARES WAR ON THE ORGANS; TO HAVE DONE WITH THE JUDGEMENT OF GOD.[1] "FOR YOU CAN TIE ME UP IF YOU WISH, BUT THERE IS NOTHING MORE USELESS THAN AN ORGAN." IT IS NOT JUST RADIOPHONIC EXPERIMENTATION BUT ALSO BIOLOGICAL AND POLITICAL, INCURRING CENSURE AND REPRESSION. BODY AND SOCIUS, POLITICS AND EXPERIMENTATION. YOU WILL NOT BE ALLOWED TO EXPERIMENT IN PEACE.

THE BWO; IT IS ALREADY ON THE WAY AS SOON AS THE BODY HAS HAD ENOUGH OF THE ORGANS AND WANTS TO PUT THEM ASIDE, OR LOSES THEM. IT'S A LONG PROCESSION: THE HYPOCHONDRIAC BODY WHOSE ORGANS HAVE BEEN DESTROYED; ONCE THE DESTRUCTION IS ACCOMPLISHED NOTHING ELSE HAPPENS—"MISS X CLAIMS THAT SHE HAS LOST HER BRAIN, NERVES, CHEST, STOMACH AND BOWELS. ALL SHE HAS LEFT IS THE SKIN AND BONES OF THE DISORGANIZED BODY; THESE ARE HER VERY WORDS[2] THERE IS THE PARANOID BODY, WHOSE ORGANS ARE ATTACKED BY OUTSIDE FORCES AND RESTORED TO OUTSIDE ENERGIES ("HE LIVED FOR A LONG TIME WITHOUT A STOMACH, WITHOUT INTESTINES, ALMOST WITHOUT LUNGS, WITH A TORN OESOPHAGUS, WITHOUT A BLADDER, AND WITH SHATTERED RIBS, HE USED SOMETIMES TO SWALLOW PART OF HIS OWN LARYNX WITH HIS FOOD, ETC. BUT DIVINE MIRACLES ("RAYS") ALWAYS RESTORED WHAT HAD BEEN DESTROYED ..."[3]). THERE IS THE SCHIZO BODY, CARRYING ON AN ACTIVE INTERNAL STRUGGLE AGAINST THE ORGANS, EVEN AT THE COST OF CATATONIA. THERE IS THE DRUGGED BODY, THE EXPERIMENTAL SCHIZO: "THE HUMAN BODY IS SCANDALOUSLY INEFFICIENT. INSTEAD OF A MOUTH AND AN ANUS TO GET OUT OF ORDER WHY NOT HAVE ONE ALL-PURPOSE HOLE TO EAT AND ELIMINATE? WE COULD SEAL UP NOSE AND MOUTH, FILL IN THE STOMACH, MAKE AN AIR HOLE DIRECT INTO THE LUNGS WHERE IT SHOULD HAVE BEEN IN THE FIRST PLACE ..."[4] AND THERE IS THE MASOCHISTIC BODY WHICH CANNOT BE UNDERSTOOD IN TERMS OF PAIN, FOR WHAT IS INVOLVED IS PRIMARILY THE BWO. IT HAS ITSELF SEWN UP BY ITS SADIST OR ITS WHORE—THE EYES, THE ANUS, THE URETHRA, THE BREASTS, THE NOSE SEWN UP, COQUETTISHLY ADDING BUTTONS WITH FOUR HOLES. IT HAS ITSELF SUSPENDED TO STOP THE ORGANS FROM FUNCTIONING, FLAYED AS IF THE ORGANS WERE SKIN DEEP, SODOMIZED, SMOTHERED, DEFECATED IN THE MOUTH SO THAT EVERYTHING IS SEALED TIGHT.

WHY THIS DREARY ARRAY OF SEWN, VITRIFIED, CATATONIZED, ASPIRATED BODIES, IF THE BWO IS ALSO FULL OF GAIETY, ECSTASY, FRISKY DANCING? WHY THESE EXAMPLES THEN, WHY ARE THEY NECESSARY? THEY ARE DEPRESSING EXAMPLES FOR A CHEERFUL HEART, EMPTIED BODIES INSTEAD OF FULL ONES. YOU HAVE DEPLETED YOURSELVES INSTEAD OF FILLING YOURSELF UP. HAVE YOU SHOWN ENOUGH PRUDENCE? PRUDENCE, NOT WISDOM, AS DOSE, AS THE IMMANENT RULE OF EXPERIMENTATION: INJECTIONS OF PRUDENCE. YOU HAVE BEEN DEFEATED IN A GREAT BATTLE.

REREADING HELIOGABALUS AND THE TARAHUMARAS (FOR HELIOGABALUS IS SPINOZA; SPINOZA HELIOGABALUS REVIVED, THE ONE HIDING BEHIND THE TERRIFYING PHILOSOPHER, THE MAD PHILOSOPHER, THE OTHER HIDING UNDER THE GUISE OF THE CHASTE LENS GRINDER. AND A VOYAGE TO THE LAND OF THE TARAHUMARAS IS EXPERIMENTATION, PEYOTE. SPINOZA, HELIOGABALUS AND PEYOTE HAVE THE SAME FORMULA: ANARCHY AND UNITY ARE ONE AND THE SAME THING, NOT AT ALL THE UNITY OF THE ONE, BUT A DEEPER UNITY.).[5] PRECISELY WHAT THE TWO BOOKS OF ARTAUD SAY: FUSIBILITY AS INFINITE ZERO, PLANE OF CONSISTENCY, MATTER WITHOUT GODS; PRINCIPLES, AS FORCES, ESSENCES, SUBSTANCES, ELEMENTS, REMISSIONS, PRODUCTIONS OR REPRODUCTIONS; THE WAYS OF BEING, OR MODALITIES, VIBRATIONS, INTENSITIES, BREATHS, NUMBERS; AND FINALLY THE DIFFICULTY OF ATTAINING THIS WORLD OF CROWNED ANARCHY, IF ONE STAYS AT THE LEVEL OF THE ORGANS—"THE LIVER THAT MAKES THE SKIN YELLOW, THE BRAIN BESIEGED BY SYPHILIS, THE INTESTINE WHICH EXPELS EXCREMENT," AND IF ONE REMAINS TRAPPED WITHIN THE ORGANISM WHICH BLOCKS THE FLOWS AND HOLDS US IN OUR WORLD HERE.

HELIOGABALUS AND SPINOZA ARE ONE AND
    THE SAME THING
  LONG LIVE THE ROSE
HELIOGABALUS AND SPINOZA MAKE THE
    SAME CHOICE
  LONG LIVE THE CROSS
THE CHASTE PHILOSOPHER WITHOUT NEED
    AND THE CRUEL EMPEROR WHICH SHITS
    ALL OVER
  HAVE THE SAME SENSE OF THE CITY
PUTTING ANARCHY IN UNITY AND THE ONE
    IN ANARCHY
  MULTIPLICITY
HOMO, EUNUCH, SADO, MASO, TRANSVESTITE
PANTHE, MODO NATURI SUBSTANTIALIST

BOTH HAVE NOTHING BUT A BODY WITHOUT
    ORGANS
AND THE VIBRATIONS THAT COME OFF IT
PITY FOR WHOEVER SIGNS HIMSELF CAESAR
    THE CRUCIFIED
FOR YOU CANNOT TRUST HIM
SINCE HE DIDN'T EVER
CALL HIMSELF HELIOGABALUS AND SPINOZA.
(SECRET SONG OF THE YOUNG ROSICRUCIANS)

WE GRADUALLY REALIZE THAT THE BWO IS NOT THE OPPOSITE OF THE ORGANS AT ALL. ITS ENEMIES ARE NOT THE ORGANS. THE ENEMY IS THE ORGANISM. THE BWO DOESN'T OPPOSE THE ORGANS, BUT THE ORGANIZATION OF THE ORGANS THAT WE CALL THE ORGANISM. IT IS TRUE THAT ARTAUD WAGES HIS WAR AGAINST THE ORGANS, BUT WHAT HE HAS REALLY HAD IT WITH AND REALLY RESENTS IS THE ORGANISM. THE BODY IS THE BODY. ALONE IT STANDS. AND IN NEED OF NO ORGANS. ORGANISM IT NEVER IS. ORGANISMS ARE ENEMIES OF THE BODY.[6] THE BWO ISN'T OPPOSED TO THE ORGANS, BUT WITH ITS "LEGITIMATE ORGANS" WHICH ARE TO BE COMPOSED AND SET, IT IS OPPOSED TO THE ORGANISM, TO THE ORGANIC ORGANIZATION OF ORGANS. THE JUDGMENT OF GOD, THE SYSTEM OF THE JUDGMENT OF GOD, THE THEOLOGICAL SYSTEM, IS PRECISELY THE OPERATIONS OF HE WHO MAKES AN ORGANISM, AN ORGANIZATION OF THE ORGANS, WHICH WE CALL AN ORGANISM, BECAUSE HE CANNOT BEAR THE BWO, BECAUSE HE HOUNDS IT, RIPS IT OPEN, TO GIVE PRECEDENCE TO THIS DREADFUL THING, THE ORGANISM. THE ORGANISM IS ALREADY PRECISELY THAT, THE JUDGMENT OF GOD, WHICH DOCTORS PROFIT AND TAKE THEIR POWER FROM. THE ORGANISM IS NOT THE BODY AT ALL, NOT THE BWO BUT A STRATUM ON THE BWO, WHICH IS TO SAY A PHENOMENON OF ACCUMULATION, OF COAGULATION, OF SEDIMENTATION WHICH IMPOSES FORMS AND FUNCTIONS ON IT, RELATIONS AND HIERARCHICAL AND DOMINANT ORGANIZATIONS, TRANSCENDENCIES ORGANIZED FOR THE PURPOSE OF USEFUL WORK. "BIND ME IF YOU WILL." WE NEVER STOP BEING STRATIFIED. BUT WHO IS THIS WE, WHICH IS NOT ME, SINCE THE SUBJECT BELONGS TO A STRATUM AND DEPENDS ON IT NO LESS THAN THE ORGANISM? WE NOW ANSWER: IT IS THE BWO, THAT GLACIAL REALITY ON WHICH THESE ALLUVIONS, SEDIMENTATIONS, COAGULATIONS, PLICATIONS AND COMPRESSIONS WHICH MAKE UP AN ORGANISM—AND A SIGNIFICATION AND A SUBJECT—OCCUR. THIS IS WHAT ENDURES: THE JUDGMENT OF GOD WHICH WEIGHS AND EXERCISES ITS WILL ON IT. IT'S WITHIN IT THAT THE ORGANS ARE COMPOSED INTO WHAT WE CALL AN ORGANISM. THE BWO HOWLS: "THEY'VE MADE ME AN ORGANISM! THEY HAVE BROKEN ME UNDULY!"

THE JUDGMENT OF GOD TEARS IT FROM ITS IMMANENCE AND MAKES IT AN ORGANISM, A SIGNIFICATION, A SUBJECT. IT IS THE STRATIFIED. AS A RESULT IT OSCILLATES BETWEEN TWO POLES, THE SURFACES OF STRATIFICATION UPON WHICH IT FALLS BACK AND YIELDS TO JUDGMENT AND THE PLANE OF CONSISTENCY IN WHICH IT UNFOLDS AND OPENS ITSELF TO EXPERIMENTATION. AND IF THE BWO IS A LIMIT, IF ONE IS NEVER THROUGH ATTAINING IT, IT'S BECAUSE THERE IS ALWAYS ANOTHER STRATUM BEHIND THE FIRST ONE, ONE STRATUM EMBEDDED IN ANOTHER. FOR IT TAKES MANY STRATA, AND NOT JUST OF THE ORGANISM, TO MAKE UP THE JUDGMENT OF GOD. THERE IS A PERPETUAL AND VIOLENT STRIFE BETWEEN THE PLANE OF CONSIS-TENCY, WHICH FREES THE BWO, RUNS THROUGHOUT AND UNDOES ALL THE STRATA AND THE SURFACES OF STRATIFICATIONS WHICH BLOCK IT, BIND IT OR FOLD IT BACK.

THERE IS NO MASOCHIST, DRUGGED, ALCOHOLIC BWO WHICH DOESN'T CONFRONT THIS PROBLEM AND THERE IS NO GENERAL SOLUTION, LIFE OR DEATH: AN OEDIPAL GREED—WHETHER ONE ABSORBS ALCOHOL, ACID OR CRACKS OF THE WHIP. YOU DON'T GO AT IT WITH A HAMMER BUT WITH A VERY FINE FILE. SELF DESTRUCTION, YES, DEATH INSTINCT, NO. TO UNDO THE ORGANISM HAS NEVER MEANT TO KILL YOURSELF, BUT TO OPEN THE BODY TO CONNECTIONS WHICH PRESUPPOSE A WHOLE PERFECT ARRANGEMENT, CIRCUITS, CONJUNC-TIONS, TIERS AND THRESHOLDS, PASSAGES AND DISTRIBUTIONS OF INTENSITIES, TERRITORIES AND MEASURED DETERRITORIALIZATIONS REMINISCENT OF KAFKA'S SURVEYOR. WHAT COULD BE MORE DANGEROUS THAN AN INTENSITY, BUT ALSO WHAT COULD BE MORE AMOROUS? MAKE PRUDENCE THE POLITICAL-EXPERIMENTAL VIRTUE, THE POWER OR POTENTIALITY OF THE BWO. THE VIRTUE OF LOVING. LET EVERYONE INVENT HIS OWN PRUDENCE, SOMETHING THE OPPOSITE OF MISTRUST, RESENT-MENT AND GLUTTONY ALL TOGETHER. ONLY I CAN KNOW IF I AM DRUNK, SAID THE CONSUL. AGAINST THE BASE ASSERTIONS OF PSYCHOANALYSIS (TO FIND YOURSELF, LOOK INTO YOUR CHILDHOOD) WE SAY: YOU DON'T KNOW WHAT YOU ARE AND YOU'LL ONLY KNOW BY EXPERIMENTING, GENTLE EXPERI-MENTATION, IF YOU ARE CAPABLE OF IT. NO ONE CAN SAY "I AM A MASOCHIST," NO ONE CAN SAY "I AM A HOMOSEXUAL," NO ONE CAN SAY "I AM A DRUG ADDICT." SOMEONE, SOMETHING AWAITS US, BUT WHAT? IT MIGHT BE SOMETHING ELSE, ONE CAN'T TELL IN ADVANCE, ONE DOESN'T KNOW IN RETROSPECT, ONE DOESN'T EVEN KNOW AT THE TIME. EXPERIMENTATION, SEARCH FOR THE BWO.

AND THEN, THERE'S ANOTHER THING: DON'T THINK THAT UNDOING THE ORGANISM IS PARTICULARLY DIFFICULT, ANY MORE DIFFICULT THAN UNDOING THE OTHER STRATA, SIGNIFICANCE AND SUBJECTI-VATION. SIGNIFICANCE AND INTERPRETATION AS CLOSE CLING TO THE SOUL AS THE ORGANISM DOES TO THE BODY. YOU DON'T GET RID OF THEM SO EASILY EITHER. AND THE SUBJECT—HOW IS IT POSSIBLE TO UNHINGE THE POINTS OF SUBJECTI-VATION WHICH FIX US, NAIL US TO A DOMINANT REALITY? TEAR THE CONSCIOUSNESS FROM THE SUBJECT TO MAKE IT A MEANS OF EXPLORATION, VOYAGE, TEAR THE UNCONSCIOUS FROM SIGNIFICANCE AND INTERPRETATION TO MAKE A TRUE PRODUCTION OUT OF IT. THE OBJECT OF A PRODUCTION—PRODUCE THE UNCONSCIOUS!—THIS IS CERTAINLY NO MORE NO LESS DIFFICULT THAN TEARING THE BODY FROM THE ORGANISM. PRUDENCE IS THE ART COMMON TO ALL THREE; AND IF IT HAPPENS THAT ONE BRUSHES AGAINST DEATH IN UNDOING THE ORGANISM, ONE ALSO DANCES ON THE EDGE OF FALSEHOOD, THE ILLUSORY, THE HALLUCINATORY, PSYCHIC DEATH BY AVOIDING MEANING AND INTERPRETATION WHICH ARE STRANGE SAFE-GUARDS AGAINST MADNESS. AND ONE RISKS UNREALITY AS SOON AS ONE LEAVES THE DOMINANT REALITY TO BECOME A NOMAD IN THE MASKED ONE. ARTAUD CAREFULLY MEASURES AND WEIGHS HIS WORDS: CONSCIOUSNESS "KNOWS WHAT IS GOOD FOR IT AND WHAT DOES IT HARM; AND THEREFORE IT KNOWS WHAT THOUGHTS AND FEELINGS IT CAN PROFITABLY ACCEPT, WITHOUT DANGER, AND WHICH ARE INJURIOUS TO ITS FREEDOM. ABOVE ALL, IT KNOWS JUST HOW FAR ITS BEING EXTENDS, HOW FAR IT HASN'T GONE YET OR HASN'T THE RIGHT TO GO WITHOUT FALLING INTO UNREALITY, THE ILLUSORY, THE UN-MADE, THE UN-PREPARED ... A PLANE WHICH NORMAL CONSCIOUS-NESS NEVER ATTAINS BUT WHICH CIGURI ALLOWS US TO REACH, AND WHICH IS THE VERY MYSTERY OF ALL POETRY. BUT THERE IS ANOTHER LEVEL IN THE HUMAN BEING, AN OBSCURE, FORMLESS ONE, WHERE CONSCIOUSNESS HASN'T ENTERED BUT WHICH SURROUNDS IT LIKE AN UNELUCIDATED EXTENSION, OR A THREAT, DEPENDING ON THE CASE, AND WHICH ALSO RELEASES ADVENTUROUS SENSATIONS AND PERCEPTIONS. THESE ARE THE SHAMELESS FANTASIES WHICH AFFECT THE SICK CONSCIOUSNESS. I, TOO, HAVE HAD FALSE SENSATIONS, FALSE PERCEPTIONS, AND HAVE BELIEVED IN THEM."[7]

IT IS NECESSARY TO RETAIN ENOUGH OF THE ORGANISM SO THAT IT CAN RECONSTITUTE ITSELF AT EACH NEW DAWN, AND TO KEEP A SMALL SUPPLY

OF MEANING AND INTERPRETATION, EVEN TO OPPOSE THEM TO THEIR OWN SYSTEM, FOR THOSE TIMES WHEN CIRCUMSTANCES REQUIRE IT, WHEN THINGS, PEOPLE, EVEN SITUATIONS FORCE YOU TO IT. AND ONE MUST KEEP SMALL RATIONS OF SUBJECTIVITY ON ONE'S DONKEY MASK IN ORDER TO BE ABLE TO COPE WITH THE DOMINANT REALITY. BE POLITE, ALWAYS BE POLITE. SCHIZO-POLITESSE, THE EXQUISITE POLITENESS OF HÖLDERLIN. BE CEREMONIOUS. MIME THE STRATA. IN SHORT, ONE DOESN'T ATTAIN THE BWO AND ITS PLANE OF CONSISTENCY BY WILDLY DESTRATIFYING ONESELF. THIS IS EVEN THE REASON WHY WE ENCOUNTER THE PARADOX OF THE LUGUBRIOUS AND EMPTIED BODIES AT THE BEGINNING: THEY HAD EMPTIED THEMSELVES OF THEIR ORGANS INSTEAD OF LOOKING FOR THE MOMENTS WHEN THEY COULD PATIENTLY AND TEMPORARILY UNDO THIS ORGANI-ZATION OF THE ORGANS WHICH WE CALL THE ORGANISM; THEY HAD FALLEN, SWIRLING, IN AN EXCESS OF SIGNIFICANCE AND INTERPRETATION, RUNNING AIMLESSLY OR, ON THE CONTRARY, IN A DODDERING STUPOR (FOR NOTHINGNESS IS STILL THE SUPREME SIGNIFIER, JUST AS SILENCE IS THE GREATEST VACANT INTERPRETATION) INSTEAD OF REPLACING THEM BY THE CIRCUMSTANTIAL ART OF AN EXPERIMENTAL POSITIVISM; THEY HAD LOST THEIR EGOS, WHICH THEY THEN SOUGHT FOR ALL THE HARDER AND MORE DESPERATELY (FOR PITY'S SAKE, GIVE ME BACK SOME MOORINGS!) SINCE THEY DIDN'T KNOW HOW TO PAY OUT THEIR NOMADIC DEPERSONALIZATION, EITHER WITHIN THEMSELVES OR WITHOUT. THERE ARE IN FACT MANY WAYS TO MISS THE BWO. EITHER ONE DOESN'T MANAGE TO PRODUCE IT, OR, HAVING PRODUCED IT SOMEWHAT, NOTHING HAPPENS UP ON IT—THE INTENSITIES DON'T CIRCULATE OR GET BLOCKED. THIS ON ACCOUNT OF THE BWO IS CONSTANTLY OSCILLAT-ING BETWEEN THE SURFACES WHICH STRATIFY IT AND THE PLANE WHICH LIBERATES IT. IF YOU RELEASE IT THROUGH TOO VIOLENT A GESTURE, BREAK UP THE STRATA WITHOUT PRUDENCE, YOU WILL HAVE KILLED YOURSELF, YOU WILL HAVE MISSED THE PLANE. (THERE IS NOTHING BUT THE PLAN, THE PROGRAM, SAID THE MILITARY MAN KLEIST TO HIS YOUNGER SISTER ULRIKE, WHO HE FELT GAVE HERSELF OVER TO HER FANTASIES TOO EASILY.) THE SAME MULTIPLE HORROR IS INVOLVED IN STAYING STRATIFIED—EITHER YOU REMAIN A PRISONER OF YOUR ORGANISM, THE ORGANISM AND ITS DOCTORS, SUBJECT TO SIGNIFICANCE, SIGNIFI-CANCE AND ITS PSYCHOANALYST, ENSNARED IN ITS RECEDENCE, BOUND TO THE DOMINANT REALITY—AND YOU DON'T EVEN FEEL IT: ONE CAN LIVE LIKE THAT AND BE CONTENT WITH ONESELF, HALF DEAD AMONG THE SYMBOLS OF POWER AND THE ICONS OF

FORCE—OR ELSE YOU DISINTEGRATE IN A SUICIDAL OR MAD BREAKDOWN AND DISRUPT THE STRATA WHICH FALL BACK DOWN ON YOU ALL THE HARDER—HOSPITAL OR CEMETERY. WHAT YOU ACTUALLY HAVE TO DO IS THIS: SITUATE YOURSELF ON A CERTAIN STRATUM, EXPERIMENT WITH THE OPPOR-TUNITIES IT OFFERS YOU, LOOK FOR A PROPITIOUS SPOT, POSSIBLE MOMENTS OF DETERRITORIALIZA-TION AND LINES OF RECEDENCE, EXPERIENCE THEM, SECURE CERTAIN CONNECTIONS OF FLOWS HERE AND THERE, TRY OUT CONTINUA OF INTENSI-TIES LITTLE BY LITTLE, ALWAYS KEEPING A SMALL PIECE OF NEW TERRITORY AVAILABLE. IT IS IN A RELATION, ACCORDING TO A METICULOUS RELATION WITH THE STRATA THAT ONE SUCCEEDS IN OPENING UP CHANNELS OF RECEDENCE AND MAKING COMBINATIONS OF FLOWS PASS THROUGH AND ESCAPE, THAT ONE MANAGES TO RELEASE CONTINUOUS INTENSITIES FOR A BWO. CONNECT, COMBINE, CONTINUE. WE ARE IN A SOCIAL FORMA-TION: SEE, FIRST OF ALL, HOW IT IS STRATIFIED FOR US, IN US IN THE VERY PLACE WHERE WE ARE; RELATE THE STRATA TO THE DEEPER COLLECTIVE MACHINIC SET-UP IN WHICH WE ARE TRAPPED; OVERTURN THE SET-UP VERY GENTLY, BRING IT IN TOUCH WITH THE PLACE OF CONSISTENCY ON THE OTHER SIDE OF THE STRATA. ONLY THEN DOES THE BWO REVEAL ITSELF FOR WHAT IT IS, CONNECTION OF DESIRES, CONJUNCTION OF FLOWS, CONTINUUM OF INTENSITIES.

THERE IS A BWO OF CAPITALISM, CANCEROUS BURGEONING MONEY, MONEY PRODUCING MONEY, CAPITAL ITSELF WITH ITS EXPANSIVE-INFLATION SUBJECTIVATION; CAPITALISM MUST CONTROL IT, ORIENT IT, KEEP IT STRATIFIED FOR ITS OWN "HEALTH", ITS OWN "ORGANISM". EVEN WHEN WE CONSIDER A PARTICULAR SOCIAL FORMATION, OR A PARTICULAR STRATIFYING MECHANISM IN A FORMATION, WE CAN SAY THAT EACH AND EVERY ONE HAS ITS BWO READY TO CORRODE, TO PROLIFERATE, TO COVER AND INVADE THE TOTALITY OF THE SOCIAL FIELD, ENTERING IN RELATION OF VIOLENCE AND RIVALRY AS WELL AS ALLIANCES AND COMPLICITIES WITH OTHER FORMATIONS, OTHER MECHANISMS AND THEIR BWOS. THE BWO OF CAPITALISM WHICH EITHER FINDS OR DOESN'T FIND ITS REGULATION IN THE STATE, BUT ALSO THE BWO OF THE STATE WHICH EITHER FINDS OR DOESN'T FIND ITS REGULATION IN INTERMEDIARY BODIES, WHICH THEMSELVES FURNISH BWOS. A BWO OF THE ARMY TAKES OVER THE STATE, ABSORBS EVERYTHING IN ITS TUMOR, ITS CANCEROUS CELLS PROLIFERATING EVERY-WHERE, IN EVERY FACTORY, EVERY SCHOOL, EVERY HOUSEHOLD. CHILE: WE HAVE THE MOST DEMO-

CRATIC ARMY IN THE WORLD, SAID THE CHILEAN. IT HAS EARS FOR THE PEOPLE AND EYES FOR THE CONSTITUTION. BUT THE BWO OF CAPITAL INFLATION BREAKS OUT ALL THE MORE VIOLENTLY WHEN THE AIM IS TO BRING DOWN A SOCIALIST GOVERNMENT: THE ARMY LOSES ITS EARS AND ITS EYES, UNLEASHES, IN ITS TURN A BWO THAT DESTROYS THE GOVERNMENT, TAKES OVER THE STATE TO RESTORE AN "ORGANIC AND HEALTHY" CAPITALISM FROM THE DEPTHS OF UTTER TERROR. COMPLEXITY OF ALLIANCES AND RIVALRIES: NAZISM FOR INSTANCE—DON'T JUST THINK OF THE GENERAL RELATION BETWEEN NAZISM AND CAPITALISM, BUT REMEMBER THE BWO OF NAZISM AND THE RAVING BWO OF GERMAN CAPITALISM BEFORE THE NAZI TAKEOVER, CONSIDER HOW THE NAZI BWO RECONSTITUTES CAPITAL'S "ORGANISM" IN GERMANY, HOW NAZISM ORGANIZES ITSELF BY UNLEASHING A BWO OF THE ARMY DISTINCT FROM THE BWO OF THE PARTY, ETC.—THERE IS A BWO OF THE FAMILY, THE SCHOOL, THE FACTORY, THE CITY, ETC.—THE ONES OPERATING IN RELATION TO THE OTHERS, INTERLOCKED WITHIN EACH OTHER, CREATING STRANGE ALLIANCES AND RIVALRIES. (THERE IS A BWO OF PSYCHOANALYSIS: THE PSYCHOANALYST HIMSELF, WITHOUT EYES, WITHOUT EARS, AND WITHOUT A MOUTH, A CANCER OF INTERPRETATION, INTERMINABLE ANALYSIS, AN INFINITY OF WORDS FOR AN INFINITE AMOUNT OF MONEY, SILENCE AS THE SUPREME INTERPRETATION, PROLIFERATION IN AN INCREASINGLY ASPHYXIATING PSYCHOSOMATIC CIRCUIT.) IN SHORT, WE BELIEVE THAT THE STRATA THEMSELVES ENGENDER BWOS. IF THE STRATA ARE A MATTER OF COAGULATION, OF SEDIMENTATION UPON THE BWO, ALL A STRATUM NEEDS IS A QUICK SEDIMENTATION TO FORM ITS SPECIFIC TUMOR WITHIN ITSELF, OR IN A CERTAIN FORMATION OF PARTICULAR APPARATUS: THE BWO OF THE STRATUM, WHICH IS STILL PART OF THE JUDGMENT OF GOD. EVERY STRATUM HAS ITS HOLES, ITS LINES OF RECEDENCE AND MOVEMENTS OF DETERRITORIALIZATION. TO BE SWALLOWED UP IN THESE HOLES, NOT IN ORDER TO REACH THE DESTRATIFIED PLANE OF CONSISTENCY BUT IN ORDER TO PLUG THEM, CLOSE THEM OFF, NOT IN ORDER TO UNDO THE STRATA WITH THE NECESSARY PRECAUTIONS BUT TO SHUT THEM UP AGAIN, EVEN TO THE POINT OF REMOVING THEIR FORM AND ARTICULATION—NOT TO MAKE "OTHER" CONNECTIONS AND COMBINATIONS POSSIBLE BUT, ON THE CONTRARY, TO ENSURE THE PROLIFERATION OF THE SAME, BLIND SCARRING, NAZI ECONOMY—NOT TO DISCOVER THE MACHINIC POTENTIAL OF DESIRE BUT TO ENSURE THE CLOSED HOLD AND POWER OF A MECHANISTIC DESIRE: SUCH ARE THE CANCEROUS OR FASCISTIC BWOS, TERRIFYING CARICATURES OF THE PLANE OF CONSISTENCY AND YET NO LESS BWO THAN THE OTHERS.

IT IS THROUGH THE BWO THAT ONE DESIRES. THERE IS DESIRE EVERY TIME THERE IS BWO OF ONE KIND OR ANOTHER. DEATH INSTINCT, YES, DESIRE EVEN INCLUDES THAT IN THE EMPTIED BWOS, AS IT DOES THE ABOLITION OF DESIRE IN CANCEROUS BWOS. HOW DOES DESIRE MANAGE TO DESIRE ITS OWN REPRESSION? HOW CAN DESIRE, THE MACHINIST, MAKE ITSELF MECHANISTIC DESIRE OF THE PROLIFERATION OF THE SAME? CERTAINLY IT IS NOT A QUESTION OF IDEOLOGY, FALSE CONSCIOUSNESS, LIES, ERROR, OR SUPERSTITION. THE BWO HAS NOTHING TO DO WITH IDEOLOGY: PURE MATTER, IT IS A PHENOMENON OF PHYSICAL, BIOLOGICAL, PSYCHICAL AND SOCIAL MATTER. DESIRE IS MATERIAL. ALL DESIRE IS DESIRE OF BWO, BWO OF MONEY, BWO OF THE STATE, BWO OF THE ARMY, BWO OF THE PARTY, BWO OF THE FAMILY, YES, ALL THAT CAN BE DESIRED, HAS BEEN, IS AND WILL BE. FASCISM IS DESIRE, CANCER IS DESIRE. THE ARMY DESIRES ITS BWO. THE POLICE DESIRE ITS BWO. THE STATE DESIRES ITS BWO. THE FAMILY DESIRES ITS BWO. DESIRE WENDS ITS WAY THROUGH THE DANGERS: IT CANNOT WARD OFF THE EMPTIED AND CANCEROUS BODIES WHICH SUMMON IT, EXCEPT BY REACHING THE PLANE OF CONSISTENCY WHICH DISSOLVES THEM AS IF IN ACID.

GILLES DELEUZE AND FELIX GUATTARI
TRANSLATED BY SUZANNE GUERLAC

NOTES

[1] TO HAVE DONE WITH THE JUDGMENT OF GOD. SEMIOTEXT(E), VOL. II, NO. 3, 1977, P. 61.

[2] JULES COTARD: ÉTARD SUR LES MALADIES CÉRÉBRALES ET MENTALES, BRAILLIÈRE, 1891. COTARD STRESSES THE DIFFERENCE BETWEEN HYPOCHONDRIAC DELIRIUM AND PARANOID DELIRIUM FROM SEVERAL POINTS OF VIEW: THE HYPOCHONDRIAC EXPERIENCES, HIS ORGANS ARE DEFINITIVELY DESTROYED WITHOUT ANY POSSIBLE RESTORATION EXCEPT BY SIMULACRUM: HE MONOLOGUES AND ACCUSES HIMSELF INSTEAD OF ENTERING INTO A DIALOGUE WITH MORE OR LESS IMAGINARY INTERLOCUTORS OR PERSECUTORS; HE IS NEGATI-

VISTIC (WITHOUT NAME, AGE, ORGANS, ORGANISM, SOUL, WITHOUT GOD) WHEREAS THE PARANOIAC IS A "GREAT ONTOLOGIST".

3   DR. SCHRIBER'S MEMOIRS, QUOTED BY S. FREUD, "NOTES ON A CASE OF PARANOIA", S.E., XII, P. 17.

4   WILLIAM BURROUGHS, NAKED LUNCH, NEW YORK: GROVE PRESS, 1959, P. 131.

5   ANTONIN ARTAUD, HELIOGABALUS, OR THE ANARCHIST CROWNED IN SELECTED WRITINGS, NEW YORK: FARRAR, STRAUS AND GIROUX, 1976. AND YET HERE, CONCERNING HELIOGABALUS, ARTAUD STILL PRESENTS US THE IDENTITY OF THE ONE AND THE MANY AS A DIALECTICAL UNITY, AND ONE WHICH "REDUCES" THE MULTIPLICITY IN "BRINGING IT BACK" TO THE ONE. HE MAKES HELIOGABALUS SOME KIND OF HEGELIAN. HE DOESN'T SEE THE MULTIPLICITY AS GOING BEYOND ALL OPPOSITION FROM THE BEGINNING, AND ABOVE ALL CANCELING ANY SUCH QUESTION, ANY DIALECTICAL MOVEMENT FROM THE BEGINNING.

6   ANTONIN ARTAUD, "THE BODY IS THE BODY," SEMIOTEXT(E), OP. CIT., P. 59.

7   ARTAUD, A VOYAGE TO THE LAND OF TARAHUMARAS, SELECTED WRITINGS, OP. CIT.

FRONTIERS BROKEN

HOLLY GOLIGHTLY MEETS THE WILD BOYS, OR WAS IT MELINA MERCOURI? "NEGRO STREETS AT DOWN, OR NOT," SHE SAID, ADJUSTING HER DARK GLASSES, "VAGINAS UNDER EVERY ARM."

MISTER MARGULIES.

DEFUNKT SEX

"AT ORGASM, THE GRIMACE AND CONTORTION OF A WOMAN'S FACE GRAPHICALLY EXPRESS THE INCREMENT OF MYOTONIC TENSION THROUGHOUT THE ENTIRE BODY. THE MUSCLES OF THE NECK AND THE LONG MUSCLES OF THE ARM AND LEGS USUALLY CONTRACT INTO INVOLUNTARY SPASM . . . THE PHYSIOLOGICAL ONSET OF ORGASM IS SIGNALED BY CONTRACTIONS OF THE TARGET ORGANS, STARTING WITH THE ORGASMIC PLATFORM IN THE OUTER THIRD OF THE VAGINA . . . ORGASMIC CONTRACTIONS OF THE UTERUS HAVE BEEN RECORDED BY BOTH INTRAUTERINE AND ABDOMINALLY PLACED ELECTRODES. BOTH TECHNIQUES INDICATE THAT THE UTERINE CONTRACTIONS HAVE ONSET ALMOST SIMULTANEOUSLY WITH THOSE OF THE ORGASMIC PLATFORM . . ."

CAMERA IN HAND, ELECTRODES IN POSITION, MASTERS AND JOHNSON, YOUR INTREPID REPORTERS, ARE ON THE SCENE, MEASURING AND RECORDING THE ACTION. THIS IS, THEY CLAIM IN THE PREFACE OF THEIR STUDY, HUMAN SEXUAL RESPONSE, "A FIRST STEP TOWARD AN OPEN-DOOR POLICY."

SEX, AT LAST, IS WIDE OPEN.

THE PATIENT IS WAITING IN KNEE-CHEST POSITION. ELECTRICALLY POWERED PLASTIC PENISES ARE READY FOR ACTION. THEY HAVE BEEN ADJUSTED TO HER SIZE. AND THEY NEVER FAIL.

THEY ARE NOT HUMAN.

THE HUMAN ELEMENT HASN'T ALTOGETHER DISAPPEARED: THE DEPTH AND RATE OF PENILE THRUST IS STILL DETERMINED BY THE INDIVIDUAL'S OWN DEMANDS. AS TENSION ELEVATES, RAPIDITY OF THRUST INCREASES.

THE MACHINE NEVER ORGASMS.

ARTIFICIAL COITAL TECHNIQUES HAVE BEEN VASTLY IMPROVED BY RADIO PHYSICISTS. PLASTIC PENISES FUNCTION AS PLATE GLASS. COLD-LIGHT ILLUMINATION ALLOWS OBSERVATION AND RECORDING WITHOUT DISTORTION. AN IMPARTIAL APPROACH TO HUMAN SEXUAL EXPERIENCE CAN NOW BEGIN.

BUT WHAT DOES AN IMPARTIAL APPROACH DO TO HUMAN SEXUALITY? WHAT DOES IT DO TO APPROACH IT LIKE ANY OTHER PHENOMENON, AND A SEPARATE PHENOMENON AT THAT, IN THE COLD

LIGHT OF THE SEX LAB, THROUGH THE NARROW LENS AND THE PECULIAR ANGLE OF THE PLATE GLASS-LIKE PENIS?

IF WE CAN APPROACH HUMAN SEXUALITY AS A RAT, A DEAD RAT, IT MAY BE THAT EVERYWHERE SEXUALITY IS LOOSING THE PLURALITY OF DIMENSIONS—THE VIOLENCE, THE JOY, THE MYSTERY, THE TERROR, THE EXUBERANCE—THAT HAVE MADE IT A TRULY HUMAN EXPERIENCE.

WE KNOW EVERYTHING ABOUT SEX, AND WE'RE NOT AFRAID TO ASK. BUT IS IT WORTH ASKING WHEN EVERYTHING WE KNOW ABOUT SEX FURTHER OBJECTIFIES IT? ERECTION, CLITORAL STIMULATION, ORAL SEX, PREMATURE EJACULATION, VAGINAL ORGASM, ANAL INTERCOURSE—WE KNOW IT ALL. WE DON'T LOOK AT THE KINSEY REPORT: WE WATCH THE JOHNNY CARSON SHOW.

WE HAVE BECOME VOYEURS OF OUR OWN SEXUAL-ITY. WE DON'T HIDE ANYTHING, ESPECIALLY FROM STRANGERS. WE WELCOME PUBLIC INSPECTION.

YOU WILL NOTICE HERE HOW THE RECTAL SPHINCTER OF THE FEMALE SAMPLE CONTRACTS AND TERMINATES, HOW THE BREASTS' AREOLAE—THIS WAY, PLEASE—RETRACT RAPIDLY AFTER ORGASM WHILE THE SEX FLUSH SUBSIDES AND HYPERVENTILATION GRADUALLY DECREASES . . .

OUR SOCIETY IS SATURATED WITH SEX. BUT IS OUR SEX REALLY SEXUAL?

BY SEXUALITY I DON'T MEAN, OF COURSE, A SIMPLE, "NATURAL" ACTIVITY BUT A COMPLEX PHENOMENON IN WHICH PHYSIOLOGICAL, MENTAL, AND SOCIAL DIMENSIONS CONSTANTLY OVERLAP. EACH CUL-TURE APPROPRIATES SEXUALITY IN ITS OWN WAY, BUT IN NO OTHER SOCIETY HAS SEXUALITY BEEN SO INTIMATELY PERMEATED WITH OR, RATHER, CONSTITUTED BY SOCIAL REPRESENTATIONS.

YANOMANI INDIANS OF VENEZUELA CODIFY SEXUALITY IN TERMS OF KINSHIP, WHICH ARE REPRESENTATIONS IN THEIR OWN RIGHT, BUT THE YANOMANI ARE NOT OBSESSED WITH THEM AS WE ARE. THEY FIND WAYS TO ACCOMMODATE THEIR MOST PRESSING INCLINATIONS, EVEN WHEN THESE DESIRES HAPPEN TO CONTRADICT THE PROHIBITION OF INCEST. LOVERS SIMPLY DECIDE TO "NAME" EACH OTHER DIFFERENTLY . . . THEIR SEXUAL

DESIRE DOESN'T STEM FROM INTERDICTION, NOR IS IT ACCOMPANIED BY GUILT OR SHAME. INDIAN MORALITY STRICTLY BANS SUCH BELATED, "CIVILIZED" REACTIONS. SEXUALITY REMAINS ESSENTIALLY FESTIVE; THE IMPLIED RULE IS "WHATEVER IS PLEASURABLE IS INTRINSICALLY GOOD." [1]

EVERYTHING CHANGES WHEN MAN FALLS PREY TO HIS "CONSCIENCE," BY FAR, AS NIETZSCHE PUTS IT, THE WEAKEST AND LEAST CERTAIN OF OUR ORGANS. MAN-THE-PREDATOR BECOMES THE "PROUD ANIMAL," ALL THE MORE INSECURE ABOUT HIS OWN DOINGS THAT HE KEEPS MEASURING THEM AGAINST A DESPERATELY IDOLIZED VERSION OF HIMSELF. FROM AN ASSERTIVE, CREATIVE ACTION, SEX GRADUALLY TURNS INTO A DOMESTICATED AND NARCISSISTIC REACTION—A TRYING TEST FOR FRAGILE EGOS.

AS SOCIETY MAKES SEXUALITY INTO AN OBJECTIVE, "AUTONOMOUS" FUNCTION, IT ISOLATES THE INDIVIDUAL EVEN FURTHER BY MAKING SEX HIS MOST PRIVATE POSSESSION AND RESPONSIBILITY WHILE RESTITUTING IT PUBLICLY AROUND HIM AS A COLLECTIVE "AMBIANCE."

TODAY SEX'S MAIN FUNCTION IS TO CATER TO THE EGO'S NEEDS, WHICH ARE NOT SO MUCH INSTINCT-UAL AS THEY ARE PROMOTIONAL. SEX, LIKE THE BODY, LIKE EVERYTHING FOR THAT MATTER, IS BEING MARKETED AT THE SAME TIME IT IS BEING "FREED."

PRIMITIVE CULTURES RUTHLESSLY BRAND THE FLESH OF TRIBESMEN TO REMIND THEM WHERE THEY BELONG. WE ARE NOT CRUEL ANY MORE—GOD FORBID—BUT WE DON'T BELONG ANYWHERE, ESPECIALLY IN OUR OWN BODY. WE ARE A PEOPLE WITHOUT A MEMORY, AND WITHOUT A FUTURE. OUR ONLY NATURAL GROUNDING, OUR REAL "STOCK" IS IN THE STOCK-EXCHANGE. OUR ONLY VALUES LIE IN THE VOLUME AND SPEED OF TRADING. THAT'S WHY OUR "BRANDS" ARE REMOVABLE TAGS.

SEX, IN OTHER WORDS, IS BEING MADE INTO A SIGN.

A SIGN REPRESENTS THE EGO FOR ANOTHER EGO. BUT WHAT IS THE EGO ITSELF, AFTER ALL, IF NOT ANOTHER REPRESENTATION? A REPRESENTATION REPRESENTS A REPRESENTATION FOR ANOTHER REPRESENTATION. CIRCULARITY OF SIGNS: "SO

TODAY IF YOU SEE A PERSON WHO LOOKS LIKE YOUR TEENAGE FANTASY WALKING DOWN THE STREET," WRITES ANDY WARHOL, "IT'S PROBABLY NOT YOUR FANTASY, BUT SOMEONE WHO HAD THE SAME FANTASY AS YOU AND DECIDED INSTEAD OF GETTING IT OR BEING IT, TO LOOK LIKE IT, AND SO HE WENT TO THE STORE AND BOUGHT THE LOOK THAT YOU BOTH LIKE. SO FORGET IT."

FORGETTING, OUR ONLY MEMORY.

THE INDIVIDUAL'S STRONGEST NEED IS TO SIGNIFY, THROUGH THE PRECARIOUS EXERCISE OF HIS SEXUALITY, HIS DEGREE OF CONTROL OF HIMSELF AND THE WORLD. HIS VERY CRAVING FOR AP- PROVAL AND RECOGNITION CONDEMNS HIM, HOWEVER, TO PERPETUAL DISCONTENT. OBSES- SIVELY HE FOCUSES ON HIS SEXUALITY AS IF SEX ITSELF COULD PROTECT HIM AGAINST THE FLOATING ANXIETY HIS OWN PERFORMANCE SIMULTANEOUSLY CRYSTALLIZES.

"TODAY WE SEEM ANIMATED EXCLUSIVELY BY FEAR. WE FEAR EVEN THAT WHICH IS GOOD, THAT WHICH IS HEALTHY, THAT WHICH IS JOYOUS," WRITES HENRY MILLER IN THE WORLD OF SEX. "AND WHAT IS THE HERO? PRIMARILY ONE WHO HAS CONQUERED HIS FEARS ... HIS SINGULAR VIRTUE IS THAT HE HAS BECOME ONE WITH LIFE, ONE WITH HIMSELF. HAVING CEASED TO DOUBT AND QUESTION, HE QUICKENS THE FLOW AND RHYTHM OF LIFE."

ALL WE ARE LEFT WITH, AT THIS POINT IS A HAUNTING QUESTION. IT COMES, APPROPRIATELY, FROM THE THEME SONG OF HUMAN SEXUAL RESPONSE, A BOSTON-BASED BAND:

WHAT DOES SEX MEAN TO ME?
WHAT DOES SEX MEAN TO SOCIETY?

THE QUESTION IS ITS OWN ANSWER. WE HAVE NOT YET CONQUERED OUR FEARS.

CASEY CAMERON, A SINGER OF THE BAND, TOLD DON SHEWEY HOW HE THOUGHT OF ITS NAME. HE WAS WORKING IN A BOOKSTORE AT THE TIME MASTERS AND JOHNSON'S BOOK WAS A BEST- SELLER: "A LOT OF PEOPLE WOULD COME IN AND ASK FOR THE BOOK RATHER FURTIVELY ... YOU COULD JUST SEE THE DISAPPOINTMENT WILT THEIR FACE WHEN THEY LOOKED THROUGH IT, BECAUSE IT WAS SO BORING. I THOUGHT IT WAS A FUNNY COMMENTARY ON THE SOCIETY; IT WAS SUCH A POP ITEM—THE FIRST BOOK WITH THE 'SEX' IN THE TITLE

THAT WAS EVERYWHERE—BUT IT HAD NO REAL MEANING TO PEOPLE."[2]

POP ITEMS DON'T HAVE TO MEAN ANYTHING TO PEOPLE. THEY ARE NOT CRYING FOR A QUESTION. FOR ALL-TOO-HUMAN QUESTIONS ("WHAT DOES SEX MEAN TO ME?"), "HUMAN RESPONSES" ARE ALWAYS UNHUMAN.

IF MASTERS AND JOHNSON'S BOOK HAD BEEN TRULY UNHUMAN AND NOT JUST OBJECTIVE, IT MIGHT HAVE BEEN QUITE EXCITING. UNHUMAN SEX AT LEAST WOULD HAVE BEEN DIFFERENT. EVEN HOLLYWOOD IS GETTING TIRED OF ROUTINE SEXPLOITATION: "MOVIE-GOERS WANT TO SEE SOMETHING SPECIAL, LIKE A SPACE SHIP COMING DOWN, AND LASER BEAMS," DECLARES AN ACTRESS FROM CLOSE ENCOUNTERS OF THE THIRD KIND. "THEY WANT TO EXPERIENCE FEAR AND MYSTERY."[3] ONLY TECHNOLOGY CAN STILL MAKE US STAND IN AWE AND EXPERIENCE ANEW THESE PRIMITIVE EMO- TIONS. ONLY WHEN IT TAKES US SOMEWHERE ELSE, IN ANOTHER SPACE, IN ANOTHER DIMENSION—"OUT OF THIS WORLD"—CAN SEX MAKE US EXPERIENCE FEAR AND MYSTERY.

ONE STEP FURTHER, AND OUR SEXOLOGISTS MAY WELL HAVE PLANTED THEIR FLAG ON THE EMERGING CONTINENT OF SEXUAL TECHNOLOGY. BUT THE BOOK NEVER GETS THAT FAR. IT NEVER REACHES THE POINT WHERE MAN'S IDENTITY VACILLATES IN THE HANDS OF THE MACHINE.

FAILING TO BE UNHUMAN, THE BOOK ALSO FAILS TO BE SIMPLY HUMAN. SOMEWHERE, UNDER THE COLD LIGHT OF SCIENCE, HUMAN SUBJECTS EXPERIENCE FAILURES OR MULTIPLE ORGASMS IN THE HANDS OF PROFESSIONAL SURROGATES OR OTHER WELL- ADJUSTED MECHANICAL MATES. BUT NOTHING IN THE BOOK BETRAYS THE SUBJECTS' SILENT CONVULSIONS. THESE ARE JUST SAMPLES OF HUMAN RESPONSES MEANT TO TESTIFY FOR A HUMANITY THAT WAS.

ANYONE, IN THE MEANTIME, CAN FIND HIS OWN BY LINGERING AMONG THIS GRAY CEMETARY OF SIGNS. ANYONE CAN MAKE UP HIS OWN SEXUAL "PROFILE" BY CHECKING THE EMPTY BOXES AND COMPARING THE EMPTY TRACES OF AN EMPTY PLEASURE TO THE VAIN PASSION OF HIS OWN IDENTITY.

WE DON'T ACTUALLY NEED TO ROAR THROUGH

REMOTE GALAXIES TO BE THROWN OUT OF OUR OWN SPACE, OUT OF OUR OWN IDENTITY. A HONDA GOLDWING 1000 WILL DO. "FEAR AND MYSTERY" DOESN'T MEAN GOING PLACES—EROTIC TRAVELOGUE—BUT BECOMING OUT OF PLACE, COLLAPSING INDIVIDUAL TIME AND SPACE IN THE VECTOR OF MOVEMENT.

IT ISN'T THE MACHINE ITSELF THAT IS EROTIC. IT IS THE VIOLENCE OF SPEED AND FEAR AND FUSION THAT GOES WITH IT. "AND THE FEELING OF UTTER EXHILARATION AS YOU GUIDE THE BIG MACHINE THROUGH TRAFFIC ..., CONTROLLING THE BEAST WITH YOUR BODY AS MUCH AS WITH THE CONTROLS ... AND THINKING HOW MUCH GREATER THIS FEELS THAN FLYING A PLANE ... ALMOST A SEXUAL THRILL."[4] WHAT IS TRULY EROTIC IS TO BE ONE WITH THE MACHINE, ONE WITH THE BEAST—FLYING AT HIGH SPEED AWAY FROM THIS DOMESTICATION OF OUR BODY AND OUR SENSES THAT WE CALL HUMANITY.

WE SHOULDN'T BE SURPRISED TO DISCOVER INTIMATELY WELDED TOGETHER IN THE MOTORCYCLE EXHILARATION, TWO "CONTRADICTORY" DIMENSIONS—BEAST, MACHINE—OF SEXUAL EXPERIENCE. THE CONTRADICTION ONLY EXISTS IN RATIONAL TERMS THOUGH. AS SOON AS A CERTAIN LEVEL OF INTENSITY (TERROR, VELOCITY) IS REACHED, SEXUALITY LOSES ITS RATIONALITY, AND CATEGORIES THEIR PERTINENCE. PURELY INDIVIDUAL DIMENSIONS, WHICH ENDLESSLY REQUIRE A MEANING ("WHAT DOES SEX MEAN ..."), DISSOLVE INTO A STATE OF UNLIMITED BECOMING.

MAN DOESN'T ACTUALLY BECOME AN ANIMAL, NOR DOES HE BECOME A MACHINE: THE FEAR AND MYSTERY OF SEXUALITY DON'T RESULT FROM MAN BECOMING SOMETHING ELSE AND ACQUIRING ANOTHER IDENTITY, THEY RESULT FROM HIS HESITATION BETWEEN GENDERS AND SPECIES— BEING ALIEN TO HIS OWN SPECIES AS WELL AS TO OTHER SPECIES; USING OTHER SPECIES IN ORDER TO GET RID OF THE LIMITATIONS AND EXCLUSIONS OF ONE'S OWN.

THIS IS, AFTER ALL, THE FUNCTION OF TOTEMISM IN PRIMITIVE SOCIETIES. CONTRARY TO CLAUDE LÉVI-STRAUSS' ASSUMPTIONS, TOTEMISM ISN'T A STRUCTURAL DEVICE BY WHICH MAN USES NATURE IN ORDER TO SEPARATE HIMSELF FROM IT. IT IS, ON THE CONTRARY, THE RITUALIZED EXPERIENCE BY WHICH PRIMITIVE SOCIETIES MAKE SURE MAN ISN'T GOING TO SEPARATE HIMSELF FROM NATURE ANYMORE THAN SETTING HIMSELF APART FROM THE OTHER MEMBERS OF THE TRIBE. TOTEMISM IS SIMPLY ONE OF THE COLLECTIVE MECHANISMS (LIKE SACRIFICE, INITIATION, CANNIBALISM) PRIMITIVE SOCIETIES USE TO PREVENT THE EMERGENCE IN THEIR MIDST OF SUCH A THING AS INDIVIDUALITY—AND WITH INDIVIDUALITY THE DIVISIONS, HIERARCHIES, OPPRESSION AND EXPLOITATION THAT MAKE UP "HUMAN" HISTORY.

WE'VE REACHED THE OTHER END OF THE LINE. WE'RE NOW BLINDLY TRYING TO BREAK OPEN THE CUMBERSOME CARAPACE OF THE EGO IN ORDER TO REESTABLISH OURSELVES AS PART OF A NATURE THAT, IN THE MEANTIME, IS FAST DISAPPEARING. AT THIS POINT TECHNOLOGY MAY WELL BE THE ONLY NATURE WE HAVE LEFT, ALTHOUGH TECHNOPHILIC INTENSITY (SPEED AND FUSION) AUTOMATICALLY LIBERATES ALL THE OTHER POTENTIALITIES OF BECOMING (BECOMING ANIMAL, OR PLANT, OR THING) THAT ARE CLOSELY CLOSETED IN WHAT THE CULTURE KEEPS CALLING—GOD KNOWS WHY—THE FREE INDIVIDUAL.

"IF WE COULD JUST LEAVE WELL ENOUGH ALONE," COMMENTS LARRY BANGOR, LEAD SINGER AND WRITER OF HUMAN SEXUAL RESPONSE, "WE MIGHT BE ABLE TO HANDLE THINGS AS EASILY AS ANIMALS DO WHEN THEY'RE JUST LICKING EACH OTHER AND PICKING BUGS." BUT THE FREE INDIVIDUAL—THAT SCARED/SACRED COW—CANNOT LIVE ALONE, OR LEAVE ANYONE ALONE SINCE HE IS ENTIRELY DEPENDENT FOR HIS EXISTENCE UPON WHATEVER JUDGEMENT, REAL OR IMAGINARY, THAT IS BEING PASSED ONTO HIM.

THE INDIVIDUAL'S LIFE IS AN ENDLESS POPULARITY CONTEST. "LOVE ME, LOVE ME," THIS ABJECT REQUEST INSTILLED BY THE CULTURE IS HAMMERED ON OUR SENSES, ON OUR "FEELINGS," AS THEY SAY, LIKE DISCO-MUSIC ON FM RADIO EVERY FRIDAY NIGHT. "BE YOURSELF, BE POPULAR, HAVE FUN": THIS IS HOW, IN THE ABSENCE OF ANY TRADITION, THE CULTURE TRAINS ITS CHILDREN. THIS IS HOW WE BRAND OUR OWN WITH THE INDELIBLE SEAL OF INSECURITY AND SUBMISSION.

IF THE INDIVIDUAL IS A SOCIAL OBJECT—A REPRESSED AND REPRESSIVE PRODUCT OF THE CULTURE—, WHY NOT AT LEAST SUBSTITUTE FOR HIM ANOTHER OBJECT (A PIECE OF FURNITURE, FOR INSTANCE) OR RATHER USE HIM LIKE AN OBJECT, LIKE AN ANIMAL, IN ORDER TO TEAR HIM AWAY FROM HIS PARALYZING HUMANITY:

"NOW TURN ME ON
AND I'LL RESPOND TO YOU
LIKE A HUMAN BEING,
BUT THAT'S NOT REALLY TRUE."

BANGOR'S UNOFFICIAL THEME SONG FOR HUMAN SEXUAL RESPONSE, HE EXPLAINS, IS ABOUT "CROSSING THE HUMAN/ANIMAL BARRIER, WHICH IS A FAVORITE THEME OF MINE. HUMANS BEING LIKE ANIMALS AND EVOLVING TOWARD FURNITURE. THE MOST NOBLE THING A HUMAN BEING CAN DO IS ACT AS FURNITURE FOR SOMEONE ELSE." SINCE WE CAN'T HANDLE THINGS AS EASILY AS ANIMALS, "THE CLOSEST WE CAN COME TO THAT IS THE FURNITURE IDEA AND THESE POOR ATTEMPTS AT ANIMAL INTIMACY THROUGH SEXUALITY—POOR BECAUSE IT'S NOT A REGULAR EVERYDAY BEHAVIOR PATTERN. IT'S MORE LIKE THIS SPORADIC BEHAVIOR ABERRATION."

"TREAT ME LIKE AN OBJECT." — "FUCK ME LIKE A DOG, LIKE THE PIG I AM." — "MAKE ME FEEL LIKE AN ANIMAL": THE WHOLE THEMATICS IS REPEATED OVER AND OVER AGAIN IN HEAVY GAY S&M. THIS ISN'T, HOWEVER, A SPECIALIZED OBSESSION. THE SYMBOL COMES UP WHENEVER PEOPLE STRIVE TO BE BROUGHT TO A PEAK AND REACH (THROUGH BEATING, OR ANY OTHER MEANS) A CERTAIN GRADIENT OF INTENSITY THAT WOULD STRIP THEM OF THEIR PSYCHOLOGICAL DEFENSES—OF THE "FREE" INDIVIDUALITY THE SOCIETY PRESENTS AS ITS MOST ENVIABLE ACHIEVEMENT.

THE EXPERIENCE DOESN'T HAVE TO BE EXCLUSIVE-LY SEXUAL. "WHEN PEOPLE SAY 'TREAT ME LIKE AN ANIMAL,' THEY ONLY WANT PART OF THE ROLE." ESTIMATES JOHN PRESTON. "THEY ONLY WANT IT IN A SEXUAL CONTEXT. IT GOES WAY BEYOND THAT."[5]

IRONICALLY, MASTERS AND JOHNSON'S EXPERI-MENTS ALSO GO WAY BEYOND HUMAN SEXUAL CONTEXT SINCE THEY LITERALLY TREAT HUMANS LIKE ANIMALS.

PRIMITIVE SOCIETIES SHOWED MORE RESPECT TO ANIMALS THAN WE DO TO HUMANS. THEY DIDN'T CONSIDER ANIMALS AS DEBASED OR INFERIOR. ANIMALS WERE DEEMED SACRED ENOUGH TO BE SACRIFICED IN A COLLECTIVE RITUAL, OR ELEVATED TO THE RANK OF TOTEM. WE DON'T SACRIFICE ANYTHING ANYMORE, ESPECIALLY NOT HUMANS. BUT WE TREAT THEM LIKE DIRT AND WE LOWER OURSELVES TO THE LEVEL OF A PAVLOVIAN DOG. THIS IS WHAT WE CALL "HUMANISM," AND "HUMAN SCIENCES."

THERE IS A VIOLENCE OF SCIENCE, BUT THAT VIOLENCE ISN'T MEANT TO BRINGING THE "SAMPLES" TO A PEAK—AT THE MOST TO GIVE THEM THE "GRATIFICATION" OF A SUCCESSFUL ORGASM. THE VIOLENCE OF OBJECTIVITY AMOUNTS TO DENYING THE ANIMAL IN MAN WHILE SIMULTANEOUSLY RELEGATING MAN TO THE STIMULUS-AND-RESPONSE STATUS OF AN AUTOMATON OR A GUINEA PIG.

THE "SAVAGE" PART OF HUMAN SEXUALITY, THE TERROR AND MYSTERY ATTACHED TO A SILENT, IRRATIONAL BEHAVIOR ABERRATION STILL RE-TURNS IN MONSTROUS, UNHUMAN FORMS WHEN-EVER REASON SLUMBERS (WE CALL THIS: THE UNCONSCIOUS), BUT OUR SEXUALITY, LIKE PETS AT HOME, OR GADGETS IN THE KITCHEN, OR THE UNCONSCIOUS ON THE COUCH, IS BY NOW SO THOROUGHLY DOMESTICATED BY THE CULTURE THAT IT CAN BE TESTED TO DEATH IN THE LAB, OR FLATTENED OUT IN THE "REAL" WORLD OF QUESTIONNAIRES AND STATISTICS WITHOUT AROUSING IN US ANY SENSE OF OUTRAGE—OR AN IRREPRESSIBLE LAUGHTER.

THE AGE OF THE CANDY SHOP

"WE SHOULD BE GRATEFUL THAT WE LIVE IN AN AGE WHEN MATURE PEOPLE HAVE A FORUM SUCH AS YOUR MAGAZINE IN WHICH TO SHARE THEIR DISCOVERIES IN THE BOUNDLESS WORLD OF PLEA-SURE."

THE PENTHOUSE LETTERS

GONE ARE THE DAYS WHEN THE ANONYMOUS AUTHOR OF MY SECRET LIFE COULD WONDER IF ALL MEN SHARED HIS STRANGE "LETCHES," HOPING THAT HIS OWN EXPERIENCE, IF PRINTED, WOULD ENABLE OTHERS TO COMPARE, AS HE HIMSELF COULDN'T.

WE KNOW FOR A FACT THAT ALL MEN, AND WOMEN TOO, SHARE HIS PASSIONS. BUT THEY AREN'T THAT STRANGE ANYMORE.

THERE ARE NO SECRET LIVES—NO MORE SECRETS,

NO MORE LIVES, AND POSSIBLY NO MORE SEX.

PENTHOUSE READERS ARE MORE THAN WILLING TO SHARE THEIR OWN DISCOVERIES IN THE "BOUNDLESS WORLD" OF SEX. THE ERA OF THE GREAT EXPLORERS, HOWEVER, IS DEFINITELY OVER.

THE SECRET VICTORIAN GENTLEMAN WAS IMBUED WITH THE IMPORTANCE OF HIS MISSION. HE TRULY LIVED FOR SEX ALONE. LIKE RENÉ CAILLÉ, HE WAS EXPLORING A FORBIDDEN CONTINENT DRESSED IN ARAB SHIRT, REACHING THE SILENT TIMBUKTU OF SEX AT THE PERIL OF HIS LIFE.

PENTHOUSE READERS DON'T GO FOR THE ABYSSES IN HUMAN NATURE. THEY ARE TOURISTS OF SEX, TAKING SNAPSHOTS AT THE WINDING AMAZONS OF HUMAN SEXUAL RESPONSE FROM THE PLANE WINDOW, TO SHOW THE FOLKS BACK HOME.

THEY DON'T EXPLORE SEXUALITY, THEY EXCHANGE RECIPES.

A READER RELATES HOW HIS WIFE DIPS HIS PENIS IN A SUGAR-HONEY MIXTURE, THEN WRAPS A TOWEL FILLED WITH ICE CUBES AROUND IT, FREEZING THIS "DELIGHTFULLY TASTY DISH." HE IN TURN PREPARES A TINY PIZZA-LIKE CREATION WHICH HE INSERTS IN HER VAGINA BEFORE BEDTIME. "I CANNOT BEGIN TO TELL YOU," HE CONCLUDES, "HOW THIS MUTUAL CULINARY CREATIVITY HAS HELPED OUR SEX LIVES." (HE ALSO ADMITS THEY GAINED MORE THAN 10 LBS.)

"A HAPPIER SEX LIFE HAS MADE ME A BETTER HOUSEKEEPER, MOTHER, AND WIFE," A READER PROUDLY ANNOUNCES BETWEEN TWO HOT HAIRBRUSH SESSIONS WITH HER HUSBAND.

DR. IRENE KASSORLA, THE "RENOWNED, INNOVATIVE PSYCHOLOGIST," JOINS IN THE HOSANNA. YES, SHE PROCLAIMS IN HER RECENT MASTERPIECE, NICE GIRLS DO, REPEATEDLY ADVERTISED ON A FULL PAGE OF THE NEW YORK TIMES, "NICE GIRLS DO HAVE SEXUAL FANTASIES . . . NICE GIRLS DO ENJOY SEX." SUCH A NICE DISCOVERY. WE'RE SURE GLAD THERE IS AN INNOVATIVE PSYCHOLOGIST TO FIGHT FOR THE CAUSE.

AFTER A DECADE OF WOMAN'S LIB, NICE GIRLS, IT SEEMS, STILL ARE "A WALKING MASS OF SENSUAL GUILT." WHAT SHOULD NICE GIRLS DO THEN? THE ANSWER IS SHORT, BUT POINTED. IT TAKES FOUR LETTERS AND A LOT OF COURAGE TO EXPLODE MYTHS ABOUT "OVERSEXED WOMEN."

WOMEN WHO ORGASM MORE FREQUENTLY, DR. KASSORLA RECOGNIZES SQUARELY, ARE BETTER ABLE TO FOCUS ON THEIR NORMAL ACTIVITIES. THEY TEND TO BE "MORE SUCCESSFUL, MORE MOTIVATED, AND MORE ABLE TO EXPRESS FEELINGS OF SELF-WORTH AND SELF-ESTEEM. THEY FEEL PEACEFUL, RELAXED, AND ENTHUSED ABOUT PARTICIPATING IN WORK AND FAMILY ACTIVITIES." (SEE ABOVE THE PENTHOUSE HAPPY SLAVE. SOME PEOPLE ARE REALLY LOOKING FOR IT.) NO ONE CAN TAKE AWAY YOUR "INALIENABLE RIGHT" TO SEXUAL FULFILLMENT, THE RENOWNED PSYCHOLOGIST CONCLUDES, SHOWING THE FLAG.

FUCKING'S THE CURE, FOLKS.

"EVERYONE IS ENTITLED TO ENJOY THE FEAST OF SEXUALITY, AND ANYONE CAN LEARN HOW TO ENJOY IT," SHE ADDS, ENCOURAGING HER "MILLIONS OF VIEWERS" (HER AD AGAIN). WHAT ABOUT THE MILLIONS OF ROBOTS ALL OVER THE COUNTRY? THEY TOO ARE PEACEFUL, AND MOTIVATED, AND "ENTHUSED" ABOUT WORK. THEY TOO COULD START CONCENTRATING ON THEMSELVES, AS SHE ADVISES HER NICE GIRLS TO DO, AND ZERO IN ON THEIR OWN PLEASURABLE SENSATIONS.

THERE IS NO GUARANTEE THOUGH THAT ROBOTS WOULD EVER ACHIEVE TOTAL SEXUAL SATISFACTION. THEY AIN'T NEUROTIC ENOUGH FOR THAT.

MAKING IT ON TOP OF THE TV SET—OR OVER THE AQUARIUM, GENITALS DANGLING IN THE WATER FOR THE FISH TO NIBBLE—ADDS "MUCH STRENGTH TO OUR SEX LIFE," PROCLAIMS ANOTHER PENTHOUSE READER WITH A SIGH OF RELIEF. THE FALTERING ERECTION OF A HARASSED BUSINESSMAN IS BROUGHT "BACK TO NORMAL" BY HIS CHANCE DISCOVERY OF THE PULSATING PROPERTIES OF A TUNING FORK. ANOTHER BEDROOM VIRTUOSO PAYS A MOVING HOMAGE TO HIS SAXOPHONE. IT HAS BECOME, HE WRITES, "A THIRD PARTY IN OUR SEX LIFE AND JUST THE SIGHT OF IT MAKES MY WIFE GO NUTS."

ARE WE WITNESSING THE DAWN OF A NEW "TROILISM"—MY WIFE, MY BATTERY AND I?

THE TECHNOPHILIC REVOLUTION IS SILENTLY GAINING MOMENTUM AMONG THE MASSES. SOON EVERYWHERE SEX WILL BE FULLY AUTOMATIZED. MILLIONS OF NICE GIRLS WILL ORGASM IN UNISON

WHILE PUTTING THE TV DINNER IN THE OVEN.

SEX ALREADY EXTENDS FAR BEYOND HUMAN REACH. WHAT REMAINS "HUMAN," HOWEVER, IS EVERYONE'S OBSESSIVE CONCERN FOR THEIR NIGHTIME DIET—THEIR "SEX LIVES."

SEX IS NO LONGER A PART OF LIFE; IT IS LIFE, RATHER, WHICH IS A PART OF SEX: "UNTIL A MAN HAS SPENT SEVERAL MINUTES SLOWLY AND LOVINGLY INSERTING HIS FINGER INTO HIS LOVE'S BEHIND TO LUBRICATE AND RELAX IT," EXCLAIMS A BORN-AGAIN MECHANIC, "HE HASN'T LIVED." YES, SEX IS LIFE—RROSE SELAVY. BUT WHAT HAPPENS TO LIFE IF SEX IS IN SHAMBLES?

"WE TRIED TO IMPROVE OUR EROTIC STIMULI TO EACH OTHER," A DISCIPLE OF PAVLOV ROMANTI-CALLY RECALLS. "I'VE MADE A CAREER OF BUILDING MY HUSBAND'S HARD-ONS . . ." ECHOES A MILITANT HOUSEWIFE. SO WE'RE LEFT WITH OUR SEX LIVES DANGLING AT THE TIPS OF OUR FINGERS, FRAIL FLOWERS OF FLESH—ROSE, EROS—WE CONSTANTLY HAVE TO RELAX AND LUBRICATE FOR FEAR IT WILL BREAK DOWN ALTOGETHER.

MY SEX LIFE. YOUR SEX LIFE. OUR SEX LIVES . . . TERRIBLE LITANY THAT ACCOMPANIES WHATEVER WE DO LIKE AN EXORCISM—OR EXAM.

"HOW'S YOU SEX LIFE TODAY?" THE THERAPIST ASKS WITH A KNOWING LOOK, HANDING HIS PATIENT A BOX OF KLEENEX.

"JUST AWFUL." — "TERRIFIC, HOPE IT LASTS." — "SOMEWHAT IMPROVED." — "NONE TOO EXCITING . . ."

"HOW MANY TIMES A WEEK?"

BLANK FACE, EYES FILLED WITH TREMBLING CIPHERS. "MY SEX LIFE . . ."

SEX HAVE MERCY UPON US.

RACHEL ENGLISH, THE AUTHOR OF MY FIRST 500, A FAST SEX AUTOBIOGRAPHY,[6] IS SOMETHING OF A PROFESSIONAL. IN ORDER TO KEEP TRACK OF HER FLEETING ARMY OF LOVERS, SHE RESORTED TO ISSUING NUMBERS. SHALL WE SAY, PARAPHRASING THE INTRODUCTION TO MY SECRET LIFE, THAT WE HAVE BEFORE US ANOTHER RECORD OF "THE EROTIC LIFE OF A PROFOUNDLY COMPULSIVE PERSON"? HARDLY SO. JUST THE ORDINARY

SWINGING HOUSEWIFE TRYING TO BREAK A RECORD BEFORE SETTLING FOR SWEET SIX-SIXTY-THREE WHO WILL SATISFY HER NEEDS "FOR LOVE AND SEX WITH THE SAME MAN."

COMPULSION HAS GONE PUBLIC, AND SEX COMPUL-SORY. SO MUCH SO THAT WE ARE LEFT WONDERING WHY ANYONE SHOULD EVEN BOTHER DOCUMENTING FIVE HUNDRED LAZY LAYS.

THERE IS A MORAL TO RACHEL ENGLISH'S ARITHMETIC THOUGH. IT POPS UP IN HER INSPIRED EPILOGUE: "AFTER FEELING LIKE THE CHILD IN THE CANDY SHOP WITH A NEW LINE OF CREDIT, ONE MAY DISCOVER THAT SEX IS A NATURAL, REPETITIVE BODILY FUNCTION LIKE EATING AND SLEEPING, AND THAT CONDITIONAL RULES ON ITS BEHAVIOR ARE UNFOUNDED."

CANDIED SEX, CANDID THOUGHT. HOW MUCH ARTIFICE DID IT TAKE US TO COME TO THIS NATURAL CONCLUSION?

TO START WITH, EATING IS NOT AS NATURAL A FUNCTION AS IT SOUNDS. MALINOWSKI OBSERVES THAT FOR TROBRIAND ISLANDERS, EATING IS IN NO WAY REGARDED AS INDISPENSIBLE TO LIFE. IN FACT, HE ASSERTS, "THEY HAVE NO IDEA THAT THERE IS SUCH A THING AS PHYSIOLOGICAL NEED FOR ALIMENTATION, OR THAT THE BODY IS BUILT UP ON FOOD." ONE EATS SIMPLY BECAUSE ONE IS HUNGRY OR GREEDY.

FOR ISLANDERS, SEX IS NOT A NATURAL FUNCTION LIKE EATING, BUT EATING AN UNNATURAL FUNCTION LIKE SEX. AND IT IS TO BE PERFORMED PRIVATELY, IN SECLUSION, JUST LIKE SEX, TO FEND OFF ANY DANGER.

SEXUALITY HAS ALWAYS BEEN A HIGHLY CODIFIED AND RITUALIZED ACTIVITY IN HUMAN AS WELL AS ANIMAL SOCIETIES WHERE MATING PATTERNS OBEY A STRICT SUCCESSION OF SIGNALS SPECIFIC TO EACH SPECIES. THE PRESENT DISCOVERY OF SEX AS A "NATURAL FUNCTION" RESULTS FROM THE BREAKING DOWN OF SOCIAL CODES, THE DECAY OF COLLECTIVE STRUCTURES, AND THE DECADENCE OF MORES UNDER THE LEVELLING PRESSURE OF KAPITAL.

ANTHROPOLOGISTS MAINTAIN THAT THE ABSENCE OF ALL RESTRAINTS, RULES, AND VALUES CANNOT

EXIST IN ANY CULTURE, HOWEVER DEGRADED OR DECADENT IT MAY BE. THEY ARE RIGHT, OF COURSE. MORAL RESTRAINTS HAVE NOT ALTOGETHER DISAPPEARED FROM OUR SOCIETIES. THE FAMILY, HOWEVER, IS TOO MORIBUND, PARENTAL AUTHORITY AND RELIGIOUS VALUES TOO FAR GONE TO BE FORCED BACK PERMANENTLY INTO AN ARCHAIC MOLD. THE BRIDE HAS BEEN STRIPPED BARE BY KAPITAL, EVEN.

WHETHER WE LIKE IT OR NOT, THE LAW OF EXCHANGE DELINEATES THE HORIZON OF THE SEXUAL REVOLUTION. NO WONDER SEXUAL REVOLUTION, TOO, IS TURNING INWARD LIKE AN INGROWN NAIL.

THE GOLDEN RULE OF LIBERAL CAPITALISM IS TO TURN A BLIND EYE TO EVERYTHING THAT'S MARKETABLE. NO MORAL TABOO CAN HOLD TOO LONG AGAINST THE INCREDIBLE PRESSURE TO INCORPORATE, INSTRUMENTALIZE, AND EXHIBIT PARTS HITHERTO KEPT OUT OF SIGHT OR CAREFULLY CONFINED TO THE MARGINS.

THE BODY OF KAPITAL IS A POLYMORPHOUS PERVERSE BODY VIRTUALLY FREED FROM ANY IMPEDIMENT, CONSTANTLY EXPLORING NEW ITINERARIES, REACHING OUT ON ALL SIDES WITHOUT COMMITTING ITSELF TO ANY—ALWAYS READY, HOWEVER, TO BRING BACK INTO THE FOLD OF NORMALITY WHATEVER "PERVERSION" IT CAN BENEFIT FROM.

CHILDREN SHOULD BE PROTECTED FROM MEN'S STRANGE LETCHES, BUT PRETTY BABIES ARE SO SEXY . . .

THIS DOESN'T MEAN, OF COURSE, THAT SEXUAL POLYMORPHISM IS INTRINSICALLY CAPITALISTIC, SIMPLY THAT KAPITAL PROVIDES THE REAL BASIS FOR ITS EXISTENCE.

KAPITAL THRIVES ON CONTRADICTIONS. ITS DYNAMISM CLEARLY LIES THERE. THE RIGHT HAND DOESN'T KNOW WHAT THE LEFT IS DOING, ESPECIALLY IF THERE ARE AT LEAST TWO DOZEN HANDS EXTENDED IN EVERY POSSIBLE DIRECTION, LIKE BUDDHA'S.

FAR FROM BEING A PRODUCT OF NATURE, THE ALLEGED NATURALNESS OF OUR SEXUALITY IS A BY-PRODUCT OF THE INCREASING ABSTRACTION OF OUR SOCIETY. SEX IS NOT NATURAL, IT IS AS HYPERREAL—AS MADE UP—AS MACROBIOTIC FOOD.

A NEW MALE COLOGNE, RECENTLY ADVERTISED IN FASHION MAGAZINES, MIXES THE ACTUAL SMELL OF PERSPIRATION WITH A CHEMICAL. GENEROUSLY APPLIED AFTER YOUR DAILY DEODORANT, IT WILL DRIVE YOUR LOVER ABSOLUTELY WILD.

THAT'S HOW WE LIKE IT: RAUNCHY, BUT CLEAN. WILD, BUT SAFE. THE REAL THING, BUT ALL MADE UP.

THAT'S HOW WE LIKE EVERYTHING: THE BEST REALITY MONEY CAN BUY.

MOANS OF PLEASURE KEEP FILLING THE AIR—ARE THEY REAL OR IMAGINARY? ARE THEY THE SUCCESSFUL SIMULACRUM OF A FEMALE ORGASM OR THE INDISCREET RECORDING OF THE ACTUAL PHYSIOLOGICAL EVENT? THE ENORMITY OF FEMALE ORGASM ON FM RADIOS IS SUCH THAT IT TRANSCENDS ANY HUMAN AGENT OR REALITY. (MALES AREN'T THAT CONCERNED WITH THEIR OWN ORGASMIC ATTAINMENTS. THEY ARE TOO BUSY MAINTAINING THE ERECT FACADE.)

FEMALE ORGASM IS A CHALLENGE TO BOTH SEXES. IT HOVERS IN THE AIR, IN THE REALM OF PURE ESSENCES, LIKE THE MUSIC OF THE SPHERES—A MAGNIFIED MODEL OF EROTIC ACHIEVEMENT FOR EVERYONE TO PEG UPON THEIR DESIRES, THEIR FANTASIES, AND THEIR GROWING ANXIETIES.

MALE ANXIETIES, HOWEVER, WILL SOON BE OVER. IN A FEW MONTHS ANYONE WILL BE ABLE TO BUY AN ERECTION, OR EVEN RENT ONE BY THE MONTH. RENT-AN-IMPLANT© AND ECONOMY ERECTION© ALREADY OPERATE IN TWENTY CITIES IN THE U.S. AND CANADA. THE DEVICE IS QUITE SIMPLE. ALL IT TAKES IS A SILICONE ROD INSERTED IN EACH OF THE CORPORA CAVERNOSA. NO ONE CAN TELL THE DIFFERENCE, EVEN UNDER CLOSE SCRUTINY. INSTALLATION IS FREE.

THERE'S ONLY ONE MINOR DRAWBACK: THE ERECTION IS PERMANENT. MANY OF OUR CUSTOMERS WON'T MIND IT AT ALL. THEY HAVE TO CATCH UP WITH THE TIMES.

WHAT HAS BECOME NATURAL FOR US ABOUT SEX IS NOT THE BODILY FUNCTION, BUT THE HIGHLY SOPHISTICATED CANDY SHOP FEELING. IS THERE ANYTHING MORE NATURAL TO THE AVERAGE

AMERICAN THAN HAVING A CREDIT LINE?

AFTER CENTURIES OF MORAL RESTRAINT, SEXUAL-ITY—AT LONG LAST—HAS COME OF AGE. THE AGE OF THE CANDY SHOP.

MICHAEL BAUMANN, A LEADER OF THE JUNE 2ND URBAN GUERRILLA GROUP IN WEST GERMANY (STILL SOUGHT ON BANK ROBBERY CHARGES), RECALLS WHAT HE LEARNED FROM SUDDENLY HAVING "AN INSANE AMOUNT OF MONEY TO SPEND." HE SOON FOUND HIMSELF BUYING A MOUNTAIN OF RADIOS, AN ENTIRE PARKING LOT OF CARS: "THE MORE SECRET THE THINGS YOU DO, THE MORE LIKELY YOU ARE TO FALL RIGHT INTO CONSUMER-ISM." HIS SECRET LIFE HAD MADE HIM A NATURAL PREY TO THE CANDY STORE SYNDROME. SOFT TERROR OF CONSUMERISM, MORE POWERFUL THAN ANY IDEOLOGY OR CONDITIONAL RULE OF BE-HAVIOR.

A GAY LIB PROPONENT, TALKING ON TV ABOUT HIS NEIGHBORHOOD GAY BARS, RECENTLY SAID, "IT'S LIKE GOING INTO A CANDY STORE AND SAYING, 'I'LL HAVE THIS ONE, AND THIS ONE, AND THIS, AND THIS . . . .'" CONSUMER SEX. SEX ON THE INSTALLMENT PLAN.

NO LONGER A CATEGORY OF EROS, EXCESS IS MERELY A DELINQUENT ACCOUNT.

IF "NATURE" DOESN'T TAKE ITS TOLL, THE GREEDY CHILD MAY BE REMINDED OF ITS EXISTENCE BY A CURT NOTE FROM YOUR FRIENDLY CANDY SHOP: "RECENT TRANSACTIONS POSTED TO YOUR ACCOUNT HAVE CAUSED YOUR BALANCE TO SUBSTANTIALLY EXCEED YOUR CREDIT LINE. THIS IS CONTRARY TO OUR AGREEMENT AND WE ARE, THEREFORE, TERMINATING ANY FURTHER USE OF OUR CREDIT CARD." SEXUAL EXCESS IS NO MORE THE APPROVAL OF LIFE INTO DEATH (GEORGES BATAILLE), JUST THE END OF THE LINE. TIME TO PAY OFF AND SETTLE FOR MORE SEDATE SEX.

FOR CENTURIES DESIRE HAS BEEN CONDITIONED TO SALIVATE LIKE A DOG WHENEVER THERE IS SOMETHING TO BE TRANSGRESSED. PROHIBITIONS, THOUGH, HAVE LOST MOST OF THEIR POWER. WERE THEY TO FADE OUT ANY FURTHER, DESIRE AS WE EXPERIENCE IT MAY WELL BREAK DOWN ALTO-GETHER.

WE'RE GETTING DANGEROUSLY CLOSE TO THAT POINT. WE MAY HAVE PASSED IT ALREADY.

GEORGES BATAILLE HAD A KEEN UNDERSTANDING OF THE DILEMMA. THAT'S WHY HE DELIBERATELY SET OUT TO INJECT MASSIVE DOSES OF SACRED INTO THE MAINLINE OF SEXUALITY IN ORDER TO HEIGHTEN THE POWER OF TRANSGRESSION. IN A SOCIETY THAT LEVELS EVERYTHING TO THE GROUND, BATAILLE FORCED SEXUAL DIFFERENCES TO COME OUT LIKE A WOUND. HIS WAS, IN MANY RESPECTS, A DINOSAUR'S ENTERPRISE, FRENETIC AND FLAMBOYANT, POSSIBLY THE LAST SUSTAINED ATTEMPT TO TURN BACK THE CLOCK OF DESIRE.

INCEST AROUSES INDIGNATION IN SAVAGES. NO SO WITH MATURE, CIVILIZED, RESOURCEFUL INDIVID-UALS WRITING TO PENTHOUSE:

"LAST SUMMER I WAS WITH MY GIRL FRIEND IN THE WOODS. WE WERE COMPLETELY NAKED AND SCREWING OUR HEARTS OUT . . . MY MOTHER [AND TEACHER] ASKED IF THEY COULD JOIN US . . . AFTER A MINUTE WE WERE ALL SCREWING. SINCE THAT DAY (AS I AM AN ONLY CHILD) I SLEEP WITH MY MOTHER EVERY NIGHT. WE SOMETIMES HAVE MY CHICK AND TEACHER SHARE OUR KING-SIZE BED WITH US."

WHAT IS TRULY AMAZING HERE IS NOT THE EXISTENCE OF INCEST—IT HAS ALWAYS EXISTED, ESPECIALLY IN PATRIARCHAL SOCIETIES—BUT THE ABSENCE OF SACRED HORROR, LET ALONE OF MORAL REPUGNANCE. BATAILLE'S MA MÈRE (MY MOTHER), A STORY OF MATERNAL CONVULSION AND DEPRAVITY, COULD SOON BE READ WITH AS MUCH PASSION AS THE DEAD SEA SCROLLS.

ANOTHER READER DESCRIBES HIS OWN PROFANA-TION IN THE SAME COOL, MATTER-OF-FACT FASHION: "SHE WAS OFFERING NO RESISTANCE, SO I EASED HER DOWN ON THE BED AND AT THE SAME TIME REMOVED MY SHORTS. I BEGAN SUCKING AND KISSING HER BREAST UNTIL SHE WAS MOANING WITH PLEASURE. I DEFLOWERED MY SISTER THAT NIGHT AND WE HAVE ENJOYED SEX TOGETHER TO THIS DAY."

INCEST HAS LOST ITS FLOWER, AND TRANSGRES-SION ITS APPEAL. ENJOY YOUR FAMILY LIFE TO YOUR HEART'S CONTENT, BUT DON'T YOU EVER ASK FOR REVULSION AND ECSTASY.

IN-SEX ISN'T AS MUCH EXCITING AS IT IS PRACTICAL: "THE THING I LIKE ABOUT IT WAS THAT IT WAS SO

CONVENIENT. I COULD GET ALL THE SEX I WANTED AND NEVER EVEN HAD TO LEAVE THE HOUSE! WHEN HE MOVED INTO AN APARTMENT, I WOULD GO OVER AND SEE HIM. NO ONE EVER THOUGHT ANYTHING ABOUT GOING OVER TO SEE MY OWN BROTHER."

HOME SEX IS SO SAFE, SO HANDY, SO MUCH FUN. AND IT CAN BE ENJOYED WITHOUT LEAVING THE HOUSE, LIKE TV. ALL IN THE FAMILY. IT'S A WONDER NO ONE EVER THOUGHT OF THAT BEFORE.

EXIT TWO THOUSAND YEARS OF AGONY. NO MORE DEADLY SIN AND BLOODY RETRIBUTION. NO MORE SACRILEGE. NO MORE TRAGEDY. MY KINGDOM FOR A KING—SIZE BED.

END OF THE LINE. END GAME.

THERE ARE NO MORE BROTHERS OR SISTERS, NO MORE GENITORS OR EVEN GENDERS FOR PEOPLE WHO ARE SIMPLY LOOKING FOR ALL THE SEX THEY CAN GET. AS RACHEL ENGLISH REMARKS POINTEDLY: "IT IS EASY TO OVERLOOK THE GENDER OF THE PERSON GIVING SEXUAL SATISFACTION WHEN SHEER GRATIFICATION IS THE MAIN PURPOSE OF THE ACT."

GENDER: "ANY OF TWO OR MORE CATEGORIES, AS MASCULINE, FEMENINE, AND NEUTER." SEXLESS GENDER. GENDERLESS SEX. NEUTER CATEGORIES. SEX, LIKE FASHION IS BECOMING A GENDERLESS SUBJECT. BLOOMINGDALE'S SPONSORS THIERRY MUGLER'S ANDROGYNOUS JUMPSUITS, FEMALE BODY BUILDERS STORM THE PROFESSION AND MALE STRIPPERS HARASSED BY UNDERCOVER POLICEWOMEN IN LAWRENCE, MASS. FILE FOR REVERSE DISCRIMINATION. IF CATEGORIES DON'T HOLD ANYMORE, INCEST SIMPLY BECOMES IMPOSSIBLE.

PANIC AMONG THE SHAREHOLDERS OF THE AMERICAN PSYCHOANALYTICAL ASSOCIATION. "STOCKS FALL ON WORRIES OVER OEDIPUS RATES," ANNOUNCES BUSINESS NEWS. IS PSYCHOANALYSIS BECOMING A SHRINKING PROPOSITION?

WHAT OTHER CATEGORIES CAN WE STILL NEUTRALIZE IN OUR BLIND, INDISCRIMINATE APPETITE FOR SEXUAL "GRATIFICATION"?

IT IS NOT JUST THE GENDER OF THE PERSON THAT IS EASY TO OVERLOOK. THE PERSON HIMSELF HAS BECOME SECONDARY TO THE ACT. ANYONE CAN GIVE YOU THE PHYSICAL SATISFACTION YOU'RE ENTITLED TO—ANYONE OR ANYTHING. SEXY SAXOPHONE, SWINGING SOAP STICKS (FORGET ABOUT THE GENDER!): THEY'D REALLY MAKE ANY WIFE GO NUTS.

EVERYONE IS EQUAL UNDER THE LAW. THE LAW OF GRATIFICATION. NOT JUST EQUAL: THE SAME. EXIT THE INDIVIDUAL, HIS BAD BREATH AND HIS TWISTED PSYCHOLOGY. ENTER THE CLONE, IMMORTAL, IMMACULATE.

SON OF SAME: AN IMAGE'S IMAGE.

NO WONDER CLONING IS NOW BEING ELEVATED TO METAPHYSICAL HEIGHTS. WE ARE ALL CHILDREN OF THE SAME GENDERLESS MATRIX. ALL HYDROGEN-BOUND TO AN ORIGINAL BASE. MOTHER DNA, THE ULTIMATE VIRGIN.

THE HUGE BODY THAT SPRAWLS OVER THE PAGES OF THE PENTHOUSE LETTERS, COLLECTING AT RANDOM BITS AND PIECES OF ITS NEW EQUIPMENT, CLAIMS TO REPRESENT "THE SEXUAL STATE OF THE NATION." THERE IS SEX—AND THERE IS PENTHOUSE SEX, THE COVER PROUDLY ANNOUNCES. SO IS THIS PENTHOUSE NATION?

A NATION OF GRATIFIED CITIZENS, A LAND OF SATISFIED CONSUMERS INVITE YOU TO CELEBRATE THE JOYS OF SEX—GENITALS AND GENDERS PRECARIOUSLY DANGLING ON THE EDGE OF BOREDOM AND BANKRUPTCY.

"A MUNDANE SEX LIFE CAN BE COMPARED TO A FROZEN TV DINNER," SUGGESTS DR. KASSORLA. "IT WILL KEEP YOU ALIVE, BUT IT'S NOT A GOURMET BANQUET SERVED IN A POSH RESTAURANT."

MILLIONS OF AMERICANS MAY WELL BE INTO GOURMET FOOD, BUT THEY ARE NOT GREAT CHEFS BECAUSE OF IT. THEY ARE SERVICING TO DEATH THEIR FAVORITE RECIPE: "SINCE THAT MEMORABLE DAY, ONE SATURDAY EACH MONTH WE HAVE HAD THE SAME SESSION," A PENTHOUSE READER EXULTS EXPECTANTLY. COMPULSION TO REPEAT, DEATH-WISH CLOTHED IN WHITE FEATHER.

THE FACT IS THAT LOTS OF PEOPLE DON'T SERVICE ANYTHING OR ANYONE ANYMORE. THE MORON MAJORITY FALLS ASLEEP ON A COLD TV DINNER.

ANY "ESCORT" IN TOWN WOULD TELL YOU THAT EVEN HER CUSTOMERS ARE NOT OVERLY EAGER TO GET DOWN TO BUSINESS. IT'S NOT THAT THEY ARE AFRAID OF SEX: THEY ARE JUST TOO LONELY, TOO BORED OR TOO DRUGGED UP TO MAKE A MOVE OF THEIR OWN. THE MOST SEXUALLY ACTIVE MERELY SIT AND WATCH WHILE THE GIRL PERFORMS WITH A HIRED STUD. WHAT THEY REALLY WANT ISN'T SEX, IT IS HUMAN PRESENCE, METERED COMPANY. NOT HEAT, JUST WARMTH. THEY BASK FOR A WHILE IN AN ATMOSPHERE OF SEXUALITY WITHOUT HAVING TO FACE ITS DRY DEMANDS.

"SEX IS HARD WORK JUST LIKE EVERYTHING ELSE," DROPS ANDY WARHOL WITH A PLASTIC GRIN. SOME STAGE CAT STRIKES. OTHERS ENVISION A SEXLESS SOCIETY.

ZERO WORK, THE WAY OF THE FUTURE?

POST-SEXUAL SEX

"I'D RATHER LAUGH IN BED THAN DO IT."

ANDY WARHOL

IT HAD TO HAPPEN IN NEW YORK. NOT IN A SEXUALLY DEVELOPING CAPITAL LIKE PARIS OR CALCUTTA. IN NEW YORK, WHERE SEX IS THE MOST ACCESSIBLE COMMODITY.

THEY DECLARED IT PUBLICLY. IT'S TOO MUCH, IT'S ENOUGH. NO MORE SEX.

IT MADE HISTORY.

NO SEX, THE LAST FRONTIER.

SEX IS SUCH A HASSLE. SUCH A BORE. SUCH A WASTE: "THINK OF ALL THE TIME AND ENERGY SPENT IN THE SEARCH AND CONSUMMATION—AND THE HANGOVERS OF SEX. THINK OF THE BOOKS I COULD HAVE WRITTEN, THE PHOTOGRAPHS I COULD HAVE TAKEN . . ."[7] FAMILIAR ARGUMENT. SO MANY

MASTERPIECES STILL-BORN IN EMPTY EMBRACES. WASTE OF TIME. WASTE OF ENERGY. WASTE OF WHITE MATTER.

AND HOW UNIMAGINATIVE. SISYPHUS STUCK ON HIS ROCKS, NIETZSCHE'S ETERNAL COMING. CUT IT OUT ALTOGETHER. NOT CASTRATION—INDIFFERENCE. SAYS STIV BATORS, LEAD SINGER OF THE DEAD BOYS: "THEY'RE JUST NOT INTERESTED. THEY'VE HAD PHYSICAL RELATIONS SINCE THE AGE OF 10, SO, BY THE TIME THEY ARE 15, THEY'RE LOOKING FOR NEW KICKS." SEX IS NOT THE ULTIMATE DOPE ANYMORE. JADED DUDES. ANGEL'S LUST.

WE'VE THROWN THE TOWEL ON THE BOXING RING. NO, THANK YOU. I'D RATHER PUT MY ENERGIES ELSEWHERE. WHY SHOULD I LET SEX, THIS VAMPIRE, THIS ANTIQUITY, POLICE THE WORLD?

IT HAD TO END UP THAT WAY.

IT IS NOT ARTAUD, NOT EVEN ABELARD. NO ANGRY VITUPERATIONS STILL SMACKING OF RELIGION. NO SACRIFICING ANYTHING. HERODIAS LIES ON THE BLANK PAGE OF HER DATE BOOK, BEAUTIFULLY STERILE. NO REPRESSION, NO SUBLIMATION. NOT EVEN CASTRATION, THAT FREUDIAN BAND AID. BUSINESS AS USUAL.

THE AGENDA IS FULL. JUST NO SEX.

THIS IS NEW YORK, NEW YORK. AND WHAT IS GOOD FOR NEW YORK IS GOOD FOR THE WORLD. LISTEN, WORLD, THE SEXLESS MESSAGE OF A SEXY CITY.

SEXLESS SEX, THE ULTIMATE WISDOM. MAKING IT BY THE SKIN OF YOUR TEETH. THE AGE OF DRACULA: "IF HELEN GURLEY BROWN WERE TO ANALYZE DRACULA, I'M SURE SHE'D SAY THAT NO SEX IS SEXY." SEX ISN'T SEXY ENOUGH. TOO MUCH OF A MOUTHFUL, NOT ENOUGH OF A BITE.

MORE AND MORE PEOPLE ARE JUMPING OFF THE TRAIN. "WE WANT OUT," POST-SEXUAL REVOLUTION-ARIES LOUDLY PROCLAIM. WHO ARE THESE NEW DEVIANTS? SHALL WE LOOK FOR THEM AMONG THE TRADITIONAL ADEPTS OF ANHEDONIA, AS PSYCHIA-TRISTS LIKE TO CALL IT? TO STATE IT MORE BLUNTLY: HAS EVERYONE GONE JUNKY OR SCHIZOPHRENIC?

BELIEVE IT OR NOT, ASEXUALITY COMES TO US FROM THE OPPOSITE END OF THE SPECTRUM—FROM THE BUSINESS COMMUNITY. SMALL ENTREPRENEURS

WITH A FUTURE JUST CAN'T AFFORD TO HAVE SEX ANYMORE. THEY HAVE TO SAVE ALL THEIR ENERGIES TO KEEP THE BUSINESS AFLOAT: "THESE PEOPLE ARE NOT LIKE COLLEGE KIDS WHO HAVE TIME FOR SEX BECAUSE THEY'VE GOT NOTHING ELSE TO DO. THESE ARE BUSY, ACTIVE PEOPLE," STEVE RUBELL, CO-OWNER OF STUDIO 54, POINTEDLY DECLARED TO ARTHUR BELL. EVEN WORKING 16 HOURS A DAY DIDN'T SAVE HIM FROM A TAXING BANKRUPTCY.

GONE ARE THE DAYS WHEN BUSY, ACTIVE PEOPLE MESSED AROUND WITH THEIR SEXY SECRETARIES. SMALL ENTREPRENEURS DON'T LEAVE THE OFFICE ANYMORE.

NELSON ROCKEFELLER IS A PRIME EXAMPLE. HE SIMPLY WORKED HMSELF TO DEATH.

NEW YORK IS STILL TOYING WITH THE IDEA OF ASEXUAL CHIC. "IT WAS JUST A JOKE," ESTIMATES RICHARD GOLDSTEIN, OF THE VILLAGE VOICE. "MOST OF THE 'ASEXUAL' PEOPLE INTERVIEWED BY ARTHUR BELL SIMPLY WERE CLOSET GAYS." JOKE OR NO JOKE, NO SEX MAY WELL HAVE REACHED EPIDEMIC PROPORTIONS IN THE SOFT BELLY OF AMERICA.

"SOME PEOPLE CAN'T WORK WHILE THEY ARE INTO SEX," CONFIDES ROBERTA, WHO MANAGES A MASSAGE PARLOR IN DOWNTOWN PITTSBURGH. "I MYSELF CAN'T WORK WITHOUT IT. IT GIVES ME A BOOST OF ENERGY." SHE ESTIMATES, HOWEVER, THAT 20% OF THE CITY IS INTO VARIOUS FORMS OF ABSTINENCE. NONE OF HER CUSTOMERS, AND NONE OF HER GIRLS, OF COURSE, HAS BEEN CONTAMINATED. MASSAGE OBLIGE. BUT NOT EVERYONE CAN TURN SEXUALITY INTO A FULL-FLEDGED PROFESSION. BESIDES, SHE ADDS, "SOME PEOPLE LIKE TO TRY A NEW THING, JUST FOR THE HECK OF IT."

IS ABSTINENCE A REACTION TO THE "OVERKILL" OF THE SEXUAL REVOLUTION?, GABRIELE BROWN, PH.D. SUGGESTS IN HER TIMELY BOOK, THE NEW CELIBACY: WHY MORE MEN AND WOMEN ARE ABSTAINING FROM SEX—AND ENJOYING IT.[8] IS THE "THRILL" GONE SOUR IN OUR SEXUALLY OPEN SOCIETY?

REVOLUTIONS ARE NEVER GOOD
NEWS FOR QUEENS.
WHEN EVERYTHING IS PERMITTED
NOTHING IS EXTRAORDINARY

PROMPTS AL CARMINES (THE FAGGOT). WE'RE ALL QUEENS AT HEART.

IN THE MEANTIME SEX HAS GROWN DEMOCRATIC. ALTHOUGH STILL AN IMMATURE INDUSTRY, THE SEX TRADE HAS BECOME "A MULTIBILLION-DOLLAR BUSINESS WITH THE CHARACTERISTICS OF MANY CONVENTIONAL INDUSTRIES—A LARGE WORKFORCE, HIGH-SALARIED EXECUTIVES, BRISK COMPETITION, TRADE PUBLICATIONS, BOARD MEETINGS, SALES CONVENTIONS," REPORTS THE NEW YORK TIMES.[9] DILDOS AND VIBRATORS CAN BE CHARGED TO VISA OR MASTERCARD ACCOUNTS, AND THE VIDEODISK BUSINESS IS PLUGGING INTO THE SEX INDUSTRY TO ACHIEVE ITS FIRST MAJOR BREAKTHROUGH.

DENNIS SOBIN, PUBLISHER OF THE ADULT BUSINESS REPORT, A WASHINGTON BASED SEX-TRADE NEWSLETTER, ESTIMATES THAT THE SEX BUSINESS HAS "THE SAME POTENTIAL FOR SALES AND PROFITS AS THE FOOD INDUSTRY. IT IS A GROWTH INDUSTRY THAT CANNOT GO BACKWARDS."

DESCRIBING THE SHOW-WORLD CENTER ON 42ND STREET WHERE "SERVICES" HAVE BEEN EXTENSIVELY RATIONALIZED, MR. WEISBROD, WHO MONITORS THE SEX INDUSTRY IN CENTRAL MANHATTAN, COMMENTS DRYLY: "IT'S SEXUAL FAST FOOD." MACROBIOTIC SEX SHOULDN'T BE TOO FAR OFF.

ARE WE GETTING CLOSE TO WHAT HENRY MILLER, LACKING A NAME FOR IT, CALLED THE LAND OF FUCK? A LAND FREE FROM SUPERSTITION, RITUAL, IDOLATRY, FEAR OR GUILT: "WHAT A MAN'S SEX LIFE MAY BE UNDER A NEW ORDER," HE EXCLAIMED, "SURPASSES MY FEEBLE IMAGINATION TO DESCRIBE." WE NOW HAVE A TASTE—JUST A TASTE—OF THE NEW ORDER. IT DIDN'T TAKE THAT MUCH IMAGINATION. IT IS THE LAND OF NOD ALL OVER AGAIN.

SEX HAS CEASED TO BE EXTRAORDINARY, EVEN FOR ORDINARY PEOPLE. PSYCHOLOGISTS REPORT THAT IT IS BECOMING AMERICA'S DOMINANT SOCIAL ACTIVITY. EVERYWHERE SEX IS TAKEN CASUALLY AS LEGITIMATE ENTERTAINMENT. "THE MIDDLE CLASS HAS THE TIME AND ENERGY AND MONEY TO PRACTICE SEX AS RECREATION," ESTIMATES DUANE COLGLAZIER, PRESIDENT OF PLEASURE CHEST LTD. AND A FORMER WALL STREET TRADER. THE

"MYSTERIOUS AND UNKNOWN, POSSIBLY FOREVER UNKNOWABLE" WORLD OF SEX IS BEING TRADED FOR DISNEYLAND. THE LAND OF FUCK RECAST IN PLASTIC PARADISE.

BUT EVEN RECREATION CAN BE A HEADACHE. COPING WITH THE NEW SEXUAL FREEDOM, THE MENTAL HEALTH PROFESSION WARNS, HAS BECOME THE NEW CHALLENGE. BUT WHAT IS NOT A "CHALLENGE" FOR THE MIDDLE CLASS? THE CULTURE KEEPS TRAINING THE INDIVIDUAL TO ASSERT HIS SUPERIORITY THROUGH A COMPARISON. PASSION OF CONFORMISM, WHO WILL EVER TELL YOUR SILENT TORTURE? MIDDLE CLASS SEX IS A REAL FIGHT WITH BLOOD AND GUTS. KEEPING IT UP BETTER THAN THE JONES': NOW THAT CARS ARE SHRINKING IN SIZE AND APPEAL, SEX LOOMS BIG IN THE NEIGHBOR'S EYE.

NO WONDER THE PENDULUM IS SWINGING WILDLY THE OTHER WAY. "THE PRESSURE FROM THE CULTURE IS VERY STRONG NOT TO BE CHASTE," ASSERTS DR. JOYCE BROTHERS. "NOBODY WANTS TO HEAR ABOUT YOUR INTEREST IN ELECTRONICS BUT ABOUT HOW MANY WOMEN YOU HAVE," SAYS CARL CLAY, DIRECTOR OF THE BLACK SPECTRUM THEATER. "THE MEDIA PROJECTS THAT SEX MUST ALWAYS BE ON YOUR MIND. EVERY RECORD SAYS, 'DO IT, DO IT, DO IT ...' THERE IS SO MUCH TO OVERCOME."[10]

SEX USED TO BE A MOLOTOV COCKTAIL AND DO IT A DECLARATION OF WAR. IT IS AMERIKA'S FRUSTRATED PENIS, SHOUTED JERRY RUBIN, THAT LED US TO VIETNAM. SEXUAL INSECURITY BREEDS IMPERIALISM ... AMERIKA'S NEW SATIETY SURELY MUST HAVE CHANGED SOMETHING. NO MORE FRUSTRATION, NO MORE INSECURITY. NO MORE HARD HATS AND CIA. JUST THE HYSTERIA ON IRAN AND BLOODBATHS IN EL SALVADOR.

WE SHALL OVERCOME SEX SOME DAY. BUT WILL WE EVER BE ABLE TO OVERCOME THE PRESSURE FROM THE CULTURE?

WE ARE PLUNGING WITH ALL OUR ENERGY INTO OPPOSITE VALUATIONS. BUT CHASTE OR PROMISCUOUS, ASEXUAL OR HYPERACTIVE, OPPOSITIONS MEAN VERY LITTLE AS LONG AS WE KEEP INTERNALIZING THE PRESSURE FROM THE CULTURE. IT IS THIS PRESSURE THAT MAKES OUR SEXUALITY SO NEUROTIC. IT IS THIS ANXIETY, AND NOT SEX PER SE, THAT BRANDS OUR MINDS. "I'M CONFRONTING ISSUES OF HOW AND WHY WE GUYS FEEL SEXUALLY INADEQUATE. AND HOW WOMEN RESPOND TO THOSE OF US WITH THOSE FEARS," DECLARED THE NEW JERRY RUBIN A COUPLE OF YEARS AGO. "I COULDN'T TALK TO WOMEN BECAUSE I WAS AFRAID TO LOOK BAD." WAS THE OLD RUBIN AFRAID TO LOOK BAD WHEN HE WENT TO CONGRESS HALF-NUDE WITH LIVE AMMUNITION? WAS THAT JUST ANOTHER "SUPERMASCULINITY TRIP" THAT THERAPY EVENTUALLY MANAGED TO CURE? "I WORRIED ABOUT MY COCK SIZE. ABOUT PREMATURE EJACULATION. WILL I GET IT UP AT ALL? I WAS OBSESSED WITH SEX."

THE "ME DECADE" REALLY DID A GOOD JOB ON OUR "AMERICAN REVOLUTIONARIES." JERRY RUBIN REMAINS AS EXEMPLARY OF THE CULTURE IN HIS NEUROTIC ABJECTION AS ACTOR RONALD REAGAN PROPPED UP TO THE LIMELIGHT OF THE PRESIDENCY.

WE DON'T HAVE SEX ANYMORE, WE HAVE "SEXUAL PROBLEMS."

EVERY SINGLE WEEK, MASTERS AND JOHNSON REPEAT IT OBLIGINGLY IN YOUR LOCAL PAPER IN CASE YOU FORGET. WOMEN'S "NEW ASSERTIVENESS" SCARES MEN INTO A "NEW IMPOTENCE," ONLY TO BE LEFT, IN TURN, STRANDED WITH AS MANY ANXIETIES. MEN ARE HAVING PROBLEMS BECAUSE THEY ARE MEN, AND WOMEN BECAUSE THEY ARE WOMEN. THE PERFECT SET-UP.

HAVING SEXUAL PROBLEMS? MALE PROGRAM OF APPLIED SEX THERAPY: "IF YOU HAVE PROBLEMS IN GETTING AN ERECTION ONCE IN A WHILE—AND DON'T WORRY ABOUT IT—YOU ARE JUST LIKE MILLIONS OF MEN." MILLIONS OF MEN CONCERNED ABOUT THEIR PERFORMANCE, DESPERATELY TRYING TO KEEP THEIR EGO 9 (ACTUALLY 5) INCHES UP. "THESE DOUBTS MAY HOUND YOU ALL DAY LONG—IN THE SHOWER, AT WORK, RIDING IN THE CAR AND ESPECIALLY IN BED," DR. DOLORES KELLER, PH.D. GOES ON TACTFULLY. "THE MORE YOU KEEP THINKING ABOUT IT, THE SOFTER YOUR PENIS BECOMES. SHE MAY SAY, 'I REALLY DIDN'T FEEL LIKE IT ANYWAY ...' SUCH COMMENTS ONLY SERVE TO MAKE YOU FEEL WORSE." SOFT MACHINE, BUT NO HARD FEELINGS.

SO ANY OLD RECIPE WILL DO. SUGGESTIONS. INSTRUCTIONS. DAILY MIRACLES OF THE TUNING FORK, OR THE TV SET.

FEMALE PROGRAM OF APPLIED SEX THERAPY: "DO YOU DAYDREAM OF THE MISSED CLIMAX AND TRY TO IMAGINE WHAT IT'S LIKE TO COME? THEN THE CASSETTE PROGRAM DEALING WITH THIS SUBJECT COULD MAKE THOSE DREAMS BECOME AN EXCITING REALITY." ONLY DREAMS COME TRUE. AMERICAN DREAMS CANNED IN A CASSETTE.

"IF ONLY SOMEONE ELSE COULD DO IT FOR ME ..."

SOME PEOPLE DO.

"HAVE YOU CHECKED OUR SURROGATE PROGRAM?" "UH." HE SCRATCHES HIS HEAD. THEN, WITH A FALTERING VOICE: "DO YOU THINK THEY COULD HANDLE THE WHOLE DARN THING ALTOGETHER? I'VE A FEELING SEX'S NOT FOR THE LAYMAN ANYMORE ..."

AS LONG AS WE HAVE NOT CONQUERED OUR FEARS AND OVERCOME THE NEUROTIC SCENARIO INDUCED BY THE CULTURE, IT MATTERS LITTLE WHETHER WE CONFRONT SEXUAL ISSUES OR RENOUNCE SEX ALTOGETHER.

MENTAL HEALTH PROFESSIONALS REALIZED IT INSTANTLY. THEY DIDN'T FEEL TOO THREATENED BY THE CLAIMS OF THE NEW CELIBATES. THERE WERE PLENTY OF REASONS FOR WORRY THOUGH: AFTER ALL, AS GABRIELE BROWN, A PSYCHOLOGIST HERSELF, READILY ADMITS, THE THERAPEUTIC FIELD HAS VIRTUALLY CEASED TO FUNCTION AS A FIELD AND HAS BECOME A SPECIALIZATION IN SEXUALITY. BUT IT COULD AS EASILY DO WITHOUT SEX AS LONG AS NO SEX COULD BE INTERPRETED AS ANOTHER SYMPTOM OF PSYCHOLOGICAL DEFENSE, OR INSTINCTUAL ABERRATION.

THERAPISTS CAN CERTAINLY GET SOME MILEAGE OUT OF ASEXUALITY. THEY CAN GET SOME MILEAGE OUT OF ANYTHING. NOTHING CAN STOP THE ADVANCE OF UPWARDLY MOBILE PROFESSIONALS.

THE CULTURE KEEPS CALLING UPON AN ARMY OF PROFESSIONALS TO DRESS UP SOCIAL TRIVIA INTO MONUMENTAL TRUTHS. THE PUBLIC SHOULD NEVER BE EXPOSED UNPREPARED TO THE HARD EDGES OF ANY EVENT. WHO KNOWS? THEY MIGHT EVEN CHOKE ON THEM. WE SURE NEED LOTS OF SPECIALISTS TO FILE DOWN EVERYTHING INTO SMOOTH, ROUNDED PILLS.

PATIENTS USED TO COMPLAIN TO THEIR THERAPISTS ABOUT THEIR SEXUAL PERFORMANCE: IMPOTENCE, PREMATURE EJACULATION, FAILED ORGASM, THE WORKS. THEY WOULD QUEUE UP AT THE OFFICE WITH THEIR LIMP ORGAN IN HAND. THOSE WERE THE DAYS.

NOT ANY MORE.

PATIENTS ARE GROWING IMPATIENT WITH SEX. "WE'RE GETTING BORED WITH THE SHOW," THEY SAY. "YOU KNOW, BEING MACHO BAGS."

"AND THEY CLAIM THEY'RE NOT REPRESSED OR IMPOTENT? SOME NERVE."

"SHALL WE START WITH A SERIES OF ELECTRO-SHOCKS, DOCTOR?"

OVER THE LAST FEW YEARS, LACK OF SEXUAL INTEREST HAS BECOME THE NUMBER ONE PATIENT SYMPTOM. SOME PSYCHOLOGISTS BEGIN TO FEEL THE PINCH. OTHERS FIGHT BACK.

DR. WILLIAM MASTERS EXAMINES THE CORPUS DELICTI. THIS IS DEFINITELY A PATHOLOGICAL PHENOMENON, HE PRONOUNCES GRAVELY, TAKING OFF HIS GLASSES TO SHOW HIS NAKED SOUL. THE PROFESSION BREATHES MORE FREELY. AS LONG AS IT IS PATHOLOGICAL ...

GUILT, GUILT, GUILT, DIAGNOSES DR. ROLLO MAY. VICTORIANS WERE GUILTY IF THEY EXPERIENCED SEX, HE STATES. "NOW WE FEEL GUILTY IF WE DON'T."

THE PROFESSION IS NOW BEAMING. WHO CARES WHERE GUILT COMES FROM AS LONG AS IT IS THERE? THERAPY, LIKE THE SEX TRADE, IS A GROWTH INDUSTRY THAT CANNOT GO BACKWARDS.

BEHIND EACH LUKEWARM BED SQUATS A SPECIALIST BUSILY TAKING NOTES. SAYS DR. HELEN SINGER KAPLAN, DIRECTOR OF THE HUMAN SEXUALITY PROGRAM AT THE NEW YORK HOSPITAL: "FOR SOME PEOPLE, SEX IS FRAUGHT WITH SO MUCH ANXIETY, ANGER AND NEGATIVE EMOTION THAT IT MAY BE A BETTER ADAPTATION NOT TO RISK IT." AND A RESIDENT PSYCHIATRIST AT BELLEVUE: "IT IS NOT UNREASONABLE TO BELIEVE THAT SOMEONE IN POLITICS OR BUSINESS TODAY IS SO ANXIETY-RIDDEN THAT HE CAN'T HAVE SEX ... IT MIGHT BE A TOTALLY APPROPRIATE RESPONSE TO AN INTENSE ENVIRONMENT." SEXOLOGISTS DON'T TAKE RISKS EITHER. IT MIGHT BE A TOTALLY APPROPRIATE

RESPONSE TO THE PSYCHIATRIC ENVIRONMENT.

THE INFLATION OF SEXUALITY HAD A LOT TO DO WITH ANXIETY TO START WITH. IT IS IN SEX THAT THE ANXIETY-RIDDEN, DEPLETED-INFLATED WESTERN EGO USED TO FIND A TEMPORARY RELIEF AND REVENGE. NOW THAT SEX IS NO SHELTER, THE EGO IS READY TO DO ANYTHING SHORT OF GIVING ITSELF UP.

NEUROSIS ISN'T THE ILLNESS IT IS SUPPOSED TO BE. IT IS ANOTHER WORD FOR NORMALITY. AND NORMALITY IS PRETTY SICK, IF YOU WANT MY OPINION. OH, NOTHING DRAMATIC, NOTHING FLAMBOYANT. ANXIETY ON A DAILY BASIS. ENOUGH PRESSURE TO KEEP THE INDIVIDUAL ON HIS TOES, BUT NOT SO MUCH AS TO ACTUALLY INCAPACITATE HIM SOCIALLY. NERVOUS ENERGY MUST BE FED INTO THE MACHINE, NOT BREAK IT DOWN ALTOGETHER.

NOW THAT THE INDIVIDUAL IS DIVORCED FROM DWINDLING "TRIBAL" STRUCTURES (FAMILY, COMMUNITY, ETC.), HE HAS A HARD TIME NOT FALLING APART IN HIS INCREASING ISOLATION. ALL THE MORE REASON TO SEXUALIZE THE INDIVIDUAL WHILE INDIVIDUALIZING HIS SEXUALITY. IT IS THE CRIPPLE LEADING THE BLIND.

ANXIETY NOW WORKS BOTH WAYS. THIS "DOUBLE BIND" CLEARLY DEFINES THE PREDICAMENT OF NORMAL NEUROTIC INDIVIDUALS—AND NOT, AS GREGORY BATESON CLAIMED, SCHIZOPHRENICS. BY LINKING TOTAL SATISFACTION TO INDIVIDUAL SELF-ESTEEM, SEXUALITY HAS BECOME JUST ANOTHER TEST, ALBEIT THE MOST EXCRUCIATING, FOR ALL TOO VULNERABLE EGOS.

DR. I.M. POTENT'S HILARIOUS COMPILATION OF 101 REASONS NOT TO HAVE SEX TONIGHT,[11] WITH ITS NON-EROGENOUS ZONES AND DIAGRAMS OF POSITIONS NOT TO HAVE SEX IN, IS A CLEAR SYMPTOM OF THE PRESENT REVERSAL OF SEXUAL TRENDS. NEUROTIC "TRAGEDY" REVEALS ITSELF FOR WHAT IT IS: A MERE SEXUAL JOKE. IT IS WOODY ALLEN THE OTHER WAY AROUND.

SEX OR NO SEX: I DON'T SEE WHY WE SHOULD BE MADE TO CHOOSE BETWEEN THE TWO. THESE KINDS OF EXCLUSIONS ALWAYS SMACK OF NEUROTICISM, WHICH IS EXACTLY WHAT WE WERE TRYING TO GET RID OF, INSTEAD OF SEX. BUT LET'S ASSUME FOR A MOMENT THAT SEXUALITY IS ON ITS WAY OUT, AND LET'S SEE WHERE THIS LEADS US TO.

WE'VE BEEN TOLD THAT WE CAN'T DO WITHOUT SEX. SURE WE CAN. MONKS DID IT—OR SO THEY CLAIM. NOW THAT MONKS ARE NO LONGER GIVEN THE PROPER "RESPECT AND ADMIRATION THEY RECEIVED EARLIER" (GABRIELE BROWN), AND THEIR LIVES EVEN CONSIDERED SOMEWHAT "UNNATURAL" BY THE GENERAL PUBLIC, TIME MAY BE RIPE TO FEED THE MONK IN US.

WE'VE BEEN SO TRAINED TO COUCH EVERYTHING IN SEXUAL TERMS, VERY RESTRICTIVE TERMS, THAT WE'RE HAVING A HARD TIME SEPARATING SEXUALITY FROM DESIRE.

IN NO WAY IS SEXUALITY THE "INFRASTRUCTURE" OF DESIRE. DESIRE DOESN'T HAVE TO BE TIED DOWN TO SEX. PEOPLE CAN LIVE WITHOUT SEX—THEY JUST CAN'T LIVE WITHOUT DESIRE. RENOUNCING SEXUALITY ISN'T THE "FINAL SOLUTION." DESIRE SIMPLY BRANCHES OUT OF SEXUALITY IN ORDER TO INVEST OTHER, LESS LOADED, TERRITORIES. THE BECOMING NON-SEXUAL OF DESIRE IS A FAIRLY EXTREME AND PRECARIOUS FORM OF POLYSEXUALITY: POLYSEXUALITY WITHOUT SEX.

THE SHAKERS' BEDTIME RITUAL (WHIRLING) IS USUALLY INTERPRETED AS A COMMUNAL TECHNIQUE FOR THE RELEASE OF SEXUAL TENSION: RENOUNCING GENITAL LOVE GIVES ACCESS TO WHAT HERBERT RICHARDSON CALLS A "NEW POLYMORPHOUS SEXUALITY."

RECENT MEDICAL DATA PROVIDES FURTHER JUSTIFICATION FOR THE INFECTIOUS WITHDRAWAL FROM SEXUALITY. NEUROLOGIST RICHARD MAYEUX FOUND THAT SOME PEOPLE "EXPERIENCE A PROFOUND AMNESIA AND DISORIENTATION FOR SEVERAL HOURS AFTER HAVING SEXUAL INTERCOURSE." IT SEEMS NO WONDER MENTAL PATIENTS COME BEGGING FOR MORE ELECTROSHOCKS. DIRTY OLD MINDS. THEY GET MORE THAN THEY DESERVE.

ATTENTION: SEX IS KILLER NUMERO UNO IN THIS COUNTRY. EVERY 80 SECONDS A CAR GOES BERSERK ON THE HIGHWAY FOR NO DISCERNIBLE REASON. ALCOHOL TEST: NEGATIVE. THE PHENOMENON BAFFLES THE POLICE. DRIVERS SHOULD BE SEVERELY PROHIBITED FROM HAVING INTERCOURSE SEVERAL HOURS BEFORE THEY HIT THE ROAD. STANDARD TESTS WILL BE ENFORCED: HEART BEAT, MUSCULAR TENSION, URINALYSIS.

POLICE DOGS, MOREOVER, WOULD SNIFF IT OUT IN NO TIME.

SEX IS NOT GOOD FOR YOU. THE SURGEON GENERAL HAS DETERMINED THAT FUCKING IS DANGEROUS TO YOUR HEALTH. FIFTY JACK RABBITS FUCKING FIFTY TIMES A DAY FOR FIFTY CONSECUTIVE DAYS CONTRACTED IT BEFORE ENTERING COMA. SEX IS CANCER PRONE. TIME TO KICK THE HABIT: "IT'S LIKE SMOKING," SUGGESTS FRANK LANGELLA. "ONCE YOU GET OVER THE FIRST THREE OR FOUR WEEKS, IT COMES EASY." IT DOESN'T COME AT ALL.

SEX AND DECADENCE

> "THE TIME HAS COME WHEN WE HAVE TO PAY FOR HAVING BEEN CHRISTIANS FOR TWO THOUSAND YEARS: WE ARE LOSING THE CENTER OF GRAVITY BY VIRTUE OF WHICH WE LIVED, WE ARE LOST FOR A WHILE. ABRUPTLY WE PLUNGE INTO THE OPPOSITE VALUATIONS, WITH ALL THE ENERGY THAT SUCH AN EXTREME OVEREVALUATION OF MAN HAS GENERATED IN MAN."
>
> — NIETZSCHE

IT IS TEMPTING TO CONSIDER ASEXUALITY A MERE BACKLASH AGAINST THE SEXUAL REVOLUTION. THE PHENOMENON, HOWEVER, IS MORE COMPLEX. IT IS MADE IN PART OF THE EXHAUSTION FROM A MOVEMENT THE CULTURE HASTENED TO MAKE SERVICEABLE, BUT IN PART ALSO OF OUR GROWING CAPACITY TO WITHSTAND SEXUAL WASTE. THESE TWO THREADS—DENIAL OF SEXUALITY, "GYMNAS-TICS OF THE WILL"—RUN SIMULTANEOUSLY THROUGH THE CLAIMS OF THE NEW CELIBACY. ONLY BY DIFFERENTIATING THE TWO ASPECTS CAN A REAL EVALUATION OF THE ASEXUAL PHENOMENON BE ACHIEVED.

"LET'S FACE IT, IT'S MORE INTERESTING TO BE CELIBATE THAN TO BE IMPOTENT," GABRIELE BROWN CONCEDES CYNICALLY. ASEXUALITY AS AN ANTIDOTE TO SEXUAL STRESS IS NOTHING NEW—A THERAPIST'S JOB. FREELY CHOSEN CELIBACY IS AN ALTOGETHER DIFFERENT STORY. WHAT MAKES ONE BECOME ABSTINENT?

"I REALLY DON'T LIKE BEING RUN BY ANYTHING—I ESPECIALLY DON'T ENJOY BEING MANIPULATED BY A PHYSICAL FEELING," SAYS ALEXANDRA, A CELIBATE WOMAN INTERVIEWED FOR THE BOOK. GIVING SEX UP IS A DECLARATION OF INDEPEN-DENCE, A POSITIVE ACT, NOT JUST THE EXPRESSION OF A MENTAL PARALYSIS. IF YOU'RE CAUGHT IN THE LABYRINTH OF SEX, YOU CAN ALWAYS INVENT A REMEDY, FORGE A NEW DEVICE. YOU CAN GROW WINGS—SIMPLY BEWARE OF ANGELISM ... ONCE ABOVE SEXUAL EXERTION, OTHER VALUES WILL EMERGE IN THE DISTANCE.

FEMALE ORGASM HAS BECOME THE PRIME CONCERN FOR BOTH SEXES. "EQUAL PAY FOR EQUAL WORK OR AN ORGASM FOR AN ORGASM," QUIPS THE NEW CELIBACY. SEXUAL PLEASURE ON THE ASSEMBLY-LINE ... THE FOCUS ON ORGASM FURTHER TIGHTENED THE ALREADY RESTRICTIVE EMPHASIS ON LOVEMAKING. WITH ORGASM LOOMING ABOVE, "THE FUTURE BECAME MORE IMPORTANT THAN THE PRESENT," COMPLAINS SARAH, ANOTHER CELIBATE. ASEXUALITY HAS NO FUTURE. BUT HAS IT GOT A PRESENT?

IF ASEXUALITY MEANS EXPERIENCING SEXUALITY IN NON-GENITAL WAYS, ITS POTENTIAL IS TRULY INFINITE. WHAT FALLS AWAY (DE-CADENS) FROM SEX, AFTER ALL, IS ONLY THE PALE CARICATURE THAT KEPT POKING THE INDIVIDUAL INTO SUBMISSION. REMEMBER JERRY RUBIN: DIDN'T HE END UP IN WALL STREET? ASEXUALITY AS A FORM OF NIHILISM IS A WAR MACHINE CAPABLE OF ATTACKING THE REACTIVE POWERS AT WORK IN OUR SEXUALITY. IF THE DESTRUCTION COULD BE MADE ACTIVE, AND NOT ANEMIC, EXUBERANT, AND NOT NOSTALGIC; IF IT WERE TO COME FROM AN OVERFLOW OF LIFE, AND NOT FROM A THINLY-VEILED DEATH-WISH, ASEXUAL-ITY COULD CERTAINLY HELP RESTORE SEXUALITY TO ITS FULLNESS.

ASEXUALITY IS A SYMPTOM OF DECADENCE, AND LIKE OTHER SYMPTOMS OF DECADENCE, IT IS AMBIGUOUS BY DEFINITION. AMBIGUITY ISN'T SUCH THAT IT REQUIRES AN ELUCIDATION—EVEN LESS A CRITIQUE: SOME ELEMENTS SIMPLY NEED TO BE "FORGOTTEN," OTHERS MOBILIZED. ONCE THE FOCUS ON GENITAL SEX IS REMOVED, A "NEW POLY-MORPHOUS SEXUALITY" COMES INTO BEING.

THE OLD POLYMORPHOUS SEXUALITY WAS FOR THE YOUNG. FREUD DESCRIBED IT AS UNFOCUSED, NON-GENITAL. HE ALSO CALLED IT PERVERSE. QUITE A SLIP OF THE TONGUE FROM THE INVENTOR OF PARAPRAXES: HAS ANYONE EVER SEEN A PER-VERSION THAT PRECEDES THE LAW? BUT THAT WAS PRECISELY THE POINT. CHILDREN ARE THE REAL PERVERTS BECAUSE THEY HAVEN'T PAID THEIR DUES. THEY ARE POLYMORPHOUS WITHOUT GUILT. NO ONE SHOULD BE ALLOWED THAT MUCH FREEDOM: A TYPICAL CASE OF "POLYMORPHOUS ENVY."

BUT WHAT IS ACTUALLY POLYMORPHOUS IN ASEXUAL SEXUALITY? THE SHAKERS' TECHNIQUE FOR THE REALEASE OF BEDTIME TENSION IS INVOKED BY HERBERT RICHARDSON AS A MODEL OF POLYMORPHOUS SEXUALITY. WHAT IS POLYMOR-PHOUS ABOUT THAT? WHIRLING AWAY FROM SEX, AT BEST, IS DANCING YOURSELF AWAY (NIETZSCHE). POLYMORPHOUS SELF, FOR SURE. NOT POLYMOR-PHOUS SEX.

MAYBE THE ATTEMPT TO SEPARATE WHAT IS SEXUAL AND WHAT IS NOT IS STILL TOO RESTRIC-TIVE. IS PHYSICAL CLOSENESS AND INTIMACY SEXUALLY POLYMORPHOUS? WHERE DOES SEX START, WHERE DOES IT END? FRANK LANGELLA HAS AN ANSWER. ASEXUALITY, HE SAYS, "IS THE FIRST STEP YOU TAKE WHEN YOU DECIDE TO BECOME NONHUMAN. THE PENIS, VAGINA, BREASTS EXIST. IF ONE WANTS TO USE THEM, ONE MUST HAVE SEX." SEX ORGANS SHOULDN'T BE WASTED. WHO KNOW? THEY COULD DRY UP AND FALL TO THE GROUND. THE NEGLECTED PENIS MAY SHRINK BEYOND RECOGNITION, LIKE A VULGAR LITTLE TWO. DAS KLINE ... WHO WANTS TO HEAR OF A NATURAL CASTRATION ANYWAY? ASEXUALITY ANNOUNCES AN "UNNATURAL" USE OF HUMAN ORGANS. BUT IS THE HUMAN BODY USED THAT NATURALLY AFTER ALL? SEXUALITY ISN'T ONLY IN SEX. SEXUAL ORGANS CAN SPROUT ANYWHERE WHEN GIVEN THE CHANCE.

MODERN SEXUALITY IS BY FAR TOO SPECIALIZED TO TAKE A CHANCE. ANATOMICAL DIFFERENCES ARE ALWAYS EXPERIENCED AS AN IRREMEDIABLE OPPOSITION, "SEPARATE FLESH ENGAGED IN ENDLESS SEXUAL CONFLICTS" (WILLIAM BUR-ROUGHS). SEX: "THE CHARACTER OF BEING EITHER MALE OR FEMALE ..." WHY NOT FEM-MALE (TRANSSEXUALS), MAN-NIMAL (THE ELEPHANT MAN), OR WOM-INERAL? WHY NOT ADD UP SINGU-LARITIES, INSTEAD OF OPPOSING DIFFERENCES? BECOMING UNHUMAN AS AN ACCESS TO NON-EXCLUSIVE CONNECTIONS—A TRULY CRATIVE ASSEMBLY-LINE.

SEXUAL ORGANS ARE BEING USED. THEY ARE BEING USED EXTENSIVELY TO NATURALIZE CULTURAL PREJUDICES. IT'S TIME TO TAKE THE ORGANS AWAY FROM THEIR CULTURAL NATURALNESS. TIME TO SUBVERT THE HIERARCHIC ORGANIZATION OF THE BODY POLITIC.

ASEXUALITY COULD LIBERATE SEXUAL ORGANS FOR OHTER PURPOSES. IT COULD ALLOW A CONSTANT RESHUFFLING OF BODY FUNCTIONS. IT COULD OPEN UP WITHIN THE COLD RATIONALITY OF ACTIVE, BUSY PEOPLE A VERTIGINOUS SPACE HITHERTO RESTRICTED TO THE MARGINS OF SOCIETY: THE IMPERSONAL BODY OF THE JUNKY, THE TORTURED BODY OF THE MASO, THE LIMITLESS BODY OF THE SCHIZO.[12]

ASEXUALITY AS A FORM OF SEXUALITY SIMPLY MEANS "NON-GOAL ORIENTED SEX," AND THAT'S THAT. IT MEANS INVENTING A BODY WITHOUT ORGANS THAT DOESN'T HAVE TO BE OBSESSED WITH GENITAL ACCOMPLISHMENT.

IT SHOULDN'T BE OBSESSED WITH GENITAL CONTINENCE EITHER. THE NEW CELIBACY, EXPLAINS GABRIELE BROWN, IS SIMPLER THAN HAVING SEX. IT INVOLVES, SHE WRITES, "DOING NOTHING."

DOING NOTHING ACTUALLY REQUIRES A LOT OF DOING. DOING NOTHING DIET: AVOID ANYTHING SPICY, INCLUDING THOUGHTS. DOING NOTHING SPORTS: EXERCISE TO DEATH, STAND ON YOUR SHOULDER TO PUMP THE ENERGY AWAY FROM THE GENITALS. DOING NOTHING EXPEDIENTS? BLOW YOUR LUST AWAY WITH COLD SHOWERS, OR SUFFOCATE IT BY SQUATTING OFER A BASIN OF COOL WATER. LAST, BUT NOT LEAST, "IT IS CLEAR THAT IF YOU WANT TO INDULGE IN CELIBACY, YOU DON'T MASTURBATE." SOME INDULGENCE.

ARE WE "GOING BEYOND" THE SEXUAL REVOLUTION, HAVE WE "GROWN BEYOND THE NEED FOR SEX"—OR ARE WE SEEKING REMISSION FOR OUR SINS? IS THE NEW CELIBACY A SECULAR WAY TO A NEW RELIGION? IT SEEMS AT LEAST TO GIVE NEW CURRENCY TO TRADITIONAL TECHNIQUES OF SEXUAL RESTRAINT. SOME FREEDOM. CELIBACY, SUGGESTS GABRIELE BROWN, IS LIKE TAKING A VACATION FROM SEX. SOME VACATION.

ANY FORM OF EXCLUSION IS REACTIVE—UNLESS IT IS SIMPLY MEANT TACTICALLY, NOT ABSOLUTELY, AS A MEANS TO "MAKE ASCETICISM NATURAL AGAIN." (THE WILL TO POWER). DISSUASION FROM SEX

PARADOXICALLY ENDS UP GIVING SEXUAL VALUE TO EVERYTHING (FOOD, EXERCISE, ETC.) THAT HADN'T YET BEEN DIRECTLY AFFECTED BY SEX. IT ALSO MEANS FALLING BACK ON AN ANTI-MASTURBATORY STAND THAT INITIALLY PLAYED A CRUCIAL ROLE IN THE HYPER-SOCIALIZATION OF SEX—WHICH THE NEW CELIBACY PRECISELY OPPOSES. IN THIS RESPECT, FAR FROM BEING AN EXIT FROM SEX, ASEXUALITY REPRESENTS ITS ULTIMATE ACCOMPLISHMENT.

SO IS FREUD'S SUBLIMATION OF SEXUAL DRIVES INTO "WORKS OF SERVICE," OR A "GENERALIZED LOVE FOR EVERYONE" FOR THAT MATTER. LOVE FOR EVERYONE? WHAT ABOUT HAIG AND PINOCHET . . . "GENERALIZED LOVE, SAME AS LOVE: SOCIAL DETERGENT." (MY DEFINITION.) THE PARANOID MACHINE CLEANS ITSELF OF THE DIRT OF INDIVIDUALISM AND COMPETITION. GUILT, GUILT, GUILT. WHAT CAN BE POLYMORPHOUS ABOUT THESE GENERALIZED PERVERSIONS?

AS SOON AS YOU TAKE A VACATION FROM THE LAND OF NOD, GOD IS WAITING FOR YOU WITH OPEN ARMS, READY TO TURN THE NEW ENERGY INTO A NEW DEAL. A NEW DEAL, A MYSTIFYING FICTION THAT EXACTLY MIRRORS THE OLD GENITAL TYRANNY. "HIGHER PLEASURES COME TO REPLACE LOWER ONES," PROMPTS GABRIELE BROWN. SOME HIGH.

THAT THE NEW CELIBACY SHOWS A STRONG INTEREST "IN RELIGION AND SPIRITUAL DEVELOPMENT" SHOULDN'T COME AS A SURPRISE. "IT WAS A GREAT RELIEF, AS WELL AS A GREAT KIND OF FREEDOM, TO BE FREE OF SEXUAL DESIRE," CONFESSES MICHAEL, WHO EXPERIENCED IN HIS YOUTH A FRUSTRATED VOCATION FOR PRIESTHOOD (WHAT COULD HE DO? HIS FAMILY WASN'T EVEN CATHOLIC . . .). RELIGION DOESN'T NEED A FROCK. THE NEW EMPHASIS ON LOVE CAN DO JUST AS WELL. TEILHARD DE CHARDIN'S "UNIVERSAL LOVE" WILL SHOW YOU THE WAY.

MANY THERAPISTS AGREE THAT THE BIG TABOO TODAY ISN'T ON SEX ANYMORE, IT IS ON LOVE: SEX IS AN EXCUSE TO AVOID INTIMACY, EMOTIONAL COMMITMENT, TRUE LOVE, ETC. "I FEEL MORE PURE, MORE WHOLE, MORE TRUE TO MYSELF AND MUCH MORE ABLE TO LOVE DEEPLY," DECLARES CELIBATE ALEXANDRA. "I REALLY ENJOY GIVING TO OTHERS BECAUSE, UNLIKE SEX, IT DOESN'T END AND THERE IS NO NEED FOR A MUTUAL PAY OFF." NO MUTUAL PAY OFF: THE AMERICAN WAY OF LOVE. A REAL BARGAIN.

DAVID THORSTAD, A SPOKESMAN FOR THE NORTH AMERICAN MAN/BOY LOVE ASSOCIATION, POINTED OUT THAT BOYS HAVE A HEALTHIER ATTITUDE TOWARD LOVE THAN A LOT OF ADULTS DO: "THEY DON'T CARRY AROUND ALL THIS LOVE BAGGAGE THAT ADULTS HAVE ACCUMULATED."[13] GABRIELE BROWN'S CONCEPTION OF LOVE, SO PURE, SO WHOLE, SO TRUE TO ONESELF, IS DEFINITELY FOR ADULTS ONLY.

"I WAS TRYING FOR AN ADULT LOVE STORY, A STORY WHERE THE PEOPLE GET TOGETHER BECAUSE THEY ARE IN LOVE RATHER THAN BECAUSE THEY WANT TO GO TO BED," DECLARES PLAYWRIGHT LANFORD WILSON. "SO MANY LOVE STORIES ARE REALLY SEX STORIES. I WANTED TO HAVE TWO PEOPLE DISCOVER . . . THAT THEY HAD FOUND THE PERFECT PERSON."[14] PURE, PERFECT, WHOLE, TRUE—THE LAND OF NOD ALL OVER AGAIN.

SO THE PENDULUM SWINGS THE OTHER WAY. AFTER LOVE—SEX; AFTER SEX—LOVE, AND BACK AGAIN. NOW THE NEW CELIBACY, SOON THE NEW MARRIAGE, OR THE NEW PRIEST.

SKIRTS OR FROCKS UP THE LEG, DOWN THE LEG, THEN UP AGAIN. SO MUCH IS NEW FOR SO LITTLE CHANGE. BUT WHO CARES? LIFE IS SHORT, AND SO IS MEMORY. SIGNS CIRCULATE, ONLY DIFFERENCES COUNT. IF THERE ARE ANY LEFT.

ARE WE HEADING TOWARD AN ASEXUAL SOCIETY? ASKS ARTHUR BELL. IT DEPENDS, OF COURSE, HOW YOU DEFINE ASEXUAL. A NON-GENITALLY-FOCUSED, POLYCENTRIC, POLYSEXUAL SOCIETY: YES, EVENTUALLY. A "NEW" ABSTINENT SOCIETY: HOPEFULLY NOT. THE REFUSAL OF SEX IS SO MUCH A PART OF RETENTIVE HABITS AND SAVINGS OBSESSIONS, IT'S BEEN MIXED UP FOR SO LONG WITH RELIGIOUS ASCETICISM AND PURITANICAL PRUDERY, WITH THE ETHICS OF WORK AND INDIVIDUAL RESPONSABILITY, ITS ROOTS GO SO DEEP IN THE AMERICAN SOIL THAT I DOUBT VERY MUCH ANY NEW VALUE CAN COME OUT OF ALL THAT. FOR ALL ITS ETHEREAL CLAIMS, ASEXUALITY IS STILL TOO EARTHY, TOO "FUNKY," TO BE TRUSTED. NOT DEFUNK ENOUGH TO BE JOYOUSLY REBORN OUT OF ITS ASHES.

IT CAN BE BORN-AGAIN THOUGH PRETTY EASILY. JUST LISTEN TO REV. JERRY FALWELL AND THE LIKE. IT CAN POP UP AGAIN RIGHTEOUSLY AS NO SEX SQUADS THROWING BOMBS AND SPREADING

MORAL TERROR OVER ALL THE 42ND STREETS OF THE LAND. (WOMEN AGAINST PORNOGRAPHY IS A CLEAR WARNING, BUT NOT A REAL THREAT. IF THEY WERE LESS LITERAL-MINDED, THEY WOULD PICKET ANNIE, NOT LOLITA ...) ASEXUALITY CARRIES AS WELL IN ITS DRY BOSOM PURE SEEDS OF SEDITION: SEXOREXIA, SEX STRIKE, CONSUMER'S BOYCOTT. BUT FOR THE MOST PART, IT WILL REMAIN A SOFT NIHILIST PHASE, A PASSING FAD.

AT LEAST WE'RE BEING GIVEN, EVEN DECLARA- TIVELY, THE POSSIBILITY OF OPTING OUT OF THE LOADED OPPOSITION BETWEEN SEXUAL REPRES- SION AND SEXUAL LIBERATION. IF THE PRESENT BATTLE OF DECADENCE WERE ONLY ABOUT THAT, IT WOULD STILL BE WORTH THE TROUBLE.

THIS BRINGS US BACK TO THE NOTION OF DECADENCE. LET ME CLARIFY IT FURTHER BEFORE I GET BACK TO SEX.

DECADENCE HAS NOTHING TO DO WITH THE ALL- TOO-LINEAR CONCEPTION OF DECLINE. DECLINE OF THE WEST. DECADENCE ISN'T DECLINE, UNLESS WE WERE TO "DECLINE" THE WEST GRAMMATICALLY, AND NOT HISTORICALLY. FAR FROM DECLINING, THE WEST IS GOING FEVERISHLY THROUGH ALL ITS CASES AND FLEXIONS. THIS EXPLAINS WHY BOTH LIBERATION AND REPRESSION ARE SIMULTAN- EOUSLY PRESENT AT THE OPPOSITE ENDS OF THE SEXUAL PARADIGM AS WELL AS IN EACH OF THE SINGULAR SEXUAL EXPERIENCES THAT KEEP SURFAC- ING IN THE CULTURE (IN THE MEDIA) AT AN EVER QUICKENING PACE: HOMOSEXUALITY, LESBIANISM, S&M, TRANSVESTISM, TRANSSEXUALITY, SOON PEDOPHILIA ... THE PARADIGM ALSO INCLUDES PELL-MELL ALL THE EXPERIMENTS WE KEEP UPROOTING—DEFUNKING—FROM OTHER CULTURES IN OUR INSATIABLE DISSATISFACTION WITH OUR OWN SORRY LOT: MEDITATION AND MARTIAL ARTS,TAO SEX AND PLATO'S RETREAT—BODY TAGS AND BODY TECHNIQUES.

THE WEST DOESN'T DECLINE, IT IS, ON THE CONTRARY, LOSING ITS SENSE OF TIMING: ITS FAITH IN PROGRESS (H-BOMB), ITS DESIRE FOR CHANGE (ZERO GROWTH), ITS HOPE FOR A POSITIVE OUTCOME (REVOLUTION). THE WEST DOESN'T DECLINE, IT KEEPS MARKING TIME. TIME NOW IS EVERYTHING BUT LINEAR. IT HAS BECOME EXCHANGEABLE, DISPOS- ABLE, REVERSIBLE, CIRCULAR LIKE EVERYTHING ELSE. WE KEEP INTERPRETING TIME AND ITS PRODUCTIONS TELEOLOGICALLY, BUT THIS SIMPLY

MEASURES OUR PRESENT INCAPACITY TO SEPAR- ATE OURSELVES FROM THE SNARES OF THE CULTURE.

OUR SOCIETY KEEPS REPEATING ITSELF OVER AND OVER AGAIN. SOMETIMES AS A TRAGEDY, SOME- TIMES AS A FARCE, BUT NOT IN A SUCCESSION (MARX): BOTH ARE PRESENT AT ONCE IN THE SAME PHENOMENON. WHETHER WE SUBMIT WILLINGLY TO ITS PATHOS, OR DERIDE ITS GRAVITY WITH LOUD LAUGHTER REMAINS A MATTER OF CHOICE. BUT ONLY LAUGHTER CAN EVENTUALLY BREAK OPEN THE HALL OF MIRRORS THAT GIVE US A FRAIL SENSE OF SECURITY—FOR WHICH WE HAVE TO PAY A STAGGERING COST IN TERMS OF POWERLESSNESS AND ANXIETY.

WE KEEP MARKING TIME PASSIVELY, REACTIVELY, ENDLESSLY PLUNGING IN OPPOSITE VALUATIONS, FEVERISHLY BURNING A WEALTH OF VALUES THAT COULD STILL TESTIFY TO AN INTENSE CREATIVITY IF WE KNEW HOW TO MARK THEM WITH THE ACTIVE POWER OF OUR IMAGINATION. AS ROLAND BARTHES ONCE SAID OF THE NARRATIVE (AND HISTORY IS A NARRATIVE, OUR BLOODY MYTH), IF WE DON'T READ A NARRATIVE OVER AGAIN, WE KEEP READING IT EVERYWHERE, UNKNOWINGLY. ASEXUALITY IS ONE OF THE MANY FICTIONS OF THE CULTURE, BUT IF WE REREAD IT CAREFULLY, INSTEAD OF TRASHING IT OUT OF THE WINDOW, WE WILL DISCOVER THAT THE HISTORY OF SEXUALITY—OR THE SEXUALIZATION OF HISTORY—IS CONVENIENTLY STAGED IN THIS CURIOUSLY AMBIGUOUS PHENOMENON.

THE ASEXUAL SYMPTOM IS EVEN MORE COMPLEX THAN WHAT RECENT HISTORIANS OF SEXUALITY WOULD BE WILLING TO ADMIT.

THE PRESCRIPTION TO EXTERNALIZE SEXUALITY IN DISCOURSE USED TO GO ALONG WTH THE OSTEN- SIBLE PROSCRIPTION OF ANY SEXUAL EXPRESSION. NOW THAT SEXUALITY SURFACES SMOOTHLY EVERYWHERE, CAN WE STILL ASSIGN IT A CRUCIAL ROLE IN THE PRESENT STRATEGY OF CONTROL, HOWEVER POSITIVE THIS CONTROL MAY BE? HOW COULD WE POSSIBLY BELIEVE THAT THERE'S ANY "TRUTH" TO BE EXTRACTED, AND POWER TO BE DERIVED, FROM ALL TOO READILY AVAILABLE ACCOUNTS OF INDIVIDUAL "SEX LIVES"? THE PROPENSITY TO SPEAK ABOUT SEX HAS BECOME SUCH AN EXPLICIT, EXPECTED, AND EXPEDIENT FEATURE OF OUR SOCIETY THAT IT TAKES A CERTAIN AMOUNT OF COURAGE TO ASSUME THAT

AN OCCULT SOCIAL INJUNCTION IS STILL AT WORK IN THE PRESENT INFLATION OF SEXUAL DISCOURSE.

WHEN MICHEL FOUCAULT'S HISTORY OF SEXUALITY CAME OUT IN PARIS, IN 1976, IT IMMEDIATELY MET WITH ANGRY OBJECTIONS. "WHAT ABOUT SEXUAL MISERY?" FRENCH CRITICS SNAPPED BACK. ON THIS SIDE OF THE ATLANTIC, HIS POSITION PARADOXI-CALLY SOUNDS, IN THE WORDS OF A NEW YORK CRITIC, RATHER "PURITANICAL." SEXUALITY MAY STILL BE PRETTY HEAVY ON THE FRENCH; IN THE NEW WORLD, IT SIMPLY DEFIES GRAVITY. SEX FLOATS AROUND AIMLESSLY LIKE A MATZO BALL IN CHICKEN BROTH, OR BACKGROUND MUSIC IN A HOWARD JOHNSON'S.

IT MAY BE THAT CROSSING THE ATLANTIC INVOLVES MORE THAN A TRANSLATION: ANOTHER SWING OF THE PENDULUM, ANOTHER TURN OF THE SCREW.

IT ISN'T THAT FOUCAULT'S ANALYSIS DOESN'T HOLD: IT HOLDS ITSELF BRILLIANTLY. BUT IT DOESN'T HOLD ANYTHING ELSE ANYMORE, ESPECIALLY NOT SEX. AT THIS POINT, SEXUALITY IS COMPLETELY DIVORCED FROM ANY "WILL TO KNOWLEDGE," ANY DESIRE FOR RATIONALITY—IF SUCH A PHILOSO-PHER'S WILL, AND SUCH A FRENCH DISEASE EVER SET FOOT IN THIS COUNTRY ON THESE TERMS. ISN'T IT PARADOXICAL THAT SUCH A STRONG INDICTMENT OF SEXUAL DISCOURSE COMES AT A TIME WHEN THIS DISCOURSE HAS GROWN SO PUBLIC AND RHETORICAL, SO FOSSILIZED AS TO LOOSE ALL CREDIBILITY? ARE WE CONDEMNED TO ENDLESSLY DEFINE IN THEORETICAL TERMS WHAT HAS CEASED TO EXIST—IF IT EVER EXISTED IN THE FIRST PLACE?

FOUCAULT'S THESIS MAY WELL BE ANOTHER ATTEMPT TO SAVE THE TRUTH ABOUT SEXUALITY AT A TIME WHEN SEX HAS OUTGROWN ANY FINALITY, EVEN A CONTROLLING FINALITY, TO PERMEATE ALL LEVELS OF SOCIETY WITH A SOFT AND EXACER-BATED EROTICISM. WE ARE NOT SEXUALLY DEPRIVED, NOR ARE WE UNDER ANY FORM OF SEXUAL SURVEILLANCE. WE ARE SIMPLY MILDLY DISINTERESTED, AS THE GROWING RECOGNITION OF ASEXUALITY CLEARLY INDICATES.

IT COULD BE ARGUED THAT MICHEL FOUCAULT'S EXCESSIVE OVERESTIMATION OF CONTROL IN SEXUALITY PARTICIPATES IN ITS OWN RIGHT IN THE RUSH TO OPPOSITE VALUES THAT LIES AT THE ROOT OF DECADENCE. AFTER HAVING SUCCESSFULLY CHALLENGED ONE OF THE MOST OBSTINATE ASSUMPTIONS OF THE CULTURE, NAMELY THAT SEXUALITY IS REPRESSED, FOUCAULT SIMULAT-

NEOUSLY PROPELS AN ALTERNATIVE CONCEPTION THAT BELONGS TO THE VERY SAME FRAMEWORK FROM WHICH HE WAS APPARENTLY TRYING TO EXTRICATE HIMSELF. DO WE REALLY GAIN THAT MUCH FROM ASSERTING THAT SEXUALITY IS REPRESSIVE RATHER THAN REPRESSED? WHAT IS, AFTER ALL, THE NOTION OF SEXUALITY AS A POSITIVE CONTROL IF NOT REPRESSION IN DRAG?

WHEN FOUCAULT SWINGS FROM A NEGATIVE TO A POSITIVE CONCEPTION OF CONTROL, HE REMAINS SQUARELY WITHIN THE SPECIFIC ECONOMY OF DECADENCE, WHICH DOESN'T PROGRESS OR REGRESS, OR EVEN LESS DEGENERATE, BUT KEEPS OSCILLATING BETWEEN ALTERNATIVE AND CON-TRADICTORY MOVEMENTS. THE HISTORIAN'S BOLD RE-EVALUATION OF HISTORY IN PENDULOUS TERMS IS PROBABLY MORE INDEBTED TO THESE VERY OSCILLATIONS THAN IT IS TO THE ACTUAL HISTORY OF THE WEST.

ASEXUALITY FULLY PARTICIPATES IN THE PRESENT EXTENUATION OF SEXUALITY IN THE CULTURE. BUT IS THIS "EXTERMINATION," AS JEAN BAUDRILLARD IMPLIES, IRREVERSIBLE? SHOULD WE DESPAIR OF SEXUALITY THE WAY WE'VE COME TO DESPAIR OF THE IDEA OF REVOLUTION? AFTER THE "END OF IDEOLOGIES," SHOULD WE PROCLAIM LOUDLY THE END OF SEX?

BAUDRILLARD DOESN'T HESITATE TO TAKE THAT STEP. EVERYTHING CONSIDERED, HE ASSERTS RUTHLESSLY, "THERE'S ONLY ONE KIND OF SEXUALITY—MALE SEXUALITY. SEXUALITY IS THIS STRONG, DISCRIMINATIVE STRUCTURE CENTERED ON THE PHALLUS, ON CASTRATION, ON THE NAME-OF-THE-FATHER, ON REPRESSION."[15] LACK AND INTERDICTION, FRUSTRATION AND GUILT, FEAR AND TRANSGRESSION ARE SO INTIMATELY WOVEN INTO THE SEXUAL FABRIC THAT DISMISSING THEM ALTOGETHER DEPRIVES SEXUALITY OF ITS ONLY AUTHENTIC ANCHORAGE. NOW THAT SEXUALITY CAN BE TOTALLY EXTERNALIZED, HE CONCLUDES, THERE'S NOTHING LEFT TO BE DESIRED. PENTHOUSE PEOPLE COULDN'T AGREE MORE: "WE FIND," WRITES A READER, "THAT ORAL PLAY, TOGETHER WITH THE USE OF VIBRATORS AND AT TIMES A DILDO, PROVIDE US WITH EVERYTHING WE COULD WISH FOR." NO MORE LACK, NO MORE FRUSTRATION, NO MORE WISH. BUT IS THE FUTURE OF SEXUALITY IN THE HANDS OF PENTHOUSE READERS? AND IS DESIRE TO BE REDUCED TO A POSH SEXUAL DEMAND?

WHAT'S COMING TO AN END, RATHER, IS THE REACTIVE CONCEPTION OF SEXUALITY BAUDRIL-

LARD STILL RETAINS FOR NO OTHER PURPOSE THAN PROCLAIMING ITS AGONY. ALREADY FREUD HAD TO FAST-FREEZE NEUROTIC SEXUALITY INTO A SCIENTIFIC MOLD FOR FEAR IT WOULD DISINTEGRATE COMPLETELY. IT IS THIS "OBJECTIVE" FRAME, GROWN MORE VACANT AND OBSESSIVE AS TIME WENT BY, THAT HELD TOGETHER A LITTLE LONGER THE FAILING GRAVITY OF SEXUALITY. NOW THAT THIS GRAVITY IS COLLAPSING UNDER ITS OWN WEIGHT, WE CAN INDEED EXPECT TO BE LOST FOR A WHILE, POSSIBLE FOR A GOOD WHILE. BUT BEING LOST AT THIS POINT MAY NOT BE AN ENTIRELY NEGATIVE SITUATION. IT MAY EVEN BE MORE FRUITFUL THAN MAKING SWEEPING ASSUMPTIONS IN PURELY OPPOSITIVE TERMS, OR PROPHETIC INTERPRETATIONS ROOTED IN THE "SYMBOLIC ECONOMY" OF PRIMITIVE CULTURES WE'VE CERTAINLY DONE OUR BEST TO EXTERMINATE.

REACTING AGAINST A REACTION MAY BE, AFTER ALL, AS MUCH A SHOW OF STRENGTH AS A SIGN OF WEAKNESS OR DEBILITY. THIS IS THE CONTEXT I WOULD LIKE TO ASSIGN TO THE RESISTIBLE ASCENSION OF THE NEW CELIBACY.

BAUDRILLARD DETECTS IN THE ECLIPSE OF SEXUALITY ONE OF THE MANY SYMPTOMS OF THE GENERAL IMPLOSION OF THE CULTURE. ONLY PRIMITIVE SOCIETIES, HE ASSERTS, CAN ACCOMODATE AMBIVALENT PHENOMENA BECAUSE IT IS IN THEIR MIDST ONLY THAT A POSITIVE REVERSIBILITY OF EXCHANGES TRULY EXISTS. IN THESE SOCIETIES THE DEAD, FOR INSTANCE, ARE NEVER EXCLUDED FROM THE SYMBOLIC CIRCULATION OF THE GROUP. THEY REMAIN ACTIVE PARTNERS IN THE MULTIPLE CIRCUITS OF EXCHANGE BY WHICH PRIMITIVE CULTURES MAINTAIN THEIR HARMONIOUS BALANCE BETWEEN LIFE AND DEATH, THE CLAN AND THE EARTH. WE, ON THE OTHER HAND, EXCLUDE THE DEAD IN A BIOLOGICAL DEATH. WE DENY THEM ANY PART IN THE SYMBOLIC CIRCULATION OF THE GROUP. INSTEAD OF MAKING DEATH A SOCIAL ACT, WE END UP MAKING OUR LIFE A LIVING DEATH.

THE ASEXUAL CLAIM COULDN'T BE AMBIVALENT IN THE SAME FASHION, HE WOULD LOGICALLY CONCLUDE. IT CAN ONLY SIGNAL THAT SEXUAL OPPOSITIONS, LIKE ALL OPPOSITIONS, CANNOT HOLD ANYMORE. THE OVEREVALUATION OF SEX, THE HYPER-PRODUCTION OF SEXUAL SIGNS, THE HYPER-REALITY OF SEXUAL PLEASURE DON'T INDICATE THE GROWING POWER OF SEXUALITY IN THE CULTURE; IT IS THE ULTIMATE FRENZY, THE LAST SEIZURE BEFORE SEXUALITY COLLAPSES ALTOGETHER. WE SEXUALIZE EVERYThiNG IN SIGHT

TO MAKE SURE SEX STILL EXISTS. INFLATED EROTIC PREOCCUPATIONS RECALL THE ROSY CHEEK OF TERMINAL TUBERCULOSIS (YES, AN OLD METAPHOR): DEATH ASSUMES THE TRAPPINGS OF HEALTH. END OF PRODUCTION. END OF POLITICS. END OF SEX.

PLURALITY OF INTERPRETATIONS IS ALWAYS A SIGN OF STRENGTH. BAUDRILLARD'S GENERAL SCHEME, FOR ALL ITS INTELLIGENCE, REMAINS A SEDUCTIVE SIMPLIFICATION. ANOTHER ATTEMPT TO MEET THE IRRESISTIBLE NEED FOR UNITY AT THE EXPENSE OF THE DISTURBING AND AMBIGUOUS CHARACTER OF THE PHENOMENA. "A NIHILIST IS A MAN WHO JUDGES OF THE WORLD AS IT IS THAT IT OUGHT NOT TO BE, AND OF THE WORLD AS IT OUGHT TO BE THAT IT DOESN'T EXIST . . . THE PATHOS OF 'IN VAIN' IS THE NIHILISTS' PATHOS." (THE WILL TO POWER). BAUDRILLARD'S COOL PATHOS MANAGES TO PRESERVE INTACT THE FACULTY TO CREATE FICTIONS. BUT HIS FICTION OF PRIMITIVE CULTURES GIVES AT BEST A NOSTALGIC TWIST TO WHAT ESSENTIALLY REMAINS A MONIST INTERPRETATION OF SOCIETY.

DECADENCE DOESN'T HAVE TO LEAD TO APOCALYPSE—NOW OR LATER. "THE DECLINE IS CONSTANTLY RESUMED, REVERSED, NEUTRALIZED, AND THIS IN MANY WAYS," WRITES JEAN-FRANCOIS LYOTARD.[16] BAUDRILLARD'S BELIEF IN AN IMPENDING DOOM EXEMPLIFIES ON THE CONTRARY THE POWER OF THE REACTIVE FORCES AT WORK IN WESTERN NIHILISM: THE ACTIVE DESTRUCTION OF VALUES, THE JOYOUS DISMISSAL OF ALL-TOO-PIOUS IDEOLOGIES (INCLUDING THE RELIGION OF MARXISM, OF COURSE) IS ALWAYS IN DANGER OF TURNING INTO THEORETICAL MORBIDITY. SKIDDING ON THE WAY, UNABLE TO GRIP THE ROAD OF PRACTICAL NIHILISM, BAUDRILLARD'S WILL TO NOTHINGNESS ENDS UP THEMATIZING ITSELF AS A COLLECTIVE DEATH-WISH.

IT DOESN'T HAVE TO END UP THAT WAY. IT DOESN'T HAVE TO END AT ALL. SEX HAS BECOME A POSITIVE PHENOMENON, BUT SIMULTANEOUSLY IT IS LOSING ITS POWER OVER OUR LIVES. NO LONGER REPRESSED, SEX IS NO LONGER REPRESSIVE. NEITHER EXTERMINATING, NOR EXTERMINATED, SEX MAY BE ON ITS WAY TO BE LEFT WELL ENOUGH ALONE—FOR A WHILE AT LEAST. ANOTHER SWING OF THE PENDULUM MAY BRING IT BACK WITH BRIGHT EYES AND ROSY CHEEKS.

THE PROBLEM WITH DECADENCE ISN'T THAT SYMPTOMS LIKE SEX DEGENERATE OR IMPLODE, RATHER THAT THEY REPEAT THEMSELVES IN MANY WAYS, THAT THEY KEEP MARKING TIME AND CHANGING PLACES, ENDLESSLY. THE PROBLEMS ISN'T THAT EVERYTHING IS COMING TO A HEAD, OR TO AN END, BUT THAT WE DON'T SEEM TO BE ABLE TO END ANYTHING ANYMORE. NEITHER GOD, NOR MAN, NOR SEX—NOR TRUTH. OUR PROBLEM ISN'T THAT WE ARE DECADENTS, BUT THAT WE ARE NOT DECADENT ENOUGH. NOT ACTIVELY, JOYOUSLY DECADENT. WE KEEP OSCILLATING BETWEEN A ROMANTIC NIHILISM, A DESPERATE ESTHETICS OF DESTRUCTION, AND A WILL TO KNOWLEDGE THAT MAINTAINS ALIVE THE TEMPTATION FOR TRUTH AT THE SAME TIME AS IT DENOUCNES ITSELF AS POWER.

THE PRESENT WEIGHTLESSNESS OF SEX REVEALS, HOWEVER, IN A NAKED FORM, LIKE THE BEACH AFTER A STORM, WHAT UNDERLIES THE PRESSURE EXERTED BY THE CULTURE ON SEXUALITY. A PRESSURE APPLIED ELSEWHERE AS WELL, IN OTHER CONTEXTS AND FOR SIMILAR PURPOSES. THIS PRESSURE IS SO BASIC, IT IS SO MUCH A PART OF THE PROCESS OF SOCIALIZATION ITSELF THAT WE MAY HAVE A TENDENCY TO OVERLOOK IT, OR ATTRIBUTE IT TO THE POWERS OF SPEECH. THIS PRESSURE HAS NOTHING TO DO WITH SEX PROPER, ALTHOUGH IT HAS FOUND IN SEX, AFTER TWO CENTURIES OF CONTRADICTORY SIGNALS, AND THE MORE RECENT PLAGUE OF POPULAR FREUDIANISM, A WELL-PREPARED COUCH. THIS PRESSURE RESIDES RATHER ON THE CONSTANT OBLIGATION TO COMMUNICATE ONESELF.

AN INDIVIDUAL, IN THIS CULTURE, IS SOMEONE WHO IS NEVER ALONE, OR SILENT. HE HAS TO COMMUNICATE AT ALL TIMES, IN ALL SITUATIONS—WITH HIS NEIGHBOR, HIS LOVER, HIS THERAPIST, HIS FEELINGS, HIS CAT, HIS PILLOW, HIS OWN SELF. AN INDIVIDUAL IS SOMEONE WHO IS ALWAYS PLUGGED ON TO THE MACHINE; SOMEONE WHO IS ALWAYS ON.

COMMUNICATION DOESN'T HAVE TO BE PRIVATE, BUT THERE IS NOTHING TOO PRIVATE TO BE COMMUNICATED: "NICE GIRLS DO TALK ABOUT SEX OPENLY WITH THEIR MATES," RECOMMENDS DR. IRENE KASSORLA. AND JERRY RUBIN AGAIN: "MINE IS THE FIRST BOOK TO ENCOURAGE MEN TO COMMUNICATE THESE INNERMOST REACTIONS." LOVERS DON'T MAKE LOVE, THEY COMMUNICATE THROUGH SEX.

PENTHOUSE READERS, OBVIOUSLY, DON'T HAVE TO BE PRESSURED INTO SHARING THEIR SEXUAL DISCOVERIES, WHILE CELIBATES COMPLAIN THAT "AS WE BEGAN TO HAVE MORE AND MORE SEXUAL EXPERIENCES TOGETHER, WE STOPPED COMMUNICATING IN OTHER WAYS . . ." THERE ARE SO MANY WAYS TO COMMUNICATE: IT IS NOT SEX, IT IS COMMUNICATION THAT IS COMMUNICATED THROUGH SEXUALITY. IT ISN'T THE GREAT AMERICAN GOAL OF CONSTANT SEXUALITY THAT PRESSURES US, BUT THE GREAT AMERICAN GOAL OF CONSTANT COMMUNICATION.

COMMUNICATION IS THE TERMINAL PAY OFF. SEX, LOVE, WORDS, EVERYTHING HAS TO BE TRADED, EVERYTHING MADE EXPLICIT IN ORDER TO ACQUIRE SOCIAL VALUE. EMPTY WORDS, THE ULTIMATE POTLATCH.

BY PUTTING EVERYONE IN A SITUATION OF DISCOURSE, IN A POSITION OF "INTERSUBJECTIVITY," THE CULTURE MAKES SURE NO ONE CAN ESCAPE THE ENVIABLE STATUS OF THE NORMAL NEUROTIC INDIVIDUAL. TO BE A LONER, A LOONY, A BACHELOR MACHINE IS WORSE THAN BEING DEAD: IT AMOUNTS TO BETRAYING THE SOCIAL CONTRACT. SUCH IS THE MAGIC PROPERTY ATTACHED TO COMMUNICATION: THE LAST SACRIFICE, THE LAST RITUAL, THE EMPTY MANA OR HAU THAT FORCE US TO RETURN THE VACANT CALL OF THE CULTURE, AND BY THE SAME TOKEN, ENDLESSLY, PAY OUR DEBT AS A FREE INDIVIDUAL.

IN A YOUNG COUNTRY LIKE THE U.S., THE BARE FACT OF SOCIAL CONTACT SUBSTITUTES FOR THE MORE DEEPLY ROOTED CONSTRAINTS THAT PREVAIL IN OTHER CULTURES. SO WE KEEP IN TOUCH, WE STAY ON BY COMMUNICATING VIRTUALLY ANYTHING TO ANYONE. WE KEEP IN TOUCH ENDLESSLY AS WE KEEP THE TV ON AT ALL TIMES WITHOUT PAYING MUCH ATTENTION TO THE PROGRAMS. WE KEEP IN TOUCH DESPERATELY BECAUSE THE CULTURE HAS STAMPED ON OUR FLESH THE DREAD OF REJECTION AND THE CURSE OF SOLITUDE.

THE MESSAGE THAT IS BEING COMMUNICATED ("TRUTH"), OR THE STRUCTURE OF COMMUNICATION ("SYMBOLIC EXCHANGE"), ARE SECONDARY TO THE FACT THAT A COMMUNICATION IS BEING ESTABLISHED, AND, HOPEFULLY, MAINTAINED. THIS IS WHAT ROMAN JAKOBSON CALLS THE PHATIC FUNCTION. THIS FUNCTION OF CONTACT IS, OBVIOUSLY, THE DEGREE ZERO OF CUMMUNICATION, BUT IT REMAINS AN ESSENTIAL FEATURE IN A

PROCESS THAT IS ALWAYS THREATENED TO BE INTERRUPTED. IT IS AN ESSENTIAL CONDITION FOR ANY INDIVIDUAL EXHANGE TO TAKE PLACE. IN THIS RESPECT, ALTHOUGH THE MESSAGE CAN HELP TO EXEMPLIFY THE POWER OF THE MEDIUM TO COMMUNICATE, YES, IT IS THE MEDIUM THAT IS THE MESSAGE.

THAT'S WHY ASEXUALITY MISSES THE MARK, IF IT EVER ATTEMPTED TO TAKE AIM. TO SUBSTITUTE ONE FORM OF COMMUNICATION (LOVE) FOR ANOTHER (SEX) CHANGES VERY LITTLE AS LONG AS WE KEEP EXTERMINATING THE MESSAGE TO LET THE MEDIUM REIGN SUPREME.

COMMUNICATON IS ALWAYS A FUNCTION OF DISTANCE. IT ALWAYS REINFORCES THE POLES AND ROLES OF INTERSUBJECTIVITY, THE "DIALECTICS" OF REPRESENTATION. THE CLOSENESS OF SEXUAL CONTACT COULD THREATEN THIS DISTANCE, LIBERATE OURSELVES FROM OUR SEPARATE FLESH, DISENGAGE THE INDIVIDUAL FROM THE ENDLESS CONFLICTS WHERE HE ACCOMPLISHES HIMSELF AS INDIVIDUAL. THAT'S WHY COMMUNICA-TION HAS TO BE STRICTLY ENFORCED AND A SOCIAL FORM OF CONTACT SUBSTITUTED TO THE SILENT EXPERIENCE OF SEXUALITY.

THERE IS NO END TO SOCIAL THERAPY. THERE IS NO END TO THE TALKING CURE. THERAPY HAS COME TO ADHERE SO CLOSELY TO SEXUALITY AS TO LITERALLY TAKE ITS PLACE. THE MOVE FROM COUCH TO BED WAS EASY ENOUGH SINCE SEX ITSELF HAS BECOME A FUCKING CURE! IT WAS UNBEARABLE THAT ANYTHING, LET ALONE SEXUALITY, SHOULD RETAIN ANY SHADOW AT THE CORE, ANY ONCE OF SERENE MYSTERY, ANY FESTIVE VIOLENCE, ANY SILENT INTENSITY. INTENSITIES TOO HAVE TO BE COMMUNICATED, ESPECIALLY BECAUSE THEY KEEP EVADING COMMUNICATION.

INTERLUDE

"NOT TO COMMUNICATE ONESELF; SILENCE; BEWARING OF CHARM."

(THE WILL TO POWER)

CHARM DOESN'T ABOLISH THE DISTANCE OF COMMUNICATION. IT SOLIDIFIES IT. IT EXACERBATES IT. IT GIVES IT ITS FINAL FORM BY ENGAGING IT IN A RICHER HALL OF MIRRORS. CONTACT DOESN'T NEED TO BE SEXUAL. BUT IT CAN BE SEXUALIZED. TURNED INTO A CHARM.

WE DON'T CALL THAT SEX ANYMORE. WE CALL IT: BEING SEXY.

BEING SEXY HAS NOTHING TO DO WITH BEING SEXUAL. BEING SEXY DOESN'T LEAD TO SEX. SEX IS DEEP AND DARK. SEXY MERELY SKIMS THE SURFACE. PRIMEVAL MONSTERS ARE NEVER TOO FAR OFF, BUT THEY ARE CONTAINED, EXORCIZED. SEX IS COMPULSIVE AND UNPREDICTABLE: WE DON'T CHOOSE OUR GENDER (YET), WE DON'T COMMAND AN ERECTION (YET). SEXY HAS NO GENDER. IT ISN'T EXPLICIT OR PHYSICAL LIKE SEX. IT IS ALL ALLUSION AND SUGGESTION. IT IS A PROMISE THAT DOESN'T HAVE TO MATERIALIZE. SEXY SIMPLY AROUSES INTEREST—AN INTEREST WE KEEP INTERPRETING SEXUALLY, LIKE EVERYTHING ELSE, BUT AT A SAFE DISTANCE FROM SEX. WE ARE "HAVING" SEX, OR WE THINK WE DO. BUT WE ARE, OR WE ARE NOT, SEXY.

SEX REQUIRES AN ACTION. SEXY DEFINES THE ACTOR. IT IS A QUALITY, AN ESSENCE THAT GIVES THE INDIVIDUAL A SPECIAL VALUE. SEX IS EXCHANGEABLE, BUT SEXY IS A "NATURAL" ATTRIBUTE. A GRACE. AN ELECTION. A USE VALUE.

WE KNOW NOW THAT USE VALUES ARE THE ROUSSEAUIST MYTH OF MARXIST ECONOMY. USE VALUES ARE MEANT TO GROUND EXCHANGE VALUES IN SOME SORT OF NATURALNESS. BEING SEXY IS THE NATURALIZATION OF SEX. IT WHITE-WASHES SEX OF ITS CRUDE FUNCTIONALITY. SEX REMAINS IN SUSPENSION, CASTING A DEEP SHADOW ON THE SEXY SURFACE. BUT THE SURFACE IS TIGHTLY SEALED, SUGARCOATED. MUMMIFIED.

SEXY IS THE VACCINE FOR SEX. IT INTRODUCES IN THE SOCIAL BODY THE DEAD VIRUS OF SEX TO PRODUCE IMMUNITY AGAINST THE SEXUAL THREAT. IT INDUCES THE FORMATION OF ANTIBODIES MEANT TO BE INTRODUCED DIRECTLY INTO THE MAINLINE OF THE CULTURE. THE FUNCTION OF THESE ANTIBODIES IS TO NEUTRALIZE THE EFFECT OF SEX, TO ALLEVIATE THE ANGUISH THAT GOES WITH IT. THESE ANTIBODIES ARE, IN THEIR REACTIVE PART, WHAT WE CALLED THE NEW CELIBACY. THIS BRAND OF ASEXUALITY CAN'T POSSIBLY BE THE FUTURE OF SEX. IT IS MERELY ITS COMPLEMENT.

BEING SEXY FREES US FROM THE PRESSURE TO PERFORM, WITHOUT RENOUNCING PERFORMANCE ALTOGETHER. BEING SEXY IS THE DEGREE ZERO OF PERFORMANCE: THE PURE PERFORMANCE OF THE EGO. ITS ENDLESS MIRROR-PHASE.

BEING SEXY IS TO SEX WHAT THE PHATIC FUNCTION IS TO THE MODEL OF COMMUNICATION: COMMUNICATION IN ITS EMPTY FORM, SEX AS A PURE, DISTANT, SOCIAL CONTACT.

IDIOSEXES

> "THERE IS NO SUCH THING AS AN IDIOLECT. AN IDIOLECT IS A PERVERSE FICTION."
>
> — ROMAN JAKOBSON

IS THERE SUCH A THING AS ASOCIAL SEXUALITIES? ROMAN JAKOBSON WOULD VIGOROUSLY DENY THEIR VERY EXISTENCE. EVEN MASTURBATION, SO OBSTINATELY TRACKED DOWN BY THE DEFENDERS OF MORAL ORDER, NEVER REFUSED TO COMMUNICATE. BETWEEN THE HAND AND THE SEX THERE SETTLED A RICH LAYER OF SIGNS, ALL THE WEIGHT OF REPRESENTATIONS.

MASTURBATION WASN'T AN ASOCIAL ACTIVITY SINCE IT REMAINED COSA MENTALE, A MANIPULATION OF MEANING AS MUCH AS A PHYSICAL ACT. IN NO WAY DID SUCH A WITHDRAWAL FROM SOCIETY INTERRUPT COMMUNICATION, IT GAVE IT ON THE CONTRARY A PERFECT FINISH. MASTURBATION WAS HUNTED DOWN SO FEROCIOUSLY BY BOURGEOIS MORALITY SIMPLY BECAUSE IT GAVE IT AN IDEAL SURFACE OF INTERVENTION. THANKS TO MASTURBATION, FOUCAULT IS CORRECT HERE, SURVEILLANCE MANAGED TO SINK DEEPER IN THE WEAVE OF THE SOCIAL FABRIC AND PENETRATE THE MOST SECRET CORNERS OF INDIVIDUAL CONSCIOUSNESS. OR RATHER STAMPED ON THE INDIVIDUAL'S CONSCIOUSNESS THE SEAL OF SECRECY.

AGAINST ALL APPEARANCES, TO MASTURBATE WAS AN EMINENTLY RESPONSIBLE ACT. RESPONSIBLE, SINCE REPREHENSIBLE. THE PLEASURE OF THE SIGNS, AND THE POUND OF FLESH, PAID THE PRICE OF GUILT.

MASTURBATION WAS NOT ONLY HUMAN, IT WAS MAN HIMSELF—THE NORMAL INDIVIDUAL CAUGHT IN THE NET OF SIGNS, ENTRAPPED IN THE STOCKS OF REPRESENTATIONS WHICH, CEASELESSLY EXTRACTED FROM HIM THE ADMISSION OF HIS DEBT AND THE TOKENS OF HIS SUBMISSION.

WHILE IT OUTWARDLY MOBILIZED ALL THE ENERGIES, THE FIGHT AGAINST MASTURBATION IN REALITY KEPT EXORCIZING A MORE UNACCEPTABLE PERVERSION. AN EXPERIMENT WHOSE OUTCOME IS SO SHATTERING THAT IT DIDN'T EVEN BENEFIT FROM THIS SUBTLE FORM OF RECOGNITION THAT IS INTERDICTION.

THE SAVAGE HAS HIS ANTHROPOLOGIST, THE JUNKY HIS CONNECTION, THE SCHIZO HIS PSYCHIATRIST. WHAT IS UPSETTING ABOUT THESE TRULY SOLITARY PERVERSIONS IS THAT THEY HARDLY PROJECT ANY SHADOW, OR ELECIT ANY ECHO SINCE THEY DON'T SEEM TO MAKE ANY ATTEMPT TO COMMUNICATE THEIR EXPERIENCE. IT IS THIS SILENCE THAT FOR US EPITOMIZES THE UNHUMAN IN MAN.

WHAT COULD WE CALL THESE UNHUMAN PRACTICES? DO WE HAVE A NAME FOR SOMETHING THAT GOES WITHOUT SAYING? WE WILL CALL THEM: IDIOSEXES.

NOTHING EXISTS OUTSIDE HUMAN COMMUNICATION, ASSERTS ROMAN JAKOBSON. LIKE IDIOLECTS, HE CERTAINLY WOULD DISMISS IDIOSEXES AS "PERVERSE FICTIONS." PERVERSE, THEY SURELY ARE. BUT ARE THEY FICTIONS? IN THEIR SUBMERGED EXISTENCE, THEY FUNCTION AS THE OBSCURE MYTH OF THE CULTURE—ITS UNATTAINABLE HORIZON.

WE ONLY KNOW THE EXISTENCE OF IDIOSEXES BY THE TRACES THEY OCCASIONALLY LEAVE BEHIND. MEDICAL REPORTS, POLICE FILES, MORGUE, WAX MUSEUM. ONLY ACCIDENTS OR DEATH MANAGE TO RETURN TO SOCIETY WHAT ESSENTIALLY IS A DISCRETE, OBSTINATE, IRREMEDIABLY SECRET ACTIVITY—A VERY QUIET KIND OF MADNESS. AND THIS SOCIALIZATION REMAINS DISCRETE AS WELL,

SO DEEP IS OUR REVULSION WHEN CONFRONTED TO SEXUAL EXPERIENCES THAT NEVER WERE MEANT TO BE BROUGHT TO LIGHT. MICHEL DE M'UZAN, TO START WITH, WAITED TEN YEARS BEFORE HE PUBLISHED HIS DESCRIPTION OF THE SCARRED MASO THAT ACCIDENTALLY FELL IN HIS HANDS.

ONE MAY WONDER IF THE VIOLENT OR MORTUARY STATUS OF THESE TRACES DON'T ALTER DRASTICALLY THE CREPUSCULAR IMAGE WE HAVE OF IDIOSEXUALITIES. FOR ONE DEADLY EXPERIENCE DEPOSITED IN THE ARCHIVES OF COLLECTIVE MEMORY, HOW MANY REMAIN UNKNOWN TO THE MEDICO-LEGAL INSTITUTION? WHAT SEEMS PRETTY CLEAR THOUGH IS THAT THE FATALITY ISN'T TOTALLY EXTERNAL TO THE IDIOSEXUAL'S EXPERIMENT. IT REMAINS ITS ULTIMATE SANCTION, IF NOT ITS EXPLICIT GOAL.

THERE IS A WORLD OF DIFFERENCE BETWEEN THE FLOATING LIBIDO, THE DISEMBODIED SEXUALITY OF THE SCHIZO AND THE TERMINAL FIXATION OF THE IDIOSEXUAL ON AN EXIGUOUS, BUT EXACTING, PRACTICE. BOTH BACHELOR MACHINES, HOWEVER, DEAL WITH GRADIENTS OF INTENSITY RATHER THAN THIS EXTENSIVE REPRESENTATION THAT NOW PASSES FOR SEXUALITY. THIS INTENSITY COULD EXPLAIN WHY ANY ATTEMPT TO ACCOUNT VERBALLY OR EVEN VISUALLY FOR THESE EXPERIENCES, THE TERROR AND FASCINATION THEY GENERATE IN US, IMMEDIATELY AFFECT IN DEPTH OUR VERY NOTION OF WHAT SOCIALIZATION IS ABOUT.

THE OBSESSIONAL FINDS A PROTECTION IN A HIGHLY RITUALIZED TERRITORY MEANT TO EXORCIZE HIS ANGUISH. THE IDIOSEXUAL IS WAY BEYOND SUCH NEUROTIC PROTOCOLS. HE DOESN'T ATTEMPT TO REGULATE HIS DESIRE BY BRINGING IT TO BEAR UPON A DISPLACED AND CIRCUMSCRIBED OBJECT (FETISH). ON THE CONTRARY, HE FOCUSES HIS DESIRE ON A SINGLE POINT IN ORDER TO REACH SUCH A PITCH OF INTENSITY THAT IT EXPLODES ALL HUMAN COORDINATES. THE IDIOSEXUAL IS PAST ANY INDIVIDUAL ANXIETY SIMPLY BECAUSE HE HAS MANAGED TO INTEGRATE IN HIS ITINERARY THE MORTAL DIMENSION OF DESIRE.

IT WASN'T EASY FOR THE MAN OF THE FORENSIC MUSEUM (BACK COVER), A LAWYER, TO CLEAR UP IN HIS BUSY TIME-TABLE A VACANT SPACE HE MAY HAVE KNOWN TO BE THE LAST. ONCE HIS FAMILY WAS SENT TO FLORIDA, HE BOOKED A ROOM IN A HOTEL AND LOCKED HIMSELF UP WITH A MON-STROUS MACHINE HASTILY PUT TOGETHER, AN ENORMOUS DILDO MADE WITH WIRE AND PAINTED COTTON WHICH HE FASTENED TO AN UPTURNED STOOL. HIS MOUTH GAGGED BY A GAS MASK, THE BODY SUSPENDED TO A SYSTEM OF PULLEYS, BRIDE IN DRAG OF THE SOMBER GUEST HE WANTED TO SEDUCE, PATIENTLY, METHODICALLY, INCH BY INCH, HE PUSHED UP HIS VISCERA A DEADLY PLEASURE. A MOST MODEST, OBSCURE, OBSTINATE PRACTICE, ON WHICH THERE IS STRICTLY NOTHING TO SAY SINCE IT REMAINS, AT LEAST FOR US, BEYOND HUMAN RECOGNITION.

CAN WE STILL CALL HUMAN SEXUALITY THIS EXPERIENCE WITHOUT A MIRROR, OR A MIRAGE, WITHOUT ANY IDENTITY TO BREAK APART, WHILE ONE AFTER THE OTHER ALL THE CATEGORIES OF SUBJECTIVITY SILENTLY CRUMBLE DOWN? ONLY A FICTION, BUT A FICTION WITHOUT AN IMAGE, AND WITHOUT A LANGUAGE COULD POSSIBLY EVOKE, WITHOUT CANCELLING, THE RADICAL EXTRANEITY OF SUCH AN IDIOSEXUAL EXPERIENCE.

DREAD OF SOLITUDE IS SO MUCH A PART OF THE CULTURE, IT SO GREATLY HAUNTS THE MIND OF EVERY INDIVIDUAL THAT THERE IS ALWAYS SOMEONE TO ACCOMPLISH THE DREAD, AND CONFIRM THE CURSE. THERE IS ALWAYS SOMEONE TO GO THROUGH THE SCREEN, THE CONTROLLING SCREEN OF PHANTASY, AND FULFILL THE HORRIFIED FASCINATION OF THE CULTURE. IN THIS RESPECT, THE LONER, THE LOONY, ALSO BELONGS. HE PAYS HIS DUES TO SOCIETY IN TERMS OF HIS OWN DEATH-WISH.

TO BELONG OR TO DIE. A MOST REASSURING ALTERNATIVE FOR A CIVILIZATION SO DISCONTENTED WITH ITSELF. THE CULTURE THUS MAKES SURE THAT ANY ATTEMPT TO SITUATE ONESELF OUTSIDE OF ITS REACH WILL END UP CONFIRMING IN AN EXEMPLARY FASHION THE VALIDITY OF ITS DREADFUL INJUNCTION.

A LAWYER BREAKING THE SOCIAL CONTRACT, A MAN OF SPEECH WALLED IN A DEAD SILENCE: CAN THE CULTURE STILL RECOGNIZE ITSELF IN SUCH A LUGUBRIOUS PARODY?

THE LAWYER'S LAST GRIMACE STILL ANSWERS TO THE SOCIAL GRIN OF THE INDIVIDUAL. WE MAY NOT

KNOW, WE MAY NOT WANT TO KNOW, BUT THE CULTURE KNOWS THAT THE GRIN AND THE GRIMACE, THE LONER AND THE INDIVIDUAL HAVE BUT ONE FACE.

"THE GRIMACE AND CONTORTION OF A WOMAN'S FACE AT ORGASM . . ."

SYLVÈRE LOTRINGER
NEW YORK, MARCH 16, 1981

NOTES

1 JACQUES LIZOT, LE CERCLE DES FEUX, ED. DU SEUIL, 1976.

2 DON SHEWEY, "HUMAN SEXUAL RESPONSE," THE SOHO NEWS, JANUARY 14, 1981.

3 ARTHUR BELL, "ASEXUALITY," THE VILLAGE VOICE, JANUARY 23, 1978.

4 MARTY RUBIN, "LAMENT FOR A LOST LOVER," MANDATE NO. 6.

5 JOHN PRESTON, UNPUBLISHED INTERVIEW WITH S.L.

6 RACHEL ENGLISH, MY FIRST 500, DELL, 1979.

7 ARTHUR BELL, OP. CIT., QUOTES FROM STIV BATORS, STEVE RUBELL, FRANK LANGELLA.

8 McGRAW HILL, 1980. QUOTES FROM DR. JOYCE BROTHERS, DR. ROLLO MAY, DR. HELEN SINGER KAPLAN, DR. RICHARD MAYEUX, HERBERT RICHARDSON.

9 THE NEW YORK TIMES, FEBRUARY 9, 1981.

10 "FATHERS AND SONS TALK ABOUT GROWING UP," THE NEW YORK TIMES, FEBRUARY 9, 1981.

11 CROWN PUBLISHERS, 1981.

12 CF. GILLES DELEUZE/FELIX GUATTARI, "HOW TO MAKE ONESELF A BODY WITHOUT ORGANS."

13 SEMIOTEXT(E) SPECIAL, ISSUE ON "LOVING BOYS," SUMMER 1980.

14 THE SOHO NEWS, NOVEMBER 5, 1980.

15 JEAN BAUDRILLARD, DE LA SÉDUCTION, GALILÉE, 1980.

16 JEAN-FRANCOIS LYOTARD, "EXPÉDIENTS DANS LA DÉCADENCE," IN RUDIMENTS PAÏENS, 10/18, U.G.E., 1977.

I AM VERY GRATEFUL TO KAREN HORNICK FOR HER HELP IN PREPARING THIS MANUSCRIPT.

63. A GYMNASIUM: TOWARD THE MIDDLE PARALLEL BARS EQUIPPED WITH LEATHER STRAPS.

64. THE CORPULENT MAN AND THE SQUAT MAN DRAG R. TOWARD THE BARS.

65. THE TWO MEN HOLD R. UPRIGHT, HER ARMS STRETCHED BETWEEN THE PARALLEL BARS.

66. ROBERTE'S HANDS, WRISTS ATTACHED BY STRAPS TO VERTICAL BARS.

67. THE SQUAT MAN, WITH SEVERAL SHORT MOVEMENTS, PULLS OFF R.'S SKIRT.

67 A. ROBERTE'S LEGS, STAMPING HER FEET STILL WEARING SHOES. ON THE FLOOR R.'S SKIRT AND SLIP.

68. ROBERTE'S FACE, HEAD LOWERED, WATCHING WHAT IS HAPPENING OUT OF THE CORNER OF HER EYE.

68 A. THE SQUAT MAN SEIZES ONE OF HER FEET BY THE ANKLE, TIES IT UP BY A LEATHER STRAP TO THE BASE OF ONE OF THE VERTICAL BARS.

68 B. THE SQUAT MAN SHOWS ROBERTE A PICTURE OF HER FINGER-PRINTS.

68 C. THE CORPULENT MAN, SEEN FROM REAR, BENDING OVER ONE OF ROBERTE'S TIED HANDS.

69. (CLOSE UP) ROBERTE'S HAND, FINGERS FOLDED ON PALM, CLOSED FIST.

70. (CLOSE UP) THE HAND OF THE COLOSSOS ON ROBERTE'S HAND, BEGINS TO UNFOLD FINGERS.

71. ROBERTE'S FACE, EYES ON THE CORPULENT MAN: EXPRESSION CHANGING FROM ASTONISHMENT TO IRRITATION: FROWNS, LOWERS EYES, PINCHED LIPS. (CLOSE UP)

72. ROBERTE'S HAND, ALL FINGERS UNFOLDED, HELD BETWEEN BOTH HANDS OF CORPULENT MAN, WHO SUCKS HER NAILS. (CLOSE UP)

73. THE PALM OF ROBERTE'S HAND TOWARD WHICH THE CORPULENT MAN BRINGS HIS MOUTH. (CLOSE UP)

74. THE CORPULENT MAN'S TONGUE ON ROBERTE'S PALM.

75. MOVEMENT OF ROBERTE'S FREE LEG: RAISING KNEE, LEG OUTSTRETCHED, FOOT THROWN FORWARD AGAINST THE CORPULENT MAN'S THIGH.

76. THE CORPULENT MAN'S TONGUE ON ROBERTE'S PALM.

77. R.'S LEG, OUTSTRETCHED FIRST, LIFTS.

77 B. THE SQUAT MAN WATCHING R.'S SEX OUT OF SHOT.

78. R.'S RAISED KNEE MOVING TO COVER SEX WITH THIGH.

78 B. ROBERTE'S FACE TURNED AWAY, HEAD THROWN BACK, EYES TOWARD CEILING, THEN LIDS LOWERED, LIPS HALF OPEN.

79. THE CORPULENT MAN'S TONGUE SLIDES OVER R.'S PALM THEN THE CORPULENT MAN COLLAPSES.

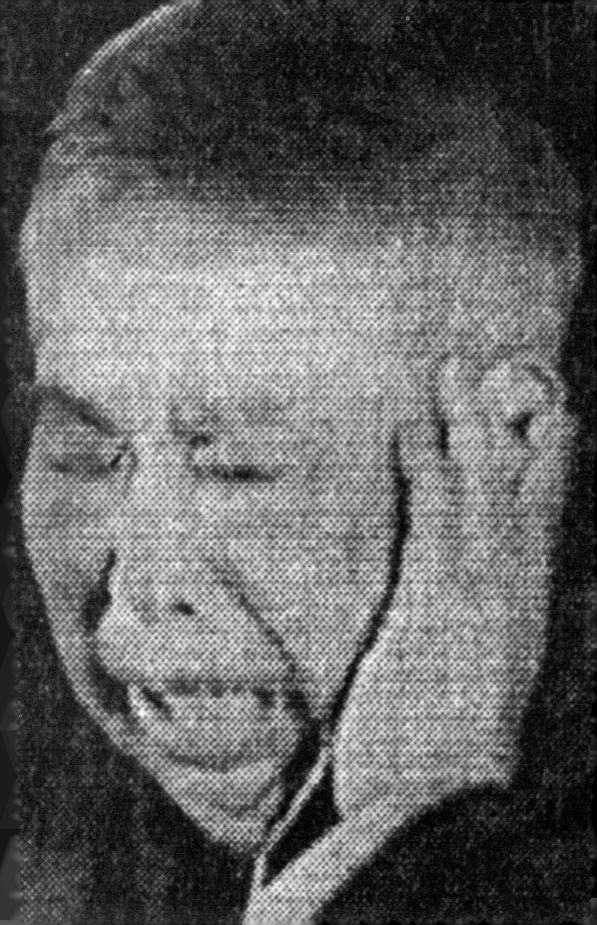

79 B. THE SQUAT MAN LIFTS THE CORPULENT MAN AND TAKES HIM AWAY.

80. ROBERTE SUSPENDED ON THE BARS.

81. THE SQUAT MAN BEGINS TO UNTIE ROBERTE, SLOWLY.

82. ROBERTE ON HER FEET, SKIRTLESS, HAIR SLIGHTLY DISHEVELLED, FACES THE SQUAT MAN.

83. THE SQUAT MAN PICKS UP ROBERTE'S SKIRT FROM THE FLOOR.

84. ROBERTE PUTS ON HER SKIRT.

85. THE SQUAT MAN OFFERS ROBERTE A GLASS OF COGNAC.

86. ROBERTE SLAPS THE SQUAT MAN.

87. WITH A GESTURE, THE SQUAT MAN PULLS ROBERTE'S SKIRT OFF AGAIN, AND PUTS HIS FOOT ON IT ON THE FLOOR.

88. ROBERTE SLAPS THE SQUAT MAN AGAIN, WHO DOES NOT FLINCH.

89. FADE OUT.

90. ROBERTE ON THE REGENCY CAFE TERRACE, EATING A CROISSANT.

91. THE GYMNASIUM, PARALLEL BARS WITH LEATHER STRAPS. FADE OUT.

92. THE FOUNTAINS ON THE SQUARE OF THE THÉÂTRE FRANCAIS.

PIERRE KLOSSOWSKI
TRANSLATION CATHERINE DUNCAN

MORE TITLES FROM SEMIOTEXT(E) / AUTONOMEDIA

DRIFTWORKS
JEAN-FRANÇOIS LYOTARD

69 WAYS TO PLAY THE BLUES
JÜRG LAEDERACH

INSIDE & OUT OF BYZANTIUM
NINA ZIVANCEVIC

ASSASSINATION RHAPSODY
DEREK PELL

SEMIOTEXT(E) NATIVE AGENTS SERIES
CHRIS KRAUS, EDITOR

IF YOU'RE A GIRL
ANN ROWER

**WALKING THROUGH CLEAR WATER
IN A POOL PAINTED BLACK**
COOKIE MUELLER

NOT ME
EILEEN MYLES

HANNIBAL LECTER, MY FATHER
KATHY ACKER

SICK BURN CUT
DERAN LUDD

THE MADAME REALISM COMPLEX
LYNNE TILLMAN

HOW I BECAME ONE OF THE INVISIBLE
DAVID RATTRAY

THE ORIGIN OF *THE* SPECIES
BARBARA BARG

AUTONOMEDIA NEW AUTONOMY SERIES
JIM FLEMING & PETER LAMBORN WILSON, EDITORS

WHORE CARNIVAL
SHANNON BELL

**INVISIBLE GOVERNANCE
THE ART OF AFRICAN MICROPOLITICS**
DAVID HECHT & MALIQALIM SIMONE

**CRACKING THE MOVEMENT
SQUATTING BEYOND THE MEDIA**
FOUNDATION FOR THE ADVANCEMENT OF ILLEGAL KNOWLEDGE

**PIRATE UTOPIAS
MOORISH CORSAIRS & EUROPEAN RENEGADOES**
PETER LAMBORN WILSON

THE LIZARD CLUB
STEVE ABBOTT

**TAZ
THE TEMPORARY AUTONOMOUS ZONE,
ONTOLOGICAL ANARCHY, POETIC TERRORISM**
HAKIM BEY

THIS IS YOUR FINAL WARNING!
THOM METZGER

FRIENDLY FIRE
BOB BLACK

CALIBAN AND THE WITCHES
SILVIA FEDERICI

**FIRST AND LAST EMPERORS
THE ABSOLUTE STATE & THE BODY OF THE DESPOT**
KENNETH DEAN & BRIAN MASSUMI

WARCRAFT
JONATHAN LEAKE

THIS WORLD WE MUST LEAVE AND OTHER ESSAYS
JACQUES CAMATTE

SPECTACULAR TIMES
LARRY LAW

FUTURE PRIMITIVE AND OTHER ESSAYS
JOHN ZERZAN

WIGGLING WISHBONE
BART PLANTENGA

THE ELECTRONIC DISTURBANCE
CRITICAL ART ENSEMBLE

X-TEXTS
DEREK PELL

THE ROOT IS MAN
DWIGHT MACDONALD

MORE TITLES FROM SEMIOTEXT(E) / AUTONOMEDIA

SOCIAL OVERLOAD
HENRI-PIERRE JEUDY

THE UNHOLY BIBLE
HEBREW LITERATURE OF THE KINGDOM PERIOD
JACOB RABINOWITZ

CRIMES OF CULTURE
RICHARD KOSTELANETZ

CAPITAL AND COMMUNITY
JACQUES CAMATTE

AUTONOMEDIA BOOK SERIES
JIM FLEMING, ED.

¡ZAPATISTAS!
DOCUMENTS OF THE NEW MEXICAN REVOLUTION
EZLN

THE DAUGHTER
ROBERTA ALLEN

FILE UNDER POPULAR
THEORETICAL & CRITICAL WRITINGS ON MUSIC
CHRIS CUTLER

MAGPIE REVERIES
JAMES KOEHNLINE

ON ANARCHY & SCHIZOANALYSIS
ROLANDO PEREZ

GOD & PLASTIC SURGERY
MARX, NIETZSCHE, FREUD & THE OBVIOUS
JEREMY BARRIS

MARX BEYOND MARX
LESSONS ON THE GRÜNDRISSE
ANTONIO NEGRI

MODEL CHILDREN
INSIDE THE REPUBLIC OF RED SCARVES
PAUL THOREZ

SCANDAL
ESSAYS IN ISLAMIC HERESY
PETER LAMBORN WILSON

POPULAR REALITY
IRREVEREND DAVID CROWBAR, ED.

THE ARCANE OF REPRODUCTION
HOUSEWORK, PROSTITUTION, LABOR & CAPITAL
LEOPOLDINA FORTUNATI

RETHINKING MARXISM
STEVE RESNICK & RICK WOLFF, EDS.

THE TOUCH
MICHAEL BROWNSTEIN

GULLIVER
MICHAEL RYAN

CLIPPED COINS, ABUSED WORDS, CIVIL GOVERNMENT
JOHN LOCKE'S PHILOSOPHY OF MONEY
CONSTANTINE GEORGE CAFFENTZIS

TROTSKYISM AND MAOISM
THEORY & PRACTICE IN FRANCE & THE U.S.
A. BELDEN FIELDS

FILM & POLITICS IN THE THIRD WORLD
JOHN DOWNING, ED.

COLUMBUS & OTHER CANNIBALS
THE WÉTIKO DISEASE & THE WHITE MAN
JACK FORBES

CASSETTE MYTHOS
THE NEW MUSIC UNDERGROUND
ROBIN JAMES, ED.

ENRAGÉS & SITUATIONISTS
IN THE OCCUPATION MOVEMENT, MAY '68
RENÉ VIÉNET

XEROX PIRATES
"HIGH" TECH & THE NEW COLLAGE UNDERGROUND
AUTONOMEDIA COLLECTIVE, EDS.

ZEROWORK
THE ANTI-WORK ANTHOLOGY
BOB BLACK & TAD KEPLEY, EDS.

THE NEW ENCLOSURES
MIDNIGHT NOTES COLLECTIVE

MIDNIGHT OIL
WORK, ENERGY, WAR, 1973–1992
MIDNIGHT NOTES COLLECTIVE